DATE DUE

AUG 31 2002	
DEC 31 2002	

GAYLORD   PRINTED IN U.S.A.

1986

The Shadow War

Foreign Intelligence Book Series
Thomas F. Troy, General Editor

The Shadow War

German Espionage and United States Counterespionage in Latin America during World War II

Leslie B. Rout, Jr.
John F. Bratzel

University Publications of America, Inc.

To our wives—who put up with us

University Publications of America, Inc.
44 North Market Street, Frederick, Maryland 21701

Copyright © 1986 by Leslie B. Rout, Jr. and John F. Bratzel

Library of Congress Cataloging-in-Publication Data

Rout, Leslie B., 1936–
  The shadow war.

  (Foreign intelligence book series)
  Bibliography: p.
  Includes index.
  1. World War, 1939–1945—Secret service—Germany.
  2. World War, 1939–1945—Secret service—United States.
  3. World War, 1939–1945—Secret service—Latin America.
I. Bratzel, John F. II. Title. III. Series.
D810.S7R58   1986   940.54'85   85–29563
ISBN 0-89093-237-9.

Printed in the United States of America

Contents

v

Illustrations

PHOTOGRAPHS *(Following page 256)*

Kapitän zur See A.D. Herbert Wichmann, commander of AST Hamburg, 1939–1945.

Heinrich Reiners, PYL ringleader in Chile, 1941–1942.

Abwehr espionage chiefs in Mexico, 1940–1945: Friedrich von Schlee-brugge, Georg Nicolaus, Edgar Hilgert, Karl Franz Rüge.

Abwehr espionage chiefs in Brazil, 1939–1943: Albrecht Gustav Engels, Friedrich Kempter (1942), Friedrich Kempter (1978), Franz Walther Jordan.

The special bomb given by Captain Mascimento to Gerardo Melo Mourao, for destroying the German freighter, *Windhuk.*

Josef Starziczny's radio equipment seized by the Brazilian police on February 10, 1942.

Marcus Baarn, the black agent sent by AST Hamburg to Brazil in 1943.

Gerardo Melo Mourão, the controversial newspaperman and scholar, convicted as sub-chief of the "Captain Garcia" ring.

The principal leaders of the PQZ ring, broken up in February 1944: Augusto Kroll, Bernardo Timmerman, Eugenio Ellinger (Juan Valdés), and Hans Graner.

Major Abwehr and SD spy figures active in Argentina, 1940–1945: Johannes Siegfried Becker, Gustand Utzinger, Hans Harnisch, Osmar Hellmuth.

Kapitän zur See Dietrich Niebuhr, naval attaché, who was chief paymaster and *ad hoc* supervisor for Abwehr operations in South America, 1940–1943.

Johannes Siegfried Becker.

Preface

It has become standard practice for various countries to accuse clandestine organizations of subverting their policies or attempting to overthrow their government. The CIA and the KGB are regularly blamed (or occasionally given credit) for all manner of activities. Some of the charges and countercharges are factual, but many are not. Ascertaining their validity, however, has often been impossible since documentation has not been available. Moreover, the few published accounts available have generally been either first-person statements or polemical diatribes.

Beginning in the early 1970s, however, classified material dealing with espionage during World War II became available in the United States. We examined it, and then looked at archives in Mexico, Argentina, Brazil, Chile, Germany, and the United Kingdom. We also conducted numerous interviews with former FBI agents, retired diplomats, and former German spies. Time has dimmed some memories and the written record has proven to be occasionally contradictory, but sufficient material is available to reconstruct an accurate history of events.

This is a comprehensive account of German–United States spy and counterspy activities in the four Latin American republics (Mexico, Brazil, Chile, and Argentina) where the Germans established major espionage networks. But to restrict the study solely to intelligence and counterintelligence activities would be to distort the historical record. Global diplomacy, battlefield developments, domestic politics, and human proclivities all had a significant effect on events. To understand any one of the parts requires an overall perspective.

Ultimately, it is our hope that this study will precipitate a reappraisal concerning the nature, complexity, and significance of clandestine operations, and will serve as a point of departure for new studies in inter-American diplomatic relations as well.

*　　*　　*

We express our sincere thanks to the following people who assisted us with the research for this book: Juan Alarcon Arcos, Dr. D.C. Allard, the Honorable Norman Armour, Dr. James Billington, the Honorable Philip Bonsal, the late Spruille Braden, Luíz Orlando Carneiro, Ricardo Ferreira, M.D., Dr. Maria Keipert, Dr. Bernd Martin, Dr. Gisela von Mühlenbrock, Paul Napier, Kathy Nicastro, Col. Oscar Reile (German Army, Ret.), Mr. and Mrs. Alberto Ramón, and John E. Taylor.

We also gratefully acknowledge the people at the following institutions for their help; they provided us with research assistance, financial aid, and/or access to their collections of documents, all of great value in the completion of this volume: the American Philosophical Society; Archiv des Auswärtiges Amt, Bonn; Arquivo Nacional, Seção do Poder Judiciário, Rio de Janeiro; Bundesarchiv-Militärarchiv, Freiburg-im-Breisgau, German Federal Republic; Centro de Pesquisa e Documentação de História Contemporanea, Fundação Getúlio Vargas, Rio de Janeiro; Department of Justice, Federal Bureau of Investigation, Office of Congressional and Public Affairs, Washington, D.C.; Department of the Navy, Naval Historical Center, Washington, D.C.; the Diplomatic and Civil Archives Division and the Modern Military Division, National Archives and Records Service, Washington, D.C.; Franklin D. Roosevelt Library, Hyde Park, New York; El Ministerio de Relaciones Exteriores, República de Chile, Santiago; El Ministerio de Relaciones Exteriores y Culto, República Argentina, Buenos Aires; and the Woodrow Wilson International Center for Scholars, Washington, D.C.

Finally, we express our utmost gratitude to Christiane Bushell, Prof. Peter Scheibert, Jack West, and Kapitän zur See Herbert Wichmann, a.D., without whom we would never have been able to write this book.

Part of Appendix A originally appeared in an article in *Cryptologia*, Vol. VII, #2 (April 1983).

1

The German Intelligence Services in Latin America

I. *The Rise of* der Kieker

> Let's see.... I must have been about seven years old.... We had a
> farm near Osorno, and were doing well.... One day, my father told
> my mother that a very important man would be passed on to our
> community, and he would spend the night at our farm. My father also
> said that while we were Chilean as well as German, if the Fatherland
> needed help, it was our duty to help. I kept thinking, if he was so
> important, why was he so short? My father towered above him.... All
> I really remember about him were his blue eyes, and that he didn't
> speak much.... He was supposed to be going over the Andes soon.
> Several years later, when I recalled this event, and asked my father
> why this man was so important, he told me that the man's name was
> Canaris.[1]

Born January 1, 1887, Wilhelm Franz Canaris was allegedly nicknamed *der Kieker* ("the Peeper") by his playmates, and in view of his
future career, a more fitting sobriquet could not have been given. Raised
in middle-class surroundings, Canaris received his commission as an
officer in the German Imperial Navy in 1908. The outbreak of World War I
found him aboard the SMS *Dresden* in Latin American waters. He participated in the victorious Battle of Coronel, and the disastrous Falkland
Islands attack late in 1914. The *Dresden* was the only German vessel to
escape destruction in the latter melee, but in March 1915, the ship was
trapped off the Chilean coast by the HMS *Glasgow*. The *Dresden* scuttled
herself, and her crew was interned on Quiriquina Island, a barren pile of
rocks about twenty miles northwest of the city of Concepción.

In August of that year, disguised as a civilian, Canaris rowed to the
mainland and traveled to Osorno, three hundred miles to the south. With

1

the aid of German sympathizers in the area, he succeeded in crossing the Andes and reached Buenos Aires in September 1915. Using a forged Chilean passport in the name of Reed Rosas, Canaris managed to convince Royal Navy interrogators that he was Anglo-Chilean. He reached Amsterdam aboard a Dutch freighter and arrived in Berlin in October, two months after his unannounced departure from Quiriquina Island.[2]

Returning to the war, Canaris was sent to Spain, where he served for two years as a secret agent, collecting ship movement data and creating supply depots for U-boats. In 1917, he forsook the life of a spy to become a U-boat commander, a position he held until the German collapse in November 1918. Canaris remained in the navy, and in the decade following the war he gained a reputation as a skilled wire puller and as a confidential agent with whom the naval power brokers could entrust special missions. In 1924, he was sent to Japan to help supervise a secret Japanese-German submarine construction project. The following year he turned up in Spain, where he participated in another clandestine submarine-building scheme and simultaneously worked to reestablish a German intelligence network in that country.[3]

Unfortunately, his constant comings and goings attracted the attention of unfriendly politicians and, when Canaris returned to Germany late in 1925, newspaper revelations ripped away his mask of anonymity and destroyed any further utility he might have had as a confidential operative. The Peeper was by now much more interested in intrigue than sea duty, but his superiors no longer had any use for a "blown" agent. They hustled him out of Berlin and posted him as executive officer aboard the old battleship *Schlesien*. Promoted to captain in 1931, he was named commander of that vessel in 1932 but was passed over for promotion in 1934. His next assignment was commander of the naval station at Swinemunde, where he could expect to complete his service and become eligible for his pension.

It was at this point, with his career seemingly over, that fate gave Canaris a matchless opportunity to escape anonymity. In 1932, Capt. Conrad Patzig had been appointed chief of the Abwehr, the military intelligence section of the German High Command. No friend of national socialism, Patzig clashed repeatedly with Reichsführer Heinrich Himmler and in 1934 began assembling an incriminating dossier against Reinhard Heydrich, commander of the Nazi party's intelligence service, the Sicherheitsdienst (SD). The problem for Minister of Defense Field Marshal Werner von Blomberg was that there was no way Patzig could win his struggle against the Nazi leadership. This made him a political liability. Blomberg wanted no problems with the Nazi party, and so he told Adm. Erich Raeder, commander of the German navy, that Patzig would have to be replaced.[4]

Canaris was certainly not Raeder's choice for the job, because the navy commander held a relatively low opinion of the Peeper. It was Patzig who stressed Canaris's cunning and skills as a negotiator and conciliator, and suggested that the latter be named as the Abwehr's next commander.

The problem developing for Raeder was that he was unable to find anyone else with the skills needed who wanted the job. Moreover, the admiral believed that he lacked the time needed to conduct an exhaustive search. In 1932, Conrad Patzig had been the first naval officer to head the Abwehr. This was one of the few interservice positions held by the navy, and if Raeder moved too slowly, Blomberg might name an army man as chief. It was this combination of circumstances that resulted in Patzig's official departure on December 31, 1934, and Canaris's appointment as Abwehr chief on his forty-eighth birthday.[5]

II. The Abwehr Organization and Command Structure

When Canaris took over the Abwehr, it was a small, relatively unpretentious command, struggling strenuously to execute its primary task of counterintelligence. But Hitler, who had a near-pathological belief in the omnipotence of Britain's MI-6, wanted a spy organization that would be as dominant in the cloak-and-dagger business as his panzers and Stukas would be on European battlefields. Such an ambition required that the Abwehr expand rapidly, simultaneously establishing worldwide intelligence stations and vast networks of agents. Canaris was, therefore, handed an opportunity given few men: to create a special organization and to stamp upon it his own personality.

An examination of the Abwehr organizational scheme suggests that, among other things, Canaris believed that compartmentalization should be pushed to its logical limits. Thus, this intelligence agency was internally divided into a host of small entities based primarily on the principles of task and/or area specialization. With the completion of a major reorganization in October 1939, Abwehr headquarters in Berlin consisted of four functional and one administrative divisions:[6]

Abteilung I — Geheimer Meldedienst (secret information or espionage)

Abteilung II — Sabotage (physical and moral)

Abteilung III — Spionageabwehr und Gegenspionage (counterespionage)

Abteilung Z — Zentralabteilung (finance and administration)

Amtsgruppe Ausland — Foreign section (service attachés)

Only Abteilungen I, II, and Amtsgruppe Ausland became involved in the direction of intelligence activities in the Americas. The most prominent of these, Abteilung I, was itself subdivided into ten sections, while Abteilung II, organized essentially on a geographic basis, had six.*

---

*The Abteilung I sections were: I-H (Heer) Ost, I-H West, I-HT (Heerestechnik), I-M (Marine), I-L (Luftwaffe), and I-T/LW (Luftwaffe Technik). The three specialist sections were I-D (Funknetze and Verkehr), I-G (Geheimsache) and I-Wi (Wirtschaft). There was also an administrative section (I-Z). The Abteilung II sections were II-Chefbüro, II-Gruppe West, II-Gruppe Ost, II-Gruppe Südost, II-Gruppe Übersee, and II-Technik. See Chart I for an English-language representation of this organizational system.

CHART I
ABWEHR HEADQUARTERS ORGANIZATION, 1939-1944

(Emphasis is given to those divisions
which had operatives in Latin America)

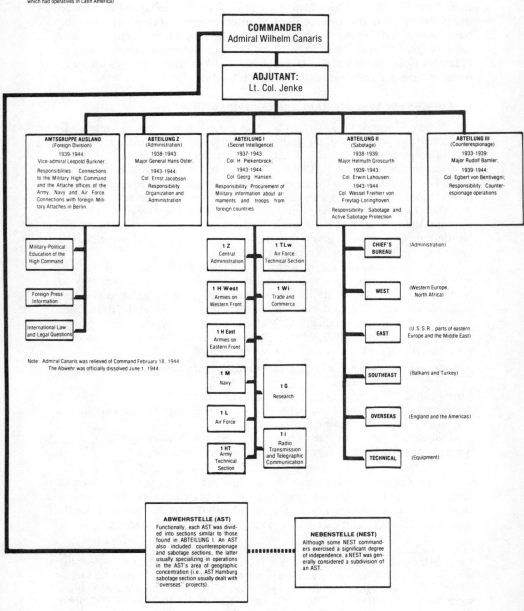

COMMANDER
Admiral Wilhelm Canaris

ADJUTANT:
Lt. Col. Jenke

AMTSGRUPPE AUSLAND
(Foreign Division)
1939-1944:
Vice-admiral Leopold Burkner:
Responsibilities: Connections to the Military High Command and the Attache offices of the Army, Navy and Air Force. Connections with foreign Military Attaches in Berlin.

ABTEILUNG Z
(Administration)
1938-1943:
Major General Hans Oster.
1943-1944:
Col. Ernst Jacobson
Responsibility: Organization and Administration

ABTEILUNG I
(Secret Intelligence)
1937-1943:
Col. H. Piekenbrock;
1943-1944:
Col. Georg Hansen.
Responsibility: Procurement of Military information about armaments and troops from foreign countries.

ABTEILUNG II
(Sabotage)
1938-1939:
Major Helmuth Groscurth
1939-1943:
Col. Erwin Lahousen;
1943-1944:
Col. Wessel Freiherr von Freytag-Loringhoven;
Responsibility: Sabotage and Active Sabotage Protection

ABTEILUNG III
(Counterespionage)
1933-1939:
Major Rudolf Bamler;
1939-1944:
Col. Egbert von Bentivegni;
Responsibility: Counterespionage operations

Military-Political Education of the High Command

Foreign Press Information

International Law and Legal Questions

Note: Admiral Canaris was relieved of Command February 18, 1944
The Abwehr was officially dissolved June 1, 1944

1 Z Central Administration

1 TLw Air Force Technical Section

1 H West Armies on Western Front

1 Wi Trade and Commerce

1 H East Armies on Eastern Front

1 M Navy

1 G Research

1 L Air Force

1 i Radio Transmission and Telegraphic Communication

1 HT Army Technical Section

CHIEF'S BUREAU (Administration)

WEST (Western Europe, North Africa)

EAST (U.S.S.R., parts of eastern Europe and the Middle East)

SOUTHEAST (Balkans and Turkey)

OVERSEAS (England and the Americas)

TECHNICAL (Equipment)

ABWEHRSTELLE (AST)
Functionally, each AST was divided into sections similar to those found in ABTEILUNG I. An AST also included counterespionage and sabotage sections, the latter usually specializing in operations in the AST's area of geographic concentration (i.e., AST Hamburg sabotage section usually dealt with "overseas" projects).

NEBENSTELLE (NEST)
Although some NEST commanders exercised a significant degree of independence, a NEST was generally considered a subdivision of an AST.

The principal task of these *Abteilungen* was to supervise the units which actually executed the sabotage and espionage operations; these were officially called Abwehrstellen (Abwehr intelligence stations), but were more commonly referred to as *Asts* (meaning *branches*). Before September 1, 1939, there were twenty-one of the posts, one in each military district (*Wehrkreis*). But as the Wehrmacht rolled across Europe, the number of *Asts* increased to thirty-three. Usually commanded by an army colonel or navy captain, an *Ast* had intelligence, sabotage, and counterintelligence divisions, and each of these was subdivided similarly to the *Abteilung* whose function it was performing. Thus, the secret information section of an *Ast* mirrored Abteilung I and possessed army (I-H), navy (I-M), air force (I-L), and economic (I-Wi) sections. An *Ast* sabotage section generally followed the organizational pattern of Abteilung II but, depending upon importance and geographic location, it might lack one or more of the subdivisions found in the Abteilung II organizational table.[7]

Every *Ast* received guidelines, specific orders, and administrative directives from the *Abteilungen* commanders in Berlin, but *Ast* chiefs could appeal any command received directly to Canaris.[8] One reason these station leaders enjoyed a semi-independent status was that each *Ast* recruited and trained its own agents, commonly called V-men (short for *Vertrauensmann*, meaning *confidential agent*). This veritable independence also resulted in the development of special expertise and regional specialization by individual *Ast* commanders. Several would specialize in the Western Hemisphere, but Asts Berlin, Hamburg, and Brussels (established in 1941) would have Latin America almost exclusively to themselves.

In order to spread their activities over a wider field, *Asts* in turn set up Abwehr *Nebenstellen*, or *Nests*, which theoretically were branch offices. In its organizational scheme and operational specialty, the *Nest* was supposed to be similar to the controlling *Ast*. But often it recruited and directed its own V-men while specializing in operational areas different from those emphasized by the allegedly controlling *Ast*. A lieutenant colonel or navy commander often commanded a *Nebenstellen*, and the two most involved with Latin America were Nest Cologne and Nest Bremen.[9]

From the espionage perspective, the most controversial *Abteilung*, both then and now, was Amtsgruppe Ausland. It was this division which exercised control over the armed forces attachés posted to the diplomatic missions outside the country. In 1933, the German foreign office reluctantly consented to allow the army and navy to once again station officers as attachés in German embassies. This agreement was struck, however, with the understanding that the attachés would not engage in clandestine activities.[10] In a number of books written about German intelligence operations in World War II, various authors have expressed sharp disagreement concerning the involvement of the attachés in espionage.[11] Moreover, in correspondence with us, several former Abwehr officers vehemently denied that service attachés in Latin America had engaged in these forbidden operations. In making their point, several of these informants stressed the notion that the republics south of the Rio Grande had almost no military or naval secrets worth ferreting out by clandestine machinations.[12]

Probably the most succinct and accurate description of the situation was supplied by Gen. Erwin Lahousen, chief of Abteilung II from 1939 to 1943. He explained that army, navy, and air force attachés who were not given espionage assignments were considered "spotless" while those who did receive them were referred to as being "stained."[13] As we shall demonstrate, by that yardstick, the attachés in Brazil, Chile, and Argentina were literally dipped in tar! They acted as paymasters, coordinators, and even organizers of espionage rings. There may have been some spotless attachés in Latin America, but given the examples cited, there is little reason to believe that this was the case.

III. The Abwehr Leader as a "Burnt Out" Case

A new agreement between the Abwehr and the foreign office governing attaché activity should have been negotiated after hostilities broke out in September 1939. Such an arrangement would have lessened friction and facilitated intelligence gathering, but the ultimate significance of this failure is that it tends to highlight other inefficiencies and organizational shortcomings. For example, why was the Abwehr so tightly compartmentalized? And how was one man (Canaris) effectively to handle the potential volume of appeals that might come from twenty-one (later thirty-three) Asts? And why were three Asts and two Nests engaged in independent and uncoordinated operations in Latin America? Paul Leverkuehn, formerly an Abwehr agent in Turkey, has written that "it would not be an exaggeration to say that the Abwehr was Canaris, and Canaris was the Abwehr."[14] Given the fact that the intelligence organization as it developed after 1935 was Canaris's creation, Leverkuehn's observation seems substantially sound. Thus, answers to some of the questions raised would lie perhaps in the character and outlook of the leader himself.

Wilhelm Canaris has been favorably treated by biographers who have written persuasively about his intellectual ability, his personal courage, and his highly developed sense of moral conduct. In addition, a number of former Abwehr officers with whom we communicated remember him as a commander who had a genuine interest in the welfare of his men.[15] On the other hand, Adm. Karl Dönitz, chief of the U-boat arm and later commander of the German navy, considered Canaris a fraud, and the Abwehr deficient.[16] David Kahn, in *Hitler's Spies*, depicted Canaris as a well-meaning but muddle-headed hypochondriac promoted to a position beyond his competence.[17] Kurt Friewald, who served under Canaris as midshipman and knew him intimately, concluded that he had a "soft heart" and as a result lacked the ruthlessness necessary "for the making of a consummate spymaster."[18] The most caustic criticism came from Lt.

Col. Wilhelm Kuebart, one of the more respected figures of World War II German intelligence. He blamed Canaris for the fact that "as an agency responsible for the collection of operational intelligence, the Abwehr proved ineffective to an extent that even the apparently well-informed enemy could not comprehend."[19]

In themselves, these pro and con judgments seem irreconcilable, but a key to this puzzle would seem to be Canaris's view of his nation's perilous position. An avowed German nationalist who by 1939 had come to hate both Hitler and the Nazi party, the Abwehr leader became increasingly melancholy because he believed that Germany could not win the war. He was further tormented by his realization that for all practical purposes, fatherland and Führer had become inextricably intertwined: they must conquer or collapse together. It was, perhaps, this glimpse of national (and probably personal) catastrophe, plus the realization that he could do little to alter the situation, which gradually immobilized the Peeper and eventually destroyed him.[20]

But the fate of the nation was not the only problem that ate away at Canaris's soul. Reinhard Heydrich and Heinrich Himmler never bothered to disguise their intentions of having the SD swallow the Abwehr. Canaris might not be able to save his beloved Deutschland, but he would defend his own organization as long as he was able. To do this, he was willing to tolerate inept intelligence officers simply because they were opponents of the Nazi party and especially the Sicherheitsdienst.[21] In a similar sense the extensive compartmentalization of the Abwehr was possibly a defensive measure intended to achieve the same end. Undeniably the system encouraged duplication, but it also meant that if the SD or some foreign intelligence service penetrated one or more sections, the affected parts could be isolated or cut away without causing the collapse of the entire organization.

Admiral Canaris certainly recognized the importance of conducting intelligence operations in Latin America. And, as we have noted, he had some idea of the conditions and difficulties Abwehr agents in the region might encounter. But as the war dragged on, defensive struggles against the SD at home and enemy intelligence organizations in Europe absorbed more and more of his time. Abwehr intelligence agents in Latin America would gradually discover that they could expect little support from the home organization—and the little they did receive would often arrive too late to make any appreciable difference.

IV. The Abwehr Organization in Latin America

Since the Abwehr was responsible to the German Military High Command, the *Asts* and *Nests* could only exist where the German armed forces were in control. In other areas, such as Latin America, no matter what the size of the individual spy ring or the significance of its work, it was administratively classified as a *Meldeköpfe* (MK); if it communicated by radio with an *Ast* controller, it became a *Funkmeldeköpfe* (FMK).[22]

The chiefs of these MKs and FMKs were V-men personally recruited by military or naval officers assigned to Ast Hamburg, Ast Berlin, Ast Brussels, Nest Bremen, or Nest Cologne. The recruiters remained the controllers of the V-men they dispatched, but the hazards of distance and probable interception and interruption of communications dictated an operational compromise. Thus, an army, navy, or air force attaché stationed in the same country often supplied funds, equipment, and instructions for the V-men and the network he had built up. Personal animosities sometimes marred relationships between the attachés, the agents in Latin America, and the controllers back in Germany so that the degree of cooperation varied from case to case. But as the war dragged on, MK-FMK survival would make personal differences increasingly irrelevant.

All the V-men sent to Latin America initially received training in the use of secret inks and special codes, but, from 1940 on, instructions in radio transmission and the microdot system became preeminent. The microdot, an ingenious invention credited to Dr. Rudolf Zapp, allowed for a photographed page to be reduced to the size of a dot, which might appear inconspicuously over the letter *i* or as a period at the end of a sentence.[23] Eight or ten dots might be hidden beneath a stamp on a letter, or attached under the flap of an envelope. By the winter of 1940, the British discovered the Germans were employing this technique and alerted their censors to carefully scrutinize letters between Latin America and Europe.[24] Eventually, scanning techniques were developed through which microdots could be more easily detected; nevertheless, the Germans continued to have great faith in them.

The quintessential mode of reportage for V-men in Chile, Argentina, and Brazil, however, became the clandestine radio transmitter. Soon after becoming Abwehr chief, Canaris realized that rapid wireless communications would shortly become indispensable. Contracts were let for a powerful but tiny transmitter-receiver; by 1938, German industry had produced the *Agentenfunk*, or *Afu* as it was generally termed. This ten to one hundred watt transreceiver had a phenomenal range and, more importantly, could fit inside a normal suitcase.[25]

The best evidence of the significance of clandestine radio reporting for the Abwehr is provided by Canaris himself. In a secret message, copies of which were supplied only to the foreign minister and the chief of the General Staff (April 25, 1940), Canaris sent precise instructions to Lt. Gen. Friedrich von Boetticher, German military attaché in Washington. The latter was told to concentrate on U.S. Army Air Force technical innovations, convoy sailings to Britain and France, and important economic developments. Boetticher was specifically ordered to avoid all activities that might smack of espionage, and not to bother with U.S. Navy or Army data. News of these developments, Canaris affirmed, was to be supplied by agents with *Afu* senders. And where were most of these agents to be found? South of the Rio Grande.[26]

One of the decisive factors influencing this decision may well have been a series of tests conducted in the fall of 1939 under Capt. Werner

Trautmann (code name: Dr. Thiele). Abwehr engineers discovered that east-west transmissions across the Atlantic were often jeopardized by sunspots, atmospheric pressures, and geomagnetic problems. In contrast, north-south transmissions (for example, between South America and Germany) proved much less troublesome.[27] Nature, in short, had shown the way. If and when the course of the war dictated the rapid expansion of espionage activity in the Western Hemisphere, Latin America would be the broadcasting and reception center for most clandestine radio communications.

V. The Abwehr's Latin American Strategy

It was not until May 1939 that the first Abwehr resident agent arrived in Latin America.[28] The timing of this event, coming barely four months before the outbreak of hostilities, demonstrates that, initially, Latin America was not high on the Abwehr's list of critical intelligence areas. Moreover, the reports sent back to Berlin by the various MKs set up in 1939 were of the same nonessential character. They dealt almost exclusively with shipments of food products and materials to Great Britain and rarely mentioned military topics.[29] So long as World War II remained primarily a European affair, reportage of this kind was about all that could be realistically expected.

The situation underwent an almost total transformation in 1940. In the spring and early summer of that year, the Wehrmacht conquered most of western Europe. The march of triumph was abruptly halted, however, when in August and September the Royal Air Force bested the Luftwaffe in the skies over southern England. Operation Sea Lion, Hitler's plan for the invasion of Britain, was shelved and, increasingly, Hilter's thoughts turned to blitzkrieg in the east. Until the Soviet Union could be subdued, the German navy's commerce raiders and U-boats would carry out the war in the west by wreaking havoc on Britain's oceanic supply lines.

It was this course of events, the increasing intervention in favor of Britain by the United States, plus the realization that the war would be a long one, which suddenly made Latin America a critical area. The U-boats needed a steady stream of ship movement information, and the German High Command wanted data concerning U.S. war production and weaponry, while the Reich itself needed certain raw materials which Latin America had in abundance. The region was to become, therefore, the soft underbelly of the United States, a safe haven for V-men smuggling vital minerals back to Germany, and a base from which others could spy on Uncle Sam and safely relay the information obtained to an *Ast* or *Nest*.[30]

Aware that this new situation required both a different outlook and tactics, Canaris sanctioned a series of psychological and technical changes in policy. In 1941, V-men in South America who were of German citizenship became eligible for reserve army officer commissions and military service awards.[31] In addition, all MKs were ordered to become

FMKs.[32] After an inauspicious beginning, the Abwehr in Latin America was finally going to become a big league operation.

Nevertheless, if Latin American republics were going to become the center for German espionage in the Western Hemisphere, the Abwehr would have other problems which could not be so easily settled. First of all, a central pool of V-men specially trained for operations in Argentina, Brazil, Mexico, and Chile did not exist, and, given the decentralized structure of the Canaris organization, it was unlikely to develop. Faced with these problems, Canaris chose an operational strategy which fitted the situation. The Abwehr would send from Europe what V-men it could, and have these train as many Latin American recruits as possible. As explained by Josef Starziczny, an FMK leader captured in 1942, the overall quality of those enlisted might not be very high, but eventually "there would be so many that it is impossible to capture them all."[33]

Given the geographical and organization problems noted, plus the need for rapid expansion caused by the changing war situation, the quantity-over-quality approach was perhaps the only one possible. Nevertheless, the Franklin D. Roosevelt administration was aware of the Abwehr build-up in Latin America and it did not intend to allow it to continue unchecked. Even more important, it had the men and the resources to, if necessary, "capture them all."

VI. Enter the Sicherheitsdienst

In 1929, Heinrich Himmler was named *Reichsführer* of the Schutzstaffel (SS), the party elite guard. Charged with the task of protecting both the Führer and other important NSDAP (Nazi party) personages from their many enemies, this former chicken farmer began the development of a special security service. The task of building the force fell to a cashiered naval officer, Reinhard Heydrich; it was this fanatical blackguard who founded the SD on July 19, 1932.

Once Hitler became chancellor (January 30, 1933), Himmler moved relentlessly to seize control of the police forces in the various German states. In his footprints followed the tireless Heydrich, who had himself named head of the secret police in Prussia that same year. Following the infamous "Night of the Long Knives" (June 30, 1934), all rival NSDAP security units were ordered merged with the SD, and the latter was reorganized as the Nazi party's intelligence and counterintelligence service.

The gradual emergence of the SD as an intelligence organization was an immense problem for the Abwehr. With the NSDAP and the German state becoming increasingly inseparable, an SD-Abwehr struggle over intelligence priorities was likely to result in an SD triumph. Canaris's first major task as organization commander was to negotiate some manner of *modus vivendi* with Heydrich and thus prevent the dreaded confrontation from taking place. In 1936, the so-called "Ten Commandments" were ratified by the two intelligence leaders. According to the terms of the agreement, the SD would concentrate its energies on political intelligence, leaving the field of military intelligence to the Abwehr.[34] But where did political intelligence end and military intelligence begin? And vice versa?

This loophole, which legitimized the SD's entrance into the business of foreign intelligence, could easily have become a noose around the Abwehr's neck, but Canaris was initially equal to the task. Rather than challenge the Himmler-Heydrich combine directly, he sought to disarm them by courting Heydrich's friendship and making a few administrative concessions. But he was ready when Heydrich decided it was time to play rough. In 1940–41, the SD chief had microphones hidden in Canaris's office and even put together a file demonstrating that the Abwehr chief was illicitly in contact with the Anglo-Americans. Heydrich had played an ace, but the Peeper was able to trump it: Heydrich apparently had Jewish ancestry, and Canaris somehow obtained evidence of it.[35] Thanks to some discreet blackmail, Heydrich was held at bay, but blunting the SD's drive for hegemony in the intelligence field would eventually prove to be a task beyond the Abwehr leader's strength.

Like the Abwehr, the SD underwent several reorganizations, the most important being that of September 27, 1939. At that time, the SD and all the German state police forces were officially merged. Created was a new umbrella organization headed by Heydrich and named the Reichs-sicherheitshauptamt (RSHA), or Reich Central Security Administration. It was divided into seven sections:

Amt I — Personnel
Amt II — Organization, administration, and legal matters
Amt III — Domestic intelligence (Deutsche Lebensgebiete)
Amt IV — Gestapo (Gegnererforschung und Gegnerbekaempfung)
Amt V — Criminal investigation (Verbrechensbekaempfung)
Amt VI — Foreign political intelligence (Ausland)
Amt VII — Ideological research and evaluation (Weltanschauliche Forschung und Auswertung)

It was Amt VI which was subsequently referred to as the Sicherheits-dienst by foreign intelligence services, and it was also the only section of the RSHA to dispatch agents to Latin America.[36] The men of Amt VI "were generally not known to the average Party member. . . . SD operatives were feared by the Gestapo with which they were . . . most closely connected. All members of the *SD* were taken into the ranks of the *SS*, and the *Amt VI* leaders abroad held an *SS* rank equivalent of Major."[37]

Amt VI was itself divided into combinations of lettered and numbered sections (see Chart II for Amt VI organizational structure). For example, VI-B originally handled the affairs of most of western Europe as well as Latin America. The head of VI-B, SS-Maj. Herman Rossner, demonstrated a real knack for selecting skilled SD operatives; it was he, and not the director of the Latin American desk (VI-B/4), SS-Lt. Ewald Geppert, who laid the foundations for SD activities in the South American republics. On June 22, 1941, Walter Schellenberg became chief of Amt VI, and two days later Rossner took command of an SS unit on the Russian front.

CHART II
R.S.H.A.
THE REICHSICHERHEITSHAUPTAMT
1939 - 1945

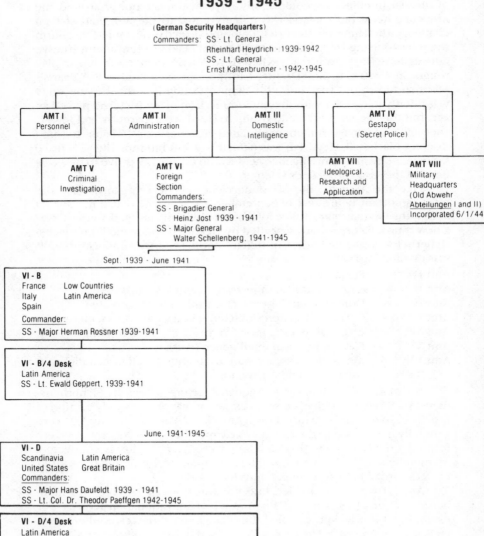

(German Security Headquarters)
<u>Commanders</u>: SS - Lt. General
Rheinhart Heydrich - 1939-1942
SS - Lt. General
Ernst Kaltenbrunner - 1942-1945

AMT I
Personnel

AMT II
Administration

AMT III
Domestic
Intelligence

AMT IV
Gestapo
(Secret Police)

AMT V
Criminal
Investigation

AMT VI
Foreign
Section
<u>Commanders</u>:
SS - Brigadier General
Heinz Jost 1939 - 1941
SS - Major General
Walter Schellenberg. 1941-1945

AMT VII
Ideological.
Research and
Application

AMT VIII
Military
Headquarters
(Old Abwehr
<u>Abteilungen</u> I and II)
Incorporated 6/1/44

Sept. 1939 - June 1941

VI - B
France   Low Countries
Italy   Latin America
Spain
<u>Commander</u>:
SS - Major Herman Rossner 1939-1941

VI - B/4 Desk
Latin America
SS - Lt. Ewald Geppert. 1939-1941

June, 1941-1945

VI - D
Scandinavia   Latin America
United States   Great Britain
<u>Commanders</u>:
SS - Major Hans Daufeldt 1939 - 1941
SS - Lt. Col. Dr. Theodor Paeffgen 1942-1945

VI - D/4 Desk
Latin America
SS - Lt. Ewald Geppert. 1941-1942
SS - Capt. Kurt Gross, 1942–1945

Note: All ranks are the highest the individual reached
during the time of service in the R.S.H.A.

In July, Latin American affairs were transferred to section VI-D under SS-Maj. Hans Daufeldt. Geppert also made the switch, but his did not prove to be particularly advantageous for either the SD or the transferee. Described by one of his subordinates as a "gangster," Geppert spoke little Spanish and had only a passing interest in the region for which he was responsible. In September 1942, Daufeldt was replaced by SS-Lt. Col. Theodor Paeffgen, who named his own VI-D/4 boss. Geppert happily moved on to VI-F (the false document and forgery section), and SS-Capt. Kurt Gross was chosen as his successor.[38]

To Paeffgen's credit, the new appointee spoke fluent Spanish and was familiar with Latin American culture. But Gross's qualifications and potential apparently blinded Paeffgen to his subordinate's cupidious instincts. Instead of building an efficient unit, Gross utilized his new appointment as a lever for obtaining fine cognac, silk stockings, and other commodities that were scarce in wartime Germany. Wags in Amt VI coined the term *Grosería* to describe the VI-D/4 chief's brazen and single-minded pursuit of prestige goods.[39] Chagrined as a result of his poor choice of section head, Paeffgen gradually took charge as sectional director, consulting Gross only when necessary.

From this recitation of administrative maneuvering and personnel misconduct, it may be deduced that Amt VI was hardly the most efficient department in the RSHA. Nor was clairvoyance its long suit, for when the war began in September 1939, there wasn't a single SD operative in all of Latin America.[40] The first to arrive was Wilhelm Hammerschmidt, press attaché for the German embassy in Chile, who reached Santiago in March 1940.[41] The key men in the SD organization for the region would be Heinz Lange and Johannes Siegfried Becker.

Lange, born in Berlin in February 1907, moved to Paraguay in 1931. An employee of Staudt y Cia. (a maritime firm), Lange remained in Asunción for eight years, returning to Germany in the summer of 1939. While the trip was made ostensibly for the purpose of visiting his friends and relatives, Lange allegedly returned carrying copies of the electrical plans for the newly constructed National Bank of Argentina in Buenos Aires. He had been expelled from the NSDAP for antiparty activity in 1928, but his arrival with the bank plans apparently earned him forgiveness. SS-Major Rossner decided that Lange was SD material and so the latter began espionage training in the fall of 1939. He returned to South America via LATI airlines (Linee Aeree Transcontentali Italiane, operated by the Italian government), reaching Rio de Janeiro on April 20, 1940. The credentials he carried established him as a representative of Hentschel de Cassel, a locomotive construction firm; his real task was to set up an SD network in Argentina.[42]

Johannes Siegfried Becker would eventually demonstrate himself to be the nonpareil among German espionage agents in the Americas. Born in Leipzig on October 21, 1912, Becker entered the army as a second lieutenant in 1933 and served honorably for several years. In 1937, he went to Buenos Aires as sales representative for Deutsche Handwerks

Gesellschaft of Berlin. The day after Great Britain declared war, Becker presented himself at the German embassy and demanded assistance in returning to the fatherland. The embassy failed to accommodate him, so on January 10, 1940, Becker stowed away aboard a Spanish vessel, the *Cuneñe*. Discovered two days later, he identified himself as Clemente Pérez, an Argentine trumpet player who was driven by the irrepressible urge to rejoin his musical colleagues allegedly performing in Madrid.

It remains uncertain whether the captain believed "Señor Pérez's" pitiable tale, but when the *Cuneñe* reached Madeira, no effort to alert the British control authorities on the island was made, an omission that helped Becker transfer unnoticed to an Italian vessel, the *Conte Grande*. After several further adventures, the stowaway reached Berlin early in April 1940. He immediately sought the reinstatement of his military commission but, again, SS-Major Rossner had different ideas. He convinced Becker that while there was no dearth of infantry lieutenants, an SD operative who could move with ease in Latin American society was of inestimable value to the Third Reich. Becker promptly transferred to the RSHA and spent seven weeks undergoing intensive espionage training. During the first week of June 1940, his instructors pronounced him ready; Rossner then named him SD chief for Latin America, with Heinz Lange as his second in command.[43]

Becker was given a broad, general assignment. He was to report on Latin American reaction to both German and British propaganda, on Anglo-American influence in the formulation of the foreign policy of the Latin American republics, and on the problems of those German commercial firms which the British had blacklisted. Military information was not an essential concern, but those bits and pieces that he came upon were neither to be ignored nor turned over to the Abwehr. Furnished with eight thousand dollars in U.S. currency, on June 8, 1940, Becker departed for Argentina via LATI airlines.[44] Thus, by mid-1940, the SD had two hastily trained agents and a press attaché gathering what was termed *political intelligence* for the entire South American continent. Hammerschmidt proved to be a timid soul, venturing into the espionage arena only long enough to recruit Eugen Hans Langer, a businessman who collected political and economic data for transmission (via diplomatic pouch) to Germany.[45] Becker and Lange, in contrast, decided that they could solve their recruitment problems in a more logical fashion; they simply invited Abwehr V-men to serve the SD as well.[46]

In the SD's organizational structure, the lines of authority were much less complicated than those of the Abwehr. Before June 1941, the order of hierarchy was Jost-Rossner-Geppert; by 1943, it was Schellenberg-Paeffgen-Gross. There were no *Asts* sending an assortment of V-men and no jurisdictional overlap. Instead, the SD appointed a single Latin American chief of espionage, a step that facilitated the rapid solution of many administrative and personnel problems. In its scope of operations, the SD also differed from the Abwehr. While the Canaris organization maintained large networks in Mexico, Chile, Argentina, and Brazil, SD activity was usually limited to southern South America.[47] SD men were told to avoid German diplomatic personnel, and not to become dependent upon assistance from German diplomatic missions, instructions which proved highly fortuitous.[48] By mid-1943, all German embassies in Latin America except Argentina had been closed, a happenstance which virtually immobilized certain Abwehr networks. But despite these unfortunate developments and increasing U.S. pressure, SD cunning and fanaticism succeeded in maintaining a German intelligence presence in the Western Hemisphere to the bitter end.

VII. Ribbentrop and Bohle: Outsiders Looking In

In addition to the Abwehr and SD, two other organizations with long tenure in Latin America were interested in entering the intelligence field. The arrogant foreign minister, Joachim von Ribbentrop, chafed at the necessity of having to depend upon the SD and Abwehr for secret information. His solution was the reinauguration on April 9, 1941, of a personal intelligence service, the Dienststelle Ribbentrop (Ribbentrop Information Station). First established in April 1934, the *Dienststelle* was an organization jointly administered by the Nazi party and the German state for the purpose of foreign affairs interpretation and propaganda. The organization led a shadow existence from March 1938 until Ribbentrop chose to revive it. Since the organization would naturally make use of diplomatic personnel, it risked crossing the thin line that separates secret diplomatic reportage from naked espionage. Andor Hencke, a durable party hack and Ribbentrop crony, was named *Dienststelle* chief. He established some operational guidelines which discouraged the cruder forms of intelligence acquisition.[49] There was, of course, no need for still another competing intelligence agency, especially one that was merely a tool intended to further the empire-building schemes of its namesake. The organization allegedly had a number of informants in Latin America, but evidence that they achieved anything is lacking.[50]

Much like Canaris, Ribbentrop's primary concern became defending his turf rather than expanding it. In particular, he was determined to see that no Abwehr or SD agents were sent abroad posing as diplomatic officers, and that the two intelligence agencies did not recruit foreign office personnel.

In an order issued March 26, 1941, Ribbentrop prohibited all employees of his ministry from doubling as Abwehr and SD agents, or aiding in espionage activities. He followed this ban with a June 19, 1941, admission that some diplomats were still secretly working for Canaris and Heydrich; as a result he specifically ordered the heads of overseas missions to report any suspected diplomat-spies.[51] Toward V-men who sought diplomatic cover, Ribbentrop proved just as obdurate. In the interest of the war effort, he might provide an individual spy with a diplomatic passport and embassy post, but only if that agent was known to the Foreign Ministry, and the head of the mission where the spy would be sent agreed to accept him.[52]

This was as far as Ribbentrop was prepared to go, but neither the Abwehr nor the SD would abide by these ground rules. The foreign minister attempted to get Hitler's support, but the Führer was apparently indifferent as to whether or not the German diplomatic corps included espionage agents. Since continued resistance might be interpreted as a failure to provide full backing for the German war effort, Ribbentrop was forced to give way. On September 11, 1941, he issued new orders allowing SD and Abwehr men to pose as diplomatic personnel, as long as they were not saboteurs.[53] Alas, even this concession was not enough, and with the Reich armies stymied on the eastern front, the time for temporizing was over. On February 13, 1942, he issued another circular which stressed the seriousness of the war situation for Germany and advised diplomatic heads of missions to cooperate with the plans and requirements of the German intelligence agencies.[54]

Ribbentrop could do nothing but accept defeat and await the time when he might exact a measure of revenge. The situation was grimly sardonic in that diplomatic personnel in Latin America had for some time been actively collaborating with German intelligence agents. In fact, had Ribbentrop known the degree of complicity of various of his charges in Brazil and Argentina, for example, he might have realized that the battle to keep his ministry "clean" had been lost before it started.[55]

The other prospective entrant into the intelligence arena was the Auslands Organisation der National Sozialistische Arbeitspartei (Auslandsorganisation or AO), which was the NSDAP outside the Third Reich. Founded in 1931 by Ernst Wilhelm Bohle, it had active branches in eight Latin American countries by 1933. Believing that these branches had intelligence-gathering potential, in 1937 Bohle ordered all *Landesgruppenleiters*, or Nazi party leaders in foreign countries, to pass on to him sensitive political and socioeconomic information about their countries of residence.[56] The United States had long considered the AO as an engine of subversion, and gradually a number of Latin American republics reached the same conclusion. In 1938, Brazil and Chile began restricting AO activities, and within four years, all the other states in the Western Hemisphere had begun arresting or deporting AO officials. These developments and the ever-tightening Anglo-American communications blockade virtually eliminated the AO as an information source.

Interrogated after the war, Bohle complained that the Nazi leadership had "never taken the AO seriously," and personally treated him with either cold contempt or untempered scorn.[57] So stark an appraisal might be judged an exercise in self-pity, but Bohle was not embroidering the facts. Like Ribbentrop, he sought to prevent the Abwehr and SD from infiltrating his organization, and, in February 1937, he wrung from Canaris an agreement not to recruit V-men from the AO's Latin American membership.[58] In Nazi Germany, however, a promise of this nature was as useful as a pledge by Count Dracula to foreswear fair necks. Even before the invasion of Poland, the Abwehr had enlisted Walter Giese (code name: Griffin), an *Ortsgruppenleiter* (city group leader) in Ecuador. Not surprisingly, neither Giese nor Canaris bothered to tell Bohle of the *Ortsgruppenleiter*'s primary shift in organizational commitment.[59]

While the Abwehr merely violated its promise, the SD seemingly preferred to rub Bohle's nose in the dirt. When Karl Arnold, *Organisationleiter* (organization leader, assistant to the *Landesgruppenleiter*) for Argentina, reached Germany in October 1940, an effort was initiated to find him a satisfactory sinecure in the AO bureaucracy. Somehow the ubiquitous SS-Maj. Hermann Rossner discovered that Arnold was in Berlin and acted posthaste. The latter was promptly named chief advisor to the SD's Amt VI/B-4 desk with Bohle being apprised of the appointment several weeks after it had been made![60] Ultimately, both the Abwehr and the SD recruited liberally from the ranks of the AO in Latin America. For Nazi zealots, service in the secret services was one of the primary methods of aiding the fatherland. Moreover, as a Nazi bureaucrat, Bohle could hardly complain about the abuse of his organization without appearing to be less than totally committed to the Reich's war effort. Like Ribbentrop, he could only hope that with the arrival of the peace that Hitler kept promising, AO fortunes in Latin America would experience a rejuvenation.

The exigencies of war and a burgeoning need for capable operatives increasingly made both the AO and the German diplomatic corps in Latin America virtual adjuncts of the Abwehr and SD. What is interesting is the degree of difference in the Abwehr and SD's treatment of the two civilian organizations. Both were circumspect in suborning diplomatic personnel. Bohle's authority was casually flouted and, ignoring his complaints, they helped themselves to his organization's membership.

VIII. Manpower, Money, and Motivation

With Hitler claiming that Aryan Germans were a master race, a question automatically arose: Would the German intelligence agencies be free to seek recruits among the miscegenated peoples of Latin America? Initially, the Abwehr accepted only *Reichsdeutschen*, fearing that the enlistment of non-Germans would cause difficulties with local governments. But once it was clear the war would be long and large numbers of agents would be needed, Canaris quietly discarded most racial and national restrictions. In addition to large numbers of *Volksdeutschen*, the Abwehr in Latin America enlisted Jews, mulattoes, and mestizos. In fact, the names of a few of these non-Aryans were even to be found on the official roster of V-men kept by controlling *Asts* and *Nests* back in Germany.[61] This is not to suggest, however, that a black man could eventually become an FMK chief; the Abwehr was willing to use non-Aryans, but only German citizens were acceptable as leaders.

Theoretically, the SD, as an elite organization and an arm of the Nazi party, should never have allowed non-Aryans to become agents. In fact, the SD's organizational scheme provided the means for resolving what might have been an embarrassing situation. Unlike the Abwehr, only the names of the agents sent to Latin America were recorded in the Amt

VI-D/4 section roster. As regional chief, Johannes Siegfried Becker had the authority to make whatever enlistment arrangements the situation required. Latin America was far away, and so long as blacks, Jews, and other "*Untermenschen*" were not listed in Germany as SD agents, the fiction of racial purity could be theoretically maintained.[62]

In availing themselves of the services of some five hundred persons,[63] the Abwehr and SD came up with a mixed assortment of recruits. Some proved earnest and resolute supporters of the Reich. Others, in contrast, had only a vague idea of what they were getting into. Predictably, perhaps, a significant minority proved to be "hot air merchants" (*Schaumschlägen*), people primarily interested in drawing a regular stipend so that they might enjoy the material pleasures they craved. American-born V-men were not, however, the only ones with an inordinate concern for tropic delights. Some of the agents trained in Germany and sent across the Atlantic as FMK leaders proved to be equally prone to temptation. Had the Germans the foresight to create an intelligence presence in Latin America prior to 1939, some effort could have been undertaken to separate the sincere from the cynics, and the capable from the incompetent. But since the regional build-up did not commence until late in 1940, the Abwehr and SD had to manage with whatever personnel they could recruit, and hope for the best.

Only in regard to financing espionage operations and providing cover identities for incoming V-men did the Germans display a spark of genius. German firms with branches in Latin America provided positions for V-men arriving from Europe, and advanced the sums needed to pay other agents and buy equipment. Aside from the symbolic loss of innocence on the part of some local executives, the companies suffered little. Receipts for the funds advanced in Latin America were sent back to corporate headquarters in Germany, and the Abwehr or SD simply reimbursed the parent firm.[64]

This clever strategy probably would have paid additional dividends if the Abwehr and SD had not spent an unconscionable amount of time battling each other. Virtually from the time Johannes Siegfried Becker reached Argentina in May 1940, the SD attempted to subvert Abwehr agents, duplicated Abwehr activities, and threatened those who made their resentment plain with disloyalty reports.[65] Even after the Reich suffered serious military reverses in 1942–43, the two German intelligence groups continued their private war despite the fact that the only real beneficiary of this internecine conflict was Anglo-American counterintelligence.

In essence, the German intelligence apparatus in Latin America was both hastily built and poorly developed. It was important chiefly because in 1940, Hitler's panzers failed to cross that ultimate antitank ditch, the English Channel. Handcuffed by its multiple deficiencies and geographical disadvantages, the prospect that this jerrybuilt complex would survive a determined Anglo-American counterintelligence campaign seemed most unlikely. But curiously enough, the Germans did have one very effective defensive weapon. No spy ring could be destroyed or rendered completely impotent unless the Latin American republic in which it operated proceeded to arrest and detain the ring membership. And, since such action might have serious internal and external repercussions, it just might not occur. This preference for procrastination was exactly what the Germans were counting on.[66]

Notes

1. This story was related by Helmuth Mügge, a Chilean citizen of German parentage, who was born on a farm near Osorno in 1908. Mügge was originally reluctant to tell us his story, but we eventually persuaded him to relate it (in Santiago, Chile, in August 1978) for publication. We also had two acquaintances in the DINA, the Chilean internal security police, check on some of the story's essentials. They subsequently informed us that they had no reason to doubt our informant's veracity.

2. On the "keiker" nickname, see Andre Brissaud, *Canaris*, English language edition (London, 1973), p. 5, and Karl-Heinz Abshagen, *Canaris* (London, 1968), p. 16, ftn. In a letter to Professor Leslie B. Rout, Jr. July 29, 1985, Kapitän zur See a.D. Herbert Wichmann questions whether the late Admiral was ever called "keiker." He argues that Canaris was nicknamed "Cica" by his crew-classmates at the Kiel Naval College. This moniker was merely a play on the family name (Canaris). Obviously, the facts about his life are still in dispute.

   On Canaris's early career and Chilean adventures, see Heinz Höhne, *Canaris: Patriot im Zwielicht* (München, 1976), pp. 24–45.

3. On Canaris's 1917–25 activities, see Brissaud, *Canaris*, pp. 6–25, *Abshagen*, pp. 17–68, and Höhne, *Canaris: Patriot im Zwielicht*, pp. 46–62.

4. On Canaris's 1925–32 activities, the best source is Höhne, *Canaris: Patriot im Zwielicht*, 62–116.

5. Slightly differing versions of how Canaris obtained the Abwehr command are found in Abshagen, *Canaris*, pp. 66–68, and Brissaud, *Canaris*, pp. 18–20.

6. On the Abwehr organization, see Gert Buchheit, *Der Deutsche Geheimdienst: Geschichte der Militarischen Abwehr* (München, 1965), pp. 106–108, 121–133, and especially, National Archives and Records Service (hereafter referred to as NARS), R.G. 165, box 982, Military Intelligence Division (hereafter referred to as MID), *Axis Espionage and Propaganda in Latin America* (Washington, D.C., 1946), pp. 24–25 (hereafter referred to as *Axis Espionage*). We are much indebted for the materials needed to construct the charts of Abwehr II to Messrs. John Taylor, George Wagner, and Robert Wolfe of the Modern Military Branch, Military Archives Division. See letter from Robert Wolfe to Prof. Leslie B. Rout, Jr., November 22, 1977.

7. The *Ast* organizational patterns and idiosyncrasies are discussed in detail in Buchheit, *Der Deutsche Geheimdienst*, pp. 112–120; David Kahn, *Hitler's Spies: German Military Intelligence in World War II* (New York, 1978), pp. 239–242; Paul Leverkuehn, *German Military Intelligence* (New York, 1954), pp. 28–32, and NARS, R.G. 165, MID, *Axis Espionage*, pp. 25–27.

8. See Buchheit, *Der Deutsche Geheimdienst*, p. 112. This was confirmed in a letter from Oscar Reile to Professor Rout, November 8, 1977. Reile is a former Abwehr officer who has written three major works on that organization's 1935–45 activities.

9. Information concerning the *Asts* and *Nests* primarily involved in Latin American operations comes from NARS, R.G. 165, MID, *Axis Espionage*, p. 25, Buchheit, *Der Deutsche Geheimdienst*, p. 121, and letter, Oscar Reile to Professor Rout, November 29, 1977. Ast Hamburg was close to the Americas, controlled a powerful radio station in the suburb of

Wohlsdorf, and was commanded by a man who had lived for some years in Latin America, Kapitän zur See a.D. Herbert Wichmann. Similarly, Nest Cologne, commanded by Lt. Col. Friedrich Rudolph (1939–41) and Lt. Col. Albrecht Focke (1941–44), controlled a large radio station at Krefeld, to which V-men from several *Asts* and *Nests* also communicated.

10. Copies of the two service attaché agreements between the German armed forces and the foreign office (2/13/33 and 9/19/35) were graciously provided by Dr. Maria Keipert of the Auswärtiges Amt (Bonn), letter 117-251.09178, December 12, 1978.

11. See Abshagen, *Canaris*, p. 74, and Leverkuehn, *German Military Intelligence*, pp. 67–68. Note that Buchheit, *Der Deutsche Geheimdienst*, p. 128, and Kahn, *Hitler's Spies*, p. 76, contradict this position.

12. Letters of September 28 and November 9, 1977, Oscar Reile to Professor Rout; former Colonel Reile mentioned that he had spoken to Kapitän zur See a.D. Wichmann and several other former Abwehr officers who did not want their names used. They all insisted that the service attachés were ordered not to engage in espionage activities. But Reile, in his prodigious study, *Geheime Westfront: Die Abwehr, 1935–45* (München, 1962), p. 327, specifically singled out Kapitän zur See Dietrich Niebühr, naval attaché to Argentina and Brazil, as chief of German intelligence in Argentina. We pointed out Herr Reile's contradictory views, and he replied in the November 9, 1977, letter that he had come to doubt the accuracy of the conclusion stated in *Geheime Westfront*. He did admit, however, that during the course of the war, some attachés may have violated the no-espionage order.

13. NARS, R.G. 59, microcopy 679, *Special Interrogation Mission to Germany, 1945–46* (Poole Mission), *Interrogation of General Erwin Lahousen*, box 2.

14. Leverkuehn, *German Military Intelligence*, p. 30.

15. Among those favorable biographers have been Abshagen, *Canaris*, Brissaud, *Canaris*, and Höhne, *Canaris: Patriot im Zwielicht*. In addition to a number of former Abwehr officers we interviewed, but who did not wish to be quoted, we have a letter to Professor Rout from Oscar Reile, November 1, 1978, which effectively summarizes what the others said: "I can say that all officers of the Abwehr . . . who got to know Canaris well, knew him as a man who knew his business, and as a human person."

16. Karl Dönitz, *Memoirs: Ten Years and Twenty Days*, 3d ed. (Cleveland, 1959), pp. 277 and 301.

17. Kahn, *Hitler's Spies*, pp. 230–231, 235–236.

18. U.S. Department of the Navy, Navy Historical Center, Washington Naval Yard, Washington, D.C. OP-29, Serial 169-C-48, Kapitän zur See Kurt Friewald, "Character Sketch of ex-Admiral Canaris," *Essays by German Officers and Officials* (n.d.), p. 4.

19. NARS, R.G. 165, AC of S, G-2 Intelligence Division, Enemy POW Information (MIS-Y) HRUSAIC IR #6, *Report on the Interrogation of Oberstleutnant Wilhelm Kuebart, 3 June 1945*, p. 3. Kuebart is listed in this revealing report as the "most efficient officer in the Abwehr," p. 1.

20. On Canaris's pessimism regarding Germany and the possibility of the Third Reich winning the war, see Abshagen, *Canaris*, p. 91, Friewald, "Character Sketch . . .," p. 6, *Report on the Interrogation of Oberstleutnant Wilhelm Kuebart*, p. 5, and Kahn, *Hitler's Spies*, p. 230. Concerning Canaris's problems and his mental turmoil, Lieutenant Colonel Kuebart is particularly informative. By 1943, ". . . although he was only in his early fifties, he [Canaris] gave the impression of being prematurely aged, broken in mind and spirit by years of constant struggle against the Foreign Office and army bureaucracy, and particularly the SD." See *Report on the Interrogation of Oberstleutnant Wilhelm Kuebart*, p. 4.

21. Ibid., p. 5. Kuebart is emphatic on this point. The same idea is implied in Kahn, *Hitler's Spies*, pp. 234–236.

22. On this general classification method and principle, see NARS, R.G. 319, United States Department of Justice, Federal Bureau of Investigation, *German Espionage in Latin America* (Washington, D.C., 1946), p. 15 (this monograph will hereafter be referred to as NARS, R.G. 319, *GELA*), and NARS, R.G. 242, ML 170 (microfilm), roll 22, *Nebenstellen Bremen— German Report Center (MK) in Argentina from 12 September 1940 to 16 February 1942*.

23. We wish to thank Morris G. Moses, a resident of Albany, New York, who in a letter of December 12, 1983, provided conclusive evidence that "Rudolf Zapp," a scientist who had German intelligence affiliations, was the primary inventor of the microdot system.

24. Accounts of how the British discovered the microdot system are found in Dusko Popov, *Spy/Counterspy* (New York, 1974) pp. 146–148, and William Stevenson, *A Man Called Intrepid: The Secret War* (New York, 1975) pp. 183–185. The chief of Ast Hamburg 1939–1945 was Kapitän zur See a.D. Herbert Wichmann. In a letter dated March 15, 1983, he related that an Ast Hamburg agent sent a letter from Latin America to Lisbon, and on the envelope he wrote "P.S. Look for the stamps." The British mail censors in Bermuda intercepted the letter, gave it a microscopic inspection, and stumbled onto the microdots hidden under the postage stamp. Wichmann's sardonic comment was, "Such is life."

25. The most detailed presentation of an *Afu* and how it was developed is found in Buchheit, *Der Deutsche Geheimdienst*, p. 121, and Höhne, *Canaris: Patriot im Zwielicht*, p. 201. A photo of an *Afu* is found in Kahn, *Hitler's Spies*, following p. 498.

26. German Federal Republic, Bundesarchiv-Militärarchiv, Freiburg-im-Breisgau, *Bestand: OKW/Amtsgruppe Auslandsnachrichten und Abwehr*, RW5/V.-118, Abw. I, NR. 24/40, p. 1.

27. This peculiar radio transmission situation is hinted at in a work graciously supplied to us by Dr. Elpídio Reali, a retired inspector with the Brazilian political police (DOPS). See Dr. Elpídio Reali, Superintêndencia de Segurança, Política e Social de São Paulo, *A rede de espionagem nacista chefiada por Niels Christian Christiansen* (São Paulo, 1943), p. 13. The details were provided in a letter from Oscar Reile to Professor Rout, November 20, 1978.

28. República de Chile, Dirección General de Investigaciones e Identificación, *Informe sobre actividades Nazis en Chile*, Tomo I (volumes are irregularly marked), pp. 13–15. Schulz-Hausmann arrived in Chile in May 1935. He went to Germany in 1938, and returned to Chile in May 1939. It was at that time that he began working for the Abwehr.

29. See NARS, R.G. 242, ML-171a, roll 23, B.-Nr. 1243/40, *I-Wi* g, n.p.; B. Nr. 2297/41, *I-M* g, 15.10; and Ast Hamburg B.-Nr. 230/41, *I-M* geb, n.p.

30. This is precisely the idea suggested in German Federal Republic, Bundesarchiv-Militärarchiv, Freiburg-im-Breisgau, *Bestand*: RW5/V.-118, p. 2. Evidence that the United States was particularly concerned about German infiltration in Latin America, and considered the Hispanic republics as a weak spot in their defense, can be seen in Mark Watson, *United States in World War II. Chief of Staff: Prewar Plans and Preparations* (Washington, D.C., 1950), pp. 95–96, and NARS, R.G. 319, *GELA*, p. 22.

31. See U.S. Department of the Navy, Naval Historical Center, Washington Naval Yard, Washington, D.C., *Files of the German Naval Staff, German Naval Attaché in Argentina* (microfilm) T-67-32010 (1), Document 182/141 (no frame number). This was a general order meant for other countries besides Argentina.

32. Orders to this effect are noted in NARS, R.G. 59, 862.20210/2439, pp. 27–28, and R.G. 319, *GELA*, p. 71. See also letter from Oscar Reile to Professor Rout, January 18, 1978.

33. See NARS, R.G. 59, 862.20210/2155, p. 1.

34. For the details of the "Ten Commandments," see Brissaud, *Canaris*, pp. 21–25.

35. The Heydrich-Canaris battle as noted here is taken from Anthony Cave Brown, *Bodyguard of Lies* (New York, 1975), pp. 157–158.

36. See NARS, R.G. 319, *GELA*, p. 20.

37. NARS, R.G. 165, box 982, MID, *German Espionage*, p. 44.

38. For the commentary on Geppert, Rossner, Paeffgen, and Gross, see German Federal Republic, Institut für Zeitgeschichte, München (Bavaria), NG-4871, *Interrogation Report of Karl Gustav Arnold*, November 20, 1946 (hereafter referred to as *Interrogation Report of Karl Gustav Arnold*), pp. 10–12.

39. Ibid., p. 13.

40. Ibid., p. 10. The Führer had indicated to Himmler and Heydrich that he wanted no agents sent to the Western Hemisphere by the SD, as he wanted nothing to interfere with German-U.S. relations.

41. On Hammerschmidt's Chilean activities, see NARS, R.G. 59, 862.20210/4-1345, p. 15, and R.G. 319, *GELA*, p. 134.

42. The story of Heinz Lange's recruitment by the SD is elaborated on in NARS, R.G. 59, 862.20210/6-1745, pp. 1–4, and *Interrogation Report of Karl Gustav Arnold*, pp. 10–11.

43. For the adventures of Johannes Siegfried Becker and his emergence as an SD agent, see NARS, R.G. 84, box 5633, 820.02 General, *Memorandum of Legal Attaché Regarding Johannes Siegfried Becker, April 18, 1946*, pp. 3–7.

44. Ibid., p. 7.

45. NARS, R.G. 319, *GELA*, pp. 134–135.

46. On SD recruitment of Abwehr aides, see NARS, R.G. 165, box 982, MID, *Axis Espionage*, pp. 48–49.

47. The SD commenced Western Hemispheric operations too late to have established networks in places like Mexico or Central America. See ibid., pp. 47–50.

48. Ibid., pp. 45–46.

49. See Kahn, *Hitler's Spies*, p. 71.

50. The only *Dienststelle* official known to be implicated in espionage was Dr. Erwin Wolf, a diplomat assigned to the German embassy in Chile. In fact, Wolf also was working for the SD, a situation of which Ribbentrop was probably ignorant. See NARS, R.G. 59, 862.20210/9-346, p. 8, and 862.20210/11-2246, pp. 13–14.

51. A copy of the March 26, 1941, order was forwarded to us by the redoubtable Maria Keipert of the Auswärtiges Amt (Bonn) German Federal Republic. This document (MBD–59) was forwarded in a letter dated December 12, 1978, 117-251.09178. The June 19, 1941, order is from NARS, *Documents Selected from German Foreign Office Records* (hereafter referred to as *DSGFOR*), T-120 series, roll 366, frames 291268 and 291269.

52. NARS, *DSGFOR*, T-120 series, roll 366, frame 291266.

53. Ibid.

54. Ibid., frames 291272–291274.

55. NARS, R.G. 319, *GELA*, pp. 39–40, 92, 134, and NARS, R.G. 165, box 982, *Axis Espionage*, pp. 24–25.

56. Concerning the AO in Latin America, the best source is NARS, R.G. 84, box 533, 820.02, *Interrogation of Ernst Wilhelm Bohle*, October 4, 1945, pp. 3–10 and 21–24. On the specific order for *Landesgruppenleiters* to supply political and economic information, see NARS, R.G. 165, box 707, G-2, WD-General Staff, SAIC/FIR/10, HTUSAIC, *Interrogation of Ernst Wilhelm Bohle*, July 26–27, 1945, p. 4.

57. NARS, R.G. 59, microcopy 679, *Records of the Department of State, Special Interrogation Mission to Germany, 1945–46* (Poole Mission), box 1, frame 011.

58. NARS, R.G. 84, box 533, 820.02, *Interrogation of Ernst Wilhelm Bohle*, October 4, 1945, pp. 45–46.

59. On Walter Giese, see NARS, R.G. 238, BDIC Pir-R, box 3, *Interrogation of Walter Giese*, September 12, 1945, pp. 1–2.

60. *Interrogation of Karl Gustav Arnold*, pp. 9–10. The best work on the AO in English is Donald M. McKale, *The Swastika Outside Germany* (Kent, Ohio, 1977).

61. Letter from Kapitän zur See a.D. Herbert Wichmann to Professor Rout, December 28, 1981. The former leader of Ast Hamburg admitted that many subagents and collaborators used by the Abwehr were certainly not Aryans.

62. See NARS, R.G. 165, G-2 Intelligence Division, Latin American Branch, Geographic Subject File, 1945–46, *German Espionage Organization—Argentina—Johannes Siegfried Becker, January 18, 1946*, pp. 11–12.

63. See NARS, R.G. 319, FBI, *GELA*, preface. The number of Axis agents identified between July 1, 1940, and December 31, 1945, was given as 832. What is not clear is how many of these persons were considered Abwehr or SD agents. On the basis of the number of persons arrested in Chile, Brazil, Argentina, and Mexico (see chapters on these countries and Appendixes B, C, and D), we arrived at a figure of roughly 500 agents.

64. See NARS, R.G. 59, 862.20210/7-745, pp. 1–10. See also NARS, R.G. 165, box 982, MID, *Axis Espionage*, pp. 24–25.

65. See in particular, NARS, R.G. 59, 862.20210/9-346, p. 8, and 862.20210/11-2246, p. 13. The basis for some of the difficulty is well explicated in NARS, R.G. 165, box 982, *Axis Espionage*, p. 46.

66. U.S. Department of the Navy, Navy Historical Center, Washington Naval Yard, Administrative Office, *Files of the German Naval Staff, German Naval Attaché in Brazil*, T-65, PG/32004, p. 187. The Germans believed that since the Latin American countries had no laws governing peacetime secret intelligence activities, months would pass before such laws would be passed, or used to prosecute those arrested. Secondly, since the espionage activities were primarily directed against the United States and Great Britain, a clever defense attorney might argue that the Latin American state was, in effect, prosecuting its own citizens for acts committed against the Anglo-American imperialists.

2

The United States Prepares: 1936–41

I. FDR Sees a Hemispheric Threat

The Chaco War, fought between Paraguay and Bolivia, began in July 1932 and resulted in one hundred thousand deaths before a cease-fire took effect on June 14, 1935. Argentina, Brazil, Chile, Peru, Uruguay, and the United States acted as mediators when the Chaco Peace Conference opened in Buenos Aires on July 1, 1935. Almost no progress had been achieved when, on December 1, 1936, Franklin D. Roosevelt was wheeled into a room where Argentine president Agustín P. Justo and the Paraguayan and Bolivian delegation chiefs awaited. (President Roosevelt was in Buenos Aires for the Inter-American Conference for the Maintenance of Peace.) After an exchange of pleasantries, he went straight to the point: The former belligerents were wasting too much time haggling over peace terms. Roosevelt saw a general European imbroglio in the offing and believed that the United States might possibly be drawn into it. A festering conflict such as the Chaco dispute might easily be exploited by the Axis, thereby diverting U.S. energies and interests away from the European theater. As a result, hemispheric questions had to be settled as definitively and expeditiously as possible.[1]

Roosevelt's reference to a possible European conflict, and his inference of possible U.S. involvement in a transatlantic struggle, took the assembled VIPs by surprise. In a letter of January 30, 1936, to the twenty other chiefs of state, FDR had suggested calling a conference to devise means to prevent threats to hemispheric peace like the Chaco War. But now that the conference had convened, there was to be a conspicuous shift of subject. The Chaco controversy was now reduced to the status of a useful tool which Secretary of State Cordell Hull might utilize in demanding the formulation of "a common attitude toward the danger rising in Europe."[2] In addressing the assembled delegates on December 2,

FDR echoed the same theme: "We in the Americas . . . stand shoulder to shoulder in our final determination that others driven by madness or land hunger, might seek to commit acts of aggression against us, will find a hemisphere wholly prepared to consult for our mutual safety. . . ."[3]

Washington's strategy was to get the Latin American republics to line up behind Uncle Sam and adopt a uniform policy if a European conflagration should take place. The key policy initiative was a proposal under which the Latins would accept the principle of compulsory consultation in case of an attack by an outside power on an American republic. Cordell Hull had dreams of carrying a large majority of the delegates with him, but Carlos Saavedra Lamas, foreign minister of Argentina, had other ideas. Certainly, he had no intention of allowing hemispheric solidarity to be equated with opposition to certain European powers, namely, Germany and Italy. Furthermore, Saavedra Lamas suspected that in the case of a European conflict, the United States might be nominally neutral, but not nonaligned.[4] He therefore let it be known that he could not support Hull's proposal.

In an effort to effect some meaningful compromise, Hull had several private meetings with Saavedra Lamas, but despite some heated exchanges, the Argentine refused to become more accommodating.[5] Faced with the prospect of forcing through a resolution which the host nation would strenuously oppose, Cordell Hull grudgingly retreated. When he departed Buenos Aires on December 23, he possessed only an innocuous pledge calling for "voluntary consultation" in case of an assault by a nonhemispheric power upon one of the American republics.[6]

Despite this setback, the United States again adopted an aggressive stance at the Eighth Pan-American Conference in Lima, Peru (December 9–27, 1938). Its delegation lobbied diligently to have the conferees accept a resolution which stipulated that continental solidarity demanded unity of action in the face of "intervention in the hemisphere by a non-American state." But once again, unrelenting Argentine opposition left the United States with the choice of forcing an ugly and divisive test of strength, or accepting another eviscerated statement of principle. Washington opted for discretion, and while the Declaration of Lima was widely touted as a major advance in common policy, all it really did was to bind the American republics to convene a foreign ministers' meeting if the peace of the hemisphere were "manifestly threatened."[7]

The Roosevelt administration would continue to seek to convince the Latin American republics of the necessity of taking stronger collective actions, and after hostilities commenced in Europe, some success in these endeavors would be attained. At the same time, the security of the United States required that stronger, more specific measures be undertaken in order to counter the possible moves of those unnamed non-American states. As early as 1936, U.S. military and naval planners had concluded that the most likely route for an attack against the United States would be via South America.[8] The distance from Dakar, Senegal, across the South

Atlantic Narrows to Natal, Brazil, is only about nineteen hundred miles, and by 1937, both Air France and Lufthansa were conducting regular airmail flights along this route.[9] U.S. naval and military planners feared a surprise German air or seaborne invasion across the narrows that could result in the establishment of bases in northeastern Brazil; subsequent attacks might then be launched against the Panama Canal or even the southern United States.[10] How exactly the Germans would first reach and then seize northeastern Brazil was problematical, but in a worst case scenario, the potential danger was deemed so grave that its likelihood had to be dealt with.

With this possibility in mind, the 1939 Atlantic Fleet exercise was an attempt to thwart a German invasion fleet bent upon assisting pro-German elements that had taken control in northeastern Brazil.[11] This test of naval capability demonstrated that the Atlantic fleet would face awesome problems if the Germans were ever in a position to launch such an attack.[12] Nevertheless, the Joint Board, the primary planning and coordinating body of the army and navy prior to the 1942 creation of the Joint Chiefs of Staff, drew up Rainbow I, a plan calling for the defense of Latin America as far south as latitude ten degrees (roughly one hundred miles south of Recife, Brazil). Franklin Roosevelt approved it in October 1939.[13] Finally, in May 1940, when Hitler's legions were sweeping across the Benelux nations and northern France, British intelligence passed on to Washington a report that German troops were headed for Dakar. This unit was to proceed to northeastern Brazil, and would act as the vanguard for a larger force that would subsequently be flown across the South Atlantic Narrows.[14]

Perhaps the fact that the Germans were smashing the Anglo-French armies so easily was the reason this report was taken at face value. In any case, FDR demanded immediate action, and in forty-eight hours (May 25–27, 1940), U.S. Army and Navy strategists concocted Operation Pot of Gold, a plan to disembark 110,000 U.S. troops in the threatened area. Certainly this plan was indisputable proof that the United States believed that the defense of northeastern Brazil was essential to its own security. Nevertheless, the Brazilians were consulted about neither Rainbow I nor Pot of Gold, and without their collaboration, these plans could easily have failed.[15] Furthermore, U.S. military and naval planners lacked the men, supplies, and transport to execute either plan and did not know when these would become available.[16] In retrospect, the United States was fortunate that the Royal Air Force stymied the German Luftwaffe in the skies over England during the summer of 1940. So long as that nation continued to resist and the English navy controlled the Atlantic sea lanes, it was never necessary to attempt to execute the highly questionable defense schemes just described.

Except for a short period in the summer of 1940 when Pot of Gold seemed necessary, FDR was never fully convinced that Hitler planned a direct assault on the Americas.[17] In his opinion, Hitler would use indirect and much more insidious means to win support and bases in the Western Hemisphere. Moreover, events taking place in Latin America seemed to support this view. For example, on May 24, 1938, a few scatterbrained swashbucklers among the crypto-Fascist Integralistas or "Greenshirts" unsuccessfully attempted to depose the Brazilian dictator, Getúlio Vargas. Then on September 3, the Nacistas or "Blueshirts," a homegrown Chilean nationalist group, failed in their attempt to seize the capital city, Santiago. There never has been conclusive evidence that the Third Reich either backed or instigated these uprisings, but Roosevelt certainly suspected such collusion.[18]

These two incidents are significant because they were precisely the type of covert or fifth column attacks that the president expected Hitler to opt for. The great fear was that Nazi elements, such as the AO, in conjunction with local pro-Fascist groups, would seize power in some Latin American state. The Nazis could then use that country as a sanctuary for Abwehr and SD agents, as a base for preparing and launching intelligence and sabotage missions, and as a springboard for campaigns of subversion against other republics.[19]

Roosevelt's concern was heightened by his conviction that an indirect, covert scheme of attack would make it difficult for the Latin American states to agree on a common course of action.[20] Moreover, if the United States took unilateral steps against a pro-Nazi state, fears of Yankee imperialism might be rekindled, thereby making Latin American cooperation harder to obtain in the future. FDR's solution to this conundrum was to fight secrecy with secrecy. In other words, the United States would make its own confidential arrangements with willing Latin American states so that the proper actions could be taken without too many troublesome questions being asked either north or south of the Rio Grande.

The first series of covert arrangements were consummated in 1939 when the United States, Pan American Airways, and the Republic of Colombia quietly removed the German management and personnel from the direction and operation of Sociedad Colombiano-Alemana de Transportes Aéreos (SCADTA).[21] Maj. Gen. David Stone, chief of the Panama Canal Zone Military District, provided the most cogent rationale for this joint intrigue when he wrote that "it is by no means unthinkable that some daredevil German Reserve Officers flying SCADTA planes would jump the gun and attempt some heroic act as damage to the Panama Canal."[22]

During the next two years, with the connivance of the governments of Ecuador, Bolivia, and Chile, the United States halted the operation of other German-controlled airlines in western South America.[23] As these organizations terminated their services, into the breach stepped Pan American and its affiliates, taking over the air routes and consolidating its position as the primary international carrier in that region.[24] Rarely have U.S. security interests and business opportunity so perfectly coalesced and, at the same time, engendered so little complaint from Latin Americans.

Air route security was important, but the most significant U.S.-Latin American scheme to counter Axis covert action began in June 1940. A small group of army and navy officers was secretly sent to nineteen Latin American republics to negotiate bilateral agreements for the defense of the Western Hemisphere.[25] In the talks that followed, the Latin Americans took the position that what they desperately required was modern weapons and technical assistance. U.S. representatives intimated that they could comply with these requests, but only if certain commitments were made in return. The United States wanted air bases in some countries, and naval and seaplane bases in others, but certain basic requirements were to be fulfilled by all. The Latin American republics would have to (1) organize or strengthen those agencies intended to combat espionage and sabotage, (2) maintain effective surveillance over suspected German agents, and (3) exchange on a prompt and regular basis with the United States all intelligence data relating to hemispheric defense.[26]

The initial series of negotiations was completed by October 28, 1940. The Latin American states were understandably cautious about entering into bilateral defense pacts until they had received more substantive assurances concerning the amount of arms they would receive. Some concerns were alleviated, however, in March 1941, when the passage of the Lend-Lease Act relieved the dollar-poor Hispanic Americans of the necessity of paying cash for the weapons received. Nevertheless, as of December 7, 1941, only Brazil, Bolivia, Nicaragua, Cuba, Paraguay, Haiti, and the Dominican Republic had concerted mutual assistance and cooperation agreements with the United States.[27] This failure to comply with U.S. plans was crucial, because without the full cooperation of all the Latin American nations, an effective hemispheric defense could never be mounted.

From December 1936 on, the Franklin D. Roosevelt administration strove earnestly to line up the Latin American republics and have them support Washington's ideas on hemispheric security. The success achieved was mixed, but in assessing the value of the agreements, several considerations seem paramount. U.S. Army and Navy planners considered the Latin American armed forces to be generally useless for anything except maintaining internal order.[28] The assorted bilateral defense agreements were of value chiefly in that they provided the United States naval and air base rights which would be indispensable in countering a potential German attack. Given these conclusions, the principal task of the Latin American republics, aside from supplying raw materials, became the combating of German espionage, sabotage, and subversive activities in their own countries. Washington had insisted on and received commitments in this regard in the Lend-Lease agreements, but whether the Latin Americans possessed either the ability or determination to perform these tasks adequately was uncertain at best.

FDR clearly wanted to believe that the security forces in the republics of South and Central America could track down and capture the V-men Hitler was sending to the Americas. But just in case, he was going to see to it that the Latin Americans would receive U.S. help in carrying out these tasks—whether they wanted it or not.

II. The State Department and Hemispheric Security

As early as October 10, 1937, Undersecretary of State Sumner Welles had called upon U.S. ambassadors and ministers in the American republics to submit special reports on the "subversive activities of non-American states."[29] The more pertinent replies were collated with other materials and presented in a study by Sheldon Chapin in February 1938. Chapin argued that since most of the republics of the hemisphere were only nominally democratic, the continued emergence of strongmen and nationalist dictators should be viewed with equanimity. Fascism in Latin America, in his view, "would be merely a new cloak for traditional Latin American personalist dictatorship." While the spread of totalitarianism might be dangerous for pan-American unity, he believed the goal of the Nazis in this hemisphere was the acquisition of "sufficient sympathy to assure, in the case of a European war, the benevolent neutrality of these Republics. . . ."[30]

Chapin's conclusions gained credence because they dovetailed neatly with those of the U.S. Army's Military Intelligence Division (MID). In 1937, Lt. Col. C.M. Bushbee had been ordered to undertake a major investigation of Axis intentions and covert capabilities in the Western Hemisphere. Bushbee had found that, although the activities of non-American nations were on the increase, there was no cause for alarm.[31] The overall message of the two reports was clear: the Nazi threat was not immediate.

Unfortunately, neither document succeeded in creating a prewar State Department consensus on the gravity of the Nazi hemispheric menace. Laurence Duggan, State Department special advisor for Latin American affairs, believed that segments of the U.S. press and some businessmen were exaggerating the Nazi threat in order to further their own special interests.[32] In contrast, George Messersmith, then an assistant secretary of state, was convinced that the Nazis had very definite plans for hemispheric conquest, and that only strong U.S. counteraction could possibly deter them.[33] In Sumner Welles's view, the Nazis planned clandestine meddling in Brazil, but an invasion would occur only after a successful coup.[34] But Adolf Berle, an assistant secretary of state, was principally concerned with the clamor that would arise in Latin America if the United States deployed military force to counter anything other than a full-fledged Nazi invasion.[35]

This diversity of opinion among U.S. policy makers precluded a serious attempt to formulate any hemispheric plans for the containment of covert Nazi activity. It was not until the Havana foreign ministers' meeting in July 1940, that the American republics formally pledged "to suppress activities directed, assisted, or abetted by foreign governments ... which tend to subvert the domestic institutions or to foment disorder in the internal political life of the Americas...."[36] Brave words, indeed, but the Latin American states did little to implement them, and the State Department still seemed unable to establish a concrete position regarding the degree and nature of the Nazi threat. Not until the appearance of *German Inroads and Plans in the Other American Republics* (September 10, 1940) would this shortcoming be remedied.

The genesis of this document was a strongly worded memorandum written by Adolf Berle on May 14, 1940. He had complained that no arrangements with the Latin American republics had been cemented regarding the "handling of 'fifth column' or other similar penetrations," and urged that something be done quickly to determine the extent of this menace.[37] *German Inroads and Plans* concluded that the nations of the hemisphere were threatened by German economic penetration, espionage, and AO-sponsored efforts "either to support a possible pro-Nazi government ... [or] to encourage revolutions which would emphasize the might ... of Germans everywhere." Overt attack by the Nazis was not even discussed, solid evidence that the State Department did not consider any Latin American invasion scenario a probability. Instead, the study stressed that the seizure of power by indirect means was the principal Nazi plan of attack.[38]

Most curious was the marshaling of evidence to prove that Berlin was conniving with Latin American nationalists to foster pro-Nazi seizures of power. The document focused on a couple of alleged plots, but grudgingly admitted that plans for Latin American takeovers by Germany were "most difficult to uncover."[39] Equally revealing was the implicit supposition that the Nazis would enjoy easy pickings among the Spanish- and Portuguese-speaking republics. U.S. officialdom was more than a little dubious concerning the competency of the Latin Americans to deal with a covert Nazi menace. Certainly, many of the states were hardly paragons of political stability, but the pessimism evinced here was hardly justified.

The growing U.S. fear concerning covert action was clearly evident in a subsequent State Department document written by Adolf Berle entitled, *The Pattern of Nazi Organization and Their Activities in the Other American Republics* (February 6, 1941). This work labeled various German groups as subversive, and specifically indicted German commercial firms as disseminators of anti-U.S. propaganda. In fact, Berle went so far as to assert that "virtually all the *Reichsdeutschen* in Latin America are sincere supporters of the Nazi regime."[40]

To what extent was Berle justified in making these sweeping condemnations? One way of answering the question is to compare AO membership with the total number of *Reichsdeutschen* in Argentina, Brazil, Chile, and Mexico. One conclusion is obvious: only rabid anti-Nazis could have totally accepted Berle's controversial judgments. The assistant secretary's sole justification seems to be that AO members exercised an inordinate amount of influence in some German communities, particularly those in Argentina. For example, in 1941, 64,319 *Volks-* and *Reichsdeutschen* belonged to the federation of German clubs spread throughout that country. But, of some 2,300 directors, club chairmen, presidents, and so forth, 1,261, or 59 percent, were AO members.[42]

A Comparison Of AO Membership and the Number of *Reichsdeutschen* in Argentina, Brazil, Chile, and Mexico[41]

U.S. Sources

Country	Date	Total Reichsdeutschen	Total AO Membership	Percentage
Argentina	1940	42,051	2,313	5.5
Brazil	1938	100,000	3,632	3.6
Chile	1938	20,000	1,311	6.5
Mexico	1940	5,761	215	3.7

German Source

Country	Date	Total Reichsdeutschen	Total AO Membership	Percentage
Argentina	1940	42,600	1,500	3.5
Brazil	1938	75,000	2,903	3.9
Chile	1938	20,000	985	4.9
Mexico	1940	5,500	310	5.6

The bases for Berle's inaccurate commentary would seem to lie in the policies and attitudes of the Roosevelt administration. Like the president and other governmental figures, Berle believed the defeat of Nazi Germany to be essential for the salvation of western civilization.[43] He was correct, but this should not blind anyone to the insidious nature of the program Berle promptly launched. *Patterns of Nazi Organization* was coded as strictly confidential and rushed to all Latin American embassies. In the document, Berle called upon ambassadorial and consular officers to commence supplying information on AO membership, AO activities, German commercial firms, suspicious Germans, and suspected acts of subversion.[44]

What he received must have given him pause; dispatches rained down upon Washington, aptly demonstrating that some diplomats were entranced with the prospect of demonstrating to the bosses both their ability to ferret out secret information and their anti-Axis sensibilities.

From Cuba, for example, came the names of school teachers, students, and a sixty-year-old unemployed mulatto, all of whom were dubbed "persons believed to hold pro-German sympathies."[45] Much more nefarious were thick dossiers sent from Mexico implicating both suspected Latins and North Americans. Among those fingered was the prominent pianist, José Iturbi, who performed for many years in U.S. café society. Señor Iturbi would probably have been amazed to learn that he was "a principal agent for Germany in Latin America."[46] Had this misinformation been publicly circulated, not only would the musician's career have been ruined, but he would have found it difficult to clear himself because the source of the accusation was not revealed in the report.

A good deal more elaborate, but not necessarily more accurate, were flow charts of Nazi party membership and espionage activities prepared in response to Berle's order. A cleverly constructed document dispatched from Argentina named Gottfried Brant as *Oberstgauleiter* (chief of *Landesgruppenleiters*) for all Latin America and Walter Wilkening as head of espionage and counterespionage for the Gestapo.[47] A similar presentation from Caracas named one C.A. Hoffmann as the chief of some thirty-four Nazi spies in Venezuela.[48] All the information just cited was wholly incorrect,[49] as was a great deal of the data dispatched in response to *Patterns of Nazi Organizations*. Perhaps the only positive development emerging from this exercise in guesswork, insinuation, and key-hole-peeping was that it may have convinced some diplomatic personnel that they, too, were playing a critical role in combating Nazi subversion. But Ambassadors Jefferson Caffery in Brazil and Spruille Braden in Colombia saw through the vapidness of Berle's project and decided that they ought to create their own intelligence organizations. Sumner Welles, however, was reluctant to have the chief U.S. representatives in Brazil and Colombia doubling as spymasters. Caffery and Braden were informed in unequivocal terms that they had better give up their cloak-and-dagger dreams.[50]

Admittedly, some U.S. diplomatic personnel certainly had the talent to operate effectively in the twilight world of espionage, but the primary mission of the diplomatic corps was the effective representation of official U.S. interests abroad. Let a few chargés get caught spying in Latin America and the probable loss of moral credibility would make the execution of the primary mission more difficult. Ultimately, the game was not worth the potential problems. But if the diplomats were expected to eschew clandestine intelligence work in Latin America, another organization would have to perform this task. Indeed, as Welles must have known, there was one organizational leader who had already claimed the job.

III. SIS: Genesis

The origin of U.S. secret intelligence in Latin America during World War II is found in a June 26, 1939, directive by Franklin D. Roosevelt, which stipulated that "all espionage, counter-espionage and sabotage matters" be handled by the FBI, MID, and Office of Naval Intelligence (ONI). The leaders of these organizations—J. Edgar Hoover, Brig. Gen. Sherman Miles, and Rear Adm. Walter S. Anderson, respectively—were ordered to create a special group to arrange for the coordination and delimitation of all U.S. intelligence activity.[51]

Not until September 1939 did the new group (usually referred to as the Joint Intelligence Committee or the Interdepartmental Intelligence Committee) meet under the supervision of Assistant Secretary of State George S. Messersmith. With skilled infighters such as Hoover and Miles determined to expand their bureaucratic empires, the achievement of a meaningful delimitation of authority agreement was problematical at best.[52] Messersmith struggled mightily to reach such an agreement. But when it became known that he was shortly to become ambassador to Cuba (which he did in February 1940), Hoover, Miles, and Anderson ceased attending the committee meetings. Instead, they sent their deputies, who spent pleasant afternoons discussing Jewish radicals, labor leaders, Communists, and mutually despised bureaucrats.[53]

Again, it was the success of the German spring offensive of 1940 which shattered the collegial lethargy the committee had fallen into. On May 21, 1940, General Miles attended his first meeting in six months and stated that a German victory in Europe presaged increased espionage activity in the Western Hemisphere. He insisted that a strict line of demarcation governing FBI, ONI, and MID activities must be swiftly drawn up. But Edward Tamm, Hoover's representative, detonated a verbal hand grenade by coolly announcing that the FBI was already considering the dispatch of undercover agents for operations in Cuba, Mexico, and Colombia.[54]

Neither objection nor approval was recorded regarding the FBI's prospective sally into the world of foreign espionage, but the next intelligence committee meeting (May 31, 1940) was the first since December 1939 at which Miles, Hoover, and Anderson were all present. Representing the Department of State was Adolf Berle, who had suggested to Sumner Welles on May 14, 1940, that the deterioration of the Anglo-French position in Europe necessitated the creation of an intelligence agency for action in Latin America.[55] At the outset of the meeting, General Miles introduced his plan for delimitation of authority between the FBI, ONI, and MID. The draft proposal gave the FBI responsibility for "all investigations of subversive activities directed by foreign countries, except in Panama and the Canal Zone," but established special priority rights for naval and military attachés. Hoover listened to Miles's proposal, and then revealed his cards. "Until a comparatively short time ago" he said, the FBI had abstained from foreign intelligence activity. Now, "upon the instructions of the President, the Bureau was arranging to detail men to Mexico City and Havana, but that this was the limit of the Bureau's operation in foreign countries."[56]

As long as the United States was not actually at war, the focus of any counterespionage activity, as foreseen in General Miles's proposal, would have to be the Western Hemisphere. Hoover's statement established that he had a presidentially sanctioned head start and a pipeline into the Oval Office. If the MID and ONI insisted on delimitation terms he didn't like, the FBI director might simply ignore them.

Aware of the implications of Hoover's declaration, General Miles immediately pressed for recognition of the special prerogatives of naval and military attachés. When discussion of this issue bogged down, the general forthwith suggested that if some covert intelligence group was to be formed, Adolf Berle (who had left the meeting to catch a train) be allowed to decide whether MID, ONI or the FBI would become its controller. The wily Hoover suavely suggested that Edward Tamm, the former's stand-in at previous meetings, be named as Berle's advisor and assistant in the selection process. The meeting ended, no blood having been spilt, but with the battle lines drawn.[57]

It is questionable whether the other conferees would have been nearly so accommodating had they known how far Hoover had already gone in staking a claim to Latin America as an FBI intelligence fief. On May 26, 1940, he had sent a personal and confidential memorandum to the White House which read, in part, "I have finally effected arrangements whereby one of my Special Agents will be in Mexico City, and he has already been able to effect contact with the most important man in Mexico so far as Nazi propaganda, espionage, and sabotage are concerned, Arthur Dietrich."[58] On June 2, 1940, Hoover forwarded another memorandum to Roosevelt which read, in part, "Special Agents of the FBI have been established in Mexico and Cuba. Each of these persons has some ostensible business connections or purpose requiring his presence in those countries."[59]

Analysis of the question of what Hoover was doing in Latin America, and what Roosevelt himself knew about it, provides for some fascinating speculation. Recall that on May 21, Edward Tamm stated that the FBI was merely weighing the possible dispatch of agents to Mexico, Cuba, and Colombia. On May 26, Hoover informed the White House that his operative would soon be in Mexico City. If this statement is compared with Hoover's May 31, 1940, presentation to the Joint Intelligence Committee, it should be evident that he was not telling the full truth to his MID, ONI, and State Department colleagues. Furthermore, the June 2, 1940, memorandum to FDR leaves no doubt that the unnamed agents were in place, and if this report is accurate, they must certainly have left the United States prior to May 31.

At our request, FBI researchers looked into the matter, and after initially giving a negative response, they later confirmed that an agent had been assigned to Mexico in an "open capacity" since "mid-1940."[60] In other words, Hoover probably made accurate reports to the White House but preferred to keep the Joint Intelligence Committee from learning anything essential about his foreign operations.

IV. The SIS Sweepstakes

Having made the necessary arrangements, Hoover had no trouble dominating the June 3, 1940, meeting and he left General Miles shaking his fist at destiny. The MID chief had insisted that delimitation of jurisdiction be given primacy on the agenda, but this demand was ignored, and the sole topic of discussion became the secret organization proposed at the previous meeting. Berle virtually wrapped up matters when, early on, he stated that "if the Military and Naval Intelligence chiefs desired the FBI to establish a Special Intelligence Service [SIS] on the east coast of South America, the State Department would be glad to cooperate."[61] Admiral Anderson said little on May 31; now he leaped aboard Hoover's wagon, indicating that the Navy would "be not only glad but anxious" to cooperate with the FBI in establishing a special intelligence force for Latin America. Only General Miles failed to give his assent, and the outmaneuvered army officer warned that he would oppose any arrangement which might compromise the authority of military attachés in the region.[62]

Ignoring this threat, the conferees voted to establish a subcommittee to study the necessity and feasibility of what was now formally referred to as the Special Intelligence Service, the identifying initials being the same as those of the British Secret Service. As for General Miles, he was temporarily silenced when, on June 6, Hoover and Anderson agreed to sign a delimitation of jurisdiction proposal. The problem was that if the SIS was actually created, the specific relationships between the new unit, MID, and ONI would still have to be hammered out. In addition, if control of the SIS went to Hoover, a provision for further negotiation might easily be transformed into a weapon for forcing the revision of any previous agreement. Since a memorandum attached to the delimitation agreement acknowledged this stipulation,[63] General Miles could be said to have gained a point, but it was the kind that J. Edgar Hoover could concede 365 days a year.

When the Joint Intelligence Committee convened on June 11, 1940, the MID chief still would not sanction the SIS, and under questioning, an irritated Berle admitted that Cordell Hull had not formally done so either. The assistant secretary was then detailed, after Miles abstained from taking on the task, to obtain both State Department and presidential approval. The committee also decided that once Berle had accomplished this mission, they would take a formal vote in order to determine which agency would become the parent organization for the SIS.[64]

No further committee meetings were held for two weeks, but one can assume that, in the interim, the struggle between MID and the FBI must have been fierce. Finally, on June 24, 1940, in the presence of General Miles, Berle telephoned President Roosevelt and asked for his decision regarding foreign intelligence activity. The president's reply was a sterling example of confusion competently organized. The FBI was assigned responsibility for "foreign intelligence work in the Western Hemisphere," but it was to act only "on the request of the State Department." MID and ONI "should cover the rest of the world, as and when necessity arises," but "under special circumstances," the State Department could also assign the FBI to perform tasks in what the president referred to as "the rest of the world" as well.[65] In reality, the only issue settled was that Hoover received the Western Hemisphere as his intelligence fiefdom. Otherwise, FDR's maddening inexactitude merely increased the chaos which already existed.

Vanquished in his bid for hemispheric intelligence control was General Miles, who, up to the last minute, apparently believed that he would either be given the SIS or some face-saving concession. In retrospect, perhaps the biggest loser was the State Department. Roosevelt's directive of June 24, 1940, suggests that he, too, assumed that the diplomatic branch would maintain ultimate control over Western Hemispheric undercover operations. But with Hoover building the service that would carry out the assignments, Welles, Duggan, Berle, et al., should have known better. As early as the fall of 1939, Assistant Secretary of State George Messersmith, the first coordinator for the Joint Intelligence Committee, had denounced Hoover as a glory hound and difficult to work with except on his own terms.[66] Predictably, perhaps, the FBI director would send Berle and the American republics section of the State Department all sorts of memoranda concerning SIS activity, but these materials generally arrived after action had already been taken. By 1942, Berle would ruefully report in his diary that incidences of effective cooperation between the State Department and Hoover had been few and far between.[67] The diplomats were ill-equipped to play rough-and-tumble with J. Edgar Hoover, and their subsequent loss of authority was the price of this inadequacy.

A more intriguing role in this series of events was played by Roosevelt himself. With his June 24, 1940, telephone directive, he approved the establishment of an undercover intelligence service designed to operate outside the United States during peacetime, probably the first time an American president had ever taken such a step. Significant also was the fact that his telephonic response was not followed up with a written executive order. The only name on the written memorandum confirming this presidential decision was that of Adolf Berle.[68] Thus, if unforeseen developments occurred, or if Hoover's agents committed a blunder which grew into an international incident, the president could maintain that he had no direct knowledge of SIS operations. Not until January 6, 1942, did FDR officially recognize the existence of the SIS.[69] Suffice it to say that Roosevelt took assiduous care to cover his tracks.

Meanwhile, at the Joint Intelligence Committee meeting of June 25, Adolf Berle announced that Roosevelt had decided the FBI would control the covert intelligence group to be created.[70] Hoover wasted no time; on July 1, 1940, the FBI officially begot the SIS.

V. The Infernal Triangle: Hoover, Miles, and Donovan

The ONI had no trouble accepting Hoover's acquisition of the SIS. For General Miles, a battle had been lost, but the struggle would recommence from new positions. At the Joint Intelligence Committee meeting of July 2, 1940, he raised the question of why a written directive establishing the SIS had not been forthcoming from the White House. Anderson and Hoover hastened to assure him that Berle's written report of the June 24 telephone conversation was sufficient authorization, but Miles remained unconvinced.[71]

Subsequently, in a special memorandum of July 23, 1940, the general went on the offensive. First, he observed that the scope of the SIS had not been defined by presidential order. Second, since the SIS was a counterespionage organization "having no experience in military intelligence," a new delimitation of authority agreement had to be signed, reserving this specialty for army attachés in the American republics.[72] Convinced that General Miles intended to regain ground previously lost, Hoover sought and received navy support for his contention that the SIS "should not be restricted in any manner in the scope of its operations." He followed up with a special letter (August 3, 1940) assuring the MID chief that the SIS would not interfere in military intelligence activities. Nevertheless, Hoover refused to sign any agreement specifically limiting SIS operations.[73]

With this rejoinder, negotiations concerning the delimitation of SIS prerogatives deadlocked, remaining so for months. In the interim, however, the MID and FBI bosses crossed swords repeatedly. On October 10 and 12, 1940, Hoover and Miles exchanged barbed letters in which each accused the other of failing to abide by previous agreements and refusing to provide promised cooperation.[74] Three days later, a Joint Intelligence Committee meeting was convened which Miles insisted be held in his office, and Hoover demanded take place in his. The general won that skirmish, but on the day of the meeting, Hoover refused to attend.[75] Exasperated by what he conceived to be a new low in petty behavior, Adolf Berle wrote despondently in his diary, "It [i.e., the Miles-Hoover struggle] can't go on. . . ."[76]

The assistant secretary might have had enough of the battle for hemispheric intelligence control, but J. Edgar Hoover was just getting ready to throw his heaviest punches. Sensing that he might need additional assistance if the general's challenge was to be beaten back, on October 29, Hoover dispatched a sizzling memorandum to the White House. In it, he excoriated Miles, charging the MID controller with sabotaging previous agreements, and he warned Roosevelt that unless General Miles was brought to his senses "unfortunate consequences" must occur.[77]

The mushrooming conflict between FBI and MID heads convinced the president that he had better intervene, but the step he took was one unanticipated by either antagonist. After the hard-working Berle managed to arrange an uneasy truce between Miles and Hoover in February 1941, FDR decided to remove Miles as MID chief, only to change his mind the following month.[78] Then on April 4, 1941, the president called a cabinet meeting, at which he declared that the U.S. intelligence program was suffering as a result of continuous FBI-MID wrangling. He allegedly proposed that Col. William J. Donovan (whom he referred to as "Mr. X") be named coordinator of information and empowered to settle inter-agency disputes.

FDR's preference for Donovan leaked out, although the minutes of this meeting did not mention any names.[79] Writing to Gen. George C. Marshall on April 8, 1941, General Miles found the choice of Donovan as referee in intelligence conflicts theoretically tolerable, but insisted that the creation of a "super agency controlling all intelligence" would also be a "calamitous" mistake.[80] On the same day, the alarmed MID leader wrote to Roosevelt himself and reiterated the objections made to General Marshall.[81] The chief executive did not bother to formulate a reply, but there can be no question as to his continued perturbation, for on July 11, 1941, William J. Donovan was officially named Coordinator of Information (COI).

Once the new spymaster took charge, Miles's worst fears were confirmed, for Donovan began working unabashedly toward the creation of a centralized, all-encompassing intelligence agency. The COI gave birth to the Office of Strategic Services (OSS) on June 13, 1942, and by 1945 the latter overshadowed both ONI and MID. But schemes to penetrate Hoover's Latin American preserve failed ignominiously. Shortly after Pearl Harbor, Donovan approached both Adolf Berle and Sumner Welles, requesting their support for a plan to put COI agents in the other hemispheric republics. Nabobs at the State Department viewed Donovan as the insolent Johnny-come-lately, determined to usurp all power for himself. They had no love for Hoover, but the devil they knew best was better than this unknown son of Satan.[82] First, Sumner Welles advised Donovan to look east and west, but not south. Then, with the FBI director adding to the din with screams of foul play, FDR issued a directive (January 6, 1942) specifically ordering Donovan to keep his operatives north of the Rio Grande.[83] After this battle, the achievement of a friendly relationship between Hoover and Donovan became as likely as a truce between the Dalton brothers and the Wells-Fargo Stage Coach lines. Donovan subsequently discovered ways to get around the president's prohibition, but he took care never to directly challenge Hoover's monopoly during the war.[84]

The 1939–42 struggle for supremacy in the U.S. intelligence community displays more than a passing resemblance to that which transpired in Germany in 1935–44. Recall that Reinhard Heydrich conceded (temporarily) the Abwehr's supremacy in military intelligence while insisting that political intelligence was the specialty of the SD. In 1940, Gen. Sherman Miles was prepared to acknowledge FBI responsibility for political or civil intelligence, but military intelligence, he adamantly insisted, was the special preserve of army attachés. In neither case did hard and fast lines clearly delineating these alleged specialities exist, and the contending parties undoubtedly realized it. The point is that in both Nazi Germany and the United States, the intelligence chiefs fought to control as much of the national intelligence apparatus as they possibly could. Where the United States was fortunate was that Hoover, Donovan, Miles, et al., eventually chose to direct the bulk of their efforts at foreign enemies rather than each other.

VI. SIS: Getting Ready for Battle

In a secret memorandum directed to the president on May 15, 1941, and signed by MID, ONI, and the FBI commanders, the SIS was described as a regimen of "undercover agents" who maintained "an extensive program of counter-intelligence, utilizing the services of American business firms operating in the Latin Americas, in operation for the purpose of maintaining a constant study of the Axis operations, propaganda, etc., in these countries."[85] Mandated by J. Edgar Hoover to commence operations on July 1, 1940, the SIS division of the FBI was commanded by Paul E. Foxworth, who immediately established a supervisory staff at FBI headquarters in Washington (see Chart III). But if the SIS planned to make the best use of business informants going to and returning from Latin America, the organization obviously needed a New York City office. In November 1940, headquarters was transferred there, space being rented in the RCA building under the prosaic cover name of the Importers Service Company.[86] Abruptly, in February 1941, administrative control of the SIS was shifted back to Washington, and while the New York office would remain open until 1945, it would henceforth serve as an outpost.

As a functioning organization, between July 1, 1940, and March 31, 1947, the SIS employed some five hundred acknowledged agents, technicians, and administrative personnel.[87] Its initial annual budget was $900,000, but by 1945, this figure had grown to $5.4 million, the 600 percent increase being a good indication of the value of this unit to the FBI.[88] Since no SIS training school existed when the first agents were assigned to Cuba and Mexico in May 1940, most of the informants selected were probably U.S. businessmen who were residents of the countries in question. Acting swiftly, Hoover dispatched other SIS operatives to Argentina and Colombia (September 1940), and Brazil, Venezuela, and Chile (October 1940).[89]

The training and preparation of these agents was spotty, and those who deigned to express an opinion bear witness to this. "I had no real idea what I was getting into, and my preparation for spying in Latin America was ass-backwards," said one former SIS man who saw service in Argentina.[90] Not bitter, but in agreement with regard to the training, was Donald Charles Bird, today a director of a large supermarket chain in Pôrto Alegre, Brazil. After graduating from the Detroit College of Law and

CHART III

SIS ORGANIZATIONAL STRUCTURE AND CONNECTION WITH THE DEPARTMENT OF STATE

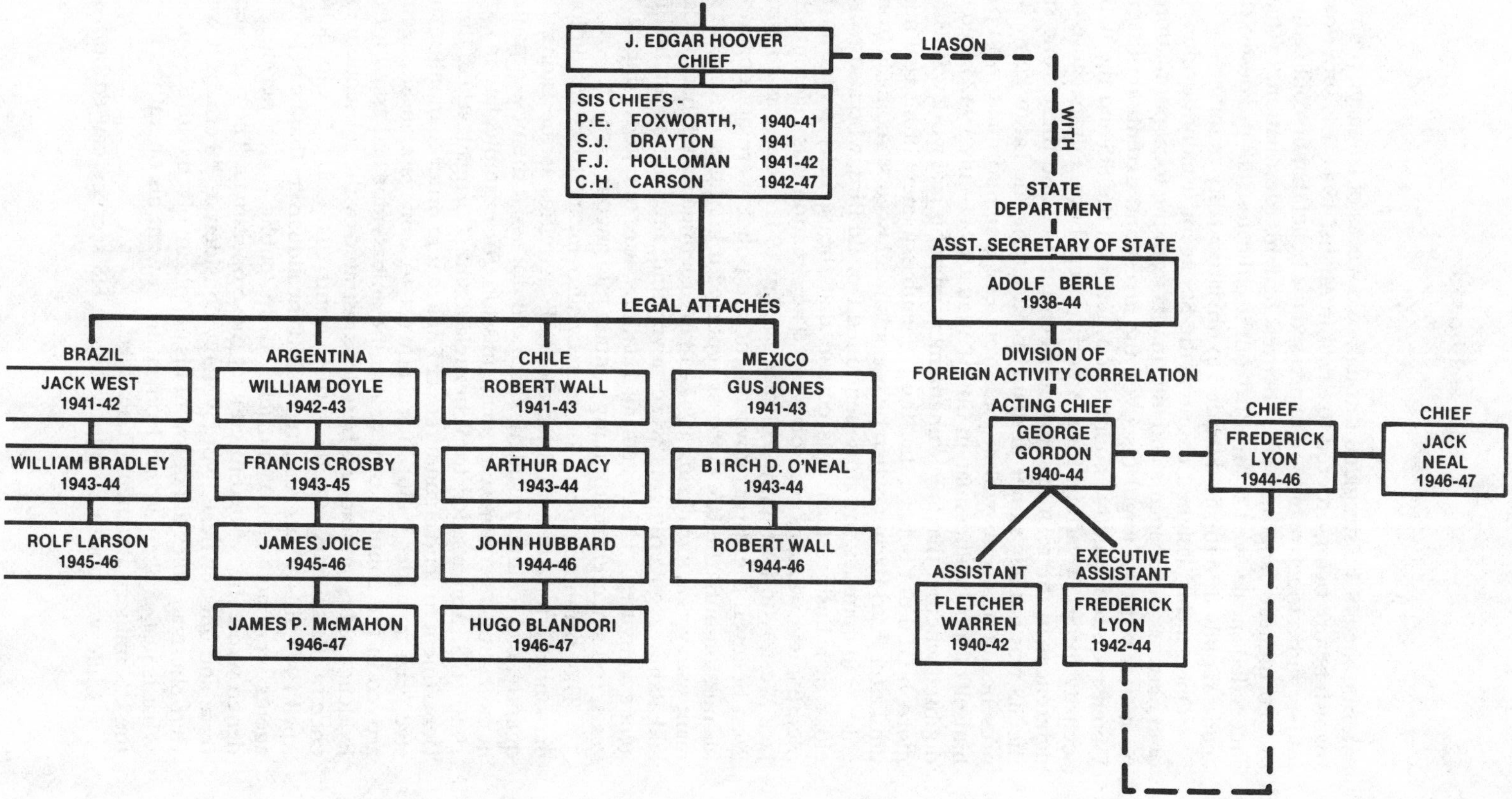

J. EDGAR HOOVER
CHIEF

LIASON WITH

STATE DEPARTMENT

ASST. SECRETARY OF STATE
ADOLF BERLE
1938-44

SIS CHIEFS -
P.E. FOXWORTH, 1940-41
S.J. DRAYTON 1941
F.J. HOLLOMAN 1941-42
C.H. CARSON 1942-47

DIVISION OF FOREIGN ACTIVITY CORRELATION

ACTING CHIEF
GEORGE GORDON
1940-44

CHIEF
FREDERICK LYON
1944-46

CHIEF
JACK NEAL
1946-47

EXECUTIVE ASSISTANT
FREDERICK LYON
1942-44

ASSISTANT
FLETCHER WARREN
1940-42

LEGAL ATTACHÉS

BRAZIL	ARGENTINA	CHILE	MEXICO
JACK WEST 1941-42	WILLIAM DOYLE 1942-43	ROBERT WALL 1941-43	GUS JONES 1941-43
WILLIAM BRADLEY 1943-44	FRANCIS CROSBY 1943-45	ARTHUR DACY 1943-44	BIRCH D. O'NEAL 1943-44
ROLF LARSON 1945-46	JAMES JOICE 1945-46	JOHN HUBBARD 1944-46	ROBERT WALL 1944-46
	JAMES P. McMAHON 1946-47	HUGO BLANDORI 1946-47	

entering the SIS, he struggled through two weeks of language training in Spanish before being ordered to Brazil in August 1941. His superiors, he told us with a touch of humor, expressed the belief that he could adjust to the Portuguese language after he reached his destination.[91] That he succeeded speaks well of Mr. Bird, but it indicates that the desire to get agents rapidly into the field tended to obviate quality training.

Once in his assigned country, the SIS agent usually developed his own network of subagents and informants from the local population. But no matter what he might discover, the arrest and detention of German V-men required effective cooperation between the SIS and the national security forces of various Latin American republics. But, because of the differences in the relationships between the U.S. and these same states, the SIS was initially rather hesitant about letting the Latins know of the presence of its agents within their frontiers. One informant, who passed himself off as a businessman in Chile (August 1941–July 1942), told us he doubted whether that government knew what his real work was. Furthermore, he did not believe that the U.S. embassy knew of his real mission until after Pearl Harbor, when he was finally allowed "to come in from the cold."[92] In contrast, the aforementioned Donald Bird, who also wore the cloak of a businessman, was certain that the security police in Pôrto Alegre knew what his real job was.[93] The situation was different still for Jack West, who journeyed to Brazil in May 1941, posing as a journalist. West believed the Vargas government and police were not cognizant of his mission until the U.S. embassy reported it in August.[94] Another informant who was active during 1942–43 in Argentina stated that the Castillo and Ramírez governments were never told anything about his intelligence activities: "U.S.-Argentine relations was not good during these years, so I sincerely doubt if my contact told anyone else."[95]

This presumed need for secrecy also meant that U.S. diplomatic personnel often knew as little about SIS activities as the Latins. Consequently, bad feelings resulted which did not assist the new organization in executing its counterespionage mission. For example, late in October 1940, U.S. Ambassador to Venezuela Frank Corrigan asked the State Department to send an undercover FBI agent in order to monitor subversive Nazi activities.[96] But, unbeknownst to Corrigan, an SIS agent had arrived in the country even before the ambassador had asked for one![97] Evidence of his ignorance is best demonstrated by the subsequent experience of the military attaché in that country, Lt. Col. C.C. Clendenen. In April 1941, this officer reported to MID headquarters that he believed FBI agents were active in Venezuela. "If the public policy permits," Clendenen wrote, he wished to contact these operatives. The reply sent was terse and unequivocal: "Not favorably considered."[98] Perhaps it was that Gen. Sherman Miles did not want his people involved with SIS operatives. What is just as likely is that Hoover didn't want his operatives known to the U.S. military attaché in Venezuela.

Chile was another country where SIS secrecy caused both ruffled feathers and strong feelings of frustration. Early in April 1941, one Clarence Moore called on U.S. Ambassador Claude Bowers. Moore indicated that he was an SIS agent enrolled as a student at the University of Chile, and asked for a letter of introduction. Bowers was first flabbergasted, then enraged. In a cable to Sumner Welles, he expressed his disgruntlement:

> As you can readily see, he [Moore] is of no benefit to us unless we are in a position to put him next to things we consider important for investigation. I can only reiterate my regret that there have been no intelligence men from home here with whom this embassy can act in cooperation.[99]

Sumner Welles was an old hand at rubbing salve into wounded egos. In August 1941 he could tell Ambassador Bowers that if he still wanted an SIS operative who would work in cooperation with the embassy, J. Edgar Hoover was now "disposed to give the most favorable consideration possible."[100] The undersecretary may have had in mind Robert Wall, who arrived in Chile late in August 1941.[101] Certainly Welles was not referring to William Caldwell, another agent who reached Chile during the same month and who was not reported to the diplomatic staff.[102] Obviously, Hoover intended to keep an ace or two up his sleeve.

New intelligence organizations invariably require time to determine the effectiveness of their operatives, work out successful operational procedures, and establish liaison with both U.S. embassy and Latin American officials. The refusal of Hoover to tell the State Department of his plans, and incidents such as the conflict with Ambassador Claude Bowers, caused friction which conceivably might have affected the SIS counterespionage effort. A solution to the problem came in the summer of 1941 with the posting of resident intelligence directors with the titles of legal or civil attaché in U.S. embassies in Latin America. The first of these officers were assigned in Brazil and Mexico in August 1941, with a similar post being created in Chile one month later.[103] In addition to coordinating the counterespionage effort in the Latin American states to which they were assigned, these attachés maintained contact with one or more embassy officials, financed operations, prepared special reports, and in general led the struggle against German intelligence.[104]

In view of the manner in which the SIS took shape, it should be evident that this organization was no better prepared for the spy-counterspy war in Latin America than either the Abwehr or SD. Furthermore, the FBI had no body of tradition nor wealth of experience in foreign espionage and counterespionage to draw on; for both Hoover and the rawest SIS recruit, it would be a case of on-the-job training. On the other hand, the SIS was operating in a region where the economic and military power of the United States was predominant. Translated into practical terms, this meant that unless SIS agents were discovered monitoring the activities of a Latin American president or his ministers, they would probably avoid arrest and imprisonment. And even if some SIS man were arrested, his Washington sponsorship made it improbable that he would "accidentally die under interrogation," or be shot "trying to escape."

Just as crucial, the SIS would also have the gods of technology on its side. On July 1, 1940, the same date as the founding of the organization, the Federal Communications Commission (FCC) created a special unit called the Radio Intelligence Division (RID). Within two years, this division had constructed twelve interception stations, one of which detected (but did not decipher) a clandestine transmission sent by an FMK in Chile on April 24, 1941.[105] Thereafter, hundreds of messages sent by V-men in Chile, Brazil, and elsewhere in Latin America were routinely intercepted.

The other unit which would prove invaluable to the SIS effort in Latin America was the cryptographic section of the FBI Technical Laboratory. According to legend, when in 1929 Secretary of State Henry Stimson ordered the suppression of the State Department's "Black Chamber," a group of codebreakers led by Herbert O. Yardley, he justified his action by insisting that "Gentlemen do not read other people's mail."[106] J. Edgar Hoover could never have met Stimson's standard, for the cryptanalysis section of the FBI Technical Laboratory was then in existence, and Hoover never saw fit to limit the scope of its activities. By 1938–39, this unit had begun work on the decipherment of German codes, but the real breakthrough occurred in 1940. William Sebold, a U.S. citizen of German ancestry, had been trapped in the Reich by the outbreak of World War II. He was pressured, browbeaten, and after the welfare of his relatives was threatened, Sebold reluctantly joined the Abwehr. After completing his training, Sebold (code name: Tramp) was directed by Ast Hamburg to return to the United States and act as radioman for a ring of Abwehr agents on the East Coast. "Tramp" did as he was told, but avenged himself by revealing all he knew to the FBI and becoming a double agent.[107]

The full significance of Sebold's defection was not only that it led to the capture of German agents in the United States, but that it was a major factor in the smashing of the Abwehr rings in Latin America as well. Sebold's cipher was given to the FBI Technical Laboratory, and Hoover's cryptanalysts soon found that most of the ciphers used by Abwehr V-men in Latin America were quite similar. (See Appendix A for descriptions of various ciphers.) With the RID intercepting the messages and the FBI Technical Laboratory decoding them, by June 1941, SIS officials were reading virtually all the Abwehr clandestine radio traffic between Latin America and Germany. Technology and a German-American's desire for vengeance had combined to give the SIS the means for unmasking a major portion of the Abwehr network operating from Mexico southward.

A former SIS operative, who would talk only if we agreed not to use his name, told us this amusing and highly informative story. Posing as a representative of a U.S. firm, he became a fast friend of a Chilean business-man. The latter invited the SIS man to dinner and following the meal and several brandies, he told the North American, "I think you work for Hoover." The SIS man was dumbfounded, but demanded to know why the Chilean thought such a thing. The reply was, "You wear a gabardine topcoat and snap brim hat like the G-men I have seen in *Time* and *Newsweek*." Reminiscing over this event, our informant observed, "I guess a lot of our boys stuck out like sore thumbs."[108]

Like many of the German V-men, SIS personnel had a lot to learn. But thanks to good fortune and technological aid, there would be time to whip the SIS organization into shape. The Germans, in contrast, obtained no SIS ciphers, and had no one like "Tramp" working inside Hoover's organization.

VII. How Good a Neighbor?

After a meeting held in J. Edgar Hoover's office on June 3, 1940, Adolf Berle wrote in his diary, "We likewise decided that the time had come when we would have to consider setting up a secret intelligence service —which I suppose every foreign office in the world has, but we have never touched."[109] These musings indicate that Berle had some misgivings about what he believed ought to be done, and well he should have. For example, the assistant secretary evidently believed that the new intelligence service would be an adjunct of the State Department. This is not what happened, and there were other potential problems as well. Suppose the new service became involved in a coup attempt or an assassination plot? Suppose it sanctioned actions which ran counter to the State Department's policies, or spied on U.S. citizens in Latin America? Would the new organization fade away after the war, or would it maintain a surreptitious existence? Admittedly in June-July 1940, the need for speed and secrecy probably seemed paramount; but eventually, someone should have asked the hard questions and attempted to create some kind of guidelines. The shame of the situation is that aside from Berle, there is no indication that anyone else who knew what was going on seems to have been greatly concerned.[110]

At the same time, in establishing a secret intelligence unit, the Roosevelt administration was making a profound statement about its Latin American policy perspectives. Recall that early in June 1940, the U.S. government decided to send a team of army and navy officers to confer with Latin American civil and military chiefs, for the purpose of establishing a mutually acceptable scheme of hemispheric defense. The consultations had not begun when FDR made his June 24, 1940, phone call establishing Latin America as Hoover's intelligence bailiwick. Furthermore, by the time the first round of these bilateral talks had been completed (October 28, 1940), SIS operatives were already in Argentina, Brazil, Colombia, Chile, and Mexico. It is therefore reasonable to conclude that the Roosevelt administration was determined to commit the SIS to secret intelligence work in Latin America with or without the consent of our "good neighbors" south of the Rio Grande. One might also ask how such a policy differed from that followed by the Abwehr or SD in the region. The answer should be evident: not much.

An objective assessment of the situation must take into consideration the fact that self-defense is the first law of nations, and, as we have established, the United States was a primary target of the Abwehr rings in Latin America. It would have been preferable for the other hemispheric republics to deal with the German V-men found within their borders without any outside assistance or interference. In sanctioning the SIS mission, Roosevelt was indicating his belief that the Latin American nations were essentially incapable of taking effective counterintelligence action or indifferent to the threat that German espionage posed. The wisdom of FDR's beliefs would soon establish itself, for in the previously alluded to 1940 bilateral defense talks, several Latin American political and military leaders admitted that they lacked the funds, the personnel, and/or the political will to deal with the problem German espionage might pose.[111] If the United States believed that not enough was being done to counter Nazi espionage, it would have to do the job itself.

In retrospect, the clandestine commitment of the SIS to Latin America marked the end of an era. The principle of nonintervention in the internal affairs of other American republics had, since 1933, become one of the cornerstones of Roosevelt's Good Neighbor policy.[112] Sending secret intelligence agents to operate in a friendly state without the knowledge of the government of said state, whatever the reason, made a mockery of the nonintervention principle. After June 24, 1940, the good neighbor concept, at least as it had been understood in the past, began the slow fade into oblivion.

Notes

1. This intriguing story was related to Professor Rout by Dr. Juan Isidro Ramírez, October 16, 1965, in Asunción, Paraguay. Dr. Ramírez was one of two Paraguayan plenipotentiary delegates to the Chaco Peace Conference, and he was also one of the Paraguayan delegates named to the Inter-American Conference for the Maintenance of Peace. This story is also found in Leslie B. Rout, Jr., *Politics of the Chaco Peace Conference: 1935–39* (Austin, 1970), p. 214n.

2. Cordell Hull, *The Memoirs of Cordell Hull*, vol. 1 (New York, 1948), p. 493.

3. U.S. Department of State, *Report of the Delegation of the United States of America to the Inter-American Conference for the Maintenance of Peace* (Washington, D.C., 1937) p. 79.

4. Carlos Saavedra Lamas, *Por la paz de las Américas* (Buenos Aires, 1937), pp. 160–161. Saavedra Lamas made it quite clear that the Argentines suspected U.S. motives. A more concise restatement of Saavedra Lamas's views can also be found in the *Baltimore Sun*, January 4, 1937.

5. Hull, *Memoirs*, vol. 1, p. 498.

6. Ibid., p. 500. A relatively dispassionate view of the results is to be found in J. Lloyd Mecham, *The United States and Inter-American Security, 1889–1960* (Texas, 1962), pp. 125–135.

7. For the initial U.S. proposal, see U.S. Department of State, *Foreign Relations of the United States—1938*, vol. 5 (Washington, D.C., 1956), p. 80. The final resolution, the so-called Declaration of Lima, called for "continental solidarity," and in Article II reaffirmed that American principles were to be defended "against all foreign intervention." The reference to "non-American states" was dropped due to Argentine insistence. See also U.S. Department of State, *Report of the Delegation of the United States to the Eighth International Conference of American States*, publication 1624 (Washington, D.C., 1941), pp. 190–191.

8. For evidence of these fears, see Stetson Conn and Byron Fairchild, *The Western Hemisphere: The Framework of Hemisphere Defense* (Washington, D.C., 1960), pp. 9–10 and 12.

9. See William H. Burden, *The Struggle for Airways in Latin America* (Washington, 1943), pp. 57-58 and 64.

10. See Stetson Conn, Rose Engelman, and Byron Fairchild, *The Western Hemisphere: Guarding the United States and Its Outposts* (Washington, D.C., 1964), pp. 9–10.

11. Patrick Abbazia, *Mr. Roosevelt's Navy: The Private War of the U.S. Atlantic Fleet, 1939–42* (Annapolis, 1975), pp. 33–49.

12. Ibid., pp. 47–49.

13. Conn and Fairchild, *The Framework of Hemisphere Defense*, pp. 9–10 and 12.

14. Mark Skinner Watson, *Chief of Staff: Prewar Plans and Preparations* (Washington, D. C., 1950), p. 95. This report was seconded by a similar report reaching Roosevelt about the end of May 1940 from Ambassador to France William Bullitt. See Orville H. Bullitt, ed., *For the President, Personal and Secret: Correspondence Between Franklin Roosevelt and William Bullitt* (Boston, 1972), p. 441.

15. See U.S. Army, Ofice of the Chief of Military History of the Army, 8-2.8BA, *Bilateral Staff Conversations with Latin American Republics*, appendix I, p. 5.

16. On the impractical nature of the Pot-of-Gold plan, plus recognition that both the Joint Board and the planning staff recognized this, see Conn and Fairchild, *The Framework of Hemisphere Defense*, pp. 33, 33n, and 273.

17. This conclusion is directly supported in Conn, Engelman, and Fairchild, *Guarding the United States and Its Outposts*, p. 13; and Conn and Fairchild, *The Framework of Hemisphere Defense*, p. 27.

18. See Alton Frye, *Nazi Germany and the American Hemisphere: 1933–1941* (New Haven, 1967), p. 105. See also William E. Kinsella, *Leadership in Isolation: FDR and the Origins of the Second World War* (Cambridge, Mass., 1978), pp.171–181. See also *Jornal do Brasil*, Rio de Janeiro, April 7, 1978. Information obtained by Dr. Ricardo Steinfuss, a Brazilian sociologist, indicates that the Mussolini government provided the Integralistas with a secret subsidy in 1937–38.

On the Nacista uprising of September 1938, see Arturo Olavarría Bravo, *Chile entre dos Alessandri: Memorias Políticas,* vol. 1 (Santiago, 1962), pp. 525–528. See also Ernst Halperin, *Nationalism and Communism in Chile* (Cambridge, 1965), pp. 44–47.

19. See Kinsella, *Leadership in Isolation*, pp. 170–171, 180–181, and Conn and Fairchild, *The Framework of Hemispheric Defense*, pp. 27 and 219.

20. Conn and Fairchild, *The Framework of Hemispheric Defense*, pp. 186–187, and Watson, *Chief of Staff*, pp. 421–422.

21. See Burden, *The Struggle for Airways in Latin America*, pp. 72–73, for an explanation of these events. The official documents demonstrate that Pan American Airways and the Colombian and U.S. governments were all involved in a scheme to destroy SCADTA and terminate German employees. See National Archives and Records Service (hereafter referred to as NARS), R.G. 59, 821. 796 Avianca/76, /125a, /188, /197, and /231. See also RG 165, entry 65, 2538-21/30 to 2538-21/61a.

22. The quoted material is from NARS, RG 165, entry 65, #2538-21/28, p. 1.

23. On the connivance between the U.S., Ecuadorean, Bolivian, and Chilean governments, the standard technique of cutting off the German airlines' fuel supplies and the role of Pan American Airways, see Burden, *The Struggle for Airways in Latin America*, pp. 67–73. The more intimate details of the deals made are found in NARS, R.G. 59, 824.796/77, /83a, /84, and /89. See also 825.79635/22, 659. Consult also R.G. 165, 2626-26/3, Report 84 from Military Attaché in Bolivia, May 26, 1941, pp. 4–5, and R.G. 226, 1222C, pp. 1–3.

24. Ibid.

25. The decision to commence bilateral staff conferences was made in June 1940. Actual talks began with all countries except Mexico in August 1940. See 8–2.8AB, *Bilateral Staff Conversations*, appendix I, pp. 1–50 for military talks. On naval talks, see appendix II, pp. 1–52.

26. Ibid., appendix I, pp. 2, 7, 9, 11, 15, 17, 21–22, 25, 27, 30, 32, 37, 40, 42, 45, and 47–48.

27. For a list of Latin American republics that had signed up for lend-lease and agreed to bilaterial defense arrangements, see NARS, R.G. 38, ONI, Division of Pan American Affairs and United States Naval Missions, entry 49, box 1, *Reports of Bilateral Staff Conversations —1942*, n.p.

28. Concerning Latin America's defenselessness on the seas, see Abbazia, *Mr. Roosevelt's Navy*, pp. 68–71, 80–81, and 84–85. On the military lack of capabilities, see Conn, Engelman, and Fairchild, *Guarding the United States and Its Outposts*, pp. 9–10.

29. This circular telegram is described in NARS, R.G. 165, 2657–201/Z, box 2069.

30. For the Chapin study, see NARS, R.G. 59, F.W., 810.00F/32, *Memorandum on Italian Fascist and German Nazi Activity in the American Republics*, February 17, 1938. The quoted material is from pp. 13 and 14.

31. See NARS, R.G. 165, box 2069, 2657–202 (1), C.M. Bushbee, *General Survey of Latin America*, November 19, 1937.

32. See Samuel Inman, Mss., Manuscripts Division, Library of Congress, Washington, D.C., Duggan to Inman, box 14, March 8, 1938.

33. George C. Messersmith Papers, Special Collections Library, University of Delaware, Newark, Delaware, 1067-n.d., Messersmith to D.N. Heiniman, July 17, 1939.

34. In January 1939, Welles raised the prospect of a German-inspired overthrow of Vargas, followed by an invasion from Africa. Recall that the 1939 Atlantic Fleet exercise was based on this same assumption. See NARS, R.G. 353, *U.S. Standing Liaison Committee, Minutes for 21 January Meeting*, file p. 4.

35. Beatrice Berle and Travis Jacobs, eds., *Navigating the Rapids: 1918–1971* (New York, 1973), pp. 206–210.

36. Elery C. Stowell, "The Habana Conference and Inter-American Cooperation," *The American Journal of International Law* 16, no. 1 (January 1941): 127.

37. U.S. Department of State, *Foreign Relations of the United States—1940*, vol. 5, pp. 14–15.

38. See NARS, R.G. 59, 862.2040/330 1/2, *German Inroads and Plans in the Other American Republics*, September 10, 1940, pp. 1 and 4. The document was forwarded from Duggan to Welles.

39. Ibid., p. 4.

40. See NARS, R.G. 59, 862.20210/414, *The Pattern of Nazi Organizations and Their Activities in the American Republics*, by Adolf Berle, February 6, 1941. The quote is from p. 12.

41. The *Reichsdeutschen* population figures are from NARS, R.G. 165, box 982, MID, *Axis Espionage and Propaganda in Latin America* (Washington, D.C., 1946), pp. VII–VIII. The source for party records is U.S. Senate, Subcommittee on War Mobilization of the Committee on Military Affairs, *Nazi Party Membership Records* (Washington, D.C., 1946), Part I, pp. 16–45, Part II, pp. 19–104, 137–143, and Part III, 14–35, 554–555 and 774. The German source is Hans-Adolf Jacobsen, *Nationalsozialistische Aussenpolitik, 1933–1938* (Frankfurt-am-Main, 1968), pp. 662 and 665.

42. See NARS, R.G. 226, 2116/C, 71036, *Hitler's Fifth Column in Latin America: Part 1, Argentina and Bolivia* (supplement to notes of 19.3.41 and 5.6.41). Passed by British censor P5985, October 17, 1941, p. 3.

43. Franklin D. Roosevelt Library (hereafter referred to as FDRL), Hyde Park, New York, *The Diaries of Adolf A. Berle*, roll 2, frame 0656.

44. See NARS, R.G. 59, 862.20210/414, February 6, 1941, pp. 1–2.

45. See NARS, R.G. 59, 862.20237/203, March 18, 1941, pp. 1–3.

46. See NARS, R.G. 59, 862.20213/2429, 15242, February 2, 1942, p. 1.

47. See NARS, R.G. 59, 862.20210/467, 2282, April 18, 1941 (chart). Prior to Pearl Harbor, U.S. diplomats usually referred to any person believed to be a German intelligence agent as belonging to the Gestapo. Thus Abwehr agents were usually referred to as Gestapo operatives.

48. See NARS, R.G. 59, 862.20210/467, 2282, April 18, 1941 (chart).

49. See NARS, R.G., 84, 820.02, box 533. *Interrogation of Ernst Wilhelm Bohle*, October 4, 1945, pp. 8–9. The last *Auslandskommissar* sent to the Western Hemisphere was Willie Koehn, who returned to Germany in 1938. No other AO leader ever received such an appointment. As for Venezuelan spies, see NARS, R.G. 165, box 982, MID, *Axis Espionage and Propaganda*, p. 40, which reports that only Abwehr II had agents in Venezuela. These were led by Ernst Gerhard Karl Roggemann, and he had no more than ten or eleven subagents.

50. Concerning Hoover's complaint about Caffery, see NARS, R.G. 165, 9794-186A/9, *Conference between Representatives of State Department, Military Intelligence, Division of War Department, Naval Intelligence and the Federal Bureau of Investigation on July 16, 1940*, pp. 7–8. On Spruille Braden's plans for becoming spymaster, see NARS, R.G. 165, MID, 311.9/16 April 17, 1941, pp. 1–4. Braden wanted a personal plane and pilot, plus five hundred dollars a month to pay informants. See also R.G. 165, MID, 310.11/16, April 21,

1941. Appended to this document is a note from Sumner Welles stating that although J. Edgar Hoover was responsible for South American operations, "the State Department will inform General Miles regarding how far the State Department wants the Ambassador to go in this phase of work." Braden was then moved out of the espionage arena. See NARS, R.G. 165, MID, 311. 14/16, April 23, 1941, pp. 1–2.

51. See NARS, R.G. 165, unnumbered letter dated June 26, 1939, Hyde Park, New York. Letter was marked "Exhibit A" (part of 9794-186A series).

52. George Messersmith Papers, University of Delaware Library, Newark, Delaware, manuscript 2018/5, n.d., pp. 1–6.

53. See NARS, R.G. 165, 9794-186A, *Conferences: FBI—December 1939 to May 28, 1940.* "Notes of Conference, FBI, February 20, 1940," pp. 2–3, and ibid., "Notes of Conference, FBI, March 26, 1940," pp. 1–2.

54. Ibid., "Conference at FBI Headquarters, May 21, 1940," p. 2.

55. FDRL, Adolf Berle Papers, box 57, Berle to Sumner Welles, May 14, 1940.

56. NARS, R.G. 165, 9794-186A/2, *Conference between Representatives of the State Department, Military Intelligence Division of the War Department, Naval Intelligence and the Federal Bureau of Investigation on May 31, 1940*, pp. 5–6 for quoted materials.

57. Ibid., pp. 6–8.

58. FDRL, Franklin D. Roosevelt Papers (hereafter referred to as FDRP), OF-10B, box 22, May 26, 1940, J. Edgar Hoover to White House (Brig. Gen. Edwin Watson), p. 1.

59. Ibid., OF-10B, box 23, memorandum of June 2, 1940, J. Edgar Hoover to White House (Brig. Gen. Edwin Watson), attached to June 3, 1940, letter, p. 5.

60. Letter from Homer Boynton, Jr., inspector, Federal Bureau of Investigation, to Professor Leslie B. Rout, Jr., December 14, 1977, pp. 1–2. We sent copies of the June 2, 1940, memorandum and the June 3, 1940, Joint Intelligence Committee minutes to the FBI. Inspector Boynton reported that "since the research conducted in response to your prior inquiries determined that no agents were assigned to undercover duties outside the country prior to June 24, 1940, I am led to believe that the statement contained on page 5 of the June 2, 1940 memorandum is in error." But in a subsequent letter dated August 8, 1979, Inspector Boynton admitted that there did indeed exist the possibility that agents were assigned to undercover duties outside the United States prior to June 24, 1940.

61. NARS, R.G. 165, 9794-186A/3, "Conference between . . . June 3, 1940," p. 2.

62. Ibid. For Admiral Anderson's comments, see p. 3; for General Miles's objections, see pp. 1, 2, and 3.

63. NARS, R.G. 165, 9794-186A/3, *Proposal for Coordination of FBI, ONI and MID*, enclosures 1 and 2, June 5, 1940, attached to "Conference between . . . June 3, 1940," pp. 1–3. The document was signed on June 6, but it was dated June 5. The proposal specifically states that no final decision had been reached concerning the control of intelligence operations in foreign countries.

64. NARS, R.G. 165, 9794-186A/4, "Conference between . . . June 11, 1940," pp.1–2.

65. Our copy was marked NARS, R.G. 165, 9794-186B/2, June 24, 1940, pp. 1–2.

66. Recall that as assistant secretary of state, George S. Messersmith was originally chosen during the summer of 1939 to act as coordinator of intelligence activities by FDR. On his views about Hoover, see George S. Messersmith Papers, University of Delaware Library, Newark, Delaware, file 2018/5, n.d., pp. 3–5.

67. Berle and Jacobs, eds., *Navigating the Rapids*, p. 404.

68. Refer again to NARS, R.G. 165, 9794-186B/2, June 24, 1940, p. 2.

69. See letter from Homer Boynton, Jr., to Professor Rout, August 8, 1979.

70. NARS, R.G. 165, 9794-186A/6, "Conference between . . . June 25, 1940," (minutes dated July 1, 1940), p. 6. Berle is reported to have said that "the President was issuing a directive for the establishment of the Special Intelligence Service." We do not know what FDR's actual intention was.

71. NARS, R.G. 165, 9794-186A/7, "Conference between . . . July 2, 1940," p. 7.

72. For General Miles's letter to Hoover, see NARS, R.G. 165, 9794-186A/12, "Memorandum for Mr. J. Edgar Hoover," July 23, 1940.

73. These issues were discussed with some heat at the Joint Intelligence Committee meeting of July 26, 1940. See NARS, R.G. 165, 9794-186A/12, "Conference between . . . on July 26, 1940" (minutes dated July 29, 1940), pp. 3–4. Hoover's reply to General Miles is found in R.G. 165, 9794-186B/4, Hoover to Gen. Sherman Miles, August 3, 1940, pp. 1–2.

74. NARS, R.G. 165, 9794-186B (G-2/9104-492), Hoover to Brig. Gen. Sherman Miles, October 10, 1940, and R.G. 165, 9794-186B/7, October 12, 1940, Brigadier General Miles to J. Edgar Hoover, MI-RES.

75. FDRL, *The Diaries of Adolf A. Berle*, roll 2, frames 0971 and 0972.

76. Ibid., frame 0972.

77. FDRL, FDRP, OF-10B, box 24, Hoover to Maj. Gen. Edwin Watson, October 29, 1940, pp. 1–4. The quote is from p. 1.

78. FDRL, *The Diaries of Adolf A. Berle*, roll 2, frames 1140 and 1197. Roosevelt told Berle that he intended to replace General Miles and was "casting about in his mind for the proper man."

79. NARS, R.G. 165, G-2, 9794-186, MID 310.11, May 29, 1941. The cabinet meeting memorandum we managed to obtain was marked "Copy for General Marshall." In the memorandum, Donovan's name is never mentioned.

80. NARS, R.G. 165, G-2, 9794-186, MID 310.11, April 8, 1941, memorandum for the chief of staff from Brigadier General Miles.

81. NARS, R.G. 165, G-2, 9794-186, MID 310.11, April 8, 1941, letter from Gen. Sherman Miles to the president.

82. Berle and Jacobs, eds., *Navigating the Rapids*, pp. 396–397. See also letter of Philip W. Bonsal to Professor Rout, May 8, 1979. Bonsal wrote: "We thought that for the activities in our field not already covered, the special qualifications of the FBI might be more useful than the as yet untried though wide-ranging qualifications of Colonel Donovan's people."

83. FDRL, FDRP, OF-10B, box 30, letter from Sumner Welles to Col. William J. Donovan, December 29, 1941. See also FDRL, Adolf Berle Papers, box 58, folder: *Hull, Cordell, January-June, 1942*. This directive was actually prepared in December 1941, but Roosevelt did not sign it until January 6, 1942.

84. William Stevenson, *A Man Called Intrepid* (New York, 1977), pp. 271–272, and R. Harris Smith, *OSS—The Secret History of America's First Central Intelligence Agency* (Berkeley, 1972), pp. 20, 20n, and 366. Smith admits that Donovan occasionally ignored FDR's order and sent OSS men to Central America. One wonders whether Roosevelt ever learned of this.

85. NARS, R.G. 165, 9794-186, MID 310.11, "Memorandum," May 22, 1941, p. 7.

86. Information on SIS leadership and headquarters location was provided in letter from Inspector Boynton to Professor Rout, January 18, 1978.

87. Letter from Inspector Boynton to Professor Rout, January 25, 1979.

88. Letter from Inspector Roger S. Young to Professor Rout, July 17, 1980.

89. Letter from Inspector Boynton to Professor Rout, August 8, 1979.

90. The quote was by Source F, an SIS agent who served in Argentina.

91. Interview, Donald Charles Bird, Pôrto Alegre, Brazil, with Professor Rout, July 18, 1978.

92. Letter from William B. Caldwell, an SIS agent, to Prof. John Bratzel, August 1, 1978.

93. Interview, Donald Charles Bird, July 18, 1978.

94. Letter from Jack West to the authors, memo 2, November 8, 1978, p. 1.

95. Source G, an SIS informant who was an Argentine rather than a U.S. citizen. The interview was conducted in Buenos Aires, August 16, 1978.

96. NARS, R.G. 59, 124.313/190, October 24, 1940, pp. 1–2.

97. Corrigan's message arrived at the State Department in November (stamped 11/2/40). Note that the first SIS agent had arrived before the State Department got Corrigan's message.

98. NARS, R.G. 165, 2610-M 69/1, 2003, March 26, 1941, and 2610-M-69, BAF/tfe, April 3, 1941.

99. Claude Bowers Papers, Indiana University, Lilly Library, Bloomington, Indiana, *Mss. I*, Bowers to Sumner Wells, April 24, 1941, p. 1.

100. Ibid., Sumner Welles to Bowers, August 16, 1941, p. 1.

101. Letter from Inspector Boynton to Professor Rout, March 28, 1979. Wall entered Chile on August 26, 1941, carrying Diplomatic Passport ESP 11738. He was simply listed as an attaché, and given Chilean Visa 162. See República de Chile, Ministerio de Relaciones Exteriores, *Oficios recibidos de la Embajada de Chile en los Estados Unidos (del I al 200) 1942*, 249/25, Michels al Ministerio, n.p.

102. Letter from William Caldwell to Professor Bratzel, August 1, 1978.

103. Letter from Jack West to the authors, memo 2, November 8, 1978. West was the first legal attaché posted to Brazil. Only in Mexico were SIS chiefs called civil attachés. See also letter from Inspector Boynton to Professor Rout, December 14, 1977.

104. On the duties of the legal or civil attachés, see FDRL, FDRP OF-10B, box 39, *Federal Bureau of Investigation, Special Intelligence Service*, March 7, 1944, pp. 1–4.

105. On the RID, see NARS, R.G. 60, annex VIII-B-2, box 5, *Statement by Mr. Phillip F. Siling of the Federal Communications Commission on United States Controls over Clandestine Radio Communications*, August 6, 1943, pp. 1-2, and NARS, R.G. 173, RID, box 5, *Testimony of George E. Sterling*, part 1, p. 14.

106. See Henry Stimson and McGeorge Bundy, *On Active Service in Peace and War* (New York, 1947), p. 188.

107. The Sebold story can be found in abbreviated detail in David Kahn, *Hitler's Spies: German Military Intelligence in World War II* (New York, 1978), pp. 331-333. The complex story of Sebold's cipher and how the FBI laboratory used it to read clandestine radio traffic emanating from Latin America was provided to us in a twelve-page memorandum from Paul Napier, a former FBI Technical Laboratory official.

108. Interview with Source J, February 4, 1980.

109. Berle and Jacobs, eds., *Navigating the Rapids*, p. 321.

110. Interview, the Honorable Philip Bonsal with Professor Rout, Washington, D.C., April 28, 1976. As for future problems with the SIS, Bonsal generalized, noting that many of the steps taken in 1940–42 "were not really thought out." In his view, however, the time for contemplative action did not exist.

111. See, for example, the admission of the Chilean chief of staff in September 1940, that the government lacked the financial means and had little inclination to deal with counterespionage problems. NARS, R.G. 165, folio 21, A-A1G-1/A-82ENs-11/EF-15/, section 4, *Chile*, pp. 10–16.

112. Irwin F. Gellman, *Good Neighbor Diplomacy: United States Policies in Latin America: 1933–1945* (Baltimore, 1979), pp. 31, 38–45. Gellman notes that while the idea of nonintervention was basic to U.S. policy in Latin America, such a vague principle would never be absolute. What Roosevelt did, however, was to sell the idea as something totally viable.

3

The Espionage War in Mexico: 1939–46

I. Introduction: Oil and Espionage

When Pres. Lázaro Cárdenas expropriated the bulk of Anglo-American petroleum holdings in Mexico on March 18, 1938, he was taking a prodigious gamble. With Washington assiduously cultivating its good neighbor image, it was unlikely that U.S. troops would enter his country, as they had in 1846, 1914, and 1916–17. Nevertheless, the directors of Royal Dutch Shell, Standard Oil of New Jersey, et al., declared that their properties had been illegally taken and instituted a worldwide blockade of Mexican petroleum. The result was a standoff: Cárdenas had the wells, but without tankers or markets, he might as well have sold the petroleum to the public and asked them to mix it with their tequila.

Determined not to bend under pressure, the Mexicans began querying Germany about increased oil sales,[1] and Adolf Hitler decided to take a hand in the petroleum poker game. Two representatives of the Reichstelle für Mineraloel (Reich Import Board of Petroleum), Karl Rekowsky and Dietrich Klamroth, arrived in Mexico City, and promptly signed a barter arrangement: in exchange for oil, the German firm of Ferostael-Essen-Ferostael would build power plants in the towns of Ixtapatango and Palmito.[2]

But one Third Reich governmental agency doing business in Mexico was not enough; a competing group also had to acquire its share of the petroleum bonanza. On the other hand, the new client did not wish to enter into direct negotiations with the Mexican government. The go-between in the complex scheme which evolved was William Rhodes Davis, a quixotic Yankee who had been involved in Mexican oil production prior to March 1938. With $3 million in funding from the Reichsbank and the blessings of Treasury (Hacienda) Minister Evaristo Sánchez Juárez and Economic Minister Eduardo Suárez, Davis was soon shipping Mexican oil

directly to Eurotank, a Hamburg-based refining concern which he allegedly owned. The director of Eurotank was Dr. Hellmuth Fetzer, a counselor assigned to represent Davis's real client: the German navy. Adm.
Erich Raeder may have believed that the Führer would not opt for a
general war until 1943, but he had no intention of having his fleet caught
with its bunkers empty. Davis signed petroleum barter agreements with
Mexico on July 6 and December 8, 1938. As a result of these deals,
500,000 tons of petroleum were made available to the German navy.[3]
Called by U.S. Ambassador Josephus Daniels Mexico's "deliverer in time
of need,"[4] Davis so impressed his Berlin paymasters that, in April 1939,
the Rekowsky-Klamroth team was recalled; Eurotank would become the
sole supplier of Mexican petroleum for the Third Reich.

With the German-Mexican oil trade increasing rapidly, in the spring
of 1939, Berlin dispatched Dr. Joachim Hertslet of the Reich Foreign
Economics Ministry to negotiate a comprehensive economic treaty with
the Cárdenas government. The suave and dapper Hertslet hosted many
social affairs, and went out of his way to demonstrate that Aryan Nazis did
not consider oil-rich non-Aryans to be hopelessly inferior. Before departing in August 1939, he negotiated a comprehensive trade pact which, had
it been ratified, might have significantly altered the course of German-
Mexican-U.S. relations. The Nazi invasion of Poland, however, spoiled this
ambitious plan.

Between March 18, 1938, and September 3, 1939, at least 1.3 million
tons of petroleum were shipped from Mexico to Nazi Germany.[5] The total
is probably greater, because the shifty Davis also consigned petroleum to
the United States, Italy, Scandinavia, and "Land's End" (British Isles),
which somehow wound up in Hamburg. According to U.S. intelligence
records, roughly 50 percent of all the petroleum exported from Mexico
during the eighteen months in question found its way into Nazi-con-
trolled refineries and storage tanks.[6] In essence, Hitler, Cárdenas, and
Davis thumbed their noses at Royal Dutch Shell and Standard Oil of New
Jersey, and got away with it.

Nevertheless, with the outbreak of the war and the establishment of
the British blockade against Germany, Davis's oil-trafficking plans disinte-
grated. Tankers destined for neutral ports were seized by the British, who
claimed that the oil was, in reality, destined for Germany.[7] In February
1940, Joachim Hertslet returned to Mexico in order to assist Davis, the
former miracle man, in slipping petroleum through. Working with Mexican minister Eduardo Suárez, Hertslet began shipping petroleum on
Japanese tankers across the Pacific. These vessels unloaded at Vladivostok, where Stalin's workers moved the product to German territory via
the Trans-Siberian Railway.[8] How much oil reached the Third Reich by
this means is unknown, but by September 1940, U.S.-Japanese relations
had deteriorated markedly, and Washington indicated to the Mexicans its
displeasure with these blockade-breaking efforts. Convinced that the
Reich had played its last card in the Mexican petroleum game, at least

until the war had been successfully terminated, Hertslet departed for Germany on September 24, 1940.

Teutonic persistence probably resulted in the successful loading of another Japanese tanker or two, but on December 20, 1940, Minister to Mexico Rüdt von Collenberg cabled Berlin that the oil traffic via Vladivostok would no longer be permitted. The Germans would still be trying to smuggle oil to the Reich in March 1941,[9] but their lack of success would only demonstrate that Hertslet had made the right move six months earlier. Meanwhile, William Rhodes Davis died mysteriously of an alleged heart attack in June 1941, and William Stephenson, chief of the British Security Coordination (BSC), has implied that his organization may have acted to quicken Davis's journey into the next life.[10] There is little question that the British certainly believed they had a few scores to settle with the man.

Naturally, the espionage problem was inextricably tied into the petroleum trade and expropriation issues. By 1939, Admiral Canaris had already decided that Mexico was to be a safehouse where Abwehr agents might prepare operations against the United States. The existence of such a privileged sanctuary depended upon the Mexican security forces maintaining a decidedly lax attitude toward German agents. Canaris counted on such benevolence, because he was sure the Mexicans understood that jailing the agents of a good petroleum customer might have disastrous economic consequences.[11]

But petroleum and German intelligence were closely linked in still another way. Karl Rekowsky would come back to Mexico two years later as an Abwehr II (sabotage) agent. Also, when he returned to Mexico in February 1940, Joachim Hertslet, while ostensibly working for the Reich Economic Ministry, had developed Abwehr connections as well.[12] The acquisition of petroleum was apparently too critical a matter to be left solely to the discretion of bureaucrats; so the bureaucrats had to join the ranks of the secret agents.

Again, the Germans were convinced that if they bought enough Mexican petroleum, their V-men would encounter few problems operating in that country. On the other hand, the idea that Abwehr agents might sneak back and forth across the Rio Grande with impunity, or use Mexico as an observation post from which U.S. developments could be charted, was something the Roosevelt administration found intolerable.[13] It is understandable, therefore, that J. Edgar Hoover would assign an FBI agent to Mexico in May 1940. Furthermore, with the creation of an SIS group in Mexico (hereafter referred to as SIS/Mexico), a secret surveillance agreement was quickly arranged with Mexican security forces. Exactly when this deal was made is unknown, but after August 30, 1940, U.S. agents regularly received copies of cables and radiograms sent and received by suspected V-men.[14]

The problem with this kind of confidential accord, however, is that until the Mexicans agreed to formalize U.S.-Mexican collaboration, it could be terminated at any time. Bilateral staff talks between U.S. and Mexican military and naval officials had begun in June 1940, and by July 30, 1940, the United States had given its assent to a preliminary pact dealing with arms deliveries, a joint regional defense board, and mutual intelligence cooperation.[15] But although the Lázaro Cárdenas and Manuel Avila Camacho regimes both sanctioned the continuation of talks, neither would formally accept any agreement reached. The real cause for Mexican reticence was the oil expropriation dispute which remained in the forefront of the national consciousness. Gradually, both the State Department and U.S. armed forces negotiators realized that the Mexicans would agree to nothing "until American claims for compensation arising from Mexico's expropriations of foreign petroleum properties should first be settled. . . ."[16]

Ultimately, the Roosevelt administration was more concerned with obtaining Mexican cooperation than in supporting the demands of Standard Oil of New Jersey and other oil companies.[17] This factor made possible a compromise which Mexico could accept, and on November 19, 1941, a comprehensive settlement satisfying U.S. land claims and providing a solution for the oil claims question was reached.[18] Foreign Minister Ezekiel Padilla went before the Mexican Senate and announced that the new agreement denoted "a marked change in the foreign policy of the United States of America."[19] As far as Washington was concerned, the payoff came on December 3, 1941, when the Mexicans agreed to previous plans calling for a joint defense board, air base rights, and intelligence cooperation. The public announcement concerning the creation of a joint defense board was made on January 12, 1942, and the lend-lease pact was announced on March 27.[20] With the announcement of an expropriation payment accord on April 17, 1942, petroleum lost its importance as a factor critically affecting the course of U.S.-Mexican foreign relations.

Although the November 19, 1941, agreement cleared the obstacles to a U.S.-Mexican military pact and secured the informal accords reached between the SIS/Mexico and the national police, certain problems continued to hamper the joint counterespionage effort. For one thing, the Mexican presidents persisted in taking a Jekyll-Hyde approach toward the problem. By May 1940, Lázaro Cárdenas had become sufficiently concerned to order Minister of the Interior (Gobernación) Luís García Tellez to begin a full investigation of German espionage activity in the country.[21] A resourceful and dominating chief executive, Cárdenas must also have known, at least in a general way, of the August 1940 communications surveillance arrangements made between the national police and the SIS/Mexico. Yet, as long as he was president, Cárdenas publicly maintained that neither German nor U.S. intelligence organizations were operating in Mexico.[22]

Nor would this situation change a great deal with the accession of Manuel Avila Camacho. In discussing the espionage issue in January 1941 with U.S. Counselor of the Embassy Pierre L. de Boal, the new president declared that he had learned that German spies were indeed operating in Mexico. But he also expressed his conviction that all these V-men had arrived from the United States, that country being their primary head-quarters! In reporting this incident to Washington, an amazed de Boal wondered whether Avila Camacho was deranged or merely misin-formed.[23] The president was probably neither, but the attitude he and Cárdenas manifested raised justifiable doubts concerning Mexico's deter-mination to grapple with its espionage problem.

In retrospect, Mexico followed paradoxical policies at home and abroad during World War II. On the one hand, that nation was one of the first Latin American states to break diplomatic relations with the Axis powers, doing so in December 1941; five months later, it declared war on Germany, Italy, and Japan.[24] Furthermore, Air Force Squadron #201, in action against the Japanese in 1945, made Mexico the only Spanish-speaking republic in the hemisphere to send forces into combat.[25] De-spite this evident commitment to the anti-Fascist cause, the Mexican government also allowed an identified Nazi spy ring to operate virtually unmolested until the end of the war. Clearly, the settlement of the petroleum expropriation problem earned the United States diplomatic and military support from Mexico in the struggle against the Axis. But when it came to counterespionage matters, Washington would discover that the Mexicans could not, or would not, hold up their end of the bargain.

II. The German Espionage Network in Mexico

A. The Boys from Ast Berlin

Although the Abwehr met with their Japanese counterparts on Mexi-can soil in 1936,[26] there was no effort until 1939 to build an espionage network in Mexico. Neither Canaris nor Foreign Minister Joachim von Ribbentrop wanted any difficulties with a Mexico whose economic poli-cies were favorable to Germany. Nevertheless, when London and Paris spurned the Führer's peace offer in October 1939, Canaris realized that the conflict might continue indefinitely; this prospect meant that the Abwehr must make haste in establishing a Mexican outpost.

It was this intelligence concern which brought Baron Karl Friedrich von Schleebrugge (code name: Morris) into prominence. Born in Prussia in 1888, the baron served on the western front for most of World War I. Between February and May 1938, he was in Mexico, claiming to be a representative of the Phoenix Sewing Machine Company of Bielefeld. Field Marshal Hermann Göring sent a letter attesting to his prowess as a peddler of these appliances, but Schleebrugge proved much more solici-tous concerning the sale of A.G. Landswerk Company products. This firm, headquartered at Landskrona, Sweden, specialized in armored cars and tanks. The baron did quite well, making both Mexican army friends and obtaining weapons contracts. He returned to Mexico in November 1938, this time representing the Lorenz Company of Berlin and hawking military communications wares. Business was none too brisk, but Schleebrugge gave many equipment demonstrations, and increased his circle of cronies among the Mexican military.[27]

Prior to September 1939, the baron transferred to the Luftwaffe, and in the Polish campaign he led a dive-bomber squadron. Evidently he distinguished himself, for, in October 1939, Baron Colonel von Schleebrugge was named a commandant of the Berlin Military Garrison. But with the Abwehr scrambling around for potential agents with experience and contacts in the Americas, the colonel found himself drafted for espionage duty. Placed under the direction of the economic section of Ast Berlin (I-Wi), the salesman-airman received only two months of training before being ordered to Mexico.

The advertising wag who coined the line, "Getting there is half the fun," could not have had Schleebrugge's itinerary in mind. Almost without exception, Abwehr agents sent to Mexico crossed the USSR by Trans-Siberian Railroad, and then by assorted vessels along the Vladivostock-Yokahama-Honolulu-California route. By the time he reached Mexico City in February 1940, the baron had not only been traveling six weeks, but had crossed the USSR in the midst of winter with a wife and two children—hardly a joyous experience under any circumstances. Upon entering Mexico, "Morris" gave his occupation as sales representative for the C. Lorenz Company and promptly began cultivating his old military contacts. With their help and the assistance of his brother, Franz Freiherr von Schleebrugge, a hardware goods businessman who had been in Mexico for thirteen years, the baron obtained an appointment in the Secretariat of Communications and Public Works. As a representative of this agency, he was thus empowered to travel the length and breadth of Mexico allegedly on government business.

"Morris" had the Mexican contacts and potentially excellent cover, but it takes more than this to establish an effective espionage network. A six-foot-tall, monocled man with a penchant for clicking his heels upon introduction, Schleebrugge drove a large, black Mercedes-Benz, and bought both a swank apartment in the capital and a fashionable home in Cuernavaca. His attractive Swedish wife, Bridget, was a quarter-century younger than her husband, and not inclined to sit at home and tend to domestic pursuits. Given his wife's preference for social prominence, plus the fact that Schleebrugge's espionage assignment did not require that he keep a low profile, it is understandable that the couple soon became well-known figures among Mexico City's international set.[28]

Col. Dr. Ludwig Dischler, commander of Ast Berlin, was well aware that while "Morris" was a logical front man, he was hardly the compleat spymaster. Instead, the man given the task of becoming the moving force behind German espionage in Mexico was Werner Georg Nicolaus (code name: Max). Born on September 26, 1898, at Charlottenburg, Germany, Nicolaus served on the eastern front during World War I and was decorated for heroism in action. After the conflict, probably because his father was manager of the Deutsche Bank in Berlin, Nicolaus obtained a position with the Banco Alemán-Antioqueño in Medelín, Colombia. As a bank officer, he made a better war hero. He served indifferently at several Colombian branches of the Banco Alemán, and while on vacation in Germany in November 1938, he received notice that his services would no longer be required.

It was this otherwise unfortuitous event which propelled Nicolaus toward his rendezvous with destiny. Encouraged by a former comrade-in-arms, Capt. Hermann Nitschke, in January 1939, Nicolaus applied for reenlistment in the German army. The rebuilding Wehrmacht greeted this authentic hero with open arms. Upon passing his physical, Nicolaus was commissioned a lieutenant, but after a short infantry school refresher course, the long arm of the Abwehr snapped him up. At forty-one, Nicolaus was a bit old to lead a field unit, but he had a flair for languages and a knowledge of Latin America which made him invaluable. After several months of training and observation trips to France, Holland, and Belgium, he was assigned to Ast Berlin's I-Wi section, his controller being Maj. Dr. Ernst Bloch. Promoted in October 1939, Captain Nicolaus was told that Mexico would be his future base of operations. He received additional training in sabotage and radio transmission before departing for his new post on January 12, 1940.[29]

As de facto leader of the Ast Berlin group in Mexico (See Chart IV), Nicolaus was directed to determine "the potential of Germany's enemies in the Western Hemisphere."[30] the major target was the United States, but "Max" was specifically prohibited from personally executing operations in that country. He was permitted to recruit agents from among the six thousand *Reichsdeutschen* presumed to be in Mexico and allotted ten thousand dollars in operational funds. Given cover as a collector for the Blaupunkt Radio Company, Nicolaus followed Schleebrugge's footsteps across the Siberian wastes and the Pacific Ocean to the Western Hemisphere. Before entering Mexico, however, he visited Max Vogel, an old banking associate in Bogotá, Colombia, and persuaded the latter to serve as a "drop," forwarding letters sent from Nicolaus to European addresses. This first task completed, "Max" arrived in Mexico City on March 30, 1940.[31]

Both *Landesgruppenleiter* Wilhelm Wirtz and Schleebrugge provided Nicolaus with the necessary entrées in capital city press, government, and military circles. As chief of the AO, Wirtz apparently expected to become the initial recruit in the network to be created, but "Max's" first selection was a businessman, Werner Barke (code name: Banco). A World War I veteran who arrived in Mexico in 1925, Barke was an employee of the Hayen-Eversbusch shipping firm and had been named honorary German consul in Tampico. After September 1939, Barke remained with this firm, but due to the British blockade, he had no significant tasks to perform. A fanatical Nazi, he spent much of his time

CHART IV

THE AST BERLIN NETWORK IN MEXICO 1940-42

COL. DR. LUDWIG DISCHLER (CHIEF, AST BERLIN)
MAJ. DR. ERNST BLOCH (CHIEF, I-Wi SECTION, ABTEILUNG-I)

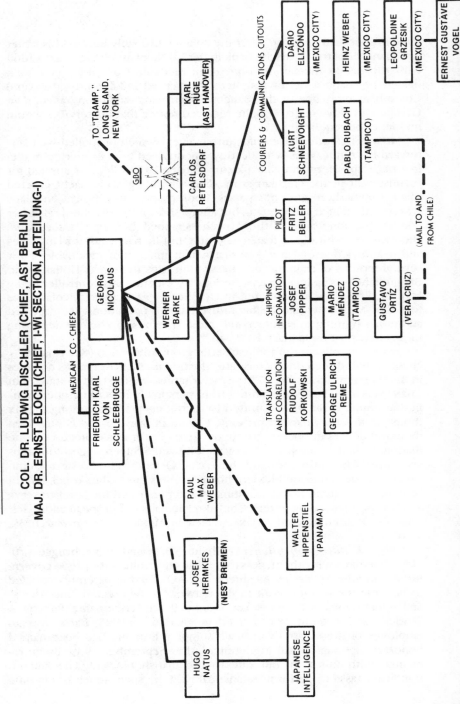

succoring German sailors on trapped ships at Tampico because of the outbreak of the war. Nicolaus visited these vessels looking for recruits, but came away most impressed by the knowledge and zeal of Barke. The new spymaster wanted information about the cargoes of arriving and departing Anglo-American ships at Tampico and Veracruz, and Barke had friends who could provide it. The relationship between "Max" and "Banco" grew so congenial that in October 1940, Nicolaus had Barke move to Mexico City and go full-time on the Abwehr payroll. The efficient and dedicated "Banco" became "Max's" chief-of-staff, making payoffs, enciphering messages, and handling reports from other members of the expanding ring.[32]

The capital city was no place to obtain shipping information, so Josef R. Pipper, Barke's old co-worker at Hayen-Eversbusch, took over that task. Arriving at Veracruz in 1925, Pipper had married a Mexican, but kept his German citizenship. Through Mario Méndez, a Mexican engineer, Pablo Rubach, a wharf and port captain at Tampico, and Gustavo Ortíz, port official in Veracruz, classified shipping information was regularly funneled to Pipper.[33]

Carlos Retelsdorf was born in Mexico in 1911 of German parents, and held both Mexican and German citizenship. An AO member re-nowned for his devotion to the Führer, Retelsdorf (code names: Glenn and Franco) was steered to Nicolaus through Wilhelm Wirtz. The young Nazi had confided in the *Landesgruppenleiter* his determination to seek a more active means for aiding the cause of the swastika. Since Retelsdorf had inherited a coffee plantation in 1934 and was independently wealthy, he would serve the Abwehr without compensation, but what most inter-ested "Max" was Retelsdorf's talent as a radio operator. When, during the fall of 1940, Canaris began encouraging Latin American agents to commu-nicate with the Third Reich via clandestine radio, Retelsdorf became Nicolaus's ace-in-the-hole.[34]

Paul Max Weber had entered Mexico as a journalist in October 1938. The German legation had requested the Cárdenas government to give him a visa and stated that his position was semiofficial. Nonetheless, Weber never carried a diplomatic passport, and his only known media activity was turning out propaganda diatribes for the Mexican AO. The holder of a doctoral degree in literature from the University of Berlin, Weber had been an exchange student at the University of Denver in 1933–34. He visited the United States again in 1939, ostensibly to consult with U.S. physicians, but the grey-eyed Dr. Weber suffered no illness that either the FBI or the Mexican police knew anything about. Contact with "Max" was established in April 1940, the omnipresent Herr Wirtz again acting as go-between. Since he spoke impeccable English and already had numerous contacts as a result of his previous residence in the United States, Paul Max Weber became the ring's expert on the United States and was charged with developing a network of informants in that country.[35]

Nicolaus was also supposed to receive assistance from Josef Hermkes (code name: Joe), a German who had served in World War I, entered Mexico in 1924, and became a naturalized citizen. That same year, he helped to organize a real estate company, an enterprise which suddenly folded in 1930 and caused Hermkes to be indicted for fraud. Not surprisingly, he returned to Germany where he remained for five years. In the interim, Hermkes joined the Nazi party, so that when he again entered Mexico in 1936, the local AO organization appointed him an *Ortsgruppenleiter* for Veracruz state. Legal trouble again made it incumbent upon Hermkes to return to Germany in 1939, but influential friends in the Cárdenas regime had him appointed honorary Mexican consul in Breslau in August of that year.[36] With the outbreak of the war, Hermkes was called up, and the details are monotonously similar. Snatched from the field army by Albert Herzog, a recruiter for Nest Bremen, Hermkes was given the equivalent of a ninety-day espionage course and ordered to Mexico along with Nicolaus in January 1940.[37]

The psychic demands upon train passengers making the trans-Siberian trip in mid-winter were probably considerable, for by the time "Max" and "Joe" reached Vladivostok, they were no longer on speaking terms. Hermkes took a different ship across the Pacific, and upon reaching Mexico in March 1940 formed a partnership with a German-Mexican, Luís Rumboldt, in the hardware sales business. Nicolaus was supposed to provide a regular stipend to Hermkes, but the former's antipathy had not abated in the interim; only direct orders from Ast Berlin made Nicolaus pay Hermkes some two thousand dollars in the fall of 1940. "Max" got his revenge, however, in that he refused to include "Joe" in any of the operations being planned or conducted. Frozen out of the picture, Hermkes remained on the Abwehr payroll, but long before the bombs fell on Pearl Harbor, he had virtually ceased to function as an intelligence source.[38]

The most useful and the last assistant sent via the USSR and Japan was Karl Franz Joachim Rüge (code number: Y2863). Another World War I veteran who sought his fortune in Latin America after that conflict, by 1933, Rüge had become general manager of Koerting Motors, Ltd., a Mexico City automobile sales concern. In August 1939, he traveled to Germany on a business trip, and six weeks later, he found himself, first, in uniform, and, shortly thereafter, in the Abwehr. But unlike Schleebrugge and Hermkes, Rüge spent eight months undergoing intensive training in microphotography. In July 1940, he was ordered to Mexico and given the task of producing microdot messages for the Nicolaus ring.

Claiming that the British blockade made a transatlantic return impossible, Rüge was able to justify his long absence and reclaim his general managership. Cover for his espionage activity was, therefore, no problem, but his financial requirements soon caused consternation. Upon his return, "Y2863" and his wife bought a new house in the posh Lomas de Chapultepec district. "Max" had been ordered to pay Rüge five thousand dollars upon arrival, but the microdot man needed even more money, for in addition to the house, he also purchased a new Cadillac sedan. Nicolaus's unfavorable comments about Rüge's propensity toward conspicuous consumption brought only sharp rejoinders from the latter. This was a situation Nicolaus would not normally have tolerated, but as he had no other microdot maker, he could only grin and bear it.[39]

Nicolaus's relationships were a good deal more cordial with an assortment of other valuable *Reichsdeutschen* and *Volksdeutschen.* Through Kurt Schneevoight, director of the Mexican subsidiary of Allgemeine Elektrizitaets Gesellschaft (AEG), a large electrical manufacturing concern, Nicolaus sent secret messages to Albrecht Gustav Engels (code name: Alfredo), an executive in Brazil and leader of a Rio de Janeiro-based spy ring. Postal contact with the PYL ring in Chile was maintained through the aforementioned Pablo Rubach, the latter either sending to or receiving information directly from Werner Barke. All legation business was handled by Hugo Natus, who passed on messages received by diplomatic pouch. Two businessmen, Richard Eversbusch, director of the Hayen-Eversbusch Steamship Agency, and Frederick Wilhelm, assistant manager for La Unión Química, provided valuable services, as did Fritz Beiler, a German aviator who had served in the Mexican army.[40]

One of Georg Nicolaus's primary tasks was to obtain information on U.S. military production, an endeavor made easier by the fact that the United States was a relatively open society. As a result, one of Nicolaus's first acts was to subscribe to some thirty newspapers and technical and economic journals published in the United States and Canada. Rudolf Richard Korkowski and eventually Georg Ullrich Reme (code name: Rurik), a United States citizen with pronounced Nazi sympathies, were enlisted to read all the publications, translating and collating the information for subsequent encipherment and dispatch back to Germany.[41] Of course, Colonel Dischler and Major Bloch at Ast Berlin also wanted figures concerning nonmilitary production as well. Data of this nature was occasionally supplied to the Nicolaus ring by two Abwehr agents in the United States, Richard Friedrich Freundt (code name: Fred) and Wilhelm von Rautter (code name: Rogers). Nicolaus also told Berlin in 1941 that he had "4 V-men north of the border" sending him a steady stream of classified information.[42] Whether this number was exaggerated or not, by the spring of that year, "Max" and his assistants were supplying classified materials concerning U.S. Navy and Army Air Force bombers and fighters, and on U.S. aluminum, petroleum, and steel production levels.[43]

Not only was the redoubtable Herr Nicolaus determined to obtain the information needed, he also took what he believed to be sufficient steps to insure that the material obtained reached the intended hands. Coded cablegrams bearing data were addressed to "Bradjob" (Ast Berlin), and the latter sent its replies to Nicolaus's post office box number 1006, addressing them to "Volco." The same titles were utilized when Nicolaus sent coded messages to Berlin via Radio Chapultepec (Radiomex), a commercial firm which beamed radiograms to foreign countries.[44] Information for which there was no great urgency or need for secrecy Nicolaus sent by airmail to specified drops in Portugal, Brazil, Chile, and Germany.[45]

Already in the fall of 1940, the Abwehr was aware that telegraphic and postal messages to and from the Americas were undergoing close scrutiny at Bermuda and elsewhere; more secretive methods would have to be used if adequate communications security was to be attained. One solution to the problem was the inauguration in January 1941 of clandestine radio transmissions by Carlos Retelsdorf. Such a procedure reduced the need to use Radiomex or to have cables and letters from "Bradjob" piling up in box 1006.

Nicolaus could also breathe easier because in April 1941, the first microdot machine finally arrived in Mexico. Included as part of an otherwise innocuous shipment of film equipment manufactured by AGFA, the apparatus was flown by LATI to Brazil and shipped to Tampico, where Frederick Wilhelm of La Unión Química took delivery of the goods. The microdot unit was listed as being a photo enlarger, a decidedly ironic twist considering what the machine actually did.[46]

Once Wilhelm had turned over the machine, Rüge and Nicolaus rented an apartment where microdot-making could be carried on without undue interference. By the end of April 1941, mail with microdots was on its way to drops in Chile, Brazil, and Sweden. The recipients of these letters either directed them to other addresses or broadcast the enclosed material to Germany via clandestine radio.[47]

Ast Berlin was encouraged to be equally circumspect in communicating with "Max." As a result, by June 1941, messages from "Bradjob" were being directed to eleven different post office boxes in the Mexico City federal district. For example, box 1744 was theoretically rented to Federico Ritter Schlegel, a *Volksdeutscher* who had moved to Guadalajara in 1937. For a financial consideration and a promise of further reward following Nazi victory in Europe, the box key was given to Dario Elizondo, a Mexican introduced to Nicolaus by the ubiquitous Wilhelm Wirtz. Heinz Weber, an employee of Bayer and Company, held a box in the name of Sánchez Paredes, while Leopoldine Grzesik, a fanatical Nazi, received mail and cables intended for "P. Barranco." All material received was turned over to "Max's" faithful subordinate, Werner Barke.[48]

But the acquisition and dissemination of sensitive information was not the only intelligence chore with which Nicolaus concerned himself. In the middle of March 1941, Werner Barke received word that an armed British freighter, the *Forresbank,* had docked at Tampico. "Banco" had made the acquaintance of Walter Joethner, a machinist on board the *Orinoco,* one of several German ships trapped in that harbor. Joethner had constructed a crude bomb, his intention being to facilitate the scuttling of the German freighters if the Mexican government made any efforts to seize the vessels. Barke sympathized with this goal but he saw in the bomb an opportunity to take offensive action. First, he persuaded Nicolaus to furnish funds so that Joethner could purchase a reliable timing device for his infernal machine. Then he convinced both men that the ersatz bomb should be tested on the *Forresbank*. On March 25–26, 1941, in the dead of night, Nicolaus and Joethner swam out to the British freighter and wired the bomb to its propeller. Setting the timing device to explode five days later, presumably when the *Forresbank* would be at sea, the apprentice saboteurs safely escaped.[49]

The homemade explosive proved to be Joethner's folly: it never detonated. But "Max" and "Banco" were not discouraged. On April 4, Ast Berlin was informed that special devices were being readied so that the trapped German vessels could be scuttled to prevent their being seized by the Mexican government. Nicolaus wanted permission to execute this plan, and to carry out the surreptitious bombing of other English freighters. Ast Berlin, however, had different ideas about the efficacy of these actions and qualms about the efficiency of the bombs being constructed. The order given by Dischler and Bloch was that "Max," "Banco," et al. were excellent agents, but that they should leave well enough alone.[50]

B. *The Man from Ast Hamburg*

With the Nicolaus-Schleebrugge ring in place, and Ast Berlin seemingly on the verge of attaining an espionage coup, other *Asts* made haste to acquire a slice of the prospective glory. The most important of these was Ast Hamburg, which already controlled groups in Brazil, Argentina, and Chile. The V-man chosen to make the trek to the land of tacos and mariachis was Edgar Hilgert (code names: Fraser and Fernández).

Born in July 1915 in Altona-Hamburg, Hilgert first entered the United States in February 1937. As a representative of A. Remy and Company, a drug firm based in Hamburg, Hilgert made several visits to the United States in 1938–39 and became well acquainted with the country that would become the chief focus of his attention. Over six feet tall with piercing blue eyes and dark hair, the gregarious Hilgert made numerous friends in U.S. and Canadian business circles before returning to Germany in June 1939.

Exactly when Hilgert joined the Abwehr is unknown, although he did mention to a colleague in 1944 that he had entered the organization in 1935 or 1936. This would mean that at the time he first entered the United States in 1937, Hilgert was already a recruit in the cloak-and-dagger business. The A. Remy drug company was known as an Abwehr front, and in September 1939, Hans Blume, general manager of the firm, was assigned to Ast Hamburg's I-Wi section. That Blume was Hilgert's company boss and became his *Ast* controller was probably no accident.

Like Nicolaus and Schleebrugge, Hilgert saw action in Poland in September 1939. Thereafter, he dropped out of sight until June 1940, when several of his North American acquaintances received letters asking them to sponsor Hilgert's efforts to gain entry into the United States. Alas, he received no takers, and, as a result, Ast Hamburg fixed "Fraser's" future base of operations as Mexico. Again, it was the long route: railroad across Siberia, steamer to Japan, and finally the Japanese liner, *Heiyo Maru,* across the Pacific. This vessel docked at Honolulu in September 1940, and since there was to be a layover of several days, Hilgert went ashore. When he was asked by U.S. immigration officials why he had been exempted from German military service, Hilgert replied that the German government had sufficient fighters, but not many who could do the specialized work of which he was capable. It could be assumed that Hilgert was referring to his cover occupation as special trade analysis expert assigned to the Banco Germánico de América del Sud branch in Mexico City. The immigration officials, however, remained unconvinced; they passed on their suspicions regarding this talented specialist to the FBI.[51]

Hilgert's arrival in October 1940 and the tribulations which ensued are proof positive that the Abwehr was probably as inefficient as some of its critics have claimed. Nicolaus had vaguely known that an Ast Hamburg representative was on the way, and he had also assumed that the new V-man would accept him as operational director of the German intelligence network in Mexico. Instead, "Max" and "Fraser" became instant enemies, the latter instructing the former that Ast Hamburg agents did not take orders from their Ast Berlin compatriots. The feisty Nicolaus salved his wounds by firing off a missive to "Bradjob" on November 5, reporting Hilgert's arrival and concluding that if the Abwehr had no one better to send to Mexico, it should cease assigning people there.[52]

As a supposedly high powered trade expert with the Banco Germánico, Hilgert had an office in the bank, but given the nature of his real work, it is no surprise that he was rarely there. What the job really provided was a suitable means for sending and relaying messages. With the help of Ewald Bork, a Mexico City *Ortsgruppenleiter* and bank manager, "Fraser" received messages from Ast Hamburg agents in other parts of the Americas, coded them, and dispatched the information to Germany via Radiomex, disguised as Banco Germánico business communiqués. Hilgert was particularly solicitous to the needs of Wilhelm von Rautter, another Remy and Company employee who under Hans Blume's tutelage had become an espionage agent. When, in April and October 1941, Rautter ran out of secret ink and needed more cash, he received letters from the German consulate in New York City, telling him when and where in Mexico City he was to meet Hilgert. Particularly since Nicolaus had previously been the recipient of the many gems of information furnished by Rautter, this agent's switch to Hilgert's direction may have been one of the more significant causes of the continuing "Max-Fraser" feud.[53]

According to instructions furnished before he left Germany, one of Hilgert's tasks was to acquire secret U.S. military information. Once on station, however, Ast Hamburg forwarded him a shopping list of specifics.

Among the materials sought, which "Fraser" was able to provide prior to September 1, 1941, were:

1. *Regional aeronautical charts of the United States at 1:1,000,000 scale. (Five copies of each were sought.)*
2. *Information on the performance and construction of Sperry gyroscopic products.*
3. *An aeronautical map (1:1,000,000 scale) of the Kenai Peninsula area of Alaska. Located near this peninsula was the town and U.S. naval base of Dutch Harbor (on Unalaska Island).* [Japanese carrier-borne aircraft attacked this town twice between June 3 and June 5, 1942.]
4. *An aeronautical planning chart of the United States of Lambert conformal conic projections.*
5. *A Great Circle Chart of the United States on Gnomonic Projection.*[54]

Hilgert's principal mission was to act as Ast Hamburg's Mexican representative, and aside from his imprudent remarks in Honolulu in September 1940, he made himself as inconspicuous as he could. Hilgert stayed away from the German legation, keeping in close touch only with Karl Rüge, whose microdot-making talents he needed, and radioman Carlos Retelsdorf. Just as significantly, Hilgert neither owned nor rented any kind of property. Between November 1940 and March 1942, he lived exclusively in apartments owned by trusted AO members, and he made sure that his name was kept off the mailbox. His only weakness appeared to be a propensity to drink, but even then, he preferred to imbibe only in the company of Ewald Bork and the AO people who provided his lodgings.[55]

The results of these precautionary measures would soon be evident. By September 1941, U.S. counterspies had managed to identify virtually all the members of the Ast Berlin ring. They also knew that Hilgert was in Mexico, but they believed that "Fraser" was merely another code name being used by Georg Nicolaus.[56]

C. *The Hardware Salesman from Nest Cologne*

Ast Münster never manifested an overwhelming interest in Western Hemispheric intelligence activity, but under the direction of Maj. Albrecht Focke (1940–44), Nest Cologne, its substation, became a significant force in transatlantic espionage activity. Focke's forte was economic intelligence, and one of his prime catches (or so he thought) was Franz Wilhelm Buchenau (code name: Saunders). Born of prosperous German parents in Torreón, Mexico in 1900, Buchenau never saw the fatherland until he arrived there to begin his secondary education in 1913. In 1920, he returned to Mexico to take a management position in Buchenau y Compañía, his father's hardware firm, but it was the age-old story; father and son simply did not get along. Franz obtained a U.S. immigration visa in 1926, and left for New York City and the golden years of the Roaring

Twenties. In 1936, it is believed that he departed the United States for Germany; two years later, he returned to Mexico via Buenos Aires, traveling on a German passport. His sojourn in the land of his birth was brief; in July 1939, he returned to Germany and began training with Nest Cologne shortly thereafter.

The story of Franz Buchenau, Abwehr agent, commences with his arrival aboard a LATI plane at Rio de Janeiro on November 2, 1940. "Saunders" carried a German passport which gave his occupation as Argentine representative of the Buchenau Company. Traveling on to Buenos Aires, he took a partner, Albert Metzger, and organized a hardware firm called El Arbolito. An Argentine *Volksdeutscher,* Metzger (code name: Alberto) proved to be both a successful hardware salesman and a faithful "cut-out" (go-between) for microdot messages subsequently sent from Mexico.[57] During the summer of 1941, Buchenau flew to Mexico City. He made contact with "Max" and surprisingly, perhaps, the two spies got along quite well together. "Saunders's" primary mission was to obtain entry into the United States, but a report for Nest Cologne sent via "Bradjob" at the end of October indicated that entry would probably be denied; Buchenau thus desired reassignment in Chile or Argentina. Nest Cologne, however, could not make up its mind. As a result, when Mexico broke diplomatic relations with Germany on December 11, 1941, "Saunders" found himself, for all practical purposes, stranded without orders.[58]

The significance of the Buchenau story lies in its inanity. Both Ast Berlin and Ast Hamburg strove diligently to find recruits who could be sent to Mexico. The operatives sent claimed to be businessmen, but with the exception of Rüge and Hermkes, inactivity in their reputed occupations made these cover identities ludicrous. Buchenau, in contrast, was a long-time Mexican inhabitant and an actual businessman. His cover was perfect, and he was operating in a country where he, and not the U.S. counterspies, would have a better knowledge of local conditions. But Buchenau wanted nothing to do with espionage in Mexico, and Nest Cologne formulated no plans for having him operate there.[59] Thus, from November 1940 on, his contributions to Abwehr intelligence were almost entirely nugatory.

D. *"Richard" and the IRA*

Winston Churchill is alleged to have said that had it been necessary, he would have made a deal with the devil to defeat Hitler. There were those among the Irish Republican Army (IRA) who would have made a pact with the Bohemian Corporal, Satan, or anyone else who could have promised the rapid termination of British rule in Northern Ireland. A leading figure among the work-with-Adolf school was Sean Russell, chief of staff of the IRA faction led by Maurice Twomey. This fiery militant had played a major role in initiating a terror bombing campaign in England early in 1939, and then journeyed to the United States on a speaking and fund-raising tour. Arrested in May of that year, Russell concluded that the

Nazis represented his best hope of gaining the aid needed to liberate Ulster. Through John McCarthy, an IRA roving ambassador, in January 1940, Russell made contact with the Abwehr and was promised funds, equipment, and sabotage training.

Reaching Berlin via Italy on May 5, 1940, Russell worked under the supervision of Capt. Hermann Goertz, studying Abwehr II (sabotage) techniques. On August 8, the IRA man boarded a U-boat; his mission (Operation Dove) was to initiate a new terrorist campaign in Ulster. Since England was then facing possible attack on her Channel coast, if Russell could mount a serious diversion, the German invasion scheme (Operation Sea Lion) might be considerably enhanced. But this activist would never throw another bomb. During World War II, U-boats carried no doctors, so that when a gastric ulcer began hemorrhaging, his fate was sealed. Sean Russell died aboard the submarine on August 14, 1940.[60]

The death of this fiery Irishman was a blow to Abwehr plans, but Northern Ireland and England were not the only places where effective sabotage missions could be mounted. Moreover, Col. Erwin Lahousen, chief of Abwehr II, had already decided to put another scheme into effect.

Karl Berthold Franz Rekowsky was born in Germany in 1899. In 1936, he entered Mexico as a representative of a newsprint concern and made several mutually satisfactory deals with the Mexican government. He also represented Reichstelle für Mineraloel in its 1938 petroleum negotiations, and made several business trips between Germany and Mexico in 1939. In February 1940, Rekowsky's intention of returning to Mexico with his family engendered a visit from Capt. Hermann Goertz. This was the same man who would become Sean Russell's controller and eventually be recognized as Abwehr II's chief specialist in Irish affairs. The captain made Rekowsky an offer he couldn't refuse: if the latter wished to go to Mexico at any time in the near future, he would have to do so as an Abwehr II operative. In the movies and the more gallant literary epics, the hero disdains to compromise his principles, but in real life it is often better to be a jackal than a lion. Besides, had Rekowsky become too defiant, his family might have been forced to pay the consequences. Code named "Richard," he was given no training in special inks, ciphers, or microdot making, but told to deliver his reports to the commercial attaché for transmission via diplomatic pouch. By LATI flight, he crossed the Atlantic to Brazil and arrived in Mexico on May 16, 1940.[61]

Through John McCarthy, Sean Russell's original contact, the Abwehr had reached an agreement whereby it promised to pay IRA militants in the United States for carrying out sabotage attacks against ships, war plants, and so forth. "Richard's" mission was to act as paymaster, with details concerning payment and reportage to be arranged when "Richard" met John McCarthy. Neither man knew the other, but Goertz solved that problem easily; a postcard was intricately cut in half; Rekowsky was given one piece, and McCarthy the other. Not until August 1940 was a meeting finally arranged in Acapulco, but the deal made was simplicity itself. The IRA elements would carry out the acts of sabotage and send newspaper clippings proving their prowess as saboteurs to a special mailbox rented by "Richard." The V-man would then pay McCarthy whenever the latter could travel to Mexico City. Abwehr II had set aside some sixty thousand dollars for this operation, and Colonel Lahousen was prepared to double the amount if the new relationship proved fruitful.[62]

Between August 1940 and April 1941, McCarthy visited "Richard" four times and received fifty thousand dollars in small bills. Meanwhile, "Richard" enthusiastically reported to Abwehr II that IRA men had comitted arson in a rubber factory in Philadelphia and wrecked the oil conduit valves of a pipeline in Texas City, Texas. Still another message, sent to Berlin on March 13, 1941, related that since the beginning of the year, sabotage attempts had been made against seventeen ships, and five of these had resulted in serious fires and other damage. "Richard" reported that although the newspaper clippings spoke of mysterious fires, accidents, and unexplained catastrophies, these were, in fact, planned acts of sabotage.[63] Rekowsky's postwar testimony suggests that he believed at least some of these claims,[64] but there is good reason to doubt many or all of them. We presented Rekowsky's testimony to an FBI spokesman, who stated the bureau had no evidence of any IRA-Abwehr acts of sabotage having been committed in the United States. His inference was clear: A group of Irish-American hustlers had conned some of the Abwehr's finest.[65]

Actually, by the spring of 1941, Canaris himself had begun to wonder about the authenticity and the efficacy of the entire IRA-"Richard" operation. Foreign Minister Ribbentrop apparently learned of it from Rüdt von Collenberg, the minister to Mexico, who stumbled upon Rekowsky's reports in the diplomatic pouch. During the winter of 1940–41, Collenberg directed several messages to the foreign office, arguing that this sabotage operation would diminish the reservoir of goodwill the Reich had built in Mexico through its timely petroleum purchases.[66] Ribbentrop, in his turn, raged at Canaris, insisting that the Rekowsky-IRA operation was a provocation which would provide Roosevelt with an excuse to declare war. But if, as Canaris had begun to suspect, the reported bombings were essentially hoaxes, admitting this fact would lay his organization open to merciless attacks by both the foreign office and the SD.[67] Such a result had to be avoided at all costs.

Meanwhile, back in Mexico City, Rekowsky was having his own problems. Although he was dimly aware of the diplomatic furor over his mission, his chief concern was that, after promising to do so, the Abwehr still refused to allow his family to join him. Alone, duped, and forced to accept a mission he never wanted in the first place, Rekowsky felt he had good reason to feel sorry for himself. Perhaps this was why he spent his evenings "flourishing large sums of American money," and "taking tourist girls to night clubs where he entertains ... extravagantly."[68] Spies, like normal persons, need rest and relaxation. But if the Abwehr decided that it was being swindled by IRA advocates in the United States, "Richard" would have to provide some convincing answers regarding his role in the affair. And if these were not deemed satisfactory, he would have neither American money to spend nor tourist girls to entertain for a long, long time.

E. *Morale and Money in Mexico*

Should a spy fight a duel? That the question comes up tends to showcase one of the more bizarre incidents in the history of Abwehr activity in Mexico. When, in September 1939, Karl Rüge was serving as a noncommissioned officer on the western front, he decided to apply for commissioned officer status and cited his position as an official in the party hierarchy. Since Rüge had joined the AO while in Mexico, Ewald Bork, an *Ortsgruppenleiter* in the federal district, was one of the persons asked to give a character reference. For some unexplained reason, a copy of Bork's confidential letter was passed on to Rüge; it portrayed the applicant as an irresponsible opportunist and intimated that his dedication to Nazism was distinctly lacking in fervor. Rüge was commissioned anyway, but he nursed a grudge which he intended to settle. Upon reaching Mexico City in September 1940, he visited Bork at the Banco Germánico and challenged him to a duel. A committee of honor was appointed from members of the German community in Mexico City, and Georg Nicolaus was placed in charge of the group.

Ewald Bork was a man on the portly side, and, in any case, bank managers are not normally skilled in either the use of firearms or hand-to-hand combat. Although he refused to retract his statements, not surprisingly, he declined Rüge's challenge. Scenting victory due to Bork's demural, Rüge circulated a letter denouncing the AO official as a sniveling coward and resigned from the Nazi party in disgust. The uproar gradually died down, but the incident soured relations between the Ast Berlin ring and Bork. More significantly, it attracted the unwanted attentions of SIS/Mexico to all the parties who were involved in the embroglio.[69]

Spending money? In addition to the cash he brought with him, between November 1940 and May 1941, Ast Berlin dispatched thirty-five thousand dollars to Georg Nicolaus for payments to subagents, bribes, purchases of materials, and living expenses.[70] Generally, the funds never came directly from Germany itself. For example, on at least two occasions, the Chase National Bank in New York received an order from the Union Bank of Switzerland to pay a specified sum to "Señor Carlos Enrique López Mann." This mysterious gentleman was to collect the funds at the Mexico City branch of the Banco Germánico. "Bradjob" then wired "Max" as to his new identity, and Ewald Bork sanctioned the handing over of the cash.[71]

After the Mexican government closed down all German consulates in August 1941, cash transfers such as that just described came under increasing scrutiny. The Abwehr solved this difficulty, however, by having branches of German companies such as Compañía General de Anilinas, a subsidiary of I.G. Farben Industries, make secret payments to German agents, the sum paid out being credited to an account in the home office. As a result, at the close of December 1941, Nicolaus could report that he still held a cash reserve of five thousand dollars.[72]

Excluding the "Richard"-IRA operation, the maintenance of the Abwehr establishment in Mexico cost more than one hundred thousand dollars annually for the years 1940 and 1941.[73] Some of this money was used by Josef Pipper and his subagents to obtain shipping information from Mexican officials.[74] Georg Nicolaus was apparently on good terms with a number of Mexican press figures, and according to U.S. documents, payments for unknown considerations were definitely made.[75] "Max" probably greased palms at the Interior Ministry as well, for he enjoyed unusual access to areas of the ministry closed to the general public.[76] Certainly he paid well to obtain one of his prizes, a transcript of the private conversation between FDR's vice president-elect Henry Wallace and Avila Camacho, held after the Mexican's December 1940 inauguration ceremony.[77]

Georg Nicolaus was relatively abstentious when it came to spending money on himself, but many of the other V-men sent to Mexico chose to live like espionage princes. Friedrich Karl von Schleebrugge's Mercedes-Benz sedan, swank home, and luxury apartment set the pace, but Karl Rüge, with his new home and Cadillac, was not far behind.[78] Others who acted as if Abwehr employment was the equivalent to a free pass on the Gravy Train were Karl Rekowsky, Paul Max Weber, and Josef Hermkes. Weber ran up outrageous debts in some of the swanker haberdasheries and night spots in the capital, while Hermkes took funds supplied by Nest Bremen and bought a business.[79]

Taken individually, the Rüge-Bork incident and the profligate spending of these V-men was hardly consequential. Added together, these acts and the general lack of discretion suggest that the Abwehr sent a pretty poor contingent of agents to Mexico. What must be remembered, however, is that the petroleum question seems to have been viewed as the controlling factor. If the Roosevelt administration had kept Mexican petroleum out of the United States while Germany was maintaining a high level of petroleum purchases, it is unlikely that the SIS/Mexico would have received significant cooperation from the Mexican police. It was not, therefore, the competence of the agents themselves, but the "black gold" halos they wore which were supposed to give them protection and make effective operations in Mexico possible.

III. The United States Counterespionage Organization in Mexico

A. Breaking into the Abwehr Network

FBI records reveal that Gus T. Jones, an agent who had worked with Mexican security forces prior to September 1939,[80] was sent to Mexico City as an undercover operative in mid-1940 to investigate German espionage activities.[81] Initially posing as a businessman, Jones was named civil attaché in August 1941, and it was he who would organize and direct the U.S. counterespionage effort in Mexico in 1940–43.[82]

In establishing the SIS/Mexico, Jones eagerly sought the assistance of U.S. citizens residing in the country, but most of his informants and contacts appear to have been Mexican nationals. In particular, his friendship with Miguel Martínez, chief of the Federal District Police, stood him in good stead. As early as July 1940, SIS/Mexico was receiving copies of suspicious communications being sent to Germany.[83] The next development was an arrangement established circa August 30, 1940, whereby SIS/Mexico received carte blanche from Mexican officials regarding interception of German postal, cable, and commercial radio communications.[84] Henceforth, copies of messages sent over Radiomex by persons deemed suspicious wound up in the hands of Gus Jones and his assistants. The same agreement gave SIS/Mexico access to Nicolaus's mailbox, thereby providing critical knowledge about "Max" and the other members of the Ast Berlin ring. Once these other agents became known, their postal boxes were also watched, and the incoming mail was carefully perused. As a result, the multi-post office box scheme that "Max" devised rapidly lost its effectiveness.[85]

With the United States close by and able to exert enormous influence, and with the British blockade having strangled the Mexican-German petroleum traffic, the German V-men simply could not have continued evading SIS/Mexico surveillance. But in addition, Schleebrugge, Rüge, Nicolaus, et al., committed several abominable blunders, which provided Gus Jones and his aides with valuable assistance. One of the more glaring and least defensible examples of German fumbling was the case of Confidential Informant 595.

Because he had spent several years there as a student, spoke the language with facility, and claimed to know the customs, Dr. Paul Max Weber was chosen by Nicolaus as the Ast Berlin ring's U.S. expert. A close friend of Weber's was William A. Bockhacker, an American citizen of German parentage, whom Weber had known since his 1933–34 school days at the University of Denver. The two men maintained sporadic contact over the next several years, during which Bockhacker moved to Los Angeles and obtained employment as an engineer in the burgeoning West Coast aircraft industry. Abruptly in an April 1941 letter, Weber dropped the mask of disinterested friendship. He reminded Bockhacker of his parental origins, his duty to the fatherland, and proposed that Bockhacker aid the Reich by supplying secret aircraft production and performance information. As a kind of afterthought, Weber hinted that the financial rewards would be substantial, but the proffered carrot did nothing to assuage Bockhacker's sense of betrayal. On April 11, 1941, he took the letter to the FBI's Los Angeles field office and told the agents all he knew about Weber.

What most interested the Hoover men was that the angry Bockhacker seemed determined to gain a measure of vengeance. The aircraft engineer was dubbed Confidential Informant 595, and instructed to become a counterfeit traitor. Eventually, a bigger fish than Weber would reveal himself, and this was the man the FBI was after. They would not have very long to wait. In May, Weber wrote his new recruit that, in the future, all replies to questions sent should be forwarded to "Mr. Volco," whose address was post office box 1006, Mexico City; the trail led directly to Georg Nicolaus, and another scheme for throwing sand into the gears of an Ast Berlin operation was put into effect.

For six months, 595 fed "Mr. Volco" tantilizing, but largely inconsequential, information while steadily collecting a handsome fee. Finally, in October 1941, Nicolaus concluded that he was being led by the nose down a blind alley, and so he allowed this latest effort at conning the Abwehr to peter out. Certainly Paul Max Weber's pretensions as a U.S. expert were shattered, but this could be no comfort to "Max." If he had ever previously doubted it, he could now be certain that U.S. counterspies knew who he was, where he could be contacted, and what he was after.[86]

Even had the Bockhacker affair not been a trap, events transpiring outside of the country had already resulted in the unmasking of most of the Abwehr's Mexico network. Painfully aware that the Anglo-Americans could and would tamper with the mails, cables, and radiograms being sent to and from Germany in the fall of 1940, the Abwehr sought to have all Latin American units establish a clandestine radio service. Carlos Retelsdorf had received a ham radio license in 1937, which permitted him to operate a five-watt transmitter, the call letters being XE1CZ. With the financial assistance of Karl Friedrich von Schleebrugge, Retelsdorf was able to install a five hundred-watt transmitter in a house in Coatepec. Station GBO began broadcasting on January 4, 1941; four days later, the RID picked up the clandestine radio's signal and, on January 9, the mysterious operator was identified as "Glenn." How had the U.S. forces moved so fast?[87]

A combination of atmospheric problems and difficulties caused by the earth's curvature combined to make it impossible for "Glenn" to contact a radio station in Germany. Attempts were also made to reach FMK "Sabine," the clandestine station inside Spain, but these endeavors also proved abortive. Thus, on January 8, 1941, "Glenn" radioed double agent William Sebold, whose station at Centerport, Long Island, was the wireless link for the Abwehr ring led by Friedrich Joubert Duquesne (code name: Joe K.). The arrangement made was that Sebold was to relay "Glenn's" messages to Ast Hamburg and vice versa.[88]

In handling messages to and from GBO, Sebold learned that "Glenn" lacked copies of both Nicolaus's and Hilgert's ciphers, but by the end of February 1941, FBI cryptanalysts had broken them and were reading the messages. As a result, potentially sensitive information could be partially edited or not relayed at all. The latter seems to have been the case with the GBO transmission of June 10, 1941, which reported that nine English battleships were undergoing repairs in U.S. navy yards.[89] Similarly, messages from Ast Hamburg to Hilgert or Nicolaus also underwent careful excision. In this way, the efforts of the Abwehr in Mexico were gradually rendered useless.

After some hestitation and probably as a result of U.S. prodding, on June 28, 1941, Ministry of Interior officials closed down Retelsdorf's Coatepec station. Somehow informed of impending developments, that same day, Edgar Hilgert cabled Ast Hamburg of GBO's impending demise and advised that Sebold be warned immediately.[90] But Gus Jones obtained a copy of this message as well and contacted Washington, whereupon Hoover decided that it was time for Sebold to end the masquerade. In a series of lightning raids carried out on June 30, 1941, the Duquesne ring was bagged in its entirety. According to one FBI agent, the round-up was like "shooting fish in a barrel."[91] Not only had the Abwehr organization in the United States suffered a crushing defeat; once Sebold began testifying, Canaris must have realized that his entire operation north of the Panama Canal was finished.

B. *Unrequited Love and Other Calamities*

Georg Nicolaus would probably have preferred to believe that the mistakes of his superiors had been the primary reason for his undoing. In fact, no one contributed more to his own network's security problems than "Max" himself. The origin of this disaster began innocently enough in the spring of 1940, when Nicolaus was introduced to Señorita Teresa Quintanilla. The lady was the sister of Don Luís Quintanilla, a counselor in the Mexican embassy in Washington, D.C.; she was also part-owner and manager of a swank Mexico City apartment house. Financially secure, Señorita Quintanilla was well connected among the capital's social elite. She professed to support fascism and was passionately antigringo, attitudes which endeared her to pro-Nazi elements.[92] Moreover, since she had shown an inclination to assist Nazis in their dealings with the Mexican bureaucracy, keeping her satisfied might conceivably contribute to the German intelligence effort. Certainly Teresa Quintanilla made no attempt to conceal her interest in the tall, blond Herr Nicolaus, and although the latter had a wife and child in Germany, not even spies could be expected to practice unrelenting continence. In September 1940, love and/or duty triumphed: Nicolaus moved in with his Mexican sweetheart.

The idyll lasted eight months. Whether the affair was essentially "sexpionage" (sex in exchange for assistance), or whether he simply tired of his señorita, at the beginning of April 1941, Nicolaus moved out. His tastes having once again gravitated toward Teutonic types, Nicolaus promptly chose a widowed German frau as his next paramour.

That Teresa Quintanilla might view such bed-hopping from a less cosmopolitan perspective was a consideration the German apparently overlooked. On April 25, 1941, the scorned woman evened scores with a devastating deposition given to security officials in the Interior Ministry. She affirmed that Georg Nicolaus had admitted that he was an Abwehr agent, and that he often discussed secret matters with Werner Barke, Paul Max Weber, and Karl Rüge. She claimed that Paul Max Weber received Mexican passports and classified information from Amelia Elena Tenorio, a lawyer in the Interior Ministry, and that Nicolaus boasted of being able to communicate with Germany by means of clandestine radio. Señorita Quintanilla did not know the name of the radio operator, but she stated that Nicolaus referred to him as "Don Carlos," and his phone number in Coatepec was 45. The Mexican police had no difficulty determining that this was the home phone of Carlos Retelsdorf.[93]

If the Quintanilla affair makes the German agents in Mexico appear criminally inept, an even harsher critique of their activity was presented to the German foreign office by Rüdt von Collenberg. On April 23, 1941, two days before Teresa Quintanilla began singing her song, the minister forwarded his observations on the local Abwehr personnel to Berlin. Karl Rekowsky was denounced as a dangerous incompetent, while Josef Hermkes was characterized as being disinclined to do anything except spend money. Karl Rüge was condemned for having revealed his mission while drunk in a Guadalajara tavern. Edgar Hilgert was criticized as being "careless in the way he was conducting himself," and thereby jeopardizing the Banco Germánico's position as a service and commercial institution. Ironically, only Georg Nicolaus earned Collenberg's respect, but as the diplomat depicted Mexico as "swimming with American spies," he believed "Max's" cover had become hopelessly compromised. In stating his conclusion, Collenberg made his position painfully clear: The bumbling V-men must be hustled out of the country as rapidly and discreetly as possible.[94]

The April 23, 1941, memorandum was etched in such uncompromising terms that if even half of what the minister said was true, the Abwehr in Mexico was obviously in its death throes. Indeed, forty-eight hours later, even Georg Nicolaus, Collenberg's choice as best of the bad, was being denounced to Mexican officials. But, as one might suspect, Collenberg did not write this communiqué before carefully assessing the situation at hand. In fact, he was well aware that some of the same fumblers he had just denounced were straining every muscle in the hope of making his recommendations come to pass.

C. Flight

If the Abwehr operation in Mexico could be compared to a sinking vessel, the first spy on board was also the first to abandon ship. Baron Friedrich Karl von Schleebrugge, acting in concert with Georg Nicolaus, was supposed to oversee Ast Berlin's Mexican operation. Initially, "Max" seemed to accept the idea that "Morris" was his operational partner and military superior, but, by the fall of 1940, the two men had become involved in bitter public quarrels, a development duly reported by

SIS/Mexico.[95] Since Nicolaus did not have to depend upon Schleebrugge for money and was essentially responsible for organizing and operating the network, he was the man most likely to triumph in the struggle for power. Increasingly, therefore, the baron came to view himself as the proverbial fifth wheel.

And if this proud but indolent man did not have sufficient troubles with his erstwhile compatriot, the Mexican government soon provided him with additional concerns. At the instigation of the U.S. embassy, in September 1940, police raided Schleebrugge's Mexico City residence allegedly looking for weapons. They found instead a powerful but unregistered radio transmitter which they confiscated.[96] Another crushing blow occurred a month later. As an official of the Mexican Ministry of Communications, Schleebrugge expected few problems when he applied to obtain a license to operate a commercial radio station; instead, his request was flatly rejected.[97] With Nicolaus having reduced his position to ceremonial chief, with the Mexican government opposed to granting his requests, and with an awareness that he was under surveillance, "Morris" made up his mind—he wanted out.

Ast Berlin was not strongly opposed to Schleebrugge's departure, but he was expected to make his own return arrangements. Unable to book a passage for himself and his family until June 1941, and suspecting that the Mexicans were planning a spy exposé,[98] Schleebrugge frantically sought Collenberg's help. Since "Morris's" exit was something the legation chief desired, he wired Berlin asking for rapid foreign office action. On April 16, 1941, Ribbentrop approached the Japanese government, and thirteen days later, Friedrich Karl von Schleebrugge, his wife, and children boarded the *Heiyo Maru* at Acapulco, the Japanese naval attaché having directed that their signatures on the passenger manifest were unnecessary.[99] By means of this ingenious strategy, "Morris" was able to give his shadowers the slip; until September 1941, SIS/Mexico believed the baron was still in the country.[100]

Schleebrugge reached Japan late in May 1941. Instead of immediately returning to the Third Reich, he decided to go sightseeing in China, and was stranded when the Russo-German war broke out. Eventually he settled in Peking where he spent the rest of the war.[101] It was hardly a fitting climax to the career of an itinerant spymaster, but it was certainly better than life in some jail or concentration camp.

The second agent who found it expedient to return to the Third Reich was the saboteur-paymaster, Karl Rekowsky. At some time during the winter of 1940–41, he became aware that he was under surveillance, a factor which did nothing to mitigate his increasing distress. Finally, on March 19, 1941, "Richard" sent a report which, although emphasizing the successes of the "northern friends" (i.e., IRA), concluded that Mexico was now too dangerous a place for further meetings and payoffs. As a new base of operations, he suggested Guatemala, and hinted that naming a new paymaster might also be a prudent step.[102]

The increasingly nervous Rekowsky also poured out his problems to Rüdt von Collenberg, and again the Japanese naval attaché was called to the rescue. On April 29, 1941, "Richard" joined Schleebrugge as an unlisted passenger on the *Heiyo Maru*. The following day, Mexican police appeared at Rekowsky's old residence to take him into custody for purposes of interrogation. "Richard" had flown the coop just in time.[103]

While Schleebrugge chose to dawdle in China and visit the Great Wall, Rekowsky sailed on to Vladivostock, and boarded the first European-bound train available. The trip was uneventful, with an apprehensive "Richard" reaching Berlin on June 20, 1941—two days before the invasion of Russia.[104] But circumstances, about which he was unaware, were now working in his favor. On May 2, 1941, Abwehr II had named Carlos Vogt, a naturalized Mexican citizen since 1934, as "Richard's" replacement, but on June 2, 1941, Admiral Canaris suddenly cancelled the whole operation.[105] Since Joachim von Ribbentrop had finally determined to go to Hitler and make the IRA sabotage campaign a fundamental policy issue, Canaris could now agree to its termination without appearing either defeatist or indifferent to Germany's greater interests.[106] Providentially, then, Rekowsky's return occurred shortly after the Abwehr had neatly managed to extricate itself from a sticky situation. A prolonged investigation of his activities would only give emphasis to an operation the organization now wanted covered up. So instead of being interrogated and jailed, "Richard" was given a tongue-lashing and told that the Abwehr no longer had any need for his services.[107] Karl Rekowsky was hardly a successful agent, but anyone who escaped potential detention in Mexico, the USSR, and Nazi Germany all in the same year must certainly have had the ear of the highest supernatural authorities.

Alas, Rekowsky's good fortune was nontransferable to the other Mexican V-men. Increasingly, these agents found themselves being shorn of their cover and subjected to the glare of unrelenting newspaper publicity. On April 30, 1941, Mexico City newspapers published what Collenberg had been afraid of—sensationalist stories naming Schleebrugge, Rekowsky, Nicolaus, and assorted AO officials as Nazi spies.[108] Next, the same day that station GBO was shut down (June 28, 1941), another series of articles was published labeling Nicolaus, Rekowsky, and Schleebrugge as spies and intimating that at least a dozen unnamed *Reichsdeutschen* were also involved in espionage activity.[109]

Even harder times were in store because, on August 8, 1941, the Mexican government ordered all German consulates closed. Shortly thereafter, antiespionage legislation was introduced in the Mexican congress. Aware that a critical juncture had been reached, Nicolaus contacted Rüdt von Collenberg and requested that the German legation not intervene if and when the Mexican police arrested him.[110] At approximately the same time, the cautious Edgar Hilgert informed Ast Hamburg via the German diplomatic pouch (August 16, 1941) that he believed the Anglo-Americans had cracked his cipher and were aware of his identity. As a result he was quitting his post with the Banco Germánico and going underground.[111]

But the sense of stoicism and determination manifested by "Max" and "Fraser" was nowhere evident in the behavior of Paul Max Weber. The latter may already have concluded that the Bockhacker contact was a trap, and that his own days of freedom were numbered. By private plane, Weber flew to Manzanillo where, on September 17, 1941, he sailed away aboard the *Heiyo Maru*. Perhaps it was his intention to remain in Japan, but instead he wound up in Saigon, then occupied by Japanese troops. Once settled in, Weber cabled Nicolaus that he still wanted to work for the Ast Berlin group at his new address. Since the distance between Mexico City and Saigon exceeds eight thousand miles, it is not clear what services Weber could still perform for Nicolaus. "Max's" reaction mirrors his probable attitude toward the absent Herr Weber: he never replied.[112]

D. *Counter-Counterespionage*

Acting informally but insisting that the matter remain confidential, on April 11, 1940, Luís García Tellez, minister of the interior, asked the U.S. Department of State for information concerning German intelligence activities in Mexico. Undersecretary Sumner Welles was consulted on this request, but the decision reached was that the petition should not be honored. U.S.-Mexican relations were still frosty as a result of the 1938 oil expropriation, and the official position enunciated by President Cárdenas was that there was no German intelligence activity being conducted in Mexico. And if these reasons were insufficient, State Department observers of Mexican internal affairs had still another. Herbert Bursley, then an officer in the American Republics section, put it most succinctly: Internal security in the Cárdenas regime was so bad that if the State Department honored the request, there was great risk "that it [information] would be used for the protection rather than the detection of Nazi . . . agents in Mexico."[113]

The 1940–41 success of the SIS/Mexico in monitoring Abwehr activity in that country was pervasive evidence that at least some Mexican police and governmental officials could keep secrets. Moreover, with the succession to Cárdenas by Avila Camacho, the Mexicans seemed increasingly inclined to cooperate with Washington in the undeclared war against the Axis. On May 21, 1941, Mexico became the first Latin American state to allow RID agents to employ mobile radio detectors on its soil, and six days later, Ambassador Josephus Daniels recommended to Washington that Gus Jones officially be named civil attaché, or U.S. counterspy chief, in Mexico.[114]

But cooperation in matters of detection tended to mask a gradually emerging and infinitely more intractable problem. On July 12, 1941, Ambassador Daniels handed to Foreign Minister Ezequiel Padilla a bulky document painstakingly denoting the intelligence activities of Georg Nicolaus, Friedrich Karl von Schleebrugge, and Paul Max Weber, and asked that these Germans be placed under arrest.[115]

Of the four Latin American nations to be discussed in this work, Mexico was the first to be treated with such confidentiality, and Foreign

Minister Padilla initially seemed prepared to act with dispatch. On July 17, he forwarded a copy of the memorandum to the attorney general for legal action. At the same time he assured Daniels that the "appropriate authorities of the Mexican government were undertaking a detailed investigation" and in "due time" the "necessary action with respect thereto" would be undertaken.[116] Washington was prepared to wait, but not for long. On August 4, a blunt message ordered the embassy to "please ascertain [the] nature of the action contemplated by Mexican authorities." Ambassador Daniels again queried Padilla (August 7), the foreign minister replying that the "alert and efficient Mexican police" were responding to the espionage situation. The next day, Daniels reported somewhat testily to Washington that he would send a detailed dispatch regarding Mexican activity only when he had some solid information.[117]

Probably no one knew it then, but both Daniels and Washington were going to wait a long, long time. On November 14, 1941, Avila Camacho decreed a tough, new espionage law.[118] On February 3, 1942, Demetrio Flores Fagoaga was named head of a new espionage bureau in the Interior Ministry, and this bureaucrat vowed that he would "rid Mexico of spies."[119] These acts may appear impressive, but between July 12, 1941, and February 27, 1942, not one of the V-men in the country was arrested, charged, or sentenced. Why?

A retired Mexican diplomat, who agreed to discuss this question if he could remain anonymous, argued that a mix of domestic and foreign issues were the key reasons no action was taken. First of all, Mexico was not at war with Nazi Germany, and the espionage operations were really directed against the United States, not Mexico. If the Avila Camacho government had carried out full-scale arrest of German agents, Berlin could have retaliated by arresting Mexicans in occupied Europe. Such a counteraction would have been extremely embarrassing since Mexico lacked the means to force the Germans to consider making an exchange. Lastly, any arrest and trial could have produced revelations of Mexican cooperation with both Abwehr agents and the SIS/Mexico; a public debate or outcry over possible collusion between regime officials and foreign agents was not to be risked.[120] What our informant seemed to be saying was that the Avila Camacho government considered itself anti-Fascist, but it did not intend to stick its neck out too far for Uncle Sam.

E. *The Hilda Krüger Affair*

U.S. officials were partially aware of the internal problems an espionage crackdown might cause, but they suspected that the principal reason for Mexican lassitude in jailing Nazi agents between July 1941 and February 1942 was two-legged and feminine. Katerina Matilda Krüger, better known by her stage name, Hilda Krüger, was born near Berlin in 1912. Five feet, five inches tall, blonde, and exceedingly attractive, she had married in 1934. A sometime motion picture actress and friend of

Joseph Goebbels, her career went into eclipse when it became known that her husband possessed a Jewish ancestor. This revelation may have been the cause for her leaving both Germany and her disgraced partner early in 1939. She moved to England, but with the declaration of war, she embarked for the United States. In January 1940, she left New York and checked into the Beverly-Wilshire Hotel in Hollywood. There she remained for several months, ostensibly attempting to obtain a film contract.

Next, Frau Krüger became enamored of Gert von Gontard, a German businessman living in St. Louis. In February 1941, she traveled to Mexico, her alleged intention being to establish residence in order to shed her spouse. But once in Mexico City, she was soon on good terms with Georg Nicolaus, Friedrich von Schleebrugge, and Paul Max Weber. Since she was continually observed in the company of these men, SIS/Mexico agents concluded that she, too, was an Abwehr operative. But hobnobbing with fellow *Reichsdeutschen* would not become her primary activity. Early that spring, Frau Krüger met Ramón Bateta, undersecretary in the Ministry of the Treasury and a member of the board of directors of the Banco Nacional de Mexico. The plans for a fast divorce and rapid return to Gert von Gontard suddenly fell into limbo, and Hilda became the undersecretary's mistress.[121]

Perhaps Señor Bateta rapidly tired of his blonde inamorata, or perhaps Hilda had her eyes on bigger game. What is evident is that the lady soon attracted the attention of Miguel Alemán, Avila Camacho's minister of the interior, and manager of the latter's successful presidential campaign. Confidential U.S. reports from the period leave no doubt about the suspicions rife in Washington. A special Treasury Department report (October 16, 1941), adopted from a secret communication of the naval attaché in Mexico, stated that Hilda Krüger: "is reported to be the mistress of Miguel Alemán, Secretary of Government in Mexico, and exercises great influence over him. . . . Her present residence is reported to be an elaborate establishment in the Colonia Roma, Mexico City, maintained by Alemán. . ."[122] An FBI evaluation states Washington's suspicions in the starkest terms: "It is reported that attempts to imprison various important Nazi agents in Mexico by government authorities has been thwarted because of the influence exercised by Hilda Krüger with high Mexican officials with whom she is reported to have been intimate, including the Secretary of Gobernación, Miguel Alemán."[123]

Given the extreme delicacy of the situation, it is not surprising that U.S. officials should employ surreptitious means to bring persuasive pressure to bear on the chief of the Interior Ministry. On January 4, 1942, the Mexico City daily, *Excelsior,* published an article in which Federal Deputy Félix Díaz Escobar, chairman of a committee investigating subversive activity, presented a list of foreigners whose presence, he believed, was inimicable to the national interest. Among those so classified was Hilda

Krüger, who Díaz Escobar stated was labeled an "active Nazi" by the U.S. government.[124]

As no such report had previously appeared either in Mexican newspapers or in the North American press, it is very likely that Díaz Escobar's information came from either British or U.S. intelligence sources. In addition, the deputy sent a copy of his list to the Interior Ministry, thereby providing a pointed reminder to Alemán that his alleged romantic attachment might have a lethal effect on his career.

The more potent bombshell exploded on February 10, 1942, when *La Prensa,* another Mexico City daily, published an unsigned article dealing with "beautiful spies" who were exerting a decisive influence over "powerful political functionaries." The most dangerous of these unnamed Mata Haris had conquered the heart and apparently clouded the brain of "one of the chief members of the Cabinet." The anonymous lady "has been seen in various public places, (i.e., with the cabinet minister) and she has been shadowed and kept under surveillance by the American [U.S.] police who have ample information on the activities of this beautiful woman of innocent face, attractive form and no few feminine wiles."[125] Lest there be any doubt about whom the mysterious sweethearts were, written in the margin of the U.S. State Department report which contained this article were the names "Hilda Krüger" and "Miguel Alemán."[126]

After further investigation, the FBI eventually concluded that whatever else Hilda Krüger may have been, she certainly was not an Abwehr agent.[127] As to her alleged exercise of influence over Miguel Alemán on behalf of German operatives in Mexico, the suspicion was probably the father of the explanation. With the advantage of hindsight, it is ludicrous to assume that an astute and ambitious politician like Miguel Alemán would have jeopardized his career for the affections of any shady lady. Furthermore, while Hilda Krüger probably sympathized with the aims and activities of the Ast Berlin coterie, her primary motivation was probably apolitical. As Alemán's mistress, she might sit out the war in comfort, secure in the knowledge that if she pleased her protector, detention or deportation was unlikely to be her fate. And it would seem she played her cards well, for there is no evidence that she was either jailed or deported from Mexico prior to the end of World War II.

F. *Score One for "Max"*

The failure of the Reich's petroleum politics, the Mexican newspaper revelations, Minister Rüdt von Collenberg's report, the hurried flight of Schleebrugge and Rekowsky, plus the closure of station GBO apparently settled matters for Canaris. Concluding that those V-men still in Mexico were either blown or useless, in August 1941, he queried Gen. Francisco Franco about the possibility of Spain's Military Information Service (SIM) assuming the bulk of the intelligence-gathering effort in Mexico and Central America. An agreement formalizing this *modus operandi* was apparently reached in the fall of 1941, but the United States' entry into the war apparently caused Francisco Franco to reconsider. In any case, there is no evidence that SIM agents in Mexico and Central America provided any data of substance to the Germans.[128]

Meanwhile, the position of the Mexican V-men continued to deteriorate. By the end of July, the Anglo-Americans were intercepting the microdot letters that Rüge was making and Nicolaus was forwarding to Latin American and European drops.[129] Furthermore, since the FBI laboratory cryptanalysts had been reading the "Bradjob-Volco" traffic since early in the year,[130] when Nicolaus was informed on November 20, 1941, that Carlos Retelsdorf's code name was changed from "Glenn" to "Franco," SIS/Mexico knew about the switch as soon as "Max" did.[131] Nicolaus was at least partially aware of this situation because he would reply to Ast Berlin that "all connections have been severed," an oblique way of stating that the "Bradjob-Volco" circuit had become, as it were, a three-person party line.[132] Since this development was one about which neither Nicolaus nor his bosses could presently do anything, "Max" chose inactivity as the prudent course of action.

With the Pearl Harbor attack and the following rupture of diplomatic relations between Mexico and Germany (December 11, 1941), Nicolaus concluded that he must continue to execute his intelligence mission despite the loss of security in his communications link. Hugo Natus, chancellor at the German legation, had been allowed to shift to the Swedish embassy in order to handle the problems of resident *Reichsdeutschen*. Through this diplomat's efforts, "Max" made contact with Capt. Kyoho Hamanaka (code name: Amanake), Japanese naval attaché. After December 8, this naval officer had been restricted to his home and placed under police surveillance. Nevertheless, as if by magic, at 11:30 P.M. on December 18, the Mexican guards wandered off, thereby allowing Nicolaus and the ever-faithful Werner Barke to enter the attaché's residence unobserved.

What then transpired laid the basis for the final triumph of "Max's" espionage career. Through "Q", an unnamed U.S. citizen working for Japanese intelligence (this may have been John Benjamin Sutton),[133] Captain Hamanaka had obtained important information regarding U.S. losses at Pearl Harbor and U.S. strategic planning for the first half of 1942. The naval attaché doubted that he could get this information to Japan, and so he wanted Nicolaus to forward it to Berlin, where the Japanese ambassador could receive it. "Max" agreed to send the information, but his inquiries concerning the identity of "Q", and whether the latter might also work for Germany, received sharp rebuffs. As a result, Nicolaus accepted the information, but decided not to tell the Japanese naval officer about the microdot system. With an assist from Hamanaka's Mexican girlfriend, he and "Max" met in a taxicab on December 29. Again the Japanese officer handed over information which he wanted dispatched. Thereafter, Mexican surveillance became more stringent and the two spies never encountered each other again.[134]

In two microdot letters dated January 3 and 14, 1942, Nicolaus communicated to Ast Berlin the following information:

1. After Pearl Harbor, the U.S. Navy's offensive activity would consist of "lightening-like" aircraft carrier raids in the South Pacific and northern Japan.
2. The American Volunteer Group (better known as the "Flying Tigers"), based in Burma and China, had only one hundred Curtiss P-40 fighter aircraft at its disposal.
3. U.S. losses at Pearl Harbor were the battleships *Oklahoma, Arizona, West Virginia,* and *Utah.* The oil storage facilities were undamaged, but 326 planes had been destroyed.
4. On December 14, 1941, the aircraft carrier *Yorktown* and battleships *Washington* and *North Carolina* transited the Panama Canal, headed for the Pacific.[135]

The accuracy of some of this information is, in certain respects, chilling. Agent "Q" accurately predicted U.S. naval strategy during the six months following Pearl Harbor, including, after a fashion, the celebrated Doolittle raid on the Japanese home islands on April 18, 1942.[136] His figures concerning the Flying Tigers were both correct and incorrect. In April 1941, FDR had secretly ordered that one hundred P-4OC fighter planes, originally intended for Great Britain, be turned over to the American Volunteer Group (AVG). But by the time the first squadrons were operational in Burma (December 15, 1941), the total strength had been reduced to roughly seventy-eight planes.[137] Five, rather than four, battleships were then resting on the bottom of Pearl Harbor, but the Naval Tank Farm, with its 4.5 million gallons of fuel had, indeed, escaped damage.[138]

Most fascinating is the report that on December 14, 1941, the *Yorktown, Washington,* and *North Carolina* sailed through the Panama Canal, headed for the Pacific. In fact, the *Yorktown* completed this passage on December 21–22, but as a result of countermanded orders, neither battleship got closer to the canal than Puerto Rico. It would seem that "Q" was guessing about certain details, but he was obviously the recipient of accurate information concerning U.S. shipping movements and orders. Probably no other agent during World War II was able to produce such high-grade reportage on U.S. naval activity.[139]

To be sure, "Max" was aware of the value of the material that had been given him, but any report he sent was likely to be intercepted. His first microdot letter was mailed to Albrecht Engels in Brazil for clandestine radio transmission. Predictably, the FBI intercepted this message, as well as the January 3 and 14, 1942, microdot letters addressed to a drop in Sweden.[140] Still, "Max" was ultimately able to outwit his adversaries, for he also supplied Hugo Natus with a microdot letter containing Hamanaka's reports. The wily diplomat successfully connived to have the letter put in the Swedish diplomatic pouch. Once in Sweden, it was delivered to another Abwehr drop box, and the Nazis got the information to the Japanese after all.[141]

But J. Edgar Hoover must have smelled a rat, because he ordered the SIS/Mexico to build a pipeline into the Swedish embassy. From July 1942, copies of cables and messages sent both by Natus and other Swedish embassy personnel in Mexico soon wound up on the FBI chief's desk.[142] "Max" had achieved his most spectacular triumph; now he would suffer the agony of defeat.

G. *Collapse*

During a 1945 interrogation, Georg Nicolaus stated that he had not been surprised when, on February 28, 1942, Mexican police arrested him as a dangerous alien.[143] In the six weeks that followed, the Interior Ministry roused itself and also apprehended Werner Barke, Josef Hermkes, Josef Pipper, and Pablo Rubach. But in detaining these persons, Mexico and the United States swiftly found themselves at odds. Nicolaus and Barke, for example, could have been charged as violators of the November 14, 1941, espionage law, but the Mexican government stead-fastly refused to level any criminal charges against those arrested. At the same time, Washington was pressing its own solution to the problem. On March 3, 1942, Ambassador George Messersmith indicated to Foreign Minister Padilla that the United States would be only too happy to take Georg Nicolaus and any other Abwehr personnel and hold them in U.S. camps for the duration of the war.[144] The Mexicans rejected this sugges-tion, too, for Berlin had made it clear that it would not accept any exchange agreement which did not provide for the return of all arrested Abwehr agents. The Mexicans then informed Washington that while those to be repatriated might be held in the United States until an exchange ship arrived, Nicolaus, Barke, et al., would have to be allowed diplomatic immunity. In other words, the V-men could not be interro-gated, "sweated," or physically "persuaded" to yield information.[145]

After some negotiation, an agreement was reached early in May 1942. It provided that the Germans to be repatriated would await the Swedish exchange ship *Drottingholm* in New York, and that these per-sons were to be outside the jurisdiction of the FBI.[146] It was with this understanding that Georg Nicolaus and 239 other *Reichsdeutsche* were taken across the border on May 28, 1942. The State Department had made an agreement with the Mexicans, but the FBI would interpret it in its own way. Hoover's agents were aided by the fact that Georg Nicolaus, ever zealous in the interests of the Third Reich, once again had his thumb on the self-destruct button. Despite his objections, before he boarded the *Drottingholm* on June 2, 1942, the FBI made him undergo a thorough search. They found a very small white packet sewed to the tongue of his right shoe, and inside it were six microdots. The FBI Technical Labora-tory deciphered the material and discovered that somehow "Max" had obtained the blueprints of an escape device being built into U.S. submarines.[147] Having obtained sufficient evidence to justify refusing the repatriation of Nicolaus, the FBI now sought permission to force him to impart desired information about his 1940–42 activities.

Conceivably the situation had been radically altered because the same day the 240 *Reichsdeutsche* crossed the border, Avila Camacho, citing U-boar attacks on Mexican tankers, called for a declaration of war against Germany. Nevertheless, the Mexicans still refused to agree to any change in Nicolaus's status, so Washington ordered him held in a U.S. detention camp.[148]

How the FBI intended to honor the agreement regarding aliens shipped by Mexico to the United States for repatriation is further demonstrated in the case of Werner Barke. When the latter was out of his room, agents effected a forced entry, and made a comprehensive search of his baggage. The most interesting item proved to be his typewriter, for after making an impression of the key facings and the machine's pattern for spacing, it was determined that most of the Mexican microdot letters had been originally typed on Barke's machine.[149] Subsequent developments would prove, however, that although the FBI had the right machine, they had the wrong man.

IV. *Culmination of the Spy War in Mexico*

A. *Abwehr Rebirth*

Sometime late in the summer of 1942, the BSC censorship station at Bermuda stumbled across a microdot letter being forwarded from Europe to an agent in Mexico City. SIS/Mexico leader Gus Jones was immediately alerted to the fact that the Abwehr was trying to contact a Mexican V-man whose code number was "Y2863," but the BSC could not determine that agent's identity.

Among the many items in the possession of the SIS/Mexico was a letter that had been mailed from Honolulu in August 1940, addressed to Frau Clara Rüge, at Schaeferstrasse 22, Berlin-Wannsee. This letter probably never left U.S. territory, for late in the summer of 1940, the postal authorities, in conjunction with the State and Justice Departments, had begun embargoing postal matter sent from and to Germany by the transpacific route. The U.S. Justice Department conjured up a legal sophistry, to wit, that "propaganda" need not be delivered since the sender was "not registered in the United States as an agent of a foreign principal."[150] The Rüge letter was hardly propaganda, but U.S. authorities treated it as such. Since the return address on the back of the envelope was Mexico City, the letter wound up in the hands of SIS/Mexico and was filed and forgotten.[151]

Subsequently, a microdot letter postmarked December 5, 1942, and sent to a Lisbon drop was intercepted. It contained several microdots, and in one of these, V-man "Y2863" asked Maj. Hermann Gusek of Ast Berlin "that my mother be informed that I and my family are getting on.

Her first name is Clara, and the last address known to me is #22 Schaeferstrasse, Berlin, Wannsee." In this fashion, SIS/Mexico was finally able to confirm that "Y2863," the mysterious microdot maker, was probably Karl Rüge.[152]

In June 1942, the Mexican police again questioned Teresa Quintanilla and she implicated both Rüge and Retelsdorf as members of "Max's" spy ring.[153] These men were taken into custody and interned at the camp for German aliens located at Perote, in the state of Veracruz. In July, however, Rüge effected his release through payment of a bribe to Interior officials.[154] He then cajoled Edgar Hilgert out of hiding, and persuaded Franz von Buchenau to lend his cooperation in executing future espionage plans. In addition, he developed a number of close collaborators among the remaining Germans and dual citizens, the most conspicuous being two businessmen, Victor Félix and Rolf Spesseger, and two coffee planters, Walter Kahle and Otto Guenther von Tuerckheim. Financial assistance came chiefly from Richard Eversbusch, a partner in the Hayen-Eversbusch Steamship Company, the same firm which had employed both Werner Barke and Josef Pipper.[155] A fanatical Nazi, Eversbusch had been honorary German consul in Tampico, as well as president of the German Chamber of Commerce of Mexico. Without his help, it is doubtful whether Rüge would have been very successful in keeping the Abwehr operation financially afloat.[156]

Certainly the most desperate need of "Y2863's" resurrected ring was a secure method of communication which the Anglo-Americans could neither interdict nor interrupt. Kahle and Tuerckheim attempted to establish another radio station, but their combined efforts were unsuccessful.[157] As a result, the Mexican V-men were forced to rely entirely upon the compromised microdot system. These messages were forwarded in duplicate to different drops in Spain, Portugal, and Sweden, but Rüge managed to establish contacts in Argentina as well. One such cut-out, a relative of Rolf Spesseger, was Wolf-Hilber Freudenberg (code name: James). Upon receipt of letters from Rüge, Freudenberg was instructed to turn these over to Lt. Martin Müller, assistant naval attaché in the German embassy in Buenos Aires. When Müller had something for "Y2863," he gave the material to Freudenberg, who relayed it by mail to a Mexico City post office box. After the war, a U.S. interrogation team questioned Freudenberg closely and concluded that he did not know what was in the letters he received or delivered. This ignorance, however, did not prevent him from being arrested in February 1944, and deported to Germany in 1946.[158]

After Fruedenberg had been blown as an intermediary, two other individuals were similarly employed between March and November 1944. At least five microdot letters were mailed by Rüge (using assorted names) to Gregorio Falcones in Buenos Aires. Señor Falcones was real enough, but the letters he received from Mexico were passed on to Alberto Metzger and José Valles. Metzger was the hardware salesman developed as a contact by Franz von Buchenau when the latter was in Argentina in 1941, while Valles had become a key link in the smuggling of strategic metals through the port of Buenos Aires. The letters these men received were given to trusted Spanish sailors, who delivered them to Abwehr agents in Spain.[159]

Implicit in this jerrybuilt system of cut-outs, multiple contacts, and message repetition was recognition of the fact that the Anglo-Americans held the upper hand: they could intercept and probably decipher any microdot message sent. This inability to establish and maintain a secure channel of communication really foreshadowed the defeat of the Third Reich, but the Rüge ring would have none of that. Their tenacious, if forlorn, effort is proof of their fanaticism and dedication. "Let the Anglo-Americans intercept our messages," they seemed to be saying, "we will keep right on sending them." In fact, between October 1942 and November 1944, the FBI intercepted twenty-two eastbound and two westbound letters containing some 359 microdots.[160] Most of these dots were not encrypted, and though the FBI saw fit to let most of them pass through, some microdots were purposely smudged to prevent the intended recipient from deciphering them. And just to make certain they were on the right track, SIS/Mexico agents broke into Rüge's home and secretly tested his typewriter, thereby establishing "Y2863's" machine as the source of the eastbound microdot letters.[161]

One reason more of the dots were not removed was probably that the information enclosed was deemed trivial. Witness the case of an intercepted message sent by Civil Attaché Birch D. ("Buck") O'Neal to U.S. Ambassador George Messersmith on February 16, 1944. It proclaimed that the U.S. ambassador was both Jewish and a war profiteer. Messersmith's scribbled reply was, "Thank you for sending this to me, as it has given me at least a bit of amusement during a busy day."[162]

An analysis of the microdots intercepted reveals that there was a good deal of data obtained from technical journals and newspapers. Special attention was paid such considerations as U.S. iron and steel manufacture and aluminum and petroleum production.[163] Valuable information was occasionally provided on the performance of military aircraft and Mexican internal politics,[164] but very little, aside from the last-named category, came under the heading of secret information. In essence, under Rüge, the espionage group concentrated on providing low-grade intelligence materials which would assist the German High Command in creating an accurate picture of U.S. political and economic developments. Evidence that Ast Berlin considered this labor to be of value came in May 1943, when "Y2863" was officially commended (by microdot, of course) for his services, promoted to first lieutenant, and awarded the Iron Cross, Second Class.[165]

B. *Freedom for Sale*

Although the Abwehr in Mexico lacked the ability to acquire anything like the data Georg Nicolaus sent out via the Swedish diplomatic pouch in February 1942, its presence and continued activity irked Washington to no end. As long as the Mexican government failed to expunge the espionage group operating within its territory, there would always remain the prospect that real damage might eventually be done. Nor should this concern be written off as the witless complaint of paranoid bureaucrats. Intercepted microdots 121 and 132, in letters dated December 5 and 12, 1942, reported that Carlos Retelsdorf had been released from Perote, and that efforts were underway to accomplish the same thing for Franz Buchenau.[166] In fact, Retelsdorf was not officially released from prison until July 1944, but from December 1942 on, he was given regular leave allegedly to visit his plantation. Particularly galling to SIS/Mexico agents, who kept him under surveillance, was that "Franco" wasted no time contacting Rüge, but spent very little time at his plantation. As for Buchenau, he had been arrested in October 1942 as a dangerous alien, but released in February 1943, "allegedly after paying a bribe of 5,000 pesos" (at that time, about $1,250).[167]

U.S. intelligence and diplomatic personnel complained bitterly about the Mexican failure to control the Rüge ring, but their protests and demands for explanation all seemed to get lost in the same place—the labyrinthian halls of the Ministry of the Interior. Angered by what he conceived of as willful negligence, J. Edgar Hoover did little to sugar-coat his criticism of the Alemán-led organization. In a full-scale assessment of the Mexican antiespionage program, he concluded that "only against the Japanese" had energetic action been taken; otherwise, Mexican spy-catching was charitably described as "unsatisfactory."[168] Lest it be assumed that Hoover was merely venting his spleen, a 1943 report by the Swedish embassy and a March 1944 analysis by the Committee for the Political Defense of the Americas (CPD)* reached the same conclusion. Indeed, the Swedish study found corruption so pervasive in the Interior Ministry that it questioned whether Alemán could have initiated a comprehensive crackdown without touching off a revolution inside his administrative bailiwick.[169]

That Mexico could not or would not deal with its espionage problem, even though the nation was at war with Germany, was a scandalous situation which could not permanently evade the scrutiny of the press. On May 5, 1945, less than a week before the Third Reich capitulated, Edgar Mowrer and Oliver Pilat began a five-part story in the *New York Post* on Nazi influence in Mexico. Among other charges of negligence, the reporters stated categorically that Rüge, Hilgert, and Buchenau had escaped detention solely as a result of payoffs to Interior officials.[170] This admittedly sensationalist account caused stirrings in both Washington

---

*This was a special five-member body created by a resolution passed at the foreign ministers' meeting at Rio de Janeiro, January 15–28, 1942. The task of this committee was to track Axis espionage activity in the Americas and to monitor the surveillance of enemy aliens by the Latin American republics.

and Mexico City, and Ambassador George Messersmith was asked to provide a critique of the allegations. Raleigh Gibson, embassy chargé d'affaires, was handed the task. His confidential report took issue with some of the newsmen's findings, but in assessing the linkage between the Interior Ministry's indifferent antiespionage labors and the charges of corruption, Gibson concluded that the accusations were "probably true."[171]

When the chargé wrote his commentary he had not yet seen the final report on the Rüge group which was delivered to the Department of State by the FBI on May 29, 1945. Both the War and Navy Departments had consistently opposed the disclosure of any secret information on Abwehr agents to Mexican officials since the release of the ill-fated July 1941 report. They argued that security was so poor that allowing the Mexican government access to secret information was decidedly counterproductive.[172] Hoover was prepared to overlook these objections, but only if the State Department would guarantee that a single copy of the bureau's final report would be personally delivered into the hands of Avila Camacho.[173] The brutal fact was that between July 1941 and the end of the war, confidence by the U.S. intelligence apparatus in the Mexican government's ability to conserve secrets had fallen to a microscopic low.

In June 1942, an unknown analyst in the Office of Naval Intelligence concluded that "the most significant benefit" to be derived from Mexico's declaration of war would be that the government must finally undertake "the effective and seriously needed control" of Axis spies "within the republic."[174] Three years later, this hope had evaporated, leaving more than a little animosity. But officially, Washington would say as little as possible about its true feelings, for by the summer of 1945, it was increasingly clear that the next president of Mexico was likely to be the oft-denounced Miguel Alemán.

C. *The Grim Charade*

Ambassador George Messersmith was caught by surprise. On June 20, 1945, he had visited Avila Camacho in order to indicate Washington's extreme displeasure with the fact that Mexico was already returning expropriated property to German businessmen. The Mexican chief executive listened politely and then served up a few of the diplomatic sophistries that Messersmith had been expecting. In the process, however, Avila Camacho stated that he would soon take steps to deal comprehensively with the Abwehr agents and collaborators that the United States had been complaining about. It was this revelation which left Messersmith perplexed. Now that the Third Reich lay in ruins, why was Mexico contemplating some comprehensive action? In his report to Washington, he was prepared to hazard a guess:

> I am not at all sure that his statement to me in this respect was not partly
> in order to remove from my mind any basis which I might have for the

belief that the action had been taken, on the initiative of the Minister of *Gobernación,* Mr. Alemán, who is now a candidate for the presidency in 1946.[175]

But telling the U.S. ambassador that a round-up would transpire in no way indicated when the desired action would take place. Indeed, three weeks after Alemán's election, thirteen months after Avila Camacho's promise, and fourteen months after V-E Day, the Mexicans finally acted. A presidential order issued July 30, 1946, specifically expelled twenty-four *Reichsdeutsche* who were charged with having "violated the hospitality of Mexico by having plotted against her security."[176] Among the first Germans arrested was Karl Rüge, who for two years had been operating a chicken farm at Tlascopec, then a Mexico City suburb. Waving a pistol and threatening to shoot anyone who entered his house, Rüge evaded detention for twenty-four hours. On August 2, a reinforced squad came to take him in. "Y2863" evaded them as well, but at the cost of his life. Police reported that he committed suicide, leaving a note stating that he would not allow himself to be shipped back to Germany.[177]

To say the least, the circumstances surrounding the reported suicide are curious, particularly since a search of his property was not officially conducted for over a week.[178] Perhaps Rüge did commit suicide, but his death could hardly have been considered inopportune by some Mexican officials.

The next in line was Edgar Hilgert, Ast Hamburg's man in Mexico. Aside from contributing a message in several of Rüge's microdot letters, "Fraser" had done little, and Ast Hamburg had criticized his perturbing inactivity.[179] Evidently, Hilgert had more romantic considerations on his mind, for during the late summer of 1943, he married Consuelo Burgos Gandulfo, a lady of prominent family. Ever the fox, he may well have concluded that marriage to a high-society woman would provide him with citizenship and a safe haven when the Third Reich collapsed. The spy and his bride moved into sumptuous quarters on the Calle Guadalajara in Mexico City, and SIS/Mexico ruefully concluded that despite its request that the Mexicans take action, Hilgert would never be deported or jailed.[180]

But the vicissitudes of politics often upset the best-laid plans of both spies and less calculating folk. Instead of becoming eligible for citizenship, after Alemán's election, Hilgert found his name on the list of those to be repatriated to Germany. On July 30, 1946, Señora Consuelo Burgos de Hilgert sent a telegram to Avila Camacho, pleading for an audience, so that she could make the case for her husband's continued residence. But the following day, his secretary, Licenciado Roberto Amoros, responded that it was "impossible to receive you at this time."[181] Once again, Edgar Hilgert went into hiding, this time on a ranch owned by his wife's family near Puebla. Demonstrating that they were entirely capable of finding a suspect when they really wanted to, federal police quickly captured

Hilgert, and provided him with an experience he had previously escaped —life in a Mexican prison.[182]

On August 15, 1946, the SS *Marine Marlin*, carrying thirteen of these "violators of Mexican hospitality," sailed from Veracruz bound for Hamburg. On board were Hilgert, Franz von Schleebrugge, brother of Friedrich, Frederick Wilhelm, the businessman who had fronted for the importation of the microdot machine, Georg Ullrich Reme, also known as "Rurik," and Hugo Natus, the diplomat who had doubled as a communications cut-out.[183] As for the other *Reichsdeutschen* scheduled for deportation in Avila Camacho's July 30 order, an August 1946 FBI report stated, "It has been reliably reported that the other subjects originally arrested for repatriation evaded such action through payment of bribes to Mexican officials."[184]

Once again, the indifferent performance of the Avila Camacho regime was something that could not be completely ignored. A *New York Times* follow-up story on October 17, 1946, stated that "big money" had changed hands, thereby permitting the other eleven deportees to avoid the transatlantic boat ride. The wire-puller in this affair was reputed to be "an importer with close government connections who had been on the Allied black list during the war."[185] This description might be said to fit Richard Eversbusch, Rüge's financier, whom the SIS/Mexico reported had paid more than ten thousand dollars to avoid being a member of the unlucky thirteen.[186]

Naturally the Mexican government reacted with some embarrassment to these allegations. On October 19, 1946, Hector Pérez Martínez, the incoming chief of the Ministry of the Interior, stated that no expulsion order had been voided, and that "several cases were now in the courts."[187] He had nothing further to add, and the Mexican government has not vouchsafed to provide further enlightenment during the past four decades.

D. *The Essence of Mexican Policy*

Almost a year before the Third Reich's utter collapse, U.S. Ambassador George Messersmith warned Washington that many of the Abwehr personnel in Mexico would be neither tried nor deported. "The German agents," he stated in a memorandum dated June 23, 1944, had received the support of the "cooperative colony" of *Reichsdeutschen* in Mexico, "and secured the good will of a great number of Mexicans of all classes of society." If the Avila Camacho government launched a real crackdown on the Abwehr, it would be necessary to arrest a good many influential foreigners who had openly collaborated with the V-men. Since any action of this kind was bound to create internal turmoil and generate negative repercussions among the German community in the country, it was too much to expect the regime to act either quickly or comprehensively.[188]

The Avila Camacho government was even more apathetic in its dealing with spies and collaborators who were either Mexican nationals or naturalized citizens. As such, Victor Félix, Walter Kahle, Rolf Spesseger, and Otto von Tuerckheim, operatives in Karl Rüge's 1942–45 network, would not have normally been subject to deportation; what is disturbing, however, is that none of these men were even arrested, detained, or held for questioning.[189]

The most curious and least explicable case of inaction, however, involved Franz Wilhelm Buchenau, the Nest Cologne agent born in Mexico, who reentered the country in 1941 using German passport number 200/40.[190] Arrested as a dangerous foreign alien in 1942 and released under mysterious circumstances in 1943, by 1945 he was claiming that because of his birth in the state of Coahuila, he should be considered a Mexican citizen. Despite his past activities, the Mexican authorities proceeded to accept Buchenau as such.[191] A trained Abwehr agent who was a German citizen and consorted with other V-men in Mexico was released from detention, never brought to trial, and finally adjudged to be a Mexican citizen. Obviously, Franz Buchenau had been persuasive, but the suspicion is rife that it was "grease" for outstretched palms which made his argument convincing.

1. *Where Are They Now?*

When we last heard of Georg Nicolaus, the FBI had discovered miocrodot messages in his shoe, and as a result, detained him in the United States (June 1942). The refusal to allow "Max" to sail on the *Drottingholm* was illegal, and when he was subsequently interrogated by the FBI, Nicolaus refused to answer any questions about his activities in Mexico.[192] What surprised U.S. officials was that the Mexicans backed Nicolaus and refused to consider changing the terms under which they had allowed the prisoner to be repatriated via the United States.[193] The FBI and other intelligence organizations would not be granted the permission to sweat Nicolaus and extract from him the information they wanted.

Realizing that he was a prisoner in a kind of limbo status, Georg Nicolaus began writing to the Swedish government insisting that his detention in the United States was illegal, and that he should be promptly repatriated to Germany or sent back to Mexico. Stockholm took up his case, but queries directed to the Mexican Foreign Ministry went unanswered. Finally, in January 1945, the Mexicans responded that Georg Nicolaus had acted in a manner "contrary to the security of the continent." As for his being returned to Mexico, the prisoner's "crimes and indiscretions" were such that prudence dictated that he remain where he was.[194] The position of the Avila Camacho government in this case suggests several possibilities, but one conclusion is indisputable: under no circumstances was Georg Nicolaus to return to Mexico. Among other things, U.S. officials had considered the possibility of using Nicolaus as a bargaining chip, exchanging him for U.S. or British agents who might fall into German hands. With the end of the war, they no longer needed Nicolaus; on December 22, 1945, he was shipped back to a ruined Reich.

Post-World War II Germany was no place Nicolaus wanted to be, and in 1950, he somehow wrangled an immigration permit for Juan Perón's Argentina. Here, Nicolaus would spend the remainder of his days, eventually acquiring a very nice home on the Calle Libertad in Barrio Florida, a suburb of Buenos Aires. He died there on July 1, 1978, at the ripe old age of 80.

It seemed that the former Abwehr agent had told all and sundry that he had been "Lt. Colonel Georg Nicolaus, chief of all German Military Intelligence in Mexico and Central America." One neighbor volunteered that "he looked like someone's grey-haired grandfather. He always said that he was telling the truth, and that he was a war hero . . . you would never have suspected by looking at him that he was a spy. . . ."[195]

Georg Nicolaus had escaped from a war-ravaged Germany as fast as he could, but Edgar Hilgert, who tried so desparately to remain in Mexico, would find life in the new Federal Republic acceptable. About 1950, he obtained a position with an aluminum products manufacturing company. In pursuit of sales, he traveled extensively in the Near and Far East, and became quite prosperous. Hilgert retired about 1970 and built a large house in the Rhineland. As of 1982, he was still there, living the life of a gentleman of leisure.[196]

Writing to Philip Bonsal in April 1943, Ambassador George Messersmith characterized Miguel Alemán as a politician who viewed World War II as an inconvenience in his personal drive to power. "He [Alemán] is the purely unscrupulous type . . . I am under no illusions in regard to him."[197] The ambassador had evidence that the Interior chief had acted as a front man for certain pro-German business interests, and by 1945, Messersmith was reportedly refusing to recognize the presence of Alemán at public meetings. This situation could have destroyed the facade of chummy U.S.-Mexican relations which had been nurtured during the conflict. Not surprisingly, Messersmith was reassigned to Argentina in April 1946, about three months before Alemán was officially elected president of Mexico.[198]

As the nation's chief executive, Alemán launched a highly ambitious public works program and headed an administration noted for its dynamism, color, and corruption.[199] Succeeded by Adolfo Ruíz Cortines in 1952, Alemán was named director-general of the National Commission on Tourism in 1958, a post he held until 1970. He died in 1983, still a controversial political figure, but indisputably a wealthy man.

V. Summary: See No Evil

In assessing the Mexican espionage and counterespionage situation during World War II, a reconsideration of the German position is critical for placing the issues in perspective. The Abwehr hoped—not without cause—that so long as Germany purchased large amounts of Mexican petroleum, its V-men would be able to operate in that country with relative impunity. With the British declaration of war on Hitler in September 1939, this traffic slowed to a trickle, and the continuation of the conflict after September 1940 made its resuscitation unlikely in the foreseeable future. Meanwhile, in 1939–41, the Roosevelt administration was shrewdly pursuing a friendly settlement of the problems raised by the petroleum nationalization, a move which undoubtedly served to enhance U.S.-Mexican intelligence cooperation. With its "black gold" protection gone, the Abwehr was forced to recognize that its Mexican operation was expendable. The idea of having Spain's SIM replace the German intelligence organization was prudent, but it came too late to have any salutary effects.

German miscalculations and failures, however, do not explain the indifferent and ofttimes contradictory counterespionage efforts of the Avila Camacho regime. Consider that while a number of important V-men were repatriated to Germany via the United States in May 1942, a considerable number remained either at liberty or under lamentably inadequate surveillance. Despite the passage of a tough, comprehensive espionage law (November 4, 1941) and the creation of a special police unit to deal with espionage (February 1942), only two persons were tried for espionage acts, and neither of these was convicted.[200] Indeed, after the war was over, the Avila Camacho regime attempted to improve its lackluster counterspy image by deporting twenty-four *Reichsdeutsche*. As we have seen, the results were hardly conspicuous, for corruption and bureaucratic inefficiency proved to be well-nigh insuperable obstacles.

On at least two occasions in 1944–45, the U.S. government seriously considered making strong but discreet protests to the Mexicans over their counterespionage lapses, failures, and inefficiencies, but ultimately, Washington chose not to do so.[201] Avila Camacho had promptly broken diplomatic relations with the Axis in December 1941 and declared hostilities in May 1942, when the outcome of the conflict was still in doubt. Furthermore, at the express request of the United States, the Mexican government removed both the Japanese aliens and naturalized citizens from their Pacific coast residences and resettled them inland.[202] Even more important from a psychological standpoint was the fact that Mexico was one of only two Latin American states to send a combat unit overseas. In essence, when the merits and demerits were added up in Washington, the Avila Camacho government came out ahead.

But even had the United States adopted a get-tough policy over the counterespionage issue, it is questionable whether the results would have been appreciably different. Except for the Communist party and other leftwing elements, popular support for Mexican participation in the war was not substantial.[203] In addition, as President Avila Camacho emphasized to Ambassador Messersmith, and as the latter regularly repeated to Washington, the German community in Mexico was highly influential and greatly respected.[204] Under those circumstances, the prosecution of prominent Germans or Mexican citizens of German origin as spies or collaborators would have been the equivalent of opening a Pandora's box of troubles and throwing away the key. Fighting the Axis outside of Mexico was noble; spy trials and investigations inside Mexico could easily have unexpected and undesirable sociopolitical repercussions. Avila Camacho was no zealot; he took the discretionary way out.[205]

In regard to U.S.-Mexican relations, perhaps the most important development of the war years was the growth of a mutual sense of trust and partnership. And for reasons of its own, the United States would soon hasten to strengthen those ties. In March 1947, Pres. Harry S. Truman visited Mexico City and made a favorable impression on both the Mexican president and the citizens of the capital. Six weeks later, the *Sacred Cow* (a forerunner of the present *Air Force One*) was dispatched to pick up Alemán and bring him to Washington. Between May 5–10, 1947, the president of Mexico addressed the U.S. Congress, received an honorary doctorate from Columbia University, and was the beneficiary of a ticker tape parade in New York City.[206]

The reader may well ask: Could this be the same Miguel Alemán who was roundly denounced by a U.S. ambassador, the ONI, the FBI, and the Department of State?[207] It was, but the United States now wanted support in its expanding struggle with the Soviets. Mexico needed developmental funds and it wished to continue sending laborers across the border (per a U.S.-Mexican agreement signed on August 4, 1942) to earn the Yankee dollar. So an informal bargain was struck: Truman would support loans to Mexico and Alemán would support the broad outlines of United States foreign policy.[208] Naturally, in the interest of furthering this new sense of collaboration, unpleasant memories of the recent past were officially banished from the scene.

Notes

1. That the Mexicans actually sought out the Germans and attempted to encourage petroleum negotiations is not generally known. See Great Britain, Stationery Office, *Documents on German Foreign Policy*, series D, vol. 5 (London, 1949–64), p. 829n. Concerning the Mexican attitude toward this traffic, see Jesús Silva Herzog, *Petróleo Mexicano: Historia de un problema* (Mexico, D.F., 1944), pp. 199–206. Evident in this work is Mexican reticence to discuss this traffic.

2. On Rekowsky and Klamroth and the efforts of the *Reichstelle*, see National Archives and Records Service (hereafter referred to as NARS), R.G. 226, XL-18534, Ref. SAIC/FIP/43, September 11, 1945, p. 2.

3. On the connections between Davis, Eurotank, and the German navy, see NARS, R.G. 226, XL-18534, Ref. SAIC/FIP/43, September 11, 1945, pp. 2–4.

4. See Josephus Daniels, *Shirt-Sleeved Diplomat* (Chapel Hill, 1947), p. 251.

5. On the total amount of petroleum shipped in 1938–39, and its destination, see NARS, R.G. 38, Chief of Naval Operations (hereafter referred to as CNO), Intelligence Division, Naval Attaché Reports, C-10-E (2294–2296), register 22854, information series A, September 10, 1939, pp. 1 and 3. See also NARS, R.G. 38, C-9-B, register 18685-A, February 18, 1939, pp. 18–19. Additional evidence that the Japanese shipped oil bound for Germany via Russia is found in *U.S. Navy*, Naval Historical Center, ONI/TAM/244, Files of the German Naval Staff, *German Naval Attaché in Mexico*, T-65 series, PG-32006, frame 13 on (1986).

6. NARS, R.G. 226, XL-18534, Ref. SAIC/FIR/43, September 11, 1945, p. 3.

7. On the measures taken by Davis to evade the British blockade, and the losses he suffered, see Klaus Volland, *Das Dritte Reich und Mexiko* (Frankfurt-am-Main, 1976), pp. 166–169.

8. Concerning Hertslet's oil shipment intrigues, see ibid., pp. 170–171.

9. NARS, Auswärtiges Amt, *Documents Selected from German Foreign Office Records* (hereafter referred to as *DSGFOR*), T-120 series, roll 1054, frames 420757 and 420741.

10. See William Stevenson, *A Man Called Intrepid* (New York, 1976), p. 295.

11. NARS, R.G. 165, Federal Bureau of Investigation, *Totalitarian Activities . . . Mexico Today* (Washington, D.C., 1942), p. 44.

12. Evidence that when Hertslet returned to Mexico in 1940, he was also working for the Abwehr (as well as the Reich Foreign Economics Ministry) was provided in a letter from Insp. Roger S. Young, FBI, to Prof. Leslie B. Rout, Jr., March 10, 1982. Proof of an indisputable connection came from *U.S. Navy*, Naval Historical Center, ONI/TAM/244, Files of the German Naval Staff, *German Naval Attaché in Mexico*, T-65, PG-32006, frame 1986, and T-65, PG-32007 (2), frame 363, and T-65, PG-32008 (4), frames 321 and 433.

13. Stetson Conn and Byron Fairchild, *The Western Hemisphere: The Framework of Hemisphere Defense* (Washington, D.C., 1960), pp. 333, 334, 351–352. See also NARS, R.G. 319, FBI, *German Espionage in Latin America* (hereafter referred to as *GELA*) (Washington, D.C., 1946), p. 22.

14. Letter from Insp. Homer Boynton, FBI, to Professor Rout, October 27, 1977, contains the explicit admission that the "FBI arranged through representatives of the Mexican goverment to obtain copies of . . . messages, all of which were in code. . . ." We date the Mexican-SIS/Mexico arrangement from August 30, 1940, because in NARS, R.G. 165, FBI, *The Mexican Microdot Case #1,* June 24, 1944, p. 42, the first intercepted message bears that date.

15. On these initial negotiations, consult U.S. Army, Office of the Chief of Military History for the Army, 8-28 *Bilateral Staff Conversations with Latin American Republics,* appendix I, pp. 34-36.

16. See Conn and Fairchild, *The Framework of Hemisphere Defense,* p. 337, for a discussion of how the oil expropriation controversy hindered U.S.-Mexican military arrangements. The quote concerning Mexican refusal to ratify a final joint defense arrangement until the oil question was settled is from William L. Langer and S. Everett Gleason, *The Undeclared War, 1940–41* (New York, 1953), p. 606.

17. Evidence of this contention is found in NARS, R.G. 59, 412.11, Oil/22, /26, and /27.

18. For the details of November 19, 1941, agreement, see U.S. Department of State, *U.S. Department of State Bulletin,* no. 126 (November 21, 1941), pp. 339–340.

19. See Conn and Fairchild, *The Framework of Hemisphere Defense,* p. 337 for the quote. The improvement in U.S.-Mexican relations thereafter is noted in Cordell Hull, *The Memoirs of Cordell Hull,* vol. 2 (New York, 1948), pp. 1140–1142.

20. On these agreements, see Conn and Fairchild, *The Framework of Hemisphere Defense,* pp. 352–353.

21. NARS, R.G. 165, FBI, *Totalitarian Activities . . . Mexico Today* (Washington, D.C., 1942), p. 436.

22. See German Federal Republic, Bundesarchiv Coblenz, R 58/1217, MA 2-25, *Reichsicherheitshauptamt VI-E, Die Latinamerikanischen Staaten: Tagebericht für das erste vierteljahr—1940* (Berlin, n.d.), p. 29. For U.S. criticisms of Cárdenas's disinclination to make public the presence of Abwehr V-men in Mexico, see NARS, R.G. 165, 10058-0-131/1, G-2, 350.05 x-3020 (9-9-40), *Subversive Activities, Mexico #1,* September 9, 1940, p. 1.

23. Franklin D. Roosevelt Library (hereafter referred to as FDRL), Hyde Park, New York, The Henry Wallace Papers, box 117, letter from Pierre de Boal to Henry Wallace, January 21, 1941.

24. Lázaro Cárdenas's opposition to Mexico's entry into the war is noted in Fernando Benítez, *Lázaro Cárdenas y la Revolución Mexicana,* vol. 3 (Mexico, D.F., 1977–78), pp. 233–234.

25. There does not appear to be a history of the 201st Mexican Fighter Squadron. Part of the story is found in Conn and Fairchild, *The Framework of Hemisphere Defense,* pp. 355–356 and 383. See also Guillermo Bois, *Los Militares y la política en Mexico 1915/1974* (Mexico, D.F., 1975), pp. 75–76, and Michael C. Meier and William L. Sherman, *The Course of Mexican History* (New York, 1979), pp. 631–632.

26. NARS, R.G. 165, FBI, *Totalitarian Activities . . . Mexico Today,* pp. 122–123.

27. On Schleebrugge's prewar activities as a salesman, see NARS, R.G. 59, 862.20212/1921, p. 2, and R.G. 319, FBI, *GELA,* pp. 22–23.

28. On Schleebrugge's activities after September 1, 1939, see NARS, R.G. 59, 862.20211/3236, pp. 1–2, R.G., 165, FBI, *Totalitarian Activities . . . Mexico Today,* pp. 207–208, R.G., 319, FBI, *GELA,* p. 23.

29. See NARS, R.G. 319, FBI, *GELA,* pp. 23–24.

30. Ibid., p. 25.

31. On the background of Georg Nicolaus, see NARS, R.G. 165, *The Mexican Microdot Case #2,* January 20, 1945, pp. 35–36 and 53.

32. On Werner Barke, see NARS, R.G. 165, FBI, *The Mexican Microdot Case #2,* p. 23, and R.G. 319, FBI, *GELA,* pp. 26–27.

33. NARS, R.G. 165, FBI, *The Mexican Microdot Case #1,* June 24, 1944, pp. 60–61, 67–68, and FBI, *Totalitarian Activities . . . Mexico Today,* pp. 180, 184–185, 188 and 194.

34. On Carlos Retelsdorf, see NARS, R.G. 319, FBI, *GELA,* pp. 36–37, and R.G. 165, FBI, *Mexican Microdot Case #2,* pp. 31–33.

35. On Paul Max Weber, see NARS, R.G. 59, 862.20212/3236, p. 7 and R.G. 165, FBI, *The Mexican Microdot Case #2,* pp. 51 and 57.

36. On Hermkes's early career and activities as a Mexican official, see NARS, R.G. 319, FBI, *GELA,* pp. 25–26 and 42, and República de Mexico, Secretaría de Relaciones Exteriores, Archivo General, *Asunto: Hermkes,* I/131/4329, *Topografía:* 35-4-44. Josef Hermkes was appointed honorary consul in Breslau on August 31, 1939; his commission was officially cancelled on October 1, 1939.

37. Information concerning Hermkes's recruitment by Nest Bremen and Albert Herzog was in a letter from Inspector Boynton to Professor Rout, February 29, 1980.

38. On Hermkes's recruitment and activity in Mexico, see NARS, R.G. 319, FBI, *GELA,* pp. 25–26, and 42, R.G. 165, FBI, *Totalitarian Activities . . . Mexico Today,* p. 169, and NARS, Auswärtiges Amt., *DSGFOR,* T-120 series, roll 733, frames 29486435 and 29686465.

39. On Karl Franz Joachim Rüge, see NARS, R.G. 319, FBI, *GELA,* pp. 34–35, and R.G. 59, 862.20212/5-2945, pp. 16–19.

40. On these agents, see NARS, 165, *Mexican Microdot Case #2,* pp. 60 and 84–85, R.G. 165, *Totalitarian Activities . . . Mexico Today,* p. 194, and R.G. 319, FBI, *GELA,* pp. 26, 39–40.

41. On Reme and Korkowski, see NARS, R.G. 319, FBI, *GELA,* pp. 31 and 41.

42. See NARS, R.G. 319, FBI, *GELA,* pp. 32, 42–43 on Freundt and Rautner. For the quoted material, see R.G. 165, FBI, *Mexican Microdot Case #2,* pp. 4, 26, and 43.

43. NARS, R.G. 59, 862.20212/5-2945, pp. 5–15.

44. NARS, R.G. 165, FBI, *Mexican Microdot Case #2,* pp. 35–36, 40–41.

45. For the addresses, see NARS, R.G. 319, FBI, *GELA,* p. 25.

46. On the installation of the microdot system, see NARS, R.G. 165, FBI, *Mexican Microdot Case #2,* pp. 41–42.

47. Ibid., p. 42.

48. On the mailbox system, see NARS, R.G. 165, FBI, *Mexican Microdot Case #2,* pp. 37–40, and R.G. 165, FBI, *Totalitarian Activities . . . Mexico Today,* pp. 159–160.

49. On the bizarre sabotage attempt, see NARS, R.G. 319, FBI, *GELA,* p. 204.

50. NARS, R.G. 165, FBI, *Mexican Microdot Case #2,* pp. 35–36.

51. On the background of Edgar Hilgert and the Hawaii incident, see NARS, R.G. 319, FBI, *GELA,* pp. 42–43, R.G. 165, FBI, *Mexican Microdot Case #2,* pp. 23–24; and see NARS, R.G. 59, 862. 20212/5-2945, pp. 24–27.

52. On the Nicolaus-Hilgert friction, see NARS, R.G. 165, FBI, *Mexican Microdot Case #2,* pp. 23–24, and pp. 28–29.

53. On the Rautter-Hilgert connection, see NARS, R.G. 165, FBI, *Mexican Microdot Case #2,* pp. 26–27.

54. NARS, R.G. 59, 862.20212/5-2945, p. 26.

55. On Hilgert's workload and cautious behavior, see NARS, R.G. 319, FBI, *GELA,* pp. 31 and 43, and R.G. 165, FBI, *Mexican Microdot Case #2,* pp. 25–27.

56. On this gaffe by the FBI, see NARS, R.G. 59, 862.20212/5-2945, p. 31.

57. On the background of Buchenau and his early activities with the Abwehr, see NARS, R.G. 59, 862.2012/5-2945, p. 31, and R.G. 165, FBI, *Mexican Microdot Case #2,* pp. 70-71.

58. NARS, R.G. 165, FBI, *Mexican Microdot Case #2,* p. 71.

59. In fact, as late as January 1942, "Saunders" still hoped to reach Chile or Argentina. See FDRL, Franklin D. Roosevelt Papers (hereafter referred to as FDRP), OF-10B, box 31, 1180, n.p.

60. On the story of Sean Russell and the Abwehr, see Carolle J. Carter, *The Shamrock and the Swastika* (Palo Alto, 1977), pp. 102–112, and Enno Stephan, *Spies in Ireland* (Harrisburg, Pa., 1965), pp. 19–23, 31–38, and 164.

61. On Rekowsky's contacts with Goertz and his induction into the Abwehr, see NARS, 862.2012/1-1548, 57, p. 1, and R.G. 238, CI-RIR/2, box 9, 1435, October 11, 1945, p. 1.

62. NARS, R.G. 59, 862.20212/1-1548, 57, p. 2.

63. NARS, Auswärtiges Amt, *DSGFOR,* T-120 series, roll 1054, frame 470755.

64. NARS, R.G. 59, 862.20212/1-1548, 57, pp. 2–3.

65. See Don Whitehead, *The FBI Story,* 7th ed. (New York, 1965), p. 249. Quote: "Throughout the war years, the FBI investigated 19,649 cases in which sabotage was suspected, but there was not one case of enemy-directed sabotage to be found." See also letter from Inspector Boynton to Professor Rout, January 18, 1978.

66. For Collenberg's denunciations of Rekowsky, see German Federal Republic, Staatsarchiv Nürnberg, *Bestand:* KV-Anklage, Nr. R-155a, Interrogations, 2856, December 17, 1947, pp. 4–5. For Rekowsky's explanations, see NARS, R.G. 59, 862.20212/1-1548, pp. 2–3.

67. See Karl-Heinz Abshagan, *Canaris* (London, 1956), pp. 186–187.

68. On Rekowsky's free-spending habits in Mexico, see NARS, R.G. 59, 862.20212/1-1548, 57, p. 3. For the quoted material, see NARS, R.G. 59, 862.20210/2293, p. 5.

69. This incident is related in detail in NARS, R.G. 319, FBI, *GELA,* p. 30.

70. Ibid., p. 42.

71. Ibid., p. 42; NARS, R.G. 59, 862.20212/5-2945, p. 32; and R.G. 165, FBI, *Mexican Microdot Case #2,* p. 52.

72. NARS, R.G. 59, 862.20212/5-2945, p. 33.

73. Ibid., p. 32.

74. Ibid., pp. 23 and 33.

75. NARS, R.G. 59, 862.20212/2340, p. 34.

76. NARS, R.G. 165, FBI, *Mexican Microdot Case #2,* pp. 57 and 59.

77. See NARS, R.G. 59, 862.20212/5-2945, p. 33, and R.G. 165, FBI, *Totalitarian Activities . . . Mexico Today,* p. 155.

78. Schleebrugge's credit was always shaky. See NARS, R.G. 238, CI-RIR/2, 1436, box 9, October 11, 1945, p. 3.

79. NARS, R.G. 165, FBI, *Totalitarian Activities . . . Mexico Today,* p. 169.

80. See NARS, R.G. 59, 862.20212/1852, strictly confidential enclosure from Pierre L. de Boal to George Messersmith, pp. 8–9.

81. Letter from Inspector Boynton to Professor Rout, August 8, 1979.

82. Ibid.

83. NARS, R.G. 59, 862.20212/1897, p. 1.

84. Letter from Inspector Boynton to Professor Rout, September 17, 1977, and NARS, R.G. 165, FBI, *Mexican Microdot Case #1,* p. 42. Refer back to note 14 of this chapter.

85. Ibid.

86. For the Bockhacker story, see NARS, R.G. 165, FBI, *Mexican Microdot Case #1,* pp. 50–51.

87. On the "Tramp"-GBO arrangements, see NARS, R.G. 59, 862.20211/3082, pp. 2–3.

88. See NARS, R.G. 319, FBI, *GELA,* pp. 36–37.

89. NARS, R.G. 59, 862.20211/3082, *Special Memorandum,* p. 50. This report was only partially correct. War records indicated that under the lend-lease arrangements, only five British battleships underwent repairs for battle damage in U.S. shipyards in 1941. These were the *Barham, Malaya, Warspite, Valiant,* and *Queen Elizabeth.* See Terry Hughes and John Costello, *The Battle of the Atlantic* (New York, 1978), pp. 108–113.

90. See NARS, R.G. 59, 862.20212/2162, p. 1.

91. The quoted material is from Whitehead, *The FBI Story*, p. 203. The Sebold-Duquesne story is related on pp. 202–203.

92. On Teresa Quintanilla's background, see NARS, R.G. 165, FBI, *Totalitarian Activities ... Mexico Today*, p. 190, and NARS, R.G. 59, 862.20212/1993, p. 3.

93. For the deposition of Teresa Quintanilla, see NARS, R.G. 165, FBI, *Mexican Microdot Case #1*, pp. 56–57.

94. For the Collenberg report, see NARS, Auswärtiges Amt, *DGSFOR*, T-120 series, roll 733, frames 294834, 294835, 294864, and 294865.

95. NARS, R.G. 59, 862.20212/1897, p. 1.

96. NARS, R.G. 59, 862.20212/1921, pp. 2–3.

97. NARS, R.G. 165, CI-RIR/2, 1437, October 11, 1945, p. 4.

98. Apparently Schleebrugge had good connections with the Mexican bureaucracy and learned that the Mexican police planned to make an example of him. See NARS, R.G. 319, FBI, *GELA*, p. 23, and NARS, R.G. 59, 862.20212/5-2945, p. 4.

99. NARS, R.G. 319, FBI, *GELA*, p. 23.

100. NARS, R.G. 165, FBI, *Totalitarian Activities ... Mexico Today*, p. 208, states that Schleebrugge did not leave the country until late in 1941. See also NARS, R.G. 59, 862.20211/3082, *Memorandum*, p. 14, which places Schleebrugge in Mexico in June 1941.

101. NARS, R.G. 319, FBI, *GELA*, p. 23.

102. NARS, Auswärtiges Amt, *DSGFOR*, T-120 series, roll 1054, frames 420754 and 420755.

103. On "Richard's" departure and narrow escape, see ibid., roll 733, frames 294831 and 294839. See also NARS, R.G. 59, 862.20212/1-1548, 57, p. 2.

104. NARS, R.G. 165, CI-RIR/2, 1437, October 11, 1945, p. 3.

105. On Carlos Vogt, see German Federal Republic, Staatsarchiv Nürnberg, *Bestand:* KV-Anklage, Nr. R-155a, Interrogations 2856, December 17, 1947, p. 6.

106. Canaris was prepared to let Ribbentrop win his fight in order to prevent the SD from charging that the Abwehr was not doing its utmost for the Reich. This infighting and political intrigue is discussed in Abshagan, *Canaris,* pp. 186–187.

107. NARS, R.G. 59, 862.20212/1-1548, 57, p. 2.

108. NARS, Auswärtiges Amt, *DSGFOR*, T-120 series, roll 733, frame 294839.

109. Ibid., frame 294849.

110. Ibid. Nevertheless, the Abwehr ordered Collenberg to intercede if Nicolaus was arrested.

111. German Federal Republic, Staatsarchiv Nürnberg, *Bestand*: KV-Anklage, Nr. R-155a, Interrogations 2856, December 17, 1947, p. 8.

112. NARS, R.G. 319, FBI, *GELA*, p. 39.

113. NARS, R.G. 59, 862.20212/1871, p. 1.

114. República de Mexico, Secretaría de Relaciones Exteriores, Archivo General, *Classificación Decimal*: III, 655.2 (72), *Topografía*, III-2418-10, May 21, 1941. A special agent of the Mexican Communications Department, José Candelaria Valdés y Valdés, was assigned to work with the undercover RID agents. On the work of Gus Jones and his appointment, see NARS, R.G. 59, 123.12/110, 339 pp. 1–2. While Ambassador Daniels had asked for Jones to be appointed in May 1941, the actual appointment occurred in August.

115. Ibid., *Topografía*, III-1329-12, *Asunto Espionaje, 1941–1942*. Ambassador Daniels passed the document to Foreign Minister Padilla on July 12, 1941. On July 17, the document was forwarded from Padilla's office to the Mexican attorney general.

116. NARS, R.G. 59, 862.20212/2184, 13321, see enclosure I.

117. NARS, R.G. 59, 862.20212/2155, 407, p. 1, and R.G. 59, 862.20212/2191, 379, pp. 1–2.

118. NARS, R.G. 165, FBI, *Totalitarian Activities ... Mexico Today*, pp. 435–436. The law provided for up to fifteen years' imprisonment for espionage activity during time of peace, and up to thirty years during time of war.

119. Ibid., p. 436. The new bureau was called the Jefatura de Servicios de Vigilancia Policía (roughly, Headquarters of Services for Police Vigilance).

120. These are the views of a retired Mexican diplomat, whom we interviewed twice during the spring of 1975, in Washington, D.C.

121. On the career of Hilda Krüger, her year in the United States, and her first months in Mexico, see NARS, R.G. 165, FBI, *Totalitarian Activities . . . Mexico Today,* pp. 177–178.

122. FDRL, Henry Morgenthau Papers, vol. 451, pp. 267–269. Attached to this report was ONI report, Serial 134-41, October 9, 1941.

123. NARS, R.G. 165, FBI, *Totalitarian Activities . . . Mexico Today,* p. 178.

124. *El Nacional,* Mexico City, January 4, 1942.

125. *La Prensa,* Mexico City, February 10, 1942.

126. NARS, R.G. 59, 862.20212/2450, 15400, p. 1. These handwritten comments are found in the left-hand margin.

127. Letter from Inspector Boynton to Professor Rout, October 27, 1977.

128. See NARS, R.G. 59, 862.20212/2250, p. 1, R.G. 59, 862.20212/2491, p. 2, and NARS, R.G. 165, MID, *Axis Espionage and Propaganda in Latin America,* pp. 85–86.

129. NARS, R.G. 165, FBI, *Mexican Microdot Case #1,* pp. 3–4.

130. Letter, Paul Napier to Professor Rout, March 17, 1981, p. 10.

131. NARS, R.G. 165, FBI, *Mexican Microdot Case #1,* p. 42.

132. FDRL, FDRP, OF-10B, box 31, 1180, n.p.

133. On Sutton and his efforts for the Japanese, see NARS, R.G. 59, 894.20212/11-1945, pp. 1–3.

134. On the "Max"-Amanake meetings, see NARS, R.G. 319, FBI, *GELA,* p. 33.

135. FDRL, FDRP, OF-10B, box 31, 1180, n.p.

136. On the accuracy of the prediction concerning the U.S. Navy's strategy, see John B. Lundstrom, *The First South Pacific Campaign: Pacific Fleet Strategy, December 1941–June 1942* (Annapolis, 1976), pp. 13–22 and 48–60.

137. Peter M. Bowers, "Heritage of the Hawk: The P-40 Story, Part 2," *Wings* 13, no. 2 (April 1983):22.

138. The sunken battleships were the *Arizona, California, Nevada, Oklahoma,* and *West Virginia.* The *Utah* was a decommissioned battleship which had been redesignated a target vessel. One hundred eighty-eight U.S. planes were destroyed, but an additional 159 were badly damaged (total: 347), a consideration which makes "Q's" figures more valid. See Paul S. Dull, *A Battle History of the Japanese Navy* (Annapolis, 1978), pp. 15–18.

139. Verification on the ship movements and dates was graciously provided by Dr. Dean Allard, chief, Operational Archives Branch, Department of the Navy, Naval Historical Center, Washington Navy Yard, Letter NAC/AR, Ser. 1168, November 19, 1979. See also Lundstrom, *The First South Pacific Campaign,* pp. 15–22.

140. FDRL, FDRP, OF-10B, box 31, 1180, n.p. Copies of "Max's" microdot letters were delivered to the White House on February 23, 1942.

141. NARS, R.G. 800.20212/306, pp. 1–2.

142. NARS, R.G. 59, 800.20212/340, pp. 1–2.

143. NARS, R.G. 59, 711.62114/9-1945, p. 1 of enclosure.

144. NARS, R.G. 59, 862.20212/2552, pp. 1–2.

145. On the U.S.-Mexican difficulties over repatriation, see FDRL, *The Diaries of Adolf A. Berle,* roll 4, frame 0835, and Stevenson, *A Man Called Intrepid,* p. 373.

146. See NARS, R.G. 84, 820.02, box 531, folder (no number): *German Nationals Deported by the Other American Republics Who Were Deported via the U.S.A.* See especially p. 51.

147. NARS, R.G. 165, FBI, *Mexican Microdot Case #1,* p. 59.

148. On Mexican refusal to release Nicolaus to U.S. custody, see FDRL, *The Diaries of Adolf*

A. Berle, roll 4, frame 0835. On U.S. legal skullduggery in detaining Nicolaus, see NARS, R.G. 59, 711.62115, AR/8-645, p. 1.

149. NARS, R.G. 165, FBI, *Mexican Microdot Case #1,* p. 44.

150. See NARS, R.G. 59, 800.20210/667, p. 2, and R.G. 59, 800.20210/667 (pages marked 7/10 and 8/10).

151. NARS, R.G. 319, FBI, *GELA,* pp. 34–35, and Stevenson, *A Man Called Intrepid,* p. 373.

152. NARS, R.G. 165, FBI, *Mexican Microdot Case #2,* p. 27.

153. NARS, R.G. 319, FBI, *GELA,* p. 34.

154. Ibid.

155. Ibid., pp. 31, 35, 36, and 38, and NARS, R.G. 59, 862.20212/5-2945, pp. 16–17, and 32–33.

156. NARS, R.G. 59, 862.20212/5-2945, pp. 33–34, and R.G. 165, FBI, *Mexican Microdot Case #1,* pp. 60–61.

157. NARS, R.G. 319, FBI, *GELA,* p. 38.

158. On Wolf-Hilber Freudenberg y Hallier and the Rüge ring, see NARS, R.G. 59, 862.20212/5-2945, pp. 20-21, and R.G. 84, 820.02, 9902, box 537, enclosure 4, May 15, 1947, pp. 1–4.

159. On Metzger and Valles, see NARS, R.G. 165, FBI, *Mexican Microdot Case #2,* pp. 8–9 and 71–72.

160. Ibid., pp. 4, 24 and 27. Copies of all the letters are found on pp. 4–61.

161. On the smudging and withholding of some microdots, see FDRL, FDRP, OF-10B, box 4, letter from J. Edgar Hoover to Harry Hopkins, February 8, 1945, p. 2. On breaking into Rüge's home and testing his typewriter, see R.G. 165, FBI, *Mexican Microdot Case #2,* p. 27, and especially R.G. 59, 862.20212/5-2945, pp. 35–60, which indicates what tests were made and what was proven.

162. NARS, R.G. 84, 820.02, box 1281, vol. 312, *American Embassy Mexico—1944, Messersmith-Bursley,* February 17, 1944, n.p.

163. R.G. 59, 862.20212/5-2945, pp. 8–11.

164. On military aircraft performance figures, see R.G. 59, 862.20212/5-2945, pp. 8–11. Reports on internal Mexican politics were provided with the assistance of Prof. Bernd Martin of Albert-Ludwigs University, Freiburg-im-Breisgau. The documents are found in German Federal Republic, Bundesarchiv-Militärarchiv, Freiburg-im-Breisgau, *Bestand:* H27/6, n.p.

165. NARS, R.G. 165, FBI, *Mexican Microdot Case #2,* p. 27.

166. Ibid., p. 29.

167. NARS, R.G. 319, FBI, *GELA,* p. 47.

168. NARS, R.G. 165, FBI, *Totalitarian Activities . . . Mexico Today,* p. 437.

169. Both views are found in NARS, R.G. 60, box 5, folio: *Committee for Political Defense Mexico: Follow-up, Latin American Section,* March 29, 1944, pp. 1–3.

170. *New York Post,* May 2, 3, 4, 7, and 8, 1945. See especially the May 2d and 3d editions.

171. NARS, R.G. 59, 862.20212/6-245, 24755, p. 3.

172. On the low opinion of ONI and MID on Mexican security procedures, see FDRL, FDRP, OF 10-B, 2620-C, box 4, Hoover to Hopkins, February 8, 1945, pp. 1–2. See also R.G. 59, 862.20212/8-2945, covering letter to Frederick B. Lyon.

173. NARS, R.G. 59, 862.20212/8-2945, cover letter, and pp. 1–2. Hoover insisted, however, that no information regarding codes, ciphers, or decodes be included.

174. NARS, R.G. 226, 16716-F, May 25, 1942, p. 1.

175. NARS, R.G. 59, 740.00115, EW/7-245, enclosed memorandum, p. 4.

176. *New York Times,* October 18, 1946.

177. See NARS, R.G. 59, 862.20212/8-1846, p. 1. The incident was also described in some detail in a letter from Inspector Boynton to Professor Rout, October 27, 1977, pp. 1–2.

178. NARS, R.G. 59, 862.20212/8-1546, p. 1.

179. NARS, R.G. 165, FBI, *Mexican Microdot Case #2*, pp. 28–29. Hilgert stayed at Rüge's farm in Tlascopac from July 1942 until May 1943. A westbound microdot message dated October 30, 1943, stated that "Fraser" (now called "Fernández") was expected to send more materials.

180. Ibid., p. 31. Hilgert moved to Mariscal 75 in Tlascopac before the beginning of 1944. On the SIS belief in his invulnerability, see NARS, R.G. 165, box 973, report R-666-45 (B-2), July 11, 1945, in folio: *Mexico—Axis and Subversive Activities—General*, p. 6.

181. República de Mexico, AGN, Archivo del Presidente Avila Camacho, *Audiencias*, III/6169, Telegrama, Señora Consuelo Burgos de Hilgert, July 30, 1946. See also reply letter from Avila Camacho's secretary, Licenciado Roberto Amoros, July 31, 1946.

182. NARS, R.G. 59, 862.20212/8-2146, p. 1, tells the story of the capture and repatriation of Hilgert.

183. Ibid., for passengers listed.

184. Ibid., R.G. 59, 862.20212/8-1546, p. 1.

185. *New York Times,* October 18, 1946.

186. NARS, R.G. 59, 862.20212/8-1546, p. 1.

187. *New York Times,* October 20, 1946.

188. NARS, R.G. 84, 820.02, box 1281, vol. 312, *American Embassy Mexico—1944*, document 18403, June 23, 1944, n.p. The same idea was expressed in R.G. 59, 740.00115, EW/7-245, p. 4.

189. See NARS, R.G. 165, *Mexico ... Totalitarianism Today*, p. 437. By a presidential decree issued July 26, 1942, Avila Camacho was empowered to expel from Mexico any naturalized citizens convicted of espionage. On the espionage activities of the persons named, see R.G. 165, box 972, folder: *Mexico—Axis and Subversive Activities*, report R-G66-45 (B-2), July 11, 1945, pp. 2-17 and 43. Also R.G. 226, 81238-C, report 4010, pp. 1–2.

190. NARS, R.G. 319, FBI, *GELA*, p. 46,

191. Ibid., pp. 46-47, and especially NARS, R.G. 165, MID, report R-666-45 (B-2), box 973, folder: *Mexico—Axis and Subversive Activities—General*, July 11, 1945, pp. 3–4.

192. Curiously, U.S. authorities described their holding of Nicolaus as "nonlegal." See NARS, R.G. 59, 711.62115 AR/8-645, p. 1. On his FBI interrogation, see letter from Inspector Boynton to Professor Rout, October 27, 1977, pp. 2–3.

193. Recall that Georg Nicolaus and the other Germans being sent back to Germany via the United States of America were to be treated as diplomats. The U.S. sought release from its pledge, and U.S. officials were angry when Mexico refused to give it. See FDRL, *The Diaries of Adolf A. Berle,* roll 4, frame 0835.

194. República de Mexico, Secretaría de Relaciones Exteriores, Archivo General *Classificación Decimal:* III/655.2 (72)/10 *Topografía* III-1329-12, roll 3, memorandum, January 16, 1945, n.p.

195. Our thanks to Señor Alberto Ramón, Señora Rosalía Ramón, and Drs. Ricardo and Alicia Ferreira of Buenos Aires, Argentina. Through their assistance, we were able to interview a number of persons who knew the late Georg Nicolaus in Barrio Florida. One such person is quoted here.

196. Information and the quote on Hilgert are from Kapitän zur See a.D. Herbert Wichmann, who was commander of the Ast Hamburg Station, 1939–1945. See letter from Herbert Wichmann to Professor Rout, August 3, 1982.

197. NARS, R.G. 84, 820.02, Secret Files, 800.1-850-4, *American Embassy, Mexico—1943*, box 1290, letters, Messersmith to Bonsal, April 27, 1943, p. 4.

198. On the poor relations between Messersmith and Alemán and the complaint in this regard by the Mexican ambassador to the United States, see letter from the late Spruille Braden to Professor Rout, December 9, 1977, p. 2.

199. See Henry Bamford Parkes, *A History of Mexico*. 3d ed., revised and enlarged (Boston, 1960), pp. 428–430.

200. We checked and rechecked NARS, R.G. 862.20212/files from 1941–46, and found no spy trial noted. Next, with the kind assistance of Dr. Gisela von Mühlenbrock, legal specialist at the Law Library, Hispanic Law Division, Library of Congress, we checked the *Diario Oficial* and Mexican court records only to draw another blank. The sole case discovered is described in NARS, R.G. 226, OSS report 83592, July 8, 1944, pp. 1–2. The persons tried were found not guilty.

201. The decision is evident in NARS, R.G. 59, 740.0015, EW.7-245, pp. 3–4, and enclosure I, pp. 2–6. See also R.G. 84, 820.02, box 1281, volume 312, *American Embassy, Mexico—1944*, 18403, June 23, 1944, n.p.

202. NARS, R.G. 60, box 5, folio: *Committee for Political Defense-Mexico*, etc., p. 2. See also NARS, R.G. 165, FBI, *Totalitarian Activities . . . Mexico Today*, p. 245. The report takes pains to point out that the Mexican government acted "in cooperation with American (i.e., U.S.) authorities."

203. See Howard F. Cline, *The United States and Mexico*, revised edition (New York, 1971), pp. 266–270, and Volland, *Das Dritte Reich und Mexiko*, pp. 178, 186–187. Suspicion in the United States that this was indeed the real situation is evinced in FDRL, *The Diaries of Adolf A. Berle*, roll 4, frame 0774.

204. See NARS, R.G. 59, 740.00115, EW/7-245, pp. 3–4, enclosure I, pp. 3–6. See also NARS, R.G. 84, 820.02, box 1281, vol. 312, *American Embassy, Mexico—1944*, 18403, June 23, 1944, n.p.

205. Ibid. To be noted is the fact that in his inaugural address in December 1940, President Avila Camacho observed that he saw his task as being one of consolidation. See also Betty Kirk, *Covering the Mexican Front: The Battle of Europe vs. America* (Norman, Okla., 1942), p. 320.

206. On Alemán and Truman, see *Time* 49, no. 19 (May 12, 1947): 21–22.

207. Further evidence of the totally scornful and negative attitude of U.S. civil and military officials toward Miguel Alemán is found in NARS, R.G. 59, MID, serial 689-41-R, December 19, 1941, pp. 1–2; R.G. 226, COI 9115, *Pro-Axis and Anti-Axis Forces in Mexico*, March 5, 1942, pp. 1–3; and R.G. 319, I.D. 227612, December 28, 1945, I.A. Files, box 1515, pp. 2–3.

208. See Cline, *The United States and Mexico*, p. 315.

4

The Espionage War in Brazil: 1939–42

I. Introduction: Getúlio's Samba

November 28, 1941, was a hot, humid day in Rio de Janeiro, with some late afternoon shower activity. But the threatening weather cleared off, and that evening German ambassador Kurt Prüfer hosted a gala dinner party. Normally, diplomats do not dispense large quantities of free food and drink solely for altruistic reasons. Whatever Prüfer's original plans may have been, a recent development had forced an important alteration. At the suggestion of Pres. Getúlio Vargas, Prüfer had invited Benjamin Vargas, the president's brother and trusted kinsman, to the affair. After dinner, Benjamin closeted himself with the ambassador and gave him this confidential message:

> He [President Vargas] had the urgent desire to remain on good terms with Germany. If he were now forced to make concessions to the United States in many fields, this did not mean any fundamental change in policy.... The President gave this assurance: he was not thinking of breaking off relations with Germany, even if America should press him to do it.[1]

No doubt Prüfer smiled and made those expressions of concurrence that are a skilled diplomat's stock-in-trade. But for him, the news from President Vargas must have had the credibility of a used car salesman's spiel. In a November 14, 1941, memorandum, he reported to Foreign Minister Ribbentrop that the Brazilian leader's only real concern was the size of the economic and military package to be paid for his allegiance. As matters then stood, Berlin could not match Washington's promises; thus, Brazil would move into the Anglo-American camp.[2]

For six years prior to these events, the Brazilian president-turned-dictator had carried on a clever double game, offering his friendship to

106

both Berlin and Washington, selling pieces of it in exchange for trade, economic development, and military equipment. In February 1935, for example, he signed a reciprocal trade agreement with the United States, the main provisions of which were free entry for Brazilian coffee and lower duties in Brazil on U.S. automobiles, machinery, and wheat. The problem, however, was that Brazil had little hard currency with which to purchase weapons or machinery in the United States, and the 1935 pact did nothing to facilitate such acquisitions.

As in the Mexican case, Adolf Hitler decided that timely actions on the Reich's part might win Latin American friends and foil Yankee planners. Brazil's size, its strategic position, and the presence of at least four hundred thousand *Reichsdeutschen* and *Volksdeutschen* were all factors which pricked his interest. But the real inducement was the prospect that coffee, cotton, iron ore, hides, and rubber might be obtained without the heavy expenditure of Germany's none-too-extensive hard currency reserves. The result was a 1936 barter agreement whereby Brazil exchanged raw materials for German arms and manufactures. U.S. exporters screamed foul, since the U.S.-Brazilian pact contained an ironclad most-favored-nation provision, but the imperturbable Brazilians blithely ignored these protests. Within two years the Third Reich had become Brazil's second best customer, and it supplanted the United States as the chief source of imported goods. This commercial breakthrough was capped by a $55 million arms contract between the Krupp works and the Brazilian government signed in March 1938.[3]

Under normal circumstances, the flouting of a U.S. commercial agreement and the purchase of large quantities of German arms would have generated some unfriendly remonstrances from Washington. That they did not was due largely to decisions made by Sumner Welles and Franklin D. Roosevelt. Neither man was overjoyed when Vargas terminated Brazil's faltering experiment with democracy in a November 10, 1937, coup. Moreover, Vargas's promulgation of the crypto-Fascist Estado Nôvo (New State) seemed to suggest that philosophically, at least, his sympathies lay with Hitler and Mussolini rather than with the democracies. Still, Brazil's strategic position in regard to hemispheric defense and its development potential dictated that the United States seek accommodation. Finally, the unsuccessful Integralista coup of May 11, 1938, convinced Roosevelt that although Vargas might not be the easiest kind of ally to justify, he was less threatening and much more dependable than Plinio Salgado and his green-shirted minions.[4]

Nor was the United States the only nation which felt compelled to recast its Brazilian policy along pragmatic lines. In the wake of the Integralista challenge, Vargas jailed German citizens and eventually insisted that the protesting German ambassador, then Karl von Ritter, be recalled. Steps of this kind usually caused Nazi Germany to retaliate, but the need for raw materials necessitated that the Aryan state take a forebearing stance towards its supplier. With both Berlin and Washington proclaiming that Getúlio Vargas was their friend, it is not surprising that the dictator and his resourceful foreign minister, Oswaldo Aranha, concluded that they could play the United States against Germany. In this way, an underdeveloped Brazil could extract the maximum price from the competitors desiring its favors.[5] Latin American leaders have long dreamed of attaining a similar bargaining position, but few have ever succeeded in doing so.

European war and the British blockade disrupted the burgeoning Brazilian-German trade, but left the Vargas regime firmly committed to expanding that traffic when opportunity permitted. This seemed a probability following the lightninglike advance of the Germans in western Europe during the spring of 1940. On June 11, the day after Mussolini declared war on France and Britain, Vargas made a fiery speech declaring that "the era of improvident liberalism, useless individualism and disorder has passed."[6] This and other ambiguous declarations were interpreted by the Nazis as proof of Vargas's conversion to fascism. However, he hastened to inform U.S. ambassador Jefferson Caffery that the June 11 speech presaged no change in Brazil's commitment to hemispheric cooperation. Then on June 21, Vargas told German ambassador Kurt Prüfer the opposite of what he had told Caffery. It will never be known to whom the Brazilian told the truth, but the signal relayed to Berlin and Washington was understood: Vargas's allegiance was for sale, and the price was going up.[7]

First off the mark with a lucrative bid were the Nazis. In a series of conferences held in July–August 1940, they promised to accept an additional $120 million in Brazilian goods and to deliver railway stock, weapons, and a Krupp-built steel mill.[8] The only problem with this proposal was that tanks, dive-bombers, and railroad cars could not be transported by U-boat; the consolidation of the deal would have to await British defeat and the raising of the blockade.

The Nazis were confident, but Vargas preferred to wait and see what kind of offer Washington would produce. It was a secret, unsigned note to Ambassador Caffery, dated July 1, 1940, which set the tone for the U.S. response. This missive concluded that "Góes Monteiro [Brazilian army chief of staff] . . . will take relatively little interest in the clash between democratic and totalitarian ideologies, but will base his sentiment and his action on a show of strength and which side can offer the most. . . . This applies probably as well to President Vargas. . . ."[9]

Fifteen days later, the U.S. ambassador sent both a synopsis of this note and a sharply worded telegram to the State Department, declaring that unless Washington outbid Berlin, Vargas could jump into bed with the Nazis. FDR decided to take no chances. On August 3, Sumner Welles promised the Brazilians large shipments of arms. Then, on September 26, an agreement was signed providing the initial credits for the construction of what became Volta Redonda, the first integrated iron and steel complex in Latin America.[10]

With the steel mill funds assured, the negotiation of agreements on other matters proceeded apace. Bilateral military and naval talks had begun in August 1940, and joint naval and military defense arrangements were reached on October 29 and November 14, 1940.[11] The next move proved to be one of the most important pre-Pearl Harbor deals negotiated with any Latin American state. In November 1940, the U.S. Army reached an agreement with Pan American Airways president Juan Trippe concerning the construction of strategic airfields on Brazilian soil. As a result, in January 1941, discussions involving the U.S. Army Air Force, Pan American Airways, Panair do Brasil, and the Vargas government began in Rio de Janeiro. (The bargaining unit was technically Panair do Brasil. This airline was at that time a wholly owned subsidiary of Pan American Airways. The U.S. Army negotiated with Pan American, and Panair dealt with Vargas.) These talks resulted in the construction of a series of airfields in northeastern Brazil, which were to be utilized by the U.S. Air Ferry Command to transport planes to anti-Axis forces in North Africa, the Middle East, and the Far East. The first aircraft to be delivered by this route reached Brazil on June 25, 1941.[12]

Not many historians seem to be aware of the critical importance of this southern air ferry route in supplying aircraft to the distant combat zones. Particularly during the winters of 1941–42 and 1942–43, when bad weather closed down the northern route (Newfoundland-Iceland-Scotland), aircraft could still reach certain combat zones via transatlantic flight from Brazilian airstrips. In fact, making these bases available was possibly Brazil's greatest contribution to the winning of the war.[13]

A stubborn Berlin, however, was not yet prepared to concede its loss in the Brazilian loyalty sweepstakes. Between March and May 1941, five German blockade runners reached Brazilian ports carrying large stocks of German manufactures. So pleased was Vargas that he proposed a trade arrangement whereby products would be shipped to Germany on Brazilian ships, via the port of Bordeaux, and he continued to entertain new German trade proposals through the summer of 1941.[14]

Unfortunately for German interests, the tightening naval blockade and the growing German preoccupation with the campaign in Russia made deliveries of goods and weapons increasingly problematic. President Vargas had done his best to leave the door ajar for further interaction, but his own military men were growing impatient. Thus, on October 1, 1941, the United States of America and the United States of Brazil signed a $100 million lend-lease contract, which pledged both nations to provide a "common defense and united resistance to aggression."[15] There is no question as to which group of nations Washington considered to be the aggressor, and, in accepting the weapons proffered, Vargas had thrown his lot with the United States. He must also have realized how Hitler would view this agreement, but that consideration did not prevent the Brazilian from continuing his efforts to obtain the arms promised in the 1938 Krupp deal. Not until November 10, 1941, did Vargas officially consider that contract as having lapsed, and still another month would pass before the Brazilian army commission sent to Germany to arrange for shipment of the weapons asked for its passports.[16] Vargas had danced enticingly, Uncle Sam had paid the bill, and now the game was over.

This tale of calculating diplomacy is not intended to give comfort to the cynical, but to furnish a background for the espionage and counter-espionage activities transpiring in Brazil in 1939–42. Admiral Canaris would send his largest contingent of hemispheric operatives to Brazil, and this was primarily because of the strategic position of that nation vis-à-vis the Anglo-American war effort. Due to naval losses and apprehension over possible Italian fleet action, between April 1940 and the summer of 1943, Britain severely restricted the movement of convoys from the Suez Canal westward to the Straits of Gibraltar. Consequently, vessels carrying goods from Southeast Asia, Australia, and New Zealand sailed independently as far as Capetown, South Africa, or Freetown, Sierra Leone. In these ports convoys were formed, and warships escorted the freighters into British home ports.[17]

Other ships, upon clearing Capetown, crossed the South Atlantic for the Río de la Plata. Here they joined steamers carrying the wheat, corn, beef, and mutton which sustained the nutrition of a war-torn England. The merchantmen proceeded singly or in small groups up the Brazilian coast, occasionally calling at Pôrto Alegre and Santos on the way to Rio de Janeiro or Recife. In these last two ports, British shipping agents and special naval personnel formed the vessels into convoys; men-of-war escorts were picked up at Trinidad and the ships proceeded to Britain. Conversely, cargo ships traveling from the United Kingdom received naval escort as far as Trinidad, but usually remained in convoy until reaching Rio de Janeiro. From that point, they were routed southward independently.[18] In essence, the partial closing of the Mediterranean made Recife, and especially Rio de Janeiro, critical ports in the British South Atlantic shipping scheme.

Given this degree of maritime activity, it is understandable that the Abwehr would establish a number of FMKs in the Rio de Janeiro area. These rings collected and collated data on shipping movements, cargoes, and ports of destination, and radioed the material to European receiving stations. Nor was shipping information the only sensitive material the German networks wanted. From the summer of 1941, data was sought and obtained concerning the number and types of aircraft being ferried across the Atlantic from northeastern Brazil. The termination of these clandestine broadcasts was definitely desired by the United States and would be the primary objective assigned the SIS unit (hereafter referred to as the SIS/Brazil).[19]

In foreign affairs Vargas had followed a zigzag course, but until late in 1941, he had remained extremely cagey about making any irreversible commitments. He would act similarly with regard to the espionage and counterespionage problem in Brazil.

From the Anglo-American perspective, by the middle of 1941, the most glaring gap in the economic blockade of Hitler-dominated Europe was the continued operation of Italy's LATI airline. After the entry of Italy into the conflict in June 1940, LATI became the swiftest and most secure means by which Axis diplomats, spies, and propaganda reached Latin America, and by which industrial diamonds, mica, and platinum were transported out. Its pilots were accused of conducting some "plain and fancy sea espionage," and while the charge was never proven, rising British losses in the South Atlantic and a doubling of LATI transatlantic flights in 1941 were all the evidence the Anglo-Americans needed.[20]

As early as April 1941, Cordell Hull had approached Getúlio Vargas, and, in the name of "hemispheric defense," sought to have LATI's contract cancelled. The secretary seemed unaware that the Italians had prepared for this eventuality. A prominent company director at LATI's Rio de Janeiro headquarters was a Vargas son-in-law, while others among Brazil's social elite held jobs with or financial interests in the Italian firm. The dictator's reply was predictable: he had no intentions of stirring up an internal political crisis in the name of hemispheric defense.[21]

Since an approach via the high road of diplomacy produced negative results, the British decided that deception became the most expedient means of achieving the desired end. After BSC chief Sir William Stephenson ("Intrepid") sanctioned the operation, a letter written by LATI president Gen. Aurelio Liotta was pilfered from the airline's files. Using this missive as a guide, Station M, a special camp in the Canadian province of Ontario where the BSC manufactured disinformation, created a typewriter which possessed all the peculiarities and defects of the instrument used by General Liotta. Another letter, ostensibly written by Liotta to Commandante Vicenzo Coppola, chief of the LATI Rio de Janeiro office, was then typed on that company's stationery. Fabricated in September, but dated October 31, 1941, the letter read in part:

> There can be no doubt that the "little fatman" [i.e., Vargas] is falling into the pockets of the Americans, and that only violent action on the part of the "green gentlemen" [i.e., Integralistas] can save the country. I understand such action has been arranged for by our respected collaborators in Berlin.... The Brazilians may be, as you said, "a nation of monkeys," but they are monkeys who will dance for anyone who can pull the string.[22]

This letter, about as subtle as a blackjack, never left North America. The BSC only made a photo negative available to those it wished to mislead. Thereafter, according to H. Montgomery Hyde's account in *Room 3603*, a BSC agent in Rio (perhaps an operative named Bernard Edge) arranged to have Commandante Coppola's house burglarized. The Italian called the police, and the incident was reported in the press—exactly as the plot required. Next, a BSC operative of Brazilian origin sought out the local Associated Press representative. Posing as a participant in the Coppola heist, and claiming to have picked up the negative inadvertently, he sold it to the American newsman. The reporter took his purchase to Ambassador Jefferson Caffery, who concluded it was genuine, and sent the negative with photo enlargements to Getúlio Vargas. Allegedly, "the infuriated President reacted exactly as Stephenson had hoped and surmised. He [Vargas] immediately cancelled all LATI's landing rights."[23]

Essentially the same story is repeated in William Stevenson's *A Man Called Intrepid*, but in this second account, the photo negative of the "little fatman" letter was "smuggled to Rio and blowups leaked to Vargas's cronies." No further explanation of how the deed was accomplished is provided, but the conclusion reached is the same as in the Hyde account: "The President [i.e., Vargas] flew into a rage, cancelled LATI's landing rights, and ordered Coppola's arrest. . . ."[24]

The principal problem with the Hyde and Stevenson narratives is that neither author cites any corroborating evidence demonstrating the decisive nature of BSC skullduggery as the primary motivational factor affecting Vargas's decision.

On the other hand, the available facts suggest that the termination of the LATI contract was essentially the result of U.S.-Brazilian negotiation and State Department intrigue. In April 1941, Vargas rejected U.S. overtures regarding the demise of LATI, but that same month, Foreign Minister Oswaldo Aranha indicated that if certain conditions were met, Washington's wishes might still come to pass. The Italian airline's importance was that it provided Brazil with air passage to the European continent unfettered by British censorship and possible interdiction. If the United States could provide additional air service which achieved the same end, LATI would become, like the pony express, an entity overtaken by the changing course of events.[25]

Prodded by Ambassador Caffery, the State Department gradually came to grips with the Brazilian reality. In August 1941, the Reconstruction Finance Corporation established a subsidiary called the Defense Supplies Corporation (DSC) with an $8 million lending authority; the DSC was charged with the removal of Axis influences from Latin American airlines. The first nail in LATI's coffin was driven in October 1941, when DSC and Pan American Airways provisionally agreed to establish a weekly New York–Belém–Natal–Cape Verde Islands–Lisbon service. In expounding on the reason for this arrangement, Cordell Hull pulled no punches; the secretary of state's October 13, 1941, cable to Jefferson Caffery indicated that he expected positive results since "the sole reason for the establishment of this new service is, of course, the elimination of LATI."[26]

The U.S. ambassador to Brazil began by applying pressure on Joaquim Pedro Salgado Filho, the Brazilian minister for aviation, and by October 24, the latter had agreed "in principle" to cancel the LATI contract.[27] By October 31, 1941, President Vargas himself had decided that the Italian airline's days were numbered, and on November 5, the Pan American-DSC contract was formally ratified.[28]

Washington expected a formal announcement of LATI's loss of its franchise when the new transatlantic service via Brazil commenced, but since the Vargas regime failed to act, the State Department forced the issue. Discussions with the Standard Oil Company had also begun in April 1941, and finally, on December 11 (the day of the formal U.S. declaration of war on Germany and Italy), Standard Oil's affiliate in Brazil announced that it would no longer sell gasoline to LATI. This move virtually immobilized the airline, and Vargas could now act without Brazil being blamed for the situation. On December 13, Pan American commenced the newly negotiated New York–Brazil–Portugal run. Ten days later, LATI had its overseas communication connection links severed, and the day after Christmas, its Brazilian properties were formally confiscated. Still, final resolution of the LATI problem would not occur until January 1942, when, at Jefferson Caffery's insistence, the U.S. Army Air Force agreed to pay Brazil $350,000 for six impounded LATI planes.[29] It would appear, therefore, that Assistant Secretary Adolf Berle and Ambassador Caffery would seem justified in concluding that the LATI shutdown was essentially a State Department triumph.

One of the more questionable aspects of the Hyde and Stevenson narratives was the presumption that insults about Vargas's girth, about the integrity of the Brazilian people, and the threat of another Integralista uprising would cause Vargas to act impulsively. It is possible that "Intrepid" and his aides knew their man, but this belief runs counter to the psychological and philosophical portrait of Getúlio Vargas presented by his several biographers.[30] In contrast, they have emphasized his cautious nature, his ability to manipulate allies and enemies, and his preference for putting off vital decisions until the passage of events virtually dictated the action to be taken. This same sense of caution and predilection for noncommitment is also evident in Vargas's general espionage and counterespionage policies. His trusted henchman, Maj. Filinto Muller, chief of all police in the Federal District of Rio de Janeiro, was directly in touch with certain Abwehr leaders in Brazil and the apparent recipient of German spy funds.[31] Furthermore, Capt. Felisberto Baptista Teixeira, chief of the Delegação de Ordem Política e Social (DOPS, the regime's principal internal security police) in the Federal District, controlled at least one double agent who successfully infiltrated a German network.[32]

With regard to U.S. intelligence concerns, Vargas requested in November 1938 that FBI agents be dispatched to Brazil in order to train the national police in counterespionage techniques. Agent Edward K. Thompson was ordered to that country in January 1939, and although he apparently performed satisfactorily, this development failed to engender close relations between U.S. and Brazilian agents and agencies. SIS/Brazil chief Jack West arrived in Rio in May 1941 and was named legal attaché in August, but he spent seven months communicating with Filinto Muller only through embassy Third Secretary Elim O'Shaughnessy. West distrusted Muller, and although he did not know whether Brazilian agents were reporting on SIS/Brazil activities, he definitely suspected it.[33]

Through his police aides, Getúlio Vargas was probably able to maintain a fair degree of watchfulness over both German and U.S. intelligence networks in Brazil. But prior to January 28, 1942, only two V-men and no

SIS/Brazil operatives had been arrested by the Brazilian police.[34] Until the calculating Vargas was ready to make a definitive move, he would keep an eye on the spies and counterspies, but do little or nothing about their activities.

II. The German Espionage Network in Brazil

A. The FMK "Alfredo" Organization

1. The Business Executive as Apprentice Spy

In the official report on Abwehr activity in Brazil, Lt. Comdr. Hermann Bohny, former naval attaché in that country, called Albrecht Gustav Engels (code name: Alfredo) "the best V-man in Brazil."[35] SIS/Brazil agent Francis Crosby interrogated "Alfredo" on several occasions, and concluded that Engels was "clever ... personable and the best-known and best-liked German in Rio de Janeiro."[36] It is an unusual spy who receives accolades from both his allies and his adversaries. The conclusion is virtually inescapable that Albrecht Gustav Engels was both an outstanding agent and an unusual man.

Born to wealthy parents on June 1, 1899, in Buchholz, Westphalia, a patriotic young Albrecht enlisted in the German army in 1916. He was wounded in 1917, commissioned a lieutenant in 1918, and mustered out in 1919. Between 1920 and 1923, he attended the Technical University of Berlin where he studied electrical engineering. During the latter years, the inflationary spiral which engulfed Germany swept away the family fortune. Determined to recoup, but convinced that the fatherland was no place to accomplish this goal, Engels took a ship to Brazil.

Arriving in Rio de Janeiro in August 1923, all he had was a few marks and a letter from a family friend to a representative of the local branch of the Siemens Schuckert Company. What followed was a Brazilian version of the Horatio Alger story. In 1931, he became the director and manager of Empresa Sul Brasileira de Electricidade, an AEG subsidiary, located in Joinville, Santa Catarina. Despite the vicissitudes of the Depression, with Engels at the helm, the company was a conspicuous success; in 1938, AEG brought him back to Rio, made him an officer in the company directorate and subdirector of its entire Brazilian operation.

AEG executives were generally given quadrennial opportunities to spend a year in Germany. Engels had made such a trip in 1934, and in February 1939, as a naturalized Brazilian citizen, he did so again. But the prospect of European hostilities caused him and his wife to terminate their holiday sooner than planned. Arrangements were hurriedly made for Albrecht and Klara Engels to return to Brazil aboard the Italian liner *Augustus*. The vessel was scheduled to leave Genoa, Italy, on September 1, 1939, but machinery breakdowns and other delays pushed the date of departure back nine days.

Unexpectedly, on the morning of his rescheduled departure, Engels received a visitor who had just arrived by plane from Berlin. This mysterious traveler, another World War I veteran named Jobst Raven, had also immigrated to Brazil in 1923, and moved to Joinville in 1931. He and Engels were acquainted, but since Raven's business ventures enjoyed scant success, the two men moved in different social circles. Returning to Germany in 1938, Raven made a short visit to Brazil in June 1939 and confided to friends that he was now a lieutenant in the German army. It is not clear how much Engels knew of Raven's military career, but for an army lieutenant to fly from Berlin to Genoa just to see him suggests that Raven was no ordinary lieutenant.

The first and last Raven-Engels conversation during World War II lasted a brief thirty minutes. The former revealed that he was now an Abwehr officer assigned to the I-Wi section of Abteilung I. He wanted Engels to act as an economic informant, sending letters concerning war production and financial developments in the U.S. and Brazil to drops in Portugal and Spain. Ever the servant of the fatherland, Engels agreed to serve; as a result, the AEG director became V-man "Alfredo," apprentice spy.[37]

Upon his return to Rio, Engels scoured *Time, Life, Reader's Digest,* and an assortment of technical publications for materials to mail to Raven. He had received no instruction in secret inks, codes, or any of the other tools of the trade a functioning spy might have been expected to master. This situation would change with the assignment in January 1940 of Hermann Bohny (then a lieutenant, senior grade) as assistant naval attaché in Brazil. Here was still another German officer who had worked in Brazil before returning to Germany in 1936. Since the attaché already knew Engels and was apprised of his assignment, they soon became comrades, both socially and in the business of intelligence procurement.[38]

2. *Exit "Leo"*

What really cemented the Bohny-Engels alliance was the bold but successful piece of deception they employed to remove Army Captain Erich Leonhardt Immer (code names: Leo and Leonardo) from the Brazilian scene. Born in Austria in May 1894, Immer was an engineer who immigrated to Brazil in 1922, and became a naturalized citizen in 1938. In August 1939, he sailed for Germany but inauspiciously returned to Brazil in February 1940. Sometime in May, he visited Engels and established his identity as I-Wi's resident spy chief in South America. That same month, he traveled to São Paulo and revealed his identity to Eduard Arnold (code name: Argus), a *Volksdeutscher* who visited Germany during the summer of 1939 and was recruited by Jobst Raven to provide economic information. Immer told both Engels and Arnold that henceforth all reports would be turned over to him. He also wanted Arnold to contact Hans Kurt Werner Meyer-Clason and arrange a meeting.[39]

In 1940, Meyer-Clason was well known as a playboy who was suspect among pro-Nazis because of his lukewarm acceptance of the Führer. Meyer-Clason was working as a cotton grader for a U.S. firm, and this fact was the basis of "Leo's" interest. In a meeting at the German Club of São Paulo in June, Immer recruited Meyer-Clason as a V-man and told him to obtain a visa for entry in the United States. When the latter agreed, Immer took out an envelope and revealed a microdot which contained instructions concerning the information desired and the names of U.S. contacts. Since this was possibly the first microdot message seen on this side of the Atlantic, it seems ludicrous that "Leo" would give the microdot to an espionage novice. The problem seems to be that Immer was determined to place an agent in the United States, and since Meyer-Clason was the only person he knew who might conceivably achieve entry, he decided to take a chance.[40]

Straightaway, Meyer-Clason applied for a visa, but in July 1940, the United States rejected his request. Chiefly to further his job prospects, he then settled in Pôrto Alegre. Once established there, Meyer-Clason contacted an optometrist named Reinaldo Vogel, confided that he was a secret agent, and sought the eye doctor's microscope in order to read the instructions that were on the microdot. Vogel and Meyer-Clason were old friends, but the optometrist was flabbergasted by what he perceived as lackadaisical security precautions. In September 1940, Vogel telegraphed the details of the incident to the German embassy in Rio, and when Bohny heard of it, he was livid with rage. The naval attaché was already at odds with Immer, for "Leo" not only refused to coordinate activities, but had indicated that his comings and goings in Latin America were none of Bohny's business. An angry Immer fired Meyer-Clason; and a furious Bohny now had an excuse for getting rid of Immer.[41]

Absolutely in accord with Bohny as to "Leo's" unsuitability was Albrecht Gustav Engels. He had known Immer before the war, but had not seen fit to make his acquaintance. Now the feisty five-foot, six-inch Immer, whose eyeglasses resembled the bottoms of two Coke bottles, was giving orders to the haughty, six-foot AEG director. It was an unbearable situation for Engels; as he later told his interrogators, Immer was not only "shallow and supercilious," but he "left the impression of being a third-class clerk." United in their mutual dislike and backed by Ambassador Kurt Prüfer, who had also complained about Immer, Engels and Bohny began concocting a plan which would speed Immer's departure while making retaliation difficult.[42]

Late in November 1940, Immer received a telegram purportedly from headquarters ordering him to return at once. He delegated command of his unit to Engels, and about December 9, took a Spanish vessel to Europe. Upon his arrival at I-Wi section, Immer received the shock of his life. There had been no cablegram. There were no new orders. And no one in Berlin knew why Immer had returned to Germany.[43]

A mortified "Leo" subsequently wrote two letters to Eduard Arnold reporting the ruse used to remove him, and vowing vengeance.[44] Unquestionably Dr. Bloch and Jobst Raven heard many an angry earful from Immer, but censuring Bohny and dismissing Engels would do nothing to strengthen their new unit in Brazil. Moreover, Immer had certainly acted stupidly with Meyer-Clason, and an agent unable to match wits with the

Engels-Bohny combination was better off back in Germany. The I-Wi operation in Brazil would henceforth be what Albrecht Engels and Hermann Bohny made it.

3. *The Apprentice Spy Becomes Spymaster*

In October 1940, Albrecht Gustav Engels was an informant who sent occasional reports to the I-Wi section of Abteilung I via mail drops in foreign countries. One year later, he was the director of an FMK replete with a back-up broadcasting station, agents in northeastern Brazil, and a contact inside the Vargas cabinet. How, in twelve months' time, did such a dramatic transformation take place?

Recall that during the fall and winter of 1940–41, the Abwehr strove to have all its Latin American MKs obtain radio transmitting capabilities, thereby becoming FMKs.[45] Berlin was, of course, particularly interested in having the Immer group make such a switch. In December 1940, Lt. Julius Stiege, of the I-M section of Abteilung I, arrived in Argentina to conduct an inspection tour of South American Abwehr units. Toward the end of the month, Stiege reached Rio de Janeiro, and he conferred with Engels and Bohny concerning the Immer affair.[46] The explanation supplied must have been satisfactory, because before he left, Stiege presented "Alfredo" with what he said was an "unbreakable code," which I-Wi section wanted utilized for radio messages. It may be that Engels understood implicitly that if he wanted to avoid any unfortunate repercussions over Immer's removal, he would be wise to agree to take charge of a clandestine radio service. By accepting the code from Stiege, he informally undertook to change MK "Leo" into FMK "Alfredo."[47]

The role of the naval attaché Hermann Bohny in this transformation also requires comment. The situation varied from country to country, but in Brazil, the military and naval attachés, actively supported by Ambassador Kurt Prüfer, viewed themselves as espionage supervisors.[48] By late 1940, Bohny had already assembled a string of informants,[49] and could have established a clandestine radio station himself. But as a member of the German diplomatic staff, he could not afford to become directly involved in activities which the Brazilian government might construe as unfriendly. He knew Engels as a capable and clever administrator with solid connections among the Brazilian elite. With Engels administering the FMK, Bohny could act as chairman of the board, gradually folding into the planned group the informants he had already recruited.

Agreeing to direct an FMK and actually establishing radio contact with an Abwehr receiving station were quite different matters. First of all, in January or February 1941, Berlin sent to "Alfredo" via microdot letter a second code based on a book entitled *Collected Works of German Authors*. (See Appendix A for examples of German ciphers.) Then on March 13, Engels cabled that CEL would be his station call letters and that he was ready to establish contact. But transatlantic radio was very uncertain at this point in time, and contact was delayed. On March 25, new instructions for broadcasting frequencies and times for transmission were sent, but these also proved unavailing. Only in June 1941 did station CEL establish regular contact with station ALD, its Reich reception station.[50] (See Chart V for the CEL network set-up.)

Since "Alfredo" knew nothing about radio transmitter construction or radiotelegraphy, Hermann Bohny handled these details; he utilized the talents of Benno Sobisch, a technician from the Telefunken Company of Brazil, and a Siemens-Schuckert engineer named Hans Muth. Both men had fought in the German Imperial Army in 1914–18, and now they were neighbors in the Santa Tereza district of Rio de Janeiro. The two complemented each other in that Muth built the transmitters and Sobisch installed, tested, and adjusted them. Most of the German FMKs in Brazil utilized Muth's transmitters, but since the agents usually dealt with Sobisch, Muth could subsequently claim that he never knew to whom his creations were sold, or for what purposes they were being used. Actually, Muth built these sets on Bohny's orders, and he usually knew who the recipients were to be.[51]

Broadcasting from his Santa Tereza home, Sobisch was the CEL radioman who first contacted Germany.[52] However, with the CEL-ALD link forged, Sobisch indicated that the "Alfredo" organization should develop its own radioman and another broadcasting base. For this task, Engels now called upon a capable and trusted henchman named Ernst Ramuz (code names: Ernesto, Mathies) and brought him to Rio. Another World War I veteran, Ramuz had earned both facial burns and notoriety as a saboteur working against the French in the Rhineland. With the police on his trail, he fled to Switzerland in 1921, got married, and the following year moved to Brazil. A decade later, Ramuz was made chief of the electrical shop at the Empresa Sul Brasileira de Electricidade. He had become friendly with Engels, and a firm, if paternalistic, bond grew between them. An indication of Ramuz's devotion is seen in the fact that when in June 1941 Engels asked that he move to Rio, Ernst left his wife and children behind and departed without knowing what his new job would entail.

Once in the capital, Ramuz learned radiotelegraphy rapidly under Sobisch's tutelage. In August 1941, CEL's transmitter was partially dismantled, and a new one was installed for Ramuz's use in a house in the suburb of Jacarépaguá. As the radioman for FMK "Alfredo," "Ernesto" faithfully sent and received network messages until arrested in May 1942.[53]

Perhaps half of all CEL transmissions dealt with Anglo-American maritime activities, and the key man for this reportage was one of Bohny's recruits, Hans Otto Meier. Beginning in March 1941, this manager of the maritime and export section for the Hermann Stoltz shipping firm delivered regular reports concerning shipping movements in the Rio de Janeiro-Santos area. With the permission of company directors Rudolf and Georg Hermann Stoltz, Meier also enlisted several employees to obtain the cargo and destination data sought. Bohny would depict Meier as "day and night, a tireless worker," and an indispensable member of the "Alfredo" organization.[54]

CHART V

THE ORIGINAL CEL NETWORK
AND SCHLEGEL SUBSTATION NETWORK

CONTROLLERS: Maj. Dr. Ernst Bloch (Chief, I-Wi Section of Abteilung I)
Capt. Jobst Raven (Asst. to Bloch, and Brazilian specialist)

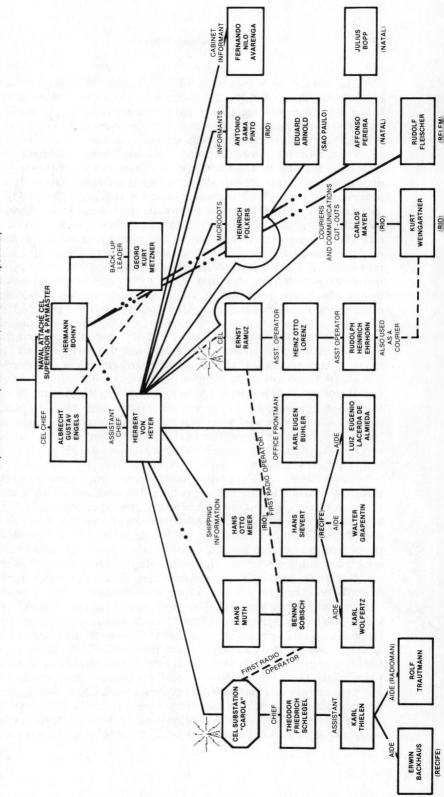

The person by whom most of this shipping data was actually received was Herbert von Heyer (code name: Humberto). Born in 1900 in
Brazil of German parents, Heyer had fought for Germany in World War I
and lived there until 1923, the same year Engels moved to Brazil. Heyer's
economic prospects did not improve until a position became available in
1938 in the Theodor Wille Shipping Company. Three years later, Herbert
von Heyer became manager of the Wille Company's steamship services. A
prewar acquaintance of both Albrecht Engels and Jobst Raven, Heyer was
nevertheless uninvolved in intelligence activity until June 1941. Four
months earlier, he left Brazil on a combination business and pleasure trip
to Spain, Portugal, and Germany. Learning of these plans, "Alfredo," who
had a high opinion of Heyer, cabled Berlin and urged that the latter be
recruited for intelligence work. What subsequently transpired reads like a
repetition of the Engels enlistment. On June 5, 1941, the day before
Heyer was scheduled to sail from Lisbon to Rio, he was visited in his hotel
by the ubiquitous Jobst Raven. Heyer promptly agreed to become another cog in the expanding engine of espionage that was FMK "Alfredo."[55]

After returning to Rio, Heyer delivered a package containing chemicals for secret inks to Engels. Rather casually, Engels suggested that the
new V-man take time off from his job and visit the northern port cities of
Recife, Natal, and Belém to recruit other informants. A comprehensive
picture of Anglo-American shipping activities could only be obtained if
regular information was supplied by informants in these ports. Possibly at
Engels's suggestion, Heyer approached Hans Otto Meier seeking the
name of a "good German" who might be trusted to carry out confidential
labors. The name given was that of Hans Sievert, and on July 4, 1941, this
representative of the Hermann Stoltz branch in Recife received a visit
from Herbert von Heyer.

Sievert, like Hans Otto Meier, had been passing on shipping information to Hermann Bohny for some time. He now agreed to work with
Heyer and also engaged two other prospective recruits, Carlos Wolfertz
and Walter Grapentin. Heyer gave the three some hasty instruction in the
use of secret inks, and when he left Recife, he was fairly confident that
Grapentin intended to build a transmitter so that Anglo-American shipping data could be relayed either to Rio de Janeiro or to Germany.[56]

Returning from his recruitment tour, Heyer was installed as FMK
majordomo. Thereafter, he received ship movement data from Meier,
Sievert, and other informants, plus mail sent to "Alfredo" from V-men in
Chile, Mexico, and the United States. Heyer also acted as group paymaster, and learned to encipher messages for Ramuz and decode replies from
ALD for dissemination among the ring members. To efficiently carry out
his local activities, he utilized several cut-outs who delivered messages,
made contacts, and provided technical assistance. These included Carlos
Meyer, a cashier at a café in Rio's business district, Kurt Weingartner, an
optometrist, and Karl Erhorn, the former first mate of a German ship sold
to Argentine interests. Another volunteer was Heinrich Folkers, who was
responsible for making microdots on a machine that was stored in the

German embassy. Hermann Bohny was in possession of this device, but the mailing of letters containing these microphotographs generally fell to Heyer.[57]

But no matter how efficient Heyer was, using his Theodor Wille office for CEL activities was patently unwise. It was Engels who came up with a well-nigh perfect solution. "Alfredo" proposed that he and Heyer join with Karl Bühler, a German they knew, to establish a hardware sales business in which all three ostensibly would be equal partners. Bühler was particularly amenable to such a suggestion because the British blockade had forced him out of business. Thanks to capital furnished by Engels, on August 22, 1941, Bühler was able to open new offices in downtown Rio de Janeiro. It is indicative of the arrangement that only the hardware salesman's name was on the lease and the post office box. Bühler was also told in no uncertain terms that his new partners would handle the mail. Various persons frequently came to the office to see Heyer, but they made few efforts to identify themselves to Bühler. Moreover, since he didn't pay the rent, he knew better than to ask searching questions.[58]

While most of the major figures in the "Alfredo" organization were *Reichsdeutsche* or *Volksdeutsche*, there were several persons of non-German origin who were collaborators. Most active among these was Antonio Gamma Pinto, a man of Luso-East Indian origin, from the former Portuguese enclave of Goa. A violent anglophobe, he was steered to Engels by Fritz Kohler, another AEG official. As a network operative and gofer, Gamma Pinto subscribed to the *Wall Street Journal*, obtained a copy of the *New York Marine Register*, collected mail from several drop boxes, and acted as bag man when payments to police or government officials were deemed necessary.[59]

As previously noted, Engels was well connected in Brazilian society, and he parlayed this association into acquiring a pipeline into the highest echelons of government. The conduit of information was apparently Fernando Nilo Avarenga, an official in the Brazilian foreign office who was then serving as a member of the presidential palace staff. Nilo Avarenga had neither blood nor ideological ties to Germany. Apparently his principal reason for passing on data to Engels was decidedly mundane: money.[60]

4. *"The Most Important Station...."*

So vital did Hermann Bohny consider the mission of CEL that he created back-up agents whose function was to take organizational command if Engels and Heyer were arrested. The man assigned as number three in FMK "Alfredo" was Georg Kurt Metzner (code name: Mary), an automobile dealer in Rio who ostensibly was serving as a courier for another Abwehr group. Arrested on March 30, 1942, Metzner never told his U.S.-Brazilian interrogators about his secret appointment, and Engels, who approved it, also kept his mouth closed.[61]

Of greater significance was the assignment of Heinz Otto Hermann Lorenz (code name: Laura) as back-up for Ernst Ramuz. Lorenz had been

third officer on the *La Coruna*, a passenger liner which sought safety in
Rio de Janeiro harbor at the outbreak of the war. He took a clerical job at
the German embassy, but his training in radiotelegraphy meant that once
Bohny learned of it, Lorenz's days as a clerk were bound to be few.
Working as an assistant to Ramuz at the station in Jacarépaguá, he became
well acquainted with many of the ring's activities and operatives. When in
March 1942, Engels, Heyer, and Metzner were all arrested, it was Lorenz
who breathed new life into the suddenly leaderless organization.[62]

Between June 1941 and March 1942, CEL dispatched 325 messages
to ALD, making it the third most active Abwehr radio transmitter in
Brazil. [63] In addition, dozens of microdot letters were forwarded by the
"Alfredo" organization to Berlin and assorted drops in Spain and Portugal.
Moreover, the "Alfredo" organization performed valuable services of a
more pragmatic nature as well. Among the most significant of these was
its participation in the escape of two cargo vessels, the *Dresden* and the
Babitonga.

Shortly before the German attack on Poland in September 1939, the
German Naval High Command dispatched several cargo vessels to Latin
American ports. The intention was to put in tactical position ships which
could provide logistical support for the commerce raiders to be un-
leashed against British sea trade. Anchored in Santos harbor, the *Dresden*
and *Babitonga* both received sailing orders on March 20, 1941. The
Dresden was the first vessel readied, but before she raised anchor and
steamed off, Hermann Bohny wanted an aerial reconnaissance conducted
to ascertain whether the British were preparing for an interception at sea.
With a Brazilian air force pilot, Lt. Franklin Rocha, at the controls, Engels
conducted a sea search, and reported to the naval attaché that the ship
could weigh anchor. On the following day, March 28, 1941, the *Dresden*
put to sea.[64]

An even more critical role was played in the sailing of the *Babitonga*.
Originally scheduled to leave Santos on April 1, the departure was
cancelled when on March 31, Engels and Rocha conducted another air
search, this time spotting two British warships just outside Brazilian
territorial waters. Bohny received this report and ordered the ship to
remain in the harbor. Not until April 24 did the *Babitonga* leave Santos,
but only after "Alfredo" and Rocha made another aerial reconnaissance
and found the sea lanes clear.[65]

On April 16, 1941, the *Dresden* rendezvoused in the South Atlantic
with the commerce raider *Atlantis*. The former reprovisioned the war
vessel, took off 329 prisoners and sailed for Bordeaux, reaching the
French port on May 25, 1941. The *Babitonga* met the *Atlantis* on May 7,
but since the sea raider then needed few supplies, the cargo vessel was
ordered to a staging area in the South Atlantic where a future contact
would be arranged. But the *Babitonga* ran out of luck. She was spotted by
British warships, and her crew scuttled her on June 21 to avoid capture.[66]

The *Babitonga*'s fate, however, does not detract from the fact that
the reconnaissance missions conducted by Engels proved eminently

valuable. Capt. Bernhard Hoppe of the *Atlantis* noted that the prisoners on his ship were rapidly depleting his supplies. By delivering additional provisions and removing the captives, the *Dresden* enabled the raider to remain at sea and wreak further havoc on the British commercial fleet. Between April 16 and November 22, 1941, when the *Atlantis* was sunk by the HMS *Devonshire*, an additional five ships were taken, bringing the total tonnage sunk to 145,000, the greatest of any German commerce raider in World War II.[67] "Alfredo's" reconnaissance missions certainly contributed to that success.

J. Edgar Hoover knew nothing about the participation of Engels and his organization in the sailings of the *Dresden* and *Babitonga*. But simply on the basis of the radio messages intercepted and decoded, he reported to President Roosevelt in February 1942 that "Station CEL ... appears to be the most important station in the chain of clandestine German radios in South America."[68] Interestingly enough, the Abwehr would have been in complete agreement with this assessment. Between June 1941 and March 1942, $112,500 was earmarked for FMK "Alfredo," making it the most lavishly financed German intelligence unit operating in Brazil. And, if more money had been needed, "Alfredo" could have gone directly to Ambassador Kurt Prüfer and requested it.[69]

B. "Salama's" Volunteer Group

1. Krefeld Calls and Espionage

Born in Berlin on June 5, 1892, Theodor Friedrich Schlegel (code name: Salama) enlisted as a private in Kaiser Wilhelm's army in 1914 and emerged as a lieutenant in 1918. After the war, he entered the steel business and, by 1935, held an executive position with Deutsche Edelstahlwerke, a steel concern headquartered in Krefeld, a town near Cologne. In November 1935, the firm ordered Schlegel to Brazil to investigate the poor performance of Companhia Stahlunion, a subsidiary operation. Upon completing his inquiry, Schlegel suggested that the unit be dissolved. Impressed with his energy and efficiency, Edelstahlwerke agreed, and decided to support the creation of a new firm, Companhia Aços Marathon, with Theodor Schlegel as chairman. Headquartered in Rio de Janeiro, the new organization enjoyed financial success until the war broke out in 1939.[70]

The circumstances are not completely clear, but as an old soldier and businessman whose trade had been injured by the British blockade, Schlegel apparently decided in 1940 to offer his services to German intelligence. A middle-aged, balding bachelor who packed over 175 pounds on a paunchy five-foot, seven-inch frame, Schlegel was well connected in commercial circles in the Brazilian capital. During the last months of 1940, Schlegel began forwarding economic data (usually culled from *Time, Life, Iron Age,* and *Reader's Digest*) by airmail via LATI to a drop in Cologne. The recipient was Capt. Georg Kraemer-Knott, an old Schlegel acquaintance and, prior to 1939, a lawyer with Edelstahlwerke. This officer, assigned to the Abwehr and posted to the I-Wi section of Nest Cologne, became Schlegel's controller.[71]

As in the case of Engels, Kraemer-Knott soon advised "Salama" that he must establish a radio transmitting capacity for future use. It was the military attaché, Maj. Gen. Günther Niedenführ, who brought the Aços Marathon executive and the Sôbisch-Muth duo together. The two technicians charged twenty contos (roughly one thousand dollars) to build a transmitter and receiver, and these were ready early in June 1941.[72]

The place of installation for the transmitter was the home of Karl Thielen (code name: Torres). A lawyer who had migrated to Brazil in 1932 and later joined Aços Marathon, he became the company's legal representative by day and Schlegel's network chief by night. He received no salary for his efforts at night, but Schlegel did pay him an additional forty-five dollars per month so that he could move into a house in a district deemed more suitable for transmitting.[73]

In theory, the existence of this set could be easily justified. Edelstahlwerke in Krefeld had a large radio station, and it communicated steel prices and received reports from its worldwide subsidiaries by radio. What company officials did not make public was that from the beginning of the war, control of communications there had passed to Captain Kraemer-Knott. Therefore, many coded messages purportedly dealing with steel sales were in fact reports intended for Nest Cologne. It was, on the surface at least, an ingenious setup.

But before either "Salama" or "Torres" could indulge themselves in dreams of espionage glory, they had to find a competent radioman. While reviewing Aços Marathon personnel records, Schlegel hit upon the name of Rolf Trautmann, who had been trained as a steel tempering technician in Krefeld. Edelstahlwerke had ordered Trautmann to Brazil early in 1939, and assigned him to Aços Marathon's São Paulo office. Once Schlegel found that Trautmann had studied radiotelegraphy for six months, he brought him to Rio de Janeiro in June 1941 and pressed him into service as network radioman.

Trautmann seems to have been nonplused by this rapid sequence of events. True, he had studied radio transmission for six months in 1936, but, in his own words, he had "forgotten how to work the dial." Again, it was Benno Sobisch who temporarily operated the transmitter in Thielen's house; only toward the end of July did Trautmann become the regular radioman.[74] Dissatisfied with his unspectacular salary (ninety-five dollars per month) and conscious of his own importance to the group, in November 1941, the radioman asked Schlegel for a raise. The ringleader's icy rejoiner was that a "good soldier" did his duty regardless of the financial rewards.[75]

Even while Trautmann had been learning to make contact with Krefeld, Schlegel was preparing for his annual trip to Germany. Bearing German passport number 406/41, he left Brazil on a LATI flight on July 24, 1941. It was sometime in August, while at the Krefeld station, that Schlegel heard with pride Trautmann's signal from Rio de Janeiro.[76]

2. *"Salama" versus "Alfredo"*

Until August 1941, all messages sent and received by Rolf Trautmann were transmitted in Rudolf Mosse business code. But, while Schlegel was visiting at Krefeld, his controller, Captain Kraemer-Knott, provided him with a variation of the code scheme used by Albrecht Engels, and based on Jerome K. Jerome's book, *Three Men on a Bummel* (i.e., a stroll) (see Appendix A). "Salama" was also told that messages in the new code were no longer to be transmitted to Krefeld, but directly to the Nest Cologne reception station. Finally, the transmitter in Rio de Janeiro received the code name "Carola," and the ring was ordered to obtain ship movement data and details of U. S. air ferry activities in northeastern Brazil. Confirmed in his belief that he was performing a valuable service for the Third Reich, Schlegel returned to Brazil, arriving in Rio on September 19, 1941.[77]

Ten days later, Captain Kraemer-Knott radioed "Salama" and ordered him to recruit an unemployed salesman named Erwin Backhaus. Since he lived in Recife, Backhaus was seemingly in an excellent position to report on U. S. airfield construction and air ferry service activity in northeastern Brazil. On October 2, 1941, Backhaus was flown to Rio de Janeiro, shown how to make secret ink from a concoction of lemon juice and pure alcohol, and ordered to send his reports by airmail to Karl Thielen.[78]

Nonetheless, it was unlikely that this one agent would supply a flood of information, and the fact is that the Abwehr was really more interested in "Carola" than in the "Salama" group's intelligence-gathering capabilities. With the Engels transmitter becoming increasingly active, a back-up or secondary source was thought to be necessary. Beginning in October 1941, Herbert von Heyer began delivering messages to Schlegel to be transmitted to Nest Cologne for delivery to Abteilung I. Between August and November 1941, at least seventy-eight messages were radioed by Trautmann over "Carola," while twenty-five were received. Perhaps half of the former originated with the Engels group.[79]

Naturally, some *Asts* and *Nests* would have taken a dim view of the practice just described, but Lt. Col. Albrecht Folke, Nest Cologne commander, and Captain Kraemer-Knott sanctioned it.[80] Until Schlegel virtually fell in their laps, that organization had had no plans for establishing an FMK in Brazil. The "Salama" ring cost virtually nothing, and as long as there was a trusted attaché like Günther Niedenführ on the spot to supervise Schlegel, the odds were good that some useful intelligence work would be accomplished.

If the rise of the "Salama" group seemed initially fortuitous, unforeseen circumstances eventually produced unfelicitous results. After his return from Germany, Schlegel, the humble volunteer of 1940, began to show signs that he had received considerable ego massaging from either Captain Kraemer-Knott or his Krefeld associates. In conversations with German embassy personnel, Schlegel stated categorically that he was the Abwehr's chief V-man in Brazil. This unfortunate bit of boasting was repeated to Albrecht Engels, and he was anything but amused. In a

November 26, 1941, message to ALD that virtually scorched the airwaves, Engels demanded a "clarification of [his] position and task, inasmuch as Schlegel has passed [himself off] as main agent."[81] The radio response indicated that Schlegel had certainly overstated his position, and it became the duty of Gen. Günther Niedenführ to stick the pin in "Salama's" balloon. The military attaché believed that Schlegel was a homosexual, and in the tongue-lashing he gave the latter, he twisted the knife by apparently making references to his suspicions of Schlegel's sexual predilections.[82] Crushed and mortified, Schlegel thereafter exhibited little zeal for espionage work. In fact, as soon as a crisis arose, the volunteer who had served without pay promptly threw in the towel.

C. *"King" and the FMK "Brazil" Organization*

1. *Forging a Transcontinental Ring*

Of the V-men who operated in Brazil in 1939–42, only Friedrich Kempter (code name: King) received the Kriegsverdienstkreuz Erster Klasse mit Schwertern (War Service Cross, First Class, with Swords). An SIS operative who interrogated him in 1942 informed us that Kempter was "a good soldier who lived by the book." Orders were orders, to be "carried out even though they might violate ethics, common sense, or personal safety." Unlike some others, Kempter never made any apologies for his wartime activities. In fact, one gets the impression that if it were 1941–42 again, "King" would still be hunched over his equipment pounding the transmitting key, asking only that the Abwehr find the information he supplied worthwhile.[83]

Too young to serve in World War I, after graduation from Tübingen University, Kempter followed Engels, Heyer, and others to Brazil, reaching Recife late in 1923. After obtaining an appointment with a German firm, Kempter married a Brazilian, María do Carmo Pessão Leal, in 1924, and three years later became chief accountant for the Banco Brasileiro-Alemão. Marital breakup and the Depression eclipsed Kempter's career aspirations, but in 1938, he landed a lucrative job as manager of the Adolfo Schafer firm, a company which supplied stock exchange data and other commercial information to German firms interested in investing in Brazil. He also took as his mistress a lady of Russian parentage named Lydia Becker, and bought a house in the Santa Tereza district.

After a decade of difficulty, Kempter's personal and business fortunes seemed to be on an upswing, but the outbreak of World War II changed all that. Hard hit by the British blockade, the Schafer Company cut back drastically on operations; Kempter was given $250 and put out on the street. Desperate for work, he wrote to the Krack-Schwenzner firm, a leading customer of the Schafer Company, and offered his services. The German outfit responded favorably, naming him as its Brazilian representative in January 1940. A month later, Kempter received another missive in which his new employers informed him that Nordisk Durium Aktiebolaget, a Swedish credit reporting house with offices in Hamburg, also wanted him to work for them. The latter company wanted Kempter to send to a Hamburg post office box information concerning the shipment of raw materials to Britain, the names and tonnages of the vessels involved, and the pertinent cargo manifests. Kempter would later tell his interrogators that "no mention was made of secret or spy work," and that he "could not foresee what was happening." That he was as bemused as he suggests is doubtful; Nordisk later sent him a letter which apprised him of the fact that since March 1, 1940, he had been enrolled as a V-man for Ast Hamburg. He was not then told that his controller was Lt. Andre von Wettstein of the Ast's I-M section. Thus commenced the espionage career of "King," possibly the best operative the Abwehr ever recruited entirely by mail.[84]

Kempter began looking around for a partner for the purpose of opening an advertising and commercial information service. Through an advertisement he placed in February 1940 in *Diario Alemão*, a German-language newspaper in Rio, Kempter met Heriberto Ottomar Josef Müller (code name: Prince), an Austrian-born businessman. The two men found themselves compatible, Müller put up $750, and he became co-owner of Informadora Rapida Limitada (Rapid Informer, Limited). The new firm opened its doors on March 1, and after several months, Kempter and Müller moved to offices on the tenth floor at 39 Rua Visconde de Inhaúma. The new location was, incidentally, across the street from Theodor Schlegel's Aços Marathon offices, and, coincidentally, superbly situated to provide "King" with a panoramic view of Rio de Janeiro's harbor. It was not until August 1940 that Kempter took Müller into his confidence and sought his partner's acceptance by the Abwehr. The arrangement struck was that Müller would handle Informadora Rapida's legitimate affairs, leaving Kempter free to deal with intelligence concerns. The actual commercial income did not pay the office rent, so from September 1940 on, Ast Hamburg provided $500 a month, thereby allowing "King" and "Prince" to effectively cope.[85]

With the Rio de Janeiro information center beginning to function effectively, Ast Hamburg moved to bring several other River Plate V-men under "King's" control. Ordered to Buenos Aires in November 1940, Kempter made contact in the Vienna Hotel with two *Reichsdeutschen,* Ottomar Müller (code name: Otis) and Hans Jacob Napp (code name: Berko). The first, a thirty-eight-year-old businessman, was a fanatical Nazi who regularly presented his views over a local radio station as part of a program called "The German Hour." Solicited to do so by another Hamburg-based firm, Schmitt and Company, he began mailing reports on British shipping arrivals and departures in January 1940. Müller soon realized that the Schmitt firm was merely fronting for German intelligence, and on February 1, a month before Kempter, Ottomar Müller went on the Abwehr payroll. Ast Hamburg was obviously pleased with his early efforts, for on April 20, Capt. Hermann Menzel, chief of I-M, Abteilung I, wired the naval attaché in Argentina, Capt. Dietrich Niebuhr, that "Otis" was a "trusted V-man" who must "work by himself."[86]

Müller's protege, Hans Napp, had knocked around Argentina and Uruguay for almost two decades. A one-time business representative, ranch foreman, and shipping clerk, "Berko" had been involved in at least one extortion scheme and was wanted by the Buenos Aires police for passing bad checks. Müller recruited him in July 1940 and, thereafter, he made regular trips to the docks and checked the newspapers for shipping and cargo information. Müller would take the data, encipher it, and cable or mail it to an Ast Hamburg drop box.[87]

As newly appointed regional chief, Kempter administered an oath (November 1940) to Müller and Napp, placing them under the Articles of War, and formally inducting them into the German military. But the fact that Kempter would have to work with these V-men did not indicate that either one was somebody with whom he intended to share a confidence or a bottle. "King" considered Napp a petty crook and Müller an idiot, but he was prepared to swallow his misgivings if this duo (referred to as MK "Argentina") provided regular and accurate information.[88]

Upon his return from Buenos Aires, Kempter found that Ast Hamburg had assigned him still another River Plate agent. The new informant was one J. Anacleto Rocco (code name: Unión), who was to be contacted through Horacio Comejo Azzi, a Montevideo artist hired by the Uruguayan government to paint harbor scenes. Kempter never met "Unión," and constantly complained to Germany about that agent's irregular responses. The mysterious and exasperating J. Ancleto Rocco was, in reality, a *Volksdeutscher* businessman named Fritz Arthur Rabe. That he chose to remain anonymous is understandable, because he was both an aspiring politician and married to a Jew. Ast Hamburg preferred to be tolerant about this situation; it told Kempter nothing about his Uruguayan sources.[89]

Roughly six months later, Kempter was informed that in addition to a southern wing, his ring was to have a western one as well. Two other Ast Hamburg agents, Walter Giese (code name: Griffin) and Heinrich Loerchner (code name: Lorenz), were soon furnishing information concerning Pacific Coast Anglo-American shipping and U.S.-Ecuadorian military and naval cooperation. Given their geographic location and the secondary nature of Ecuador's military and economic position, the kind of information "Griffin" and "Lorenz" could provide was certainly limited. Still, what these two operatives lacked in quality, they attempted to make up in quantity. Between April and December 1941, materials from the Ecuadorian informants were found in forty messages sent by Kempter to Ast Hamburg. "Unión," in contrast, was not nearly as active.[90]

2. *The rise of FMK "Brazil"*

In keeping with Abwehr policy in the Americas following the aborted invasion of Britain, Ast Hamburg wanted its South American networks to develop a radio broadcasting potential. Consequently, in December 1940, Kempter received a message from Nordisk Durium, which suggested that he secure a radio operator and establish a clandestine station. When he agreed, he received another message telling him to contact a "Mr. S," a technician for Telefunken in Rio de Janeiro. He also received, through the German diplomatic pouch, instructions for a code based on the book, *The Story of San Michelle*, written by Axel Munthe.[91]

After making some initial inquiries, Kempter determined that the man he sought was Benno Sobisch. This technician had apparently been alerted by Bohny, because he knew what Kempter wanted and an agreement was swiftly reached. Kempter agreed to pay 35 contos ($1,750) for the installation of a transmitter and receiver. Furthermore, since he knew nothing at all about radiotelegraphy, Sobisch agreed to supply instruction and operate the transmitter until Kempter could do so by himself.[92]

On March 18, 1941, the Kempter station, known as LIR, successfully contacted station MAX at Ast Hamburg and broadcast its first message.[93] (See Chart VI, which depicts the setup of FMK "Brazil.") In April, Sobisch installed the radio equipment in Kempter's home and attached the antenna. The former continued to perform much of the broadcasting until June 1941; thereafter, Kempter did his own telegraphy. Such was the origin of the first and longest continually operating Abwehr station in Brazil.

In executing his mission, Kempter visited the Rio waterfront almost daily and became a habitué of the bars frequented by sailers, buying drinks, promising female companionship, and paying for information. But the expanding radio work load, plus local intelligence activities, made finding an assistant a necessity. The man selected was Karl Eugene Haering (code name: Timken), a fifty-three-year-old sales representative born in Stuttgart. As a result of his experiences in a World War I prisoner-of-war camp, Haering was violently anti-British. Cognizant of the latter's hatred, Kempter recruited him in March 1941 and proposed that Ast Hamburg put "Timken" on its payroll. Mysteriously, the controlling station displayed a reluctance to do so, finally ruling in August 1941 that Kempter could use Haering, but he would not be registered as an Ast operative.[94]

As second-in-command of FMK "Brazil" (also referred to as FMK "Rita" by Ast Hamburg headquarters), Haering proved extremely efficient. He subscribed to a number of magazines and journals so that LIR could match other networks in sending U. S. economic and political data to the Abwehr. He put post office box 171 at Kempter's disposal, and when Kempter sought another, Haering paid Josef Pessek, a piano teacher, to rent box 3136. Like Heyer, Engels's trusted aide, Haering was paid no salary for his work. Kempter's promise of big representation contracts after the war was the only recompense Haering expected to receive.[95]

The last agent added to Kempter's network was Carlos Fink (code name: Star), a *Reichsdeutscher* businessman living in Recife. On August 28, Ast Hamburg suggested that Kempter find an informant in the "hump" of Brazil. Six weeks later, he flew to Recife and enlisted the services of Fink, a Theodor Wille Company representative with whom Kempter had

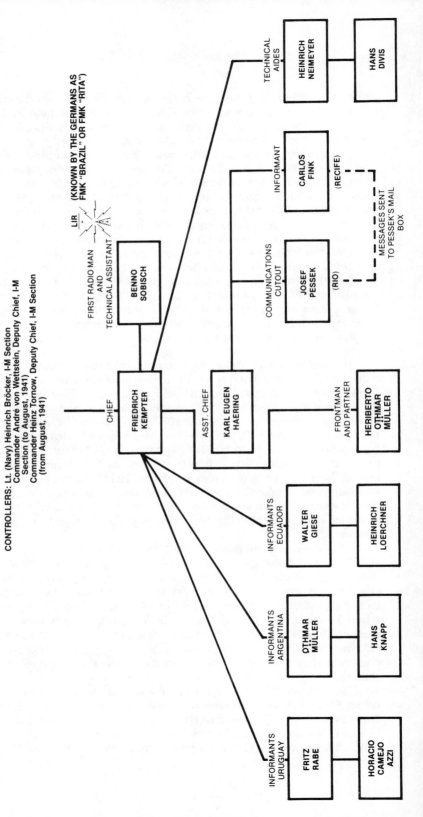

CHART VI
LIR RING

CONTROLLERS: Lt. (Navy) Heinrich Bröcker, I-M Section
Commander André von Wettstein, Deputy Chief, I-M
Section (to August, 1941)
Commander Heinz Tornow, Deputy Chief, I-M Section
(from August, 1941)

LIR (KNOWN BY THE GERMANS AS FMK "BRAZIL" OR FMK "RITA")

FIRST RADIO MAN AND TECHNICAL ASSISTANT

BENNO SOBISCH

CHIEF

FRIEDRICH KEMPTER

ASST. CHIEF

KARL EUGEN HAERING

TECHNICAL AIDES

HEINRICH NEIMEYER

HANS DIVIS

INFORMANT

CARLOS FINK

(RECIFE)

COMMUNICATIONS CUTOUT

JOSEF PESSEK

(RIO)

MESSAGES SENT TO PESSEK'S MAIL BOX

FRONTMAN AND PARTNER

HERIBERTO OTHMAR MÜLLER

INFORMANTS ECUADOR

WALTER GIESE

HEINRICH LOERCHNER

INFORMANTS ARGENTINA

OTHMAR MÜLLER

HANS KNAPP

INFORMANTS URUGUAY

FRITZ RABE

HORACIO CAMEJO AZZI

done business in the past. "King" wasted no time; he offered Fink fifty dollars per month plus expenses for information concerning the arrival and departure of Anglo-American merchant vessels and the units of Adm. Jonas Ingram's South Atlantic Fleet.[96]

Nevertheless, Fink's enlistment was somewhat different because it was effected under duress. He agreed to work for Kempter only after the latter indicated that refusal to do so might have unfortunate consequences. The good businessman knows when he has been given the final offer; better to be a spy than to someday return to an unfriendly fatherland.

3. *The True Believer as Achiever*

Of at least 563 messages transmitted to MAX between March 18, 1941, and March 13, 1942, the majority were fairly innocuous shipping reports. A typical message as logged by Ast Hamburg on June 5, 1941, read:

> MK Argentina [i.e., Müller, Napp] reports on June 2 via FMK Brazil [Kempter]:
> On May 29, the English steamer *Andalucia Star* left Buenos Aires for England.
> On May 30, the English steamer *Avila Star* left Montevideo for England.[97]

Lieutenant Commander von Wettstein in the I-M section of Ast Hamburg could check these ships, speculate on their cargoes and probable ports of destination, and draw certain conclusions about when and where convoys might be forming. If and when the information was passed on to U-boat headquarters at Brest, France, appropriate action could conceivably be taken. Insufficient evidence exists to sustain the argument that a U-boat was ordered to attack a convoy because of shipping information supplied in a clandestine Brazilian broadcast.[98] Yet this was precisely what Kempter and Ast Hamburg hoped to accomplish, once Adm. Karl Doenitz could assign a flotilla of U-boats to South American waters.

Decidely more dangerous was a February 14, 1942, report from Kempter which stated that

> Official secret Atlantic route for all ships to U.S.A. from South America after leaving the north coast of Brazil inside territorial waters from Cayenne [French Guiana] to Caracas [La Guaira, Venezuela], then direct to the strait between Cuba and Haiti, then directly to Charleston ... and then two miles inside the lightships to Baltimore.

The FBI indicated that this was both secret and accurate information which probably had been purchased. It recommended that the navy make an immediate change of route; otherwise, the most likely result would be more sunken vessels and drowned sailors.[99]

Another coup achieved by Kempter was the acquisition of the tide tables for the English Channel. The request for this information was sent to Ast Hamburg agents all over the world during the summer of 1940, and "King" was the first V-man to acquire the charts desired. Station MAX would later inform him that "Berlin [i.e., Abwehr High Command] expressed a special recommendation to you for the tide tables."[100] Having been successful once, Ast Hamburg ordered the acquisition of more navigational maps and tide tables in June 1941, this time for the east coast of the United States. Kempter could not obtain these in Brazil, but for V-men like him, the difficult task only took a little longer. Ottomar Müller in Buenos Aires was instructed to have someone order the maps from the United States. After they were received in Argentina, Müller airmailed them to Kempter. The latter prevailed upon Dr. Heinrich Niemeyer, director of the Zeiss Company subsidiary in Rio, to make microphotographs of these maps. On July 3, 1941, the materials were forwarded to Germany via LATI. Eleven days later, Ast Hamburg acknowledged receipt of the goods and commended Kempter.[101]

Of FMK "Brazil's" several informants, Giese and Loerchner in Ecuador proved to have the best governmental connections. Their most astounding feat was the purloining of a copy of a secret memorandum from Pres. Carlos Arroyo del Río of Ecuador to his foreign minister, Julio Tobar Doñoso. Dated December 26, 1941, this document divulged that Ecuador would break diplomatic relations with Germany following the closure of the Rio de Janeiro Foreign Ministers' Conference. Kempter radioed the details to Germany on January 14, 1942, a development duly noted by the FBI, which demanded that Arroyo del Río be told that the Abwehr had a pipeline into his office.[102]

In contrast to Kempter's success as an espionage chief was the relatively small sum Ast Hamburg paid to keep the network in operation. Prior to Brazil's break in relations with Germany (January 29, 1942), Kempter's funding came to about fourteen thousand dollars. Most of this money was sent by cable to either the Banco Alemão Transatlántico or the Banco Alemão-Brasileiro da América do Sul, but during July 1941, some three thousand dollars was provided by the Theodor Wille Company.[103] Aside from certain expense payments, Kempter never paid his Argentine, Uruguayan, or Ecuadorian informants. Ast Hamburg took care of these problems, a practice which allowed the voice of LIR to concentrate on intelligence matters to the exclusion of the more wearisome details.

In essence, FMK "Brazil" was international in scope, small in membership, and arguably the most effective supplier of sensitive information. Like Engels, Kempter received no formal espionage training, but his well-developed cunning and strong sense of duty made him an extremely capable adversary. Information he supplied to us would seem to reinforce this conclusion:

> Here is a top-secret for the then enemy [i.e., British, U.S.A.] agents. . . .
> All their messages sent from Recife [October 1941] to the U.S.A. and the U.K. during my stay there were read by me, before their transmission by the post office or even by their consulates. . . .[104]

Was Kempter exaggerating? In any case, the Anglo-American counter-spies were fortunate that leaders of most of the other FMKs proved considerably less capable.

D. *The "Lucas"-"Kuntze" Organization*

1. *An Unpopular Spy*

If one had to guess Elpídio Reali's occupation prior to his retirement, lawyer or businessman might be the typical response. The gentleman does hold a legal degree, but for most of his life, he was a police officer. What this smiling, self-effacing Brazilian does not look like is a former assistant chief of DOPS, the dreaded political police of Getúlio Vargas's Estado Nôvo. Today, Reali lives in a fashionable apartment building in midtown São Paulo. We went to the city to interview this retired police-man because he had been primarily responsible for the arrest of Josef Jacob Johannes Starziczny (code names: Lucas, Lucassen), a cochief of another Abwehr ring. Reali had a good deal to say about the investigation, apprehension, and interrogation of "Lucas." Most enlightening, however, was his ultimate comment: "He [Starziczny] was a scientist, not a spy. They [Abwehr] should never have sent him to Brazil."[105]

Mention Starziczny to Friedrich Kempter, and the name elicits both loathing and invective. In "King's" opinion, Starziczny was "one of the 'second-line spies'," a security risk and a fool who threw money around on "luxury cars" and "loose women." Hermann Bohny's final report on Brazilian operations depicts Starziczny as the least capable of the FMK leaders and a disgrace to the time-honored profession of espionage.[106] Why did the Abwehr ever send someone like this to act as a chief of one of its Brazilian intelligence networks?

A descendant of Polish parents and born in Upper Silesia, Starziczny served as a seaman with the German navy in World War I and attended the Technical University of Breslau in 1918–22. He graduated with honors as a mechanical engineer, and during the next eleven years, he took out patents on designs for rotating boilers attached to steam tur-bines. In 1938, he became a founder and partner in Work and Science, Ltd., a London-based firm created to market Starziczny's patents through-out the British Empire.

War clouds checked company manufacturing plans, and after much procrastination, on September 1, 1939, Starziczny, his wife, and adopted daughter sailed from England to Denmark. Seventy-two hours later, the family entered Germany, and the Abwehr quickly laid claim to his serv-ices. Assigned originally to Ast Kiel, and then transferred to Ast Hamburg, he was given a job with the I-i section (communications), headed by Lt. Col. Werner Trautmann, a man with whom Starziczny had been friendly at the University of Breslau. Trautmann (code name: Dr. Thiele) was one of the Abwehr's leading radio specialists, and he put Starziczny to work creating codes and making experimental transmissions.

The new recruit had taken the code name "Lucassen" while still at Ast Kiel, and seemed reasonably satisfied working with his old university comrade, until once again his situation was suddenly and unfavorably altered. In July 1940, Starziczny was transferred to Ast Hamburg's I-L section (air force), commanded by Lt. Col. Joachim Ritter. This officer ordered him readied to parachute into England for the purpose of establishing a clandestine radio station. Starziczny liked England, but he had no desire to return in the manner Ritter had prescribed. He complained vehemently that since he was already known there, he would be easily recognized and captured. Ritter doggedly insisted that orders had to be executed. But Trautmann pulled the necessary wires, and his now frantic colleague was transferred to Ast Brussels. This bit of administrative shuffling may have saved Starziczny's life, but it came too late to save his health. In August, he was felled by a bad case of stomach ulcers, and it was November before he was transferred back to Ast Hamburg and reassigned to section I-i.

In mid-January 1941, the chief of the I-M section of Ast Keil, Lt. Comdr. Friedrich Weisshuhn (code name: Weigelt), in company with Trautmann, held a conference with Starziczny and ordered him to prepare for a mission in the New World. Specifically, he was to create a radio transmission center for Otto Uebele, whom Weisshuhn described as the "chief agent of the German Navy in Brazil." Once this job was completed, Starziczny was to travel to the United States and develop another station there. Once again, the engineer evinced no enthusiasm for a field assignment, noting among other things that "he did not speak Spanish." In any case, "Weigelt" was uninterested in Starziczny's linguistic shortcomings, and Trautmann warned his friend that the illness of August-November 1940 was viewed at headquarters as being induced by cowardice. Starziczny had to accept this mission or face unmentioned, but obviously severe, consequences.

In February 1941, both Weisshuhn and Trautmann accompanied Starziczny to Paris, and the following month, the naval officer took the V-man aboard the *Hermes*, a steamer loading at Bordeaux for Brazil. He was given an updated passport as Niels Christian Christiansen, a Danish engineer, a letter for Otto Uebele, fifty-two hundred dollars in cash, two microdots with radio construction information, a revolver, and an *Afu.* Lastly, Weisshuhn solemnly warned Starziczny to destroy his radio transmission records, cipher, and microdots if capture appeared imminent. The *Hermes* sailed on March 14, evaded the British blockade and, after an uneventful trip, reached Rio on April 6, 1941.[107]

2. *Creating the "Lucas"-"Kuntze" Ring*

"Lucas" had expected to be met either by Otto Uebele or a representative of Theodor Simon, chief of the Theodor Wille Company branch in Rio. Instead, his first contact upon docking was with Hermann Bohny, who initially claimed to know nothing whatsoever about his mission. While the naval attaché subsequently acknowledged receipt of a telegram verifying the new V-man's arrival and sent Albert Schwab to sneak him past the immigration authorities, "Lucas" and Bohny became instant enemies. It was another Bohny trustee, Hans Buckup, who accompanied Starziczny to Santos, and only on April 10 did Starziczny finally meet Otto Uebele, honorary German consul and owner of the Theodor Wille branch in that port. "Lucas" promptly handed over the letter he was carrying. Written by Heinrich Diedrichsen, general manager of the Theodor Wille Company home office in Stettin, it ordered Uebele to pay "Niels Christian Christiansen" (as Starziczny would be known in Brazil) $250 monthly, and to make up to $5,000 available for expenses.[108]

It was immediately thereafter that the transatlantic voyager received his second shock. Otto Uebele, a millionaire whose code name was "Kuntze," and who had served with German intelligence during World War I, announced that he was too old and too busy to play cloak-and-dagger games again. He paid Starziczny the $250 and bade him return to Rio de Janeiro with a trusted aide and employee, Dr. Heinz Treutler, who would assist in setting up a radio station.

But no sooner had Starziczny returned to Rio de Janeiro when he was introduced to a second person whom Otto Uebele had assigned to work with him. This turned out to be Albert Schwab (code name: Spencer), the same man used by Hermann Bohny to sneak Starziczny past the Brazilian immigration authorities. By this time it must have dawned on Starziczny that Otto Uebele, who was "too old" and "too busy," already had a network of agents in place, and that the Santos coffee broker had prepared for his arrival with some care. In essence, Starziczny was to help an already existent network expand its activities and become more efficient in executing them. And since his stay in Brazil was to be temporary, he was expected to cause his paymaster, Otto Uebele, as few difficulties as possible.[109]

Starziczny spoke no Portuguese, so it became the task of Schwab and Treutler to recruit persons who might be willing to work with him. The first two enlisted were Karl Muegge (code name: Moss), a rotund traveling salesman specializing in rubber products, and Hans Japp (code name: Fritz), a Chilean *Volksdeutscher* who had lived a decade in Brazil. In April and May 1941, Starziczny taught these men and Otto Uebele's son, Hans Ulrich Uebele (code names: Mendes and Kuntze, Jr.) his own code, based on the book *No Antro da Vida (In the Cave of Life)*, and the use of two kinds of secret ink. Nevertheless, the major concern of the V-man from Asts Hamburg and Kiel remained the rapid establishment of a functioning radio station. It was Albert Schwab who solved this problem, and in a predictable fashion. Through Bohny, he made arrangements with the Sobisch-Muth team, and for fifteen hundred dollars, the necessary equipment was provided. Contact with Hamburg was initially made on May 17, and on May 25, station CIT officially went on the air, its transmission center being the living room of the Muegge house.[110] Easily understood are the objections of Gertrude Muegge, who stayed out in front of the house, fearfully watching for the police. She probably breathed a sigh of relief when Starziczny decided to move the transmitter to Sobisch's home; that residence would be the source of all CIT broadcasts until early July 1941. (See Chart VII for a depiction of the CIT network.)

With the radio connection achieved, what was now needed was a steady flow of information regarding Anglo-American shipping. Schwab, who was head of the shipping section of the Theodor Wille Company in Rio, had no problems fulfilling this requirement. Data concerning minerals shipped to the United States and Britain was furnished by Galdino Franco Medeiros, an official in the port customs house, while shipping details were furnished by José Ferreira Días, a Wille Company stevedore, and Urquiza de Sant'ana, chief dock inspector and de facto captain of the port. Hans Japp surreptitiously photographed Anglo-American shipping in Rio harbor and made himself useful by coding reports that Schwab did not find time to do.[111]

Meanwhile, in Santos, Hans Ulrich Uebele took charge of the gathering of shipping information. A part-time aviator and something of a playboy, "Kuntze, Jr." never went to the docks himself; his information procurors were Heinrich Bleinroth (code name: Lead) and Wilhelm Gieseler (code name: Greenwood). Bleinroth, a secretary to the German consul, controlled a string of lesser agents, while Gieseler ran a waterfront bar and acted as contact man for two U.S. seamen informants, John Vogel and Otto Boettcher. Both "Lead" and "Greenwood" communicated with the younger Uebele through Emil Wohlman, manager of the Theodor Wille office in São Paulo. In addition to Fritz Weissflog (code name: White), a rancher-pilot, Paulo Timm and Georg Karl Metzner ("Mary") also brought money and messages to "Lucas" and returned with receipts and instructions from him.[112]

More informants were going to be necessary if accurate data was to be obtained concerning Anglo-American shipping at Recife and air ferry activity in northeastern Brazil. On orders from Otto Uebele, Karl Muegge flew to the city of Salvador on June 6, 1941, where he recruited Werner Stark (code name: Fontes). The director of a shipping agency which was experiencing severe financial difficulties, Stark agreed to report Anglo-American shipping movements for a fee of $25 a month. Moving to Recife, Muegge enlisted the assistance of a well-known Nazi, Karl Hans von den Steinen (code name: Hendrick). Son of the local German consul, von den Steinen was eager to earn his spurs as a spy, but his price was much higher than "Fontes's"—$250, plus a fee of $25 a month. In addition to shipping reports twice a week, "Hendrick" also promised information concerning airfield construction and details on the number and types of aircraft being ferried to Africa.[113]

Having tasted success in northeastern Brazil, the "Lucas"-"Kuntze" group moved to develop observers in the extreme south of the country as well. In July, the indefatigable Muegge flew to the cities of Pôrto Alegre and Rio Grande, where he added Werner Dratwa (code names: Paulo, Antonio) and Friedrich Wilhelm Wilkens (code name: Francisco) to the spy ring's roster. Muegge knew both these individuals from his traveling

CHART VII

CIT RING
CO - DIRECTORS
**COMMANDER FRITZ WEISSHUHN - AST KIEL
LT. COLONEL WERNER TRAUTMANN - AST HAMBURG**

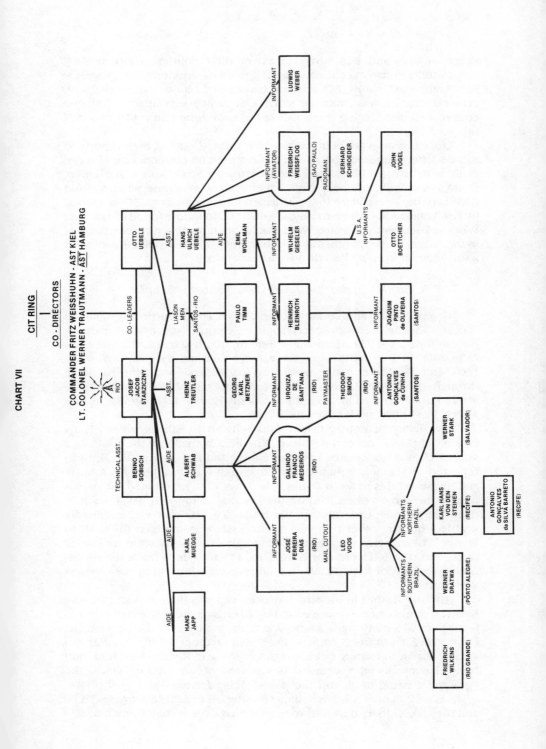

salesman days and was fairly certain of their political sympathies. A successful business executive, "Paulo" agreed to work only for expenses, but "Francisco," whose AO activism had earned him detention in 1939, claimed that he was probably still under police surveillance. Muegge coaxed him into joining the organization promising him a $15 a month salary.[114]

Once this network of informants was formed, getting their reports to Rio de Janeiro undetected also became a preeminent concern. Muegge dealt with this problem by demonstrating to Stark, von den Steinen, Dratwa, and Wilkens a secret ink which they were to use when writing their reports. These were to be airmailed to post office box 3006, owned by Leo Voos, a Rio de Janeiro businessman and longtime friend of Muegge. When subsequently arrested, Voos insisted that he never knew what was in the letters. This was possibly true, but Muegge also provided Voos with a small fee for keeping his curiosity under control.[115]

3. Battles against the Enemy and between the Spies

Given its size and far-flung character, it is not surprising that the "Lucas"-"Kuntze" network scored some noteworthy successes. For example, on June 24, 1941, Hermann Bohny met with Starziczny at the Club Germania. In Rio and Santos, three more German freighters, *Hermes*, *Lech*, and *Frankfurt*, were now fully loaded and preparing to break through the British blockade to return to France. The naval attaché wanted Starziczny to arrange for a reconnaissance flight similar to the March 1941 effort undertaken by Engels.

Starziczny promptly dispatched Schwab to Santos, where Hans Ulrich Uebele had procured a plane. With Fritz Weissflog at the controls, a sea search was undertaken between Santos and Rio on June 25. Schwab reported to Starziczny that no British man-of-war was lying in ambush, and he passed this news to Bohny. The latter then sanctioned the departure of the three vessels, and on the evening of June 28, 1941, each of them sailed independently for Bordeaux. The *Hermes* was eventually scuttled, but the other two vessels successfully completed the dash to France. The manganese, industrial diamonds, cotton, platinum, and other materials unloaded were worth millions, a factor which made the reconnaissance flight of June 25, 1941, a notable contribution to the German war effort.[116]

Another feather in the spy network's cap was the job performed by Karl von den Steinen. He moved swiftly to engage the services of Antonio Gonçalves da Silva Barreto, a newpaperman employed by the Recife daily, *Diario de Pernambuco*. In September and October 1941, Silva Barreto visited the aerodromes being constructed near Recife, Fortaleza, and Natal. He produced a detailed description of the landing fields, the equipment being used, and the planes being ferried—and took photograhs as well. "Lucas" dispatched these materials to Ast Hamburg via LATI, and they were disseminated throughout the German High Command.[117]

These credible efforts were balanced by this same group's uncommon ability to generate misinformation. For example, on November 8, 1941, Fritz Weissflog telephoned Starziczny and urged him to come to São Paulo immediately. After he arrived, Weissflog excitedly reported that an informant, "infiltrated into the American Embassy," had reliable information regarding a Washington-sponsored coup against Getúlio Vargas. A week later in messages numbered 341, 342, and 343, Starziczny reported this bizarre tale to Ast Hamburg. He credited its origins to Weissflog, but embroidered it with additional sensational detail, claiming that the Argentine government was Washington's partner in the alleged conspiracy. Furthermore, if Vargas resisted, Argentina's acting president, Ramón Castillo, would send troops to polish off the pudgy dictator.[118]

Hardly was this tropic fantasy off the airwaves when on November 17, Starziczny radioed of mounting U.S. labor strife, the details of which had come from "an absolutely reliable informant who sits in the U.S. Embassy." This message caused consternation in Washington, and the SIS/Brazil was ordered to find the leak and to plug it posthaste. Months later, under interrogation, Starziczny admitted that this secret embassy informant was a figment of his imagination. He had invented this source "in order to enhance his value in the eyes of his superiors . . . and because he felt that he was losing the confidence of his assistants."[119]

One reason "Lucas" resorted to wholesale deception of both his principals and underlings was that he felt himself to be under enormous pressure. A cause for his growing distress was the implacable opposition manifested by the leaders of the Engels organization. In May 1941, both Bohny and Engels visited Starziczny and inquired exactly why he had been sent. They were unimpressed with his response. The "Alfredo" organization chiefs made their position unmistakably clear: they insisted that "Lucas" submit to their orders, a proposal which Starziczny rejected.

But the Engels-Bohny combine was not prepared to take no for an answer. In June, they buttonholed Starziczny again and showed him a telegram allegedly from the Abwehr, ordering a halt to his activities and making Bohny the recipient of all CIT radio codes and equipment. This was a variation on the Immer trick of December 1940, but this time the victim refused to be duped. Starziczny agreed to obey the order, provided he received verification from Lieutenant Colonel Trautmann at Ast Hamburg and Lieutenant Commander Weisshuhn at Ast Kiel. The reply from Germany was the expected: "Lucas" was to maintain a separate and distinct organization. Jubilant, Starziczny made haste to inform Otto Uebele of the failure of the Bohny-Engels strategem; "Kuntze" cautioned his coleader that henceforth, he could expect "Alfredo" and the naval attaché to show him no quarter.[120]

Outmaneuvered and thwarted, Bohny and Engels dropped their masks and declared open hostilities. Georg Kurt Metzner, the messenger and bagman traveling the Santos-Rio axis, was, in reality, a secret member of Engels's organization, and Bohny ordered him to report on "Lucas's" activities. Metzner also may have persuaded Paulo Timm to spy on Starziczny for the purpose of acquiring information which might be incriminating.[121] These acts, though distinctly unfriendly, were nothing in comparison to the knockout punch that Bohny was readying. Aware that Benno Sobisch had made his facilities available to "Lucas," the naval attaché ordered Sobisch to make his home off-limits to that V-man; as a result, Station CIT was off the air from July 7 to August 6, 1941. And when a perturbed Starziczny was finally able to return to the airwaves, it would again be Gertrude Muegge's turn to be upset; for until December 1941, it was her house that would be the base for CIT broadcasts.[122]

4. *The V-man and the Lady*

This sordid game of rule or ruin in Rio de Janeiro did nothing to move forward Abwehr aims in Brazil; nevertheless, the chief cause of "Lucas's" problems was distinctly of his own creation. When he returned to Rio after meeting Otto Uebele in April 1941, he spent several days at the Central Hotel. There, as "Niels Christian Christiansen," he encountered a thirty-seven-year-old woman named Ondina Batista Peixoto de Oliveira. The exact circumstances under which the V-man and the senhorita became intimate are unclear, particularly since "Christiansen" was a guest at the hotel only a short time before he moved to Rua Francisco Sá 5, Apartment 82 (Copacabana), the same building where Engels lived. Although Senhorita Peixoto de Oliveira later told police that her occupation was housekeeper, her only apparent talent was that she knew English, a language which the non-Portuguese speaking Starziczny understood. Still, her other charms must have been considerable, because when the already married Starziczny moved to his luxury apartment, he brought her along, calling her his "fiancée."[123]

In July, possibly prodded by his sweetheart, Starziczny told the Uebeles of his need for a motorcar. Otto owned an automobile distributorship, and Georg Karl Metzner, manager of its Rio branch, arranged for Starziczny to obtain a new 1940 Oldsmobile. In addition, Metzner paid the necessary bribe so that a driver's license could be obtained with no questions asked. But, a new car and a Copacabana address were still not enough to satisfy the acquisitive instincts of the amorous couple. Among other things, Senhorita Peixoto de Oliveira began complaining that the apartment was not commodious enough. With the capable Metzner once again making the arrangements and signing the papers, in August 1941, Starziczny and his fiancée moved into a fashionable, two-story house in the Leblon district. Had it been left to the two lovers, they might have lived there happily ever after.

A new auto, fancy apartment, and new home cost, both then and now, a good deal of money. According to "Lucas's" records, between April 7, 1941, and March 10, 1942, he spent more than thirty thousand dollars.[124] Compared with the parsimonious Friedrich Kempter, who spent less than half this amount in two years of operations, Starziczny was a most expensive spy. Recall that Otto Uebele had been ordered to provide "Niels Christian Christiansen" with up to five thousand dollars for operational expenses. By September 1941, Starziczny had already received seventeen thousand dollars from this source, and was demanding that Ast Hamburg and Kiel send even more money.[125] The espionage occupation paid well, but not enough to keep Starziczny and Ondina Peixoto de Oliveira living in the style to which they had so quickly become accustomed. The logical solution to the problem was obvious: they had to cut their expenses. But for a spy in love, passion dictated that reason be damned. To escape this financial dilemma, Starziczny decided to reduce agent payments. Thus, Albert Schwab, who had been receiving one hundred dollars a month, found his September salary slashed to twenty-five dollars. Probably through Bohny, Schwab registered his complaint directly with Ast Hamburg, but the fact is, he was lucky. Wilhelm Gieseler in Santos was promised a salary but never got it, while Muegge had to cease paying Dratwa and Wilkens in southern Brazil, Stark in Salvador, and von den Steinen in Recife. Even this desperate and imprudent juggling proved inadequate, for by December 1941, Metzner was threatening to repossess the Oldsmobile because Starziczny was in arrears.[126]

5. *Crack-up*

As a result of this loathsome behavior on the part of a coleader, the "Lucas-Kuntze" ring was bound to experience increasing stress and eventual defection. The first to go was Heinrich Treutler, the man originally assigned by Otto Uebele as Starziczny's assistant. In July 1941, Treutler and Starziczny quarreled violently, and an exchange of blows was averted only through the judicious intervention of Hans Japp. According to Starziczny, Treutler's blatant misuse of funds could no longer be tolerated, but the latter insisted that interference in FMK affairs by Senhorita de Oliveira was the cause of the conflict.[127] Whatever the truth of these accusations, the fact was that the lady in question knew entirely too much about "Lucas's" activities; if she spoke carelessly to the wrong people, Schwab, Muegge, Japp, and their families could find themselves in deep trouble.

The final confrontation came in October 1941. Both Albert Schwab and Karl Muegge were pressing "Lucas" with their concerns over Ondina Peixoto de Oliveira's involvement in the group's intelligence work and their own needs for more money. After several acerbic exchanges, the harried "Lucas" threatened his aides with arrest by the Gestapo unless they ended their complaints. Frightened and angry, Muegge took his grievance to Hans von Cossel, head of the AO in Brazil and commercial attaché in the German embassy. Cossel assured him that Starziczny had clout with neither the German secret police nor the Nazi party. His bluff called, in December 1941, both Muegge and Japp severed their connections with the spy ring. Of the original Rio nucleus, only Schwab was left, and since Starziczny knew that he was a Bohny collaborator, the sharing of confidences became increasingly unlikely.[128]

Even more ominous was the attitude being manifested by his erstwhile ally, Otto Uebele. Radio CIT had reestablished contact with Ast Hamburg on August 6, 1941, and on August 20, Lieutenant Commander Weisshuhn ordered "Lucas" to travel to the United States and establish a clandestine radio station there.[129] But "Lucas" continued to put off making preparations for a departure in September, and Otto Uebele concluded that in addition to wishing to remain with Senhorita Ondina Peixoto de Oliveira, "Lucas" would not leave because he was just plain scared.[130] The tempestuous affair with the Brazilian woman, Treutler's dismissal, plus Starziczny's amazing ability to make money disappear, had soured Otto Uebele. Still, if the unstable Starziczny was forced to go to the United States, he was almost certain to be caught; if that happened, "Lucas" would probably implicate Uebele and jeopardize the security of the painstakingly built spy network. It was wiser to keep the radioman in Brazil where his blundering, unpredictable ways would be controlled—at least until his services could be dispensed with.[131]

On September 23, 1941, Otto Uebele called Starziczny to Santos and ordered him to begin immediately constructing an emergency radio station in nearby São Vicente. It was very clear to Starziczny that with the completion of the emergency station, his usefulness would inevitably be reduced. Initially, the inability to surreptitiously obtain parts seriously disrupted building plans. Later, though, on December 12, 1941, Gerald Schroeder (code name: Tip-Tap), who was to run the new unit, complained to "Kuntze" that "Lucas" seemed almost totally uninterested in making the station operable.[132] Since Starziczny probably viewed his situation as being similar to that of a man being told to dig his own grave, his perceived lack of enthusiasm was undoubtedly real.

In January 1942, the "Alfredo" and "King" groups continued to function effectively, but the "Lucas-Kuntze" network, suffocating in a miasma of fear and suspicion, was on the verge of collapse. The cause of the conflict was Starziczny, a V-man who could not speak the language, whose knowledge of Brazilian culture was miniscule, but who was doing his best to avoid leaving that country. It was as if some mirthful myrmidons had concocted a recipe for disaster, mixed it mischieviously, put it on the stove, and then sat around waiting for it to boil over.

E. *Frank Walther Jordan and the LFS Network*

Franz Walther Jordan (his actual name) was neither a World War I veteran nor a university graduate. But, as a twenty-year-old youth in the Depression-ridden Germany of 1930, he reached the same conclusions as Engels, Kempter, et al.: it was time to get out. Between 1930 and 1938, Jordan was a naval seaman (discharged in 1932 for fighting), a newpaperman in the Far East, and a traveler in the United States. He joined the Nazi party while in Shanghai in 1933, but it was not until November 1939 that the Third Reich indicated a particular need for his services. At that time, he was visited in his Hamburg home by an Abwehr recruiter who called himself Albert Herzog. The man was, in reality, a Nest Bremen agent named Walter Frischmuth, who controlled V-man Josef Hermkes, who was in Mexico. He solicited Jordan's entry into the German intelligence service, and when Jordan concurred, he was told to await a special directive.[133]

Early in 1940, Jordan was ordered to a special school for spies in Berlin. For three months, six days a week, ten hours a day, he studied radiotelegraphy, codes, and radio repair. He does not seem to have been assigned a code name, but he selected as his code book Karl Haushofer's *Geopolitics*. In Jordan's official deposition, there is no indication as to what his duties were between April, the time he left the intelligence school in Berlin, and December 1940, when he was supposedly informed of his Brazilian assignment. More than likely he was assigned to Nest Bremen in some capacity, and since he spoke passable Portuguese when he reached Brazil, it is probable that he spent part of this period studying that language.[134]

On February 3, 1941, Franz Walther Jordan was taken to the offices of Johannes Bischoff, an army captain attached to Nest Bremen who was also a director of one of the largest cotton brokerage houses in Europe. The Bischoffs were hardly neophytes in the game of espionage. It has been alleged that they allowed German agents to pose as company representatives in World War I, and Johannes had long been hoping to develop V-men who could also double as legitimate business representatives. Jordan's mission in Brazil was characterized by the fact that he was to act both as a spy and as a Bischoff representative, purchasing raw materials which eventually might be slipped through the British blockade.[135]

During his February 3, 1941, conference with Bischoff, Jordan received a passport in the name of Frank Walter Jordan. He also received merchant seaman's papers, a pen filled with secret ink, six microdots, his codebook, sixteen hundred dollars in U.S. currency, and his *Afu* transmitter. In addition, Bischoff furnished him with a list of Brazilian contacts who were to be greeted with the phrase, "Greetings from Rupker." Finally, he was ordered to board the steamer *Lech*, then loading at Bordeaux. This vessel sailed on February 8, 1941, and on March 3, she became the first German vessel to reach the port of Rio de Janeiro from Europe since September 1939. On hand to greet the *Lech* was a crowd of cheering *Reichsdeutsche* and *Volksdeutsche*. The presence of this milling throng and numerous ship visitors provided perfect cover for Jordan's disembarkation. Since Fritz Brinkmann, the ship's captain, had already given him the equivalent of two hundred dollars in Brazilian money, the Nest Bremen V-man was ready to begin his mission.[136]

One of the names on the list given Jordan was Dr. Hans Holl, an engineer and naturalized Brazilian citizen. Holl, who was a rising star in the Brazilian Ministry of Aeronautics, was visiting relatives in Germany when the war broke out in September 1939. Recruited by Johannes Bischoff, he returned to Brazil with the understanding that he would be required to assist a V-man who would "organize a maritime and intelligence service in Brazil." When on March 4, 1941, "Frank Walter" (as Jordan identified himself) came to his door and announced that he brought salutations from "Rupker," Holl knew that he was now expected to make good on his promise.[137]

Like the farmer's daughter-turned-princess in the fairy tale *Rumpelstiltskin*, Holl no longer wished to fulfill the commitment made. But being cognizant of the fact that the Abwehr might avenge itself upon his German relatives, he had arranged to provide a substitute. On March 5, Holl took the spy to the offices of a *Reichsdeutscher* named Herbert Max Winterstein.

A resident of Brazil since 1926, Winterstein had held several insignificant jobs, losing the last in January 1941. Nevertheless, on March 5, when Holl took Jordan to meet him, Winterstein was occupying a spacious office in downtown Rio de Janeiro and was now listed as a broker for Continental Produktion Gesselschaft, a Hamburg import-export firm controlled by the Bischoff family. As a visitor to Germany in 1938–39, Winterstein may have been recruited by the Abwehr, but evidence is inconclusive. What is certain is that by March 1941, he had made a lucrative deal with the Bischoff interests, and during the Holl-Jordan visit, he formally agreed to replace Holl as Jordan's liaison.[138]

Winterstein quickly settled Jordan in his home and told family and friends that the visitor was a seaman of the *Lech*. He also helped the V-man sneak his luggage off the ship, and purchased a radio receiver for use in conjunction with Jordan's *Afu* sender. Jordan wasted little time setting up his equipment, and using the call letters LFS, he attempted to reach the receiving station at Ast Hamburg. These efforts proved unavailing and during the month of May, the *Lech* began making preparations to return to Europe. Jordon's cover story seemed about to disintegrate, and at the same time, he was getting no closer to making radio contact with Germany.

It became Winterstein's task to solve these problems, and he did so with some alacrity. Through his friend José Falção Teixeira, a Brazilian businessman, an apartment was rented, but "Walter Frank" (as Jordan was now known) continued to be frustrated by communication difficulties. He moved again. Ironically enough, it was in a house owned by a German Jewish family named Gross that on or about June 15, 1941, Jordan finally made contact with Ast Hamburg. But after a month, aware of the family's anti-Nazi opinions and suspecting that they had discovered his equipment, "Frank Jordan" (his name there) moved again. Between June 1941 and March 1942, he would change his address three additional times. Known in these other places as Frank Walter, Walter Frank, and Jordan Walter, the V-man kept moving in an effort to throw both real and imagined counterspies off his trail.[139]

Another name on the list Johannes Bischoff had given Jordan was Paul Georg Engmann, a *Reichsdeutscher* businessman. After a visit from "Walter Frank," Engmann supplied the address of Afonso Digeser, who lived in the suburb of Jacarépaguá. Both Digeser and his spouse were Third Reich sympathizers, and they allowed Jordan to mount his equipment and put up an antenna next to the house. Thus, from the end of June 1941, the V-man was able to send and receive with some regularity. But convinced that it was not wise to live in the same place where he was broadcasting, Jordan limited the Digeser home to being his base of operation.[140]

A working radio station was only as effective as the information sources it possessed, and Jordan initially had none. What he needed was a person who could easily acquire information about Anglo-American shipping activities in Rio de Janeiro harbor. José Falção Teixeira knew a lawyer named Amaro Souza Carneiro, who recommended one José Gnecco de Carvalho. A kind of troubleshooter for an import-export company, Gnecco was twenty-three years old, living beyond his means, and desperately seeking ways to supplement his income. Souza Carneiro brought Jordan and Gnecco together, and a deal was struck: the new recruit would obtain information on Anglo-American ships—their cargoes, armaments, and destinations—and deliver it to the offices of either Falção Teixeira or Souza Carneiro, where Jordan would pick it up. Nonetheless, in August 1941, Jordan decided that too many people passed through Falção Teixeira's office, and that some of them might be police. As a result, the suite of another attorney, Mauro de Souza Machado, became a drop, Gnecco leaving envelopes signed "Occeng" (Gnecco spelled backward), which Souza Machado knew better than to open.[141]

The chief reason these Brazilians stood ready to aid Jordan was that all of them (with the possible exception of Gnecco) were Integralistas, members of the green-shirted party which Vargas had suppressed. If the Brazilian dictator favored the Anglo-Americans, then helping the Germans was necessary in order to save Brazil and thwart the founder of the Estado Nôvo. Profit and patriotism being such an appealing mix, these Integralistas could discover no reason to resist them.[142]

Perhaps Jordan was pleased that non-Germans were performing the bulk of the necessary labor, but Winterstein wanted to balance the Brazilian contingent with some German blood. Right off the street, in October 1941, he plucked Walter Moll, a man with a checkered background who was then a "salesman in the public squares." Moll agreed to help a person who was "working for Germany." He began by duplicating José Gnecco's task of reporting shipping movements. Jordan found his reports satisfactory and his companionship satisfying; thus in January 1942, he made Moll the ring's second-in-command. At thirty dollars a month, Jordan believed that he had obtained a faithful, albeit cheap, assistant. From Moll's perspective, the amount paid was more than double what he previously earned hawking wares of questionable value on nondescript street corners.[143]

Perhaps the most unique characteristic of the Frank Walter Jordan ring was its anonymity. Hermann Bohny knew indirectly that Jordan was somewhere in Rio de Janeiro, but no contact was made, for the Nest

Bremen agent had strict orders to avoid contact with other Abwehr operatives.[144] This separation enabled Jordan to avoid the petty feuds and intrigues which poisoned relations between the other groups. In addition, Jordan proved himself a most penurious fellow; the forty-three hundred dollars Nest Bremen paid him by the end of December 1941 made this V-man probably the least expensive German spy chief in Brazil.[145]

Still, from the point of view of results, the Jordan group was, on balance, unsuccessful. Working through Winterstein and using funds supplied by him, Jordan purchased a large quantity of Brazilian cotton and arranged to have it loaded aboard German freighters in Brazilian ports. Unfortunately for the Reich, Nest Bremen, and Jordan, none of these vessels broke through the Anglo-American blockade or reached a German-controlled port.[146] In addition to shipping information, Jordan was also the recipient of secret Brazilian air force data supplied by Hans Holl. The trouble was that the Nest Bremen V-man's *Afu* simply couldn't do the job; between June 1941 and March 1942, only about fifty-nine LFS messages were received by the Ast Hamburg reception station.[147] Conceivably this situation might have been remedied had Jordan or Winterstein known about Benno Sobisch and Hans Muth. But Jordan would have known about this pair only if he had contacted Hermann Bohny, an action which he had been cautioned not to take. As a result, Jordan's greatest asset—his anonymity—also proved to be a service liability.

F. *"Grillo" and the JOH-RND Network*

1. *Spying for the Family's Sake*

When the LATI westbound transatlantic flight landed at Recife on July 31, 1941, Othmar Gamillscheg (code name: Grillo) thought he could finally relax. After six years in Germany, he was returning to Brazil, and he had every intention of remaining. Unfortunately for Gamillscheg, Inspector Renato Medeiros of the Recife DOPS suspected that a German passenger on a LATI westbound flight was either a spy, a diplomat, or a Nazi party bigwig; otherwise, permission for such a trip while Germany was at war would not have been granted. The police officer gave Gamillscheg's name to an SIS agent, who forwarded it to Washington. Meanwhile, on August 1, 1941, ALD radioed CEL, "Grillo arriving by LATI." This message was intercepted by the RID and decrypted by the FBI laboratory. When this data was passed to the SIS, it did not take long for researchers to point the finger of suspicion at Othmar Gamillscheg. For the Abwehr, it was the ultimate disgrace: the new secret agent was discovered even before he reached his post.[148]

Gamillscheg traveled to Brazil for the first time in 1919. A native of Bohemia, he fought as an Austro-Hungarian army officer in World War I. Embittered as a result of the Hapsburg Empire's defeat, he and other former army officers emigrated to Brazil and established an agricultural colony in São Paulo state. Eventually, Gamillscheg became involved in the import-export business, and in 1926 he was named director of the Junkers Aircraft South American mission, headquartered in Rio de Janeiro. He married María Soares de Oliveira, fathered a daughter, and settled down to a comfortable existence. Alas, the Depression put an end to his prosperity. Consequently, when, in May 1935, he was offered a position in Germany as a salesman for the Roechling Steel Company, he snapped it up. By 1938, he was export sales manager, but with the outbreak of war in September 1939, Gamillscheg promptly sought to return with his family to Brazil. But he was not allowed to leave. He was fifty years old, but the consideration most important to the Third Reich was that he was a trained army officer. Once he passed his physical examination, all possibilities of escape seemed to evaporate. He was pressed into service and accepted a commission, and, by December 1940, he had risen to the rank of major.[149]

The Abwehr, meanwhile, was actively seeking V-men who could successfully operate in Latin America. Both Gamillscheg and his wife saw this development as their best chance of leaving Germany. Early in 1941, he approached Abwehr authorities in Berlin and offered his services. Gamillscheg knew something about airplanes, and since U.S. airfield construction was rumored to have begun in northeastern Brazil, he proposed that he return to that country and obtain the facts. His offer was accepted, and Gamillscheg became "Grillo," a V-man assigned to the I-L (air force) section of Ast Berlin. Like Starziczny, however, he was to work under a dual control, for his orders were to contact the receiving station of Ast Brussels, a newly created unit commanded by Col. Heinrich Servaes.[150] His cover identity was that of Brazilian representative of United German Aviation Industries, a firm with which he had purportedly become connected in January 1941. Gamillscheg was to work on postwar transatlantic air routes and negotiate the sale of German aerial equipment to Brazilian purchasers. How German material was to get through the British blockade, or how soon Germany would be able to deliver it, was never really explained. Presumably, if the Wehrmacht's string of European victories continued, both Vargas and the potential purchasers would politely refrain from asking such questions.

In July 1941, Gamillscheg found himself winging southward over the Atlantic, but to his sorrow, his request to take his wife and daughter with him had been rejected. Ast Berlin wanted Senhora Gamillscheg to remain behind so that "Grillo" could write innocent-looking letters to her which contained intelligence information written in secret ink.[151] So long as the family was separated, the steady interchange of mail was deemed less likely to draw unwarranted attention. Implied at the same time was a conditional response to "Grillo's" request: If he performed satisfactorily, his wife and daughter might again stroll with him along Copacabana beach. And if he became recalcitrant or blundered badly, the hoped-for reunion might be a very long time in coming.

On August 8, 1941, seven days after "Grillo" landed in Rio de Janeiro, Herbert von Heyer, identifying himself as "Humberto," paid a visit. Gamillscheg was informed that the military attaché, Major General Niedenführ, would provide him financial and political support, but if Gamillscheg wanted his material transmitted, he would have to give his coded messages, call letters, and frequency information to Heyer.[152] Naturally, Gamillscheg protested, but he might as well have saved his breath. When on October 14, 1941, JOH successfully contacted RND in Brussels, the man behind the telegraph key in Brazil was either Heinz Lorenz or Walter Ramuz, the radiomen for the "Alfredo" organization.[153] In effect, "Grillo" became a subordinate to that organization, and JOH a CEL substation.

Gamillscheg had no intention of becoming another V-man who was handcuffed due to Albrecht Engels's determination to be Brazilian lord of the spies. In an angry message to RND on November 21, 1941, "Grillo" reported that some unmentioned action on the part of Engels had compromised his cover identity. Therefore, "the best thing would be to put him [Engels] under my command. Even the General [Niedenführ] advised [that] his [Engels's] conduct [was] wrong."[154] These recommendations were passed on in "Grillo's" personal code, one which Hermann Bohny described as being decidedly primitive.[155] This conclusion implies that not only Anglo-American counterspies, but CEL agents as well, easily unraveled the mysteries of the cipher system Gamillscheg thought was unbreakable (see Appendix A). Not surprisingly, then, Engels soon learned of "Grillo's" recommendations and, since he did not consider his conduct wrong, he began arranging a well-orchestrated response calculated to repay Gamillscheg in kind.

In the meantime, "Grillo" busied himself with the selection of a collaborator. This turned out to be Adalberto Wamser (code name: Werner), a former Austro-Hungarian army officer and long-time friend. Wamser later claimed that Gamillscheg's cover was so implausible that he guessed his friend was a spy long before Gamillscheg admitted the fact. The arrangement made between the two was that Wamser would do the recruiting, while Gamillscheg stayed in the background.

Between October and December 1941, the new aide delivered two recruits, whose activities seem as questionable as they were short-lived. The first was Manoel Mesquita dos Santos, a Portuguese newspaperman then working in Rio de Janeiro, and a personal friend of Wamser. Incredibly, Wamser did not seek dos Santos out; the latter approached Wamser and stated that he wanted a job working for German intelligence! Eventually, Gamillscheg accepted dos Santos's request as genuine. Given the code name of "Tomé," the newspaperman was to sail to Lisbon, and then travel to Lourenço Marques (now called Maputo), the capital of Mozambique. After establishing himself, he was to send secret ink letters to Gamillscheg and copies to an Abwehr drop in Lisbon. Information was to be obtained about Red Sea convoys, South African political developments, and all "British, American, and De Gaullist aircraft" seen in the area. With his ticket and $250 for expenses, on January 7, 1942, "Tomé" sailed for Lisbon. What subsequently occurred has never been explained, but the FBI account is most succinct: "Whether dos Santos ever left Portugal is not known."[156]

The second recruit Wamser dredged up was a lawyer named Elias Napoleão Días da Silva. Starziczny, Engels, and Kempter all had agents in the northeast of Brazil, but "Grillo" planned to do them all one better: Días da Silva (code name: Panama Man) was to go to the Canal Zone. The latter received instruction in the use of secret inks, a special code, $1,100 in cash, and was ordered to report on Panama Canal shipping. On February 7, 1942, Días da Silva sailed from Rio de Janeiro, but he never reached his destination. When his ship reached the port of Belém, "Panama Man" was allegedly arrested and returned to his place of embarkation. Gamillscheg probably had no idea that Elias Napoleão Días da Silva was, in fact, a double agent under the direction of the Federal District DOPS chief, Capt. Felisberto Teixiera. In any case, the failure of the mission ended any dreams "Grillo" may have had for becoming a spymaster extraordinaire.[157]

2. Time Clocks and Homecomings

Did Gamillscheg take any positive steps aimed at the accomplishment of his original mission? His only known achievement was the November 1941 delivery of drawings of U.S.-built airfields at Belém, Fortaleza, and Recife. Ast Berlin commended "Grillo" for his efforts in obtaining what were touted as secret materials. In fact, this harried V-man obtained the drawings from the German embassy in Rio de Janeiro.[158] Meanwhile, this middle-aged, itinerant spy continued to seek his family's return, but after he refused an assignment to create a radio station in Argentina (November 1941), the replies to his inquiries became increasingly noncommittal. Angry and frustrated, on December 26, 1941, Gamillscheg forwarded a message to RND which bordered on insubordination. He stated that the eventual release of his wife and daughter had been at least implicitly promised, and he warned Ast Brussels that no further steps should be taken to delay or prevent the reunion of the family Gamillscheg.[159]

This challenge to authority definitely irritated his controllers, and several reports from Engels depicting "Grillo" as a fumbling fool also seem to have had their effect. Early in January 1942, Gamillscheg was notified by radio that he had been suspended. Since no other Abwehr ringleader in Brazil was so punished in 1940–42, this move generated a crisis. A flurry of messages traveled back and forth, until on January 14, Gamillscheg was informed that the suspension had been lifted.[160] The V-man was not exactly restored to good graces, but he could again hope that his loved ones might soon be allowed to join him.

Why Asts Berlin and/or Brussels changed their minds remains a matter of speculation, but there is one consideration which very likely played a part in effecting this reversal. Brazil was contemplating the rupture of diplomatic relations with Germany. A message to Joachim von Ribbentrop on January 14, 1942, from Ambassador Kurt Prüfer made it clear that it was only a matter of time before Vargas acted.[161] Once the break occurred, getting new V-men into Brazil would become virtually impossible, a contingency which made those already there doubly valuable. Moreover, merely by reuniting Gamillscheg and his family, the Abwehr could satisfy a disgruntled agent and execute a critical mission at the same time.

The great day for Gamillscheg finally arrived on March 7, 1942, when a Portuguese vessel arrived in Rio carrying María Soares de Oliveira Gamillscheg, their daughter, and an innocuous-looking clock. The previous day, "Grillo" received a message from "Carlos" (probably Colonel Servaes, commander of Ast Brussels) telling him of his family's imminent arrival and of an important timepiece being carried in the luggage. The day after the ship docked, Herbert von Heyer immediately took possession of the clock. After he returned it, the assistant chief of the "Alfredo" group told Gamillscheg that hidden behind the front piece had been several microdots bearing instructions and assigning tasks for "Grillo" and other V-men in Brazil.[162] These would be the last set of general orders to get through the sea blockade prior to the SIS-inspired roll-up of the Abwehr FMKs. Not by doing anything spectacular, but simply by having a wife whom he wanted to get out of Germany, Gamillscheg performed his greatest Abwehr service.

G. *"Antonio" and the INC-MNT Network*

1. *The Station That Couldn't*

The early histories of Werner Christoph Waltemath and Franz Walther Jordan are replete with strong similarities. Waltemath was one year older, but both spent their youths in Hamburg, neither was able to enter a university, and both departed Weimar Germany in 1930. Waltemath settled in the city of São Paulo, but unlike Engels or Gamillscheg, he found Brazil no El Dorado. A sometime ditchdigger, salesman, and bookkeeper, Waltemath's most auspicious achievement in Brazil was his marriage to a *Volksdeutsche* named Vera Griese in 1936. Two children were born before Waltemath took his family and returned to Germany in February 1939. Resettling in Hamburg, he obtained a well-paying position with an import-export firm interested in the Brazilian market. Finally, it seemed, Werner Waltemath was about to obtain for himself a modest measure of economic prosperity.

It was Adolf Hitler who ruined these dreams of socioeconomic ascension by invading Poland. Waltemath was able to send his wife and children back to Brazil, but the Reich refused his requests to leave the country. On May 1, 1940, he was inducted into the army and saw eight months of service as a radiotelegrapher and field communications man. Waltemath tried to obtain a discharge from the army. He became a V-man only when it was clear that there was no other way he could get out of Germany. By volunteering to serve with an Abwehr that desperately needed Brazilian agents, Waltemath simultaneously escaped front-line service, earned himself exit papers, and fattened his wallet.[163]

In March 1941, Waltemath was assigned to the I-L section of Ast Münster, Maj. Karl von Bauer (code name: Francisco) being designated as his controller. Since he was already trained in radiotelegraphy, Waltemath's course of instruction dealt chiefly with the making and use of secret inks and radio construction. Dubbed "Antonio," Waltemath was given a thoroughly unique mission: He was to build a radio station in São Paulo, but he was to start transmitting only after he received special orders to do so. He became, in effect, the first "deep cover" agent sent to Brazil. The very nature of his assignment indicates that the Abwehr already suspected that its first-line FMK leaders were known, or could be easily apprehended; hence the creation of alternative stations became a top priority.[164]

Possessing one thousand dollars, a novel called *Pagel in Glück* (literally, *Pagel in Good Fortune*) as his codebook, and two microdots bearing instructions for building a radio station, "Antonio" boarded a LATI airliner in Rome on June 2, 1941. Also aboard the plane was Hans Christian von Kotze (code name: Fred), an agent who was allegedly being sent on a leather-purchasing mission for a state trading company. Unknown to Waltemath, Kotze was also an I-L operative from Ast Münster and the contact man he was supposed to work with once his radio became operational. Possessed of a sadistic streak, Kotze badgered Waltemath all the way across the Atlantic, until the latter finally admitted that he was a trained radio operator. When the plane reached Rio, the wily "Fred" indicated that he had known of "Antonio's" mission all along and would keep in touch because he soon expected to have information to transmit.[165]

Once in São Paulo, Waltemath bought a new house for his family, intending to install his transmitting station there. He surreptitiously purchased radio parts, and with the help of Carlos Bosbach, a *Volksdeutscher* technician, he began assembling them. By the end of October 1941, he had built his transmitter, bought a receiver, and sent a cablegram to Bauer announcing "birthday greetings to Peter." This was the agreed-upon signal indicating that Waltemath was ready to transmit, but he soon found that he had acted prematurely. Radio station INC (Waltemath) regularly but unsuccessfully attempted to contact station MNT (Ast Münster), and frenzied adjustments proved unavailing. Secret ink letters from Waltemath to Bauer in November 1941 and January 1942 related this tale of woe in more detail, but nothing done or suggested on either side of the Atlantic produced any improvement.[166]

2. "Springbok" Trips "Antonio"

What Waltemath did not know was that, like Othmar Gamillscheg, his cover had been blown even before he went on the airwaves. The awful truth was that the trusted Carlos Bosbach was secretly an informant for the São Paulo DOPS. But Waltemath and the Abwehr organization in Brazil had another security problem as well; Hans Christian von Kotze was a British double agent, and most likely the one code named "Springbok."[167] Perhaps the BSC thought that Kotze might disarm both Brazilians and Germans by flaunting his propensity toward dissipation, but if this was the case, he went too far. In addition to running up a string of unpaid debts, Kotze gambled, drank heavily, and made little pretense of carrying on any useful activity. He lived openly with two women and even strove to seduce the wife of the BSC resident chief. Ambassador Prüfer complained to Berlin, and on August 15, 1941, after only two months in Rio, Kotze was told by Hermann Bohny that he would soon be undertaking an intelligence mission elsewhere.[169]

For this proposed operation, the Abwehr gave Kotze a new identity as "Johannes van Hughes," but the BSC apparently did not want "Springbok" assigned outside the Western Hemisphere. As a result, in November 1941, when he was supposed to leave for South Africa, he disappeared. Hermann Bohny eventually learned that the missing Kotze had gone to Canada, his excuse for disobeying orders being that he hoped to atone for his Rio debaucheries by staging an espionage triumph in another part of the Western Hemisphere.[170]

Shortly before he was supposed to embark upon his South African mission, Kotze visited Waltemath in São Paulo. He had obtained the new address by contacting Gustavo Griese, Waltemath's brother-in-law, a partner in the S. Capellosi Trading Company. Kotze showed "Antonio" his passport as "Johannes van Hughes," and directed that the reports he sent to Brazil were to be radioed to Germany. Kotze also provided Waltemath with a code based on the book *The Martyrdom of Man*, and then he departed, never to meet him again. In actuality, the British intent was to pump misinformation into the Abwehr via Waltemath's radio, while discovering as much as possible about German intelligence operations in Latin America. "Springbok" fooled the Abwehr once; with this new gambit the BSC was obviously hoping that the charade could be successfully continued.[171]

On January 28, 1942, the day before Brazil broke relations with Germany, Waltemath received a message from Hans Morgener and hurried to the German consulate offices in the city of São Paulo. Another diplomat who doubled as an Abwehr operative, Morgener (through an intermediary) gave Waltemath one thousand dollars in cash. To that date, Waltemath had received twenty-five hundred dollars in U.S. and Brazilian currency; but due to the imminent diplomatic rupture, no additional funds would be forthcoming from this source.[172] In February, therefore, Waltemath redoubled his efforts to contact MNT. Under his living room floor, he constructed a secret transmission cellar, and attached a new and more sensitive antenna to his house. Nightly, he broadcasted his call letters, but as before, his labors produced no useful results.

Unable to make contact, and baffled by his inability to do so, Waltemath was the recipient in February 1942 of a secret ink letter from his controller, Major von Bauer. The missive had apparently been transported across the Atlantic by a Spanish sailor, who mailed it in Brazil after his ship docked. The message stated that Waltemath was known to Anglo-American intelligence, that Kotze was the traitor, and while Bauer wished him well, that it would be advisable for "Antonio" to " 'go underground.' "[173] The Ast Münster control officer did not say so specifically, but his meaning was clear: With his identity known and his transmitter uncooperative, Waltemath had, for all practical purposes, been written off.

H. *Janos Salamon and the HTT-ORE Network*

1. *Magyars in Brazil*

The most bizarre group sent to Brazil was also the only FMK operated by non-Germans. The HTT radio ring was dominated by Hungarians, the leader of which was a former merchant marine captain named Janos Salamon (code names: José, Joszi). He was recruited for espionage work by Hungarian army intelligence, his original controllers being László Veghi Vócykondy (code name: Viragh) and Alexandre Adríansky (code name: Akos). These men shared operational supervision of Salamon with Hugo Sebold (code name: Hugh), an Abwehr officer assigned to the I-L section of Ast Vienna. The HTT radiomen initially hoped to transmit to Budapest; since this proved impossible, contact was achieved with a Nest Cologne receiving station whose call letters were ORE. Between August 21, 1941, and January 22, 1942, sixty-two messages were received by that source.

Janos Salamon received no more than a modicum of espionage training. He knew how to use secret inks, but the tasks of radio transmitting and message coding were handled by an assistant, Sandor Mocsan (code names: Miki, Alexander). The latter used a mechanical leg, and, because of it, nursed a definite inferiority complex. The two men hardly made an auspicious team, but perhaps their incompatibility was not as evident in Hungary as it would be in Brazil.

The mission of "José" and "Miki" was to obtain information about U.S. airfield construction and aircraft ferry activities in the Brazilian northeast. For protective purposes, Salamon and Mocsan were given diplomatic passports and assigned to the Hungarian legation in Rio de Janeiro. As cover, Salamon was named Brazilian representative of a newly created state trading concern, Companhia de Navegação Pôrto Livre de Budapeste (Budapest Free Port Navigation Company). Once he reached Rio, he was to establish a Brazilian subsidiary of this organization, which was called the Companhia Pôrto Franco Nacional de Budapeste para América do Sul (Budapest National Free Port Company for South America). To those who cared to listen, Salamon proposed to stimulate Hungarian-Brazilian trade by shipping purchased goods across the Pacific! Unless the Soviet Union rapidly succumbed to German hammer blows, this scheme made no sense whatsoever, and the longer the Soviets resisted, the more improbable Salamon's project became. One problem "José" would not have, however, was obtaining a reliable transmitter. A machine was disassembled and carried across the Atlantic as part of Mocsan's diplomatic baggage. When the two arrived at Rio on July 5, 1941, they flashed their diplomatic passports, whisked their unopened luggage through customs, and were ready to start constructing a broadcasting station.[174]

As a prospective spymaster, Salamon proposed to enlist as subagents Hungarian nationals and persons of Hungarian origin who were citizens of Brazil. His initial target was Rosa de Balàs Weisz. The lady married Victor de Balàs in 1931, obtained a legal separation in 1935, and went on to carve out a successful career for herself as a lawyer. Well known among capital city barristers, she handled much of the legal work for the Hungarian legation, and it was there that Salamon met her in July 1941. "José" had known Victor de Balàs in Europe, and this proved to be his entrée. Rosa de Balàs befriended him and introduced him to other Hungarians in the city. Whether she knew Salamon was a spy is debatable. Certainly she knew what kind of persons he was looking for, because she promptly introduced him to Ellemer Nagy.[175]

Since migrating from Hungary in 1927, this electrical engineer had dabbled in Integralista party politics, and seemed perpetually in a state of financial distress. What Salamon needed was someone who would find a location for the transmitter, install it, act as back-up radioman, and recommend other persons who might become informants. In exchange for $150 a month, plus rent for a new house for himself and his mistress, Nagy did all those things. He became the first and best recruit Salamon found during his tenure in Brazil.[176]

Of the other persons enlisted by "José," the most flamboyant was María Tereza Calvacanti Ellender, a well-known journalist employed by LATI airlines. She had toured Hitler's Europe at Fascist expense both in 1940 and 1941, and was a member of the Comité Cultural Brasil-Italia. Salamon met this lady through his acquaintance with LATI officials, but why he decided she (code name: Mary) would be a useful agent befuddles the imagination. Her pro-Fascist press publications had made her notorious, and São Paulo DOPS commenced shadowing the lady in October 1940, and in July 1941 tapped her phone.[177] Moreover, to recruit her, Salamon had to obtain the permission (through Ast Vienna) of a General Piccola, an official in the Italian Intelligence Service.[178] Senhora María Calvacanti Ellender was a controversial personality, a non-Hungarian, and someone apparently in the employ of another secret service. She was too conspicuous to be useful as an operative.

Worst of all, her accomplishments for HTT proved to be largely imaginary. When, in August 1941, the Abwehr was informed that she could obtain entry into the United States, it ordered Salamon to pay her five hundred dollars a month plus expenses, and promised "special compensation" if "Mary" performed "good work." Nothing happened until, on December 11, HTT reported that "Mary" had established a "relationship" with Brazilian air cadets being sent to the United States for training. The flight trainees were slated "to hook in through Mary and report on technical developments and airfleet movements." But suddenly, on January 5, 1942, Salamon reported that the cadets' trip was cancelled, and that "Mary's" journey to the United States was also shelved. Rather abjectly, "José" radioed that he had already paid Senhora Calvacanti Ellender one thousand dollars, but he still hoped "the result [would] correspond to expenditure."[179]

The only mission actually undertaken by "Mary" was an alleged tour of the airfields in the Brazilian northeast being used to ferry aircraft to Africa and the Far East. When informed of the trip, station ORE ordered that she obtain data regarding aircraft types and numbers, aircraft destinations, and U.S. plans to expand the air ferry service. On November 10, 1941, she flew from Rio to Recife, returning to the capital ten days later. That evening, HTT radioed that "Mary" saw "underground hangars" being constructed at the new airfield near Recife. Suffice it to state that neither the U.S. Army Air Corps nor Panair do Brasil ever contemplated such a project.[180]

The other non-Hungarian agent recruited was a Rio de Janeiro DOPS officer, Jofre Magalhães dos Santos. Salamon made the contact through Ellemer Nagy, and offered Magalhães dos Santos $150 monthly to become northeast representative of Companhia Pôrto Franco Nacional. This enlistment proved as useless as the liaison with María Calvacanti Ellender. Magalhães dos Santos arrived at Recife on December 7, 1941, and in a message sent nine days later, he reported that the Brazilian army was sending extra infantry companies to guard airfields at Belém, Fortaleza, Natal, Recife, and Salvador.[181] But if he planned to imitate "Mary's" tactics for wringing top dollar out of Salamon, he was too late. After January 15, 1942, the Hungarian stopped sending him any money.

2. *The Spymaster as Con Man*

Although the informants he recruited seemed eager to collect Salamon's money, they were petty chiselers compared to the man who was paying them. On September 30, 1941, the father of Rosa de Balàs died, leaving her a small salad oil factory. In October, she sold the factory to Salamon for twenty-two contos (eleven hundred dollars). "José" assured the Abwehr that the salad oil firm would make a good front for HTT activities. He also reported that the asking price, plus expenses, was one hundred contos, or five thousand dollars. Through Engels, on October 18, some fifteen thousand dollars was delivered to Salamon for this purchase, and also to pay the salaries of some expensive new agents he claimed to have recruited.[182] In addition to Rosa de Balàs, whom he bragged he could handle, Salamon told ORE about several imaginary agents: "Paulo," who had DOPS connections, "Nelson," who had important naval contacts, and "Gutíerrez," who made mysterious journeys to foreign countries. In the end, the Abwehr wasn't the only party duped; information from the decoded messages was forwarded to the SIS/Brazil, which spent time and money chasing these phantoms.[183]

Why did Salamon go to such extremes to fool his bosses? The answer seems to be that initially he saw espionage as a means of lining his pockets while staying out of the front lines. But unforeseen developments forced a redefinition of his goals. In September 1941, Sebold of Ast Vienna discovered that Salamon had been a member of the extreme, right-wing Arrow-Cross party in Hungary.[184] Thereafter, the German officer was openly hostile, a development which meant that if the Hungarian was to continue living the good life in Rio de Janeiro, he would have to make his services indispensable.

Salamon took a risk on September 20, 1941, when he sailed to Recife and, five days later, flew to Natal. During this period of time, he stomped around the airfields being constructed asking probing questions and justifying his actions by claiming to be a U.S. citizen. Not surprisingly, his curious conduct drew the attention of DOPS, and Salamon was arrested when he returned to Recife on October 2. Taken into custody, he produced his diplomatic passport, but the police found that Salamon had registered at hotels in Natal and Recife using a second, nondiplomatic passport. The latter identified Salamon as "Janos Saros," and although the Hungarian was allowed to slide out of an embarrassing situation, his cover was now irreparably damaged.[185]

The Brazilian police had chosen to be lenient in this two-passport incident, but one prominent party decided upon the opposite course of action. Miklos Horthy, Jr., head of the Hungarian legation, had been suspicious of Salamon and Mocsan ever since he discovered that they were not regular members of the national diplomatic corps; the Recife embarrassment became the excuse needed for getting rid of both of them. Moreover, since he was a son of the national dictator, Adm. Miklos Horthy, Sr., he had the clout to do so. In December 1941, the younger Horthy began telling Brazilian government and police officials that Salamon and Mocsan had completed their researches and were no longer attached to the Hungarian legation. He also intimated that if they refused to leave Brazilian territory soon, the Vargas government should throw them out.[186]

Horthy's campaign generated resistance from Salamon, but it persuaded Sandor Mocsan that his departure had already been delayed too long. Moreover, the two spies had quarreled violently over the false information an increasingly apprehensive Mocsan was being ordered to transmit. Without telling his erstwhile chief, on January 8, 1942, Mocsan boarded the Spanish liner *Cabo de Esperanza Buena* and sailed for Lisbon. He was traveling as a Hungarian diplomat, but when the ship reached Port of Spain, Trinidad, on January 22, British officials secretly took Mocsan off the vessel and placed him in detention for the rest of the war.[187]

In January 1942, Janos Salamon sought legal help from Rosa de Balàs in order to obtain a permanent residence visa. Consequently, Miklos Horthy, Jr., warned the lady barrister not to take the case, intimating that once Salamon returned to Hungary, he would face charges of treason. On January 26, 1942, Brazilian police again took Salamon into custody. On February 3, he was released with the understanding that he must leave Brazil as soon as possible. Salamon took passage for Lisbon aboard the *Cabo de Hornos* on February 17, 1942. As he was certain that the Abwehr intended to repay him for his duplicity, Salamon's intention was to remain in neutral Portugal where, out of harm's way, he could sit out the war. On March 12, 1942, the *Cabo de Hornos* docked at Port of Spain. Salamon was taken into custody as a spy and sent to a United Kingdom detention camp.[188]

The Abwehr spent twenty thousand dollars on HTT over a period of six months, an amount which, on average, made Salamon and his associates an even more expensive proposition than the prodigal Starziczny. In any case, it was money thrown to the winds, and although Janos Salamon pocketed the bulk of these funds, he had only harsh words for his former employers. For example, he told British interrogators that the Abwehr "did not trust its own agents."[189] He was probably correct in his assessment, but given the example he provided, was there any reason why it should have been otherwise?

III. *Mounting the Counterespionage War in Brazil*

A. *The Cryptographic Victory*

In Brazil, there would be no double agent like William Sebold, handling the messages from and for station GBO in Mexico, and turning over copies to the FBI. Nevertheless, the Achilles heel of the FMKs in Brazil proved to be the radio messages being transmitted to Germany. Recall that RID intercept stations in the United States began functioning in July 1940. On April 28, 1941, an RID station in Maryland picked up signals from a station in Europe, using the call letters MAX, that was attempting to contact a station presumed to be somewhere in eastern South America. LIR-MAX thus became the first Abwehr radio circuit detected that had one of its terminals in Brazil.[190]

Copies of the signals were turned over to the cryptologists of the FBI laboratory and to similar specialists working for Henry Morgenthau's Treasury Department. Thanks to the information on Abwehr cryptographic practices made available by William Sebold, the FBI laboratory had few problems breaking the codes used by the Brazilian V-men and reading the messages being sent.[191] Beginning on July 15, 1941, the Treasury Department's code breakers provided weekly summaries of the decoded messages to MID, ONI, and COI. The record of RID interceptions is as follows:

Station	Date of First RID Intercepts of Brazilian or German Station Broadcast[192]
CEL-ALD	7/4/41 (CEL) & 6/7/41 (ALD—Berlin)
(SCHLEGEL) "CAROLA"	8/29/41 (Nest Cologne—no intercept date)
LIR-MAX	5/4/41 (LIR) & 4/28/41 (MAX—Ast Hamburg)
CIT	6/3/41 (CIT) & 7/1/41 (Ast Hamburg)
INC-MNT	No effective contact established
LFS	9/21/41 (LFS) & 9/26/41 (Ast Hamburg)
JOH-RND	10/14/41 (JOH) (Ast Brussels—no intercept date)
HTT-ORE	8/21/41 (HTT) (Nest Cologne—no intercept date)

The interception and stripping away of the codigraphic security of the Brazilian FMKs were gains the importance of which cannot be overemphasized. However, the hard, thankless task of identifying the agents, of separating the suspects from true ring members, could not be accomplished by technical means. Moreover, since the Abwehr's largest hemispheric operation was in Brazil, the SIS had to mount its major counterespionage offensive there and send perhaps its best men to do that job.

B. *West Goes South*

It is probably not coincidental that one month after the Vargas regime received the first steel mill construction credits and a U.S.-Brazilian preliminary defense agreement was reached, the first SIS operative reached Brazil.[193] Who that agent was and what he accomplished is not known. In any case, the war against the Abwehr FMKs did not shift into high gear until the arrival of an SIS officer named Jack West. A six-foot Texan and law school graduate, West had been selected for SIS duty in February 1941. He spoke Spanish rather than Portuguese, but acting chief of the SIS Spencer J. Drayton was unconcerned. He told West to "go on down there and get the job done," and while the Texan had no experience as a controller of counterspies, he never let on that he had any qualms about his assignment.[194]

Posing as a journalist, the new agent disembarked in May 1941 with orders to secretly deliver any significant information he might uncover to Ambassador Jefferson Caffery. In the ensuing three months, however, J. Edgar Hoover decided that closer embassy cooperation was necessary for his operatives. As a result, in August 1941, West went "inside" and was named the first legal attaché in South America. As the chief of SIS/Brazil, eventually he had fifty-four agents under his command. Some, like Donald Bird in Pôrto Alegre and Arthur Baker in São Paulo, posed as businessmen, while maintaining informal relations with the local police; others were underground personnel known only to West.[195]

Almost as vital to the U.S. counterespionage capabilities in Brazil as the RID interceptions and FBI laboratory decipherments was the assistance of Jack West's prize informant, a Brazilian citizen known only as "Tom." The latter had contacts in the government, the army, various embassies, and a myriad of Rio de Janiero business organizations. Without the information provided by this secret but highly efficient source, SIS/Brazil would have spent many additional months working to achieve the break-up of the Abwehr's Brazilian networks.[196]

Although West and "Tom" made a superlative team, successful counterespionage activity in Brazil ultimately required support from other U.S. diplomatic officials. The Vargas government was quite aware that the SIS/Brazil was ferreting out Abwehr operatives in the country, but public acknowledgement of Brazilian cooperation in this secret struggle might easily have elicited a major uproar among nationalist elements. In practical terms, it meant that even though West had a pseudodiplomatic post in the embassy, only a regular State Department staff person could officially act as liaison with Brazilian security forces. The man selected by Ambassador Caffery was the embassy third secretary, Elim O'Shaughnessy.

Descriptions of the late O'Shaughnessy vary significantly from person to person. One source notes that he was a flamboyant, affected man who knew nothing about counterespionage but loved to take part in activities he viewed as conspiratorial. Another view was that while he smoked cigarettes from a long cigarette holder and sought to appear as a lady's man and bon vivant, he was in fact a sharp-witted character who preferred that others believe him only semicompetent. The essential consideration is that O'Shaughnessy was well regarded by Brazilian police in Rio de Janeiro and São Paulo, and was considered simpatico by the Brazilian elites. He proved himself invaluable as a middleman and negotiator in sensitive situations.[197]

With the SIS man acting as coordinator and planner, the West-"Tom"-O'Shaughnessy triumvirate dominated the U.S. counterespionage effort in Brazil. Nevertheless, they did not always confide in each other, nor did they necessarily agree on operational tactics. For example, on one occasion, West passed to O'Shaughnessy a particularly choice piece of information which may well have come from "Tom." The third secretary was intrigued. How had West, a man who had been in the country a comparatively short time, obtained such an important piece of intelligence? The response was classic: "I [West] said that a little of this [rubbing thumb and forefinger together to indicate money] went a long way. Elim was mildly shocked and said that the Department [of State] would never countenance such a thing, and expressed doubts about the value of information obtained in such an approach." Stunned or not, the third secretary soon reappraised his position, for "within a matter of months, Elim himself was paying for information."[198]

Proof that the dollars spent and the hard labor of SIS/Brazil were producing tangible results was soon forthcoming. Toward the end of November 1941, Maj. Filinto Muller conferred with the German military attaché, General Niedenführ, and suggested that the Abwehr radio networks in Brazil be shut down. According to Muller, Anglo-American intelligence was intercepting the radio messages, and the SIS/Brazil agents knew who the FMK leaders were. By disengaging now, an exposé that could only have unfortunate repercussions for the Third Reich might be avoided. This advice was ignored, chiefly because Niedenführ and Bohny distrusted the Brazilian police chief.[199] Nevertheless, the information divulged was exceedingly accurate. A November 29, 1941, secret communiqué from Hoover to Roosevelt demonstrates that West and his aides had already identified Friedrich Kempter, Janos Salamon, and Herbert von Heyer.[200]

C. Summary: Scraping the Bottom of the Barrel

In his final report on Abwehr operations in Brazil, Hermann Bohny asserted that many of the V-men assigned to Brazil should never have been sent. They lacked sufficient understanding of the Brazilian cultural milieu, and some of their cover identities were so ludicrous that they could just as well have done without them.[201] In voicing this criticism, Bohny was perhaps criticizing the policy which allowed any interested *Ast* or *Nest* to send agents to Brazil. But whatever his feelings and intentions, this critique provides a springboard for analyzing what was perhaps the Abwehr's most glaring problem.

When the war started, what the Canaris organization wanted was information concerning the shipment of foodstuffs, minerals, and other raw materials from Brazil to Great Britain. Gathering this kind of intelligence required no great training, and businessmen-informants like Engels or Kempter could accomplish this task with relative ease. But that was before Operation Sea Lion was shelved and before the Battle of the Atlantic began in deadly earnest. Suddenly, in late 1940, the Brazilian MKs were asked to supply ship movement information and transmit it by clandestine radio. These demands placed a strain on the existing networks and necessitated the recruitment of additional, but not necessarily competent, informants. Then in 1941, the problem was compounded by the German air force's desire to learn about airfield construction and air ferry activities in northeast Brazil. It was, therefore, no coincidence that all the V-men sent after June 1, 1941—Kotze, Waltemath, Gamillscheg, and Salamon—were all controlled by I-L (air force) section officers.

The Abwehr rushed in agents to report on these developments, but consider who was sent: Gamillscheg, whose primary concern was getting out of Germany; Waltemath, whose motivations were similar; Salamon, the Hungarian hustler; and Hans Christian von Kotze, the probable double agent whose sexual exploits resembled those of the fabled James Bond. The assignment of such V-men to Brazil reveals a great deal about the Abwehr's manpower problems. There had been no preparation for a long war, and now the Germans had little choice except to throw into the breach anyone who could be persuaded to accept a Brazilian assignment.

No organization of any kind likes to be caught in that kind of bind, but by 1941, this is essentially where the Canaris outfit found itself.

To be sure, the Germans were quite aware of these and other problems that the unexpected emergence of Brazil as a theater of importance was causing them. The hope seems to have been that even if many of the V-men proved worthless or were quickly blown, some of them would still conceivably avoid detection and/or be able to continue operations.[202] Nevertheless, fresh agents would have to be continually recruited and somehow dispatched to Brazil without being detected. Finding new agents was still a possibility, but after LATI folded, getting them to Brazil became virtually impossible.

Notes

1. See Great Britain, Her Majesty's Stationery Office, Auswärtiges Amt, *Documents on German Foreign Policy: 1918-1945* (hereafter referred to as *DGFP*), series D, vol. 12 (London, 1949–64), p. 895.

2. U.S. Department of the Navy, Naval Historical Center, Washington Naval Yard, *Files of the German Naval Staff, German Naval Attaché in Brazil* (hereafter referred to as *GNAB*), T-65-I, PG/32004, pp. 148–149.

3. On Vargas's strategy of advancing Brazil's prospects by allowing both Washington and Berlin to court her, see Roberto Gambini, *O duplo jôgo de Getúlio Vargas; Influência americana e alemã no Estado Nôvo* (São Paulo, 1977), pp. 89–117; Stanley Hilton, "Military Influence on Brazilian Economic Policy: 1930–1945; A Different View," *Hispanic-American Historical Review* 13, no. 1: (February 1973) 76–78; and Hilton, *Hitler's Secret War in South America*, 1939–1945 (Baton Rouge, 1981), pp. 18–24. On the growth of German trade and the agreements signed, see A Republica do Brasil, *Comercio Exterior do Brasil, 1937–1939*, Servico de Publicações (Rio de Janeiro, 1940), pp. xiv, xvi, xx, xxii-xxiii; and Frank D. McCann, *The Brazilian-American Alliance: 1937–45* (Princeton, 1973), pp. 148–51.

4. Concerning Roosevelt's fear of the Integralistas and his faith in a dictatorial Vargas, see U.S. Department of State, *Foreign Relations of the United States—1937*, vol. 5 (Washington, 1954), pp. 312–315 (hereafter the series is referred to as *FRUS*). Other works discussing this dilemma and decision are John Morton Blum, *Roosevelt and Morgenthau* (Boston, 1970), pp. 180–181, and McCann, *The Brazilian-American Alliance*, pp. 68–69.

5. On Germany's remarkable restraint in dealing with Brazil, see Great Britain, *DGFP*, series D, vol. 5, pp. 843–845. See also *FRUS—1938*, vol. 5, pp. 413–420.

6. For the speech and quote, see Lourival Coutinho, *O General Góes Depõe*. 2° a Edição (Rio de Janeiro, 1956), p. 367.

7. See *FRUS—1940*, vol. 5 (1961), pp. 618–623, and *DGFP*, vol. 9, p. 659. The Vargas course in diplomacy is carefully plotted in Stanley E. Hilton, "Brazilian Diplomacy and the Washington–Rio de Janeiro 'Axis' during the World War II Era," *Hispanic-American Historical Review* 59, no. 2 (May 1979): 208–209.

8. On the German offers, see *DGFP*, series D, vol. 10, pp. 131, 177–178, and 426.

9. For the quoted material, see National Archives and Records Service (hereafter referred to as NARS), R.G. 165, G-2, Regional File, 1933–44 Brazil, 5700–5930, box 200, July 1, 1940, p. 1.

10. *FRUS—1940*, vol. 5, pp. 49–50, 612–613. On the steel mill negotiations, see also Rio de Janeiro, Fundação Getúlio Vargas, Arquivo Getúlio Vargas, GV 40.01.09.

11. John F.W. Dulles, *Vargas of Brazil: A Political Biography* (Austin, 1967), p. 214, emphasizes the idea that without the steel mill agreement, the military and naval discussions would not have gone as they did. On the details of these agreements, see United States Army, Office of the Chief of Military History for the Army, 8-28, BA, U2, C1, *Bilateral Staff Conversations with Latin American Republics*, Appendix 1, pp. 5–7, and NARS, R.G. 38, Entry 49, *Summary of Naval Conversations and Agreements with American Republics*,

copy 6, "Conversations between Captan A.F. Beauregard and Vice-Admiral José Machado da Castro Silva, September 10, 1940," pp. 4–9.

12. On the planning for these airstrips, the negotiations behind their construction, see Wesley F. Craven and James L. Cote, eds., *The Army Air Force in World War II*, vol. 1 (Chicago, 1948), pp. 319–342. The best history concerning the negotiation of the airfield construction contracts is in McCann, *The Brazilian-American Alliance*, pp. 222–239.

13. See Craven and Cote, *The Army Air Force in World War II*, vol. 1, pp. 318–322, and vol. 7, pp. 46–50.

14. On the German blockade runners and German strategy, the best study is by Reiner Pommerein, *Das Dritte Reich und Lateinamerika: Die deutsche politik gegenüber Süd und Mittelamerika: 1939–1942* (Düsseldorf, 1977), pp. 203–208, 212–215.

15. *FRUS—1941*, vol. 6, pp. 528–539. The quoted material is found on p. 534.

16. Arquivo Getúlio Vargas, GV 41.11.10 (letter is actually dated November 10, 1941); and Stetson Conn and Byron Fairchild, *The Western Hemisphere: The Framework of Hemisphere Defense* (Washington, 1960), p. 271.

17. See S.K. Roskill, *The War at Sea, 1939–1945*, vol. 1 (London, 1954), pp. 271–274; and, in particular, Terry Hughes and John Costello, *The Battle of the Atlantic* (New York, 1977), front and back covers.

18. Hughes and Costello, *The Battle of the Atlantic*, front and back inner covers, adequately depicts the African–South American convoy routes. Specific information on routing and ports of call comes from Harold Midkiff, Interview, Brasilia, D.F., Brazil, June 28, 1978. In 1941, Midkiff was a naval officer attached to ONI, and assigned the task of directing convoy traffic in and out of Rio de Janeiro harbor.

19. NARS, R.G. 242, ML-170, microfilm roll 22, n.p., indicates German intent. U.S. plans were delineated by Jack West, legal attaché in Brazil 1941–43, in a letter to Prof. Leslie B. Rout, Jr., October 21, 1980.

20. The background of the LATI affair is found in Conn and Fairchild, *The Western Hemisphere*, p. 247; H. Montgomery Hyde, *Room 3603: The Story of the British Intelligence Center in New York in World War II* (New York, 1962), pp. 144–145; William Stevenson, *A Man Called Intrepid: The Secret War* (New York, 1975), pp. 267–268. A Brazilian interpretation of these events is found in Hélio Silva, *1942: Guerra no Continente*, vol. 12, *O Ciclo de Vargas* (Rio de Janeiro, 1972), pp. 319–321. The quote on sea espionage is from the Franklin D. Roosevelt Library (hereafter referred to as FDRL), *The Diaries of Adolf A. Berle*, roll 3, frame 0287.

21. For these initial negotiations, see NARS, R.G. 59, 832.796/380, no. 197, pp. 1–2. The Brazilian view of these negotiations is summarized well in Silva, *1942: Guerra no Continente*, pp. 319–322.

22. A copy of the original letter is found in Hyde, *Room 3603*, pp. 145–146.

23. Ibid., pp. 146–147.

24. See Stevenson, *A Man Called Intrepid*, p. 269.

25. See NARS, R.G. 59, 832.796/299a, no. 178, and 832.796/300, no. 291, pp. 1–2. See also Silva, *1942: Guerra no Continente*, p. 321.

26. NARS, R.G. 59, 832.796/597, no. 941, pp. 1–2.

27. NARS, R.G. 59, 832.796/607, no. 1566, p. 1.

28. Arquivo Getúlio Vargas, GV 41.10.30/2, letter.

29. For the oil company negotiations, see NARS, R.G. 59, 832.796/299a, no. 178, and 832.796/597, no. 741. On the purchase of the planes for $350,000, see NARS, R.G. 165A-727, G-2 Regional File, 5900–5920, November 23, 1942, p. 12. Berle's statement concerning the State Department's success is in FDRL, *The Diaries of Adolf A. Berle*, roll 3, frame 0856. For Caffery's claim, see his NARS, R.G. 84, File 120.1, no. 10284, *Embassy Accomplishments Report on Concessions and Privileges Gained from Brazilian Matters Relating to Hemisphere Defense, United States and United Nations Military and Naval Operations and Other Things*, February 27, 1943, p. 15.

30. See Richard Bourne, *Getúlio Vargas of Brazil, 1883–1954* (London, 1974), p. 198; Dulles, *Vargas of Brazil*, pp. 173 and 219; and Robert Levine, *The Vargas Regime: The Critical Years: 1934–1938* (New York, 1970), pp. 176–177.

Even his enemy, Affonso Henriques, in *Ascenso e Quedo de Getúlio Vargas*, vol. 1 (Rio de Janeiro, 1966), pp. 459–461, pays tribute to Vargas's political abilities as a master manipulator.

31. *GNAB*, T-65, PG 32004, p. 184.

32. See *A República do Brasil*, Arquivo do Tribunal de Sergurança Nacional, Rio de Janeiro, Processo 3.093, *Niels Christian Christiansen e Outros* (hereafter these volumes will be cited as Processo 3.093, *NCCEO*), 16 vols. (titles on volumes vary slightly). The admission in question is in vol. 14, box 228, p. 3088 (pagination in most volumes is irregular).

33. See Arquivo Getúlio Vargas, GV 15.11.38, letter. For the U.S. side of these negotiations, see Donald B. Schewe, ed., *Franklin D. Roosevelt and Foreign Affairs*, second series, January–August 1939, vol. 12 (New York, 1979), p. 113. On Thompson, see NARS, R.G. 59, 832.105/23, p. 1, and 832.105/29, p. 1. On Jack West, see letters, Jack West to Professor Rout, memo 2, November 8, 1978, and March 21, 1980.

34. NARS, R.G. 319, *German Espionage in Latin America* (hereafter referred to as *GELA*), (Washington, 1946), pp. 62–63, and R.G. 59, 862.20210/1917, p. 4. The two V-men arrested were released in less than a week.

35. See *GNAB*, PG-32004, p. 199.

36. See NARS, R.G. 59, 862.20210, Engels, Albrecht Gustav/71, part 4, n.p.

37. The history of Albrecht Engels and his enlistment as a spy by Jobst Raven is told in Processo 3.093, *NCCEO*, vol. VI, box 227, pp. 1081–1083.

38. Additional information on Jobst Raven and Hermann Bohny is found in NARS, R.G. 319, *GELA*, pp. 52 and 55.

39. On Immer's contact with Engels and Arnold, see NARS, R.G. 59, 862.20210, Engels, Albrecht Gustav/71, part 4, n.p.

40. Personal letter from Curt Meyer-Clason, of Munich, to Professor Rout, September 3, 1979. A less flattering presentation of Herr Meyer-Clason's personality (i.e., the playboy aspects) is presented in *Folha da Tarde*, Pôrto Alegre, Rio Grande do Sul, March 30, 1942.

41. A detailed description is found in NARS, R.G. 84, 820.02, box 547, *Hans Kurt Werner Meyer Clason, Declaration before the Delegacia de Ordem Política e Social*, Pôrto Alegre, March 5, 1942, pp. 2–4. For the Immer-Bohny scrap, see NARS, R.G. 59, 862.20210, Engels, Albrecht Gustav/71, part 4, n.p.

42. On Immer's appearance and photo, see NARS, R.G. 319, *GELA*, p. 54. On Immer and the unfavorable comments by Engels, see NARS, R.G. 59, 862.20210, Engels, Albrecht Gustav/ 71, part 4, n.p. For Prüfer's complaints about Immer, see NARS, *Documents Selected from German Foreign Office Records* (hereafter referred to as *DSGFOR*), T-120 series, roll 223, frame 157146.

43. The best narratives of the Bohny-Engels removal of Immer are found in NARS, R.G. 59, 862.20210, Engels, Albrecht Gustav/71, part 4, n.p.; R.G. 319, *GELA*, pp. 54–55; and *GNAB*, P.G. 32004, p. 212.

44. See NARS, R.G. 84, 820.02, no. 7578, box 547, *Declaration of Edward Arnold Before the Delegacia de Ordem Política e Social*, March 5, 1942, pp. 3 and 7.

45. NARS, R.G. 173, R.I.D., box, *Testimony of George E. Sterling*, part 1, pp. 14–24.

46. NARS, R.G. 59, 862.20232/1-2446, p. 2; R.G. 319, *GELA*, p. 143; and *GNAB*, P.G. 32004, p. 212.

47. For the Stiege statement, see NARS, R.G. 59, 862.20232/1-2446, p. 2. Hilton, *Hitler's Secret War,* pp. 32–33 and 35, states that "Johann Siegfried Becker" persuaded Engels to establish a clandestine radio station and supplied Engels with both a transmitter and a microdot machine. Since Engels told his share of falsehoods while being interrogated by Brazilian and SIS/Brazil agents, almost any story is plausible. We support a different version of the origins of Engels's clandestine station and the acquisition of the microdot machine. In

NARS, R.G. 59, 862.20210/1-2446, p. 2, Engels confessed, after the war was over, that the microdot machine had always been in the German embassy. In *GNAB*, P.G. 32004, p. 192, Bohny points out that he controlled the machine and that an agent named Heinrich Folkers had been the microdot maker.

Hilton apparently did not consult Johannes Siegfried Becker's deposition (NARS, R.G. 84, 820.02-General, box 533 [Suitland, Maryland], pp. 1–50), in which Becker fails to mention Engels or Bohny. What Becker does emphasize in his deposition is that in 1940–41, he was primarily concerned with building up an SD ring in Brazil (pp. 12–15) which was to be directed by Heinz Lange. Becker's story is verified and expanded upon by Karl Gustav Arnold, the special SD adviser for Latin American Affairs. Arnold's deposition is in German Federal Republic, Institut für Zeitgeschichte, München, NG-4871, G2-BL. PH., *Interrogation of Karl Gustav Arnold*, November 20, 1946, pp. 10–11.

Finally, in 1948, Albrecht Engels submitted a sworn deposition in which he stated that all that he attributed to Becker had been the work of Lt. Comdr. Hermann Bohny. See A República do Brasil, Brasilia, D.F., Arquivo Superior Tribunal Militar, Apelação 1422, Processo 3.293, *Tulio Regis Nascimento e Outros*, vol. 6, pp. 1185–1186.

In summary, we believe Engels knew Johannes Siegfried Becker, and that he probably discussed important issues with him. But we doubt whether an SD chief who was struggling hard to get his own radio service operable would turn over a radio transmitter and the only microdot machine known to be in Brazil to an Abwehr organization.

48. *GNAB*, PG 32004, p. 182.

49. Ibid., pp. 170–171, 193, and 203.

50. This code information was supplied in a letter from Kapitän zur See a.D. Herbert Wichmann to Professor Rout, April 6, 1982. Wichmann, the Chief of Ast Hamburg, stated that he obtained the information from "old comrades of Abwehrstellen Berlin." On these efforts to get a station functioning and the cable contacts, see *DSGFOR*, T-120 series, roll 1054, frames 420750, 420752, and 420756. On intercepts, see NARS, R.G. 59, 862.20210, Engels, Albrecht Gustav/71, part 4, n.p., and part 15, n.p.

51. For Muth's connection with Bohny, see *GNAB*, PG 32004, p. 212. On the backgrounds of Sobisch and Muth, see Processo 3.093, *NCCEO*, vol. 9, box 227, pp. 2214–2218 and NARS, R.G. 319, FBI, *GELA*, pp. 57–58.

52. See NARS, R.G. 59, 862.20210, Engels, Albrecht Gustav/71, part 4, n.p.

53. On Ramuz's early life in Germany and Brazil, see Processo 3.093, *NCCEO*, vol. 6, box 227, pp. 1029–1038. For the quoted material, see *GNAB*, PG 32004, p. 170.

54. On Hans Otto Meier's general activities, see ibid., and Processo 3.093, *NCCEO*, vol. 16, box 228, pp. 3469–3470.

55. On Heyer's background and recruitment, see NARS, R.G. 59, 862.20210/2339, pp. 1–2. See also Processo 3.093, *NCCEO*, vol. 1, pp. 137–140.

56. On Sievert's previous recruitment by Bohny, see *GNAB*, PG 32004, p. 170. For a full description of Heyer's northeastern trip, see NARS R.G. 59, 862.20210, Engels, Albrecht Gustav/71, part 4, n.p.

57. Folkers was undetected by the SIS/Brazil, but a history of his activities is found in *GNAB*, PG 32004, pp. 191 and 195–196. For the official deposition of Carlos Meyer, see Processo 3.093, *NCCEO*, vol. 3, box 227, pp. 550–551 (also marked 00139–00140). For the deposition of Kurt Weingartner, see ibid., vol. 6, box 228, pp. 1097–1098 (00184–00185).

58. On Bühler's interrogation and his arrangements with Engels and von Heyer, see NARS, R.G. 84, 820.02, no. 7771, *Statement Made by Karl Eugene Bühler in the Special Police Department of the Federal District at Rio de Janeiro, June 8, 1942*, pp. 1–5.

59. For Gamma Pinto, see NARS, R.G. 59, 862.20210, Engels, Albrecht Gustav/71, part 4, n.p.; R.G. 59, 862.20232/1-2446, p. 5; and R.G. 319, FBI, *GELA*, pp. 60–61.

60. NARS, R.G. 59 832.00/4278, p. 1, and 832.00/4289, p.1.

61. On Georg Karl Metzner's secret appointment, see *GNAB*, PG 32004, p. 190.

62. The best report on the activities of Heinz Lorenz is his statement to the Brazilian police; see Processo 3.093, *NCCEO*, vol. 3, box 227, pp. 538–545.

63. FDRL, Franklin D. Roosevelt Papers (hereafter referred to as FDRP), OF-10-B, box 37, FBI, *Latin American—Clandestine Radio Stations Utilized by the German Espionage System*, February 1942, p. 6.

64. On the *Dresden* affair, see Pommerein, *Das Dritte Reich*, p. 215. On the roles of Rocha and Engels, see *GNAB*, PG 32004, pp. 172 and 224.

65. *GNAB*, PG 32004, pp. 172 and 224.

66. See August K. Muggenthaler, *German Raiders in World War II* (Englewood Cliffs, N.J., 1977), pp. 103-105; and Pommerein, *Das Dritte Reich*, p. 215.

67. Muggenthaler, *German Raiders*, pp. 16, 104–105.

68. FDRL, FDRP, OF-10B, box 37, FBI, *Clandestine Radio Stations*, p. 6.

69. On funds available and received, see *GNAB*, PG 32004, p. 187, and NARS, R.G. 59, 862.20210, Engels, Gustav Albrecht/71, part 14, n.p.

70. On the background of Schlegel, see *NCCEO*, vol. 6, box 227, pp. 968–973.

71. Schlegel told varying stories as to how he began working for the Abwehr. The most credible version is found in NARS, R.G. 59, 862.20210, Engels, Albrecht Gustav/71, part 3, n.p. Hilton, *Hitler's Secret War*, p. 55, suggests that Schlegel may have been recruited when he visited Germany in 1939.

72. *GNAB*, PG 32004, pp. 211 and 213, and NARS, R.G. 59, 862.20210, Engels, Albrecht Gustav/71, part 3, n.p.

73. On Karl Theilen, see NARS, R.G. 319, *GELA*, p. 62.

74. NARS, R.G. 59, 862.20210, Engels, Albrecht, Gustav/71, part 3, n.p.

75. On Trautmann's recruitment, travails, and complaints, see NARS, R.G. 84, 820.02, no. 7578, *Declarations Made by Rolf Trautmann, May 4, 1942*, pp. 1–2.

76. NARS, R.G. 84, 820.02, no. 7578, *Declarations Made by Theodor Frederich Schlegel*, May 5, 1942, pp. 1–2.

77. NARS, R.G. 862.20210, Engels, Albrecht Gustav/71, parts 3 and 10, n.p. For the code book and the system, see R.G. 59, 862.20210/2338, pp. 1–3.

78. Ibid., R.G. 59, 862.20210, Engels, Albrecht Gustav/71, part 3, n.p.; and NARS, R.G. 319, *GELA*, p. 63.

79. NARS, R.G. 59, 862.20210, Engels, Albrecht Gustav/71, part 3, n.p.; and R.G. 319, *GELA*, p. 63.

80. NARS, R.G. 59, 862.20210, Engels, Albrecht Gustav/71, part 3, n.p.

81. On this event (Schlegel's denial but apparent boast) plus Engels's message, see ibid. For additional evidence that Schlegel made such a boast, see NARS, R.G., 84, 820.02, *Deposition of Neils Christian Christiansen, August 28, 1942*, p. 5.

82. On Neidenführ's actions and suspicions, see *GNAB*, PG 32004, p. 213.

83. See *Jornal do Brasil*, Rio de Janeiro, June 17, 1978, and letter from Source Z, March 21, 1980.

84. For Kempter's life and Abwehr recruitment, see NARS, R.G. 59, 862.20210/1324, no. 7021, enclosure no. 2, pp. 3–5. On his controller, see letter, Kapitän zur See a.D. Herbert Wichmann to Professor Rout, December 28, 1981.

85. On Kempter and Heriberto Müller, see NARS, R.G. 59, 862.20210 Kempter, Federico/18, no. 7082, pp. 2–3. See also 862.20210/2439, p. 7.

86. On Ottomar Müller's recruitment and background, see R.G 84, 820.02, box 537, no. 9883, *Enclosing Results of Interrogation of Ottomar Müller, German Deportee from Argentina, May 13, 1947*, pp. 1–2. On Menzel's message to Niebuhr, see U.S. Navy, Naval Historical Center, *Files of the German Naval Staff, German Naval Attaché in Argentina*, T-67, PG 32009, p. 107.

87. On Hans Napp, see NARS, R.G. 59, 862.20210/1459, no. 4903, enclosure 1, pp. 1–2.

88. On Kempter's relationship with Müller and Napp, see NARS, R.G. 59, 862.20210 Kempter, Federico/18, no. 7082, p. 15, and 862.20210/2099, no. 7551, pp. 4–5.

89. On "Unión"—his real name and occupation—see NARS, R.G. 59, 862.20210/4-945, file 64, 21361, pp. 1–5. For a manifestation of Kempter's anti-Semitic views, see NARS, R.G. 59, 862.20210, Kempter, Federico/18, no. 7082, p. 24.

90. On "Griffin" and "Lorenz" and their messages, see NARS, R.G. 59, 862.20210/2439, pp. 15–22. For a comparison with the sporadic traffic from "Unión," see 862.20210/4-945, pp. 5–8.

91. See NARS, R.G. 59, 862.20210/1325, enclosure 2, pp. 1–2, and 862.20210, Kempter, Federico/18, pp. 19–20. On Kempter's code book, see Brasil, *Vida Policial*, vol. 4, no. 46 (April 1942), p. 29, and NARS, R.G. 319, FBI, *GELA*, p. 77.

92. NARS, R.G. 319, *GELA*, p. 71.

93. Ibid.

94. On Karl Eugene Haering and his activities for Kempter, see NARS, R.G. 59, 862.20210/1325, enclosure 4, pp. 1–2.

95. Processo 3.093, *NCCEO*, vol. 6, box 227, pp. 933–935.

96. On the recruitment of Fink, his special shipping code, and Kempter's threat, see NARS, R.G. 59, 862.20210/1325, enclosure 2, p. 6; 862.20210, Kempter, Federico/18, pp. 15–16 and 23.

97. See NARS, R.G. 59, 862.20210/2439, p. 8, and R.G. 242, *Records of Nebenstellen Bremen*, roll 22, n.p.

98. NARS, R.G. 59, 862.20210/2092, no. 2485, enclosure, n.p.

99. NARS, R.G. 59, 862.20210/2439, pp. 14–15.

100. Kempter boasted of his achievement in *Jornal Do Brasil*, June 17, 1978.

101. For the details of this event, see NARS, R.G. 59, 862.20210, Kempter, Federico/18, pp. 13–14.

102. NARS, R.G., 862.20210/2439, p. 20.

103. Ibid., p. 8; and R.G. 319, FBI, *GELA*, p. 77.

104. Letter from Friedrich Kempter to Professor Rout, October 18, 1978.

105. Interview with Dr. Elpídio Reali, São Paulo, Brazil, July 6, 1978.

106. Letter from Friedrich Kempter to Professor Rout, July 31, 1978; for Bohny's views, see *GNAB*, PG 32004, pp. 206–207.

107. The materials on Starziczny's life between 1898 and 1940 and all the quotations are from Processo 3.093, *NCCEO*, Appendix 1, box 228, pp. 00007 and 00011–00013.

108. For the letter to Uebele, see NARS, R.G. 59, 862.20210 Christiansen, [Niels] Christian/110, no. 1555, plus enclosures. See also 862.20210/2664, pp. 28, 82–83. Jobst Raven was connected by marriage to the Uebele family. Lieutenant Commander Weisshuhn was a nephew of Diederichsen. It is almost as if Starziczny's mission was some kind of family affair.

109. The best description of the first meeting with Otto Uebele, the assignment of Treutler, and the elder Uebele's strong desire to have the radio station located in Rio rather than Santos, is found in NARS, R.G. 59, 862.20210/1930 1/2, pp. 13 and 23–27. See also the special document provided by Elpídio Reali, Superintêndencia de Segurança, Política e Social de São Paulo, *A Rede de Espionagem Nazista chefiada por Niels Christian Christiansen* (hereafter referred to as *A Rede*) (São Paulo, 1943), pp. 18–19.

110. See Processo 3.093, *NCCEO*, vol. 1, box 226, p. 111, vol. 6, box 227, pp. 1040–1041, and vol. 8, box 227, pp. 1640–1644. See also R.G. 319, FBI, *GELA*, p. 68, and *A Rede*, pp. 49–50, for the beginning of radio contact with Ast Hamburg.

111. See Processo 3.093, *NCCEO*, vol. 1, box 226, pp. 110–114, 118, 223–224.

112. On the São Paulo branch of the ring, see NARS, R.G. 59, 862.20210/1930 1/2, pp. 14–16, and especially *A Rede*, pp. 62–81. On Gieseler's U.S.A. contacts, see NARS, R.G. 84, 820.02, *Gieseler, Wilhelm*, pp. 1–6 (report is dated March 31, 1943).

113. On the recruitment of Stark, see *A Rede*, pp. 21 and 90–91, and NARS, R.G. 84, 820.02/891, Stark, July 13, 1942, pp. 1–3. On von den Steinen, see *A Rede*, pp. 80–81, and NARS, R.G.59, 862.20210, Christiansen [Niels] Christian/134, pp. 3–6.

114. On the agents in the south, see *A Rede*, pp. 22, 92–94, and NARS, R.G.59, 862.20210/ 1930 1/2, p. 31. On Wilkens's past activities in the Nazi party, see Aurelio da Silva Py, *A 5ª Coluña no Brasil: A Conspiração Nazi no Rio Grande do Sul* (Pôrto Alegre, 1942), pp. 95–111.

115. On Leo Voos, see Processo 3.093, *NCCEO*, vol. 1, box 226, pp. 147–148; vol. 8, box 227, p. 1651; and NARS, R.G. 59, 862.20210, Christiansen [Niels] Christian/134, pp.4 and 6.

116. The reconnaisance flights and the story related here are found in detail in Processo 3.093, *NCCEO*, vol. 6, box 227, pp. 1019–1020, and NARS, R.G. 59, 862.20210/1930 1/2, pp. 10–11.

117. On the efforts of Silva Barreto and Karl Hans von den Steinen, see NARS, R.G. 59, 862.20210, Christiansen, Niels Christian/134, pp. 3–9, and *A Rede*, pp. 81–86. For these materials, as circulated by the German High Command, see German Federal Republic, Auswärtiges Amt, Bonn, *Akten Betreffend, Büro des Staatssekretärs*, Brasilien, 21 April 1939–28 February 1942, band 1 (Iv D 4-D.NR 2517 0/41), pp. 235108–235112.

118. *A Rede*, pp. 25 and 38.

119. Ibid., and NARS, R.G. 59, 862.20210/1930 1/2, p. 2. For orders to the FBI regarding the suspected leak, see 862.20232/362 2/3, p. 1.

120. R.G. 59, 862.20210/1930 1/2, pp. 27–28. Uebele was convinced that Bohny and Engels were out to destroy not only "Lucas," but the Santos-based wing of the organization as well.

121. On the actions of Metzner and Timm, see *A Rede*, pp. 53–54 and 80, and NARS, R.G. 59, 862.20210/1930 1/2, p. 32.

122. NARS, R.G. 59, 862.20210/1930 1/2, pp. 32–33.

123. See Processo 3.093, *NCCEO*, vol. 1, box 226, p. 103, for de Oliveira's testimony. See also NARS, R.G. 59, 862.20210/1930 1/2, p. 28.

124. On the new car, the bribe, the new house, and payments, see *A Rede*, pp. 23–24, and NARS, R.G. 59, 862.20210/1930 1/2, pp. 31–32.

125. Ibid., pp. 24, 32, and 34. See also R.G. 319, FBI, *GELA*, p. 68.

126. On nonpayments to Schwab and his complaints via Bohny, see Processo 3.093, *NCCEO*, Appendix 2, box 228, pp. 00102 and 00108. On nonpayments to others, see NARS, R.G. 59, 862.20210/1259, p. 3. On nonpayment of Metzner, R.G. 84, 820.02, no. 7578, *Declarations Made by George Kurt Metzner, March 27, 1942*, p. 2.

127. *A Rede*, pp. 23 and 50, and *GNAB*, PG 32004, pp. 204–205.

128. *GNAB*, PG 32004, pp. 204–205. Schwab had worked with Bohny in one capacity or another since 1940. Ibid., p. 203. See also, Processo 3.093, *NCCEO*, Appendix 2, box 228, pp. 00108 and 00109.

129. NARS, R.G. 59, 862.20210/1930 1/2, pp. 32–33, and *A Rede*, p. 24.

130. Letter, Hans Ulrich Uebele to Professor Rout, September 10, 1981. Hans Ulrich recalled that once his father concluded that Starziczny was afraid to go to the United States, he was finished with him. His chief intention thereafter was to gradually ease "Lucas" out.

131. Ibid. For other evidence of Uebele's distrust of Starziczny, see NARS, R.G. 59, 862.20210, Christiansen [Neils] Christian/77, pp. 2–3, and 862.20210/1930 1/2, p. 35.

132. *A Rede*, p. 71. Starziczny was already believed by the Uebeles to be dragging his feet. See also NARS, R.G. 59, 862.20210/1930 1/2, p. 35.

133. German records indicate that Jordan's correct name, to his superiors, was Franz Walther Jordan. See NARS, *DSGFOR*, T-120 series, roll 750, frames 354843–354846. Herzog's real name was supplied in a letter from Homer Boynton, Jr., Inspector, Federal Bureau of Investigation, to Professor Rout, February 29, 1980.

134. See NARS, R.G. 84, 820.02, no. 7578, *Declaration Made by Herbert Max Winterstein, Before the Special Police in the Federal District*, May 25, 1942, p. 2.

135. On the Bischoff connection and its implications, see NARS, R.G. 319, FBI, *GELA*, pp. 80–81. On the Bischoffs and international espionage, see Ladislas Farago, *The Game of Foxes*, Bantam edition, third printing (New York, 1973), pp. 167, 297, and 630. On the

Bischoffs' espionage plans from the beginning of the war, see NARS, R.G. 319, FBI, *GELA*, pp. 189–190.

136. Ibid., p. 81.

137. For the Hans Holl story, see NARS, R.G. 59, 862.20210/1859, pp. 10–11, and R.G. 84, 820.02, no. 7578, *Statements Made by Hans Holl, May 27, 1942*, pp. 1–4.

138. On Paul Max Winterstein, see NARS, R.G. 59, 862.20210/1859, pp. 9–10, and R.G. 84, 820.02, no. 7578, *Declaration*, p. 3. See also R.G. 319, FBI, *GELA*, pp. 79–80, which gives a more realistic determination of Winterstein's activities.

139. See NARS, R.G. 59, 862.20210/1859, p. 1, for his first contact with Germany, and p. 6 for Jordan's changes of address. The best commentary concerning Jordan's frequent juggling of aliases is found in A República do Brasil, Arquivo do Tribunal de Segurança Nacional, Rio de Janeiro, Processo 2.996, *Frank Walter Jordan e Outros*. (hereafter referred to as FWJO), volume 2, box 228, pp. 345–346.

140. On Afonso Digeser, and transmissions from his home, see Processo 2.996, *FWJO*, vol. 2, box 228, pp. 360–361.

141. On the members of the LFS ring, see NARS, R.G. 59, 862.20210/1859, p. 7; *FWJO*, vol. 2, box 228, pp. 298–299 and 360–365; and NARS, R.G. 59, 862.20210/2251, no. 10001, p. 1.

142. On the opposition of the Integralistas to Vargas after 1938, see Hilton, *Hilter's Secret War*, pp. 86–87, and Edgard Carone, *O Estado Nôvo (1937–1945)* (Rio de Janeiro, 1977), pp. 193–215.

143. On Walter Moll, see NARS, R.G. 59, 862.20210/1859, pp. 8–9. The quoted material is on p. 8. See also R.G. 319, FBI, *GELA*, pp. 82–83.

144. NARS, R.G. 59, 862.20210, Engels, Albrecht Gustav/71, part 5, n.p.

145. On Jordan's finances, see R.G. 319, FBI, *GELA*, p. 77.

146. On the efforts to run cotton through the British blockade, see ibid., pp. 79–80, and R.G. 84, 820.02, no. 7578, *Declarations Made by Herbert Max Karl Ernst Winterstein*, p. 3.

147. On the passing on of secret Brazilian air force data, see Processo 2.996, *FWJO*, vol. 2, box 228, p. 358. For the message total, see FDRL, FDRP, OF 10-B, box 37, *Clandestine Radio Stations*, pp. 14–15, and NARS, R.G. 59, 862.20210/1859, pp. 2–3.

148. For the activities of Renato Medeiros, see NARS, R.G. 59, 862.20210/1860, p. 2. On "Grillo's" arrival and the message interception, see NARS, R.G. 59, 862.20210/1379, pp. 21–27.

149. For the background on Gamillscheg, see Processo 3.093, *NCCEO*, vol. 3, box 226, pp. 431–432 (pages numbered irregularly).

150. On "Grillo's" station and his direction, see *GNAB*, PG 32004, p. 208. Information on Colonel Servas was provided by Herr Oskar Reile in a letter to Professor Rout, November 1, 1978.

151. Concerning the conflict over the separation from his family and the plans of the Ast Berlin directors, see NARS, R.G. 59, 862.20210/1860, p.6.

152. On Neidenführ as Gamillscheg's Brazilian supervisor, see *GNAB*, PG 32004, p. 208.

153. On the arrangements with Heyer and Gamillscheg's radio problems, see NARS, R.G. 59, 862.20210/1860, pp. 5–6.

154. FDRL, Harry Hopkins Papers, box 141, *Brazil: Totalitarianism Today*, p. 109.

155. *GNAB*, PG 32004, p. 208.

156. On Adalberto Wamser, see NARS, R.G. 59, 862.20210/1860, pp. 12–13. On Mesquita dos Santos, see ibid., pp. 6–8, the quoted material being on p. 7. See also, Processo 3.093, *NCCEO*, vol. 3, box 226, pp. 432–433.

157. On da Silva, see Processo 3.093, *NCCEO*, vol. 3, box 226, pp. 433–434, and NARS, R.G. 59, 862.20210/1860, pp. 6 and 8–9. See also note 32 in this chapter.

158. NARS, R.G. 59, 20210/1860, p. 7.

159. Ibid., p. 9

160. Ibid., and see Processo 3.093, *NCCEO*, vol. 3, box 226, pp. 435–437. The stories vary

slightly in detail, and there does not exist a third source against which the story can be checked.

161. German Federal Republic, *Akten zur Deutschen Auswärtigen Politik, 1918–1945* (series E: 1941–1945) vol. 1 (Göttingen, 1969–1979), pp. 224–225.

162. On the message and the clock incident, see NARS, R.G. 59, 862.20210/1860, pp. 9–10.

163. On Waltemath's background, see NARS, R.G. 59, 862.20232/920, enclosure 2, pp. 1–2.

164. Ibid., p. 3. Compare with R.G. 59, 862.20232/970, pp. 2–5. On his section and *Ast* assignment and controller, see *GNAB*, PG 32004, pp. 208–209. On his special mission, see NARS, R.G. 59, 862.20232/970, p. 8.

165. On Kotze's assignment and his connection with Waltemath, see *GNAB*, PG 32004, p. 208, and NARS, R.G. 59, 862.20232/970, enclosure 3, p. 2.

166. On Waltemath's radio problems, see NARS, R.G. 59, 862.20232/970, pp. 18–20.

167. NARS, R.G. 319, *GELA*, p. 93.

168. On "Springbok's" Brazilian antics, see Hyde, *Room 3603*, p. 222.

169. On Kotze's knowledge of and introduction to the leaders of the Bohny-Engels ring, see *GNAB*, PG 32004, pp. 192, 208–209, and R.G. 59, 862.20210, Engels, Albrecht Gustav/71, part 4, n.p. The message that he would be reassigned was given by Hermann Bohny to Kotze.

170. *GNAB*, PG 32004, p. 209. Bohny informed Abwehr headquarters that he was convinced that Kotze was a traitor.

171. On these meetings between Kotze and Waltemath, see NARS, R.G. 59, 862.20210/920, enclosure 2, pp. 2–3.

172. On Hans Morgener and the Abwehr, see *GNAB*, PG 32004, p. 170. On his relations with Waltemath, see NARS, R.G. 59, 862.20232/970, p. 29. On the total received, see R.G. 319, FBI, *GELA*, p. 93.

173. On this last message from Bauer and the specific instructions given, see NARS, R.G. 59, 862.20232/970, p. 26.

174. For the background on Salamon and Mocsan, the messages sent, their controllers, and their cover identities, see NARS, R.G. 59, 862.20210/1917, pp. 2–4, and R.G. 319, FBI, *GELA*, pp. 84–86.

175. On the Rosa Belàs story, see Processo 3.093, *NCCEO*, vol. 3, box 226, pp. 454–456.

176. On Ellemer Nagy, see ibid., pp. 464–467.

177. On María Tereza Calvacanti Ellender's background, see NARS, R.G. 59, 862.20210/1917, pp. 10–12. On the activities of DOPS, see Processo 3.093, *NCCEO*, vol. 4, box 227, pp. 578–581.

178. On Piccola and the alleged link with the Italian intelligence service, see NARS, R.G. 319, *GELA*, p. 87.

179. For details concerning this incident, see NARS, R.G. 59, 862.20210/1917, p. 14.

180. On the underground hangars report and the U.S. denial, see NARS, R.G. 59, 862.20210/2469, n.p.

181. For the statements and activities of Jofre Magalhães dos Santos regarding his work for Salamon, see NARS, R.G. 59, 862.20210/1917, pp. 16–18, and Processo 3.093, *NCCEO*, vol. 3, box 226, pp. 439–440.

182. For costs and payment from Engels, see R.G. 59, 862.20210, Engels, Albrecht Gustav/71, part 4, n.p.

183. NARS, R.G. 59, 862.20210/1917, pp. 23–27, and R.G. 59, 862.20210/2469, n.p.

184. NARS, R.G. 319, FBI, *GELA*, p. 87. See also C. A. MacCartney, *A History of Hungary, 1929–1945*, vol. 2 (New York, 1967), pp. 294–295, for a partial history of the quixotic Arrow-Cross party.

185. On the passport debacle in Recife, see NARS, R.G. 59, 862.20210/1917, p. 4.

186. NARS, R.G. 59, 862.20210/1917, pp. 6–7.

187. On Mocsan's difficulties with Salamon and his arrest, see ibid., pp. 3, 5–6; R.G., 59, 862.20210/2469, n.p.; and Processo 3.093, *NCCEO*, vol. 4, box 227, pp. 763–764.

188. On Salamon's last days, see NARS, R.G. 59, 862.20210/1917, pp. 5–7, 20–22. Evidence that the Abwehr would have punished him had he returned is in Processo 3.093, *NCCEO*, vol. 3, box 226, p. 441.

189. NARS, R.G. 319, FBI, *GELA*, p. 88.

190. The source of these dates and other information is FDRL, FDRP, OF-10-B, box 37, FBI, *Clandestine Radio Stations*, p.1.

191. See NARS, R.G. 59, 862.20210/599, /627, /629, /642, /650, /661, /662, /678, and /679.

192. FDRL, FDRP, OF-10-B, box 37, *Clandestine Radio Stations*, pp. 1–26.

193. On the first SIS arrival in Brazil, see letter from Inspector Boynton to Professor Rout, December 14, 1977.

194. Letter from Jack West to Professor Rout, July 20, 1979.

195. Memo 2, from Jack West to Professor Rout, November 8, 1978. See also letter from Arthur J. Baker to Professor Rout, February 3, 1979, and interview, Pôrto Alegre, Brazil, July 18, 1978, Professor Rout with Donald Charles Bird.

196. On "Tom," see Memo 2, Jack West, November 8, 1978.

197. These descriptions of Elim O'Shaughnessy came from a former foreign service officer, who gave the information with the stipulation that his name would not be used, and from Harold Midkiff, Brasilia, D.F., Brazil, June 15, 1978 (interview with Professor Rout).

198. Letter, Jack West to Professor Rout, January 25, 1979.

199. *GNAB*, PG 32004, pp. 184 and 199.

200. FDRL, FDRP, OF-10-B, box 29, letter J. Edgar Hoover to Maj. Gen. Edwin M. Watson, secretary to the president, November 29, 1941.

201. *GNAB*, PG 32004, p. 185.

202. See NARS, R.G. 59, 862.20210/2115, p. 1.

5

Climax of the Espionage War in Brazil: 1942–55

I. Introduction: Guns for Spies

Late in 1941, shortly after the Pearl Harbor attack, the Republic of Chile invoked the Havana Declaration of Reciprocal Assistance and Cooperation and called for a special convocation of the American republics. This declaration had been formulated at the Second Foreign Ministers' Conference, held in Havana on July 21–30, 1940. It stated that any act of aggression by a non-American state against any signatory of the declaration, which the United States was, would be considered an act of aggression against all the other signatories as well. On January 12, 1942, Washington sent Undersecretary of State Sumner Welles to Rio de Janeiro, the convocation site. The undersecretary arrived in Brazil with instructions "to persuade all the other American governments that it was essential to sever diplomatic relations ... in order to end Axis espionage and subversion activities in this hemisphere."[1]

Pres. Franklin D. Roosevelt and Secretary of State Cordell Hull expected some trouble from Argentina but assumed that, if Buenos Aires resisted this initiative, the government of Acting Pres. Ramón S. Castillo would find itself isolated.[2] Since 1933, the Roosevelt administration had assiduously labored to bury the image of the United States as the bully boy of the Americas. This conference would demonstrate whether the Latin American republics would support a U.S. proposal over the possibly violent objections of one of their own. In that sense, the Third Foreign Ministers' Conference became the crucible in which the viability of the much ballyhooed Good Neighbor Policy would be tested.

Long before the conference opened on January 15, Welles concluded that the unwavering support of Brazil was essential if the United States was to attain a diplomatic success. But, from the commencement of the proceedings, Getúlio Vargas began transmitting confusing signals. On the sixteenth, the Brazilian leader declared himself completely behind the United States,[3] but the following day, he complained loudly of his nation's military weakness and Washington's failure to supply the promised arms. Brazil "would not be treated as a small Central American power," Vargas warned, and Welles quickly demonstrated that he got the message. Acting with unusual dispatch, FDR cabled Vargas on January 19 that "the flow of material will start at once."[4] This difficulty overcome, Welles believed he could count on Brazilian support. Alas, he was not expecting the events which would take place in the afternoon of January 23.

Several days previously, pressure on the Argentine Delegation had become so intense that Foreign Minister Enrique Ruíz Guiñazú, whom Welles castigated as "one of the stupidest men to hold [that] office,"[5] offered to telegraph his chancellery and request new instructions. This move by the Argentine diplomat may have been merely a diplomatic ploy, because Acting President Castillo's reply was mulishly inflexible.[6] This telegram, received on the morning of January 23, declared that Argentina would accept no resolution calling for a break in diplomatic relations with the Axis powers. Welles would either have to confront the Argentine challenge or allow Buenos Aires to dictate the nature of the final resolution.

But before the undersecretary could decide whether to sound the charge or truckle before Argentine obstinance, Getúlio Vargas pulled the rug out from under his feet. On January 18, Vargas had told Welles privately that Brazil's decision to stand with the United States "implied inevitably that she would soon be actually at war."[7] Five days later, Vargas was insisting that although he was still Uncle Sam's loyal supporter, pressure from worried Brazilian generals had forced an agonizing reappraisal of the situation.[8] The promised arms had not yet arrived, and since support for U.S. conference aims would result in tension with Argentina, the security of southern Brazil would be endangered. Clearly backpedaling from his previous position, Vargas indicated that he hoped that Welles would make every effort to avoid a showdown and resultant crisis.[9]

As a skilled interpreter of diplomatic nuance, Sumner Welles had no trouble interpreting the Brazilian president's implications. If he persisted in demanding a resolution that required all the Latin American states to sever diplomatic relations with the Axis, he would do so without Brazilian support. But, if Welles acquiesced to Argentine intransigence he would violate the spirit and, most likely, the letter of his diplomatic instructions. Claiming that the inter-American consultative system would have been destroyed had he executed his original orders, Welles held his nose and accepted an innocuous Argentine-sponsored resolution which merely recommended the rupture of diplomatic relations.[10]

As for President Vargas, he continued to vacillate, apparently intending to maintain diplomatic relations with the Axis. But Foreign Minister Oswaldo Aranha would have none of this. Arguing that he had pledged his word to Roosevelt in early January 1942, the foreign minister threatened to resign unless Vargas supported his policy.[11] Thus, on the evening of

January 28, 1942, Brazil severed relations with the Axis, but Vargas made sure that the United States recognized that his action bore a price tag. Exactly forty-eight hours later, Finance Minister Artur Costa Souza was bundled off to Washington, his mission being "the procurement of [the] necessary armament."[12]

The lend-lease pact with Brazil signed on October 1, 1941, called for the delivery of $100 million in military goods and equipment. In addition to requesting the immediate dispatch of tanks and antiaircraft guns, Costa Souza made it clear that his president believed that his loyalty had been undervalued; in other words, the entire contract would have to be renegotiated. Secretary of State Hull and the U.S. Army consultants considered these Brazilian demands both brazen and exorbitant, but Sumner Welles thought otherwise, and he had Roosevelt's ear. In the undersecretary's opinion, "We cannot afford to treat Brazil any longer as the War Department has been treating her now that she is coming into the war on our side."[13]

The agreement signed on March 3, 1942, doubled the lend-lease package to $200 million and provided that part of New York City's antiaircraft defense system be shipped to Rio de Janeiro between March 7 and 30, 1942.[14] Perhaps the most amazing aspect of this renegotiation is that these arrangements were made even though U.S. Army field commanders were screaming for more antiaircraft equipment. Needless to say, in March 1942, the chances of a German bombing attack on Rio de Janeiro were, at best, exceedingly remote.

Ultimately, the issue was that in the arms-for-policy support game, Uncle Sam had to pay or else run the risk of Brazil adopting a more neutral policy. Given the crucial importance of the airfields being completed in the northeastern part of that country, this was a gamble not worth taking. Vargas apparently concluded during the Third Foreign Ministers' Conference that he could once again utilize his country's strategic position in order to extract from the North Americans the additional weapons he wanted. As a result of the canny manipulation of his options, the Brazilian army would emerge as the most powerful military establishment in Latin America.

Naturally, Washington expected some conspicuous examples of collaboration in exchange for its favors, and there is evidence that an expanded and more comprehensive counterespionage policy was a quid pro quo. On March 5, 1942, two days after the revised lend-lease treaty was signed, Welles wrote a short memorandum to Adolf Berle which expressed the belief that "the new lend-lease agreement will certainly encourage stronger action ... against the [German] espionage rings."[15]

Actually, Brazil had already taken forceful action aimed at curtailing Abwehr activity. At the suggestion of the United States, Oswaldo Aranha had prevented the January 30, 1942, departure for Buenos Aires of Maj. Gen. Günther Niedenführ, German military attaché assigned to Brazil and Argentina. The foreign minister's feeble and highly legalistic excuse for refusing an exit visa was correctly interpreted by the Germans as being

U.S.-influenced.[16] Indeed, with Niedenführ both stranded and under surveillance, it became impossible for the military attaché to assist those agents in Brazil (especially Schlegel and Gamillscheg) who depended on him. By incapacitating a key agent, U.S. policy makers hoped to disorient the entire Abwehr organization in South America.

Undoubtedly, Welles and Roosevelt were gratified by Brazilian cooperation in the Niedenführ affair, but a 100 percent increase in military funding was expected to buy more accommodation than that. Three days after the new lend-lease agreement was signed, Ambassador Caffery brazenly requested that the Vargas government actually arrest German ambassador Kurt Prüfer, Major General Niedenführ, and Press Attaché Walter von Cossel on espionage charges.[17] From intercepted radio messages, the SIS/Brazil and the State Department knew that Prüfer and Niedenführ were deeply involved in Abwehr activities, but why Cossel was included on this diplomatic hit list remains inexplicable.[18]

Normally, when a diplomatic official is accused of espionage activities, he is declared *persona non grata*, given his passport, and ordered to leave the country. Moreover, in the spring of 1942, the Germans again held the military initiative in Russia and North Africa, and their U-boats were running amuck in the Atlantic. With justification, the Nazis could have considered the proposed arrests as violations of diplomatic immunity, retaliated against the Brazilian diplomatic staff still in Germany, or even claimed that Prüfer's arrest was grounds for a declaration of war. It is not surprising, then, that Minister of Justice Francisco Campos judged the U.S. proposal legally indefensible and refused to have anything to do with it. In addition, Maj. Felinto Muller, chief of police in the Federal District, threatened to resign if ordered to carry out the arrests. These two responses were enough; assuming he ever gave the plan serious consideration, Vargas now had sufficient excuse to reject it outright.[19]

But, the lucky Vargas never realized how fortunate he actually was. The fact is that the U.S. proposal and Muller's threatened resignation were all known in Berlin even while they were being discussed in Rio de Janeiro. Evidence is lacking concerning the source of the leak, but the finger of suspicion points toward Muller, the police chief having been identified by Ambassador Prüfer as an informant of General Niedenführ.[20] If the previous episodes imply that the Abwehr operatives in Brazil were generally zealous incompetents, this particular incident is incontestable proof that the V-men could and did occasionally gain access to truly sensitive information.

Perhaps Washington was disappointed with Vargas's refusal to make the desired arrests, but the Brazilian dictator soon found other ways to satisfy his arms supplier. On March 9, 1942, permission was granted for Robert Linx, an FCC-RID official, to establish a U.S.-controlled radio monitoring unit on Brazilian soil.[21] A week later, Jack West drew up a list of eighty-four to eighty-seven spies to be arrested and gave it to Third Secretary Elim O'Shaughnessy,[22] and between March 18 and 20, 1942, DOPS in the Federal District went into action. It was the first major

roundup of Abwehr agents in Latin America, and it was also further
evidence that Getúlio Vargas's support and cooperation was directly
related to every bullet, tank, and gun the new lend-lease agreement
provided.

The acid test of U.S.-Brazilian collegiality, however, would come only
after some fifty alleged spies were behind bars. Brazilian law provided no
penalty for espionage activities conducted while the country was not at
war. Nevertheless, the SIS/Brazil and the embassy, despite the paucity of
proofs submitted and the influence of powerful personalities, ". . . managed to exert sufficient counterpressure to keep the individuals incarcerated. . . ."[23]

But Ambassador Caffery and Jack West were still worried about
Filinto Muller's "pro-German sympathies" and "lack of enthusiasm" in
ferreting out fugitive agents.[24] The Federal District chief of police was too
well ensconced, however, for Yankee machinations to accomplish his
removal unaided. Luckily, though, angry quarrels, first with Oswaldo
Aranha, and later with the acting minister of justice, Vasco Leitão da
Cunha, greased the skids. As part of a major cabinet shuffle, on July 17,
1942, Muller was removed, and then kicked upstairs to a position on the
staff of Minister of War Gen. Eurico Gaspar Dutra.[25] Six days later, Col.
Alcides Etchegoyen replaced Muller as commander of all police forces in
the Federal District. The new chief promptly informed U.S. embassy
officials that, for the time being, he was going to leave the spy hunting to
SIS/Brazil operatives.[26] Thus, a bit of good luck, patience, and some
indirect pressure resulted in the departure of a troublesome police
official and a free hand for the SIS/Brazil.

All these events transpired against a background of steadily increasing U-boat attacks on Brazilian shipping. Between February 15 and May
18, 1942, seven Brazilian merchantmen were torpedoed and sunk. Then
on May 19, the German Naval High Command informed Foreign Minister
Ribbentrop that it was initiating unrestricted warfare in Brazilian coastal
waters.[27] During the next ninety days, a dozen more vessels were destroyed as a result of U-boat attacks. This continuing sea slaughter in-
flamed Brazilian public opinion, and Vargas found himself in the fateful
position he had hypothesized for Sumner Welles on January 18, 1942:
facing war with Germany. With the Nazis having fired what was deemed
to be the first shot, the portly president could announce, on August 22,
and without trepidation, that a "state of belligerency" existed between
the United States of Brazil and the Third Reich.[28]

II. The Twilight of the Abwehr Networks

A. The Disillusioned

During the last week of November 1941, both Albrecht Engels and
Maj. Gen. Günther Niedenführ criticized Theodor Schlegel ("Salama"),
with Niedenführ adding snide comments about what he believed to be
Schlegel's sexual preference. Though forced to suffer these blows in

silence, Theodor Schlegel retaliated by becoming the first V-man in Brazil to quit Abwehr service. But six months later, he told police that "the [radio] station was operated by the free will of the deponent [Schlegel] . . . and not under the express orders from Germany, for which reasons transmissions could cease or begin again whenever the deponent deemed it desirable."[29]

Initially, the chance of disengaging with honor seemed distinctly possible. For some months, radioman Rolf Trautmann had been complaining that the increasing number of transmissions from clandestine radios in the Rio de Janeiro area was bound to generate a counterintelligence reaction. If a crackdown occurred, broadcasting from Karl Thielen's home would definitely become a dangerous proposition. Atmospheric conditions during the first two weeks of December 1941 made transmitting to Germany virtually impossible,[30] and they also provided the perfect excuse for going off the air and moving the transmitter elsewhere. Earlier, Schlegel had struck a bargain with Klaus von Dellinghausen, a *Reichsdeutscher* businessman and colleague in the iron and steel trade, that if ever it became necessary to move the transmitter, it could be taken to a farm controlled by Dellinghausen. "Salama" decided that the time had come, and on December 12, 1941, Trautmann removed "Carola" from the Thielen home and departed for Dellinghausen's farm approximately 250 miles northwest of the capital city.[31]

Schlegel would later justify his action as being a security step, and the course of events would initially make him appear eminently wise, for on December 18, 1941, Erwin Backhaus, his agent in Recife, was arrested by the local DOPS. Since October, Backhaus had mailed Schlegel several mediocre reports on shipping movements in that port city, but the quality of these communications had little effect upon Backhaus's burgeoning sense of his own importance. He bragged of his secret work for the Reich in the local German community, and word of his patriotic exploits eventually reached the ears of the police.[32] Backhaus thereby attained the dubious distinction of being the first operational V-man arrested in Brazil, but his detention proved temporary. Either he convinced his interrogators that his clandestine missions were purely fictitious, or DOPS decided that an espionage arrest was then politically imprudent. Whatever the reason, on December 23, Erwin Backhaus was released and sent to his home.

Meanwhile, the German consulate in Recife learned of the jailing and flashed the news to the embassy in Rio. Schlegel was informed the same day Backhaus was arrested, and panicked. With "Carola" disconnected, he contacted Nest Cologne via CEL, and on the evening of December 18, urgently requested "the emergency code key."[33] Schlegel was convinced that Backhaus would talk freely, and that eventuality suggested that his own arrest was imminent. His directors at Nest Cologne apparently drew similar conclusions for on December 26, 1941, they ordered "Salama" via ALD to make a full report on recent events, and added that if his position became untenable, he was to withdraw to the west, but only after holding out for as long as possible.[34]

Schlegel preferred to believe that the December 26 message from Nest Cologne justified completing the disengagement process upon which he was already embarked. Not surprisingly, Hermann Bohny had a different interpretation of what the December 26 message sanctioned and the kind of response the situation now required. On December 30, 1941, the naval attaché called Schlegel to the embassy where a confrontation ensued. Undoubtedly Bohny suspected something, because he demanded the report requested by Nest Cologne and insisted that Schlegel explain why "Carola" had been inactive for a month. After a half-hearted attempt at evasion, Schlegel declared that since Backhaus may have talked, he (Schlegel) believed that he should withdraw from active Abwehr service. In response, the naval attaché noted that the charges against Backhaus were unproven, and he insisted that Schlegel present his special report for Nest Cologne posthaste.[35]

If nothing else, the verbal exchange with Bohny made it evident to Schlegel that getting out of the Abwehr with honor was not going to be easy. That he was still determined to do so, however, is evident from a January 2, 1942, message which was transmitted to Nest Cologne via CEL. Again, Schlegel castigated Backhaus for compromising his secret identity, but intimated that it might still be possible for him to serve in some minor capacity. Lastly, he assured Nest Cologne that "Carola" would soon be reactivated.[36]

The final episode in the story of the "Salama" ring began on January 5, 1942, when Benno Sobisch arrived at the Dellinghausen farm in the state of Minas Gerais with an electronics expert named Gustav Edward Utzinger (in reality, an SD agent named Wolf Franczok) and over fifteen hundred pounds of equipment. Sobisch had transported by train a transmitter, two receivers, six large batteries, and the parts for a dynamo. Since he was certain that the farm lacked sufficient electric current to power the transmitter, he brought Utzinger along to assemble the dynamo and get it functioning. Utzinger accomplished this in forty-eight hours and promptly returned to Rio.

It was now up to Sobisch and Trautmann to get "Carola" on the air. For over three weeks they strove diligently, but without success. Sobisch finally decided that the iron ore deposits in the surrounding mountains made sending and receiving impossible. Disgusted and convinced that no transmitter could be made to function on the Dellinghausen farm, on January 30, 1942, Sobisch left the place. Sixteen days later, during the Rio de Janeiro carnival celebration, he suffered a sudden heart attack and died.[37]

Schlegel had hoped to withdraw honorably, but after Sobisch quit the Dellinghausen farm, he decided to effect his disengagement by any means available. The most persuasive evidence for this conclusion is the several messages forwarded to Nest Cologne between February 14 and

March 8, 1942, via Friedrich Kempter's LIR. The first of these affirmed that "despite [a] change in climate [i.e., location] 'Carola' is again in danger." Establishment of a new transmission base was declared impossible for at least three weeks. A second message sent on February 19 called for Nest Cologne "to listen for 'Carola' daily starting March 1," gave the station's new call letters as ZEP, and asked that Cologne use KLN. Finally, on March 8, a cryptic report sent via CEL noted that "we are trying again to lodge 'Carola' elsewhere."[38]

The tendentious nature of these communications is obvious because after Sobisch returned to Rio de Janeiro, Trautmann buried "Carola" and entrained for the federal capital on February 8. In fact, the entire time that "Salama" was exhorting Nest Cologne to listen for "Carola's" signal, the transmitter was buried in the soil of the Dellinghausen farm. Following Rolf Trautmann's return to Rio de Janeiro, Schlegel offered the former radioman fifty dollars a month to keep an eye on "Carola" and his mouth shut—for the duration of the war. The offer was acceped, and on February 17, Trautmann again departed for the Minas Gerais property.[39]

Schlegel's determination to put an end to his intelligence career was a wise decision, but it came too late. Back in September 1941, the SIS/Brazil noted his return from Germany and thereafter he was under surveillance.[40] The 1941 radio messages sent by Trautmann were intercepted by RID, decoded by the FBI Laboratory, and since these were signed either "Schlegel" or "Salama," SIS/Brazil had no trouble identifying their man.[41] Lastly, Sobisch's journey to the Dellinghausen farm with nearly a ton of equipment had not gone unnoticed. Between the second week of February and the end of March 1942, DOPS in the state of Minas Gerais searched the place several times looking for the buried equipment which Trautmann was guarding.[42]

Thus, "Salama's" February 14, 1942, message had been correct: "Carola" was in danger. But by that time Schlegel had become, for all practical purposes, a counterfeit spy. Unfortunately for him, he would not end up in a counterfeit jail.

B. *The Determined*

With the development of the Cold War, the popular reading public has been both titillated and terrified by tales of ruthless special agents whose primary task is the merciless liquidation of designated adversaries. In contrast, the cloak-and-dagger struggle in Brazil in 1941–42 was remarkably free of bloodshed. Indeed, the only example of an assault on a spy with a deadly weapon was the "attack" on Friedrich Kempter ("King") on January 31, 1942. As he told the story, at 10:00 P.M., he was sitting in his living room reading a magazine when "a gun was heard to go off and the bullet passed right by my forehead, lodging in the wall." Kempter did not know who fired at him, but he blamed the British Security Coordination for the presumed attempt on his life.[43]

Checking this story against other sources of information reveals that the truth is more fantastic than Kempter imagined. There definitely was a shot fired on the night of January 31, 1942, but it was not the work of either the BSC or someone who was determined to eliminate Kempter. The gun was actually fired by Maj. Filinto Muller, the erstwhile chief of police in the Federal District. He and Kempter were good friends, with the policeman being well aware of the intelligence activities of the latter. On the night in question, either BSC or SIS/Brazil agents were watching Kempter's home hoping to catch him in the act of transmitting. Muller fired the shot as a warning in order to make sure that on this occasion, "King" stayed off the air.[44]

This incident also tends to emphasize the increasing problems besetting the Kempter ring. In September 1941, "King" told his Buenos Aires subordinate, Ottomar Müller ("Otis"), that the Abwehr wanted him to set up a radio transmitter. "Otis" hadn't the faintest idea of how to accomplish this, and his fumbling efforts to buy equipment were rebuffed by suspicious suppliers. Unwilling to admit his failure, Müller simply made excuses. When, in October, Ast Hamburg radioed its suspicion that British intelligence had "Otis" under surveillance, Kempter decided that he was free to take drastic action. On the twenty-fifth of the month, he told "Otis" to cease activity immediately and turn over all equipment and records to his assistant, Hans Napp ("Berko"). "Otis" was to become inactive, with Napp taking charge of the ship reporting work which Kempter wanted continued.[45]

The new arrangement was communicated to Ast Hamburg on November 14, 1941, but it lasted less than three months. On January 27, 1942, Kempter wrote Napp that all contact between the two must cease immediately. LATI, the Italian airline, was already defunct, and Condor, the German-controlled line, was in jeopardy; sending airmail letters via Pan American or some other non-Axis airline was considered too risky. "Berko" was instructed that, henceforth, his information was to be taken to Capt. Dietrich Niebuhr (code name: Diego), naval attaché at the Germany embassy in Buenos Aires.[46] This change in the routing of data took place smoothly enough, but it left "King" short of informants on Anglo-American shipping in Argentine waters.

The reduction in the scope of ring reportage was compounded because at roughly the same time, Kempter also lost the services of the western wing of his organization. Walter Giese ("Griffin") had been declared *persona non grata* by the Ecuadorian government on September 5, 1941. Giese had friends among the country's elite, and for four months he successfully fought this executive order. Finally, the Arroyo del Río regime presented him with two alternatives: He could depart immediately or face internment as a dangerous alien. On January 6, 1942, Giese left Ecuador and, after sojourns in Chile and Argentina, set sail in April for Europe. His partner in espionage, Heinrich Loerchner ("Lorenz"), continued sending reports of Pacific Coast sailings and mineral shipments for another month. But since Ecuador had broken relations with Germany on January 29, 1942, the inevitable roundup of *Reichsdeutschen* soon included Loerchner as well. Interned in March 1942, he was shipped to the United States as part of a U.S.-Ecuadorian program for the detention and interrogation of dangerous enemy aliens. Never officially charged with being an Abwehr operative, "Lorenz" nevertheless sat out the war in a North Carolina internment camp.[47]

In addition to the loss of these Argentine and Ecuadorian ring members, the Recife observation post was also shut down. On January 6, 1942, "King" received his last shipping report from Carlos Fink ("Star"). A known Nazi sympathizer, Fink was an obvious target once the local DOPS officials, anticipating Brazil's break with Germany, began arresting suspicious *Reichsdeutschen*. On January 27, 1942, Fink was jailed and questioned closely for several hours. He confessed to being an Abwehr agent, but the governor of the state of Pernambuco, Agammenon Magalhães, a known Integralista, suppressed the confession.[48] Kempter did not learn of this event, for in answer to a February 14, 1942, query, he told Ast Hamburg that "connections with 'Star' [are] broken off, reason unknown."[49] In short, another arm of the Kempter organization had been lopped off.

As if the gradual collapse of this carefully constructed network was not trouble enough, Kempter soon found himself at odds with Albrecht Gustav Engels ("Alfredo"). On January 30, 1942, because money could no longer be sent via Banco Transatlántico, Ast Hamburg radioed Kempter that a messenger identifying himself as "Max" would soon deliver seventy-five hundred dollars. Two weeks passed, and with his funds running low, Kempter fired off several angry messages to his superiors, even asking that "Alfredo" be authorized to lend him the needed money. On February 22, Engels gave Kempter twenty-five hundred dollars, but the latter complained that a minimum of five thousand dollars more was needed.[50]

Ast Hamburg apparently made some pointed inquiries about "Alfredo's" payment policies, because on March 4, 1942, the CEL boss shot off a testy retort denouncing Kempter as an ingrate and "a pain in the head."[51] What remained unexplained was why Engels, who had the money, waited so long to pay Kempter.

In two years, Kempter had come full circle. In March 1940, he had been a veritable one-man spy ring supplying Ast Hamburg with reports of shipping movements in Rio de Janeiro harbor. In the summer of 1941, he was the linchpin in a transcontinental network providing a multiplicity of services via the FMK "Brazil" radio circuit. By March 1942, Kempter was once again reduced to reporting shipping movements in Rio de Janeiro harbor.

Grimly sardonic is the fact that it was his transmitter, the instrument which made him so valuable, that was also the cause of his undoing. In June 1941, the FBI laboratory began decoding LIR-MAX messages.[52] As fate would have it, this was the same month in which Engels, possibly for competitive reasons, denounced Kempter as a security risk. In refuting these charges, Kempter radioed Ast Hamburg information on his background, general habits and activities. On June 19, 1941, his controller, naval Lt. Comm. Andre von Wettstein, replied that "on the basis of your performance to the present, I have never doubted you."[53] Ast Hamburg had decided that "King" was not a security risk; yet with the RID intercepting these messages, and the FBI laboratory decoding them, that is exactly what Kempter had become.

C. *The Demented*

Euripides once wrote: "Those whom the gods would destroy, they first make mad." By March 1942, Josef Starziczny, known as "Niels Christiansen" to his mistress and "Lucas" to Ast Kiel and Ast Hamburg, had traveled a considerable distance down the road toward mental derangement. Quarrels over money and the meddling of his mistress, Ondina Batista Peixoto de Oliveira, had caused "Lucas" to lose both his broadcasting base and the services of his trusted lieutenants, Karl Muegge and Albert Schwab. Not until January 16, 1942, would "Lucas," transmitting from his own house, reestablish contact with Ast Hamburg.[54]

Meanwhile, his chronic need for funds made Starziczny increasingly desperate, and gave his enemies the means to bring him to heel. On January 15, 1942, the alienated Albert Schwab told him that Hermann Bohny wanted to see him immediately. The two men met that evening and the naval attaché wasted no time; he offered Starziczny two thousand dollars to get rid of his mistress. Bohny proclaimed himself convinced that Senhorita de Oliveira was a member of British intelligence,[55] and either she went or Starziczny would be fired. Starziczny, however, could not be swayed by either threats or blandishments; the meeting ended on a hostile note.

Nevertheless, he must have had second thoughts about his stance, because the following day, when he radioed Ast Hamburg and asked for money, he was told that either Otto Uebele ("Kuntze") or Bohny would take care of his financial needs. In light of his most recent disagreement with the naval attaché, "Lucas" could be fairly certain that Hermann Bohny would not be generous. This situation made him doubly dependent upon his co-chief, Otto Uebele.

A terse message from Ast Hamburg on January 17, 1942, assured "Lucas" that Uebele would pay him $1,000 a month or more, 30 percent of which was for personal expenses and 70 percent for organizational costs. "Kuntze" had already arranged to pay the sum of $1,050 through Georg Metzner in Rio, but when, on January 27, Starziczny visited this middleman, he was given only $800. Without telling Uebele, Metzner subtracted $250 from the intended payment, money still owed for the new Oldsmobile that Starziczny had purchased in July 1941. The financial juggling provoked angry denunciations from the surprised recipient, but Metzner retorted that Starziczny's cavalier attitude toward time payments could no longer be tolerated. The two men parted in anger, with "Lucas" especially rueful of the fact that in one month's time, he would have to go to Metzner once again.[56]

Starziczny's belief that he was being persecuted was reinforced by events transpiring in February 1942. On February 2, Otto Uebele had advised his co-leader that due to increased counterespionage activity, it was time for "Lucas" to destroy his code, bury his transmitter, and go into hiding.[57] During that same week, Bohny and Engels offered to buy "Lucas's" code and transmitter. Starziczny refused, but on February 13, he received an unexpected visit from Mr. and Mrs. Georg Metzner. "Lucas" assumed that this unannounced social call was, in reality, Otto Uebele's method for checking on him. But, later in the evening, Starziczny "surprised Mrs. Metzner in his kitchen ... he saw that she had a small bottle containing a white liquid which he suspected was poison, and [he believed] that ... Mrs. Metzner [was] trying to poison his food."[58] Before coming to Brazil, "Lucas" was told by his friend and co-controller, Lieutenant Colonel Trautmann, that the Gestapo had perfected a poison which took effect eight hours after ingestion, and left no trace. Starziczny was convinced that he was marked for murder, but who ordered the assassination? Was it Otto Uebele, Hermann Bohny, or both?

On February 17, two days after this unsettling visit, Starziczny received another shock when he heard that Benno Sobisch had died suddenly of a heart attack. The deceased was known to have a loose tongue when inebriated, and Starziczny suspected that Sobisch had been murdered by Muegge, Schwab, or Georg Metzner. In fact, Sobisch died of natural causes,[59] but after the kitchen incident, Starziczny believed that he had become dependent for his pay upon a man who was planning to murder him.

In the end, though, it was not Starziczny's torrid romance and profligate spending which proved to be his undoing; rather, it was a silly mistake. Since late September 1941, both Otto and Hans Ulrich Uebele had been prodding Starziczny to complete installation of a transmitting station near Santos. The radioman had procrastinated, a contingency which did nothing to improve his relationship with his Santos-based allies. On December 12, 1941, Starziczny was called to that city and after some desultory discussion with the Uebeles, he decided that a wavemeter was needed to determine why the transmitter would not function. On the fifteenth of the month, Starziczny went to a radio equipment shop in São Paulo co-owned by Juvenal Sayão to purchase the needed equipment. He was told that there was no wavemeter in stock, but one could be ordered if the purchaser left an address. Starziczny wrote on a piece of paper, "O. Mendes, Hotel Santos, Santos."

A team of psychiatrists would have had a field day trying to determine why Starziczny pulled this name out of the hat. "Mendes" was one of the code names used by Hans Ulrich Uebele, and "O," perhaps, was for "Otto," the first name of the elder Uebele. What aroused Juvenal Sayão's suspicions, however, was the fact that Starziczny could not speak Portuguese. The conversation had to be conducted in English, and the store-keeper considered it inconceivable that a person with a Portuguese surname could not speak the language. Moreover, the attack on Pearl Harbor had just occurred, and the police were asking dealers to report all radio equipment sales made to suspicious persons. Sayão promptly tele-phoned DOPS headquarters in São Paulo, and reported that "a person who spoke English with a German accent" had attempted to buy a wavemeter. Inquiries to the Hotel Santos revealed that no "O. Mendes" was regis-tered. DOPS headquarters placed agent Elpídio Reali in charge of the investigation, and Juvenal Sayão was ordered to inform him if "O. Mendes" ever returned.

Interestingly enough, when Starziczny reported his radio shop deba-cle to his Santos colleagues, initially it generated little concern. But when the Uebeles learned, through police contacts, that the "O. Mendes" incident had sparked a DOPS investigation, their apprehension mounted. This was the principal reason why, on February 2, Uebele had urged Starziczny to cease his broadcast activities and drop out of sight.

But, if Uebele was concerned about network security, he should have started with his son, because it was Hans Ulrich Uebele who compounded Starziczny's blunder. Deciding that the police had forgotten about "O. Mendes," he telephoned Domingo Squarzi, a Santos radio equipment dealer, on February 15, 1942, and offered to pay fifty dollars for a wavemeter. Squarzi did not have one, but in order to make the sale, he telephoned his fellow dealer, Juvenal Sayão, in São Paulo. Sayão promptly contacted Elpídio Reali, who immediately went to Santos. Squarzi was questioned and although he did not know "O. Mendes," his sales records revealed that a radio transmitter had been sold to the Theodor Wille Company branch in Santos in August 1941. Further inves-tigation of state licensing records demonstrated that the Theodor Wille Company had never requested a license to operate a radio. The conclu-sion was obvious: The transmitter was destined for clandestine operation.

Three weeks later, on March 5, 1942, DOPS went into action. Squarzi was arrested, as were all his companions, in a determined effort to prevent news of his incarceration from leaking out. Since interrogation by DOPS could be both mentally and physically debilitating, Squarzi chose not to be discreet; he quickly fingered Hans Ulrich Uebele as the man who bought the transmitter and ordered the wavemeter.

The hunt now entered its final stage. That same day, DOPS arrested Hans Uebele and, on March 6, he was brought to São Paulo for intensive interrogation. Initially evasive, the younger Uebele finally acknowledged that he had given the transmitter to Gerhard Schroeder to hide. The arrest of Schroeder and five other network operatives swiftly followed before the sought-after transmitter was found in the home of Severino Jovino Bento, a former Integralista who worked for the city government of Santos. But Juvenal Sayão advised that none of those arrested was the mysterious "O. Mendes," and so on March 7, DOPS returned to the task of loosening Hans Uebele's tongue. The younger Uebele stopped short of fingering Starziczny, but he did identify "O. Mendes" as an important German engineer who specialized in gas generators.

On the same day Reali and a squad of DOPS agents went to Hans Uebele's office at the Theodor Wille Company branch in Santos. There, in a folder marked "Gas Generators," he found several letters signed "N. Christensen [sic], Civil Engineer, Rua Campos da Carvalho #318, Leblon [District], Telephone 45-01-47, Rio de Janeiro."[60] Thirty-five years later, we discussed these events with the retired Elpídio Reali, and inquired as to his explanation for his success. His laconic reply was, "Luck."[61]

Certainly the younger Uebele's blunder spelled *finis* for the "Lucas"-"Kuntze" ring, but Starziczny's actions provided him with no excuse for recrimination. He had been told to bury his transmitter, to destroy his codes and papers, and to drop out of sight. Instead, on February 13, 1942, he rented a safe deposit box at the Banco do Credito Mercantil and stored his records and documents there. Why did Starziczny act so imprudently? Among other things, he was a vain man, and he apparently hoped to maintain his records as proof of his outstanding service to the Reich.[62] His actions also seem to have been prompted by a more pragmatic motive. Convinced that the Gestapo was going to make him pay for his lies, distortions, and tempestuous love affair, Starziczny made his records his best defense. Let Himmler's blackguards or anyone else attempt to liquidate him or his mistress, and the Abwehr organization in Brazil would be blown sky-high. Moreover, if the SIS/Brazil or BSC got to him first, the same documents might be his ticket to preferential treatment.

D. *The Defiant*

On January 30, 1942, Frank Walter Jordan warned Germany "that [the] police shall seize all [the] radio sets of Axis agents." Believing himself to be shadowed, the voice of LFS reported that transmissions would be terminated "until the spy complex has blown over." The next message radioed on February 17, 1942, stated that "the mail [is] unsafe; please don't use obvious code key."[63] Jordan was probably guessing. But on March 6, after sending a ship movement report to the Ast Hamburg radio station, he removed his transmitter and receiver from Afonso Diegeser's home. Shortly thereafter, he buried them in the basement of a house owned by Hugo Fleischer, Diegeser's friend and business partner. Convinced that his arrest was imminent,[64] Jordan acted as Starziczny should have by attempting to drop out of sight. Jordan hoped to avoid detention and start broadcasting once circumstances were again fortuitous.

The determination to serve effectively at whatever personal cost was also evinced by Albrecht Gustav Engels and the members of the ring which he and Hermann Bohny had assembled. Indeed, while other Abwehr units in Brazil were disintegrating or shrinking in size due to increased surveillance, the "Alfredo"-Bohny organization was actually expanding. New recruits for the ring included Ellemer Nagy and Jofre

Magalhães dos Santos, castoffs of Janos Salamon's defunct HTT group. Both men talked to Gustav Glock, German embassy secretary, who referred them to Herbert von Heyer ("Humberto"). The latter instructed Nagy to keep the HTT transmitter to serve as a back-up instrument. Meanwhile, on January 29, 1942, Magalhães dos Santos met with "Humberto" and "Alfredo." Heyer was not happy with the work of Hans Sievers and wanted someone in Recife who would be more active. Magalhães dos Santos took the job, received some brief instruction in the use of secret inks, and twenty-one hundred dollars. In February, he departed for Recife, but Heyer never received any reports from him. For Magalhães dos Santos, the espionage game was simply a fast way of making money.[65]

Another Brazilian the Engels-Bohny group claimed to have recruited after January 28, 1942, was Sylvio Romero, Jr., son of a famous littérateur and a retired diplomat,[66] but the most fascinating inductee was an army captain, Tulio Regis do Nascimento. Born in 1908, do Nascimento followed in his father's footsteps, and entered the Brazilian military. Commissioned as a second lieutenant in 1928, he fell ill that same year, suffering from tertiary syphilis and an excessive dependency on drugs. After he was married in 1934, his drug addiction resurfaced, and the doctors diagnosed him as suffering from "psychic manifestations of depression"; not surprisingly, the marriage lasted less than a year.

Committed to an army hospital, do Nascimento recovered sufficiently to be posted to a coastal artillery unit in 1936. During the next four years, he became an aviator, a director of a factory which made artillery fire control units, and was promoted to captain. Seemingly on his way to success, in 1941 he entered the Brazilian Army Technical School, only to have psychological problems lay him low again. On December 5, 1941, Army medics diagnosed do Nascimento as suffering from mental exhaustion and assorted psychoneuroses. They prescribed sixty days of treatment, pronounced the captain "able to travel," and placed him on leave, at least until he completed his treatment.[67]

Given the medical history of Captain do Nascimento, it is unlikely he could have remained in the Brazilian army without the intervention of his father, a respected colonel. But the Brazilian army was not the only organization to turn a blind eye toward the captain's physical and psychological infirmities. Because he was a pro-Axis sympathizer, in late December 1941 or early in January 1942, do Nascimento queried his close friend and German embassy counselor Walther Becker about Abwehr service. He offered to organize an all-Brazilian ship reporting service in Rio de Janeiro, so Becker turned do Nascimento over to Hermann Bohny. It was this spymaster who assigned do Nascimento the code name "Captain García" and put him in contact with Engels. As we have seen, the naval attaché was becoming increasingly pessimistic concerning the survival of the FMKs operating in Brazil. He viewed "Captain García" as the director of an all-Brazilian spy network which would eventually become an independent operation.[68]

Meanwhile, the rupture in Brazilian-German relations on January 28, 1942, served to make the CEL-ALD link even more critical. Bohny, Niedenführ, and Ambassador Kurt Prüfer had been moved to the city of Petrópolis where they were supposed to be kept under close confinement. In fact, German embassy personnel maintained contact with Berlin via Engels's clandestine radio. So heavy did this traffic become that in an effort to prevent the CEL transmitter from remaining on the air too long, Heyer utilized Kempter's radio from January 25 to February 23 to assist in the transmitting work.[69]

In keeping with its increased intelligence importance, the Engels-Bohny group also became the primary recipient of new Abwehr operational funds. In two separate payments during January 1942, over seventy-two thousand dollars in assorted currencies were delivered to Engels by Bohny and Capt. Dietrich Niebuhr, the naval attaché in Buenos Aires.[70] After diplomatic relations were broken, embassy secretary Gustav Glock shifted over to the Spanish embassy, where he acted as liaison for *Reichsdeutschen* in Brazil. He also served as secret contact man for "Alfredo," issuing funds being held by the new keeper of the financial reserve, Walther Becker.[71] With over seventy-two thousand dollars in new funds, and with Kempter and Starziczny increasingly dependent upon him for financial support, Albrecht Gustav Engels had finally become de facto controller of the Abwehr in Brazil. Unfortunately for him, he would have little time to savor his triumph.

III. The Roll-Up Commences

A. *Jack West's Gambit*

Since March 1941, Brazilian FMKs had transmitted hundreds of messages to Germany similar to this one:

> #59 MK Argentina Reports on December 30 (1941) via FMK Brazil:
> December 25 - in Buenos Aires from England: English refrigerator
>   ship, *Viking Star*—6445 tons
> December 26 - in Buenos Aires from Cardiff: English steamer, *Salter-
>   gate*—3940 tons
> December 26 - leaving Buenos Aires en route for New York: Ameri-
>   can liner, *Brazil*—20,614 tons
> December 26 - leaving Buenos Aires for Rio (de Janeiro): Norwegian
>   steamer, *Scebeli*—3,025 tons[72]

Former naval captain Herbert Wichmann, commander of Ast Hamburg from 1939 to 1945, assured us that the Abwehr considered these reports valuable.[73] Nonetheless, until Hitler sanctioned U-boat attacks in the coastal waters of the Americas, the value of these messages remained theoretical rather than real. This circumstance changed when on January 16, 1942, the German navy launched Operation Paukenschlag (Drum Beat), a concentrated onslaught against merchant shipping along the U.S.

coast. This was followed by Operation Newland which extended the U-boat war into the Caribbean. In less than three months of methodical slaughter, German submarines sank more than one million tons of shipping.[74]

With these new developments in the U-boat war, the arrest of the Brazilian V-men became a necessity. Jack West's conclusion was that piecemeal action was useless; a hard, sweeping blow that would put all the FMKs off the air at once became SIS/Brazil's goal.[75] But despite increasingly open cooperation between Washington and Rio de Janeiro, the SIS/Brazil remained dependent upon the national police forces for the arrest of the German V-men. Unfortunately, many Brazilian police officials, like Filinto Muller, were either hostile or indifferent to the U.S. counterespionage effort.

Just as crucial, a number of DOPS chiefs were independently proceeding with investigations which were definitely in conflict with SIS/Brazil plans. Possibly the most significant of these was transpiring over fifteen hundred miles south of Rio de Janeiro in the city of Pôrto Alegre, where on January 29, 1942, DOPS chief Plinio Brunal Milano took Hans Kurt Meyer-Clason into custody. The scapegoat in the Immer microdot fiasco of August 1940, Meyer-Clason was denounced as a Nazi, a suspicious person, a useless playboy, and the son of a German general. Furthermore, after forty-eight hours of continuous interrogation, Plinio Milano obtained what he described as "a confession that delineated the work of the German High Command ... especially in Brazil."[76]

In light of SIS/Brazil's conclusion that Meyer-Clason had not been involved in Abwehr activities for almost sixteen months, the veracity of this conclusion was, to say the least, questionable. Thirty-six years later, Meyer-Clason, now a distinguished linguistic scholar, detailed for us how this deposition was obtained:

> Prisoner stands naked with outstretched arms, against the wall. As soon as [his] arms sink, [he receives] knee of interrogator into scrotum, stomach, kidneys ... burning cigarette into the flesh, fist into the face, until prisoner falls. Then injections until final fall.

Meyer-Clason also asserted that he was blindfolded when he signed his confession.[77]

Implicated by this confession was Eduard Arnold ("Argus"), the man who brought Meyer-Clason and Immer together back in 1940. Arnold had continued functioning as a drop for the Bohny-Engels network and had received additional messages from Immer. Plinio Milano was determined to pursue his investigation, and since DOPS in São Paulo was amenable, Arnold was arrested on February 27, 1942, and held incommunicado. Taken to Pôrto Alegre, he was confronted by Meyer-Clason, and after "three days of exhaustive interrogation," on March 5, 1942, Arnold signed a confession implicating himself, Engels, and Heyer.[78]

Meanwhile, Chief Fabio Conejo of the Recife DOPS had also become active. About February 20, he arrested the Bohny-Engels area informants,

Hans Sievert and Walter Grapentin. Five days later, these men were reputed to have confessed, and on March 5, Conejo sent a telegram to Filinto Muller asking the Federal District police chief to question Herbert von Heyer. Nothing was done regarding this request, or one from Plinio Milano to have Engels and Heyer extradited to Pôrto Alegre.[79] But since neither of these investigations was likely to produce the total radio blackout desired, Jack West and his aides had no interest in seeing them continued.

There did exist, on the other hand, one investigation which did have SIS/Brazil backing.[80] Elpídio Reali and Juvenal Sayão had arrived in Rio on March 8, 1942, and spent the next day working out arrangements with Captain Felisberto Teixeira, the head of the DOPS in the Federal District. Shortly after 8:00 A.M. on March 10, 1942, the São Paulo DOPS agent knocked on the door of a white house with blue shutters at Rua Campos de Carvalho 318. Plainclothes operatives had taken up positions controlling entry and access to the block. The fugitive could not escape. Reali knocked at the door, which was answered by Ondina Peixoto de Oliveira. Establishing that "Dr. Christiansen" was at home, he and other DOPS agents immediately pushed into the house. "Christiansen" was taken without a struggle and was promptly identified by Juvenal Sayão. The captive seemed relieved, and, for Reali, the chase was finally over.

A thorough search of the house yielded a rich harvest. Discovered were "Lucas's" transmitter, receiver, code book, and microdot instructions, as well as an undestroyed message dated March 9, which reported the arrival in Rio of the *Queen Mary*. The São Paulo DOPS man called Elim O'Shaughnessy and the British ambassador and suggested that the ocean liner-turned-troopship change course on its voyage to Sydney, Australia. The captured equipment had to be left behind, but Elpídio Reali was satisfied; Starziczny and Senhorita Peixoto de Oliveira were his prisoners, and on March 11, he hustled them off to São Paulo.[81]

All of these arrests and interrogations were supposedly secret, but somehow Albrecht Engels learned of Meyer-Clason's and Arnold's incarcerations; on March 17, he reported this information to ALD and speculated that the Anglo-Americans certainly knew of the microdot process.[82] It is also likely that the Sievert-Grapentin arrests and interrogations were reported to an Abwehr source, because on February 20, 1942, Ast Hamburg radioed Kempter that "Brazilian police know Vesta's work and probably all those who had connection with Vesta," "Vesta" being the name used by Herbert Von Heyer, when he sent messages through Kempter, Gamillscheg or Schlegel.[83]

There was still another important reason why Engels now had to take emergency measures. On March 11, he telephoned Starziczny to tell him that he was replacing Bohny and Uebele as paymaster, and that up to thirty thousand dollars in new financing would be made available. But when he rang the Leblon house, an unknown person answered. The stranger asked who was calling, so Engels hung up. Since he had no faith in Starziczny's ability to remain silent under police interrogation, Engels concluded that his own arrest was imminent. Heinz Lorenz ("Laura") was called in and ordered to activate a back-up organization, while Ernst Ramuz was told to prepare to move the CEL transmitter from its Jacaré-paguá location. Finally, on March 16, Engels delivered eighty-nine thousand dollars plus his code book and papers to Gustavo Glock.[84]

Meanwhile, Jack West was putting the final touches on a plan for a massive spy roundup. Early in March, he received an important report from "Tom," his secret informant, which filled in some of the blanks concerning the true identities of certain ring leaders and V-men. Convinced that the Germans were preparing to go underground, West decided to take immediate action. Through Elim O'Shaughnessy, a list of roughly eighty-four persons was submitted to Captain Teixeira about March 16.[85] Forty-eight hours later, the arrests began and by the evening of the twenty-second, Engels, Heyer, Kempter, Schwab, Muegge, and over twenty others were in custody. In the case of Kempter, the police bagged his equipment and much of his money as well. DOPS officers could have seized Heyer's code key and secret inks, but the latter had given these to his Japanese landlady shortly before his arrest. The lady delivered the materials to Klara Engels, and Bohny personally disposed of them.[86]

Between March 10 and 18, 1942, CEL, LIR, and CIT went off the air, but the SIS/Brazil had failed to achieve its goal; part of the Abwehr espionage network was still intact and determined to survive.

B. *Confess—Or Else*

Assisted by the SIS/Brazil, in the eight weeks after March 18, 1942, DOPS captured virtually all the integrants of the Engels, Kempter, Jordan, Schlegel, Starziczny, and Gamillscheg rings. In contrast, the interrogation effort was, in the opinion of U. S. representatives, scandalously mishandled. After a month of questioning, Engels and Heyer had provided little information, a circumstance which West and Caffery did not perceive as accidental. They considered DOPS chief Felisberto Teixeira "physically incapable" of getting the job done, and were also convinced that Filinto Muller was somehow acting to hinder the process.[87] On April 28, 1942, West and Caffery moved to outflank this suspected opposition by placing in the hands of Foreign Minister Oswaldo Aranha, Pres. Getúlio Vargas, and the air force minister, Gen. Eduardo Gomes, copies of CEL-ALD messages.[88] The U.S. representatives were pleased by the expected angry reactions of these Brazilian leaders, and by the offer of cooperation which came from Amaral Peixoto, governor of the state of Rio de Janeiro.[89] These developments evidently tipped the scales decisively, for on May 1, Engels was shifted from DOPS headquarters in the Federal District to the DOPS headquarters in Niterói, then the capital of the state of Rio de Janeiro. This meant that Engels was no longer under the jurisdiction of either Captain Teixeira or Major Muller. Rather, "Alfredo" received the undivided attentions of Carlos Ramos de Freitas, an officer of dubious reputation. He was subject to several days of hard treatment, being kept in a darkened cell, denied sanitary privileges, and prevented from sleeping.[90] Under the effects of this brutalization, Engels began telling his interrogators what they wanted to know.

Physical violence might eventually produce the desired results, but in the case of Josef Starziczny, the most significant breakthrough was achieved by more subtle means. Elpídio Reali decided that psychological tactics were most likely to make his prize prisoner cooperative. This DOPS agent kept Starziczny in a dark cell, questioned him constantly, and intimated that he might not be able to protect Senhorita de Oliveira from sadistic policemen. But Reali's trump card was his offer that the spy and his mistress could be reunited, given a clean, lighted suite, and allowed to console each other; all Starziczny had to do was talk.[91] It was this combination of promise and implied threat to his mistress that broke "Christiansen." On April 2, he revealed his real name and supplied information which resulted in the immediate arrest of Otto Uebele, Georg Metzner, and others of the Santos–São Paulo group. This was an excellent start, but Reali had become curious about what a Yale key on the prisoner's key chain opened. Initially, Starziczny refused to say, but Reali warned him that if he wished the solace of his mistress, he had better comply. Starziczny finally admitted that the key fit a safety deposit box, and on April 10, 1942, Reali went to Rio de Janeiro and opened box number 619 at the Banco do Credito Mercantil. Its contents included all the messages sent and received by "Lucas" since May 1941, records of money paid to agents or received from Otto Uebele and Theodor Simon, plus reports from network informants all over Brazil.[92] The official record does not mention, however, the presence of a diamond bracelet reputedly worth over five thousand dollars.[93] Starziczny may have intended to give this to his mistress, but, just as likely, he may have considered it a hedge against the day when the Abwehr might stop paying him. The recovery of these documents was followed on April 11 by a new confession from Starziczny, who then offered his services to the Brazilians![94]

The sophisticated methods used on Starziczny must be contrasted with the sometimes systematic brutality inflicted upon prisoners elsewhere. In Recife, Erwin Backhaus, arrested on December 18, 1941, but released five days later, was rearrested on April 4, 1942. He was kept in a cell six feet long, three feet wide, with no bed, and continuously interrogated. Not unnaturally, he fingered his compatriots, and DOPS in the Federal District arrested Theodor Schlegel and Karl Thielen on or about April 8. Capt. Felisberto Teixeira supposedly gave agents Machado Lima and Francisco Milton Monza veritable carte blanche in allowing them to extract information from some of the captives. Schlegel had a hernia, but this did not prevent the police from beating him into unconsciousness, nor giving Thielen a strong dose of the same medicine. Determined to preserve his health, Thielen agreed to go to the Dellinghausen farm and show DOPS where "Carola," the "Salama" group's transmitter, was buried.[95]

Unfortunately, these were not the only V-men upon whom DOPS officers were allowed to indulge their baser instincts. Franz Walther

Jordan, who was arrested on March 23, suffered dislocated fingers, while Herbert Max Winterstein had it recorded in his official disposition that he had been tortured by Filinto Muller.[96] Elpídio Reali insists that no one ever proved that he physically abused a prisoner,[97] but someone in the São Paulo DOPS unit meted out cruel and unjustifiable punishment to Carlos Wollfertz. A subagent of Hans Sievert's Recife group, Wollfertz fled to São Paulo in March 1942, only to be arrested on or about April 5. The police interrogated him in the nude for two days, allegedly pouring cold water on this unfortunate captive and keeping an electric fan aimed at him, running at top speed. Wollfertz was reported to have suffered both physical collapse and temporary mental derangement.[98]

The most unusual story of prisoner resistance is that of Friedrich Kempter. This spy refused to be interrogated nude or unshaven; the police compromised by letting him shave before being questioned. The food served, Kempter recalls, was "full of rocks" and, for several days, he simply refused to eat. As a spy network chief and possessor of valuable information, SIS/Brazil was concerned about his health and sought to intervene in the situation. Eventually, a DOPS officer dressed Kempter in decent clothes and escorted him to a nearby restaurant for steak and french fries. As Kempter recalls, it was "one of the better meals" of his life.[99]

The most effective response to police brutality was engineered by Albrecht Engels. Unknown to either SIS/Brazil or DOPS, between April 10 and 30, 1942, he smuggled four reports to Hermann Bohny via his wife and chauffeur. These reports revealed the locations of $32,500 in assorted currencies still available for intelligence operations, and confirmed that the codes of Kempter, Starziczny, and Gamillscheg had been broken. In addition, he detailed the tortures being inflicted upon various V-men, and reported that both Starziczny and Hans Muth had made incriminating confessions.[100] After the reports of these indignities to Abwehr agents reached Berlin, vehement denunciations were delivered through the Spanish embassy to Foreign Minister Oswaldo Aranha. The Brazilian reply, on July 2, 1942, was that continued U-boat attacks on Brazilian ships and the "sacrificing of Brazilian lives" made the German protests invalid.[101] This was a properly nationalist reply, guaranteed to win support from the populace, but from a historical perspective, the torture of some agents cannot be so easily explained away.

SIS/Brazil personnel were involved in some of the interrogations, and information regarding the torture of some prisoners was forwarded to Washington.[102] In explaining their predicament, SIS/Brazil sources argued that the primary U.S. concern was to put the known V-men in jail and keep them off the airwaves. U.S. counterspies concluded that if they intervened too frequently on behalf of the prisoners, the political police might become less cooperative. These were contingencies nobody in Washington wanted to face. The only discreet course of action left was to look the other way when the men of DOPS became too heavy-handed.[103] Thus, if J. Edgar Hoover, Sumner Welles, and Adolf Berle were ignorant of what was transpiring in the Brazilian jails, it was essentially because they preferred not to know.

C. *The Roll-Up Is Consolidated*

On March 26, 1942, Jofre Magalhães dos Santos received a very terse but vital communication from his mistress in Rio de Janeiro, Diny Gaal. The information relayed was that Ellemer Nagy (code name: Berto) had been arrested, and Diny also implied that the espionage game was becoming too dangerous for people who were in it chiefly for the money. Magalhães dos Santos had been living well in Recife, but with Engels in jail, no more money was forthcoming. He made the mistake of returning to the capital on April 11, where DOPS promptly arrested him.[104]

By this time, the survival prospects of the V-men still at large were very grim. Nevertheless, a handful of Abwehr survivors struggled on. Of the two groups still operating at the end of March, the most important in terms of clandestine radio activity was the Heinz Lorenz ("Laura") back-up group. The other members of this rump network were Othmar Gamillscheg ("Grillo"), Carlos Meyer, a restaurant manager, Ernst Ramuz, radioman, and Kurt Weingartner, an optometrist and businessman. Following the arrest of Engels, Lorenz decided that the first order of business was the acquisition of a transmitter for Othmar Gamillscheg, who had been seeking his own for over six months. In January 1942, Lorenz received an ersatz apparatus from Hermann Bohny, and before he was arrested, Albrecht Engels named Gamillscheg as that instrument's recipient. By March 29, "Laura" had arranged for Gamillscheg to commence broadcasting from Kurt Weingartner's farm located at Campo Grande, a suburb approximately six miles west of the capital city. "Grillo" then cabled Ast Brussels via a drop, saying that he expected to start broadcasting on April 15.[105]

Although his name was on the list submitted by Jack West to DOPS in the Federal District, the political police ignored Gamillscheg until Adalberto Wamser was arrested on March 25. After the usual rough treatment, Wamser admitted that "Grillo" was Gamillscheg, but Felisberto Teixeira's men did not make the arrest until April 6, 1942. The recipient of the same kind of punishment meted out to Wamser, Gamillscheg suffered a nervous collapse,[106] but recovered sufficiently to name Weingartner and Lorenz as his collaborators. So it was that after six months without his own transmitter, Gamillscheg received one, only to be jailed before he could tap out a single message.

The reestablishment of radio contact with Germany remained the top priority, but everything now depended upon Ernst Ramuz. Since arriving in Rio de Janeiro in May 1941, this man had remained loyal to Engels, but not to his spouse, Stefanie. Freed from wifely surveillance, Ramuz became enamored of Henriqueta de Barros Pimental, the sister-in-law of Carlos Meyer. Senhorita Pimental apparently met Ramuz in August 1941, shortly after Ramuz moved from Chaves Farias 84, in the São

Christovão district, to Rua Tres Ríos 320, in surburban Jacarépaguá. She was aware that Ramuz made clandestine broadcasts, but claimed to know nothing of their contents, her lover having insisted that "one could not trust women."[107]

The emotional life of Ernst Ramuz entered a crisis following the November 1941 arrival of his wife Stefanie and their two children. His marital relationship continued to deteriorate, for he wanted his family to remain at the São Christovão address, while he spent the bulk of his time with his transmitter and paramour in Jacarépaguá. Senhora Ramuz was unhappy with these unorthodox conjugal arrangements, and as she was an unrelenting critic of his espionage activities, Ramuz decided that there was no reason for maintaining the pretense of domestic tranquility. Early in February 1942, Senhorita Pimental moved all her belongings into the Jacarépaguá house; the woman who knew how to keep her mouth shut officially replaced the wife who could not.[108]

This uneasy triangle remained intact until the arrest of Engels and Heyer on March 18, 1942. Both Bohny and Lorenz suspected that the Anglo-Americans knew where the CEL transmitter was located, and they wanted it promptly relocated. During the last week of March, Ernst Ramuz and the Senhorita moved into a house owned by Carlos Meyer at Rua Couto 526, in the Rio de Janeiro suburb on Penha. On April 3, 1942, Kurt Weingartner, Carlos Meyer, and Ramuz joined forces to move the radio to the Penha address, where they buried it under a floor in the house. This expedited change of address placed on additional strain on Ernst Ramuz's financial resources, for he was in no position to pay rent on three different residences. His solution to the problem was to abandon the house in Sao Christovão, and move Stefanie and his children to the residence he had recently vacated in Jacarépaguá.[109]

The operational plan of Heinz Lorenz called for a resumption of broadcasting from this new address once the Brazilian spy furor had died down. After a suspension of roughly six weeks, contact was reestablished with ALD, and on May 1, a message signed by "Laura" advised that a detailed account of events was already "en route via Diego" (Dietrich Niebuhr) in Buenos Aires. The reconstruction of the spy network was described as proceeding "slowly," and the most urgent need was "a new key [code]." A reply to this signal came four days later; ALD advised that a new code was en route "from Diego to BEH [Bohny]."[110]

The new code apparently reached Brazil by Spanish diplomatic courier from Argentina, and was passed on to Lorenz by Gustavo Glock. On May 6, Berlin received the first message in the new key. Alas, the joy at headquarters in reestablishing a connection was tempered by the information received; it indicated that Engels was in a Niterói prison, no longer under the protection of "strong friends" and definitely "on his own."[111]

After almost a week of "interrogation" in Niterói, Engels could stand no more; on May 11, 1942, he named Ernst Ramuz as his chief radioman. He also admitted that he knew about the radio station in Jacarépaguá, but insisted that he did not know where Ramuz was.[112] Whereas it took eleven days after Adalberto Wamser's arrest for DOPS in the Federal District to pick up Othmar Gamillscheg, within twenty-four hours of Engels's confession, Ramos de Freitas and state of Rio de Janeiro DOPS agents were pounding on the door of Ramuz's old residence at Rua Chaves Farias 84. The Ramuz family was long gone, but neighbors remembered that a moving van with the name Androinha on the side had borne the family furniture away. DOPS agents checked company records, and found that the Ramuz family was now ensconced in the Jacarépaguá residence. When they visited the house, Ramuz's son, Walter Augusto, was discovered on the premises. Ramos de Freitas threatened the young man with incarceration unless he revealed where his father was, and Walter Augusto made haste to comply. Taken to the suburb of Penha in an unmarked police car, he pointed out the house at Rua Couto 526. For squealing on his father, the DOPS agent rewarded Walter Augusto with bus fare back to Jacarépaguá.[113]

Arrested on May 12, 1942, Ernst Ramuz offered only a minimum of resistance before naming his fellow V-men. Within forty-eight hours, Kurt Weingartner and Carlos Meyer had also been detained. The tightening net left Lorenz with no place to go; on June 15, 1942, police picked him up when he returned to his old apartment to obtain clothing and money. Two days previously, a radio station in Germany using the call letters RDH began broadcasting "blind" in a desperate effort to reach someone attached to the "Laura" group. The message confirmed that the report to "Diego" mentioned in the May 1, 1942, transmission, had just been received in Berlin. It also asked that Lorenz and his group obtain details concerning a bauxite supply contract between the Brazilian government and the Reynolds Metals Company. Finally, the sender added: "We are very proud of your excellent work...."[114] Abwehr chiefs had rarely lavished praise on their Brazilian operatives in the past. The trouble was that when this broadcast was made, Ramuz, Weingartner, Meyer, and Lorenz were in no position to hear it.

D. *The Misadventures of "Captain García"*

After he returned to Germany in May 1942, Lt. Comdr. Hermann Bohny touted Capt. Tulio Regis do Nascimento ("Captain García") as a brilliant recruit whose future success would necessitate the taking of extraordinary security meaures. Abwehr agents entering Brazil should contact the captain only by leaving a message in Portuguese, which included the phrase, "Regards from the navy," at the do Nascimento family apartment in Rio. Whoever received the message was to be told, "I am looking for the book that Heitor left." After two days, "Captain García" would send a reply to the address provided with the number 1673 written in the lower left-hand corner. When the meeting finally took place, the V-man was required to say to "Captain García," "Greetings from Federico Américo."[115]

In keeping with other efforts aimed at protecting the identity of
Abwehr agents in Brazil, this circumspect but rather jejune procedure
proved utterly futile. Possibly at Bohny's suggestion, late in January 1942,
do Nascimento wrote a letter to Gen. Lehman Miller, chief of the U.S.
military mission in Brazil. In this message, do Nascimento cited his
responsibility in the establishment of Brazil's only fire-control equipment
factory, and requested that he be allowed to tour U.S. war manufacturing
plants. In particular, the captain wished to visit the Sperry Corporation to
observe a demonstration of U.S. artillery fire control equipment in action,
and emphasized that his request had the support of Gen. Gasper Dutra,
Brazilian minister of war.

News that "Captain García" might soon be making the proposed tour
was flashed by CEL to ALD on February 20, 1942, and intercepted by the
ubiquitous RID. As deciphered by the FBI laboratory, the message read:

> Local Captain in our service departs for the U.S. in two weeks in
> commission (on Mission?) on invitation of Lehman Miller. He will be
> active ... at Sperry, in arsenals and aircraft factories. Have approved
> trip and $3,000. He received [secret] ink. Alfredo.[116]

The U.S. Army promptly rejected this initiative,[117] and the evidence
reveals that "Captain García" was blown from the start; but amazingly,
there is an even more sardonic twist to this incident. In intercepting and
decrypting the February 20 message, either the RID or the FBI specialists
established the second word of the text as *Hauptmann*, meaning "captain" in German. It is understandable that working from this hypothesis,
the FBI concluded that the "local Captain in our service" and Captain do
Nascimento, who had specifically sought to visit the Sperry plant, were
one and the same officer.[118] But under intensive interrogation, both
Herbert von Heyer and Albrecht Engels stubbornly denied having sent
the message as translated. They insisted that the word intended was
Vertrauensmann and that for purposes of simplication and abbreviation,
the word *Vauptmann* was usually substituted. Given the similarity of
Vauptmann and Hauptmann, one is left with the strong suspicion that do
Nascimento's unmasking was largely the result of a translation error made
by either the RID or the FBI, rather than a more typical Abwehr foul-up.

Through his cousin, Alexandre Konder, a lawyer who ran a bookstore in the capital city, do Nascimento wangled an introduction to
Gerardo Margela Melo Mourão, a journalist, author, and undercover
member of the outlawed Intregalista organization. Mourão had allegedly
been hired by the Germans to conduct the "Hora Portuguesa," a Nazi
propaganda broadcast emanating from Berlin and beamed at Portugal and
Brazil. On July 7, 1940, DOPS in Recife arrested him probably because
the Vargas government didn't want Mourão to conduct the program.
Quite likely, the detention and the interrogation which followed increased the antipathy Mourão already felt for the Estado Nôvo.[119]

Gerardo Melo Mourão and "Captain García" (the only name, other than "Tulio," by which the newspaperman claimed he knew do Nascimento) first met in Konder's bookstore in January 1942, but not until April did the captain express a need for his services. Mourão was going to Buenos Aires on assignment for *Gazeta de Notícias*, a Rio newspaper, so "García" suggested that journalism and espionage be combined. Before he left the capital, Mourão received $200 to deliver both a ciphered letter and a message written in scret ink which was hidden in a package of cigarettes. These were to be delivered either to Thilo Martens, the general manager of Norddeutscher Lloyd, a German shipping firm, or to someone named "Otto" (perhaps Horacio Ortelli, an MK Argentina V-man) whose last name was not known, nor address given.

Arriving in Buenos Aires on April 10, 1942, Mourão delivered the materials to Martens. He received $150–$200 for expenses from an unknown German, and thirty days later, he returned to the Brazilian capital. The evening of his return, Mourão contacted "Captain García" and reported that "Number 19 has arrived." Whatever the meaning of this cryptic message, do Nascimento was apparently satisfied, for he paid Mourão another $100 for his troubles.[120]

This successful delivery signaled the reestablishment of a fragile but functioning communications link between Brazil and Argentina. Hermann Bohny had ordered this courier mission,[121] but on May 7, 1942, the naval attaché was repatriated aboard the Portuguese ship, *Serpa Pinto*, a development that left supervision of the "Captain García" ring to embassy counselor Walther Becker. This diplomat-turned-emergency spymaster wanted another courier mission to Buenos Aires undertaken, ship movement data, and fresh details concerning U.S. naval and air installations in the Brazilian northeast. Captain do Nascimento promised to accomplish these tasks, but the arrangement of details and the making of contacts fell to Mourão, who became, for all practical purposes, "García's" major domo. The journalist recruited a few Integralista friends to execute these endeavors, but little in the way of useful intelligence information was ever obtained.[122] Nevertheless, this flurry of activity set the stage for the commencement of the most ambitious operation attempted by "Captain García" and his associates.

Anchored in Rio de Janeiro's Guanabara Bay was the seven-thousand-ton German freighter *Windhuk*. This vessel had been loaded in preparation to run the British sea blockade, but after December 7, 1941, the Brazilian government refused to issue the necessary clearance papers. Since it was rumored that the vessel was to be turned over to the United States, the Germans wanted the *Windhuk* sunk. In addition, if the ship could somehow be destroyed, the act would serve to show the BSC, SIS, and DOPS that the Abwehr in Brazil was still a force to be reckoned with.

The decision to sink the *Windhuk* was made prior to Bohny's departure, [123] but not until June 1942 did Walther Becker broach the subject to do Nascimento. Furthermore, it would be mid-July before Mourão received specific orders to carry out a sabotage mission. His initial task was to buy two alarm clocks, four batteries, and a box of flares; with these either do Nascimento or Walther Becker constructed a crude time bomb.[124] "García's" next move was to order that the infernal device be placed in the hold of the *Windhuk*, the hope being that following the explosion, the resultant cargo fire would destroy the ship. On August 10, 1942, Mourão approached Alvaro da Costa e Souza, an Integralista friend previously recruited to report on ship movements, and proposed that the latter execute this mission, or find someone else who could. Mourão allegedly promised a six thousand dollar payoff if the *Windhuk* was wrecked, and showed Costa e Souza an impressive roll of bills as proof. The latter may not have been enthused about sabotage, but he wanted the cash. He agreed to carry out the operation, and took possession of the bomb.[125]

However, as a result of a growing U-boat offensive in Brazilian coastal waters, and an escalation of German-Brazilian tensions, Costa e Souza soon began reassessing his commitment. On or about August 15, Costa e Souza contacted DOPS chief José Ramos de Freitas in Niterói and reported that German agents were planning to sink the *Windhuk*. Not surprisingly, Costa e Souza failed to mention to the police that he was the designated saboteur. Apparently, his intention was to curry favor with DOPS while simultaneously acquiring as much of the proffered six thousand dollars as he could without actually setting fire to the ship.[126]

After August 31, 1942, Brazil was unequivocally at war with the Third Reich, so that if do Nascimento and his men continued their activities, they ran the risk of being tried as traitors. "Captain García" appeared relatively untroubled by these events, but Gerardo Melo Mourão was absolutely convinced that DOPS was shadowing him. On September 7, he contacted Fr. Joel Ribeiro, a priest who had acted as a drop, and pleaded with the cleric to give him a cassock so that he might be able to elude the police and flee Brazil. Fr. Ribeiro was a friend and Integralista sympathizer, but lending a potential fugitive clerical garb, and thereby directly implicating the national clergy, was an idea whose time had not yet arrived. Bluntly, the priest told Mourão that he would have to find some other disguise.[127]

Two days later, Alvaro da Costa e Souza played his last card in the quest to gain a payoff without actually executing the sabotage mission. He contacted Mourão and insisted that war between Germany and Brazil had seriously altered the situation. No explosive device could be placed on the *Windhuk* without full payment prior to the execution of the job. On the evening of September 10, "Captain García" and Mourão met to discuss this new demand and other matters. After some inconclusive discussion the two men separated, but DOPS officers who had been watching moved in and arrested Mourão. The others connected with the ring were quickly taken into custody, and on September 13, the police asked Capt. Tulio Regis do Nascimento to present himself at DOPS headquarters in the Federal District. He had been under suspicion ever since the FBI and RID intercepted the fateful message transmitted by CEL on February 20, 1942.

Now with Brazil formally at war with Germany, arresting an army officer for espionage became the politically justifiable act it might not otherwise have been.[128]

On September 17, 1942, Ambassador Kurt Prüfer and embassy counselor Walther Becker left for Europe aboard the steamer *Cuiabá*. One month previously, the ambassador had presented do Nascimento with cash, secret ink, a personal code, and named him "Controller-General of the German information services in Brazil."[129] Yet, when the ship sailed, it is likely that both Prüfer and Becker were aware that the "Captain García" group had been liquidated. Despite frenzied efforts, the Abwehr in Brazil was virtually kaput.

Captain do Nascimento once remarked to his mistress, Ysette Bittencourt Días, that if he wanted to go to Germany, "a submarine will come here to fetch me."[130] Only a megalomaniac could have believed that during the midst of the convoy war on the Atlantic sea-lanes, the Germans would have sent a submarine just to pick him up. In retrospect, a mentally stable version of "Captain García," commanding a carefully chosen group of Integralistas, could have been a most effective spy ring. Instead, the Abwehr paid out eighty-five hundred dollars[131] and got a man who suffered from a variety of mental illnesses, one of which might be described as U-boats on the brain.

E. *"Antonio" and "Springbok": The Last Skirmish*

When we last mentioned Werner Waltemath ("Antonio"), the "sleeper" agent with the unresponsive radio, his controller, Major Karl von Bauer, had told him as tactfully as possible to find some place to hide and to hope for the best. The Abwehr may have decided that Waltemath was expendable, but the BSC had plans for resuscitating this discarded V-man. The key figure in the British plan was Hans Christian von Kotze, a double agent whose Abwehr code name was "Fred," whose BSC code name was probably "Springbok," and who departed Brazil as "Johannes van Hughes." In November 1941, the Abwehr ordered Kotze to South Africa, but his BSC controllers sent him to Canada instead.

For three months, Waltemath heard nothing. He built a special cellar underneath his living room for his useless radio and became a partner in a chemical supply business with his brother-in-law, a *Volksdeutscher* named Paulo Gustavo Griese. Unexpectedly, there arrived a letter postmarked February 4, 1942, from "John van Hughes," who declared that he was now a representative of Vickers and Benson Ltd., an import-export company located in Toronto, Canada. Utilizing the code previously worked out, Hughes and Waltemath exchanged at least thirteen letters and ten telegrams between February 4 and August 1, 1942.[142] These communications appear to be inane and repetitive discussions of such mundane matters as the sale and price of peanuts, Jockey Electric Grinders, vitamins, and male sex hormones, but in reality, they masked a grimly serious business. Hughes intended to use Waltemath as his long-distance radioman and to supply him with a mixture of falsehood and fact that would confuse and bedevil German intelligence. The genius of the scheme, however, lay in the fact that its success did not depend solely on "Antonio's" balky transmitter. Hughes made it clear that with or without the "Midwest Electric Company" (i.e., Waltemath's radio), he expected the data supplied to be passed on to "Mr. Rubin," the latter being a crudely inverted and phonetic spelling of the last name of the German naval attaché in Argentina, Capt. Dietrich Niebuhr. Since von Kotze had established a reputation as a degenerate spendthrift, "Mr. Rubin" would deem it logical that the same man, whatever he chose to call himself, would expect hefty commissions for the "peanuts" (i.e., intelligence data) he shipped.[133]

With the opportunity to become a functional V-man again, Waltemath threw caution to the wind. By unknown means, he contacted Niebuhr in March 1942 and reported that information on Anglo-American convoy sailings could be supplied by Hughes, who was now in Toronto. The naval attaché weighed this communication, and on March 26, 1942, he cabled the I-M section at Abwehr headquarters in Berlin that "V-man John van Hughes" was offering to sell convoy information: Did the Abwehr wish to make a purchase, and if so, how much was to be made available?[134] What reply Niebuhr received is not known, but despite several pointed hints from Hughes in letters to Waltemath, no funds were forthcoming. Still, the BSC agent and his controllers had no reason to be dissatisfied; a connection of sorts had been established, and if the "peanuts" delivered were judged satisfactory, the campaign of misinformation might still be effectively carried out.

Towards the end of May, and then at the end of June 1942, Hughes arranged for an assortment of documents to be delivered to Waltemath. The materials included newspaper and magazine clippings concerning U.S. aircraft, a report on the Canadian army, and a small photograph map of the city of Toronto.[135] All of this data was hidden inside several catalogues of sample goods which Vickers and Benson Ltd. was allegedly submitting for Waltemath's perusal.

Since some "peanuts" had been delivered, it was now incumbent upon Waltemath to take some responsive action. First, he took all the materials received to a photographer friend named Hans Mueller, who made two sets of thirty microphotographs. With German-Brazilian diplomatic relations sundered, Waltemath knew that the Vargas government would not allow a Third Reich passport holder to make a São Paulo–Buenos Aires round trip. Therefore, he asked his brother-in-law and business partner, Paulo Griese, to deliver the materials to Alfred Voelkers, a German businessman who occasionally acted as a front for Niebuhr.[136] Since Griese had helped to build the radio cellar under the Waltemath house, he knew about his brother-in-law's espionage activities. A set of microphotographs was sewn into the shoulder of his overcoat, and on July 10, 1942, Griese left São Paulo for Buenos Aires.

The trip to the Argentine capital was uneventful, but the delivery of the microphotographs proved exasperating. No one at the address given Griese had ever heard of Voelkers, so on July 17, the Brazilian went directly to the German embassy and asked for Capt. Dietrich Niebuhr. "Mr. Rubin" had no intention of conferring on demand; instead, he sent his aide, Lt. J. Martin Müller, to look into the matter. Müller heard Griese's tale, took the microphotographs and directed the Brazilian to return on the eighteenth at 5:00 P.M.; Voelkers would be at the embassy awaiting his arrival.

The Germans probably feared that Griese was a double agent, because when the Brazilian met Voelkers, the latter had little to say except that Griese was to remain in Buenos Aires until he received further instructions. Not until August 13 did Voelkers take him to a meeting with Niebuhr at the German embassy.

One reason that the naval attaché may have let Griese twiddle his thumbs for several weeks was that he was waiting for instructions from the Abwehr. Once the meeting began, Niebuhr gave Waltemath the same advice as Karl von Bauer had: as a blown agent, Waltemath must "go underground."[137] Hughes was denounced as a double agent; all further contact with the traitor was expressly forbidden. After giving Griese the bad news, Niebuhr did provide one faint ray of hope. If a letter on H. Capelossi Company stationery was received with the name "Anita" in the body and the clause "Mr. Rubin sends regards" towards the end, then Waltemath could again become active. Griese was given $200 to cover his expenses, $250 for Waltemath, and a new "drop" address for contacting Voelkers. The meeting ended and, the following day, the Brazilian flew back to São Paulo.[138]

Obviously Niebuhr wanted the Waltemath-Hughes connection broken, and although there is no evidence that "Antonio" ever received a letter on Capelossi Company stationery, he nevertheless wrote responses to Hughes dated September 6, 1942, and January 5, 1943. In the second letter, Waltemath complained about the materials received and stated that as a result, "we abandon further proposals." Hughes's feisty reply of February 19, 1943, was that additional "samples of peanuts were forthcoming," and that Waltemath had failed to "properly invoice the goods" and to "keep in communication."[139] With this exchange, the Hughes-Waltemath correspondence had ceased to serve any tactical purpose.

On June 1, 1943, São Paulo DOPS arrested Werner Waltemath and Paulo Griese, but this was not the end of the former radioman's saga. In Britain, MI-6 had been very successful in persuading captured Abwehr V-men to radio misleading information back to their German controllers. Brazil wanted to do the same, and so Waltemath was forced into becoming DOPS' first "turned" Abwehr agent. He was given a working radio and ordered to contact the Ast Münster station, but the Germans refused to be deceived. Finally, the inadvertent release of the Waltemath story to the national press in August 1943 put an end to this scheme. DOPS' intention of creating its own version of the British "double-cross" system would have to await more propitious circumstances.[140]

F. *The Abwehr as Equal Opportunity Employer*

During the year 1942, Adm. Karl Doenitz's submarines sank over 6.2 million tons of shipping.[141] In particular, the waters off the Brazilian coast proved to be the scene of easy pickings, with Lt. Comdr. Heinrich Schlacht in *U-507* single-handedly sinking ten ships in less than two months (October–November 1942).[142] Yet even with at-sea refueling, the journey to the Brazilian coast remained arduous, with the crews suffering seriously from the heat, the confined quarters, and the consequent deterioration of the quality of the food. Doenitz was acutely aware of these problems; still, he looked to 1943 with confidence. For the first time, he would be able to maintain a sizable fleet of U-boats in the North Atlantic and off the African and South American coasts at the same time.[143] Grimly ironic, however, was the fact that just when the Germans could look toward mounting a sustained campaign in Brazilian waters, ship movement data via clandestine radio had become unavailable. Could this information source be successfully reestablished?

William Marcus Baarn was an illegitimate child of African ancestry born on July 10, 1908, in Paramaribo, Dutch Guiana (now the Republic of Surinam). He received little formal education, but it was enough to convince him that the normal channels for social ascendancy would likely be closed to him. In 1937, he stowed away aboard the Dutch freighter, *Venezuela*, and reached Rotterdam. During the next four years, while attempting to make a name for himself as a singer and nightclub entertainer, he worked periodically as a doorman and dishwasher. In December 1941, an Abwehr agent known as Jack Schwartz (or Zwartz) pressed him to accept a job with German intelligence. Baarn claims that he refused this and several additional offers made in 1942, but deteriorating conditions in the Netherlands and the nightly passage of British bombers overhead made it obvious that Nazi-dominated Europe was no longer a place for an aspiring nightclub celebrity. In January 1943, he accepted the Schwartz proposition and was sent to Ast Hamburg for training.

Almost immediately, Baarn commenced the comprehensive study of codes and radio telegraphic procedures. Taken under the wing of "Dr. Cadmus" (possibly Col. Werner Trautmann of the I-i section of Ast Hamburg), Baarn was given intensive training in transmitter usage and repair. He refused his first two assignments, in South Africa and Zanzibar, settling for his third choice, Brazil. He was given the code name "Emma" and the 1938 Oxford edition of the Holy Bible as his code book. Sent to Paris on May 1, 1943, he was installed in a villa at 7 Boulevard les Sablons, in the seventeenth arrondissement. Understandably, the Abwehr never expected anything like philosophical loyalty or a conversion to the Third Reich's principles from Baarn. But if they could show him the affluence that he craved and promise him more where that came from, William Marcus Baarn, the first black man assigned by the Abwehr for Latin American operations, might prove to be an effective V-man.[144]

On or about May 16, 1943, Baarn was told to go to the Bois de Boulogne where, at a certain corner, an automobile would stop and pick him up. "Emma" did as he was told, and in the automobile, he met his eventual partner in the Brazilian mission, Wilhelm Heinrich Koepff. A World War I veteran born in 1900, Koepff's personal history resembled that of Albrecht Gustav Engels. Faced with a marginal future in Weimar Germany, he left for Peru in 1925. An instant success in the import-export business, Koepff became wealthy and was elected a director of the German Chamber of Commerce in the city. He joined the AO, visited Germany in 1935 and 1938, and returned an enthusiastic supporter of the Third Reich. But after the war started in Europe, the British blacklisted Koepff's firm. A shuffle of dummy directors and a change of name helped for two years, but after the United States added the company to its own blacklist, begun in May 1941, Koepff's business collapsed.

After Peru broke relations with Germany on January 29, 1942, Koepff pressured Ramírez Núñez, a police official, to have his name placed on the list of dangerous aliens to be repatriated. On April 13, 1942, he and other *Reischdeutschen* were shipped to New Orleans, and, after making a promise not to take up arms against the Allied nations, they were allowed to leave for Europe aboard the *Drottingholm* on June 1, 1942. Arriving in the fatherland, he was initially approached by Lt. Hans Jorgensen of Ast Stettin. Since Koepff was willing to serve, he was given the code name "Hedwig," and on October 30, 1942, Commander Hermann Wiebe, Ast chief, officially enrolled him in the I-M section of that station.[145]

After performing a few inconsequential services, in March 1943, Koepff was called to Berlin. Here he met Lt. Comdr. Ernst Wehner, an officer attached to I-M, Abteilung I, who knew Koepff personally, and had been a businessman in Peru for several years. A clandestine Brazilian landing operation was apparently Wehner's brainchild; as an aid to the V-men to be landed, he had had constructed a careful replica of Guanabara Bay, showing the Copacabana and Gavea beaches.[146] Once Koepff agreed to the assignment, intensive radio telegraphy and radio construction training began. The code book given him was *Sorte Grande* (or, loosely, *Great Fortune*), a novel by Armando Ferreira. He spent two weeks working with Ast Hamburg authorities establishing his radio technique and style so that the Germans could be certain who was sending. Pronounced ready for his mission, he departed for Paris where he subsequently rendezvoused with Baarn.[147]

With both men together, final arrangements for the operation were completed. Baarn was given five thousand dollars in U.S. currency, British pounds, and Brazilian cruzeiros, an *Afu*, and a passport which identified him as a seaman. After reaching Rio, he was to mingle with the Afro-Brazilian population, get a job as a stevedore, and begin broadcasting in two months. Koepff was given eight thousand dollars in assorted currencies, an *Afu*, a revolver, a special case of secret inks, and was told to keep an eye on Baarn. Koepff was to pose as a businessman, and it was hoped that he would use his money to purchase the necessary identification documents from corrupt policemen. Neither man was given the name of a Brazilian contact to reach, but Koepff was told that in case of emergency, he might report his plight to the Spanish embassy.[148]

The vehicle for the transport of the V-men to Brazil was not one of Admiral Doenitz's vaunted subs, but a sixty-three-foot yawl with diesel motors, the *Passim*, built in 1929 and confiscated from a French millionaire. The skipper of the boat was Heinz Garbers, a German sailor who had crossed the Atlantic from Hamburg to New York in 1938 in a forty-foot boat. The vessel carried six light machine guns, but its major defense was its unobtrusive appearance, as well as a full set of international flags.[149] After one aborted attempt, the *Passim* sailed on June 9, 1943, from the port of Arcachon in southwestern France. The course taken ran southward past the Canary Islands, and then southwest toward Brazil. The voyage was highlighed by the development of an infected boil on Koepff's leg and increasing tension between the German and the black man, the representative of the "master race" providing a steady diet of taunts and insults which Baarn resolved to repay.

Off the Brazilian coast, the *Passim* changed its name to the *Santa Cruz*. As it neared the coastal waters of Rio de Janeiro State, it became the Argentine fishing boat, *Santa Barbara*. Garbers was supposed to take his charges directly into Guanabara Bay and land them on one of the capital city's beaches, but he decided that this would be too dangerous. On August 9, 1943, the *Santa Barbara* dropped anchor off the beach near Gargaú, a village in the northeastern part of Rio de Janeiro State. Shortly after midnight, Baarn and several crew members scrambled into a large rubber boat, the black spy and his equipment safely reaching the beach. He buried his radio and set out for the village. An hour later, Koepff attempted to land in another rubber raft, but it capsized near shore. Koepff's radio was recovered, but he lost much of his personal gear, and the infected leg was further injured. He decided to stay on the beach until dawn and then proceed from Gargaú to Campos, a larger town, where he hoped to get medical attention.

In the end, all the careful training and the precautions taken went for naught. The morning after he landed, Baarn turned himself in to the police, and following the detention of Koepff as a suspicious person, Baarn denounced him as well. The German denied all charges until, on August 11, he was moved to the DOPS station in Niterói. There, "persuasion" similar to the kind used on Albrecht Engels soon induced his full confession.[150]

When news of the capture of Koepff and Baarn was revealed to U.S. officials, Jack West, who had been reassigned to Cuba, was ordered back to Brazil to assist William Bradley, then chief of SIS/Brazil.[151] The trip proved inconsequential, for, as Jefferson Caffery reported to Washington, Brazilian army intelligence wanted no outside assistance in arranging the scheme it was planning. Efforts to use Werner Waltemath as a double agent had failed; with one of the new captives, Brazilian army intelligence was determined to achieve the success which previously eluded it.[152] In fact, the Brazilian plan was flawed from the beginning. Koepff admitted that Baarn was a better radio operator, and the black man was telling all who would listen that he had intended to surrender as soon as he got free of the clutches of the Nazis. The SIS/Brazil believed Baarn's claim;[153] nevertheless, the Brazilians decided to use Koepff as their "turned" agent. The error made was soon evident, because on September 4, 1943, Koepff, who had no intention of betraying the Third Reich, attempted suicide by cutting his throat.[154] He failed, but it was painfully obvious to the chagrined Brazilians that they had bet on the wrong spy.

Rueful, perhaps, the Brazilians wasted no time being considerate of Koepff's mental state. As soon as he was physically able, he was forced to practice radio telegraphy until another radioman had successfully managed to copy his "fist."[155] The counterfeit "Hedwig" then attempted to raise Ast Hamburg, finally making contact toward the end of October. False or misleading shipping data, laced with occasionally accurate figures on U.S. war production, were fed to the Hamburg reception station, but in December 1943, the Abwehr requested information on the defenses and minefield placements in Rio de Janeiro harbor. Since the Brazilians had no intention of providing this information, contact was gradually broken off, with intermittent exchanges continuing until early June 1944, when the Brazilians gave up. And on June 29–30, 1944, the newspapers were allowed to publish the Koepff-Baarn story.[156]

Finally, the precautions taken to keep this espionage double-cross secret proved utterly useless. In August 1945, U.S. Army intelligence officers, examining captured German records, discovered that the Abwehr had known all along that Koepff and Baarn had been captured.[157] In essence, the Brazilians had attempted to fool the Germans; they wound up duping only themselves.

The failure of the Koepff-Baarn mission and the circumstances under which it was executed indicate both the bankruptcy of Abwehr policy and the desperation of its leaders. It was probably clear in Berlin that this mission had virtually no chance whatsoever to succeed. But to admit that fact publicly, or to argue that it was now senseless to send new agents to Brazil, could have earned the declarer a treason charge, assignment to the Russian front, or a private session with the Gestapo. Thus, agents who had virtually no chance to succeed were sent to Brazil in order to obtain shipping data which Germany's decreasing offensive capabilities made useless in any case.

IV. Justice?

A. The Making and Testing of an Espionage Law

Once the Abwehr agents and their collaborators were in jail, the question became: What was the regime to do with them? The Mexican solution had been to bring no legal charges, to dispatch some dangerous personnel to the U.S., and to ignore the rest for the duration of the war. But if different and more stringent action was envisaged, Brazil initially was no better off than Mexico, for the legal machinery to deal with contemporary espionage problems did not exist.

Conscious of this deficiency, on January 17, 1941, Getúlio Vargas created a commission of civilian and military jurists and charged them with the task of formulating a new military legal code which could deal with modern war and espionage. The commission was still in the process of developing a new code when ship sinkings and the imminent prospect of war with Germany made time the essential consideration. It remained for commission chairman Cardoso de Castro, chief of the Supreme Military Tribunal, to present a proposal upon which Vargas might immediately act. The result was Decree-Law No. 4,766 of October 1, 1942, Articles 19 to 25, which prohibited the unauthorized entry into the country by a secret agent, the installation and use of a clandestine radio transmitter, and the delivery of classified materials to the agents of a hostile power.[158]

The heart of this legal catch-all was Article 67, which stated that this law "will be retroactive in relation to crimes against the internal security [i.e., of the state], from the date of the rupture of diplomatic relations [January 28, 1942] with Germany, Italy, and Japan."[159] The language of this article appears straightforward enough, but putting it into effect required some adroit legal maneuvering. Article 122 of the Constitution of November 10, 1937, specifically guaranteed that penalties established in a new law could not be retroactively applied to the same act committed prior to the passage of said law. Had this protection remained in effect, Article 67 of Decree-Law No. 4,766 would plainly have been unconstitutional, but the legal experts on the regime's payroll were equal to the task. On August 31, 1942, Decree-Law No. 18,358 rendered Article 122 null and void, so that when Decree-Law No. 4,766 went into effect on October 1, there would be no question of inconsistency with the existing constitution.[160]

The purpose of the law, stated candidly, was to put all Abwehr agents, real or suspected, behind bars, and to keep them out of circulation for the remainder of the war. In order to test the new law's interpretation by the judges of the Tribunal of National Security (TSN) and to gauge the evolving tactics of defense lawyers, the government started by prosecuting its least complicated case; this was the suit against the Theodor Schlegel ("Salama") ring. All these men were *Reichsdeutschen*, their transmitter had been found, and the FBI decodes provided solid evidence of their post-January 28, 1942, activity.

There would be few public tears shed for the half-dozen men named in the case. Their trial, held in the TSN court in the federal capital, began on October 17, 1942, and the proceedings were short, sharp, and sweeping. On November 19, 1942, Theodor Schlegel was found guilty and was sentenced to fourteen years' imprisonment. On December 9, 1942, the five other defendants received eight-year sentences. All legal appeals were denied, and the sentences were officially reaffirmed on December 17, 1942.[161] (For the names of all those convicted, see Appendix B.)

A different situation would develop when, on January 18, 1943, official charges were brought against Frank Walter Jordan and the LFS group. The scene of the trial was the same as in the Schlegel case, with Antonio Pereira Braga as judge and José María McDowell da Costa as state prosecutor. The Nest Bremen V-man was sure to be convicted, but the five Germans involved with him made strenuous efforts to avoid his fate. Walter Moll, for example, could not deny that he had collected ship movement data after January 28, 1942, but he insisted that the materials he provided for Jordan came from the daily newspapers. Afonso Digeser admitted that Jordan built an antenna on his property and transmitted from a room in his house, but argued that he knew nothing about the V-man's activities. Hugo Fleischner, in whose cellar Jordan's *Afu* was found, admitted burying the suitcase in which the receiver was stored, but claimed that he was told that its contents were old books. Had Herbert Max Winterstein known that Frank Walter Jordan was a spy? Yes and no, was the response of this cagey individual. Winterstein maintained that while he knew that Jordan was a German agent, he believed that the latter was only interested in the purchase and shipment of strategic raw materials.[162]

These arguments, shrewdly prepared by lawyers Lauro Fontura and Jamil Feres, were tactically sound since Jordan obligingly testified that Fleischner knew nothing of the radio in the suitcase, and that Digeser had never been told anything about LFS broadcasting activities.[163] This strategy might have been completely successful had it not been for the recalcitrant engineer, Hans Holl. This defendant admitted his arrangement in Bremen with Johannes Bischoff, and insisted that Herbert Winterstein knew beyond a shadow of a doubt that Jordan was an Abwehr agent.[164]

As for the five defendants of Brazilian origin, they claimed that Decree-Law No. 4,766 was inapplicable since they had ceased to have any relationship with Frank Walter Jordan after January 28, 1942. Of these men, José Gnecco de Carvalho had been arrested on March 23 with shipping data in his pocket, and so the sincerity of his defense was immediately suspect. The others, however, uncompromisingly maintained their innocence.[165]

The TSN deliberated for several weeks, and on April 14, 1943, it sentenced Jordan to twenty-five years, Walter Moll to eight years, and José Gnecco de Carvalho to four years. All the other defendants were found innocent, but their jubilation was short-lived. Ambassador Jefferson Caffery expressed a distinct distaste for the lenient judgments, and clemency for Integralistas did not sit well with Vargas, either. The Brazilian government appealed the verdicts, and on May 28, 1943, a TSN appeals court dispensed some harsher sentences. Jordan found his sentence reduced to twenty years, but Walter Moll's rose to fourteen and José

Gnecco's four-year term was doubled. More significantly, eight-year terms were also meted out to Afonso Digeser, Hans Holl, Herbert Winterstein, and Eduardo Pacheco do Andrade.[166]

On the basis of the Schlegel and Jordan cases, it would be assumed that the TSN courts would show no mercy to *Reichsdeutschen*, and would cast a jaundiced eye upon known or suspected Integralistas. But, could Decree-Law No. 4,766 be implemented if the prosecution could not prove that a defendant had been active after January 28, 1942? And what action would the Vargas government take if persons they viewed as spies were found not guilty by the courts? With the biggest espionage trial in Brazilian history about to commence, answers to these questions would soon be forthcoming.

B. *"Words, Words..."* and Three Other Trials

Espionage indictments were handed down on April 13, 1943, for fifty-one Germans and/or dual citizens, thirty-three Brazilian nationals, five Hungarians, one Chilean, and seven persons who were outside the country. Eighty-five of those accused were men, and twelve were women, five of them being the wives of indicted agents.[167] Nearly all of the ninety-seven being tried were allegedly associated with Engels, Kempter, Starziczny, or Gamillscheg, and when the trial opened in Rio de Janeiro on April 30, 1943, a wide variety of defense tactics were tried. Albrecht Engels, for example, seemed determined to do his best to befuddle the prosecution. As early as May 1942, he attempted to shift some of the responsibility for organizing and directing the ring he and Bohny had led onto the shoulders of a shadowy figure he referred to as "Alfredo Becker." Jack West believed that "Alfredo Becker" was Engels's alter ego. Still, DOPS agents spent over four months searching for the man. Finally, on February 1, 1943, the political police reported that "Alfredo Becker" was not to be found in Brazil. Nevertheless, the TSN chiefs decided to take no chances; they listed "Alfredo Becker" as twenty-sixth on the list of persons named in the indictment.[168]

Next, Francis Crosby of SIS/Brazil had a brainstorm. After several interviews with Engels in 1942–43, he concluded that the mysterious "Alfredo Becker" was, in reality, Johannes Siegfried Becker, an SD agent sent to Argentina in May 1940.[169] Becker entered Brazil in December 1940, but remained there only intermittently until he departed in October 1941. In any case, on October 11, 1948, Engels was again in court, and with the war over, he testified that "Alfredo Becker never existed, that it was a name [he] invented to safeguard the identity of [Naval] Attaché Bohny." Tortured by DOPS, and convinced that his trial was a pro forma affair, Engels stated that he had had no qualms about misleading his tormentors.[170]

Friedrich Kempter chose to hamstring the prosecution by giving sworn statements denying that his assistants provided him with any information after January 28, 1942.[171] But Joséf Starziczny sought to curry favor by implicating almost anyone and everyone he had come into contact with in Brazil. This tactic earned him no judicial clemency, but it kept him separated from his erstwhile cohorts and, therefore, alive. Kempter and others considered Starziczny a traitor and refused to speak to him. Given the opportunity, they would have made short work of the man they considered to be a stool pigeon.[172]

Others among the accused used a variety of strategems in their desperate efforts to escape long penal sentences. Otto Uebele, Jofre Magalhães dos Santos, Theodor Simon, and a host of others insisted that they had ceased all espionage activity prior to January 28, 1942. Heinrich Bleinroth pleaded that he was only a minor figure in the CIT network. Paulo Timm claimed that he never realized what Starziczny was actually doing. Eduard Arnold and Hans Kurt Meyer-Clason eventually chose to throw themselves upon the mercy of the court.[173]

Meanwhile, the female defendants in the case found it efficacious to employ variations on a similar theme. "My only crime was being a wife," insisted Dorothea Metzner, spouse of Starziczny's contact man. "I could not abandon my man," pleaded Helene Lohse, the mistress of Kurt Weingartner. "We should not confuse Cupid with Mars," argued María Pita Soares de Andrade, lawyer for Ilona (Diny) Gaal, the mistress and lookout for Jofre Magalhães dos Santos.[174] In a macho-oriented Brazilian society, the implied argument that a woman who loyally supports her husband or lover is simply doing her duty proved to be an effective one.

Certainly the briefest and most caustic defense presented was that of José Ferreira Dias, the stevedore who supplied shipping information to both Alberto Schwab and Hans Otto Meier. Impressed neither by his attorney's denunciation of Decree-Law No. 4,766 nor the prosecutor's vigorous presentation, Dias told Judge Pereira Braga his assessment of the entire proceeding: "Words, words, words."[175]

After almost five months of testimony and legal arguments, on October 6, 1943, TSN Judge Pereira Braga handed down his decision and pulled a major surprise. In a long, sometimes rambling explanation, the judge concluded that although he believed that the spy ring leaders ought to be punished, the retroactive aspect of Article 67 had to be taken literally. Since the state had not proven that the majority of those charged had committed any acts of espionage after January 28, 1942, he dismissed the indictments against seventy individuals.[176]

Such lenient judgment did not find favor with Ambassador Jefferson Caffery. On October 7, 1943, he cabled the State Department: "I am taking steps to keep them [i.e., the acquitted] under arrest anyhow, and shall probably be able to have them sentenced." The U.S. ambassador followed up this prediction of bad tidings with an October 8 message which read, in part: "I repeat, [the absolved] will be kept in jail."[177]

Certainly, Caffery's entreaties carried a great deal of weight with President Vargas and Foreign Minister Aranha, but no Brazilian government could allow the United States to appear to be dictating to the national judiciary. Most important, perhaps, was the fact that in October

1943, a Brazilian expeditionary force was undergoing intensive training in preparation for combat. Heavy casualties had to be expected, and under such circumstances, the unconditional release of a significant number of questionably loyal persons was guaranteed to raise the ire of the armed forces.[178] On the other hand, influential special interests were working behind the scenes, striving to gain the release of some persons the TSN judge had found guilty.[179] What the Vargas regime needed was a decision that would either please or disarm the divergent interests which were unhappy with the Judge Pereira Braga's October 6 ruling.

Possibly, Vargas gave the TSN appeals court some signal as to what findings the regime would favor, for the decision announced on October 29, 1943, was both a judicial travesty and a political masterstroke. As a guiding principle, the five judges of the appeals panel argued that in matters dealing with the "high and inalienable interests of the defense of the fatherland," personal rights or legal technicalities were secondary in their importance. Specifically, "small divergences in the appraisal of the retroactive application of the law cannot permit that confessed spies continue to act against the national security."[180] Whether or not said spies had been tortured to obtain their statements was immaterial; whether said acts ceased on January 19, or 29, 1942, was also unimportant. How much further back in time Article 67 could be made to stretch was not clear. But the judges left no doubt about one thing: it would be stretched to fit the situation.

But once having stated their principle, the judges ingenuously seized the middle ground. They reduced two sentences, absolved an additional person, and found twenty-one of those Pereira Braga had judged innocent to be guilty of espionage. This left forty-nine persons, or two-thirds of those ordered released on October 6, nominally free.[181] (See Appendix B.)

Neither Caffery nor the State Department was overjoyed with this decision either, but there seemed to be no compelling reason to insist on additional legal stringency. Moreover, after conferring with Vargas and Aranha, on November 7, 1943, the ambassador cabled Washington that "most of those acquitted . . . will be held in prison for the duration of the war."[182] Since the aim was to have those considered security risks placed in detention for the length of the conflict, this "means of security" as Caffery described it,[183] gave the United States de facto accomplishment of its goals. The largest spy trial in Brazilian history ended with most of the legally guilty as well as the legally innocent behind bars, precisely the same situation in which they had been before the trial started.

Commencing on May 16, 1943, but ending before the aforementioned trials, were the legal proceedings instituted against Capt. Tulio Regis do Nascimento and his confederates. When the prosecution commenced its case, thrown into the dock with "Captain García" were Albrecht Engels, several men of his organization, and three absent parties: Kurt Prüfer, Walther Becker, and Hermann Bohny. In all, some twenty persons were cited in this indictment.[184]

In a desperate effort to save his son, Col. Flavio Quieroz do Nascimento took the witness stand and testified that Tulio's mental illness rendered him incapable of making sound judgments and, therefore, he was not legally responsible for his acts.[185] This unconventional (for a spy) and impassioned plea failed to sway the judges. On June 28, 1943, Captain do Nascimento, Gerardo Melo Mourão, and Albrecht Engels received thirty-year terms; the three members of the former German diplomatic party in Brazil (Prüfer, Becker, Bohny) twenty-five-years each, while nine other defendants received twenty- or twenty-five year sentences. The appeals court, citing diplomatic immunity, dropped charges against German embassy officials on July 27, but confirmed all other sentences.[186] (See Appendix B.)

The trial of Captain do Nascimento, Engels, et al., lasted slightly longer than six weeks, but in roughly one month's time, the proceedings against Werner Waltemath and three others were completed. Following an appeal, on December 28, 1943, Werner Waltemath and Paulo Griese received sentences of twenty-seven and one-half and twenty-five years respectively, with Hans Christian von Kotze, alias Johannes van Hughes, receiving the same sentence as Waltemath. To be sure, DOPS was well aware that the man who called himself Hans von Kotze was a BSC agent; what the Vargas regime wanted to impress upon British intelligence with this in absentia sentence was that von Kotze would not be welcome in Brazil at any time soon.[187]

Finally, in October 1944, the trial of William Marcus Baarn and Wilhelm Koepff began under some unusual circumstances. In May 1942, naval attaché Hermann Bohny deposited five thousand dollars in a special account controlled by a lawyer named Fritz Beiler, for the purpose of paying for the defense of jailed agents.[188] By 1944, however, these funds were gone, and the Reich was supplying money for legal defense through the Spanish embassy. The initial surprise came when the Spanish ambassador to Brazil informed the TSN that Berlin would provide the money for Koepff, but not for Baarn.[189] Apparently, non-Aryans could be recruited into the Abwehr, but they could count on little support if they were caught. It is more likely, however, that the Germans knew Baarn was a traitor to their cause and were not interested in assisting in his defense.

José Julio Parise-Iglesias, Baarn's court-appointed lawyer, sought absolution for his client by introducing examples of the spy's cooperation with Brazilian security forces. The press took up the issue until Brazilian army staff headquarters issued a statement denigrating the efficacy of Baarn's assistance. Privately, an army staff official admitted to Rolf Larsen, then legal attaché, that although the black man freely gave information, the army feared that Parise-Iglesias's defense tactics would lead to public support for a soft sentence. The result would be, in the army's opinion, a weakening in the national resolve to carry on the war.[190]

The eventual court ruling would seem to demonstrate that in Brazil in 1945, the will of the army was not to be thwarted. On April 9, 1945, TSN judge Pedro Borges absolved Baarn, but sentenced William Koepff to a twenty-five-year stretch. Six weeks later, on May 22, 1945, a TSN appeals court gave both agents twenty-seven and one-half years. For better or worse, the native of Dutch Guiana never served his time in an ordinary jail. He had been under psychiatric observation since early 1944, and in July 1945, he was committed to the sanitarium for the criminally insane at Bangú, outside of Rio de Janeiro. As far as can be ascertained, he may still be there.[191]

C. *The "Body Count" Game*

Certainly the harsh sentences meted out by the TSN judges made the Vargas regime appear avowedly anti-Nazi and determined to deter other V-men from entering Brazil. Furthermore, the reports of two U.S. officials did much to further these notions even though they did little to enlighten anyone as to the actual situation. For example, on November 11, 1943, Ambassador Jefferson Caffery informed the State Department that 57 persons convicted of espionage activity had received a total of 990 years in prison. A similar report, dated sixteen days later, raised the number to 63 agents and the aggregate to 1,074 years in sentences.[192] Finally, J. Edgar Hoover reported to the White House that as of May 22, 1944, 1,193 persons "who had been the subjects of investigation by SIS representatives" had been arrested, 218 had been charged, and 86 of these convicted, resulting in the imposition of 1,298 years in jail sentences.[193]

Predictably, neither the Hoover nor Caffery reports said anything about the legitimacy of what had been done or the inequitable sentences meted out. For example, a most egregious error was committed in the case of Georg Metzner, Uebele's man, who provided Starziczny with living expenses in January–February 1942. Presenting an explanation which strained the limits of credibility, Judge Pereira Braga concluded that even though Metzner made his last payment to Starziczny after January 28, 1942, this could not be considered as financing espionage activity because the funds had been set aside by Otto Uebele prior to the break in diplomatic relations.[194] The TSN appeals court apparently agreed with the logic of this conclusion, for it also ruled that Metzner was not guilty.

Equally illogical was the acquittal of María Tereza Calvacanti Ellender by both Judge Pereira Braga and the TSN appeals court. Better known as "Mary" when she was on the payroll of Janos Salamon's HTT ring, Senhora Ellender was arrested by São Paulo DOPS on April 25, 1942, and, on the basis of the HTT radio intercepts, charged with espionage. Some fourteen months later, on June 19, 1943, her lawyers defended her in court by emphasizing her cultural contributions as a newspaper columnist and arguing that she had not violated the provisions of Decree-Law No. 4,766.[195] Note that Fritz Weissflog and Karl Haering, among others, made the same argument concerning their legal culpability, yet they received twenty-year sentences for their efforts.[196] Certainly the judges seemed loathe to convict Brazilian women and sentence them to jail as spies. Ultimately, her sex, rather than her connections, national origin, or defensive arguments, may well have been the chief reason why María Calvacanti Ellender escaped a lengthy prison term.

The most disturbing reversal of a judgment concerns Hans Muth, the engineer who constructed the radios used by Kempter, Engels, Starziczny, and Schlegel. Once arrested, Muth steadfastly maintained that all arrangements concerning the delivery and payment for the transmitters were handled by the deceased Benno Sobisch. Furthermore, Muth argued that he never met the spies who used his creations and did not knowingly construct transmitters for espionage purposes.[197] Had the TSN officials been able to read Captain Bohny's record of the Abwehr's activities in Brazil,[198] Muth's argument would have been relegated to the waste basket; as matters stood, however, his unchallenged protestations of innocence retained a dubious credibility. Nevertheless, Judge Pereira Braga, who had been exceptionally benign toward Georg Metzner, sentenced Hans Muth to twenty-five years on October 6, 1943. The following day, Muth's lawyer, A. de Senna Valle, citing errors in court procedure and malicious treatment on the part of the prosecution, appealed the decision. Subsequently, the TSN Appeals Court overturned Pereira Braga's decision, and made Hans Muth a free man, subject, however, to the rigors of continued security measures.[199]

The key to this unexplained and highly controversial decision would seem to be Muth's long-time status as telecommunications instructor for both the Brazilian army and navy. In fact, on June 15, 1943, four captains and several other naval officers placed in the court record a letter which stated that Hans Muth, in their opinion, "had never practiced any suspected act of espionage against Brazil."[200] It may well be that behind-the-scenes pressure exerted by naval officers, and perhaps, by army officers as well, produced Muth's acquittal. In working for the Brazilian armed forces since 1937, Muth had performed the repair and instructional tasks assigned him without charge.[201] His legal salvation aptly demonstrates that those who perform free services may eventually receive payment in full nevertheless.

This compilation of facts and speculations regarding the 1942–45 Brazilian spy trials suggests that the proceedings and sentences were intended to accomplish several different, but interconnected, goals. In jailing the spies and having them convicted, the Vargas regime was attempting to inculcate in the Brazilian people an awareness of the extent of Nazi subversion and a determination to make the sacrifices necessary in waging war against the Third Reich.[202] Secondly, the entire process would seem partially designed to demonstrate to the world (and the United States in particular) that although Vargas's Brazil was not democratic, its anti-Nazi credentials were both authentic and incontestable.[203]

Bearing these considerations in mind, it is quite logical that the primary targets became Engels, Kempter, do Nascimento, Schlegel, Starziczny, and other ring leaders. For these men there would be draconian, attention-getting jail sentences, and the same for the in absentia German embassy personnel, specifically Hermann Bohny, Walther Becker, and Kurt Prüfer. The Vargas government recognized that the strictures of diplomatic immunity made the twenty-five-year terms meted out to these men mere formalities, but the Brazilian man-in-the-street did not necessarily know this, and the regime did not publicly report that the sentences had been dropped.[204]

Following the same logic, it is understandable that once the number of those arrested became impressive enough, and the trials themselves had been utilized to gain every possible propaganda advantage, the Vargas regime lost interest in the myriad of secondary agents and collaborators. If some of these were innocent but went to jail, or if some were guilty but escaped punishment, that was just too bad; the advancement of the national interest took precedence over issues of justice for individuals. Of course, the determination of what exactly the national interest was could change quite rapidly, a consideration which may help explain why, after the bulk of the spies had been sentenced and imprisoned, the jails rapidly began releasing these same enemies of the state.

V. Aftermath

A. *The Revolving Door*

An admitted informant of the CIT ring, Galindo de Medeiros had been absolved by Pereira Braga, but given a seven-year sentence by the TSN appeals court on October 29, 1943. Perhaps the fact that he was a native Brazilian, or the possibility that as a customs official he had powerful friends, made a difference. In any event, his appeal was taken up by the Brazilian Supreme Court and, eventually, a writ of *habeas corpus* was issued. Then the Supreme Court decided that de Medeiros had committed no crime and on August 29, 1944, he was set free.[205]

The next convicted spy upon whom the Supreme Court would look favorably was the prominent and controversial Otto Uebele. This spy ring co-leader had been found not guilty by Judge Pereira Braga, who ruled that Uebele had commited no proven act of espionage after January 28, 1942. The TSN appeals court decided otherwise, and gave Otto a comparatively light eight-year sentence. Considering the twenty-five- and thirty-year stretches Engels, Starziczny, Kempter, and other ring leaders received, Otto was fortunate indeed. Both of the courts and the police seemed to have been impressed by his wealth and his possession of the Medal of the Southern Cross, the highest award that can be granted by the Brazilian government to a foreign national. Certainly, Uebele spent little time behind bars either before or after his conviction.[206] With Carlos Cyrillio Júnior, a lawyer described as a consummate wire-puller, masterminding his appeal, Otto Uebele's case was before the Brazilian Supreme Court in December 1944. Early in 1945, the agent known as "Kuntze" obtained the full abrogation of his sentence, and although his health and bank account had suffered grievously, he was free.[207]

Following the end of the war in Europe in May 1945, the appeal of Max Winterstein, formerly of Frank Walter Jordan's LFS ring, was the first to obtain a favorable adjudication. On September 10, 1945, the Supreme Court, in its strongest statement yet, ruled that the plaintiff had been convicted "without proofs" and "contrary to the literal interpretation of the law."[208] A bitter confrontation over Decree-Law No. 4,766 between the Supreme Court and the TSN was shaping up, but another event made this problem moot. On October 29, 1945, army officers deposed Getúlio Vargas. With the former strongman now a private citizen, the authoritarian state machinery he created could not long survive; Decree-Law No. 8,186 brought the TSN to an ignominious end on November 19, 1945. Thereafter, all requests for appeals and writs of *habeas corpus* would be heard by the Supreme Military Court. This change generated a veritable blizzard of requests for pardons, retrials, and reconsiderations of sentences. The Military Court moved cautiously, but in December 1945, writs of *habeas corpus* resulted in the releases of Wilhelm Gieseler and Hans Holl, to be followed on January 2, 1946, by Hans Ulrich Uebele.[209]

Meanwhile, with Brazil on the road to democracy, the new view of legal devices like Decree-Law No. 4,766 was best exemplified by Article 145 of the Constitution of 1946, Section 2 of which specifically prohibited the imposition of retroactive federal laws. A general exodus from the jails would not commence, however, until two 1947 court cases reduced the status of Decree-Law No. 4,766 to that of a veritable dead letter. In the first of these, Hans Kurt Meyer-Clason would finally obtain the favor of the gods of fortune. First exonerated by Judge Pereira Braga on October 6, 1943, he was subsequently crushed by a twenty-year sentence handed down by the TSN appeals court. As of April 1947, he was languishing in prison when he was approached by an enterprising lawyer named Alcibiades Delmora Noguiera de Gama, who offered to take up his case.

After he succeeded in gaining the consent of the Supreme Military Court to a review on July 7, 1947, Noguiera de Gama presented a compact but devastating brief. The attorney never attacked Decree-Law No. 4,766 directly. Instead, he argued that since his client was arrested and jailed on the morning of January 29, 1942, and diplomatic relations with the Axis had been severed during the evening of January 28, Meyer-Clason had had less than twenty-four hours to commit acts of espionage. What evidence had DOPS presented demonstrating that Meyer-Clason had committed an act of espionage between the evening of the twenty-eighth and the morning of the twenty-ninth? According to the lawyer, the official record revealed none whatsoever. The court obviously found the argument efficacious, for it ordered Meyer-Clason released. As the first of the spies arrested in the January 1942 roundup, he had spent over five years behind bars; on August 14, 1947, he was finally free.[210]

The Meyer-Clason case established that unless DOPS presented evidence that proved an alleged spy had been active after the evening of

January 28, 1942, that person could probably be released. It also set the stage for the precedent-setting Fritz Weissflog decision. An active member of the Starziczny-Uebele group, Weissflog was still another defendant who had been acquitted on October 6, 1943, but subsequently given a twenty-year sentence by the TSN appeals court. In commuting this sentence on December 24, 1947, the Supreme Military Court concluded that Weissflog had been convicted for participating in the reconnaissance flight which resulted in the departure of the German vessels *Lech, Frankfurt,* and *Hermes* from Brazilian waters. But, as this incident transpired in June 1941, the limitation stated in Article 67 of Decree-Law No. 4,766 made that statute inapplicable. Undeniably Weissflog's aerial investigation was of considerable benefit to Nazi Germany, but since no statute prohibiting this action then existed, no legal transgression had been committed.[211]

This reversal implied that the Gaspar Dutra government would do nothing to defend the legitimacy of all-purpose security laws enforced during the Estado Nôvo years, and so, by 1948, even individuals whose activities fell within the parameters of Decree-Law No. 4,766 were seeking new trials or requesting amnesty. Preeminent among those who would gain their freedom during that year were Gerardo Melo Mourão and Friedrich Kempter.[212] Clearly, if the commutation of their twenty-five and thirty-year sentences could be justified, the release of other spy ring leaders must soon follow.

By 1949, only Albrecht Engels, Joséf Starziczny, Herbert von Heyer, Wilhelm Koepff, Tulio Regis do Nascimento, and five others were still in prison. Engels obtained his release in 1953, Koepff in 1955, and Joséf Starziczny in 1958.[213] If these legal reversals took place with a minimum of public outcry, there would be one publicized case which, for a decade, would claim more than its share of press attention. After several appeals on various grounds, Tulio Regis do Nascimento was ordered released in January 1948, only to have the decision reversed and his sentence reconfirmed. In March 1950, the Supreme Military Tribunal reduced his term to twelve years, but he kept fighting. His case and the continuing controversy surrounding it generated intense passions among army officers, some of whom considered his conduct disgraceful, while others believed him to be more sinned against than sinner. Finally, on April 24, 1954, the Brazilian Supreme Court, facing up to the implications of the previous releases, declared Decree-Law No. 4,766 unconstitutional. Captain do Nascimento was put at liberty in July 1954, and declared free in March 1955.[214]

It seems that none of the Abwehr agents or collaborators convicted in the Brazilian courts served an entire prison sentence. This observation only reemphasizes the legal burlesque these trials really were. But some of the issues associated with wartime espionage in Brazil had moral as well as legal repercussions, the fact of which some Brazilians would become uncomfortably aware.

B. *The Stanley Hilton–Gerardo Melo Mourão Affair*

In 1977, Editora Civilização Brasileira, a distinguished publishing house in Rio de Janeiro, published Stanley Hilton's *Suástica sobre o Brasil: A História da Espionagem Alemã no Brasil, 1939–44.* Using TSN records, microfilmed German Foreign Office papers, Nest Bremen records, and other papers found in the U.S. National Archives, Hilton produced a history of Abwehr activity in Brazil. The work is quite sketchy concerning the organization and activities of the SIS/Brazil,[215] but it is a relatively dispassionate effort. In contrast, the expanded English language edition (entitled *Hitler's Secret War in South America: Espionage and Counter-Espionage in Brazil, 1939–1945,* published by the Louisiana State University Press, 1981) contains a preface which is at once both angry and argumentative in tone and style.[216] Nevertheless, it was the Portuguese language effort which drew the most intense criticism, Hilton's chief antagonist being Gerardo Margela Melo Mourão, whom the professor listed as a member of the "Captain García" ring.

Following his pardon and release from prison in August 1948, Mourão went on to become a leading poet, a deputy in the National Congress and, ironically enough, an advocate of the political machine founded by Getúlio Vargas, the Brazilian Workers party (PTB). Mourão's World War II activities had not been the subject of press discussion since 1969.[217] Apparently, the appearance of *Suástica sobre O Brasil* raised new fears and reopened old wounds. In any case, the Brazilian initiated a series of attacks on Hilton which climaxed in a confrontation on the pages of one of Brazil's most prestigious newspapers, *Jornal do Brasil.* On January 21, 1978, Mourão stated in an interview that "the history of Brazil cannot be written by an agent of the CIA who is neither a Brazilian, nor a historian." Three days later, in another interview, Mourão added that in releasing the book, Editora Civilização Brasileira was "trying to sell the *paper* [our italics] of an incompetent at the cost of my reputation."[218]

Angered by Mourão's broadsides, Hilton hurled some venom-tipped shafts of his own. In a rebuttal entitled, "I am not a CIA agent, but Mourão continues to be a Nazi," he defended his work as an historian, and argued that "unfortunately, the cultural nazism still defended by Senhor Melo Mourão suggests that the personality and the world view (Weltanschaung) which caused him to work in support of the victory of the Nazi regime during the early years of the world war have not been substantially modified since that sad epoch."[219] Taking the offensive in this tabloid war of words, Hilton published additional articles taking Mourão to task,[220] and defending the conclusions reached in *Suástica sobre O Brasil.* The North American professor had reason to be vexed by the turgid comments directed at his work and the undisguised *ad hominem* attack; but since he chose to cross swords with a prestigious national literary figure, he should have expected the brickbats that subsequently came his way.[221]

The name-calling indulged in both by Hilton and Mourão produced no enlightenment and made both participants appear more than a little pompous. In an interview he granted to us, Mourão stated that violence to his person and threats against his "wife" persuaded him to sign the confession attributed to him. He also laid special emphasis on the fact that his trial and conviction had been judged as unconstitutional in 1948, and implied that said confession was a compendium of lies.[222] In contrast, Stanley Hilton's position was that although torture may have been used to elicit the desired depositions, this did not in itself mean that Mourão's confession (or that of anyone else) was necessarily false.[223]

It would seem that the history of Mourão's 1942 activities, as related in Hilton's book, and also on these pages, is essentially correct. We make this judgment on indirect, but persuasive, evidence. While some of those convicted refused to discuss their activities or confessions, several others reviewed English or Portuguese accounts of their 1940–42 activities and verified for us their essential reliability.[224] If these confessions are basically accurate, there is no evident reason to assume that DOPS fabricated a totally fallacious deposition solely to convict Mourão. Moreover, in neither of the January 1978 *Jornal do Brasil* articles nor in his interview with us did Mourão specifically deny taking part in the intelligence activities attributed to him. What he implied was that the question of innocence or guilt was a good deal more complicated than the degree of his collaboration or noncollaboration. Was it?

The key in the lock and partial solution to this problem was found in the *Jornal do Brasil*'s Rio de Janeiro newspaper morgue. In a file marked *"espionagem,"* we discovered some articles by, and communciations directed to, a well-known newspaperman of leftist and nationalistic views, Edmar Morel. During the 1947–50 period, Morel wrote for two small capital city newspapers, *Panfleto* and *Diretrizes,* and in them waged a battle against the release of those convicted as spies. Taking an unabashed advocacy position, Morel ignored the processes used to extract the confessions, and implied that Kempter, Mourão, Uebele, et al., were obtaining their releases through corruption or deception.[225] But by 1979, this writer had seemingly shifted his position almost 180 degrees. In a newspaper article on December 21, 1978, he rebuffed Hilton and declared himself to be in total support of Mourão. Morel insisted that Mourão had "the right to have his sympathies, since the Axis powers, among other things, were fighting against Anglo-American imperialism which enslaves, and still enslaves a great part of the world." In praising the poet-author, Morel provided a clue as to why his opinions seemed to have changed so radically: "He [Mourão] had lived long enough to see that the monstrosities of Nazism were no different than the atomic bomb dropped on Hiroshima. He had lived long enough to see the nefarious crimes perpetrated [by the United States] against the populations of Korea and Vietnam."[226] More significantly, Morel reported that Mourão had repented of his Nazi sympathies on the pages of *Diretrizes,* embraced democracy, and declared himself to be a good Brazilian. He was neither a diehard nor "closet" Nazi, and certainly not someone to be denounced and indicted by the representative of a country whose hands were not clean.

We were unable to find the 1948 copy of *Diretrizes* referred to, but the *espionagem* file in the *Jornal do Brasil* morgue contained an undated communication to "Edmar Morel," signed "Gerardo Margella Mello Mourão," which may be the confession in question. The beliefs and opinions expressed are highly revealing:

> No other Brazilian journalist has attacked the famous Nazi spies [probably meant sarcastically] like you have. As for me, I assume the entire responsibility for [my] Germanophile activities which happened before Brazil entered the war. I wanted the victory of Germany, judging that only the Axis could free us from the bolshevisation . . . and establish for semi-colonial countries like ours, a healthy equilibrium in the face of Anglo-American imperialism . . . I feel a desire to say I was wrong . . . if I still thought merely in political-economic terms, I would continue supporting the Axis flag. Today I think in Christian terms. I thank God for the defeat of the Axis.

Mourão also denounced the "Big Three" (the United States, Great Britain, and the Soviet Union), declared that he had quit the Integralista movement in 1943, and suggested that if Morel were interested in justice, he should condemn the Estado Nôvo's judicial system as well as the "famous Nazi spies."[227]

The late heavyweight champion, Joe Louis, expressed the feelings of millions when he declared that the United States was fated to win World War II "because we are on God's side."[228] In contrast, the statements of Mourão then, and Morel now, reveal that Brazilians of nationalistic bent do not view the U.S. victory over the Axis as being either an unalloyed triumph or of universal benefit. Their preeminent concern was, and is, an independent Brazil free from economic domination by the Anglo-Americans. In our view, those Brazilians who cooperated with the Abwehr because they believed that Nazi victory would result in deliverance from economic dependency were pitifully naive. Still, they will continue to receive the sympathy of other nationalistic Brazilians who view such collaboration as technically guilty, but morally innocent.

Finally, this issue of motivation carries with it still another consideration of some relevance. Friedrich Kempter, for example, made it quite evident to us that while he never joined the AO, he felt no remorse about working for Nazi Germany during World War II. Having been away from Germany almost fifteen years when he was arrested, Kempter was in no way responsible for such abominations as Dachau or Buchenwald. But, unlike Mourão, he does not "thank God for the defeat of the Axis." For Kempter, Germany's error was that it took on more enemies that it had the capacity to defeat.[229]

We are not in the business of apologizing for German spies or pro-Axis sympathizers. Nevertheless, the motivational factors which led

Friedrich Kempter and Gerardo Melo Mourão to cooperate with the Abwehr are clearly different. There will always be disagreement, even among men of good will, over the degree to which motivation mitigates the culpability of an act. We believe that those who pass on the question of Mourão's relative guilt or innocence must give the motivational factor serious consideration. The conclusion they reach will not be as important as their realization that black or white answers cannot be applied in problems like this one.

1. Where Are They Now?

Released in 1953, Albrecht Gustav Engels recouped his financial fortunes, becoming, among other things, part owner of a lucrative automobile dealership. Throughout the 1970s, he maintained residences in Germany and Brazil.[230]

The Brazilian government seized the assets of the Theodor Wille Company in 1943, a contingency which, along with war-related losses, legal expenses, and court costs, ruined Otto Uebele. After his 1945 release, he strove energetically to improve his blighted economic prospects. Evidently, he met with some measure of success, for when the reorganized Theodor Wille Company reopened for business in 1954, Otto Uebele was named honorary president. He died in 1956, but his son, Hans Ulrich Uebele, is today a successful entrepreneur in the southern state of Santa Catarina.[231]

Commercial endeavor has not been the only field in which former agents have made names for themselves. After leaving Brazil in September 1942, diplomat Walther Becker was financial counselor at the German embassy in Madrid until 1945. He was rehabilitated by the diplomatic corps of the Federal Republic of Germany in 1951, and named ambassador to Egypt in 1955, serving in this post until 1959. He retired with full honors, and died in March 1973.[232]

Gerardo Melo Mourão's greatest success as a man of letters occurred in 1980. Three of his books of poetry (O Pais dos Mourões, 1963; Peripécias de Gerardo, 1972; and Rastro de Apolo, 1977) were united in a single, illustrated volume entitled Os Peãs (The Peons), published by Edições GDR in agreement with the National Book Institute, a branch of the Brazilian Ministry of Education and Culture. In 1981, Mourão was again a newspaperman, this time as a foreign correspondent assigned to the People's Republic of China.[233]

Although he has the most prestigious reputation, Mourão is by no means the only person connected with German intelligence in Brazil during World War II who has become successful as a man of letters. Conspicuous among the Germans has been Hans Kurt Meyer-Clason who in the 1980s lives in Munich. Known internationally as an interpreter, analyst, and translator (into German) of Portuguese poetry, Meyer-Clason traveled to Brazil on several occasions in the 1970s, and has lectured on poetry at the Federal University of Rio Grande do Sul in Pôrto Alegre.[234]

Friedrich Kempter remained in Brazil for two decades after his release in 1948. Subsequently, he settled his family in the Hamburg suburb of Wandsbek-Marienthal, where, in 1980, he was earning a reasonable livelihood as a Portuguese-German translator.[235]

After his release in 1958, Joséf Starziczny settled in the city of Niterói. He allegedly owned and operated a radio repair shop there during the 1960s. He was, nevertheless, more fortunate than Hermann Bohny. The former naval attaché died in a French prisoner-of-war camp on May 26, 1945;[236] the circumstances of his death and exactly how he ended up in the camp are unclear.

Perhaps the only things the survivors have in common are their bitter memories of the tortures inflicted upon them by DOPS and their agreement that the TSN trials were monstrous travesties.[237]

VI: Summary: Payment for Services Rendered

DOPS agents like Elpídio Reali demonstrated unusual investigatory capabilities, and the SIS/Brazil under Jack West proved its competence in the heat of struggle. Add the inestimable assistance of the RID in intercepting the German messages, plus the success of the FBI laboratory and Treasury Department code breakers in decrypting them, and the battle against the Abwehr became a rout. Nonetheless, the Germans did recruit some resourceful operatives, and the capture and imprisonment of Kempter and Engels, in particular, cannot debase the energetic efforts of these men and their occasional successes. Indeed, take away the technological advantage, and it becomes interesting to speculate on how much longer DOPS and the SIS/Brazil would have had to struggle in order to defeat their German adversaries.

While the United States and the Vargas government cooperated effectively in smashing the Abwehr network in Brazil, the treatment of the V-men by DOPS and the TSN trials highlight the fact that these allies did not share the same ideals. This difference in outlook is convincingly evidenced by the following incident.

On December 8, 1944, J. Edgar Hoover directed a report to Harry Hopkins and Franklin D. Roosevelt, which advised that a U.S. citizen in Rio de Janeiro had recently written a letter to a friend outside Brazil criticizing the Vargas regime. DOPS intercepted this letter, and its agents arrested the unnamed individual and roughed him up. Yet, when queried by U.S. embassy officials about this incident, the political police expressed themselves as "overjoyed at having been able to ... do a favor for the American government." Why was the arrest and pummeling of a U.S. citizen salutary? An SIS operative who investigated the matter informed Hoover that "it was determined that the police had learned that the American arrested was a Republican, and that they considered this good cause for his arrest. The Brazilian police ... feel that any political party which is not in office in the United States must necessarily be the enemy of the United States government, comparable to the outlawed Brazilian

parties such as [the] Integralistas and the Communists."[238] The Estado
Nôvo was not a democracy, and Vargas had made it clear early on that
weapons shipments and economic aid meant more to him than moral
scruples. Allowing DOPS officers to savage spies, Brazilians, and U.S.
citizens who were Republican party members, were simply not matters of
significant concern.

The United States was determined to achieve the military defeat of
the Axis powers, and Brazilian support was deemed vital. Thus, FDR
could speak eloquently of the Four Freedoms, but as Undersecretary
Sumner Welles pointed out in March 1942, with Vargas, the issue was
essentially payment for sevices rendered. Between 1942 and the end of
1945, Brazil received $366 million in military aid and $550 million in
economic assistance, these being the largest amounts granted any Latin
American republic.[239] In the end, Vargas more or less got what he wanted,
and the United States more or less got what it wanted. But those officials
in the Roosevelt administration who knew what was happening in Brazilian jails often found it expedient to look the other way.

Notes

1. Sumner Welles, *The Time for Decision* (New York), p. 225. Welles also alludes to the gravity of the espionage problem and its significance to U.S. policy makers in his *Seven Decisions That Shaped History* (New York, 1950–51), pp. 99, 106, and 112.

2. Agreement on this point and its inclusion in Welles's instructions can be seen in U.S. Department of State, *Foreign Relations of the United States—1942* (hereafter the series is referred to as *FRUS*), vol. 5 (Washington, 1963), p. 27.

3. Ibid., p. 28.

4. For Vargas's statement, see National Archives and Records Service (hereafter referred to as NARS), R.G. 59, 740.0011 European War 1939/1861, no. 21, section 4, p. 11. For Roosevelt's reply, see NARS, R.G. 59, 832.24/634, p. 1.

5. Welles's comment concerning Ruíz Guiñazú is found in *Seven Decisions That Shaped History*, p. 100.

6. See Enrique Ruíz Guiñazú, *La política argentina y el futuro de América* (Buenos Aires, 1944), pp. 83–90. Ruíz Guiñazú insists that he never intended to sign any agreement breaking relations with the Axis.

7. This statement is found in NARS, R.G. 59, 740.0011 European War 1939/1861, section 4, p. 11. Note that most of this document is included in *FRUS—1942*, vol. 5, but the section noted here was not included.

8. The words of caution from the Brazilian army are found in Fundação Getúlio Vargas, Rio de Janeiro, Brazil, Arquivo Getúlio Vargas, GV 42.01.24/3, letter from Minister of War Eurico Dutra.

9. The events of January 23, 1942, are discussed in detail in Welles, *Seven Decisions That Shaped History*, pp. 110–111, and Gary Frank, *Struggle for Hegemony in South America: Argentina, Brazil and the United States during the Second World War* (Miami, Fla., 1979), pp. 14–15.

10. See Welles, *Seven Decisions That Shaped History*, pp. 118–119. For the actual resolution, see *FRUS—1942*, vol. 5, p. 42. On Cordell Hull's objections to Welles's actions, see Cordell Hull, *Memoirs of Cordell Hull*, vol. 2 (New York, 1949), pp. 1148–1149.

11. Evidence that Aranha had pledged his word concerning some manner of diplomatic action can be seen in Arquivo Oswaldo Aranha, OA, 42.01.07/1, a letter from Franklin D. Roosevelt to Aranha. See also NARS, R.G. 59, 710, Consultation, 3/133, no. 2224, p. 1. A discussion of Aranha's threat to resign unless Vargas took action is found in Frank D. McCann, *The Brazilian-American Alliance, 1937–1945* (Princeton, 1974), pp. 256–258.

12. See NARS, R.G. 59, 832.24/651, p. 1.

13. NARS, R.G. 59, 740.0011, European War 1939/1861, section 6, p. 15.

14. For the details of the negotiations and Welles's role in aiding the Brazilians, see Stetson Conn and Byron Fairchild, *The Western Hemisphere: The Framework of Hemisphere Defense* (Washington, D.C., 1960), pp. 314–316. Concerning equipment withdrawals from U.S. defenses, see *FRUS—1942*, vol. 5, pp. 654–655.

15. This note was found attached to an unnumbered document in the Suitland, Maryland, Document Center. See NARS, R.G. 84, 820.02, Brazil, 1933–1944, G-2 Regional File

5900–5920, box 260. It was one of several stuck inside (misplaced?) document 10284, dated February 27, 1943.

16. For Aranha's tendentious explanation and justification, see Arquivo Oswaldo Aranha, OA 42.03.11/1. For German views, see NARS, R.G. 59, 862.20210/820, no. 286, p. 1. On the U.S. initiation of the action, see NARS, R.G. 84, 820.02, Brazil 1933–1944, G-2 Regional File 5900–5920, box 260, document 10284, entitled: *Embassy Accomplishments Report on Concessions and Privileges Gained from Brazil in Matters Relating to Hemispheric Defense, United States and United Nations Military and Naval Operations and Other Things* (hereafter referred to as *Accomplishments*), p. 19.

17. For a record of this request, see NARS, R.G. 59, 862.20210/2421, unsigned to Gordon (FAC), 3/4/42. See also NARS, R.G. 59, 862.20210/Stubbs, Edgar/8, and 862.20210, Grough, Max/12.

18. Cossel is also listed as an agent in NARS, R.G. 165, box 982, M.I.D., *Axis Espionage and Propaganda in Latin America* (Washington, 1946), p. 27.

19. This rejection was reported in NARS, R.G. 59, 862.20210/2421, p. 1.

20. The German report of this incident is found in NARS, R.G. 242, ML-171a, roll 23, Ast Hamburg B. 1018/42 IMg. On the previous reports by Muller to Niedenführ, see German Federal Republic, Bonn, Auswärtiges Amt, Büro des Staatssekretärs, *Akten betreffend: Brasilien,* band 1, April 21, 1938–February 28, 1942, pp. 157294-157295.

21. See NARS, R.G. 173, RID, box 5, *Testimony of G. S. Sterling,* part 1, p. 19.

22. Conversation between Jack West and Prof. Leslie B. Rout, Jr., November 3, 1980. West was not certain whether the number of agents listed was eighty-four or eighty-seven.

23. See NARS, R.G. 84, *Accomplishments,* p. 19.

24. Ibid.

25. On Muller's problems and his enforced departure as police chief, see Arquivo Vargas, GV 42.03.01. See also *Accomplishments,* p. 19, where Caffery hints that he had a hand in the removal, and NARS, R.G. 59, 832.105/145, pp. 1–2.

26. NARS, R.G. 59, 711.32/136, p. 1, and 832.105/47, p. 1.

27. See German Federal Republic, Bonn, Auswärtiges Amt, *Akten zur deutschen auswärtigen politik:* 1918–1945, series E, vol. 2 (Göttingen, 1969), pp. 381–382.

28. Hélio Silva, *1942: Guerra no continente* (Rio de Janeiro, 1972), pp. 373–383. This was not technically a declaration of war, and so on August 31, 1942, in Decree No. 10, 358, "a state of war in all the national territory" was declared.

29. See NARS, R.G. 84, 820.02, no. 7578, box 547, *Declarations Made by Theodoro Frederich Schlegel,* p. 4.

30. On the problems caused by atmospheric conditions in Rio de Janeiro in December 1941, see NARS, R.G. 84, 820.02, no. 7578, box 547, *Declarations Made by Rolf Trautmann,* p. 1.

31. Ibid., p. 2, for Trautmann's arrangements. On the Schlegel-Dellinghausen connection, see Processo 3.093, *Niels Christian Christiansen e Outros* (hereafter referred to as *NCCEO*), vol. 8, box 227, p. 1570.

32. On Erwin Backhaus and his activities and his ill-advised behavior, see U.S. Department of the Navy, Naval Historical Center, Washington Naval Yard, *Files of the German Naval Staff, German Naval Attaché in Brazil* (hereafter referred to as *GNAB*), T-65, PG-32004, p. 213. See also NARS, R.G. 59, 862.20210, *Engels, Albrecht Gustav/71* (hereafter referred to as *Engels/71*), section 3, n.p.

33. *Engels/71,* section 3, n.p.

34. Ibid.

35. On the Schlegel-Bohny quarrel, see *Engels/71,* section 3, n.p., and *Declarations Made by Theodoro Frederich Schlegel,* p. 3.

36. For these messages, see NARS, R.G. 84, 820.02, box 547, *Memorandum, Rio de Janeiro,* January 5, 1943, p. 2.

37. On the Sobisch-Utzinger trip, and the effort to get "Carola" operating on the farm controlled by Dellinghausen, see *Declarations Made by Rolf Trautmann*, pp. 2–3, and *Declarations Made by Theodoro Frederich Schlegel*, pp. 3–4.

38. For these messages, see *Engels/71*, section 3, n.p.

39. *Declarations Made by Rolf Trautmann*, p. 3.

40. Ibid., and *Declarations Made by Theodoro Frederich Schlegel*, p. 4.

41. See NARS, R.G. 59, 862.20232/486, p. 2. That the Germans were aware that Schlegel was under surveillance is noted in *GNAB*, T-65, PG-32004, p. 186. Message translations and the identification of "Salama" and/or "Schlegel" can be found in *Engels/71*, section 3, n.p.

42. *Declarations Made by Rolf Trautmann*, p. 3, and *Declarations Made by Theodoro Frederich Schlegel*, p. 4. See also NARS, R.G. 59, 862.20210/1384, no. 1447, p. 1.

43. This incident is related in NARS, R.G. 59, 862.20210, *Kempter, Frederico/18*, p. 13.

44. *GNAB*, T-65, 32004, p. 199. On the long friendship between Kempter and Muller, see *O Jornal do Brasil*, July 17, 1978.

45. For the Ottomar Müller-Hans Napp shift of jobs and authority, see NARS, R.G. 84, 820.02, Folder: 820.02-1947, no. 9883, box 537, pp. 1–3, and NARS, R.G. 59, 862.20210/2439, pp. 30–31.

46. For the January 27, 1942, messages, see NARS, R.G. 59, 862.20210/2439, p. 39. On Knapp's transfer to Dietrich Niebuhr's control, see La República Argentina, Ministerio de Relaciones Exteriores y Culto, Archivo de Relaciones Exteriores, *Guerra entre Estados Unidos y los paises del Eje,* dispatch 1, vol. 8, appendix 2, 1943, pp. 8–9.

47. On the trials and travails of Walter Giese, see NARS, R.G. 59, 802.20210/2439, pp. 18–21. On Heinrich Loeschner, see NARS, R.G. 319, *German Espionage in Latin America* (hereafter referred to as *GELA*), pp. 76–77 OG, and R.G. 59, 862.20210/1945, pp. 1–4.

48. For the details of Fink's arrest and eventual release, see NARS, R.G. 59, 862.20210/1334, pp. 3–5.

49. See NARS. R.G. 59, 862.20210/2439, pp. 25–26.

50. On the Engels-Kempter friction in January 1942, see ibid., pp. 8–9.

51. Ibid., see also *Engels/71,* section 6, n.p.

52. See NARS, R.G. 59, 862.20210/2439, p. 1. The first decode of a Kempter message was achieved about June 12, 1941.

53. Ibid., p. 9.

54. All messages sent and received on that day are found in Superintêndencia de Sequrança, Política e Social de São Paulo, *A Rede de Espionagem Nazista chefiada por Niels Christian Christiansen* (hereafter referred to as *A Rede*) (São Paulo, 1943), pp. 26 & 41.

55. See *GNAB*, T-65, PG 32004, p. 206.

56. The amount to be paid and Metzner's financial juggling are carefully explained in NARS, R.G. 59, 862.20210/1930 1/2, p. 36.

57. For these events, see ibid., and *A Rede*, p. 26.

58. For the quote, see NARS, R.G. 59, 862.20210/1930 1/2, p. 36. On the secret poison, see *NCCEO*, Appendix 1, box 228, p. 38.

59. *A Rede*, p. 26.

60. This entire story and the quoted material are found in *A Rede*, pp. 2–5, and *NCCEO*, Appendix 1, box 228, pp. 29–37.

61. Interview, São Paulo, Dr. Elpídio Reali with Professor Rout, July 6, 1978.

62. *Ibid.*

63. For these messages from Jordan, see NARS, R.G. 59, 862.20210/1859, pp. 3–5.

64. Ibid., pp. 4–5.

65. See *NCCEO*, vol. 3, box 227, pp. 441–443 and 462–484, for testimony by Magalhães dos Santos and Nagy concerning the events decribed. See also *Engels/71*, section 4, n.p.

66. On Romero's alleged recruitment, see NARS, R.G. 59, 862.20210/1218, p. 2.

67. For do Nascimento's medical history to 1941, see *A República do Brasil*, Arquivo Superior Tribunal Militar, Brasilia, D.F. Processo 3.294, *Tulio Regis do Nascimento e Otros* (hereafter referred to as *TRNO*), vol. 4, pp. 505–506, and vol. 5, pp. 9–10.

68. On Bohny's beliefs concerning the future utility of "Captain García," see *GNAB*, T-65, PG 32004, pp. 196–197.

69. See NARS, R.G. 84, 820.02, box 547, *Memorandum of January 5, 1943*, pp. 2–3, R.G. 59, 862.20210/2439, pp. 4–6, *Engels/71*, section 6, n.p.

70. On the hurried deliveries of money in dollars and Argentine pesos to Engels in January 1942, see *Engels/71*, section 13, n.p. See also *GNAB*, T-65, PG-32004, p. 157, which also explains how the money was changed into cruzeiros.

71. On the work of Glock and Becker after the rupture in diplomatic relations, and the financial role played by Walther Becker, see *GNAB*, T-65, PG-32004, pp. 167–168, and NARS, R.G. 59, 862.20232/1-2446, p. 3.

72. See NARS, R.G. 242, ML-170, roll 22, n.p.

73. Letter from former Abwehr officer Oskar Reille, Mölln, Federal Republic of Germany, to Professor Rout, January 30, 1979. Reille contacted Wickmann, and forwarded his reply.

74. On the destruction of shipping during the first six months of 1942 off the U.S. coast, see Terry Hughes and John Costello, *The Battle of the Atlantic* (New York,1977), pp. 196–202.

75. Letter from Jack West to Professor Rout, October 21, 1980.

76. Hans Kurt Meyer-Clason's arrest and interrogation are discussed in detail in Estado do Rio Grande do Sul, *Vida Policial*, vol. 4, no. 44 (March 1942), pp. 27–29.

77. The quoted material and the blindfolded confession are from a letter from Hans Kurt Meyer-Clason (now known as Curt Mayer-Clason) to Professor Rout, September 3, 1979.

78. On Arnold's arrest and confession, see *Vida Policial*, vol. 4, no. 44 (March 1942), p. 30, and NARS, R.G. 84, 820.02, box 547, *Declaration of Edward Arnold before the Delegacia de Ordem Político e Social, Pôrto Alegre, Brazil*, March 5, 1942, pp. 1–9.

79. For these arrests and the attempted extradition of von Heyer, see NARS, R.G. 84, 820.02, no. 12486, box 547, *Addenda to Dispatch #11871 Regarding Axis Espionage, Sabotage, Propaganda, etc. Activities in Brazil*, August 25, 1943, pp. 2–5.

80. In November 1941, Elim O'Shaughnessy contacted Elpídio Reali and sought his support in regard to future counterespionage activities. Interview with Elpídio Reali, July 6, 1978.

81. This full story is from *A Rede*, pp. 5–6.

82. NARS, R.G. 59, *Engels/71*, part IX, n.p.

83. NARS, R.G., 59, 862.20210/2439, p. 5.

84. NARS, R.G. 59, 862.20232/1-2446, p. 3. In his official confession dated September 30, 1942 (862.20210, *Engels, Albrecht Gustav/44*, p. 2), Engels stated that these materials were delivered to the mysterious "Alfredo Becker." By 1946, he was ready to admit that he had lied.

85. NARS, R.G. 59, 862.20232/807, pp. 1–3, and telephone conversation with Jack West, November 3, 1980.

86. *GNAB*, T-65, PG-32004, p. 193.

87. See NARS, R.G. 59, 862.20210/1259, pp. 1–2, and 862.20210, *Engels, Albrecht Gustav/123*, p. 1. On the general distrust of Muller, Jack West expanded in detail in a phone conversation, November 3, 1980.

88. These decodes, and the final decision as to which ones would be released, were decided by Jack West, according to his letter of November 21, 1980. The decodes released to Brazilian government sources (particularly the air force) were probably those found in the Franklin D. Roosevelt Library (hereafter referred to as FDRL), *Henry L. Morgenthau Papers*, vol. 462, pp. 109–111. On releasing the decodes, see NARS, R.G. 59, 862.20210/1360, pp. 1–2, 862.20210/1126, pp. 1–2, and 862.20210/1147, no. 942, pp. 1–2.

89. On Governor Peixoto's cooperation, see NARS, R.G. 59, 832.105/45, pp. 1–2. Peixoto apparently had some scores to settle with Felinto Muller.

90. On Engels's treatment in Niterói, see NARS, R.G. 59, 862.20210, *Engels, Albrecht Gustav/23, Memorandum,* p. 1. On the criminal background of Ramos de Freitas, see Arquivo Oswaldo Aranha, OA, 42.02.00, letter to Aranha from Francisco de Sossa Netto. Ramos de Freitas would later be charged and convicted of attempting to extort money from prisoners charged with espionage. See Processo 3.093, *NCCEO,* vol. 8, box 227, pp. 1689–1691 and 1781–1783.

91. Interview with Elpídio Reali, July 5, 1978.

92. See *A Rede,* pp. 9, 11–12. See also Processo 3.093, *NCCEO,* vol. 8, box 227, pp. 1701–1703.

93. The presence of this item, not mentioned in the general listing of materials seized, was pointed out to us in a letter from Jack West to Professor Rout, January 25, 1979.

94. See NARS, R. G. 84, 820.02, box 1929, *Deposition of Niels Christian Christianen, Memorandum of Reginald Castleman,* August 28, 1942, pp. 2–3 and 11.

95. On the beatings and tortures, see *GNAB,* T-65, PG 32004, pp. 199–200, and NARS, Auswärtiges Amt, *Documents Selected from German Foreign Office Records* (hereafter referred to as *DSGFOR*), T-120 series, roll 750, frames 355245 and 355251. See also NARS, R.G. 242, ML-156, box 6, n.p.

96. See *GNAB,* T-65, PG 32004, p. 194, and U.S. Department of the Navy, Naval Historical Center, Washington Naval Yard, *Files of the German Naval Staff, German Naval Attaché in Argentina* (hereafter referred to as *GNAA*), T-67, PG-32010, p. 227. See also A República do Brasil, Arquivo do Tribunal de Segurança Nacional, Rio de Janeiro, Processo 2.996, *Frank Walter Jordan e Outros* (hereafter referred to as *FWJO*), Processo 2.996, vol 1, box 228, pp. 285–286.

97. Interview with Elpídio Reali, July 6, 1978.

98. *GNAB,* T-65, PG-32004, p. 198

99. On Kempter's trials and travails, see *O Jornal do Brasil,* Rio de Janeiro, June 17, 1978. The quote on the quality of the meal is from a letter from Friedrich Kempter to Professor Rout, July 31, 1978.

100. *GNAB,* T-65, PG-32004, pp. 198–199 and 212.

101. See Stanley Hilton, *Suástica sobre O Brasil: A história da espionagem Alemão no Brasil, 1939–1944* (Rio de Janeiro, 1977), p. 291.

102. On the informing of Washington policy makers, see NARS, R.G. 59, 862.20210/2339, p. 5, and *Engels, Albrecht Gustav/23, Memorandum,* p. 1.

103. Jack West talked frankly about this situation, and the impossibility of doing much about the treatment meted out to prisioners in a phone conversation, November 3, 1980.

104. See NARS, R.G. 59, 862.20210/1917, pp. 16–17.

105. On Bohny's supervision of this backup unit, his instructions to Lorenz and Engels's instructions, see *GNAB,* T-65, PG-32004, pp. 168, 171, and 188. See also Processo 3.093, *NCCEO,* vol. 6, box 227, pp. 1111–1115, and NARS, R.G. 59, 862.20210/1860, pp. 6 and 12.

106. NARS, *DSGFOR,* T-120 series, roll 750, frames 355222, 355223, and 355245.

107. On the Ernst Ramuz–Henriqueta Pimental affair, see NARS, R.G. 84, 820.02, no. 7771, box 547, *Transmitting Statements Made by Members of the CEL Clandestine Radio Ring,* June 26, 1942 (hereafter referred to as *Statements*). See specifically, *Statement Made by Henriqueta de Barros Pimental in the Special Police Department of the Federal District of the Rio de Janeiro,* p. 1.

108. On the Ramuz family's domestic troubles, see *Statements.* Specifically, see *Statement Made by Stefanie Ramuz in the Special Police Department,* etc., p. 1, and *Statement Made by Walter Augusto Ramuz in the Special Police Department,* etc., pp. 1–2.

109. On these events and the changes in address, see Processo 3.093, *NCCEO.* vol. 3, box 227, pp. 547–549, and vol. 6, box 227, p. 1114.

110. On the May 1, 1942, message, see *Engels/71,* part 4, n.p. On the message of May 5, see NARS, DSGOR, T-120 series, roll 750, frame 355254.

111. On the 'Sonder-Schleuss' and its arrival in Brazil, see *GNAB*, T-65, PG-32004, pp. 167–168, and NARS, *DSGFOR*, T-120 series, roll 750, frame 355254.

112. NARS, R.G. 59, *Engels/23, Memorandum,* p. 1.

113. On Walter August's adventure, see NARS, R.G. 84, 820.02, no. 7771, box 547, *Statements,* and specifically, the *Statement of Walter Augusto Ramuz,* pp. 1–2.

114. See NARS, R.G. 59, 862.20210/1866, n.p.

115. See *GNAB*, T-65, PG-32004, p. 196.

116. See NARS, R.G. 59, 862.20210/2076, p. 1 for the quoted material, and pp. 1–2 for the background.

117. Ibid., p. 2.

118. See NARS, R.G. 59, 862.20210, *Engels, Albrecht Gustav/72,* pp. 2–3.

119. For an accurate description of Mourão's elevated position in the underground Integralista organization, we have an undated letter, ostensibly signed by Mourão, and addressed to Edmar Morel. This letter was found in the newspaper morgue of *Jornal do Brasil*, and was provided on June 30, 1978, by Senhor Luíz Orlando Carneiro, then managing editor of this prestigious paper. On the background of Gerardo Melo Mourão, see Processo 3.294, *TRNO,* vol 3, pp. 408–409.

120. For details of the Buenos Aires trip, see Processo 3.294, *TRNO,* vol 1, p. 34 and the following unnumbered pages. See also NARS, R.G. 59, 862.20210/2076, no. 3353, pp. 1–2, and *GELA*, p. 139.

121. See NARS, R.G. 59, 862.20210/2324, p. 4, and Processo 3.093, *NCCEO,* vol. 6, box 227, pp. 1114 and the following unnumbered page.

122. On Mourão, do Nascimento, and Becker, and the intelligence activities conducted, see NARS, R.G. 59, 862.20210/2324, pp. 4–12, and Processo 3.294, *TRNO,* vol. 1, pp. 35, 51–53, and vol. 2, pp. 127–131.

123. See *GNAB*, T-65, PG-32004, p. 174.

124. The description of the bomb, how it was supposed to work, plus a picture of same is found in NARS, R.G. 59, 862.20210/2728, p. 1.

125. See ibid, p. 11.

126. See NARS, R.G. 59, 862.20210/2392, pp. 1–2, and Processo 3.294, *TRNO,* vol. 1, p. 38 and the following unnumbered page.

127. Mourão's fears and request for a cassock are noted in Processo 3.294, *TRNO,* vol. 1., pp. 63–64.

128. See NARS, R.G. 59, 862.20210/2324, p. 1, and 701.6232/6-1148, pp. 1–2.

129. Processo 3.294, *TRNO,* vol. 3, p. 435.

130. NARS, R.G. 59, 862.20210/2076, *Statement Made by Ysette Bittencourt Días, September 16, 1942,* p. 1.

131. See Processo 3.294, *TRNO,* vol. 3, p. 431. This sum was paid him by Ambassador Kurt Prüfer and embassy counselor Walther Becker.

132. NARS, R.G. 59, 862.20232/920, enclosure 4, n.p. See, in particular, enclosure 3, pp. 3 and 5, which notes that Kotze's full code name in Canada was "John George van Hughes." This factor is relevant because in the correspondence listed in enclosure 4, Hughes signed the letters "J. Hughes," "John," and several other ways.

133. On British plans, see NARS, R.G. 59, 862.20232/970, p. 21. On Hughes's demand for money, see, for example, 862.20232/920, enclosure 4, n.p., telegram of July 24, 1942.

134. See *GNAA*, T-67, PG-32010, p. 203.

135. See NARS, R.G. 59, 862.20232/970, p. 23.

136. For the story on Alfred Voelkers, Niebuhr, and Paulo Griese, see *GELA*, p. 94.

137. For the quoted material, see 862.20232/970, pp. 25–26.

138. A full history of this incident is found in ibid., pp. 25–26.

139. NARS, R.G. 59, 862.20232/920, enclosure 4, letters, January 5, and February 19, 1943.

140. On the British double agent methods, see J.C. Masterman, *The Double Cross System in the War, 1939 to 1945* (New Haven, 1972). See also NARS, R.G. 59, 862.20232/970, p. 1. This is a report from the FBI relating to Waltemath's attempted employment as a double agent.

141. David Mason, *U-Boat* (London, 1958), pp. 257–258.

142. On Schlacht's one-man war off the Brazilian coast, see Hughes and Costello, *The Battle of the Atlantic,* pp. 206–207 and 258.

143. Ibid., p. 257.

144. The story of Baarn's early life and Abwehr recruitment is from *GELA*, pp. 95–96, and *Vida Policial,* vol. 6, no. 20 (May 1944), pp. 47–48.

145. See *GELA*, pp. 96–97, and NARS, R.G. 59, 862.20232/962, pp. 7–10, and 862.20232/943, pp. 1–2.

146. Materials on Wehner's background were available through Dr. Sonnenthal, *Deutsche Dienststelle,* Ref. V/V, no. 239, October 10, 1980, letter to Professor Rout. Wehner was actually assigned to the I-M, *Abteilung I*, Abwehr headquarters. See, in particular, *Vida Policial,* vol. 7, no. 72 (December 1944), p. 34.

147. See *GELA*, p. 97.

148. *Vida Policial,* vol. 6, no. 70 (May 1944), p. 48. See also NARS, R.G. 59, 862.20232/1057, pp. 25–37. It is quite possible that Heinrich Koepff was given the name of a German business representative who would provide a "cover" identity for him until forged identity documents were obtained. See *ibid.*, pp. 110–120.

149. On the *Passim*, its fittings and equipment, see NARS, R.G. 59, 862.20232/981, enclosure A, n.p.

150. On the capture of Koepff and Baarn, see *GELA*, pp. 97–98, and NARS, R.G. 59, 862.20232/7-144, pp. 3–4, and 862.20232/7-1945, pp. 1–3. See also the account in *O Jornal,* Rio de Janeiro, June 29, 1944, and *O Globo,* June 30, 1944.

151. Letter from Jack West to Professor Rout, memo 2, November 8, 1978.

152. NARS, R.G. 59, 862.20232/975, pp. 1–2,

153. See NARS, R.G. 59, 20232/7-1945, p. 2.

154. See *GELA*, p. 98, and NARS, R.G. 862.20232/960, p. 1.

155. See NARS, R.G. 59, 862.20232/1.004, pp. 1–2.

156. On the "Hedwig" messages, see NARS, R.G. 59, 862.20232/1.017, p. 1. For copies, see NARS, R.G. 238, ML-171a, roll 23, n.p. A more comprehensive listing of "Hedwig" messages is found in Department of the Navy, Naval Historical Center, Washington Navy Yard, Washington, D.C., TM 16 (microfilm) *Reports of the Intelligence Sub-Office, Bremen,* n.p. All these documents bear the number 166. For press reports, see the newspapers mentioned in note 150.

157. See NARS, R.G. 59, 862.20210/8-1845, pp. 4–5.

158. This commission and its membership are listed in Roi Pessoa, *Es pionagem e os meios juridicos sequrança nacional* (Rio de Janeiro, 1966), pp. 81–83. How Cardoso de Castro's draft became Decree-Law No. 4,766 is related in detail in ibid., pp. 82–84. For a comprehensive discussion of Decree-Law No. 4,766, its constitutional origins and its retroactive aspects, see Almirante Alvaro Rodrigues do Vasconcellos, "Inconstitucionalidade da aplicação retroáctiva da Lei penal," *Revista de Jurisprudência Brasileira,* vol. 97, (October–November 1952), pp. 13–19.

159. The quote is from Galdino Siquiera, "Revisando-Edmondo De Robillant," *Revista de Jurisprudência Brasileira,* vol. 97 (October–November 1952), p. 42.

160. The legal maneuvers decribed here are both praised and condemned in ibid., pp. 42–48.

161. See *GELA*, pp. 61–63, and NARS, R.G. 59, 862.20210/2111, p. 1.

162. For the defensive arguments and statements of these individuals, see Processo 2.996, *FWJO,* vol. 1, box 228, pp. 285–286, 288–289; see also vol. 2, pp. 352–355.

163. For Jordan's statements, see ibid., vol. 2, p. 356.

164. On Hans Holl's declarations and disagreements with Winterstein, see ibid., pp. 358 and 365–366.

165. For the defenses of these Brazilians, see ibid., vol. 1, pp. 85–86, and vol. 2, pp. 353, 358–359, 364, and 365.

166. On the sentences meted out, see ibid., vol. 2, pp. 373–374.

167. A listing of all those being tried in the process, plus the charges against them are to be found in Processo 3.093, *NCCEO*, vol. 1, box 226, pp. 37–75 (hand marked). A description (often prejudicial) of those to be tried and their nationality is found in *NCCEO*, vol. 8, box 227, pp. 1635–1657.

168. On Engels's reference to "Alfredo Becker," and Becker's alleged role as organizer of CEL, see NARS, R.G. 59, 862.20210, *Albrecht Gustav Engels/23, Memorandum,* enclosure 1, p. 1. For Jack West's opinion on "Alfredo Becker," see ibid. On the search by DOPS agents for "Alfredo Becker," see Processo 3.093, *NCCEO*, vol. 8, box 228, p. 1631, and vol. 14, box 228, pp. 3528–3529 and 3537.

169. On Francis Crosby's questioning of Albrecht Engels, and the admission of the latter concerning the creation of the Engels-Bohny ring, see NARS, R.G. 59, 862.20210, *Engels/71,* Part 4, n.p. After the war Engels dropped his references to Becker entirely. See NARS, R.G. 59, 862.20232/1-2446, pp. 1–5.

170. On these postwar revelations, see Processo 3.294, *TRNO*, vol. 4, pp. 1185–1186 and the unmarked pages after each of these.

171. See Processo 3.093, *NCCEO*, vol 13, box 228, pp. 2825–2827 and 2861–2862.

172. On Kempter and his desire to punish the turncoat Starziczny, see the letter from Friedrich Kempter to Professor Rout, July 31, 1978, p. 2.

173. On Starziczny's declarations implicating his cohorts, see Processo 3.093, *NCCEO*, vol. 11, box 228, pp. 2282–2287. For the defense of Bleinroth, Timm, Meyer-Clason, Arnold, and others, see ibid., vol. 15, pp. 3176, 3190, and 3280–3282.

174. Ibid., vol 15, pp. 3197, 3217, and 3220.

175. Ibid., p. 3245.

176. Ibid., pp. 3358–3363. See also NARS, R.G. 59, 862.20210/2590, p. 1.

177. See NARS, R.G. 59, 862.20210/2589, p. 1, and 862.20210/2590, p. 1. The quote is from /2590.

178. The best history of the Brazilian expeditionary force and its importance to Brazil is Manoel Thomaz Castello Branco, *O Brasil na II grande guerra* (Rio de Janeiro, 1960), pp. 123–589.

179. The Germans, for example, sought the release of Albrecht Gustav Engels. See NARS, R.G. 59, 862.20210, *Engels, Albrecht Gustav/86,* p. 1. On August 8, 1943, Aranha of Brazil received a cable (through the Spanish) offering to exchange a Brazilian dipomat for Engels. This offer was rejected.

180. See Processo 3.093, *NCCEO*, vol. 15, box 228, p. 3390.

181. Ibid., pp. 3399–3404.

182. See NARS, R.G. 59, 862.20210/2643, p. 1.

183. NARS, R.G. 59, 862.20210/2661, p. 1.

184. Processo 3.294, *TRNO*, vol 1, pp. 2–3 and 14.

185. Ibid., vol. 4, pp. 505–506.

186. On the sentences meted out, see NARS, R.G. 59, 862.20210/2419, p. 1, and 862.20210/2643, pp. 1–2.

187. For the Waltemath-Griese trial and sentencing, see NARS, R.G. 84, 820.02, no.14023, December 29, 1943, p. 1, and *GELA*, pp. 92–94. For proof that the Brazilians knew Kotze was actually a BSC agent, see *Vida Policial,* vol. 4 (March 1944; in special supplement 3), p. 44.

188. *GNAB*, T-65, PG-32004, p. 187.

189. NARS, R.G. 50, 862.20232/7-1945, p. 1.

190. On the Brazilian army's objection to clemency for Baarn and the report of Rolf Larsen, see ibid., pp. 2–3.

191. *GELA*, p. 98.

192. See NARS, R.G. 59, 862.20210/2643, pp. 1–3, and 862.20210/2661, p. 1.

193. FDRL, Harry Hopkins Papers, box 141, May 22, 1944, FBI Report, J. Edgar Hoover to Harry L. Hopkins.

194. See Processo 3.093, *NCCEO*, vol. 15, box 228, p. 3356.

195. On María Tereza Calvacanti Ellender, see Processo 3.093, *NCCEO*, vol. 8, box 227, p. 1472. The legal defense is presented in ibid., vol. 9, box 228, p. 1896.

196. On Weissflog and Haering, see ibid., vol. 8, box 227, pp. 1473–1474, and vol. 13, box 228, pp. 1908–1909.

197. On Hans Muth's denials, see *GELA*, p. 58, and Processo 3.093, *NCCEO*, vol. 6, box 227, pp. 1078–1080.

198. *GNAB*, T-65, PG-32004, pp. 186 and 198. Muth is portrayed by Bohny as a drug addict (i.e., 'Äther-Säufer,' literally "ether eater").

199. See *GELA*, p. 58, and Processo 3.093, *NCCEO*, vol. 16, box 228, pp. 3356–3357. For the appeal made by his lawyer, see ibid., p. 3367.

200. Ibid., vol. 15, box 228, p. 3243.

201. Ibid.

202. An excellent example of how the espionage issue was manipulated in order to arouse public opinion can be seen in the *Folha da Tarde*, Pôrto Alegre, Rio Grande do Sul, March 30, 1942, and *O Jornal*, Rio de Janeiro, December 22, 1943. See also NARS, R.G. 84, 820.02, no. 10284, box 1931, *Two Confidential Reports*, p. 14, which details the close relations between the United States embassy, the Brazilian Department of Press and Propaganda (DIP), and the newspapers, which were censored by DIP.

203. Evidence that the Brazilians were succeeding in favorably influencing U.S. opinion in this regard is seen in a memorandum from J. Michael Hanley, Foreign Activity Correlation Division, to Adolf Berle, assistant secretary of state, dated February 15, 1943. See NARS, R.G. 59, 862.20210/2272 (memorandum was attached to this document).

204. See Processo 3.093, *NCCEO*, vol. 15, box 228, p. 3405. The TSN appeals court specifically cancelled Bohny's sentence "in virtue of [his] diplomatic immunities." See ibid., p. 3405.

205. Processo 3.093, *NCCEO*, vol. 16, box 228, p. 3547.

206. Uebele had been placed under house arrest due to his allegedly poor health. See NARS, R.G. 84, 820.02-Uebele, box 1931, n.p. On his award of the Medal of the Southern Cross, see Processo 3.093, *NCCEO*, vol. 11, box 228, p. 2350.

207. On the roles of Carlos Cyrilio Júnior in obtaining Uebele's freedom, see *Diretrizes*, Rio de Janeiro, vol. 10, no. 1278, February 8, 1949. His son, Hans Ulrich Uebele, noted that the process eventually bankrupted his father. See the letter from Hans Ulrich Uebele, Iberama, Santa Catarina, Brazil, to Professor Rout, February 2, 1981.

208. See Processo 2.996, *FWJO*, vol. 2, box 228, p. 435.

209. For these releases, see Processo 3.093, *NCCEO*, vol. 16, box 228, pp. 3436–3437. A letter from Hans Ulrich Uebele to Professor Rout (February 2, 1981) provided the date of Hans Ulrich's release.

210. Copies of official release papers and Noguiera de Gama's brief were kindly supplied in a letter from Hans Kurt Meyer-Clason to Professor Rout, September 3, 1979.

211. Superior Tribunal Militar, "Requerente Fritz Weissflog," *Revista de Jurisprudencia Brasileira*, vol. 80 (September 1948), pp. 145–147.

212. On Mourão's release on August 30, 1948, see Processo 3.294, *TRNO*, vol. 5, p. 1068. For Kempter's release as part of a Christmas 1948 general amnesty, see *Jornal do Brasil*, June 17, 1978.

213. Information on Engels was found in Processo 3.294, *TRNO*, vol. 6, p. 1105, and vol. 7, pp. 1562–1563. On the sentence reduction for Wilhelm Koepff, see Superior Tribunal Militar, "Revisão Criminal—Wilhelm Heinrich Koepff," *Revista de Jurisprudencia Brasileira*, vol. 97 (December 1952), pp. 135–136.

214. On the do Nascimento imbroglio, see Processo 3.294, *TRNO*, vol. 8, pp. 1616, 1617, and 1720.

215. Essentially, what Hilton failed to do was to consult with SIS/Brazil personnel concerning their activities in the country in 1941–42. For example, in *Suástica sobre O Brasil*, p. 243, Hilton calls Elim O'Shaughnessy both an FBI agent and a legal attaché. O'Shaughnessy was neither.

216. In the introduction of *Hitler's Secret War in South America*, pp. 9–10, Hilton refers to an interview given by Professor Rout, to *Jornal do Brasil*, September 15, 1978, in excessively caustic terms. Hilton charged that Rout "dismissed *Suástica* as invalid because its geographic and thematic focus was limited . . . and because I had not approached my subject 'with sympathy.' Curiously too, he defended Mourão, stating that he had not found any document incriminating him and charging implicitly that I had distorted the evidence. But more seriously, Rout indicated that he had experienced difficulty in retracing my steps in some official records because of the repercussions of *Suástica*—certainly a deplorable circumstance."

Professor Rout replies:

(a) Concerning my alleged dismissal of *Suástica*, in the *Jornal do Brasil* article, I argued that since the Abwehr mounted significant operations in at least four countries, presenting the issue "only in terms of one country, distorts the question. . ." Insofar as Hilton generalizes about Abwehr operations in the Americas from the perspective of the Brazilian experience, he has read my comments correctly. On the other hand, *Suástica* as a study of Abwehr intelligence in Brazil, or controlled from Brazil, is not necessarily invalid or incompetent. Hilton, unfortunately, seems unable to admit even the possibility of this limitation.

(b) Concerning my alleged defense of Gerardo Melo Mourão, Hilton notes that I had found "no proof" that Mourão was a "German agent." In the next paragraph of the newspaper interview, which Hilton ignores, I explain what was meant by that statement. Reference was made to the oft-quoted final report of Lt. Comdr. Hermann Bohny (*GNAB*, PG-32004, T-65, pp. 168–224), which Hilton never consulted. I stated specifically that in this document there are the names of eighty-six Abwehr-acknowledged agents and nowhere did I find the name of Gerardo Melo Mourão. Capt. Tulio Regis do Nascimento was perhaps the only non-German listed as a "paid agent."

(c) As for the controversy stirred up in *Suástica*, precisely what it appears to have done was to make it impossible for me to obtain certain documents not referred to in Hilton's work. For example, a month after arriving in Brazil in 1978, I received Telex 469, G11592 USIS BR, July 12, 1978, to USICA, Rio [Dan] Traub, [ILZA] Viegas: "Itamarati source states Minister Brandao's letter of May 6 incorporates Minister Lins's views regarding Rout's access and it would be fruitless to direct another request to him at this time. The subject is considered as sensitive at present, particularly as a result of Hilton's recent book."

217. On the last previous commentary, concerning Melo Mourão's espionage activities, see *Ultima Hora*, Rio de Janeiro, April 1, 1969.

218. For these initial attacks by Gerardo Melo Mourão on Stanley Hilton and *Suástica*, see *Revista do Homen*, vol. 4 (October 1977), and *Veja*, vol. 10 (December 28, 1977). The bitter remarks quoted in the text are from *Jornal do Brasil*, January 21 and 24, 1978.

219. For Hilton's blistering reply, see *Jornal do Brasil*, January 21, 1978.

220. For an example of Hilton's counterattack, see *Jornal do Brasil*, February 18, 1978.

221. An example of a favorable review of *Suástica* is found in *Jornal do Brasil*, December 31, 1977. For reviews of an unfavorable and derogatory nature, see *Jornal da Tarde*, Rio de Janeiro, February 1, 1978, and *Jornal do Brasil*, March 11, 1978.

222. Interview, Rio de Janeiro, Gerardo Margela Melo Mourão with Professor Rout, June 30, 1978. Mourão's original confession is found in Processo 3.294, *TRNO*, vol. 1, pp. 33–41. In

testimony on August 20, 1948, Mourão repudiated almost everything admitted in the early confession. See Processo 3.294, *TRNO*, vol. 6, pp. 1068–1070. Evidence of the setting aside of the verdict against him is found in *Jornal do Brasil*, January 24, 1978.

223. See *Jornal do Brasil*, February 25, 1978; the same idea is implied in the article which appeared on February 18, 1978.

224. We note, in particular, a letter from Friedrich Kempter, October 18, 1978, acknowledging the correctness of the account of activities, a letter from Hans Kurt Meyer-Clason, September 3, 1979, acknowledging the correctness of the account of his activities, and a letter from Hans Ulrich Uebele, February 2, 1981.

225. For his anti-Nazi views and his obstinate opposition to releasing any convicted agents, in Edmar Morel's writings, see *Diretrizes*, February 1 and 10, 1949, and *Panfleto: Reportagem da Dia*, Rio de Janeiro, August 20, 1948.

226. The quoted material is from an article by Edmar Morel in *Tribuna de Imprensa*, Rio de Janeiro, December 21, 1977.

227. The undated communication addressed to "Edmar Morel," and signed in the margin, "Gerardo Margella Mello Mourão," was one of the documents found in a file marked *"espionagem."* In gaining access to this file, we would like to acknowledge the invaluable support of Senhor Luíz Orlando Carneiro, who was the managing editor for *Jornal do Brasil*.

228. See Joe Louis, with Edna and Art Rust, Jr., *Joe Louis: My Life* (New York, 1978), p. 174.

229. Letter from Friedrich Kempter to Professor Rout, July 31, 1978. Kempter implies as much in the newspaper article about his life and work in *Jornal do Brasil*, June 18, 1978.

230. Information on Engels's personality is from source Y, a former Abwehr agent who now lives in Morelia, in the state of São Paulo, and who was in prison with Engels in 1943–46. He talked to Professor Rout, with the understanding that his name would not be used. A second source is a letter from Friedrich Kempter to Professor Rout, July 31, 1978. On Engels's subsequent activities, see the letter from Luíz Orlando Carneiro to Professor Rout, August 22, 1981.

231. Information on the Uebeles is from the letter from Hans Uebele to Professor Rout, February 2, 1981.

232. On Walther Becker, see the letter, A 177-251.09/77, Auswärtiges Amt, Dr. Maria Keipert to Prof. Peter Scheibert, Marburg/Lahn, German Federal Republic, April 17, 1978.

233. Letter from Luíz Orlando Carneiro to Professor Rout, August 26, 1981.

234. Letter from Hans Kurt Meyer-Clason to Professor Rout, September 3, 1979.

235. Letters from Friedrich Kempter to Professor Rout, July 31 and October 18, 1978.

236. Information on Starziczny is from Hans Ulrich Uebele's letter. On Hermann Bohny, see letter, *Deutsche Dienststelle*, Ref. V.V, Berlin, Spiller to Professor Rout, November 16, 1978.

237. See, in particular, the Meyer-Clason, Uebele, and Kempter letters. Source Y also argues that the Vargas regime saw the trials as a means of seizing millions of dollars of German commercial property.

238. See FDRL, FDRP, box 40, OF-10B, letter from J. Edgar Hoover to Harry Hopkins, December 8, 1944.

239. See United States of America, Export-Import Bank of Washington, *First Semi-Annual Report to Congress for the Period of July–December, 1945* (Washington, D.C., 1945), pp. 20, 41–43, and U.S. Department of State, *Twenty-Third Report to Congress on Lend-Lease Operations*, Publication 2707 (Washington, D.C., 1946), p. 27.

6

The Espionage War in Chile:
1939–47

I. Introduction: The Politics of Espionage

Pedro Aguirre Cerda was hardly a world-renowned political leader, but his death on November 25, 1941, touched off a battle for succession more suited to some mythical Balkan state than a democratic Latin American republic. The chief candidates for the Chilean presidency were Carlos Ibáñez, a former dictator with right-wing backing, and Juan Antonio Ríos, a Radical Party wheelhorse who was leading the Alianza Democrática, a coalition of Radical, Liberal, and Socialist Party elements. It appeared that the election scheduled for February 2, 1942, would be close, and since Ríos was alleged to be more supportive of the western democracies, the Winston Churchill government proposed a joint U.S.-British purchase of the election for him.[1]

This proposal was vehemently opposed by Laurence Duggan, the State Department's senior advisor for Latin American affairs, and Assistant Secretary Adolf Berle. They viewed the proposal as a repudiation of the Good Neighbor Policy and an unmitigated invitation to disaster,[2] but other prominent U.S. officials disagreed. COI chief William Donovan, in a report dated January 17, 1942, agreed that

> the election of Ibáñez to the Presidency of Chile would constitute a serious danger to American interests . . . and consequently to the entire American war effort. . . . The candidature of Ríos should be covertly assisted by holding at his disposal sufficient funds to insure his election. . . . Steps should be taken to insure by all means available, including bribery if necessary, that the armed forces would not support any attempt at a coup d'etat on the part of Ibáñez. . . . [3]

Donovan's brief for purchasing the election suggested that a covert agency (possibly his own), with an expense fund of $250,000, could accomplish the task of keeping Ibáñez out of the Casa Moneda, the executive office of the Chilean president. Vice-President Henry Wallace made it known that he supported Donovan's scheme and attempted to persuade Franklin D. Roosevelt to accept it. FDR might have used questionable means in persuading the public of the necessity of fighting the Nazis, but it is to his credit that he rejected this proposal.[4]

Nevertheless, the British had been at war over two years, and they were neither easily dissuaded nor particularly concerned with Good Neighbor niceties. On January 21, 1942, Sir William Campbell, counselor of the British embassy, suggested a variation on the election purchase proposal to Adolf Berle. This time, all the U.S. need do was look the other way; Sir William Stephenson, of British Security Coordination, would perform the actual dirty work. But neither Berle nor anyone else at the State Department wanted anything to do with this gambit.[5]

What Berle, Duggan, and other U.S. officials did not know, but may have suspected, was that the Germans, as well as the British, were greatly interested in determining the outcome of the Chilean presidential contest. On December 4, 1941, Ambassador Freiherr von Schoen suggested to Berlin that significant contributions made early might buy good will.[6] The German Foreign Office experts analyzed the proposal, and suggested making $100,000-$150,000 contributions to both the Ríos and Ibáñez coffers. Foreign Minister Joachim von Ribbentrop hesitated because he was convinced that any revelation of German meddling would result in undesirable and definitely disadvantageous repercussions. Concluding that January 1942 was too late for a financial contribution to have a decisive effect, Ribbentrop rejected the influence-purchasing operation.[7]

One can only imagine Ribbentrop's anger and exasperation when he later discovered that the Abwehr had decided that Ibáñez was the man of the hour, and was secretly subsidizing the Chilean's campaign for the presidency. The payments were apparently made through the German air attaché, Maj. Ludwig von Bohlen, whose personal relationship with the former strongman stretched back over a decade.[8] But despite his displeasure, the German foreign minister would have reason to feel smug, for the infusion of Abwehr funds failed to further Ibáñez's hopes. On February 2, 1942, Ríos won handily, taking about 56 percent of the popular vote.[9]

It is possible that the British did surreptitiously make a sizable contribution to the Juan Ríos electoral campaign, but if they did, returns on their investment proved meager indeed. On March 28, 1942, Foreign Minister-designate Ernesto Barros Jarpa met with German ambassador Freiherr von Schoen and stated that Chile would follow a policy of strict neutrality in the war then raging.[10] Five days later, Schoen conferred with Ríos himself, and the President explained that Barros Jarpa had been given the Foreign Ministry portfolio principally because for years he had represented both the U.S.-owned copper companies and ITT in Chilean litigation. Ríos claimed to be convinced that Washington would acquiesce to Chilean neutrality if a man long trusted by U.S. interests was in charge at the Foreign Ministry. After this interview, Schoen informed

Berlin that the Abwehr had wasted its gold. Nevertheless, Germany had won the battle; Chile intended to do nothing that might precipitate a diplomatic break with the Reich.[11]

That the new regime would adopt a neutralist stance should hardly have been a surprise in Washington. Brazilian foreign minister Oswaldo Aranha had warned Sumner Welles in March 1942 that political expediency would dictate the adoption of precisely this policy position.[12] Of the parties which comprised Ríos's Alianza Democrática, only the Socialist party openly favored the Anglo-American cause. This meant that the ruling coalition was quite likely to shatter if the president endorsed anything other than a "traditionally independent [i.e. neutral] foreign policy."[13]

Not surprisingly, there was strong public sentiment for noninvolvement,[14] and there existed still another reason for hedging foreign policy bets. On December 8, 1941, the Japanese ambassador had threatened that if Chile cast its lot with the U.S., an attack by a Japanese naval force could be expected.[15] Particularly in 1942, with the Nipponese war machine still surging triumphantly across the Pacific, there was no reason to doubt that Japan could make good on the ambassador's threat. Moreover, since Chile was supplying the United States with valuable copper and had granted that nation nonbelligerent status, there was nothing more the North Americans could expect—at least not until the war situation changed unequivocally in their favor.[16]

In contrast to the skillful reading of the Chilean intentions by German ambassador Frieherr von Schoen and Brazilian minister Oswaldo Arahna, U.S. policy makers long persisted in their belief that the Ríos government would arrest and convict the Abwehr agents operating in the country and break diplomatic relations with the Axis powers. Washington's problems were rooted, in part, in the philosophical predilections of its ambassador to Chile, Claude Bowers. Despite the outspoken disagreement of Military Attaché Col. John Wooten and Counselor of the Embassy Donald Heath, Bowers stubbornly maintained that a democratic Chile would recognize its moral responsibilities and thereby take the two actions noted.[17] Bowers's faith in the integrity of the Chileans was commendable, but both his descriptions of events and the interpretation he gave them left much to be desired.

But even if Bowers had been inclined to present a more realistic picture of the situation in Santiago, State Department policy makers would hardly have been appeased. Sumner Welles believed that Bowers's lack of Latin American experience made him unfit for the post, while Philip Bonsal, chief of the American Republics desk, evinced his low opinion of the ambassador's capabilities on more than one occasion.[18] Bowers was probably aware of his low standing with Welles and the State Department's Latin American establishment, and based on his personal friendship with Franklin D. Roosevelt, he took to sending many of his reports directly to the White House. Bowers was a favorite with southern Democratic congressmen whose support Roosevelt needed; consequently, FDR displayed exceptional forebearance towards his sometimes irrepressible ambassador. At length, however, the President grew weary of wearing the mask, and early in December 1941, he agreed to an arrangement whereby Welles and Duggan wrote the replies to the reports Bowers sent to the White House. Since FDR personally signed these responses, Bowers apparently never realized that his criticisms of Sumner Welles and other State Department figures were being read and replied to by the undersecretary and his aides.[19]

The Abwehr decision to create a major network in Chile was based not so much on any need to have one there, but upon the fact that one could be established there relatively easily. With a resident population of 25,000 *Reichsdeutschen* and 125–130,000 *Volksdeutschen,* the country was a reservoir of potential recruits. Moreover, even though the German racial and cultural community represented only 3–4 percent of the total Chilean population in 1941, it exercised a socioeconomic influence far in excess of its size. For example, of the eight radio broadcasting stations then operating in the capital of Santiago, four were German-owned.[20] Thus, German intelligence perceived Chile as a "safe house," where agents could be recruited and trained, and as a communications center, through which information could be relayed or delivered for broadcast to Germany. These factors made Chile's Pacific Ocean location a matter of minor importance.[21]

As much as in Mexico and Brazil, the problems of espionage and counterespionage in Chile became tightly interwoven with internal political and external diplomatic considerations. But to the surprise and growing irritation of the United States, Juan Ríos proved tenacious in his determination to maintain a neutralist foreign policy stance and quite disinterested in taking any action against the German espionage organization. A combination of U.S. pressure and political circumstance would force the abandonment of neutrality in January 1943,[22] but the diplomatic reversal of policy did not signal the emergence of a new attitude toward counterespionage cooperation. For example, in May 1943, the unexpected detection of a new Abwehr clandestine radio caused consternation in the SIS/Chile organization. To counteract this threat, Legal Attaché Robert Wall requested Chilean manpower assistance for increased investigative work. In answer to this query, an official of the Dirección General de Investigaciones e Identificaciones (DGII), the internal security police, suggested that Wall draw up a list of known Nazi sympathizers and AO members and submit it to him, whereupon those persons would be promptly arrested. Whether the people jailed were responsible for the new wave of clandestine radio activity was immaterial; evidently a bit of cosmetic spy-catching was all the security police were interested in becoming involved in.[23] Disgusted with this lackadaisical attitude, on July 19, 1943, the military, naval, and legal attachés sent a joint report to Washington describing their discontent with Chilean policy. In their opinion, the Ríos regime simply wasn't interested in combating German intelligence activity; only because that government wanted U.S. loans was it prepared to make "some small gesture" which could be "used to create favorable publicity in the United States."[24]

It is not clear that the U.S. Army or Navy intended to do much about the situation, but J. Edgar Hoover certainly did. Long unhappy over Chilean counterspy apathy, the FBI director started pulling his agents out of the country. As far as he was concerned, his men could be put to better use in a nation where they would receive greater cooperation.[25]

Once it became evident that Hoover was serious about dismantling the SIS/Chile apparatus, Ambassador Bowers decided that only a desperate appeal would change hearts and minds in Washington. In an October 1943 cable marked "very confidential," the ambassador argued:

> It is my firm conviction that the abandonment of [our] espionage service in Chile at this time would be a distinct contribution to the ... attempt to wipe out all democratic institutions in South America. . . . The activities of the active Axis agents who overrun Chile cannot be properly restrained or even observed due to the fact that the Chilean police [DGII] has [*sic*] such inadequate facilities. . . . As a consequence, there should be no (repeat no) further reduction of the agents here. . . .[26]

Hoover eventually reconsidered the withdrawal of his agents, and the U.S.-Chilean cooperation in the fight against German espionage improved dramatically in 1944. Still, after the war, captured German records revealed that in December 1941 both Juan Antonio Ríos and Carlos Ibáñez secretly contacted German ambassador Freiherr von Schoen and aggressively solicited campaign contributions.[27] What this discovery suggests is that Ríos's alleged sympathies for the Anglo-American cause, and the similarity of Chilean political institutions to those in the United States, were factors of minor consequence.[28] Internal political exigencies, the desire to gain the executive office, plus the reluctance of the Chilean public to become involved in the conflict were the critical determinants. Idealistic declarations of democratic solidarity might make headlines, but they would not get German spies arrested; and that would have been true whether Ríos or Ibáñez wore the presidential sash.

II. The PYL Story

A. "Casero" the Great

Born in Tübingen, Germany, on June 25, 1903, Friedrich Tadeo von Schulz-Hausmann (code name: Casero) was too young to serve in the German Imperial Army during the First World War. And, like many of the Brazilian V-men discussed, he concluded that Weimar Germany was no place for an aspiring young man to seek his fortune. He became associated with the North German Lloyd Shipping Line, and from 1931–35, he served the company as its agent in Panama and Ecuador. In May 1935, he was named general agent for the Pacific coast of South America, and director of Campañía Transportes Maritimos, the Lloyd Line's Valparaíso affiliate. His career as a spy did not commence until after he visited Germany during the summer of 1938. Apparently recruited by the I-M section of Ast Hamburg, Schulz-Hausmann returned to Valparaíso in May 1939 carrying seventy-five thousand dollars in cash and orders to create an Abwehr network on the west coast of South America. Thereafter, he began easing employees out of the Lloyd Line offices in Peru and Chile, replacing them with persons who might serve as informants or area agents. Thus, when war broke out in September 1939, "Casero" already had a fledgling network, and he could commence activity as soon as he received specific orders.[29]

Schulz-Hausmann's first assignment was the preparation of seven German steamers trapped by the war in Chilean ports for escape across the Pacific. Capt. Dietrich Niebuhr, naval attaché in Buenos Aires, was in overall charge of the plan, but it fell to Schulz-Hausmann "to pull all sorts of strings and engage in judicious bribery with the various [Chilean] officials in order to obtain fuel and other materials necessary for the departure of the ships."[30] "Casero" proved more than equal to the task. Between December 1939 and August 1941, all these steamers were secretly loaded, and one by one, sailed to Japan or Vladivostock. The cargoes were either sold or shipped to Germany over the Trans-Siberian Railway, and while the vessels never returned to the fatherland, the value of the cargoes and the sale prices for the ships were worth millions of dollars to the Germans.[31]

Another major operation involving "Casero" was the smuggling of officers and technicians from the pocket battleship *Graf Spee* back to Germany. After the battle of the River Plate, from December 13–17, 1939, the German warship was scuttled, and some one thousand crew members were interned in Argentina and Uruguay. Again, it was Captain Niebuhr who contrived elaborate plans for their escape. Some fugitive sailors were put aboard Spanish ships in Buenos Aires, while others were surreptitiously guided to Schulz-Hausmann, who fed and housed them until they could be smuggled onto departing Japanese or Russian freighters. These activities transpired without a hitch until October 4, 1940, when four *Graf Spee* officers, carrying false passports, were apprehended by Chilean police while boarding a Japanese vessel.[32]

When news of the arrests became known, "Casero" panicked and sought refuge in the German embassy. But as the storm quickly subsided, Schulz-Hausmann regained his nerve and returned to the business of assisting other escapees. By June 1941, about fifty *Graf Spee* officers and technicians had boarded vessels in Chilean harbors, and returned to Germany via Vladivostock and the Trans-Siberian Railway.[33] Moreover, two of the officers who exited South America via the Chilean escape route became U-boat commanders, subsequently running up impressive scores of sunken ships.[34]

In addition to his shipping and sailor escape efforts, Schulz-Hausmann collaborated with Fritzhof Groth, manager of the Condor-LATI airlines office in Santiago, in supplying platinum and other scarce metals for the German war machine. Theodor Barth, a mine operator in Colombia, smuggled platinum to Chile, where Groth and Schulz-Hausmann repackaged it for clandestine shipment. Platinum was critical to the manufacture of war-related materials, and with the British in control of the seas, virtually all other commercial channels were closed. Between August 1940 and February 1941, twenty-five separate one-pound packets of platinum reached the Reich via Condor Airways to Brazil, and LATI across the Atlantic.[35] By 1942, Germany would pay nearly eight dollars per gram, twice the standard price, for black-market platinum shipped from Buenos Aires, a clear indication of the value to the Reich of these precious metals shipments.[36]

These activities, all of which were accomplished in less than two years after the invasion of Poland, stamp Schulz-Hausmann as one of the most versatile Abwehr agents in the Americas. Nevertheless, Dietrich Niebuhr considered him to be conceited and perverse and did not shrink from reiterating these views to other Abwehr personnel.[37] The naval attaché's dislike was heightened when, in June 1941, Schulz-Hausmann applied for the job of director of Bromberg and Company, a Buenos Aires-based German concern. Niebuhr and others in the German embassy in Argentina wanted Heinrich Volberg, a press attaché and leading local Nazi, to have this position, but in September 1941, company directors in Germany appointed Schulz-Hausmann.

The backers of Volberg viewed this action as a calculated affront; they retaliated by making Schulz-Hausmann an outcast among Buenos Aires *Reichsdeutschen*. Reacting to the frigid treatment, the embattled Schulz-Hausmann gave the pink slip to a number of Volberg's friends on the company's staff, but it was the naval attaché who had the last laugh. "Casero" could do little except gnash his teeth when, as a result of the successful escape of the seven ships from the Chilean waters, the Abwehr gave the lion's share of the credit to Niebuhr.[38] Moreover, the latter seems to have avenged himself upon the truculent V-man in yet another way. Although the SIS continued to view Schulz-Hausmann as a dangerous spy, after he arrived in Buenos Aires in October 1941, he does not seem to have received another significant Abwehr assignment. It may be that as a result of Niebuhr's denunciations, Ast Hamburg concluded that "Casero" was either untrustworthy or blown. In any case, although Schulz-Hausmann lived until December 1945, as far as intelligence work was concerned, he was operationally dead after October 1941.[39]

B. *The PYL-REW Circuit*

Friedrich von Schulz-Hausmann's best known achievement as a spymaster was the establishment of a Pacific coast clandestine radio reporting service. Known to the Germans as FMK "Valparaíso," or FMK "Condor," this station was better known to the U.S. counterintelligence as PYL, with the Ast Hamburg reception station being referred to as REW.[40] (See Chart VIII for a representation of the PYL network.) The origin of

CHART VIII

PYL RING

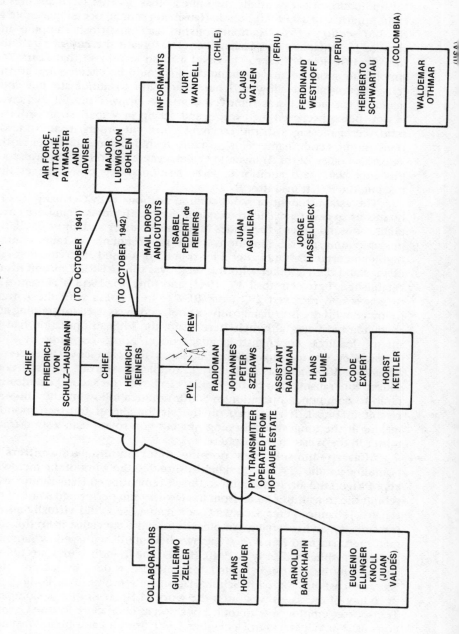

CONTROLLERS: Lt. Heinrich Bröcker
Lt. Commander Andre von Wettstein, I-M Section (to August, 1941)
Commander Heinz Tornow, I-M Section (from August, 1941)

CHIEF — FRIEDRICH VON SCHULZ-HAUSMANN

(TO OCTOBER 1941)

(TO OCTOBER 1942)

CHIEF — HEINRICH REINERS

REW

PYL

RADIOMAN — JOHANNES PETER SZERAWS

PYL TRANSMITTER OPERATED FROM HOFBAUER ESTATE

ASSISTANT RADIOMAN — HANS BLUME

CODE EXPERT — HORST KETTLER

AIR FORCE, ATTACHÉ, PAYMASTER AND ADVISER — MAJOR LUDWIG VON BOHLEN

INFORMANTS

KURT WANDELL   (CHILE)

CLAUS WATJEN   (PERU)

FERDINAND WESTHOFF   (PERU)

HERIBERTO SCHWARTAU   (COLOMBIA)

WALDEMAR OTHMAR

MAIL DROPS AND CUTOUTS

ISABEL PEDERIT de REINERS

JUAN AGUILERA

JORGE HASSELDIECK

COLLABORATORS

GUILLERMO ZELLER

HANS HOFBAUER

ARNOLD BARCKHAHN

EUGENIO ELLINGER KNOLL (JUAN VALDES)

this radio circuit is essentially the same as that of other German rings in Latin America. In 1939–40, Schulz-Hausmann sent an occasional cable to the I-M section of Ast Hamburg, giving data on British shipping and cargoes in Valparaíso and Callao (Peru).[41] Toward the end of 1940, the Abwehr instructed "Casero" to build a radio station so that faster and supposedly more secure communications could be effected, but fortuitous circumstances allowed Schulz-Hausmann to anticipate the command. A transmitter was removed from the *Osorno,* one of the seven vessels being prepared for escape, and set up in Valparaíso in order to send secret messages to the escaping ships. On orders from "Casero," Hans Blume (code name: Flor), a radio technician and manager of the Valparaíso office of the Transradio-Chilena cable and telegraph firm, took this unit, and with additional parts, fashioned the powerful set that became the PYL transmitter.[42]

The establishment of radio communications with Germany was by no means an easy task. The tremendous distance from Ast Hamburg (over eight thousand miles), the Andes Mountains barrier and, most of all, the unstable atmospheric conditions, made the frequency of radio contact highly uncertain.[43] "Only after a lot of milling around . . . trying first one change and then another with the set"[44] was the PYL-REW circuit firmly established. Between April 17, 1941, and June 15, 1942, PYL sent 429 messages and received 287 from REW.[45] In keeping with the pattern followed with the Brazilian groups, a book code was used for sending and receiving messages, although, here again, the Chilean operation had its unique features. An English language novel, *South Latitude,* by F. D. Ommanney, was used to decipher messages from Germany; *The Letters of Katherine Mansfield,* as edited by J. Middleton Murray, was the code source for transmission to the Reich.[46] PYL was the second clandestine radio to commence operation in South America following the LIR-MAX circuit in Brazil. It remained on the air for almost fourteen months, making it the longest functioning Abwehr-controlled clandestine transmitter in the Western Hemisphere.

"Casero" himself knew nothing about building transmitters or pounding a radio key, but he skillfully directed the work of the men who kept PYL on the air. In addition to the aforementioned Hans Blume, who rebuilt the transmitter taken from the *Osorno* and performed some of the repairs, Johannes Peter Szeraws (code name: Esco) did virtually all the transmitting and receiving. An officer and radio specialist from the German merchantman *Frankfort,* Szeraws became ill with yellow jaundice and was hospitalized early in 1940. He became friendly with Hans Blume, and when the *Frankfort* sailed for Japanese waters in March 1941, Szeraws cast his lot with Schulz-Hausmann's group. The coding and decoding of messages was often the work of Horst Kettler, a Compañía Transportes employee who took a position as code clerk for the German consulate in Valparaíso in December 1939. Szeraws and Blume installed the radio transmitter in a cottage on a small estate near Quilpué, a town about ten miles east of Valparaíso. Hans Hofbauer (code name: León), an accountant who also worked for Compañía Transportes, owned the estate. Hofbauer's only work for the ring was the care and feeding of Szeraws, and silence concerning the former sailor's radio activities.[47]

Although he had nothing to do with building or installing transmitters, and he was not involved in either the German steamer escape or the *Graf Spee* sailor return operation, Heinrich Reiners (code name: Tom) would nevertheless attain his share of espionage notoriety. A former Compañía Transportes employee, Reiners opened his own freight shipping office in Valparaíso early in 1939. The outbreak of war diminished his prospects of entrepreneurial success, and blacklisting by the British finished them. According to Reiners, his bankruptcy and desire for revenge were the forces which propelled him into the PYL organization. In May 1941, Reiners became the organization's major recruiter, traveling to port towns in northern and southern Chile to enlist friends and German sympathizers as informants concerning ship movements. On June 12, 1941, "Casero" sent a message to REW criticizing both Reiners and Blume as "lacking experience and connections," and therefore, incapable of replacing him. "Tom" must have done a great deal of maturing in a relatively short period of time, for when Schulz-Hausmann left Chile in October 1941, he named Heinrich Reiners as chief of the PYL ring.[48]

The sextet of Blume, Szeraws, Kettler, Hofbauer, Reiners, and Schulz-Hausmann made up the PYL nucleus, but there were a dozen others who acted as collaborators and aides. For example, mail sent from Europe to Chile was received by Juan Aguilera, an office worker at Compañía Transportes.[49] The post office box in the name of Isabel Pederit de Reiners (code name: Señorita) was the reception point for agent mail coming from Mexico, Brazil, and China. The wife of Heinrich Reiners would subsequently insist that she had nothing to do with any espionage ring, and that she never opened any of the letters which went to her post office box. Her role in the ring was probably limited to acting as a cloak for her husband, but it is difficult to believe that she was completely ignorant of what was going on.[50]

Among the most important informants and aides mentioned in the PYL radio dispatches were the Compañía Transportes representative in the port of Coquimbo, Kurt Wandell, and the North German Lloyd representatives in Callao, Peru, Claus Watjen (code name: Vasquez) and Ferdinand Westoff (code name: Quezón).[51] Also eminent among this group were Eugenio Ellinger Knoll (code names: Juan Valdés, Martín Flores) and Arnold Barckhahn (code name: Junior), both of whom acted as couriers and special assistants to Schulz-Hausmann. The difference was that Knoll, who served as a guide in the *Graf Spee* sailor escape operation, also took orders from intelligence chiefs in Argentina. "Junior," in contrast, limited his activities to performing those general utility services the Chilean leadership might require.[52]

There was one other prominent associate of the PYL ring, but his position was different from any of the others. This man was Luftwaffe attaché Maj. Ludwig von Bohlen (code names: Bach, Rivera, Papi, Uva). A

World War I veteran, former magistrate, and expert in Chilean jurispru-
dence, Bohlen had reentered the German armed forces as a lieutenant in
1937. Rising to the rank of major by November 1940, he was given
command of a mobile antiaircraft battery and posted to East Prussia. Early
in 1941, Bohlen concluded that the increased movement of German
troops into Eastern Europe indicated only one thing: forthcoming hostilities with the USSR. Since he had served as an army officer on the eastern
front in World War I, Bohlen wanted no part of another Russian adventure. Able to pull a few strings, and aided by the connections of one Fritz
Busch, a wealthy businessman with Abwehr ties, Bohlen obtained the
post of air force attaché in Chile. He left Berlin to take up his new
assignment exactly one day before the start of the Russian campaign.[53]

In escaping the rigors of eastern front warfare, Bohlen exhibited a
talent for survival and a flair for maximizing his career options. Initially,
however, he must have wondered whether his transoceanic journey out
of the potential line of fire had been a wise move after all. While Bohlen's
controller was Lt. Col. Ernst Arno Kleyenstueber, his regional superior
was Capt. Dietrich Niebuhr, and so Bohlen called on the naval attaché
while en route to Santiago.[54] Arriving in Buenos Aires on June 28, 1941,
Bohlen met not only Niebuhr, but Friedrich Schulz-Hausmann as well.
The latter was in the Argentine capital interviewing for the Bromberg and
Company post, and as soon as the two attachés were alone, Niebuhr
began castigating Schulz-Hausmann as conceited, conniving, and insuffer-
able. Obviously, the naval attaché had little regard for "Casero," but, as
Bohlen would discover, the feeling was fully reciprocated.[55] Also, the
July–October 1941 relationship between Schulz-Hausmann and Bohlen
in Chile, though not as contentious as that between Schulz-Hausmann and
Niebuhr, was by no means friendly. The major had brought four hundred
thousand dollars with him to finance covert operations. In exchange for
some financial assistance, he would be allowed to receive and send
messages via the PYL transmitter, but that was essentially all. Both
Schulz-Hausmann and, after he departed, Heinrich Reiners took pains to
impress upon Bohlen that they received their marching orders from Ast
Hamburg alone.[56]

Each Abwehr network in Latin America had its own particular eccentricities, and an understanding of these provides the clearest insight
into each organization's inner dynamics and goals. For example, the PYL
leadership consisted entirely of *Reichsdeutschen* working or living in
Valparaíso who, with the exception of Johannes Szeraws, had known each
other for several years and worked for Compañía Transportes. Secondly,
with the possible exception of Schulz-Hausmann, none of the members
received any specialized espionage training in Germany. No doubt the
group received and sent secret ink letters, but prior to 1942, it had no
microdot specialist available to it. Thirdly, four of the five PYL principals
—Schulz-Hausmann, Heinrich Reiners, Horst Kettler, and Hans Blume—
were card-carrying members of the Chilean AO.[57] The emergent picture
is that of a small, tough intelligence group that was short on experience,

but long on energy, enthusiasm, and knowledge of the society in which it would operate.

Bearing this appraisal in mind, to what degree was the information provided by the PYL transmitter vital to the German cause? Information on ship sailings, cargoes, and their destinations reached Germany a good deal more rapidly via radio than by cable, but Doenitz's U-boats lacked the range to operate effectively off the Chilean coast. Thus, ship movement details radioed over PYL, while indirectly useful, were not as important as similar information being supplied by Kempter's FMK "Brazil." Of greater value to the Abwehr, probably, was the data supplied on Chilean iron and copper exports to the United States. Ludwig von Bohlen was specifically instructed to make sure that this kind of information reached Germany. The German High Command realized that Chilean ore shipments were crucial to U.S. war production. Therefore, knowledge of how much was being exported to the United States was useful intelligence.[58]

But, data on ore shipments aside, the great value of the PYL transmitter lay in its utility. For example, after station GBO was closed down late in June 1941, George Nicolaus, Edgard Hilgert, and the other V-men in Mexico began mailing or cabling their reports to Isabel Pederit de Reiners's post office box in Valparaíso. Particularly after the destruction of the Brazilian FMKs in March 1942, Abwehr agents all over Latin America were directed to dispatch their messages and reports to Chile so that the radio station at Quilpué could relay them. Even before then, mail and cables from agents as far away as Shanghai arrived at the Valparaíso drop for transmission by PYL.[59] Ultimately, the messages themselves tell the real story. Of 429 messages sent to Ast Hamburg between April 1941 and June 1942, 293 (68 percent) included data provided by some non-Chilean source or from some agent who was not a part of the PYL organization.[60] As a source of information about Chile or Pacific coast activities, the station was of limited value; as a general clearinghouse and relay station for German agents in Latin America and elsewhere in the world, it was priceless.

III. The First Counterespionage Campaign in Chile

A. The Hunt for PYL

On April 28, 1941, the RID monitor in Millis, Massachusetts, detected a faint signal from a station that was attempting to cloak its transmissions by operating on the same frequency as the transatlantic radio-telephone circuit. This station used the call letters REW again and again, but when the sender stopped to listen, signals from another station on a different frequency, employing the call letters PYL, were also picked up by the RID. Since the two stations were found to be sending at approximately the same time daily, RID officials concluded that they were attempting to contact one another. In the espionage world, a secret is sometimes as perishable as a snowflake. In this case, the PYL-REW circuit, the second Abwehr radio link to become operational in South America, became the first one to be detected by a U.S. radio direction finding unit.[61]

Particularly since FMK "Valparaíso" had only made contact with Ast Hamburg on April 17, the efficiency and effectiveness of the RID monitors is evident. This rapid interception process was neatly complemented by the deciphering activities of the codebreakers at the FBI Technical Laboratory. By September 1941, decoded PYL messages were being regularly circulated among a restricted group of State Department and armed forces intelligence personnel.[62] This meant that despite German efforts to safeguard spy network security, the code names, drops, cutouts, and true identities of the PYL ring members were soon known to the SIS.

Once the V-men were identified, steps might have been taken to inhibit or terminate their activities. However, in a multiparty democracy like Chile, the possibility of negative political repercussions long ruled out anything except the most timid course of conduct. In 1938, the country had elected Pedro Aguirre Cerda, leader of the Popular Front coalition, to the presidency. Less than a year after he took office, the outbreak of European war would cause serious dissension within the coalition.[63] While Aguirre Cerda and some of his colleagues in the Radical party (which was not what its name implied) were privately sympathetic to the European democracies and the Socialist party was openly favorable to them, the Communists labeled the conflict a struggle between rival imperialisms and occasionally collaborated with the Nazis.[64] If Aguirre Cerda intended to keep his contentious factions together, he could not afford to do anything which would make Chile appear non-neutral. And since the arrest or prosecution of German agents would have done precisely that, this step was out of the question. Thus, in December 1939, although Britain's MI-6 passed to the DGII reliable information regarding the activities of Schulz-Hausmann, "these vacuous Chileans," as one British diplomat described them, filed the information and apparently forgot about it.[65]

British unhappiness with Aguirre Cerda would soon be matched in Washington. The Roosevelt administration was deeply concerned over the issue of hemispheric defense, and on September 3, 1940, secret talks between a commission of U.S. Army, Navy, and Air Force officers and the Chilean chief of staff, Gen. Oscar Escudero, began in Santiago. An agreement was reached in October 1940 calling for $50 million in arms aid by the United States in exchange for unspecified naval cooperation, and a Chilean promise "to strengthen the agencies charged with the surveillance and control" of Axis espionage groups.[66]

But hardly was tentative accord reached by the negotiating parties when General Escudero began introducing reservations. Although he acknowledged that Chile was undertaking a counterespionage commitment, he insisted that the nation "did not have funds for increasing the organizations for surveillance and control." In other words, if the United

Kapitän zur See A.D. Herbert Wichmann,
commander of AST Hamburg, 1939–1945.
(Courtesy of the subject.)

Heinrich Reiners (c. 1938). (Courtesy of the FBI.)   Heinrich Reiners (1981). (Courtesy of the subject.)

Reiners became PYL ring leader in Chile, 1941–1942.

Friedrich von Schleebrugge

Georg Nicolaus

Edgar Hilgert

Karl Franz Rüge

Abwehr espionage chiefs in Mexico, 1940–1945. (All photos courtesy of the FBI.)

Albrecht Gustav Engels. (Courtesy of the Library of Congress.)

Friedrich Kempter (1942). (Courtesy of NARS.)

Friedrich Kempter (1978). (Courtesy of *Jornal do Brasil*.)

Franz Walther Jordan. (Courtesy of the Library of Congress.)

Abwehr espionage chiefs in Brazil, 1939–1943

The special bomb given by Captain Mascimento to Gerardo Melo Mourão, for destroying the German freighter, *Windhuk.* (Courtesy of NARS.)

Josef Starziczny's radio equipment seized by the Brazilian police on February 10, 1942. Note AFU (suitcase radio) at the far right. (Courtesy of *Jornal do Brasil*)

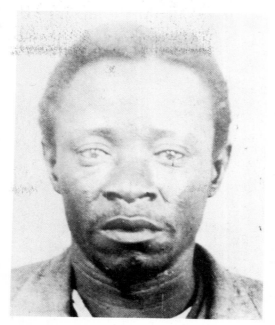

Marcus Baarn, the black agent sent by AST Hamburg to
Brazil in 1943. (Courtesy of the FBI.)

Gerardo Melo Mourão, the controversial newspaperman and scholar, convicted as sub-chief of the "Captain
García" ring. (Courtesy of *Jornal do Brasil.*)

The principal leaders of the PQZ ring, broken up in February 1944. The spies are Augusto Kroll, Bernard Timmerman, Eugenio Ellinger (Juan Valdés) and Hans Graner. (Courtesy of NARS.)

Johannes Siegfried Becker (Courtesy of NARS.)

Gustand Utzinger. (Courtesy of the Library of Congress.)

Hans Harnisch (Courtesy of NARS.)

Osmar Hellmuth. (Courtesy of *La Prensa*.)

Major Abwehr and SD spy figures active in Argentina, 1940–1945

Kapitän zur See Dietrich Niebuhr, the naval attaché who was chief paymaster and *ad hoc* supervisor for Abwehr operations in South America, 1940–1943 (Courtesy of El Archivo de la Nacion Argentina, Buenos Aires.)

Johannes Siegfried Becker (Courtesy of El Archivo de la Nacion Argentina, Buenos Aires.)

States wanted an effective Chilean counterespionage agency, the United States would have to pay the bill. This thinly disguised demand for security funds raised hackles in Washington, but events rapidly rendered all negotiations moot. Aguirre Cerda had personally authorized these secret discussions, but as soon as he realized that no free weaponry would be immediately forthcoming, the Chilean president promptly rejected the bilateral defense accord.[67]

Despite this failure to concert an agreement concerning the provision of military hardware, the counterespionage issue would be promptly resurrected. In February 1941, Aguirre Cerda and General Escudero confidentially asked U.S. ambassador Claude Bowers to request that the FBI send a team of instructors to Chile to assist in the training of DGII officers in counterspy techniques. Bowers immediately sanctioned the proposal, but Adolf Berle, chief for State Department intelligence concerns, scuttled it. Fearing some future disavowal which would leave the United States holding the bag, Berle insisted that the Chilean president must provide a written request for the training agents. Citing internal political instability, Aguirre Cerda adamantly refused to put anything on paper, and so this initiative, like the previous one, produced no tangible results.[68] Until his sudden death in November 1941, Aguirre Cerda would publicly deny the existence of German espionage agents in his country, while privately bemoaning the fact that he was not sure whether his assertion was true or false.[69]

From Washington's perspective, counterespionage needs required that steps be taken with or without Chilean consent. In October 1940, J. Edgar Hoover ordered the first SIS agents into Chile,[70] but the struggle against PYL did not gain any momentum until legal attaché Robert Wall reached Santiago on August 26, 1941.[71] Before Juan Ríos's election in February 1942, SIS/Chile-DGII cooperation remained both insignificant and, at all times, unofficial.[72] Thereafter, the situation silently but significantly changed. Fearing a possible Japanese attack, on March 20, 1942, the Chilean president formally accepted a standing offer to establish U.S.-manned coast artillery batteries for the defense of Chile's major harbors.[73] In consummating this defense arrangement, Juan Ríos must have realized that even though the United States had a vital interest in maintaining the copper ore traffic, a quid pro quo of some kind was expected. It may be coincidence, but less than a week after he accepted the weapons, Ríos ordered DGII chief Enrique Frías to collaborate with the SIS/Chile.[74] Promptly, the SIS/Chile and DGII agents inaugurated a jointly administered twenty-four-hour watch on the Compañía Transportes office in Valparaíso. All employees and office visitors were shadowed, phones were tapped, and mail opened surreptitiously. Some of these actions were of questionable legality, but they produced the confirmations needed.[75] Moreover, in April 1942, Ríos sanctioned the entry of John DeBardeleben, an RID specialist who was bringing portable radio direction-finding equipment to facilitate the hunt for the PYL transmitter.[76]

Despite the pro-U.S. moves, the Chilean president continued to affirm his neutrality in the worldwide conflict, and locating the transmitter took a good deal more time than had been originally thought. Damage to John DeBardeleben's equipment and a snafu in shipping replacement parts meant that it would be May 10, 1942, before the RID specialist was able to conduct signal-search location operations.[77] In any case, the PYL ring was not sitting idly by, waiting for the U.S. and Chilean searchers to methodically close in for the kill. In April 1942, Johannes Szeraws was told to cut down the number of days on which he transmitted, and to stagger his broadcasting schedule. Next, Heinrich Reiners ordered that a special crate and cart be constructed so that the PYL transmitter could be made portable. The result was the creation of the first mobile Abwehr radio in the Americas. Broadcasting from the Hofbauer estate continued, but Szeraws occasionally moved his equipment by truck and transmitted from the Valparaíso home of Guillermo Zeller as well.[78]

This strategem, apparently intended to throw the hunters off the trail, provided only temporary relief. DeBardeleben would complain of the "difficulties of terrain" (i.e., around Quilpué), but in his report of June 15, 1942, he stated that two broadcasting locations had been found.[79] The RID man was quick, but Reiners and his cohorts proved just a step faster. On June 1 or 2, Szeraws reported that he had seen a car near the Hofbauer property carrying what he believed to be mobile radio-location equipment mounted on its roof.[80] The last PYL message to Ast Hamburg was received on June 6, 1942. Szeraws attempted to renew contact from Zeller's house on several occasions during the period June 7–15, 1942, but he was heard only by RID interceptors. After the latter date, the PYL transmitter was put back in its crate and stored in a corner of the Zeller basement.[81]

Meanwhile, Ambassador Claude Bowers, impressed with the progress being made in the pursuit, decided to take personal charge of coordinating its diplomatic aspects. On May 2, 1942, he sought permission from Cordell Hull to ask the Chileans to arrest the PYL spy ring members as soon as DeBardeleben had located the transmitter. The secretary of state cautiously approved this plan on May 16, and Robert Wall was given the task of compiling a compendium of facts which would provide the Ríos government with sufficient evidence to institute detention and prosecution proceedings.

After DeBardeleben presented his June 15, 1942, report to Bowers, the ambassador cabled Washington that he was ready to set his plan in motion.[82] The next move in what was rapidly coming to resemble a chess match was a June 25 DGII raid, instigated by Robert Wall, on the home of Guillermo Zeller. The premises were searched, but nothing was found; however, shortly after the police departed, Zeller foolishly telephoned Ernesto Seeman, a suspected ring member, and observed that "luckily they [the police] did not search very good especially in the basement. . . ."[83] The DGII men who conducted this investigation may not have been very thorough, but they had tapped the phone, and on June 27, a veritable ransacking of Zeller's home was conducted. This time, the crate bearing the radio was found, but either the forces of caution or the powers of financial persuasion prompted the investigators not to open it. Wall was extremely upset when he learned what had occurred; perhaps he realized that this had been the last chance he would have to lay his hands on the assembled PYL transmitter.[84]

At that moment in time, however, the hope of obtaining full Chilean cooperation did not seem to depend entirely upon the seizure of the spy transmitter. On June 30, 1942, at a special meeting between Ambassador Claude Bowers and Chilean foreign minister Ernesto Barros Jarpa, Robert Wall handed the latter one copy of the multipaged document he had been working on since May 16. The long memorandum, entitled "German Espionage Agents in Chile," named eighteen persons as German spies, and included seventy decoded PYL-REW messages as proof that the ring directed by Schulz-Hausmann and Heinrich Reiners was "not only a threat to Chile, but a source of peril to the entire policy of hemispheric defense...."[85] Although the document did not specifically request that Ríos promptly arrest and prosecute the PYL group, this is what Washington wanted, and essentially what Bowers had suggested he could deliver. The U.S. ambassador also took pains to impress upon the foreign minister that the document was top secret. Barros Jarpa, in his turn, promised to take the necessary procedures, but warned that the document could be acted upon only by Minister of the Interior Raúl Morales.

Wall, Bowers, and their Washington superiors had planned well, but the Germans again succeeded in dodging the bullet. On June 28, the PYL transmitter, which the DGII searchers inexplicably failed to find, was removed from the Zeller house and partially disassembled. Arnold Barckhahn took the radio in its crate to a fruit store owned by Juan Cuneo and, affirming that it was an old sewing machine, hid it in the back of the store. Heinrich Reiners took the radio crystal and several other parts and committed them to the safekeeping of a shop owner named Otto Buchholz. Thus it was that the longest operating Abwehr transmitter in the Americas finally ceased operation.[86]

In one sense, SIS/Chile had succeeded, for PYL was finally and permanently off the airwaves. What Robert Wall and J. Edgar Hoover did not know, however, was that on July 2, Maj. Ludwig von Bohlen received a copy of the secret spy memorandum handed to Barros Jarpa on June 30.[87] Now that the Abwehr knew what SIS/Chile was doing, and so long as Bohlen's connections held up, future U.S. counterspy operations could be anticipated and parried.

IV. Stalemate

A. *The Spy Memorandum as Turning Point*

From Washington's perspective, the beauty of the June 30, 1942, memorandum was that it was at once both an exposition of Abwehr activity in Chile and an implicit demand that the Ríos regime initiate a program of espionage arrests. The inherent assumption seemed to be that once Chile began detaining German agents, that nation must eventually align itself with the coalition of states battling the Axis powers.[88] Alas, this scenario ignored the possibility that while Ríos might sanction surveillance collaboration with SIS/Chile, he had no intention of taking the kind of steps which might lead to the abandonment of neutrality. Not surprisingly, on July 8, 1942, when Barros Jarpa sent a copy of the spy document to Minister of the Interior Raúl Morales, the former made no recommendations, and the latter ordered neither interrogations nor detentions.[89]

Conscious of his optimistic forecasts of May and disappointed that the Chileans exhibited no sense of urgency, Claude Bowers attempted to subtly expedite action. On July 13, he saw Barros Jarpa and tentatively suggested that if the Chileans arrested the persons named in the June 30, 1942, memorandum, the ensuing trial with its revelations would provide a plausible justification for diplomatic rupture with Germany. Barros Jarpa was noncommittal, but Bowers did not intend to let the Chilean off the hook. On the seventeenth, the North American again pressed for action, but this time the foreign minister pulled a surprise; he eschewed all responsibility and declared that the inactivity was the fault of Minister Morales.[90]

By this time the U.S. ambassador was more than a little peeved with what he considered to be Chilean stonewalling. On July 25, the diplomatic mask slipped a bit, and harsh words were exchanged, with Barros Jarpa reputedly agreeing to take the matter directly to President Juan Ríos.[91] He may have done so, but the only official response Bowers received during the next three months was that the matter was still under investigation by the minister of the interior.[92]

Diplomacy having produced meager results, it became the task of SIS/Chile to discover what the Ríos government really intended to do about the June 30, 1942, spy memorandum. In August, Robert Wall reached an understanding with the new DGII commander, Jorge Garreton, and obtained the following information: The Chilean government—or at least the Ministry of Interior—did not consider the spy memorandum to be a sufficient basis for either conducting interrogations or making arrests![93] In essence, the detection and surveillance collaboration between DGII and SIS/Chile in March–June 1942 was evidence of the Ríos regime's desire to collaborate. So, too, the official silence and continuing procrastination after June 30, 1942, was evidence that the collaboration received was all that a neutral Chile intended to give.

Juan Ríos apparently wished to believe that even if he took no decisive action regarding the spy memorandum, he had collaborated sufficiently for the United States to become reconciled to the situation. If so, he ignored the observation of the Chilean emissary in Washington, Ambassador Rodolfo Michels, who viewed his government's inaction on the espionage issue with growing trepidation. In a July 18, 1942, communiqué, Michels reported that Sumner Welles and other State Department officials were continually complaining that Chile had "done little to curb Axis subversion and espionage." Based on these criticisms, Michels concluded that in Washington, the issues of German espionage and the rupture of diplomatic relations had become fused. Unless the Ríos government managed to separate them or take conclusive action against the V-men, "the Government of the United States will insist upon, and will act to determine the definition of our international position. . . ."[94]

B. *The Cable Capers*

In persuading Heinrich Reiners to end PYL's activities, Ludwig von Bohlen argued that the ring's membership was known to the North Americans, and that any arrests followed by "an espionage trial [would] lead to a break in [diplomatic] relations." The Ríos government, in the attaché's opinion, did not desire to initiate a spy prosecution; thus, if PYL became inactive, possible provocation would disappear. Moreover, Bohlen could give assurances that ship movement and other intelligence information would continue to reach Germany by means of cables coded in his personal cipher, over Transradio Chilena.[95]

The Axis use of the telecommunications system in Latin America had been an issue for U.S. policy makers since 1940, and they used a variety of approaches in dealing with it. The usual method was to approach a Latin American government and negotiate a confidential agreement whereby copies of Axis diplomatic cables or any suspected spy cables were regularly supplied to SIS officials. Arrangements of this nature had been made with Mexico in August 1940 and with Brazil in December 1941.[96] At the third foreign ministers' meeting at Rio de Janeiro in January 1942, Sumner Welles pushed successfully for the adoption of Resolution XL, which called for the execution of "immediate measures" intended to sever telecommunications connections between the Western Hemisphere and the Axis.[97]

Most American republics promptly complied, but neither Chile nor Argentina took action or indicated when they would do so. The United States was not disposed to wait for these nations to make up their minds, and so overt moves gave way to covert ones. In March 1942 the SIS began receiving copies of pertinent cables from a source inside Transradio Chilena, and the FBI laboratory rapidly decoded these messages.[98] During the same month, the FCC commenced the interception of all cable traffic to and from Chile and thereafter provided daily summaries to the MID, ONI, and FBI.[99]

Knowing what the German embassy was sending was gratifying, but if the Germans utilized a cypher which defied FBI laboratory cryptanalysts, the advantage the United States enjoyed would be lost. Furthermore, a most pressing consideration was the U-boat carnage then being conducted off the eastern seaboard of the United States. Since the intercepted information still got through and was thought to contribute to the ship sinkings, the only real solution was to shut it down completely.

Washington's policy had been to continue intercepting the cables while seeking to have the Ríos government close the telecommunications circuits to the Axis powers. But in June 1942 Bohlen's intercepted cables revealed an increasing amount of ship movement data.[100] While the Chileans still had to be the prime movers in the situation, they would now be pushed, rather than merely pressed, to take action. Claude Bowers was alerted, and on July 11, 1942, he received a special memorandum for presentation to Foreign Minister Ernesto Barros Jarpa.

When the two men met by appointment four days later, Bowers stated that all cable traffic between Chile and the Axis was being intercepted and decoded by Anglo-American intelligence. He showed Barros Jarpa copies of nine deciphered messages which, in the opinion of the United States, demonstrated the glaring misuse of diplomatic privilege by several German embassy staff members. The U.S. ambassador laid special emphasis to the shipping information sent by Ludwig von Bohlen and insisted that "it is more urgent than ever before that Chile undertake action to sever the telecommunications circuit which it now maintains with Axis territory. . ."[101]

Undoubtedly, Barros Jarpa was taken aback by these revelations. He received another jolt when he asked for copies of the decoded cables, for Bowers made a vague comment about a "possible leak," and a more pointed one concerning Chilean failure to arrest any of the persons mentioned in the June 30, 1942, memorandum.[102] No materials would be handed over, a development which starkly demonstrates the impact which the failure of the Ríos regime to act was having on U.S.-Chilean diplomatic relations.

It may be that Bowers believed that his indications of Washington displeasure over Chilean policy might elicit a more conciliatory response on the telecommunications issue; if so, he would again be sadly mistaken. Indeed, the tactics of Barros Jarpa reveal how a skillful diplomat can go round and round, but nonetheless wind up in the same place from which he started. On July 17, 1942, the foreign minister formally offered to terminate the dispatch of coded cablegrams from Chile to Axis-controlled territories. Ambassador Bowers's reply was that the proposed action, although helpful, was still unsatisfactory, for the Germans could still send out valuable information whether it was coded or not.[103] This objection apparently did not faze the Chileans, for on August 12, 1942, a decree prohibiting the use of coded cablegrams was promulgated by President Ríos.[104]

The effect of the new law may or may not have been foreseen by the Chileans, but it was certainly the opposite of what the United States expected. Despite the decree, Axis diplomats continued using Transradio Chilena in order to send coded cables to their capitals. On the other hand, U.S. businessmen were denied the same privilege, and their complaints were soon heard in the halls of Congress.[105] On September 3, 1942, an angry Cordell Hull censured Bowers, and demanded to know why, in light of the August 12 decree, Axis diplomats could send ciphered messages, but U.S. businessmen could not. A harried ambassador took up the issue with both Barros Jarpa and Ríos, but neither man claimed to know why Transradio Chilena was acting so strangely.[106] The foreign minister unenthusiastically agreed to look into the difficulty, and Bowers finally got the message: Chile did not intend to act as the United States desired.[107]

The State Department had tasted frustration in its attempt to maneuver the Ríos government into arresting German agents, but in the telecommunications matter, an alternative plan had long been under consideration. This project called upon the corporations which owned Transradio Chilena to order the connection with the Axis cut. Discussions to this effect began in April 1942 with RCA (U.S.A.) and, a month later, with Cable and Wireless, Ltd. (Great Britain). In the talks with company officials State Department representatives argued that it was "psychologically bad . . . for British and American communication companies to allow stations over which they have financial control . . . to facilitate the stream of intelligence between South America and the Axis detrimental to the best interests of the Allies."[108]

The principal stumbling block in this situation was that 50 percent of the stock in the consortium which owned Transradio Chilena was held by French and German interests. But because of U.S. dominance in the Americas, the five-member board which controlled the consortium's subsidiaries in the Western Hemisphere was usually chaired by a U.S. citizen. As a result, the vote of two North Americans and the single British board member gave the Anglo-Americans a three-to-two advantage and, despite Franco-German protests, on July 6, 1942, this majority voted to support the State Department's wishes.[109] The next step was to have RCA and Cable and Wireless, Ltd., acting in the name of the consortium, order the local Transradio Chilena board of directors to terminate all its circuits with Germany, Italy, and Japan.

Since it feared the Chilean government might object to any drastic action and retaliate accordingly, RCA was loath to ask its representative and local Transradio director, Alfred Jory, to convene a meeting for the purpose noted. However, State Department threats soon convinced the company that Washington could be infinitely nastier than Santiago.[110] Thus, Jory was ordered to get on with the task of producing a majority, and to hold the necessary meeting as soon as he had one. On September 29, 1942, he informed his superiors that three other board members would also vote for closure of the circuits, and that the board meeting would be held on October 6. On September 30, RCA ordered Jory to proceed and instructed him that if the Chilean government objected, it was to be told that unless Transradio Chilena acted as the parent organization wished, parts for the maintenance of operations would no longer be supplied.[111]

Naturally, the Ríos government objected, but some weeks previously it seems to have guessed what the State Department was plotting. In response to a hypothetical query from Bowers concerning a closure of the telecommunications circuits by the consortium owners, Barros Jarpa made it clear (September 17, 1942) that he wanted no punitive action taken. Breaking the connections, he stated, would rob Chile of a justification it might use "at some future date" if the government decided to break diplomatic relations with Germany, Italy, and Japan.[112] As a result, when, on September 30, 1942, Bowers informed Barros Jarpa in a general way what actions the Transradio board was about to take, the Ríos regime was not caught off balance. Instead, it prepared a plan for dealing with that contingency. Three members of the seven-man Transradio Chilena directorate were Chilean nationals, and on October 5, Señores Valenzuela and Balmaceda, the two Chileans supporting the closure resolution, received personal phone calls from Juan Ríos. The president stated that his wish was merely a request, but he made it clear that he wanted the October 6 meeting postponed at least twenty-four hours. Jory objected to any delay, but he had to agree or watch his majority dissolve. On the morning of the sixth, Ríos again phoned the two Chileans and gave them their marching orders. They could support a resolution prohibiting the transmission of coded telegrams to Axis territory, but uncoded cables would be transmitted without restriction. Jory objected, but to no avail; it was this resolution that the board of Transradio Chilena passed on the afternoon of October 8.[113]

The results of this vote were clear: Juan Ríos had called the RCA–State Department bluff, and conceded no more than Barros Jarpa had offered on July 17, 1942. Moreover, despite the action taken by Transradio Chilena, the Axis embassies could still send coded cables to Argentina, where other officials relayed them to Berlin, Rome, or Tokyo.[114] These developments had to be especially galling to the United States, for on August 12 at Bowers's suggestion, President Roosevelt had sent a message to Ríos promising to protect his regime from attack by "an Axis power," or by "elements instigated and dominated by Axis spies."[115] FDR had made his pledge contingent upon Chile's breaking of diplomatic relations with the Axis. But, with Ríos not arresting German spies and continuing to play coded cables charades, it seemed unlikely that he would send Axis diplomats packing. With momentous battles then being fought in and around Guadalcanal and in the rubble of Stalingrad, Washington decided that it was time to get tough.

C. *Sumner Welles Ends the Impasse*

The only Abwehr agent captured and executed for espionage in Latin America during World War II was an Ast Hamburg operative, Heinz August Luning (code number: A-3799).[116] Luning began posing as a Dutch Jewish refugee upon reaching Havana, Cuba, on September 2, 1941. During the next twelve months, he sent forty-seven secret ink letters to drops in Spain and Portugal. These letters dealt with ship sailings and cargoes, and precisely because many of these messages were sent during a period in which U-boats were active in the Caribbean (February–July

1942), Luning was deemed a dangerous agent. Arrested on August 31, he was tried secretly in Havana, found guilty on September 18, and executed by a military firing squad on November 10.[117]

The demise of "A-3799" intersects with German espionage activity in Chile because, in his confession, Luning revealed that in April 1942 he received a cable draft for $1,507.50 from a Chilean named Manuel Tapía. He also received several cables from another Chilean, Carlos Robinson, who demanded to know whether a transmitter had been obtained, and gave signals information and call letters for contacting Ast Hamburg.[118] Luning's statement was sent to Claude Bowers towards the middle of September, and SIS/Chile leader Robert Wall promptly forwarded it to Minister of the Interior Raúl Morales. After he read the report, Morales declared that if effective action could be taken against the German spies in Chile, it would " 'change the whole panorama of the Government's international policy.' " Commenting on Morales's observation, J. Edgar Hoover reported to the White House that "the Minister of the Interior and the official of the Chilean Bureau of Investigation [Jorge Garreton, chief of the DGII] were in agreement that the apprehension of the espionage agents and a successful prosecution of them would afford President Ríos of Chile a sufficient motive for breaking relations with the Axis."[119]

Although Jorge Garreton had been on close terms with SIS/Chile since August 1942, the interior minister remained an unknown quantity. The June 30, 1942, spy memorandum had been turned over to his office of July 8, but despite Morales's subsequent declarations, there is no evidence that he made any effort to substantiate its claims.[120] The interior minister was comparatively young (thirty-six years old), ambitious, a protégé of Juan Antonio Ríos, and on old enemy of Ernesto Barros Jarpa.[121] Possibly Morales sensed that U.S. pressure must eventually force Ríos to break relations with the Axis, and by placing himself in the vanguard of the rupture movement, he could simultaneously become cabinet strong man, and even old scores with the foreign minister.[122] U.S. officials could not have cared less about his motives. For here at last was a major cabinet official who seemed interested in arresting German spies, and was prepared to use this issue as a means of forcing the long-desired diplomatic break.

One reason for U.S. optimism was that once the Luning confession was made available to Morales, he quickly demonstrated that he would act with dispatch. On or about September 18, DGII forces secretly arrested Carlos Robinson and three Reichsdeutschen, Wilhelm Dorbach, Ludwig Russ, and Alfred Klaiber. After what was described as "the severest interrogation," Robinson and Russ fingered Alfred Klaiber, manager of the Banco Germánico branch in Santiago, as the source for the draft sent by Manuel Tapía and the instructions cabled by Robinson. But, much to Bowers's annoyance, DGII interrogators were "too easily discouraged in their interrogation of Klaiber," who would only admit that he received his instructions from Francisco Müller, a Banco Germánico executive in Barcelona, Spain.[123]

In fact, Klaiber was not an Abwehr agent,[124] and was probably only doing what he was told. In company with Russ and Dorbach, he would later face deportation proceedings, but in the meantime, this case would be made to serve other political ends. On October 1 and 2, 1942, a reporter named Benjamin Subercaseaux published sensational articles in *El Mercurio,* Santiago's leading daily, charging that German spies in Chile were sending data to the fatherland via clandestine radio, and that this information had resulted in U-boat sinkings of Allied shipping.[125] Since both the Klaiber-Luning connection and the June 30, 1942, spy memorandum were kept secret from the public, and the Ríos government had steadfastly denied or ridiculed all allegations of German espionage in the country, the articles caused a sensation.[126] Barros Jarpa immediately denounced the *El Mercurio* articles as detrimental to national security interests and he demanded Subercaseaux's arrest.

The next move was Morales's and he proceeded to sandbag Barros Jarpa and initiate a cabinet crisis. On October 7, he complied with the foreign minister's request by issuing a warrant for the newspaperman's arrest. But that same day, he called a general press conference and outlined, in a totally erroneous and confusing manner, the arrest of Alfred Klaiber and his associates and their connection with Heinz Luning.[127] This was the first admission by a Chilean government official that the Germans were supporting or conducting espionage operations from Chilean soil, and it made Barros Jarpa's demand for the newspaperman's arrest appear stupidly vindictive. Even more important, the revelations plus the open conflict between two cabinet officials had immediate, unsettling political repercussions. On October 8, the Radical party's executive board called for Barros Jarpa's removal while the Chilean House of Deputies passed a resolution of support for both Morales and Subercaseaux.[128]

Chile is noted for its earthquakes, and by the evening of October 8, Juan Ríos may have felt that a fissure was opening beneath his feet. That very day, he and Barros Jarpa had just repulsed the Yankees on the coded cable issue, but Morales's actions, plus the rebellion brewing in both the Chilean Congress and the president's own party, were threatening to break up the fragile parliamentary coalition upon which the regime depended. Some kind of foreign policy realignment would have to occur, and Ríos intended to control it, but another event transpiring thousands of miles to the north forced his hand. On the night of October 8, 1942, Sumner Welles, then serving in the capacity of acting secretary of state, made a fiery speech before the twentieth National Trade Convention in Boston, Massachusetts. Making no effort to appear conciliatory, he charged that two of twenty-one American republics had not severed diplomatic relations with the Axis, and therefore, had not met commitments undertaken at the Rio de Janeiro Conference of January 1942. Futhermore, Welles argued that as a result of ship movement reports being sent by German agents in the two states, vessels of nine American republics had been sunk. He concluded his remarks on the situation with the following observation: "I cannot believe that these two republics will continue to permit their brothers and neighbors in the Americas to be stabbed in the back by Axis emissaries operating in their territory. . . ."[129]

The following day, an angry Barros Jarpa immediately denounced the speech as a tissue of distortions and misrepresentations, characterizing it as unwarranted intervention into Chilean internal affairs.[130] Then on October 11, President Ríos, citing the Welles speech as evidence of an unfriendly attitude in Washington, canceled his impending visit to the United States. Ambassador Claude Bowers exceeded himself in searching out examples of Chilean support for the undersecretary's remarks, but the fact remains that he was not previously consulted, and would always consider the speech ill-timed and unfortunate.[131] Seemingly, the tough talk from the usually politic Welles was proving more counterproductive than helpful.

Nevertheless, after a show of injured pride, economic, military, and political considerations dictated that the Ríos regime must strike a conciliatory pose. The lend-lease agreement had yet to be signed, the country was totally dependent upon the United States for petroleum shipments, and negotiations for a needed $100 million loan from North American banks were entering a delicate stage.[132] Thus, the same day that Ríos announced the termination of his travel plans, Ambassador Rodolfo Michels was ordered to discover the price of accommodation with Uncle Sam. On October 12 and 13, 1942, long discussions were held with Sumner Welles, and three days later, Michels cabled his observations and findings to Santiago.

If nothing else, this ambassador's report demonstrates that he had excellent contacts in the U.S. capital. First, Michels revealed that for some time, a draft of Welles's offensive speech had been circulating through the State Department, and it had been sanctioned by, among others, Vice-President Henry Wallace. Wallace himself told Michels that the October 8 speech had been painful to make, but that the United States had waited long enough for Chile to act on its own. It was the ambassador's surmise that since Chile had done little about the espionage problem, and failed to sever diplomatic relations, the October 8 bombshell had been partially intended to force Ríos to cancel his prospective visit. Michels also warned that the continuing "allusions to acts of espionage by Welles" made the situation unequivocally clear: Unless the regime took conspicuous action soon, there would be no loan, no weapons, less fuel oil, and more unfriendly speeches.[133]

Evidently Ríos had already decided to make certain changes, for on October 16, the same day that Michels's observations were cabled to Santiago, the first assurances that arrests would soon be made were passed to legal attaché Robert Wall by the DGII (October 16, 1942).[134] Thereafter, events unfolded almost as if they had been placed on a programmatic schedule. On October 17, the Chilean cabinet declared itself hopelessly divided over what to do about the espionage issue, a development the president had undoubtedly foreseen. Three days later, the ministers officially resigned, and on the twenty-second, Ríos publicly announced that "Chile will be at the side of the American nations."[135] On the twenty-fourth, a new cabinet was named; Raúl Morales kept his post, but Ernesto Barros Jarpa was among those replaced. In fact, the minister of the interior must have known for several days that he would be reappointed because on October 23, he ordered the DGII to commence the detention and interrogation of some eighteen persons named in the June 30, 1942, memorandum.[136]

Ten days after the new cabinet was named, Raúl Morales held a general press conference in which he admitted publicly that Barros Jarpa had sent the spy memorandum to his ministry on July 8, 1942. Morales insisted, however, that it had been "humanly impossible" to proceed with dispatch toward verifying the charges made in the memorandum "even though he [Morales] had wished to do so."[137] No explanation was given as to how the document had been validated, or why it had been impossible for more than three months to arrest or even interrogate the persons named in it. With more time, perhaps, a credible explanation could have been fashioned, but the United States had dropped the other shoe and denied the Chileans that opportunity. On October 22, the State Department officially forwarded the June 30, 1942, memorandum to the Emergency Advisory Committee for the Political Defense of the Americas (CPD).[138] On November 3, the day before Morales held his press conference, the CPD made public for the first time the contents of the spy memorandum, an act to which the Chilean representative on the committee took violent exception.[139]

Particularly since it was Sumner Welles's October 8, 1942, address which dramatically helped to accelerate the redirection of Chilean foreign policy, certain questions remain: What was the undersecretary's major objective? Did he fully believe the charges he made about the ship sinkings? First of all, the cessation of cabling activity, especially by Maj. Ludwig von Bohlen, was apparently his primary goal.[140] The Chilean actions in this regard were considered inadequate; the Ríos government was to be coerced into prohibiting the use of the telecommunications circuits to the Axis powers.

Where Welles could be faulted, however, was in his insistence that reports being sent from Chile were directly responsible for the sinking of vessels flying the flags of American republics. When asked for proof of the connection concerning messages from Chile and Argentina and ship sinkings by U-boats, Welles was deliberately vague and misleading, for he could not reveal that the coded cables were being intercepted and decrypted.[141] Unless the undersecretary had access to information that is still secret, we must attribute his intentional misinformation to the tense war situation then prevalent in the USSR, North Africa, and the South Pacific.

Already noted is the probability that one of the aims of the October 8, 1942, speech was to indicate to Juan Ríos that since Chile was still officially neutral, he was not welcome in Washington. It was hardly subtle, but Ríos obviously got the message.[142] Perhaps another signal sent to Santiago with the speech was that the Chilean president would be wise to drop Barros Jarpa, chief spokesman for Chilean neutrality.[143] Immediately following Welles's speech, the foreign minister denounced it as an "offense to the national dignity," and insisted that no information emanating from Chile could possibly be responsible for the sinking of ships in the Caribbean Sea or the Atlantic Ocean.[144]

After his departure from the Ríos cabinet and the publication of the June 30, 1942, memorandum by the CPD, Barros Jarpa raised the level of invective by lambasting Welles unmercifully in print. The former foreign minister insisted that the October 8, 1942, speech represented "the apex of the worst days of United States diplomacy," and dared Welles to produce proofs that vessels of the American republics had been sunk as a result of intelligence messages sent from Chilean soil.[145]

There can be no doubt whatsoever that Barros Jarpa had a legitimate point to make, but another assessment of the situation helps to put it in a more meaningful perspective. Sir Charles Orde, British ambassador to Chile, scrupulously withheld a final judgment in the Welles–Barros Jarpa dispute until he could make the kind of reasoned, dispassionate analysis which is in keeping with the best British examples of this genre of reportage. Orde was aware that the cable traffic for which Ludwig von Bohlen was responsible was the nub of the problem. He also knew that Barros Jarpa could blaze away fearlessly, for Sumner Welles would never publicly reveal the cable interception secret. With typical British understatement, Orde concluded that there was "an element of conjecture" in Welles's claim that ships had been sunk as a direct result of messages sent from Chile. Nevertheless, the "dangerous behavior of Barros Jarpa," particularly after he was removed from office, was inexcusable and boorish. In the sense that the undersecretary's speech helped to end Chilean inaction, Orde's sympathies rested with the U.S. diplomat.[146]

While proving a direct cause-and-effect relationship is always tenuous, the likelihood is strong that as a direct result of Welles's speech and the public release to the CPD of the spy memorandum, on November 23, the Ríos government introduced in the Chilean Senate a comprehensive antiespionage bill.[147] This legislation was debated secretly and passed into law on December 31, 1942. After further debate and a shabby effort to extort additional concessions from the United States,[148] on January 20, 1943, Chile severed diplomatic relations with the Axis powers.

The achievement of this goal brought rejoicing to the halls of the Department of State. Laurence Duggan would write: "All is well that ends well. The break has occurred and Chile is once more a 100% member of the American community of nations."[149] What Duggan did not seem to realize was that while the espionage and diplomatic relations issues had been considered as fused, the termination of the latter did not provide a solution for the former. And soon enough, succeeding events would force Duggan to make a decidedly less optimistic reappraisal of the situation.

D. The "Friends" of PYL

1. Those Who Escaped

By the time that the DGII began making arrests on October 23, 1942, it was already too late to catch most of the major figures in the PYL ring. Again, it was the crafty Ludwig von Bohlen who was responsible for seeing to it that the DGII dragnet would pull in only the small fry. After Bohlen showed Johannes Szeraws ("Esco") a copy of the June 30, 1942, memorandum, the former sailor prepared to shake the dust of Chile from his feet. In September 1942, the resourceful air attaché made arrangements with a group of smugglers who took Szeraws across the Andes Mountains into Argentina. Subsequently, "Esco" went on to become a leading figure in the SD network that operated there.[150]

Next to go was Heinrich Reiners ("Tom") who, despite pointed suggestions from Bohlen, remained in Santiago until public controversy developed over Sumner Welles's speech. On October 12, 1942, he left his wife and boarded the international train for Buenos Aires. Reiners remained in the Argentine capital until he was able to sail for Europe in 1943. He spent the rest of the war serving with German intelligence, apparently as an integrant of the Nest Bremen organization.[151]

Happy-go-lucky Hans Blume ("Flor") almost didn't make it. Despite his firing by Transradio Chilena in August, and the knowledge that he, too, was named in the June 30, 1942, document, Blume ignored Bohlen's urgings until October 22, 1942. Informed that the DGII was about to make arrests, Blume took refuge in the German embassy in Santiago. Early in December 1942, Bohlen paid Adolfo Graf, a ski instructor, $260 to take "Flor" out of Chile by way of an unguarded Andes pass. Subsequently, he, too, became an important cog in the SD apparatus in Argentina.[152]

Bohlen also attempted to locate Eugenio Ellinger Knoll, but that V-man was comfortably ensconced in a Santiago apartment with his mistress and out of contact with the other PYL principals. When Knoll learned on October 28 that the DGII had begun making arrests, he left his paramour and headed for Argentina. Approximately four days after his departure, his lady love concluded that he would not soon return and therefore would not continue to support her in the style to which she had become accustomed. The angry and distressed señorita told all she knew to the DGII, but Knoll had covered his tracks well. He and his sweetheart had shared many an intimate moment; still, the only name by which she knew him was "Juan Valdés."[153]

With the flight of these four and the arrest of numerous subagents, the PYL ring passed into history. But one man who shed no tears over the demise of the network was Major Bohlen. In a special report forwarded to Abwehr headquarters in July 1943, the air attaché intimated that the inherent weaknesses of the PYL group condemned it to collapse. In Bohlen's opinion, the most salient shortcomings were the following:

1. The codes used by PYL-REW were too easily broken by the Anglo-American cryptologists.

2. Before they left Chile, Reiners, Blume, and Szeraws failed to destroy all the ring's materials and equipment.
3. Too many people (he named Reiners, Szeraws, Blume, Hofbauer, Kettler, Valdés, and Barckhahn, "as well as a girl") knew about the transmitter on the Hofbauer estate.
4. Too many PYL members were lacking in discipline, and others like Barckhahn confessed, thereby implicating others.
5. Too many people failed to heed warnings to flee Chile.[154]

Utterly lacking in this report is any evidence of concern for those who faced possible conviction in Chilean courts for their work with the PYL organization. One reason may have been that as a trained lawyer, Bohlen was aware that no espionage statute existed that could be applied in this case. Therefore, unless the Ríos government sought to obtain a reinterpretation of existing law or chose to employ extralegal tactics, the persons arrested were unlikely to receive lengthy jail sentences. In fact, thanks to some behind-the-scenes maneuvers, it soon became evident that nobody would serve any penal time at all.

2. Cover-up

Beginning on the evening of October 23, 1942, the Valparaíso section of the DGII arrested twenty-four persons who were questioned by the interrogation unit headed by Sub-Commisario Milton Suau Canning (see Appendix C). The methods of interrogation and the tactics employed revealed elements of apathy, guile, and brutality. Some of those arrested, like Juan Aguilera, whose name was used on a drop box controlled by Schulz-Hausmann, were questioned briefly and then released.[155] The police concluded that Aguilera and other minor functionaries knew little of the network's activities, and so there was no reason to detain them. Among the others questioned but swiftly freed was Guillermo Zeller, and the leniency demonstrated in his case was hardly justified. Zeller, whose home had been used as both a broadcasting site and a hiding place for the PYL transmitter, admitted knowing Johannes Szeraws the first time he was questioned, but subsequently denied it. An SIS/Chile observer noted this contradiction and called it to DGII attention, but the police failed to interrogate Zeller again.[156]

The most glaring and inexplicable example of poor police work took place as part of the investigation of Otto Buchholz, a *Reichsdeutscher* businessman. On October 26, Buchholz brought a box containing several parts of the PYL transmitter to a Valparaíso police station. How had Buchholz obtained the radio equipment? He explained that it was delivered to his place of business sometime in August 1942 when he was out to lunch. Who received the box? Two employees whose names Buchholz no longer remembered. Could these employees be found? Buchholz had no idea where, and had somehow mislaid the employment records. This German further insisted that he had brought the box to the police only because he had read about espionage activity in the newspaper. Inexplicably, the DGII apparently accepted this tale and never bothered to interrogate Buchholz.[157]

Of the twenty-four people taken into custody, three appear to have been subjected to physical abuse. On October 24, Hans Hofbauer ("León") was arrested, and he was interrogated three times during a forty-eight-hour period. He admitted to an awareness of Szeraws's transmitting activities, but steadfastly insisted that the broadcasts from Quilpué were innocent messages sent to other ham operators. This answer was considered inadequate by his questioners, who brought increasing pressure to bear on the hapless Hofbauer. It was after the third session that he signed a statement confessing his knowledge that the broadcasts were "intended to serve the interests of the German government."[158]

Arnold Barckhahn's experiences would be similar, except that additional means would be used to loosen his tongue and sharpen his memory. Arrested during the evening of October 23, Barckhahn insisted that any imputation that he was involved with German intelligence was a lie. But after a second quizzing on the next day, he stated that he "was remembering things and connecting these with some of the questions that had been asked." At this point, one of his interrogators told Barckhahn that he had acted as a spy, but if he were indeed "a patriot," he would now tell all he knew. The combination of nationalist appeal, the long hours of questioning, and physical abuse apparently took its toll; "Junior" cracked and became the José Starziczny of the Abwehr in Chile. He elaborated on his role in the PYL organization, named other ring members, and listed payments made and missions undertaken.[159]

The most immediate effects of Barckhahn's confession were the discovery of the rest of the PYL transmitter in a box in the store owned by Juan Cuneo, and the November 3, 1942, arrest of Horst Kettler. The latter gave evasive answers to the questions put to him, but after a night in the hands of the Valparaíso DGII, he recalled taking an envelope left for him at the German consulate to Johannes Szeraws at Hofbauer's Quilpué estate. He admitted watching Szeraws operate the transmitter, but he denied any knowledge of what was in the envelope and could not explain what impelled him to deliver it.[160]

Even while the DGII was still interrogating suspects, on October 26, 1942, the judicial inquiry into the PYL ring's activities began in the Valparaíso Court of Appeals with Justice Rodolfo González presiding. Under Chilean judicial procedure, González had complete control of the proceedings. He could summon, interrogate, examine, and cross-examine witnesses, and call in experts to give additional testimony. He kept his own record of the proceedings which was allegedly secret, and his written opinion would establish whether or not a crime had been committed, and who ought to be indicted.[161]

After eight days of hearings and examinations of the suspects, González declared that sufficient evidence existed to justify the holding of Horst Kettler and Hans Hofbauer.[162] In the six weeks that followed, he sanctioned the house arrest of Isabel Pederit de Reiners, denied diplomatic to Horst Kettler, and declared Reiners, Blume, and Szeraws fugitives from justice.[163] Proceedings were temporarily slowed by charges of brutality, lodged by Hans Hofbauer's lawyer, Jorge Guarello. This attorney argued that his client's October 25 statement had been obtained by torture, an allegation denied by Sub-Commisario Milton Suau Canning. González concluded that, for the moment, the statement was admissible evidence and that he would rule on the brutality issue at a later date. Records fail to indicate that he ever did.[164]

In December 1942, Horst Kettler and Hans Hofbauer were released on bail and, with six others, were ordered confined to small towns away from Valparaíso until further notice.[165] The rest of the suspects were released with the understanding that they would remain in Valparaíso and its vicinity. All that remained, seemingly, was for González to close the investigations and issue his opinion.

Tied to the question of who was guilty was an interrelated and equally thorny problem: In terms of Chilean law, of what crimes were these German agents and collaborators guilty? Especially since Chile was not at war and the intelligence activities under scrutiny were not necessarily directed against it, this was by no means a mere legal quibble. A secret DGII memorandum dated November 3, 1942, concluded that if any of the suspects were indicted, they could only be tried for violating Article 147 of the May 1941 Regulation of Broadcasting Decree. Issued by the minister of the interior, this law provided that "he who installs a clandestine radio station [whether it be] fixed, portable, or movable, in addition to a fine and confiscation of the apparatus on the part of the government, will suffer the penalty of minor confinement to its maximum degree."[166] Under Chilean law, this meant that convicted persons would be imprisoned for no more that three years.[167] This last contingency was of some concern to the State Department, whose legal experts had conducted their own study of the legal mechanics and concluded that the 1937 Law of Internal Security could also be used to prosecute those whom Justice González might indict in his opinion. Since violation of this statute was a major crime, those found guilty were certain to be jailed for at least five years—or, presumably, until the war was over, which was the goal sought by the United States.[168]

Alas, these speculations failed to take into consideration the possibility that hemispheric security might be very low on the agendas of both Justice González and President Ríos. Although the former ceased hearing testimony in the case in January 1943, nine months later, much to the disgust of U.S. officialdom, no decision had yet been rendered. In Brazil, for example, the trial of the Abwehr V-men had been executed with dispatch and with satisfactory (i.e., from a U.S. perspective) results. In Chile, it began to look as if the proceedings might never end, and that no indictments would ever be handed down.

One reason for González's snail-like pace of deliberation may have been that he was probably coordinating his actions with machinations of the Ríos government. Note that in November 1942, González had rejected the German embassy's contention that Horst Kettler possessed diplomatic immunity. After he was released on bail in December 1942, Kettler was confined to the town of Buín, but not before the justice again rebutted the German claim that Kettler enjoyed diplomatic protection.[169] But unexpectedly, on September 13, 1943, Minister of the Interior Raúl Morales issued a secret order freeing Kettler from relegation in Buín and placing him under house arrest in Santiago.[170] Then, without any explanation, on September 28, 1943, Kettler was suddenly given diplomatic status and repatriated as part of the departing German embassy staff two days later. The SIS/Chile report emphasized the conclusion that this otherwise inexplicable bit of juggling had been facilitated by the payment of large sums of money to Chilean officials.[171]

Raúl Morales's secret order of September 13, 1943, also sanctioned the return to Valparaíso of Hans Hofbauer, who, like Kettler, had been relegated to the town of Buín. Whether Hofbauer would also have been granted diplomatic status is not clear, but as the latter owned considerable property in Chile and had not lived in Germany for two decades, he may not have desired repatriation. In any case, the leniency displayed by the Ríos government may well have led Hofbauer to appraise his legal predicament from a highly optimistic perspective.[172]

The significance of the Hofbauer-Kettler incident is that it reveals a good deal about the intentions of the Ríos government in the PYL case. In December 1943, for example, SIS/Chile learned from a friendly source that DGII authorities had actually obtained signed confessions from both Horst Kettler and Hans Hofbauer.[173] Therefore, unless Justice González intended to throw out these declarations, Kettler and Hofbauer would have had to be indicted. Thus, by letting Kettler go, the Chilean government not only conspired in the escape of a suspect who had already confessed, but it assisted the Third Reich in reclaiming the services of a talented operative. These events made it evident that while diplomatic relations with the Axis were broken, and the PYL organization was smashed, convicting the V-men was going to be a very iffy proposition.

Even before the controversial departure of Horst Kettler for Germany, a number of U.S. diplomatic officials had become fully convinced that the Ríos regime was determined to avoid convicting anyone involved in the PYL case. Nevertheless, it was not until September 1943, when Ambassador Claude Bowers was conveniently away from Santiago, that a stringent effort was made to force the Chileans to show their hand. First, Acting Ambassador Donald Heath cabled Washington on September 13 (the same day of the secret orders on Kettler and Hofbauer) and proposed a two-pronged attack. Chilean foreign minister Joaquín Fernández had departed Chile a few days previously and was scheduled to arrive in the United States to discuss an economic aid package. Heath intended to call upon the acting foreign minister in Santiago and express the opinion that the completion of the PYL trial "would appear ... dramatically apropos in connection with Fernández's arrival in the United States." Since the major Chilean intent was to obtain financial and technical assistance in the construction of a steel mill, Heath wanted Cordell Hull to impress upon Fernández that cooperation in the PYL case was essential if Chile expected U.S. economic assistance.[174]

In meetings on September 18 and 20, 1943, Hull listened to the Chilean requests but remained noncommittal, insisting that "it was better to say too little rather than too much."[175] But there is no question that at least one of those accompanying Fernández in the negotiation sessions got the message. In a confidential dispatch dated October 6, 1943, Rodolfo Michels, who acted as a translater for Fernández, told his superiors that the assistance they sought would probably not be forthcoming. The ambassador acknowledged the predominance of internal political issues, but concluded that "we cannot hope to achieve the assistance we need unless the problem of the German agents is soon resolved. . . ."[176]

Between October 1943 and April 1944, U.S. officials expressed increasing frustration over the espionage inquiry still ostensibly going on in Valparaíso. An investigative report by Comdr. John Rockwell, the naval attaché in Santiago, condemned the Ríos administration's handling of the case.[177] Then, on January 17, 1944, Claude Bowers again conferred with Joaquín Fernández. He noted the Brazilian handling of their spy trials and virtually pleaded with the foreign minister to name an approximate date when the PYL judgment would be rendered. Unfortunately, Fernández was either unwilling or unable to give any indication of his government's intentions.[178]

Since the patient approach had produced no discernable results, the CPD was once again called in to exert moral pressure. On March 6, 1944, the CPD published a document which concluded that "the effective control of spies was the most pressing measure" facing the Chilean government. The report then went on to cite the PYL case as proof that the Ríos regime was failing to perform its hemispheric security obligations.[179] Commenting on the CPD's conclusions, State Department advisor Laurence Duggan would weigh in with his share of invective,[180] but it was J. Edgar Hoover who delivered the sharpest thrust of all. In an April 1944 memorandum addressed to Adolf Berle, the FBI chief flayed Ríos and his colleagues, calling them a band of morally bankrupt politicos who had never intended a vigorous prosecution of the PYL case. Hoover's vitriolic communication ended with this cryptic observation: "It might be thought that democracy [Chile] would have possessed a better perception of its interests."[181]

The tenor of these memorandums and reports suggests that sometime in 1944, another confrontation similar to that which followed the Sumner Welles speech of October 8, 1942, could have transpired. But another development militated that the State Department, Hoover, et al. step lightly. During Febuary 1944, the existence of another Abwehr ring in Chile was revealed to the public, and a new spy investigation was soon under way. Since the Ríos government seemed determined to prosecute the PQZ group, as the new ring became known, it behooved the United States not to cause trouble by complaining about inaction in the PYL case.[182] Furthermore, the crafty Chileans made it easier for the North Americans to swallow the bitter with the sweet. On April 12, 1944, they issued new indictments against Heinrich Reiners, Hans Blume, and Johannes Szeraws, and they included the prosecution of these spies as part of the new investigation. There was no evidence whatsoever that these three were involved in PQZ operations, but by taking this action, the Chileans were implying that no matter what Justice González's final decision was, the regime remained determined to prosecute the principal PYL operatives.[183]

With these actions taken, the PYL melodrama could finally be allowed to end. On December 6, 1944, over two years after proceedings were initiated, Rodolfo González issued his opinion. In it he declared that the May 1941 law banning clandestine radio broadcasts had been violated, but only those involved in the actual installation and operation of the PYL transmitter were guilty of any crime. This meant that Szeraws, Blume, and Reiners were guilty, but since they could not be found, they could not be imprisoned. Of those questioned and arrested during the PYL investigation, only Horst Kettler and Hans Hofbauer were guilty of any culpable crime. On January 9, 1945, an appeals panel reviewed González's conclusions and approved them.[184]

These actions could have terminated the judicial process, but Hans Hofbauer's lawyers immediately asked González to reconsider his decision. In addition to arguing that their client had committed no crime against Chile, they noted that Hofbauer was the only person among those found guilty who would probably serve time. González took the request under advisement, and on August 17, 1945, three days after Japan capitulated, he ruled in the defendant's favor.[185] In Washington, only J. Edgar Hoover manifested more than token interest in this final turn of events. He ordered legal attaché John Hubbard to contact González and discover the rationale for this decision. In his report, the SIS/Chile chief explained that while the justice believed that the May 1941 radio law allowed the government to seize the equipment of those who violated its provisions, he considered the law unconstitutional insofar as it gave the state the right to level penal punishments against violators. Hubbard considered this explanation disingenuous hair-splitting, but the war was over.[186] The PYL case ended with five Germans found guilty, one German appealing the sentence, and nobody imprisoned.

Ultimately, the judicial deception commonly known as the PYL case was the responsibility of Juan Ríos. The motives of the Chilean president in conducting his slow charade were multiple, but the only book which has thus far attempted a full analysis of his presidency gives emphasis to his deep and prolonged resentment of U.S. pressure.[187] Eventually Ríos might have independently taken some action against the PYL principals, and he would undoubtedly have broken relations with the Axis powers sometime before World War II was over. The trouble was that Sumner Welles's October 1942 speech and the resulting political crisis forced Ríos to take actions he was at best loath to take, long before he wanted to take them.[188] It is our conclusion that since he was unable to avenge himself directly against the irrepressible Yankees, Ríos utilized the PYL case as a means of quietly demonstrating that pressure exerted upon him would yield counterproductive results.

Nevertheless, Juan Ríos recognized that his country desperately needed U.S. credits and technical aid. Moreover, if Washington decided that he wasn't cooperating in the fight against German intelligence, it was unlikely to provide the economic and technological assistance sought. Fortunately, the Germans were prepared to give Ríos another opportunity to demonstrate to the United States just how anti-Axis his regime could be.

V. The Emergence of PQZ

A. "Victor," "Dunkel," "Ina," and "Pedro"

When the Mexican police closed down GBO in June 1941, the Abwehr network in that country was permanently put out of the clandestine radio business. In Brazil, when DOPS smashed the FMKs in and around Rio de Janeiro, Heinz Lorenz and the CEL group tried to keep operating, but in mid-May 1942, the Brazilian connection with Germany was utterly destroyed. The PYL-REW circuit was terminated in June 1942. Then, suddenly on May 5, 1943, RID radio direction finders in the United States began picking up the signals of a clandestine radio station in Chile using the call letters PQZ.

This was a disturbing development, particularly since the PYL organization had been broken up, and there had been no detected clandestine radio activity in Chile for almost a year. The greater shock would come when the intercepted signals were delivered to FBI Technical Laboratory cryptologists; they found that the Abwehr had come up with a code they could not easily break.[189] The lack of signal security had been a decisive factor in the collapse of the GBO, PYL, and the Brazilian FMKs. The emergence of PQZ meant that the FBI and, in particular, SIS/Chile were facing a tough, new opponent against whom the decoding tactics so useful in the past would no longer be effective.

The spymaster responsible for the Abwehr's rejuvenation in Chile was Maj. Ludwig von Bohlen ("Bach"), the same man who somehow obtained a copy of the June 30, 1942, memorandum forty-eight hours after Barros Jarpa had received it. What the U.S. investigators did not learn until the war was over was that Bohlen knew that the cable traffic between Chile and Germany was being intercepted and that his personal cipher had been decrypted.[190] Thus, the Luftwaffe major decided that if the new espionage group he was building (i.e., PQZ) was ever broken up by U.S. counterspies, it would not be because the FBI analysts were reading his messages. Indeed, PQZ operatives would be occupants of Chilean jails for months before the FBI laboratory was able to decipher the first transmissions sent over the PQZ-URK (Chile–Ast Hamburg) circuit.[191]

The success of Ludwig von Bohlen as a spymaster was no accident, for even though the attaché post was attained primarily through political jockeying, Bohlen was, in many respects, the man made for the job. Born of German parents in Valparaíso in 1896, he spent his first fourteen years of life in Chile and spoke flawless Spanish. A World War I veteran, he subsequently earned a law degree, and in 1928 was sent to Chile by the German Ministry of Justice to study judicial theory. He became personal secretary to Carlos Ibáñez, then dictator (1927–31) and later perennial presidential candidate (1938, 1942, and 1951). Assigned to a specially created legal commission in 1929, Bohlen helped to write sections of a new Chilean penal code. He occasionally lectured at the National Law School, and taught students who later became judges, diplomats and administrators.

Bohlen returned to Germany in 1931. After he reentered army service in 1937, he was occasionally assigned to accompany junketing Chilean military men. In this capacity, Bohlen became intimate friends with a number of officers, foremost of whom was Manuel Tovarías, later commander-in-chief of the Chilean air force. Thus, Bohlen's success with PQZ would be the result not only of a safe code, but his background and contacts, factors which made him a redoubtable foe.[192]

After his return to Chile in July 1941, Bohlen rapidly concluded that he would have to create his own spy ring. His first recruit was a *Reichsdeutscher* businessman and acquaintance, Albrecht Heise (code name: Victor). The latter obtained a post office box and took out subscriptions to several U.S. journals featuring military aviation, which he turned over to Bohlen. "Victor" would continue acting as front man for the air attaché until the latter departed in September 1943.[193]

Next to join the fledgling organization was a husband and wife team, Wilhelm and Anne Hellemann. When Bohlen met the pair in November 1941, they were not happily married. A bon vivant with a small bankroll, Wilhelm viewed Anne as a rock of stability and a meal ticket. What the woman saw in him is not immediately evident, but for some time they had been spending increasingly disenchanted evenings together. Bohlen shrewdly sized up the couple and, after entertaining them royally, enlisted them as agents. Mrs. Hellemann (code name: Ina) was fluent in English and German, and it became her task to take the magazines obtained by Albrecht Heise, clip out the information Bohlen wanted, and translate it into German for dispatch to the Reich. She did an outstanding job, and soon became Bohlen's girl Friday, making arrangements for the purchase of a safe house for emergency radio operations, contacting other ring members, and passing on the attaché's orders.[194]

Wilhelm Hellemann's work was of a different nature, but initially of major significance. He (code name: Dunkel) was trained to use secret ink, taught a simple code, and, in April 1942, sent to northern Chile to recruit informants to provide shipping data. Wilhelm enlisted five Chileans and two *Reichsdeutschen* in the ports of Tocopilla, Coquimbo, and Iquique. Beginning in May 1942, these observers received twenty dollars a month for sending their reports to "Dunkel" at post office box 3290 in Santiago. The sketchy quality of some of these reports drew sharp criticism from Bohlen, who intended to cable shipping information to Germany. The attaché's annoyance was increased by Hellemann's nagging requests for funds, but Bohlen eschewed precipitous action lest it result in heightened domestic friction for Mrs. Hellemann.[195]

Among the skills Wilhelm Hellemann claimed he was developing (one he believed justified his requests for more funds) was that of radio operator, but Bohlen was uninterested because he had already found his man. This was Guillermo Kunsemüller, born of German parents on December 23, 1906, at Antofagasta, Chile. He returned with his parents to Hamburg, Germany, in 1928, and seven years later, volunteered for pilot officer training in the Luftwaffe. The application was rejected since Kunsemüller was a dual citizen and had not renounced his Chilean citizenship. He enlisted in the Luftwaffe in 1936 as an aviation mechanic, but two years of service convinced him that a mechanic's career was not a back door into pilot training, and it certainly was not the career he wanted. By declaring himself a Chilean citizen, Kunsemüller was able to obtain a release from the Luftwaffe, and complete his education as an aircraft engineer. Still, his rejection of German citizenship made him a kind of pariah, unable to work in the occupation for which he had been trained. Married in March 1941, Kunsemüller was reduced to doing odd jobs and working in his father's drug store.[196]

Unhappy with his lot, Kunsemüller became convinced that the solution to his problems lay in escaping from the Reich. According to his subsequent testimony, in July 1941, he answered a Hamburg newspaper advertisement placed by an import-export firm soliciting the services of young men who were interested in working in foreign commercial activity. It was in this manner that he met a man called "Dr. Scholz," who was a recruiter for what Kunsemüller would later refer to as "the Institution" (i.e., the Abwehr). Allegedly, "Dr. Scholz" told him that the only way he could expect to leave Germany with his German wife was as a V-man. Claiming that he had no other alternative, Kunsemüller decided to become a spy.[197] Under the auspices of the I-L (air force) and I-i (communications) sections of Ast Hamburg, he began training in radio telegraphy, coding, and radio construction. Completing these studies in October 1941, Kunsemüller was placed under operational control of Ast Hamburg section I-T/LW (technical development), commanded by a "Dr. Nautsch," who was, in reality, Maj. Hans Naumann. He was given the code names "Pedro," "Roberto," and "Alfredo," but it was by the first that he would become infamous. He and his wife boarded a boat in Lisbon on November 5, 1941, and reached Santiago five weeks later.[198]

Immediately following his arrival in the Chilean capital, Kunsemüller contacted Heinrich Reiners, who gave him one hundred dollars for immediate expenses and turned him over to Ludwig von Bohlen. PYL had no real use for "Pedro," but for the air attaché, the arrival of an *Ast*-trained radioman was a godsend. Major Kleyenstueber, Bohlen's controller, had indicated that a second radio station should be established, and the network Bohlen was creating would certainly need a trained operative; "Pedro's" arrival solved both problems at once. Moreover, Schulz-Hausmann had left the air attaché with a ship's transmitter that, if modified and repaired, could be pressed into service. Szeraws and Kunsemüller had some problems with the set, but they finally succeeded in mounting it and getting it to function in a home rented by the latter in the Santiago suburb of La Cisterna. On March 10, 1942, a PYL message to REW stated that "Pedro" would be ready to commence broadcasting within twenty-four hours. The following day, Kunsemüller made contact with Ast Hamburg, and the NOI-GES circuit came into existence.[199]

Undoubtedly, "Dr. Nautsch" back at Ast Hamburg was gratified with the commencement of broadcasts by NOI, but in sending Kunsemüller to Chile, he had other plans as well. By means of secret decrees and other covert acts, since October 1940 the Chilean government had been purchasing small amounts of military aviation equipment in the United States.[200] Furthermore, in April 1942, the U.S. and Chile consolidated plans for training Chilean pilots in the United States.[201] How much the Germans knew of these negotiations and accords is not known, but the Abwehr rightly assumed that Kunsemüller's technical training would make him a prized recruit for the Chilean air force. Therefore, "Pedro" was ordered to enlist as an officer in that service arm and learn all he could about the characteristics of U.S. military planes, training methods, and radio equipment techniques. He was also to enlist the aid of sympathetic Chilean air force personnel, especially those who might be sent to the United States for training, for these men could obtain information which Kunsemüller might not otherwise be privy to.[202]

This was a well-conceived scheme, one which indicated that the Abwehr, after floundering around in Mexico and Brazil, was learning from its mistakes. But there would be unexpected snags which would jeopardize aspects of the plan's operation. In December 1941, Kunsemüller applied for entry into the Chilean air force as a lieutenant. Apparently there were suspicions about both his suitability and his motives, for when he was accepted for service in the technical branch on March 27, 1942, he was only given the rank of corporal. The failure to obtain the commissioned officer's rank would make the cultivation of officer contacts more difficult, but Chilean authorities assured Kunsemüller that upon completion of his training, he would be promoted to the rank of ensign, roughly equivalent to a U.S. Army Air Force warrant officer, first class. Moreover, since his first assignment was to the El Bosque Air Station outside of Santiago, "Pedro" had no problems conducting clandestine broadcasts from his home.[203]

Between March 11, 1942, and July 16, 1942, thirty-two messages were exchanged over the NOI-GES circuit.[204] Kunsemüller experienced great difficulty in contacting Ast Hamburg with his seventy-watt merchant ship transmitter, and he complained to Ast Hamburg that, as yet, he was receiving little useful information.[205] In mid-July, Major Bohlen solved these problems by having Johannes Szeraws reclaim the set. Bohlen explained that the June 30, 1942, memorandum proved that the NOI-GES messages were being intercepted and decoded. Since the transmitter's discovery or "Pedro's" capture "would certainly have accelerated Chile's break with Germany," Bohlen wanted NOI off the airwaves.[206] Kunsemüller was, nevertheless, to remain in the Chilean air force and continue gaining the confidence of his superiors and extending his network of contacts.

In October 1942, the PYL organization was broken up, but neither the DGII nor SIS/Chile made any moves against "Victor," "Ina," "Dunkel," or "Pedro." True, the SIS knew that "Pedro" operated NOI but it did not know his real identity. Bohlen had been circumspect in using the names of his network members in the messages sent over PYL radio, NOI radio, or by coded cable.[207] Still, since he had been identified as "Bach" in the oft-mentioned June 30, 1942, memorandum, Bohlen knew he was under surveillance and would be repatriated whenever German embassy personnel were kicked out of the country. What this meant was that hurriedly, but unobtrusively, he must complete the construction of the network he was building. Obviously this could not be done without the aid of an unsuspected assistant. The man tapped for the job was "Salvador."

B. *"Salvador" and His Lieutenants*

On January 22, 1943, Major Bohlen held a private interview with Bernardo Francisco Timmerman (code name: Salvador) and told him that he had been selected as future chief of the Abwehr in Chile. With German-Chilean relations severed, Bohlen planned to disengage himself gradually from espionage activities and assist "Salvador" in working into the leadership role. The air attaché might leave, but in Timmerman's capable hands, intelligence activities would continue without a hitch.[208]

In selecting Bernardo Timmerman, a dual citizen, as network chief, Bohlen was partially responding to orders he had received earlier in the month from Abwehr headquarters.[209] Canaris and his staff had finally recognized the fact that future intelligence operations in Chile would have to be conducted by Chilean citizens, for they were unlikely to be confined by decree to some isolated town or expelled simply by government fiat. There remains, however, the question of why Timmerman specifically got the nod. Possibly the attaché was strongly influenced by the fact that Timmerman's first cousin was Elizabeth Timmerman von Leiswitz, wife of the first secretary of the German embassy.[210] Furthermore, Hildegaard von Plate Timmerman, another of Bernardo's cousins, was Bohlen's secretary and mistress, and it was this woman who brought the two men together.[211] Their initial meeting took place in March 1942, and since both of them were deeply interested in photography, this commonality of interests served to deepen the relationship. Timmerman was an expert in the field, so that the attaché promptly recruited him to make reproductions of the photos found in the journals supplied by Albrecht Heise for shipment by diplomatic pouch to Germany.[212] A combination of familial connections, personal friendship, and a record of excellent, gratuitous service seems to have influenced Bohlen to choose Timmerman as his successor. "Salvador" would prove to be a hard-working, if not a particularly brilliant, spymaster.

Born on August 18, 1912, in Concepción, Chile, of a *Volksdeutscher* father and a *Reichsdeutscher* mother, Bernardo and his family did the same as the Kunsemüllers: after World War I, they left Chile and settled in Germany. Bernardo received special training in photography in Munich and Dresden from 1931 to 1934, and after two years' service in an infantry regiment, he returned to Chile. Because of his photographic expertise, he obtained a position with the Wilhelm Reichmann firm, distributors of Zeiss optical and photographic equipment. In 1938 he married Gertrude Bethke Basle, who, like Bernardo, had one German parent.[213]

After "Salvador" started working for Bohlen as a photographic specialist in 1942, he became increasingly involved in other intelligence activities as well. At Bohlen's suggestion, Julius Mahn, another embassy official, taught Timmerman Bohlen's cipher and the use of secret ink. After the aforementioned January 1943 conference took place, "Salvador" spent a great deal of time learning a new cipher system (see Appendix A) which had been delivered to Bohlen shortly before Chilean-German diplomatic relations were broken.[214] The attaché also made arrangements for Timmerman to meet Guillermo Kunsemüller, whom he hadn't known previously, Albrecht Heise, and the Hellemanns.[215] Taking charge of this basic nucleus, it became "Salvador's" task to enlarge the organization and obtain a steady stream of data on ship movements, mineral shipments, and U.S. military aviation.

The first step taken by Timmerman was the recruitment of an unemployed engineer named Augusto Kroll (code name: Pita). Born near Oberhausen, Germany, on March 27, 1899, Kroll was a World War I veteran who obtained his engineering degree and left Germany during the Great Depression. Arriving in Chile in 1933, Kroll applied for naturalization in 1938 and soon after received a Chilean passport. He met Bernardo Timmerman that same year, and the two became fast friends. Still, it was not until April 1943 that Kroll agreed to become a member of PQZ, doing so because, as a former soldier, he felt an obligation to aid the fatherland. (See Chart IX for a depiction of the PQZ network.) That Chile had broken relations with Germany made no difference; as he later told his interrogators, his adopted nation and the land of his birth were not at war.[216]

Kroll's role within PQZ would rapidly come to resemble that which Herbert von Heyer performed for Albrecht Gustav Engels. As "Salvador's" major domo, he was in charge of many PQZ ring activities, but the concept of organization was rather different from that used in Brazil. Timmerman subscribed to the theory that group security could be per-

CHART IX

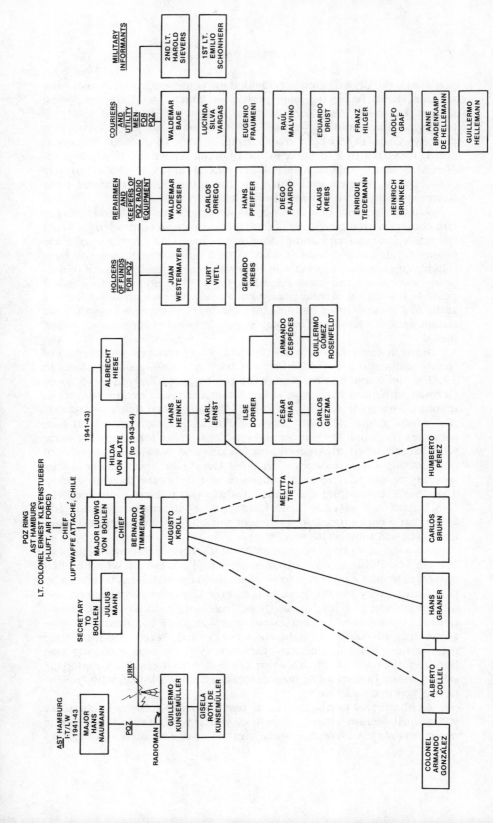

petuated if the organization was divided into independent, self-sustaining sections, Kroll being the only person in contact with the individual section leaders.[217] One such section, as it were, consisted solely of Guillermo Kunsemüller, whom Kroll took pains to avoid contacting directly. Once PQZ began transmitting in May 1943, Kroll delivered coded messages to a lockbox in the building where the newspaper, *El Mercurio*, had its offices. Kunsemüller picked up his $150 a month pay plus expense money, and delivered the messages he received from Germany to the same box for Kroll's pickup.[218]

Another scheme of indirect communication was employed to maintain contact with the members of the second section controlled by Kroll. His immediate assistant and general utility man was a Jew named Hans Graner (code name: Manolo), who worked only for expenses, and later told his captors that national socialism was an acceptable political philosophy "except for the ideas regarding Jews."[219] In an effort to confuse possible shadowers, Graner occasionally made the pick up and deliveries at the *El Mercurio* office building box, but his primary task was to act as a cutout between Kroll and a V-man named Humberto Pérez (code name: José).

Born in Asunción, Paraguay, in 1915, Pérez was a newspaperman of strong nationalist views who found himself stranded in Buenos Aires in 1942, without much in the way of future prospects. Early in 1943, some German nationalist friends, who knew that Pérez had been a radio telegraphist during the Chaco War (1932–35), suggested that a mysterious "Dr. Alves" might need his services. The alleged doctor was, in fact, Johannes Siegfried Becker, Sicherheitsdienst chief for South America, who had returned to Argentina in January and was in the process of constructing a new network there. "Dr. Alves" paid Pérez ninety dollars monthly to act as a reserve radioman from February through August 1943. Sometime during this period, Ludwig von Bohlen contacted Brig. Gen. Friedrich Wolf (code name: Palta), military attaché in Argentina, and asked that a back-up radioman be sent to Chile. Wolf contacted Becker, and Pérez was soon on his way.[220]

Arriving in Santiago on August 23, 1943, Pérez presented himself to Ludwig von Bohlen, who passed him on to Timmerman, who bundled him off to Kroll. Contact was to be maintained through Hans Graner, who paid Pérez every month, gave him a small transmitter, a receiver, and funds for finding an apartment. "José" was not to do any broadcasting until Kunsemüller was either captured or forced off the airwaves. Quite aware that his services might soon be needed, Pérez lost little time making new demands, and by October 1943 he was receiving two hundred dollars a month. This was more than Kunsemüller's espionage salary, but no one seems to have complained since a V-man with "José's" talents was irreplaceable.[221]

Neither Pérez nor Graner knew that Augusto Kroll was in charge of still a third section, the chief agent of which was Alberto Collel (code name: Alberto). A Chilean national, this man was recruited in June 1943 even though he was simultaneously working as an agent for Col. Armando González, chief of Chilean military intelligence. Kroll was aware of Collel's other controller, but nevertheless, considered him a useful operative. Initially, he assigned Carlos Otto Bruhn as liaison between himself and Collel, but Bruhn backed out in September 1943; therafter, Kroll made his contacts with Collel personally.[222]

No PQZ leader controlled as many sections as Augusto Kroll, but there existed two others, one of which was directed by "Salvador" himself. In March 1943, Wilhelm Hellemann was decreed a potentially dangerous German alien and ordered relegated to the town of San Fernando in southern Chile. The network of seven observers he had created in Iquique, Coquimbo, and Tocopilla could not be allowed to become moribund. Instead, Hellemann gave the key to post office box 3290 to Bohlen, who turned the key and the responsibility for this unit over to Timmerman. Thereafter, as the reports arrived, "Salvador" sent out the payments and requests for specific information.[223]

Valparaíso was Chile's largest and most important harbor, and, as always, the German navy wanted information concerning the cargoes, arrivals, and departures of Anglo-American ships. Timmerman solved the problem in October 1943 by selecting an electrical engineer named Hans Joachim Heinke as leader of the Valparaíso section. Born in Magdeburg, Germany, on August 31, 1912, Heinke was an engineering whiz kid. Two years after graduating from Cologne University in 1937, he was appointed chief technical adviser and salesman for the A.E.G. subsidiary in Chile. The recruitment of this individual had its grimly ironic aspects. In July 1941, Hans Heinke had presented himself at the German embassy and asked to be given a task serving the fatherland which would be commensurate with his talents. Ludwig von Bohlen dismissed the request at the time, but the deteriorating military situation made the reject of 1941 a prize recruit of 1943. The air attaché recommended Heinke to Timmerman, and when the engineer gave an affirmative response, his services were snapped up.[224]

It would not, however, be Heinke's task to enlist and manage informants in Valparaíso itself. This was the responsibility of Ilse Blanca Dorrer (code name: Traum), a *Volksdeutsche* woman who spent a year in Germany in 1941–42, and subsequently became secretary to Friedrich Kaven, a member of the German consular staff in Valparaíso. In September 1943, Kaven provided Señorita Dorrer with a list of Chileans in that city friendly to German interests and obtained her assent to work for German intelligence. In October 1943 for the first and only time, Timmerman took Heinke to Valparaíso and introduced him to "Traum." The arrangement worked out was that she would obtain the shipping information and hold it for Heinke. Shortly thereafter, Heinke recruited as his cutout to Ilse Dorrer, another *Volksdeutscher*, named Karl Ernst (code name: Colonel). Two to three times a week, the woman took the material gathered by her informants and mailed it to a post office box in Valparaíso rented to Ernst. "Colonel" then traveled to Santiago and gave the materials to Heinke. Any instructions or funds for Señorita Dorrer were delivered by Ernst upon his return to Valparaíso. In addition to $100 a month for Ernst, Timmerman provided $200 to $250 monthly for the payment of Ilse Dorrer and her informants. Heinke, like "Salvador," was expected to work only for expenses.[225]

In addition to these five sections, Timmerman developed a number of independent informants and aides who were directly responsible to him. Ricardo Krebs, Juan Baldomero Westmayer, and Kurt Vietl were men who functioned as keepers of funds and equipment.[226] Did the PQZ chief want facts and figures concerning Chilean copper and iron ore shipments to the United States? Carlos Frías, an employee in the office of the Director General of Statistics, provided these.[227] Lucinda Silva Vargas, a professor of romance languages at the University of Concepción, made trips to Peru and Bolivia and furnished written reports on U.S. bases, particularly in Peru.[228] Would transmitters have to be moved or hidden? Waldemar Koeser and Johannes Möller were glad to lend their services.[229] Useful, too, was cousin Hilda von Plate Timmerman who, following the closure of the German embassy, continued to represent Reich interests, first at the Spanish embassy and then at the Swiss legation. In addition to passing on orders received by diplomatic pouch, she kept her ears open and was able to alert some agents in time so that their arrests could subsequently be avoided.[230]

Part of Ludwig von Bohlen's success in 1941–43 lay in the fact that because of his contacts in high places, he could find out what SIS/Chile and the DGII were doing and take effective countermeasures. Bernardo Timmerman sought protection of a similar nature and in the process enlisted some interesting informants. Beginning in October 1943, Armando Cespédes, subcommisario with the DGII branch in Valparaíso, went on the payroll at approximately one hundred dollars a month. A similar fee was paid to another security officer, who U.S. sources allege was Guillermo Gómez Rosenfeldt, DGII prefect of police in Valparaíso.[231]

Of this mélange of ring members and part-time informants, easily the most unusual was Alberto Collel. As previously mentioned, this otherwise nondescript character was working simultaneously for both Timmerman and the chief of Chilean military intellegence, Col. Armando González. What made Collel the nonpareil among PQZ operatives was that he somehow managed to wangle his way onto the staff of secret informants maintained by the U.S. military attaché, Col. Wendell Johnson. Whether the latter ever received any useful information from Collel, only the colonel can say.[232] On the other hand, this triple agent did supply Timmerman with several U.S. government pamphlets, information concerning other personnel working for the military attaché, and flowery gossip concerning the supposedly sordid lives being lived by U.S. diplomatic and military personnel in Santiago.[233] Probably Collel never learned anything that was critical to U.S. diplomatic or counterintelligence operations, but his minor penetration of U.S. security was important because it was one of the few achieved by Abwehr forces in Latin America.

Some idea of the size of the PQZ network and the varied scope of the data it collected and collated can be inferred from the fact that it consisted of perhaps a dozen key members, and fifty or more collaborators, contacts, and paid informants. It had eyes and ears in the DGII, in the armed forces, in every major Chilean port, and was probably the largest Abwehr network in the Americas.[234] Its significance in the greater scheme of things can be partially assessed from the fact that in 1943, although Bohlen and Timmerman spent $26,452 on espionage expenses,[235] PQZ was never strapped for cash. Before his September 1943 repatriation, Bohlen left Timmerman with $200,000 in Chilean, U.S., and Argentinian currency, and told him that if needed more, Brig. Gen. Friedrich Wolf in Buenos Aires would meet additional requests.[236] This "spybank" was almost double the amount made available to the leading spymaster in Brazil, Albrecht Gustav Engels, and is still another indication of the importance of the PQZ to the Abwehr.

By the end of 1943, PQZ and Karl Rüge's group in Mexico were the last Abwehr networks still functioning in the Americas. In that sense, PQZ's continued operation became increasingly important, not simply because of what it achieved, but because its continued existence implied that Germany still had a chance to win a war which, by the end of 1943, it was clearly losing.

C. The PQZ Success Story

Since 1940, the Abwehr had been pushing its Latin Ameican units to develop informants in the United States who could obtain secret military information and somehow transmit it back to Germany.[237] In this regard, Georg Nicolaus's Mexican group had been a miserable failure, and while the Brazilian groups of Joséf Starziczny, Friedrich Kempter, and Albrecht Engels developed several informants, these had become known and promptly arrested.[238] In contrast, the PQZ group would infiltrate an informant inside military installations in the United States, have that agent obtain secret data and return safely to Chile.

The prized informant for PQZ was Emilio Schonherr, a Chilean air force lieutenant, who befriended Guillermo Kunsemüller while the two men were serving at the El Bosque Air Base outside Santiago. As part of a special pilot training program, Schonherr was ordered to commence flight training in the United States in July 1942. The lieutenant told Kunsemüller of his orders, and the latter agreed to pay Schonherr for information on U.S. military planes, their armament, flying characteristics, and performance. Schonherr received advanced flight instruction at Corpus Christi Naval Air Station and at the U.S. Army Air Force centers at Foster and Kelly Fields, all in Texas. Never hesitant in expressing his admiration for German military figures like Field Marshals Feodor von Bock and Erwin Rommel, Schonherr was otherwise discreet, for his U.S. service record related that he had "no unusual interest in confidential matters."[239] Army Air Force security men slipped up in this case, for although Schonherr had no espionage training, he knew how to hide his activities and get what the Germans wanted. He pumped other Chileans and friendly U.S. pilots for information about the planes they flew, and surreptitiously borrowed aircraft familiarization and repair manuals dealing with specific U.S. aircraft. The result was the compilation, by August 1943, of a bulky report on the training given U.S. fighter and bomber pilots, fighter pilot tactics as taught in training schools, and on the speed, range, and armament of assorted U.S. combat aircraft.

Apparently Schonherr feared that he might be caught with this data, and so he gave his report to an unknown Chilean officer who personally delivered the document to Kunsemüller. That the PQZ leadership was satisfied with what they received is manifested by the fact that on August 26, 1943, Augusto Kroll deposited $250 in a special account for Schonherr. The lieutenant returned to Chile on December 31, 1943, a trained fighter pilot and proven Abwehr informant. In January 1944, he presented a second report to Kunsemüller, received another payment, and was put on a special payroll controlled directly by Bernardo Timmerman.[240]

Among the aircraft on which Schonherr provided accurate profiles were the following:

Aircraft	Model(s)	Type	Nicknames
P-38	H	Twin-engine fighter plane	Lightning
P-39	Q	Single-engine fighter plane	Airacobra
P-40	K and N	Single-engine fighter plane	Warhawk
P-61	A	Twin-engine night fighter	Black Widow
PB2Y	2	U.S. Navy 4-engine patrol bomber	Coronado
B-25	G and H	Twin-engine medium army bomber	Mitchell

By August 1943, the P-39 and P-40 were obsolescent fighter aircraft, but still in combat in North Africa, the Pacific, and on the Russian front. The P-38 and PB2Y-2, in contrast, were first-line aircraft, while the P-61 was still being tested and would not see combat until August 1944. The Abwehr had employed far too many hot air merchants in its Latin American effort; for a change it received accurate information, and got it rather inexpensively.[241]

Emilio Schonherr was not the only Chilean officer who helped PQZ to acquire sensitive data about the U.S. Army Air Force. Additional information concerning lend-lease equipment and its distribution among

Chilean units came from 2nd Lt. Harold Sievers, a young infantry officer whose code name, "Erwin Rommel," provides some indication of his ideological preferences.[242] Although SIS/Chile eventually learned of "Erwin Rommel's" activities, it never did discover who was responsible for another leak of military information to PQZ. As part of the Lend-Lease Act signed in February 1943, an army air force training mission was sent to Chile to teach preflight, basic flight training, and aircraft engine maintenance and repair procedures. In May 1943, two books and training manuals in English were presented as gifts to Gen. Manuel Tovarías, commander-in-chief of the Chilean air force. These manuals, plus two others containing classified information belonging to a training mission member, were surreptitiously taken to Timmerman, photographed, and then returned to their owners. Not until after the PQZ ring was broken up did the fact that the manuals had been pilfered become known.[243]

Hardly inconsequential among the other coups scored by the PQZ ring was the acquisition of plans or blueprints dealing with the Panama Canal defenses built in 1940–41. Suspected as the culprit in this operation was the Chilean ambassador to Panama. How he obtained these plans is still unknown, but the suspect managed to ship them back to Chile via the diplomatic pouch. Later, the ambassador reclaimed the plans, which were being held for him by a member of his family, and sold them to Ludwig von Bohlen. The air attaché believed the documents authentic, for he paid the Chilean's price: ten thousand dollars.[244]

The information supplied by Schonherr and Sievers, the data from the "borrowed" manuals, plus figures on copper production were transmitted in part on the PQZ-URK radio circuit. But Timmerman left nothing to chance; he microfilmed all materials and shipped them by courier to Brigadier General Wolf, German attaché in Argentina.[245]

Finally, there would be one triumph which PQZ achieved thanks to an assist from a Chilean official. Ludwig von Bohlen was scheduled to leave Chile with members of the German diplomatic party, but he had certain documents (perhaps the Panama Canal plans) which he did not want examined. Early in September 1943, both the U.S. and British ambassadors called upon Foreign Minister Joaquín Fernández and obtained a pledge that all German diplomatic baggage would be examined by DGII officials, in the presence of U.S. and/or British observers.[246] One way or another, Washington and London intended to find out what secrets the Germans might be taking out of Chile.

The air attaché, however, had even more powerful contacts than the Anglo-Americans, a fact which the latter would later ruefully admit. On September 29, 1943, the last members of the German diplomatic staff left Chile via international train to Buenos Aires. Before doing so, their luggage was examined and sealed—all except for the baggage of Major Bohlen. Indeed, DGII examiners found the air attaché's bags sealed and supposedly examined personally by Chilean air force commander Manuel Tovarías. The latter let it be known that since he had checked his friend's bags, no one else need look into them. As the DGII had no intention of disregarding the expressed wish of an air force general officer, Bohlen sailed through without his luggage being opened.[247]

D. *Sicherheitsdienst: The Abwehr's Friendly Enemy*

It might be assumed that a spy network which had achieved what no others in the Americas had accomplished would be highly prized. Furthermore, the creator of such an organization, Major Bohlen, should have been richly rewarded. This would not be the case, for both the PQZ organization and the former air attaché would be under attack by another German intelligence organization from January 1943 on. On the twenty-third of that month, Dr. Erwin Wolf, the second secretary in the German embassy in Santiago, paid a call on Bohlen. A member of Dienststelle Ribbentrop as well as an SD agent, Wolf was no ordinary diplomatic paper shuffler; when he spoke, spymasters found it politic to listen.[248]

The second secretary had come to inform Bohlen that an SD operative named "Victor Vougha" was in the Chilean capital, and Wolf urged the attaché to aid the agent with all means possible. Shortly thereafter, Bohlen met Victor Vougha, who came quickly to the point: The SD man wanted a regular supply of funds, the new code that Bohlen was using, a coding machine, and a radio transmitter. Bohlen didn't like Vougha's aggressive manner, didn't want any competition in Chile, and believed the demands made were ridiculous. He forwarded his objections to Berlin, and was undoubtedly discomfited when he was told to comply with the SD agent's requests.[249]

Who was the mysterious Victor Vougha? He was, in fact, Heinz Lange, the first SD field agent sent to Argentina in May 1940. As second-in-command to Johannes Siegfried Becker, Lange left for Brazil in January 1941, his orders being to create an SD-controlled clandestine radio network in that country. Lange's efforts there were a complete failure, and when the Brazilian security forces began arresting Abwehr V-men in March 1942, he fled to Paraguay.[250] A long-time resident of that country, Lange had many contacts there. As a result, in October 1942, he obtained a legitimate passport in the name of Victor Vougha, signed by Cap. Melo Vargas, private secretary to the chief of police of Asunción. The real Vougha was a "sickly clerk" working in the Asunción office of the Banco Germánico. Whether he knew that someone else was using his name is debatable, but with this new identity, Heinz Lange was ready to reenter the cloak-and-dagger wars.[251]

After moving to Argentina, Lange met with his former boss, Johannes Siegfried Becker, on January 15, 1943, in Mendoza. The latter had departed for Germany in October 1941, and had returned to Argentina clandestinely only a few days before. Becker decided that, notwithstanding Lange's miserable performance in Brazil, he was to move on to Chile and establish an SD radio station and agent network in that country. Lange knew nothing about Chile, but Becker, who wanted him out of Argentina, promised that Eugenio Ellinger Knoll ("Juan Valdés") would be sent to provide assistance.[252]

By the time Ellinger returned to Santiago in March 1943, he found that Lange was receiving funds from Bohlen through Lange's mistress, Melitta Tietz, and had found a radioman in former bank clerk Heriberto Schlosser. Over the next eight months, the most important collaborator recruited was Aristides Parodí, first secretary of the Paraguayan legation in Santiago. This diplomat provided the SD men with false papers, updated passports, information gleaned from the embassy cocktail circuit, and the use of a car with diplomatic license plates.[253]

Using a Chilean priest, Fr. Francisco Martínez, as a drop,[254] Lange established postal contact with Johannes Becker, but plans for the radio station went awry. Bohlen reluctantly provided a transmitter, but despite repeated attempts, Schlosser never reached either Germany or one of the clandestine stations established in Argentina. At length, weary of failure and told by Aristides Parodí that Schlosser's signals were being intercepted by U.S. detection units, Heinz Lange dropped out of the spy wars for the second time in three years. In December 1943, he and his mistress, in company with Heriberto Schlosser and his wife, joined a group of Chilean contrabandists and crossed the Andes into Argentina. Eugenio Ellinger Knoll remained behind to direct the small number of collaborators the group had recruited. He buried the transmitter and coding machine on property owned by his mistress, Renata Ebensperger. The Chilean SD group, which began its activities inauspiciously, terminated them the same way.[255]

Heinz Lange's misadventures in Chile are of importance only because of the problems they caused PQZ, and because of the insight they provide concerning the nature of continuing Abwehr-SD conflict. Lange obtained money, a code machine, and a transmitter from Bohlen, but even this was not considered enough. Since the small ring he gathered around himself had virtually no access to secret information, military or political, Lange also had to obtain worthwhile data from PQZ. Thus, one of his first moves was to insinuate Melitta Tietz into the Abwehr organization. As a member of Hans Heinke's section, she was able to obtain some shipping information, while at the same time reporting on the political reliability of the PQZ agents with whom she came into contact.[256]

A similar operational scheme was worked out with Humberto Pérez ("José") who, as the PQZ backup radioman, received orders and payments from Augusto Kroll. When Pérez arrived in Chile in August 1943, both Bohlen and Kroll told him that although he had served with the SD in Argentina, as a member of an Abwehr group, he must have no contact with the SD in Chile. Pérez had agreed to this order. But Becker had instructed him to report to Lange as well, and the latter naturally wanted contact with Pérez continued. The arrangement worked out was that any secret information PQZ obtained which Pérez heard about was to be passed on to Lange. Secondly, Pérez was to provide reliability reports on those PQZ members whom he came in contact with.[257]

It is the viciousness and self-defeating nature of the Abwehr-SD conflict which leaves the most indelible impression. Unless Bohlen, Timmerman, et al. provided Lange with the equipment he needed and information of importance so that he appeared competent to his Berlin superiors, he would report them as being half-hearted supporters of national socialism. Naturally, Bohlen and Timmerman resented this blackmail, and although they had to accept a known leak in Melitta Tietz, they did all they could to isolate Lange's lover. The result was that the SD man received virtually nothing of significance to report, and naturally, he blamed Bohlen for his failure.[258]

In January 1944, after he had escaped to Argentina, Heinz Lange wrote a long report on his sojourn in Chile in which he denounced Bohlen as being anti-Nazi. SD headquarters had already decided that espionage would never be Lange's forte, but the charges against Bohlen gained credence when they were repeated by Dr. Erwin Wolf, the air attaché's erstwhile colleague in the German embassy in Chile. When Lange's report and Wolf's confirming statements were presented to SS-Capt. Kurt Gross, chief of the SD's Latin American division, the latter declared that Bohlen was unreliable, and would be ineligible for any further foreign territorial assignments.[259]

This report would prove critical because on Febuary 12, 1944, Hitler ordered Adm. Wilhelm Canaris removed from his position and sanctioned the absorption of the Abwehr by the SD.[260] Even though Bohlen did not come directly under the authority of SS-Captain Gross in the new intelligence structure, the rap laid on him by Lange, Wolf, and Gross ruined his career. Bohlen was promoted to lieutenant colonel in March 1944, but the post he strove to get, that of air attaché in Spain, was given to another officer. His recommendation for the War Service Medal, First Class was denied, a real insult when it is recalled that spymasters like Friedrich Kempter received much more prestigious awards. Distressed by his evident pariah status, Bohlen sought to discover why his work for German intelligence seemed so unappreciated. Eventually Hedwig Sommer, SS-Captain Gross's private secretary, took pity on him and told Bohlen of Lange's denunciation, Wolf's confirmation, and Gross's condemnation.[261]

Ludwig von Bohlen had been judged unreliable by those who passed as unswerving followers of the Führer. His past services kept him out of the Gestapo's clutches, but that was all the gratitude he was going to get.

VI. The Second Chilean Counterespionage Campaign

A. The Tell-Tale "Fist"

The heart of the PQZ ring which Ludwig von Bohlen planned was to be the clandestine radio station operated by Guillermo Kunsemüller. The instrument believed necessary in order to make consistent contact with Germany was a new model *Afu*, and this was brought from the Reich as part of the diplomatic luggage of a Chilean consul. Before this diplomat returned to Santiago in June–July 1942, the deal he struck with the

Abwehr was that he would receive a fee and turn over the transmitter to a man who would identify himself as "Condor." Nevertheless, a communications snafu took place somewhere along the line, because for several months, no one appeared to claim the transmitter and make the payment. Apparently the revelations of the PYL case and the prospect of a break in relations with Germany caused the Chilean diplomat to lose all interest in further cloak-and-dagger escapades. In November 1942, he contacted the German embassy and threatened to destroy the *Afu* unless someone appeared to claim it. Bohlen was belatedly informed, and it was he who obtained the transmitter and made the payment. The radio was passed to Timmerman, who delivered it to Kunsemüller in February 1943.[262]

Using the new code Bohlen had obtained and equipped with the latest Abwehr equipment available, Kunsemüller was seemingly ready to establish contact with Germany. On April 27, 1943, he succeeded in contacting Ast Hamburg, and eight days later, PQZ and URK exchanged their first messages. The new *Afu* was a 100-watt machine, and considered extremely efficient, but Kunsemüller soon discovered that it lacked the power to consistently overcome the atmospheric and other problems existing along the eight-thousand-mile circuit between Santiago and Hamburg. He continued signaling as often as he thought consistent with security conditions, but not until June 18, 1943, would URK reply that it had received a second message.[263]

Frustrated and angry, Kunsemüller demanded that a more powerful transmitter be immediately made available. As a temporary measure, Bohlen secured a 150-watt instrument which was delivered to the radioman in July 1943. The PQZ-URK connection was reestablished on the twenty-first of the month, and a modest abatement in transmission problems was experienced. The last message sent by PQZ occurred on October 27, 1943; thereafter, atmospheric conditions over the Andes forced a cessation of transatlantic contact. Not until February 1944 was regular communication expected to resume.[264]

Bernardo Timmerman's long-range solution to the radio problem was the construction of an instrument as powerful as the old PYL transmitter (i.e., 300 watts). He hired several technicians who worked feverishly on the project, but the war made necessary parts almost impossible to obtain. Moreover, to avoid alerting Chilean authorities, virtually all purchases of materials were made cautiously and surreptitiously. The new radio was supposed to have been ready in March 1944, but Kunsemüller was impatient and would not wait. In December 1943, he obtained Timmerman's permission to make contact with the radio network that Johannes Siegfried Becker had created in Argentina. Using the call sign COX2, Kunsemüller made repeated broadcasts in December 1943 and January 1944, all to no avail.[265]

The sardonic nature of the situation was one which few novelists could have created without straining their credibility. The defeat of PYL and the other Abwehr rings in Latin America had been achieved in large measure because the RID and the FBI Technical Laboratory had intercepted the radio messages, cracked the codes, and thereby identified many of the ring members. PQZ's signals were intercepted in May 1943, but a year would pass before the FBI laboratory would decipher the first messages. Thus the identity of the network's members remained secure. But because of the difficulties experienced with the radio equipment, the information obtained could rarely be transmitted. The sad result was that while Kunsemüller attempted to contact both Ast Hamburg and the Becker network in Argentina over three hundred times between May 1943 and January 1944, only twenty-two messages, all over the PQZ-URK circuit, were exchanged.[266] Undaunted by these technical hazards, Bernardo Timmerman made microfilm copies of all the data obtained and sent them by courier to military attaché Gen. Friedrich Wolf in Buenos Aires. But after he was captured, Timmerman expressed his disgust over the broadcasting situation by noting that "in [his] judgment, this [PQZ radio] service was a total failure. . . ."[267]

Paradoxically, U.S. counterspies, even though they couldn't read the messages, benefitted simply because Kunsemüller was such a hard-working failure. Just as each person has individual fingerprints, each radio telegrapher develops a style of sending that is distinctive and serves as an accurate means of identification. Even when he consciously attempts to alter his sending technique, analytical study by telegraphic experts can overcome such deception, and identify the sender by his transmitting style, or "fist."[268] In the case of PQZ, it was the RID which provided the help the SIS needed. From a PYL message of March 9, 1942, U.S. counterspies knew that someone named "Pedro" would start broadcasting on the NOI-GES circuit and began studying his transmitting style. They had three months to do so before broadcasting ceased in July 1942.

Ten months would pass before new clandestine signals were detected coming from Chile on May 5, 1943. Three different RID stations picked up PQZ, and from Kunsemüller's continuing efforts to reach URK the monitors were soon able to confirm that "Pedro" was back in business. As George E. Sterling, chief of the RID, stated in a secret report to a congressional committee:

> The very day the agent went on the air after a year, we knew who he was, and by [directional] bearings fixed the appropriate location of his transmitter close to Santiago, Chile. The RID man in that country was immediately notified, and working alone . . . the second time we picked up his [Kunsemüller's] signal, he [RID agent] located the house where the transmitter was in operation. That, I believe, is a record.[269]

This rather glib statement fails to make clear that George Fellows, the RID agent in Santiago, was able to pick up PQZ on his mobile radio direction finder only in July 1943. It was the length of time "Pedro" stayed on the airwaves, frantically trying to contact URK, which aided Fellows. He eventually was able to report that Kunsemüller's residence at Ossa 191, La Cisterna, in Santiago was PQZ's broadcasting base.[270]

With "Pedro's" identity apparently established, SIS/Chile kept the radioman and all unknown visitors under close surveillance. Eventually, Kunsemüller's phone was tapped, his mail opened, and a surreptitious search of his home was conducted,[271] but these actions produced no significant results. The shadowers did note that Kunsemüller and Augusto Kroll were seen using the same lockbox in the *El Mercurio* office building, and so the latter's phone was also tapped.

One evening in September 1943, an unidentified woman calling from Kroll's house told another friend that Herr Timmerman had just received a message stating that unspecified materials "had arrived safely in Lisbon." Kroll had been seen having lunch on one occasion with Bernardo Timmerman, and so SIS/Chile concluded that the Herr Timmerman who sent things to Lisbon and the man dining with Kroll might be the same man. Thus, after months of gumshoeing and listening in on phone calls, a Kunsemüller-Kroll-Timmerman connection was established.[272]

This was highly circumstantial evidence, and the situation would not soon improve, because early in October 1943, SIS/Chile surveillance plans collapsed. Somehow Kunsemüller discovered that his house was being watched, and with an audacity rarely exhibited by Abwehr agents, he sneaked out of his back door and took a photograph of the SIS/Chile agent watching his house.[273] Thereafter, Kunsemüller took to ducking suddenly into doorways, doubling back along his route, and generally acting as if he knew he was being tailed. Since PQZ went off the air after October 27, 1943, it was not necessary for Augusto Kroll to deliver messages for transmission, and Kunsemüller kept away from members of the ring he knew. Although the surveillance of the radioman and those who visited him continued, SIS/Chile would not achieve another significant breakthrough.

The FBI in Washington would liked to have spent more time working on the PQZ code, collating additional information and discovering more about other members of the ring, but late in January 1944 its hand was forced. Eager to fatten his purse, Kunsemüller had become a smuggler as well as a spy. As a member of a group of contrabandists led by Edmundo Menge, he participated in the trafficking of semiprecious stones, florescent lights, and radio tubes from Chile to Argentina. J. Edgar Hoover could not have cared less about these criminal ventures, but in January 1944 he received two unsettling reports. The first was that certain DGII officers were threatening both Menge and Kunsemüller with arrest unless a $2,500 payoff was promptly made. The second report, apparently obtained by an SIS/Chile informant, was that the spy-smuggler, for multiple reasons, was preparing to flee to Argentina in February 1944.[274] Convinced that either Kunsemüller's departure or his arrest by Chilean police would " interrupt the investigation in regard to the [PQZ] organization's espionage activity," Hoover decided that he must move quickly.[275] The evidence available was compiled in a thirty-one-page document, and presented to the State Department on February 5, 1944, under the title, "Radio Station PQZ—Santiago, Chile."

In comparison with the oft-mentioned PYL memorandum of June 30, 1942, the PQZ document of February 5, 1944, was more elaborate, more detailed, but not nearly as accurate. For example, Augusto Kroll was listed as the leader of the PQZ ring, and members of the Menge gang were listed as spy ring members or collaborators. Moreover, of some sixty-one persons subsequently arrested by Chilean police for being involved in the PQZ affair, only four of these were mentioned in the February 5, 1944, memorandum.[276] The irony of the situation is that the June 30, 1942, spy memorandum, which named most of the members of the PYL organization and included eighty decoded messages, would not be acted upon by the Chilean government for almost four months. The hastily assembled, highly inaccurate February 5, 1944, memorandum named only four PQZ agents or collaborators, and included no decoded messages whatsoever. Yet, less than twenty-four hours after this document was handed over to Chilean authorities, the DGII began detaining suspects. Clearly the Ríos government had decided to execute a startling change in its counter-espionage policy.

B. *The Blow Falls*

At 4:00 P.M. on February 14, 1944, Ambassador Claude Bowers handed Foreign Minister Joaquín Fernández an abridged copy of the February 5, 1944, spy memorandum. That same afternoon, Fernández turned the report over to the DGII director, Jorge Garreton, who immediately sought arrest warrants from the court of appeals in Santiago. The first judge approached refused to comply, and given the lateness of the hour, it was unlikely that a more amenable magistrate would act before the next morning. Disregarding the procedural problem, the Ríos government opted for immediate action. Jorge Garreton was ordered to commence making arrests, and the legal details were to be dealt with later.[277] At 9:00 A.M. on February 15, DGII officers in Santiago were ordered to seize Guillermo and Gisela Kunsemüller; forty-five minutes later, these two were in custody and being held incommunicado.[278] After a continuous grilling on February 16, Kunsemüller implicated Kroll and Timmerman.

Arrested on February 17, Augusto Kroll proved to be another tough customer. He denied all charges, admitting only that a German official, whose name he did not know, left a box to keep for the duration of the war, which he had never opened. Angered by his refusal to admit being a spy, and his feigned ignorance concerning Abwehr activities in Chile, DGII interrogators called upon certain "allies" to assist in the loosening of Kroll's tongue. First, the prisoner was denied food and water for almost twenty-four hours. As to what happened next, SIS/Chile's report is terse:

> The condition of the cells in the various jails in Santiago is bad. . . .
> Almost every subject in this [PQZ] case has quickly broken down,
> and has given as a reason—failure to resist the attacks of the vermin

that infest the cells. It was noticeable that Kroll, after a short time in
jail, had large bites over his hands....[279]

After his session with the rodents on the night of February 18–19, 1944,
Kroll named all the PQZ members under his supervision and agreed to
lead the police to the places in his yard where radio equipment was
buried.

At the same time Augusto Kroll was arrested, Bernardo Timmerman
was also supposed to be taken into custody, but the ring leader was then
vacationing in the southern Chilean town of Petrohué. A DGII official was
sent to arrest him, but Timmerman somehow learned of what had happened in Santiago. He was boarding a plane to Argentina when he was
apprehended by the DGII on February 19.[280] Taken back to the capital the
same day, Timmerman made a long, rambling confession in which he
stated that his code name was "Pancho," that "Salvador" was still at large,
and that he was only a minor figure in the PQZ organization. Even a night
in the vermin-ridden cells failed to change his story, but on the morning
of the twentieth, DGII director Jorge Garreton tried a different tack.
Conducting the interrogation himself, Garreton told Timmerman that
unless he became more cooperative, the Timmerman residence would be
ransacked, and "broken down, piece by piece."[281]

Whether it was this threat by itself, or a combination of physical
abuse, lack of sleep, and so forth, Timmerman cracked. That afternoon, he
showed DGII agents the secret locations that they had expected to find.
Buried in the garden under a concrete slab were $55,000 in PQZ reserve
funds and another transmitter. In the basement of the house, hidden
behind a fake wall, the police found a laboratory and storage closet
containing photographic equipment, hundreds of feet of microfilm, Chilean government passports, official ministry stamps, and the spy network's
store of invisible ink. In the library, the DGII also found the books used
for the code, and in a flower vase they found the hidden code wheels for
the PQZ coding machine.[282]

On February 21, 1944, Bernardo Timmerman made a new confession
in which he named other members of the ring. Hans Heinke was arrested,
and he led the police to a rock quarry where the network's archives and
still another radio transmitter were buried in the side of a hill. Subsequent
arrests in February–March 1944 boosted the DGII's haul of PQZ money
and equipment to five transmitters, four receivers, and $201,000 in U.S.
dollars, Argentinian pesos, and Chilean pesos.[283] In fact, these arrests were
conducted with such speed, secrecy, and precision that only three
members of the ring managed to escape to Argentina.[284] The PQZ organization had been smashed and, with its demise, the last Abwehr network in
South America passed into history.

The success achieved against one German intelligence organization
indirectly resulted in the destruction of the SD group as well. Not until
Febuary 22, 1944, was the story of the arrest of the PQZ agents revealed

in the press,[285] but Eugenio Ellinger Knoll learned of these events two days earlier, and assumed that Humberto Pérez had also been apprehended. If Pérez talked, Knoll knew he would be a hunted man, so it was time once again to flee to Argentina. Nevertheless, a new passport would be necessary to avoid detection, and so he contacted a shady underworld figure named Jorge Dumont. The latter took a down payment of $350, and on February 21 contacted legal attaché John N. Speakes, who may have given Dumont a heftier fee. A trap was laid on February 24, and shortly after 12:30 A.M. on the twenty-fifth, Knoll picked up both the passport and a convoy of DGII shadowers. A running gun battle ensued in which Knoll was cornered and eventually captured.[286]

If capturing Knoll seemed relatively easy, keeping him alive proved much more difficult. The SD man had told Dumont that he carried a small vial of TNT around his neck, and would blow himself up rather than endure captivity. The DGII discovered that the dangerous vial contained nothing but patent medicine, but once behind bars, the prisoner attempted to commit suicide by beating his head against the stone wall of his cell. Obviously, he did not want to talk, but his belated resistance was of no avail. The DGII record enigmatically states that to induce Knoll's cooperation, "it was necessary to adopt all the means of security that the situation required."[287] Whatever those may have been, within one day after Knoll's capture, he was talking and the SD in Chile was finished.

In comparing the PQZ spy hunt of 1944 with the fumbled PYL effort of 1942, a number of differences are evident. In 1942, even though the group membership was known, the timid and dilatory moves of the Chilean government allowed most of the ring leaders to escape. In 1944, following Kunsemüller's confession, the Chilean police moved fast enough to bag Kroll, Heinke, and Timmerman. Once the chiefs were in police custody, the paralyzed network was then swiftly rolled up. The same thing happened with the moribund SD group. By grabbing Eugenio Ellinger Knoll and making him talk, it became relatively easy to pick off the other ring members. Interestingly enough, neither the SIS/Chile nor the DGII had known of Knoll's presence in Chile, and not until he was arrested did they learn that "Juan Valdés" and "Martín Flores" were now also in custody.[288] Luck played an important role in the counterespionage victories of March 1944. For the Germans, the luck was all bad.

C. *Some of the Guilty Go Free*

Another way in which the PQZ case differed from its PYL counterpart was that the public revelation of the existence of the Bohlen-Timmerman group touched off a violent reaction on the part of the press. On February 23, 1944, *El Siglo*, the Communist party tabloid in Santiago, called for the execution of Timmerman, Kunsemüller, and other ring leaders. *El Mercurio* on the same date ran a nine-page spread on the PQZ ring and demanded that, once and for all, the regime wipe out all vestiges of German espionage in the country. Perhaps the most typical sentiment expressed would be found on the pages of *La Nación* which, in a March 8, 1944, editorial, insisted that "the machinations of the German spies can no longer be tolerated. All true Chileans will realize that this danger to the national security must be eliminated."[289]

The demand for retribution manifested in the press would be matched by an apparent transformation of attitude on the part of the Juan Ríos government. The same day of the initial press revelations, judicial action commenced under Justice Luís Baquedano in the Santiago Court of Appeals. February 23 was also the day that Minister of the Interior Raúl Morales held a press conference and assured the assembled reporters that the prosecution of Nazi agents would be energetic and comprehensive. He also insisted that the guilty parties, no matter what their socioeconomic position, would be made to stand before the bar of justice.[290]

Considering the past record of the Ríos regime, brave words of this nature might normally be dismissed as political posturing. But the subsequent actions of the government suggested that this time it meant business. On March 3, 1944, after several days of testimony, Justice Baquedano freed nine persons arrested by the DGII and ordered the incommunicado status of the rest lifted. This action infuriated Juan Ríos, who believed these decisions inimicable to the policies he wanted pursued. On March 8, the president summoned Dr. Humberto Trucco, chief justice of the Supreme Court, and demanded that he "put some iron" into Baquedano's spine. In addition, Ríos ordered that the incommunicado status of prisoners be reestablished and warned that any persons released by Baquedano might be rearrested on presidential orders. Convinced that Ríos wasn't bluffing, Humberto Trucco indicated that the courts would act in a manner that would facilitate government foreign policy. Evidently, he saw to it that the presiding magistrate received the proper instructions, for on March 9 Baquedano suddenly reversed his incommunicado ruling, and acquiesced while the DGII rearrested several persons previously released.[291]

A complex of reasons seems to have dictated this reversal in the policy of the Ríos regime. In 1942, when the PYL case became a public issue, the Chilean people desired neutrality, and Ríos wanted to ensure that he did not align his nation with the losing side;[292] caution in prosecuting German V-men was therefore deemed prudent policy. But by February 1944, with Mussolini defeated and Germany in retreat on all fronts, it no longer mattered what Berlin thought about Chilean actions. This contingency made the prosecution of the PQZ members both safe and, depending upon how it was handled, a political bonanza. For example, between March and June 1944, the Ríos government received several reports from Rodolfo Michels and Manuel Bianchi, ambassadors to the United States and Great Britain, respectively, which emphasized that actions taken against the spies created favorable impressions in both Washington and London. In particular, Bianchi insisted that counterespionage campaigns like those carried out against PQZ were the only way to erase the suspicion that Chilean opposition to the Third Reich was opportunism of the most blatant kind.[293]

Certainly Ríos was happy about the international propaganda advantages the arrest and prosecution of the German agents brought his administration; nevertheless, the most basic consideration, as evidenced in the *La Nación* editorial of March 8, 1944, was fear concerning Chilean internal security. Guillermo Kunsemüller, a trained Abwehr agent, had entered the Chilean air force. This action caused outrage, not only because it was an insult to the national honor, but also because it raised the question of how many other Chilean air force officers and men were either Abwehr agents or sympathizers. A break with past attitudes was thus dictated because the operations of the PQZ ring, unlike those of PYL, were perceived as a threat to Chile as well as a threat to the United States. It was this realization more than anything else which changed hearts and minds in Santiago.[294]

The crucial test of the Ríos government's new attitude came quickly; and interestingly enough, the issue would be the involvement of the national military. From papers found in the Kunsemüller home, the DGII was soon aware of the role played by Lt. Emilio Schonherr, while receipts found in the Timmerman residence implicated both Lt. Harold Sievers ("Erwin Rommel") and Schonherr.[295] During the first week of April 1944, the two junior officers were subjected to intense questioning. Sievers admitted that he had supplied information concerning lend-lease equipment, but insisted that he had done so "in a totally innocent manner."[296] Schonherr, in contrast, denied any wrongdoing; the DGII thought otherwise, and after it made its report, the air force officer was suspended from flight duty.[297]

The most important army officer known to be implicated was Col. Armando González, named in the confession of Alberto Collel. Invited to testify in the PQZ case on April 12, 1944, González admitted that he had given "certain publications" of the United States and British embassies to Collel for delivery to Augusto Kroll.[298] Had only three officers been involved, the Ríos government might have remained undaunted, but the March 1944 recovery of the PQZ archives, buried by Hans Heinke, inplicated other officers as well. In a March 26 dispatch to Washington, Claude Bowers explained that "there are so many high ranking Chilean Army officers involved in the PQZ spy case that these officers will have to be turned over to a military court."[299] Among those alleged to be involved was Gen. Carlos Fuentes, the chief-of-staff of the Chilean army,[300] and that possibility caused the U.S. ambassador to query Joaquín Fernández about the government's proposed course of action. "In strictest confidence" the foreign minister admitted the complicity of "certain Army officers." These discoveries had caused the government to have second thoughts about military trials and a possible confrontation with the armed forces. Fernández explained that implicated officers would be removed through retirement and by "other means."[301]

The decision to eschew the prosecution of military personnel left Luís Baquedano in the middle, and the judge had no intention of becoming the fall guy. On May 13, 1944, he suddenly announced that the involvement of army officers meant that the spy case would have to be reassigned to a military judicial court.[302] Matters became stickier when, two days later, Gen. Fuenzalida O'Ryan, chief of the Chilean Military Court of Santiago, rebuffed Baquedano and told the press that there was no evidence to support the supposition that any military personnel had been involved in espionage activities.[303] Since Kunsemüller—to name but one person—was still technically an air force member, this statement was patently ludicrous. Still, General O'Ryan's attitude indicated that the Chilean military would neither try nor convict any of its own, and they were prepared to face a constitutional confrontation to make this point. The jurisdictional dispute was eventually solved by the Supreme Court which, on June 25, 1944, ruled that Baquedano's authority was sufficient to try the case and that he had primary jurisdiction.[304] In short, the justice would have to deal with the PQZ "hot potato" as best he could.

The Juan Ríos regime enjoyed good relations with the Chilean officer corps and felt a distinct need for the military's support.[305] If it wished to maintain that backing, then it could not allow the image of the military, as the incorruptible guardians of national security, to become tarnished. Discreet methods were used to remove Lt. Col. Armando González from his post in October 1944, but the former chief of army intelligence did not step aside quietly. In a withering attack published on November 4, 1944, in *El Chileno*, a nationalist newspaper, González accused the United States of spying against Chile, and denounced the DGII as a group of Yankee stooges.[306] González's charges caused a national scandal, but the government took no action against him, and he retired with full honors. As for Lieutenants Schonherr and Sievers, they avoided all legal prosecution and kept their commissions.[307]

But the military was not the only element whose support, or silence, Ríos eventually deemed critical. Note that on March 11, 1944, Armando Cespédes, the sub-commisario on Hans Heinke's payroll, was arrested and promptly confessed that he had passed on information and accepted payoffs.[308] A problem developed, however, in the case of DGII prefect Guillermo Gómez Rosenfeldt, who also received funds from Heinke via Ilsa Blanca Dorrer. In April 1944, Claude Bowers queried Joaquín Fernández on the government's intentions regarding Gómez Rosenfeldt. The foreign minister acknowledged the police prefect's involvement, but replied that no action could be taken "because of the possible embarrassment of the government."[309] A minor figure like Cespédes could be thrown in jail and made to pay for his crimes, but Gómez Rosenfeldt would resign with full pension. Apparently he knew too much and could cause the government a great deal of trouble.

With allowances being made for the military and the police, consideration had to be given civilian political interests as well. This time, Alberto Collel, who simultaneously served the U.S. military attaché, the

Abwehr, and Chilean army intelligence, would be the prime recipient of special favors. Arrested on February 26, 1944, Collel, in a controversial confession, admitted spying for the Germans, but claimed that he had only done what Col. Armando González told him to do.[310] Collel was behind bars one day short of two months when, on April 25, 1944, he was suddenly released. He was never indicted, and there would be no public explanation of why he was allowed to go free. Collel's escape from prosecution caused concern in the U.S. embassy precisely because that agent had wormed his way into the confidence of the U.S. military attaché, Col. Wendell Johnson. SIS/Chile boss John Speakes sought an answer from his confidential informants, all of whom gave the same response: Señor Arturo Alessandri.[311] This politician was the only Chilean elected to the presidency twice during the twentieth century (1920 and 1932), and he remained a man of considerable personal prestige. Collel was a blood relative of Alessandri's, and this factor was apparently the reason for the former president's intercession.

Still, it took something more than past glory for Alessandri to achieve Collel's release. Alessandri had thrown his weight behind Ríos in the February 1942 electoral battle against Carlos Ibáñez, and he would be a candidate in the special senatorial election to be held in August 1944. Ríos was in Alessandri's debt, but he would be supporting another politician in the upcoming senatorial contest. Still, if Alessandri won the seat (which he subsequently did), Ríos was certain to need his vote at some future date. The shrewd political move was to pay Alessandri back; Collel's freedom was one way of doing so.[312]

On March 26, 1944, Joaquín Fernández had admitted to Claude Bowers that exceptions would be made for the military, but he had insisted that "the civilians involved [in the case] would be prosecuted to the limit."[313] The Alberto Collel situation demonstrated that the foreign minister had spoken too soon. The ultimate government policy was that it would only prosecute those Abwehr spies and collaborators who could give it no trouble.

D. *Some of the Guilty Are Found Guilty*

Even after the Chilean government decided not to prosecute various military men and other VIPs, the PQZ case continued to be an exercise in intrigue which at times bordered on farce. Between February 15 and September 1, 1944, the DGII and Justice Luís Baquedano questioned some ninety persons and arrested sixty-one (thirty *Reichsdeutschen,* twenty-six Chileans, one dual citizen, one Italian, two Paraguayans, and one Spaniard) as part of the continuing investigation.[314] This number included Fr. Francisco Martínez, the priest who acted as a drop for the Heinz Lange group, but neither the police nor the judiciary wanted problems with the Roman Catholic Church. Not surprisingly, Martínez, arrested on April 2, 1944, was released the same day. So, too, was Richard Ulrich, a *Reichsdeutscher* businessman who was taken into custody on

April 1. DGII interrogators were understandably chagrined when, after twelve hours of questioning, they found that the joke was on them; they had arrested the wrong man.[315] Also conspicuous among those arrested was Isabel Pederit de Reiners ("Señorita"), who had been put under house arrest in the PYL case and would now be jailed as part of the PQZ investigation. She earned the dubious distinction of being the only person to suffer confinement in both spy cases.[316]

Among the more unique aspects of the case were the legal tools brought to bear in this probe. As in the PYL affair, the court would seek to determine whether the Radio Transmissions Decree of May 15, 1941, had been violated. But for the first time, a Chilean magistrate would also be attempting to establish whether those arrested had violated the new External Security Law of December 31, 1942. This statute, specifically created to deal with instances of peacetime espionage, prohibited the transmission outside of Chile of "news of any usefulness to those countries at war with the nations of the American continent and their allies." It provided a minimum of one and-a-half years of imprisonment and a maximum of ten, but since it was vaguely worded (i.e., "news of any usefulness") and had never been previously invoked, it was certain to be challenged by defense lawyers.[317]

Still, it was the tragicomic maneuvering, fumbling, and string-pulling which made this judicial investigation one for the books. Consider that some two hundred thousand dollars in espionage funds had been seized by DGII officers and held as evidence to be used in the prosecution case. Nevertheless, when Justice Baquedano asked that these funds be turned over to the court as evidence, a serious snag developed. On March 14, 1944, DGII chief Jorge Garreton sent a secret memorandum to the magistrate reporting that fifty-five thousand dollars of the funds had mysteriously disappeared.[318] The most likely culprits were DGII officers, a consideration which caused Garreton no end of embarrassment. This development also necessitated that Baquedano exercise discretion in raising questions about the funds used to finance PQZ operations. In effect, the judge became an indirect accomplice for the prosecution.

A crisis of a more complicated and satirical nature developed over the twenty-two PQZ-URK messages intercepted by the RID, but which the FBI laboratory had been unable to decipher. The Chileans wanted the messages in order to establish irrefutably that intelligence reports had been transmitted from Chile to Germany by clandestine radio. Fortunately, the confessions of Timmerman and Kunsemüller provided the key for decoding the messages;[319] all Washington had to do was provide them. Claude Bowers enthusiastically endorsed this step, and on April 20, the RID intercepts were received in Santiago.

No sooner had the messages arrived when the ambassador received another order prohibiting him from turning them over to the Chileans. Rear Adm. John Schuirman, then ONI chief, cited past examples of poor Chilean security methods and objected to the release of the intercepts. Made aware of the navy's opposition, Claude Bowers blew his top. In an

April 25, 1944, cable he raged that "Chile is not a country controlled by a dictator, but a democracy that functions under legal process. For a prompt and complete prosecution of the case, the Chilean judicial authorities must have (repeat, must have) legal evidence against the spies in the form of the intercepted radio messages."[320] Bowers again vented his spleen on April 27, 1944, insisting that "Chile is making the most drastic and sweeping onslaught on an espionage ring that has been made in any American country." If Washington failed to cooperate, then it could only blame itself if those being investigated eventually escaped punishment.[321]

These howls of dismay evidently forced a reassessment at the Department of the Navy, for on May 8, 1944, Admiral Schuirman withdrew his objections.[322] But the most outrageous aspect of this episode occurred on August 14, 1944, when in response to the query of a defense attorney, Justice Baquedano declared that he was still unable to read the PQZ-URK messages![323] It may be that the Chilean cryptologists had trouble deciphering the messages, but it is difficult to understand why, three months after the United States turned the messages over, the presiding judicial authority still had not received any decodes. In the end, despite all the fury and controversy, the PQZ-URK messages never played a major role in the investigation.

Alas, these were not the only aspects of the PQZ investigation which indicate that the objectivity of the judicial process was seriously flawed. The DGII apparently placed listening devices in the rooms where the prisoners conferred with their visitors and legal representatives. Furthermore, these police refused to allow those jailed to talk with their lawyers except in the presence of a DGII agent.[324] And if arbitrary and extralegal machinations by the police were not enough, there was also the disturbing attitude evinced by Juan Ríos himself. In a private interview on June 15, 1944, with U.S. naval attaché Capt. J.P. Rockwell, the president stated that he was doing everything he could to cooperate with the Allies. So determined was Ríos to demonstrate his anti-Axis credentials that he affirmed categorically that "he would, when necessary, even ignore Chilean laws to see that the Nazi spies are punished and disposed of properly."[325]

Very early during the inquiry process, the defense lawyers seem to have decided that their clients were likely to be convicted, so any legal trick, tactic or strategem became fair play. On February 29, 1944, for example, Roberto Álvarez Pratt, defending Elena de Graner, wife of Hans Graner ("Manolo"), introduced a variation on a classic macho argument: Wives of spies committed no crime if they merely supported their husbands and were not directly involved in espionage activities. This argument found favor with Justice Baquedano, who admitted that he was not inclined to vigorously prosecute the female spouses of those implicated.[326] With a single exception, he would prove that he was as good as his word.

For male prisoners, of course, no similar legal-cultural escape hatch existed. Nevertheless, the strategy developed by *Volksdeutscher* Oswaldo Koch set the pace and provided an example which other attorneys emulated. Prominent in Santiago legal and government circles, Koch had previously defended several of those persons implicated in the PYL affair. In exchange for a prepaid thirty-five hundred dollar fee, a liberal expense account, plus the recognition that a debt was being paid, he undertook the defense of Bernardo Timmerman.[327] It was while serving as the latter's counsel that Koch made some startling and seemingly indiscreet comments about his client and the case to intimate friends. According to Koch, not only was Timmerman guilty, but he was an idiot as well; as such, he was an odds-on favorite to be indicted and then convicted.[328] On the other hand, Koch stated that a number of Chilean military personnel had been on Timmerman's payroll and that these officers were not going to be indicted. He sensed a whitewash and voiced the view that "due to government manipulation, the trial was not being properly conducted."[329]

Koch's commentary to assorted intimates explains to a significant extent his courtroom tactics. Constantly he hammered away at the same theme: his client's confession had been obtained by illegal means and his civil rights had been consistently violated. But as to Timmerman's actual guilt or innocence, in court Koch displayed an amazing skill in avoiding the consideration of that question. In conducting the defense along those lines, Koch obviously hoped to make DGII treatment of prisoners the major issue. By law, he was not to reveal any testimony given or actions taken by the court until after Justice Baquedano had released his opinion.[330] Still, if the idea could be promoted that mysterious leaks concerning police brutality might occur, ways and means might be found to obtain clemency for his client. It was a calculated risk, but a regime which chose not to prosecute guilty military men might also decide that Koch's silence was worth a shorter stretch in the penitentiary for Timmerman.

The tactics employed by other defense lawyers soon indicated that they believed Koch's maneuvers might be efficacious for their clients as well. The result was an unchecked outpouring of invective aimed indirectly at the United States, directly at the Ríos government, and specifically at the DGII chief, Jorge Garreton. Garreton denied having extorted confessions or having tortured prisoners, but by June 1944, U.S. observers knew that, under the continuing drumfire of charges, he was beginning to feel the pressure.[331] Not surprisingly, before the investigation ended, the Chilean policeman managed to have himself sent to Argentina where he passed some time in an abortive attempt to effect the extradition of several Chileans who had fled to escape the PQZ probe.[332]

The U.S. Department of State was, of course, vitally interested in the legal pyrotechnics emanating from Santiago. After the first arrests on February 25, 1944, Acting Secretary of State Edward R. Stettinius praised Chile for taking "another significant step in the defense of the hemisphere." But less than a week after this declaration, on March 2, Stettinius was privately excoriating the Chilean government for not prosecuting the case more vigorously. Afraid that the PQZ case might go the way of the

dormant PYL investigation, he ordered Claude Bowers to pressure Foreign Minister Joaquín Fernández into speeding up the proceedings.[333]
Acting sometimes under orders and sometimes in an unofficial capacity,
the U.S. ambassador urged Fernández on several occasions to have Justice
Baquedano complete this investigation as soon as possible.[334] Both
Bowers and the policy makers in Washington were keenly aware that the
DGII had used illegal means to obtain information.[335] What unnerved
them, however, was that if the inquiry lasted too long, the irregularities
might become public and cause the PQZ investigation to collapse. It was
this last contingency which had to be avoided at all costs.

Finally, on October 25, 1944, after eight months of bickering over
jurisdictional rights, charges of torture, and the validity of the evidence
gathered, Justice Luís Baquedano closed the case. He proposed indictments against thirty-four persons, submitted his findings to the prosecuting attorney, Dr. Pelegrín Sepúlveda, and eventually forwarded these joint
observations and recommendations to an appeals court tribunal.[336] All
these procedures took time, and it was not until June 6, 1945, that
Baquedano declared the judicial process completed. In his written opinion, presented the following afternoon, he noted that several of the
prisoners had been tortured by the DGII, but denied that the brutality
inflicted affected the validity of the charges made.[337] Found guilty of
violating the Radio Transmission Decree of May 15, 1941, and the External Security Law of December 31, 1942, were eighteen Chileans, six
Germans, one dual citizen (Timmerman), and one Paraguayan (Humberto Pérez). All told, those found guilty were sentenced to serve a total
of fifty-nine years and fifty-three days in prison.[338] (See Appendix C.)

The sentences meted out were nothing if not arbitrary. Bernardo
Timmerman was the head of the PQZ ring, but he received a shorter
sentence than Guillermo Kunsemüller. Humberto Pérez, who entered the
country as a spy and also functioned as a conduit for information, was
condemned to eighteen months behind bars. In contrast, Walter Thieme
and Jorge Epensberger, who worked with Heinz Lange and attempted to
install a working transmitter in Thieme's home, both received double the
sentence given to Pérez. Armando Cespédes, the corrupt DGII official who
supplied information to Ilse Dorrer, received the same 541-day sentence
as she did. So did Franz Hilger, who was nothing more than a part-time
drop for Ludwig von Bohlen. When one considers that Heinz Lange's
drop, Fr. Francisco Martínez, was never even indicted, the discrepancy
becomes blatant. Justice Baquedano's apparent *modus operandi* was to
give longer sentences to persons he considered top ring leaders, and slap
the others with eighteen-month terms regardless of whether they were
actively or passively involved in espionage activities.[339] This was hardly
justice in its more classical form, but in light of the long delays, the
shameful compromises and the unlawful police tactics utilized, perhaps it
is amazing that any convictions were gained at all.

With the pronouncement of sentence, all those found guilty suffered
the suspension of their civil rights, plus the loss of all properties and

monies seized by the state.[340] They were, however, permitted to appeal their convictions to a special tribunal that would consist of three Santiago Court of Appeals justices. J. Edgar Hoover informed the State Department, MID, and ONI that, in his opinion, "it is improbable that the sentences ... will be changed."[341] But between June 7 and October 3, 1945, the war against Japan ended, and that event undermined the FBI chief's conclusions. On the latter date, the appeals tribunal handed down rulings which modified twelve sentences and set five persons at liberty. (See Appendix C.) Among other changes, Guillermo Kunsemüller's term was cut to three years, Bernardo Timmerman's to two, and Hans Heinke's to eighteen months and a day. Augusto Kroll and Eugenio Ellinger Knoll also had their time of imprisonment cut to eighteen months, but since these two men had been in custody since February 1944, the tribunal declared their prison terms completed. The net result of these decisions was that, barring additional pardons, no German agents were in Chilean jails after December 31, 1948.[342]

In justifying this radical revision of the June 1945 sentences, the tribunal noted several procedural errors, but in general it failed to make a real case for the actions it took. Through an informant, SIS/Chile learned that the magistrates unanimously felt that the DGII had grievously abused the prisoners' civil rights. Another factor mentioned was that on April 14, 1945, Chile had formally declared war on Japan, a development which gave policy matters precedence over rights issues; with the war over, that situation was reversed. Perhaps the October 3, 1945, reversals were the appeals tribunal's way of saying that, in the end, justice had prevailed over expediency.[343]

The remission of punishment mandated on October 3, 1945, accurately presaged events to come. Ill heath forced Juan Ríos to step down from the presidency on January 17, 1946. Thereafter, the issue of German espionage would not disappear entirely, but the Chileans would display a marked talent for ignoring certain aspects of it. Consider that in July 1947, at the request of the Argentine government, the DGII searched for and apprehended Fernando Baulenas Salas, a former member of Johannes Siegfried Becker's SD ring who had fled to Chile.[344] Of course, Baulenas Salas did not enter the country alone; he confessed that his companions had been Hans Blume, Johannes Szeraws, and Heriberto Schlosser, all key figures in Abwehr or SD activities in Chile in 1941–43. Before Baulenas Salas was deported, U.S. intelligence (CIA?) learned that he had informed the DGII where he believed this trio was, but the police made no further arrests.[345]

Concerned over the Gabriel González Videla government's apparent failure to pursue the matter, in November 1947, counselor of the U.S. embassy Edward Trueblood forwarded a polite inquiry to the Chilean Foreign Office. The response he received on January 21, 1948, noted that detention orders were pending against Hans Blume, Johannes Szeraws, and Heriberto Schlosser, but observed that the police were still unable to locate these fugitives. Since Trueblood doubted that the DGII was looking very hard, on February 2, 1948, he asked the State Department for additional instructions. The official record fails to indicate that he ever received any.[346] Obviously, the Chileans were not particularly concerned about the presence or activities of these former agents. And with the Cold War on, Washington was now more interested in Communist activities than in the whereabouts of former Nazi spies. The matter was quietly allowed to lapse.

1. Where Are They Now?

After 1947, a significant number of the former German spies who fled the country resettled in Chile. As of 1981, Hans Blume was running a business in Valparaíso, while Guillermo Kunsemüller was living in Santiago. Heinrich Reiners returned to Chile via Venezuela in 1949 and runs an import-export business headquartered in the Chilean capital. Contradictory information concerning Bernardo Timmerman was given to us, the most reliable source asserting that although he has retired, his family continues to hold numerous agricultural and residential properties in central and southern Chile.[347] Ludwig von Bohlen, born in Chile in 1896, returned to that country from West Germany in 1972. Ten years later, he was still alive, but no longer able to move around without some assistance.[348] For the most part, these men have experienced few problems in Chile, and they hold few grudges. Unlike the situation in Brazil, the spy issue is—and evidently has been for some time—a closed book.

VII. Summary: A Back Seat on the Gravy Train

Recall that in an October 1942 dispatch, Rodolfo Michels, Chile's ambassador to the United States, stated flatly that unless Chile severed relations with the Axis and broke up the PYL spy ring, $100 million in private loans the Ríos government sought would not be forthcoming. In January 1943, diplomatic relations with the Axis were broken, but the half-hearted Chilean counterespionage effort remained a source of conflict between Santiago and Washington. This did not prevent Foreign Minister Joaquín Fernández from going to the U.S. capital in September 1943 and asking for funds to build a steel mill. Cordell Hull remained noncommittal, and again it was Rodolfo Michels who was the bearer of unwelcome news: Unless the government vigorously prosecuted German agents, it could forget about obtaining the mill.

The Ríos government was always reluctant to face unpleasant alternatives, but by February 1944, the probability of Axis defeat, plus public indignation following press revelations about the PQZ ring, made a counterespionage policy shift relatively painless. Moreover, once it began taking forceful action against PQZ V-men, the Chilean leadership immediately put itself in a stronger position to press its economic development program on a heretofore unresponsive United States. Thus, in a February 29, 1944, dispatch stamped "strictly confidential," Foreign Minister Joaquín Fernández ordered Ambassador Michels to step up publicity concerning the PQZ arrests, and to use this sign of collaboration as a lever in hopes of obtaining U.S. commitments for loans to build a steel mill and other forms of heavy industry.[349]

Four days later Michels replied, accepting these suggestions but emphasizing the possibility that the war in Europe might end before Chile received the full quotient of lend-lease goods promised or any of the desired loans. The ambassador speculated that these difficulties might be overcome only "if some South American government—Chile for example —would offer more cooperation . . . [in order] to facilitate in a positive manner, the resolution of the [U.S.] Pacific campaign. . . ." Michels's words were carefully chosen, but his meaning was clear. By offering bases to the U.S. Navy, or declaring war on Japan, Chile still had a chance to obtain the items it sought. And, as a kind of afterthought, he intimated that the swift and forceful prosecution of the arrested spies was one way the regime would continue to aid its own cause.[350]

Juan Ríos had not heeded Michels's suggestions in 1942–43, but his subsequent actions in 1944 were quite in line with the ambassador's suggestions. On May 5, 1944, he personally sanctioned the dispatch of Wilhelm Hellemann and several suspected German agents to the United States for detention and interrogation.[351] Nevertheless, the changes in Chilean foreign policy elicited little in the way of a sympathetic reaction on the part of the United States. The most candid explanation for this failure was provided by Philip Bonsal, chief of the American republics desk, who on May 17–18, 1944, visited Santiago and discussed economic issues with Joaquín Fernández. The foreign minister presented a long exposition on foreign policy in which he touched on the progress of the PQZ trial, suggested that Chile might declare war on Japan, and sought firm trade and aid commitments. Bonsal personally believed that a war declaration was no more than an excuse for Chile to press Washington for more aid and weapons. He shyly countered by recalling the desperate days of 1942, and then drove home the point: "At the time, when we most needed Chile's assistance, that assistance had not been forthcoming." Warming to his topic, Bonsal added that in 1942, Chilean neutrality and its related policies had "somewhat handicapped" the U.S. war effort. Since that time, Chile had broken diplomatic relations with the Axis and arrested the PQZ agents, but the United States expected "a very high degree of cooperation in the future in order to overcome that [earlier] handicap."[352]

Subsequent developments suggest that Bonsal's blunt commentary shocked the Chileans, and forced a more realistic appraisal of their situation. Recall that on June 15, 1944, President Juan Ríos solemnly promised U.S. officials that he would break national laws in order to convict the German agents. Roughly one year later, on June 7, the PQZ trial ended with twenty-six Chileans and foreign nationals receiving prison sentences. But despite this evidence of changes in policy, the hearts and minds of U.S. policy makers were not appreciably affected. In August 1944, for example, the State Department rejected a Ríos request for more lend-lease aid and ruled that unless Chile came under direct attack, there would be no further arms shipments. All told, Chile received only $7 million of the $50 million in lend-lease weaponry it originally was scheduled to receive.[353]

Concerning economic assistance, the Ríos government garnered little except promises until, perhaps coincidentally, Justice Luís Baquedano handed down indictments in the PQZ case. Between December 30, 1944, and September 30, 1945, the Import-Export Bank made $40 million in loans available, half of which came in a grant on September 12 for the purchase of steel mill equipment. But the aid given should be put in perspective. Chile received a total of $47 million in aid from 1942 to 1945. Brazil, on the other hand, received $550 million during the same period, with $80 million of that amount coming in 1945.[354]

Basic to the situation would seem to be the fact that DOPS in Rio de Janeiro arrested Albrecht Gustav Engels in March 1942. No spymaster of equal stature would be captured by the DGII in Santiago until February 1944. Getúlio Vargas acted in 1942, when the Axis was still on the march in Europe and in the Pacific, and the United States needed all the help it could get. In contrast, PYL ring leaders like Hans Blume, Heinrich Reiners, and Johannes Szeraws all escaped arrest and imprisonment. Furthermore, by the time Guillermo Kunsemüller and Bernardo Timmerman were jailed, the final defeat of the Axis was in sight and the United States no longer felt any gratitude toward Latin American late-comers.

After much hesitation, Juan Ríos finally jumped aboard the Allied victory wagon. But by the time he got on, the better seats had been taken, a development which left his government at a disadvantage in the struggle to obtain a larger slice of Uncle Sam's largess. Clearly, internal conditions militated against Ríos's climbing aboard much sooner than he did. Still, the half-hearted and dilatory counterspy measures he pushed until February 1944 probably resulted in the loss of arms and economic assistance which Chile would otherwise have been able to obtain.

Notes

1. The Franklin Delano Roosevelt Library (hereafter referred to as FDRL), Hyde Park, New York, *The Diaries of Adolf A. Berle,* roll 3, frames 1002, 1003, and 1048.

2. Ibid., frame 1048.

3. See National Archives and Records Service (hereafter referred to as NARS), R.G. 226, OSS, C.O.I. 24520, pp. 8–10. The quoted material is from p. 10.

4. FDRL, *The Diaries of Adolf A. Berle,* roll 3, frame 1048.

5. Ibid., frames 1002–1003.

6. See NARS, R.G. 59, 862.20225/5-1546, p. 1.

7. See German Federal Republic, Auswärtiges Amt, *Alten zur deutschen auswärtigen politik:* 1941–1945, series E, vol. 1 (Göttingen, 1969), pp. 37–38 and 210–211.

8. Ibid., pp. 210–211.

9. The Ríos-Ibáñez race is described in John Stevenson, *The Chilean Popular Front* (Philadelphia, 1942), pp. 57–119, and also Florencio Duran Bernales, *El Partido Radical* (Santiago, 1958), pp. 171–180. A short, cogent explanation of some of the issues involved in the race is found in Paul W. Drake, *Socialism and Populism in Chile, 1932–1952* (Urbana, 1978), pp. 268–269.

10. See NARS, *Documents Selected from German Foreign Office Records* (hereafter referred to as DSGFOR), T-120 series, roll 691, frames 312342 and 312343.

11. See ibid., and NARS, R.G. 84, 820.02, FMG-1, box 53, *Interrogation of Freiherr von Schoen,* January 24, 1946, pp. 2–3.

12. See NARS, R.G. 59, 862.20210/1324, personal cable no. 19, p. 1.

13. Our view of the Ríos government, its party problems, and wobbly support was formed while reading Drake, *Socialism and Populism in Chile,* pp. 256–258; Bernales, *El Partido Radical,* pp. 171–195; Frederick M. Nunn, *The Military in Chilean History: Essays in Civil-Military Relations: 1810–1973* (Albuquerque, 1976), pp. 262–263; Arturo Olivarria Bravo, *Chile entre dos Allessandri: Memorias Políticas* (Santiago, 1965), vol. 2, pp. 3–48; and Frederick B. Pike, *Chile and the United States: 1880–1962: Emergence of Chile's Social Crisis and the Challenge to United States Diplomacy* (South Bend, 1963), pp. 247–248. The best source, however, is the still little known—see NARS, R.G. 226, written by "X," OSS 19655, *Recent Developments Since the Ascension of President Ríos,* pp. 1–9.

14. Strong evidence of this conclusion is seen in NARS, R.G. 59, 825.00/1850, no. 3117, pp. 1–2, and R.G. 226, no. 1306, R. and A. Report, no. 610, *Factors Influencing Chile's Policy Toward the Axis,* pp. 1–5. In his letter of June 24, 1976, to Prof. Leslie B. Rout, Jr., Ambassador Donald Heath argues that, in 1942, there was not a single major politician in Chile who did not favor an international policy of neutrality.

15. Concerning the Japanese threat, see NARS, R.G. 38, Office of the Chief of Naval Operations, entry 49, book 1, folder: *Chile-General Hemisphere Defense, Staff Conversations and Related Correspondence,* May 1940 to March 1942, ONI, no. 2804, from naval attaché, December 30, 1941, n.p.

16. Evidence of this assertion is from the Claude Bowers papers, Indiana University, Bloomington, Indiana, *Mss. II*, letter to Sumner Welles, December 23, 1941, pp. 1–3, and letter to Welles, February 4, 1942, pp. 1–2.

17. See NARS, R.G. 165, box 970, folio: *Chile-Submarines: 4180–31*, Report of Colonel John Wooten to MID, June 27, 1942, pp. 2–3. Also, letter to Professor Rout from Ambassador Heath, June 24, 1976. As for Bowers's belief that patience and an absence of pressure would cause the Chileans to recognize some nebulous moral responsibility as a democratic Western Hemisphere state, see Bowers, *Mss. II*, letter to Sumner Welles, March 16, 1942, pp. 1–2, and letter to Sumner Welles, April 16, 1942, pp. 1–3.

18. Concerning Welles's opposition to the latter as ambassador to Chile, plus the need for southern democratic support, which was a major reason FDR made the appointment, see letter to Professor Rout from Ambassador Heath, June 24, 1976. See also NARS, R.G. 59, 825.00/1598, p. 6, for Bonsal on Bowers.

19. NARS, R.G. 59, 825.00/1599, p. 1. See also unnumbered confidential memorandum from Welles to Duggan attached to this document, as well as the note from FDR sanctioning this action.

20. For these figures, see NARS, R.G. 165, box 985, MID, Special Study Group Report, January 14, 1942, *Axis Propaganda and Activities in Latin America*, n.p.

21. NARS, R.G. 226, OSS, CID, no. 24520, p. 1. See also letter, Kapitän zur See a.D. Herbert Wichmann to Professor Rout, March 30, 1983.

22. Interview, Santiago, Chile, August 31, 1978, Professor Rout with retired Chilean diplomat, Tobias Barros Álvarez. This gentleman was the son of Tobias Barros Ortíz, the last Chilean ambassador to Nazi Germany and first cousin of Ernesto Barros Jarpa. Álvarez had talked of these events with Barros Jarpa and other Chilean diplomats of the period, and noted Ríos's attitude. A further indication of Ríos's anger and resentment of U.S. pressure is directly indicated in the work of his biographers. See Luís Palma Zúñiga and Julio Iglesias Meléndez, *Presencia de Juan Antonio Ríos* (Santiago, 1957), pp. 157–161.

23. NARS, R.G. 165, box 494, Chile: G-2 *Regional File, 1933–1944, Chile 5900–5940*, Military Attaché Col. Wendell Johnson to MID, May 29, 1943, pp.1–2. This was the MID copy of the report.

24. Ibid., p. 2.

25. See NARS, R.G. 862.20210/2640, no. 1947, p. 1.

26. See NARS, R.G. 59, 862.20210/2640, no. 1950, p. 1. The "attempt to wipe out all democratic institutions" refers to Bowers's belief that a plot was being hatched in Argentina to wipe out all democratic regimes existing in Latin America.

27. NARS, R.G. 59, 862.20225/5-1546, p. 1.

28. This conclusion is concurred with in U.S. Department of the Army, Center for Military History, Washington, D.C., Historical Section, Caribbean Defense Command, *Chile and the War Effort*, 8-2.8, B.E., C-1 (Washington, 1946), pp. 1–3.

29. Schulz-Hausmann's party designation was verified in República de Chile, Dirección General de Investigaciones e Identificación, *Informe Sobre Actividades Nazis en Chile* (hereafter referred to as DGII, *Informe*), vol. 1 (volumes are irregularly titled and numbered), pp. 12–13. For the background of Schulz-Hausmann, see NARS, R.G. 319, *German Espionage in Latin America* (hereafter referred to as *GELA*) (Washington, D.C., 1946), p. 101. On his return as an agent and evidence of the sum carried, see NARS, R.G. 165, MID, *Axis Espionage and Propaganda in Latin America* (Washington, D.C., 1946), p. 31.

30. The escape operation of the seven steamers is described in NARS, R.G. 59, 862.20210/12-1445, p. 12, and 862.20210/9-346, pp. 3–6.

31. See NARS, R.B. 59, 862.20210/9-346, pp. 3–4, and R.G. 226, OSS II, 10837-C, serial 64-42, pp. 1–2.

32. The sources for the *Graf Spee* crew escape operation are NARS, R.G. 59, 862.20235/4-1046, no. 2540, pp.1–2, and R.G. 165, box 976 (no document number), *Clandestine German Radio PYL, November 26, 1942*, pp. 5–6. For a Chilean perspective, see DGII, *Informe*, vol. 1, pp. 14–17.

33. NARS, R.G. 59, 862.20225/155, pp. 1–2, and 862.20235/4-1046, no. 2540, p. 2.

34. For names of these escaping officers, consult Sir. E. Millington-Drake, ed., *The Drama of Graf Spee and the Battle of the Plate* (London, 1964), pp. 385, 390, and 473–480.

35. About these shipments from Chile, see NARS, R.G. 165 (Suitland, Maryland), G-2, *Chile Regional File, 1933–44,* box 494, naval attaché report dated July 24, 1943, p. 1.

36. About the critical nature of platinum for the production of war-related items, and the German need for it, see NARS, R.G. 59, 740.00112, *Platinum*/18A, p. 3. On the value of the shipments and the $7.80 figure, consult 740.00112, *Platinum*/1-3144, p. 1. A one-pound package (453.6 grams = 1 pound), at $7.00 a gram, was worth about $3,175. Thus, 25 pounds would have been worth more than $79,000. At 1980s prices, the value of these shipments would have been more than $400,000.

37. The friction between Schulz-Hausmann and Niebuhr is described in NARS, R.G. 59, 862.20210/9-346, p. 3.

38. Ibid., pp. 3–5. For the *Graf Spee* sailor escape, and the steamer escape, Niebuhr received the War Service Cross, Second Class, with Swords. Schulz-Hausmann received only the War Service Medal.

39. See NARS, R.G. 89, 862.20210/2010, p. 4, and *GELA*, pp. 67–68. U.S. sources never doubted Schulz-Hausmann had continued his espionage involvement, but they failed to explain what he did to assist German intelligence while in Argentina. Compare with La República de la Argentina, Ministerio de los Relaciones Exteriores e Culto, *Guerra entre Estados Unidos y los Paises del Eje,* vol. 20, dossier 26, no. 273, *Policia Federal-Coordinación Federal,* p. 10. The Argentine police never proved that Schulz-Hausmann had been involved in any German intelligence operations after he became a resident of their country.

40. For the German name of the organization operating in Chile and the transmitter it operated, see NARS, R.G. 242, *Records of Abwehrstellen Bremen,* ML-172, reel 24, n.p. The first relevant data on PYL was found in FDRL, Franklin D. Roosevelt Papers (hereafter referred to as FDRP), OF-10B, box 37, *Radio Group PYL-REW,* pp. 9–17.

41. See, for example, NARS, R.G. 242, ML-171a, reel 23, n.p., and *GELA,* p. 101.

42. On the development of the radio station PYL, slightly contradictory stories are found in NARS, R.G. 59, 862.20210/9-346, p. 4, and in 862.20210/11-2246, no. 7839, p. 6. The latter source identifies Blume as the builder of the transmitter. See also NARS, R.G. 173, RID, box 5, *Testimony of G. E. Sterling,* part 1, p. 20.

43. A discussion of atmospheric conditions and the problems of transmitting from Chile are discussed in NARS, R.G. 59, 862.20210/11-2246, no. 7839, p. 6. According to Maj. Ludwig von Bohlen, the transmitter could only be used effectively during certain seasons.

44. See NARS, R.G. 59, 862.20210/9-346, p. 4.

45. The data on the number of messages sent and the number received over the PYL-REW circuit was supplied in a letter from Roger L. Young, FBI, assistant director in charge, Office of Congressional and Public Affairs, to Professor Rout, July 23, 1981. It should be noted that these dates differ somewhat from German sources, which give the dates of the first and last messages received by Ast Hamburg as April 18, 1941, and June 6, 1942. See NARS, R.G. 242, ML-172, reel 24, n.p. FDRL, FDRP, OF-10B, box 37, *German Clandestine Transmitters in Latin America,* p. 9, indicates that the first PYL message intercepted by U.S. sources occurred on April 28, 1941.

46. The books used in the coding procedure are noted in a letter from Roger L. Young to Professor Rout, July 23, 1981.

47. For the activities of these four men, see *GELA,* pp. 102–111, and NARS, R.G. 60, box 1, *Official Record of the Consultative Visit of the Emergency Advisory Committee for Political Defense in the United States* (hereafter referred to as box 1, *Record—Emergency Advisory Committee*), envelope 1, resolution 14, pp. 92–93 and 100. A good discussion of the activities of these men is found in República de Chile, Dirección General de Investigaciones e Identificación, *Proceso seguido en Valparaiso, conocido con el nombre de PYL Ano: 1942* (hereafter referred to as DGII, *Proceso seguido en Valparaiso*), vol.11, pp. 29–42.

48. Reiners explained why he joined the Abwehr and his financial hardship in a letter to Professor Rout, October 15, 1978, p. 1. Reiners's story is detailed in *GELA*, pp. 106–107, and in box 1, *Record—Emergency Advisory Committee*, pp. 91, 92, and 100.

49. About the activities of Juan Aguilera and his explanation of the same, see NARS, R.G. 165, box 967, *Clandestine German Radio "PYL"—October 31, 1942* (unnumbered document), p. 5, and FDRL, FDRP, OF-10B, box 38, no. 2427-A, letter from J. Edgar Hoover to Harry L. Hopkins, October 13, 1942, p. 3.

50. See *GELA*, p. 108, box 1, *Record—Emergency Advisory Committee*, pp. 90–91, and especially NARS, R.G. 84 (Suitland, Maryland), no. 64-3112, *Radio Station PYL-Chile*, J. Edgar Hoover to Assistant Chief of Staff, G-2, January 4, 1946, pp. 2 and 4.

51. See NARS, R.G. 59, 862.20210/2715, p. 1, 862.20210/2247, pp. 1–3, R.G. 165, box 967, *Clandestine German Radio "PYL"—November 6, 1942*, pp. 14–15, and *GELA*, pp. 104–105.

52. A confession explicitly outlining Barckhahn's activities is found in DGII, *Proceso sequido en Valparaíso*, vol. 11, pp. 8–16. About Knoll, see República de Chile, Dirección General de Investigaciones e Identificación, *Declaraciones de los implicados en Proceso "Contra Timmerman y otros"* (hereafter referred to as DGII, *Declaraciones de los implicados*), vol. 43, n.p.

53. Bohlen was quite explicit about his desire to escape action on the Russian front, and his use of friends to obtain the Chilean attaché post. See NARS, R.G. 59, 862.20210/11-2246, no. 7839, pp. 1–2.

54. Information concerning Lt. Col. Ernst Arno Kleyenstueber (chief of I-L, Abteilung I, Berlin) was provided by a letter from Roger Young to Professor Rout, October 8, 1981. The connection with Niebuhr is detailed in NARS, R.G. 59, 862.20210/9-346, p. 4.

55. The friction between Schulz-Hausmann and Niebuhr has been previously detailed. See also NARS, R.G. 59, 862.20210/9-346, pp. 4–5.

56. Bohlen describes his role of PYL ring financier and how he brought $400,000 into Chile in NARS, R.G. 59, 862.20210/11-2246, pp. 2–3 and 7–8, and 862.20210/9-346, pp. 5, 9–10, and 16.

57. DGII, *Informe*, vol. 1, pp. 2, 11–17, lists party members, date of entry into the AO, and the place of enlistment.

58. About business orders and the need for information concerning mineral shipments, see NARS, R.G. 59, 862.20210/11-2246, p. 10.

59. Concerning messages sent from Mexico, Shanghai, the U.S.A., and other areas to "V-Post Señorita," see NARS, R.G. 59, 862.20225/5-2845, pp. 5–8 and 15–16. Consult also NARS, R.G. 84, no. 64-3112, *Radio Station PYL-Chile*, Hoover to Assistant Chief of Staff, G-2, January 4, 1946, pp. 7–8.

60. We are grateful to the FBI, which supplied copies of these messages. Excerpts from roughly 20 percent of these messages can also be found in box 1, *Record—Emergency Advisory Group*, pp. 100–103.

61. The story of the detection of the PYL-REW circuits is related in NARS, R.G. 173, RID, box 5, *Testimony of G. E. Sterling*, pp. 14–15.

62. Samples of these decoded messages are found in NARS, R.G. 59, 862.20210/629, p. 2 and 862.20210/678, p.2.

63. Concerning the political problems and the instability of the Popular Front government of Aguirre Cerda in 1938–41, see Great Britain, Public Record Office (hereafter referred to as PRO), F-0371, 24194-06063, Registry A no. 3323G, pp. 112–113, and Bowers, *Mss. II*, letter to Sumner Welles, March 14, 1941. There are several other notable sources dealing with Popular Front politics. See Ernest Halperin, *Nationalism and Communism in Chile* (Cambridge, 1965) pp. 42–52, and Stevenson, *The Chilean Popular Front*, pp. 57–119. The most interesting source was a letter from Sir Richard Allen to Professor Rout, September 20, 1977. Sir Richard, a well-known scholar, was a diplomat in the embassy in Santiago, 1938–42. He referred to Aguirre Cerda's administration as well-meaning but unfortunate.

64. Corroboration of Communist, Socialist, and Radical party behavior in regard to the war is found in República de Chile, DGII, *Informe*, vol. 1, pp. 33–35, and Bowers, *Mss. II*, letter

to Sumner Welles, October 22, 1941. See also NARS, R.G. 59, 862.20210/882, p. 1. Bowers goes into further detail (and adds a dash of vituperation) in *Chile Through Embassy Windows: 1939–1953* (New York, 1958), pp. 64–65.

65. See República de Chile, DGII, *Informe,* vol. 1, pp. 12–13, and Great Britain, PRO, F-0371, 24194-01906, Registry A no. 3390/1/51, p. 221.

66. The first secret talks between U.S. military and naval officers (who arrived in mufti) and their Chilean counterparts took place in June 1940. See Bowers, *Mss. II,* letter, Franklin D. Roosevelt to Claude Bowers, June 11, 1940. The September 1940 events related here are from NARS, R.G. 165, folio 21, A-ALG-1/A-82/EN3-11/EF-15, section 4, *Chile,* pp. 10–16. Consult, in addition, NARS, R.G. 38, Office of the Chief of Naval Operations, E-49, August 23, 1946, book 2, folder: *Chile-General-Hemisphere Defense, Staff Conversations and Related Correspondence,* pp. 11–17.

67. For Aguirre Cerda's objections, see NARS, R.G. 165, folio 2, 2-ALG-1/A-82/EN-3-11/EF-15, section 4, *Chile,* p. 16.

68. For the Berle-Bowers-Chilean government negotiations on assistance to the DGII, consult NARS, R.G. 59, 862.20210/427, p. 1, and Bowers, *Mss. II,* letter to Sumner Welles, April 16, 1941.

69. On the dual policy regarding espionage, see NARS, R.G. 59, 701.6224/24, no. 355, p. 1. Another source on the Aguirre Cerda regime's basic refusal to publicly recognize the presence of German spies in the country is Bowers, *Chile Through Embassy Windows,* pp. 63–64.

70. The October 1940 initiation of SIS operations in Chile was affirmed in a letter from Inspector Homer Boynton, FBI, to Professor Rout, August 8, 1979.

71. Robert Wall received visa no. 162. He was listed simply as an attaché. See República de Chile, Ministerio de Relaciones Exteriores (R.R.E.E.), *Oficios recibidos de la Embajada de Chile en los Estados Unidos del 201 al 400-1941,* n.p.

72. Concerning the period between September 1941 and February 1942, Source H, who was in Chile during this period, noted: "Hell, the politicians were too afraid to take any chances that might get them bounced out.... After Aguirre (Cerda) died, everything stopped anyway. We soon realized that nothing was going to be decided by anybody until after the election."

73. The story of the provision of special military aid for Chile outside the normal lend-lease channel is detailed in NARS, R.G. 226, 2430C, box 148, pp. 1–2, which reports that the first military equipment arrived on March 16, 1942. According to República de Chile, Ministerio de R.R.E.E., *Archivo Confidencial-Sección Clave, Oficios Recibidos-Embajada en E.E.U.U. —1942,* no. 3410/76, Michels to the Foreign Ministry, June 4, 1942, n.p., the Chilean ambassador reports that the agreement was concerted on March 3, 1942. It was Sumner Welles who, for some unknown reason, did not wish the agreement announced until March 20, 1942.

74. Juan Ríos confirmed this, without giving a specific day, in Bowers, *Mss. II,* Memorandum of Conversation with President Juan Ríos and Foreign Minister Ernesto Barros Jarpa, May 18, 1942, p. 2. Specific evidence from Chilean sources that joint surveillance and other activities took place in March 1942, is found in DGII, *Proceso seguido en Valparaíso,* vol. 11, appendix 2, *Vigilancias V-1, Informe* no. 13, p. 237, *Vigilancias V-3, Informe* no. 14, p. 238, *Vigilancias V-4, Informe* no. 4, p. 239, and *Vigilancias V-5, Informe* no. 6, p. 240.

75. DGII, *Proceso seguido en Valparaíso, Vigilancias V-3, Informe* no. 14, p. 238, specifically notes that Blume's house was searched and two radio antennas were found. No mention of a search warrant is made here. See also ibid., *Vigilancias V-1, Informe* no. 25, p. 255, which relates the story of the surveillance and check of mail from certain post office boxes. Specific recognition on the part of the U.S. officials of illegal actions being carried on in the PYL investigation is found in NARS, R.G. 59, 862.20225/765, p. 1.

76. For DeBardeleben's arrival and work, República de Chile, Ministerio de R.R.E.E., *Oficios recibidos de la Embajada de Chile en los Estados Unidos del 201 al 400-1942,* no. 1770/256, Michels to the Foreign Ministry, April 16, 1942, n.p., and NARS, R.G. 59,

862.20210/1003, p. 1, 862.20210/1103, p. 1, and R.G. 173, RID, box 5, *Testimony of G. E. Sterling*, pp. 19–20.

77. See NARS, R.G. 59, 862.20210/1390, pp. 1–2.

78. See NARS, R.G. 59, 862.20210/1665, p. 3. On the use of the Zeller residence for clandestine broadcasting, see 802.20210/2857, pp. 66–67, and R.G. 173, RID, box 5, *Testimony of G. E. Sterling*, p. 21.

79. For the quote, see NARS, R.G. 59, 862.20210/1390, p. 1. About finding the transmitting sites, see 862.20210/1655, enclosure 1.

80. NARS, R.G. 59, 862.20210/9-346, p. 12.

81. That signals by Szeraws were transmitted until June 15, 1942, was verified in a letter from Roger L. Young to Professor Rout, July 23, 1981.

82. About Bowers's declarations, Hull's responses, etc., see NARS, R.G. 59, 862.20210/1390, pp. 1–2, 862.20210/1930, p. 1.

83. The Zeller affair is reported in full in NARS, R.G. 173, RID, box 5, *Testimony of G. E. Sterling*, p. 21. The quoted material is also on the same page.

84. Ibid., and NARS, R.G. 59, 862.20210/2857, p. 66.

85. See NARS, R.G. 60, box 1, *Record—Advisory Committee*, pp. 85–104, for the memorandum. The quote is found on p. 96. A Spanish language copy of this memorandum was found in the Archives of the Chilean Foreign Office. The folio had no number, but was marked "1942—Espionaje Alemán en Chile—Conf." In *Chile Through Embassy Windows*, p. 107, Bowers gives the FMK Valparaíso station call letters as PSY [*sic*]. In addition, on p. 108, he fails to mention that the June 30, 1942, memorandum was actually the work of Legal Attaché Robert Wall.

86. The dismantling of the PYL transmitter is described in NARS, R.G. 59, 862.20210/2857, pp. 45–46 and 48–50. Consult, in addition, R.G. 165, box 962, *Clandestine German Radio—PYL—October 31, 1942: Statement of Arnold Barckhahn Gutman*, pp. 2–3, and FDRL, FDRP, box 38, OF-10B, 2427-A, memorandum, J. Edgar Hoover to Harry L. Hopkins, October 13, 1942, pp. 4–5.

87. NARS, R.G. 59, 862.20210/9-346, pp. 5 and 12, and 862.20210/11-2246, p. 8.

88. Observations of Source H who further observed that "we believed that if this [spy memorandum] didn't smoke them [the Chilean authorities] out, nothing would."

89. Evidence of the July 8, 1942, delivery of *German Espionage Agents in Chile* to the minister of the interior is found in República de Chile, Ministerio de R.R.E.E., *Archivo Confidencial-Oficios-Canje Diplomático: Chileno-E.E.U.U.-1942,* no. 36, July 8, 1942, E. Barros Jarpa to the Minister of the Interior, p. 1.

90. The conclusion of Bowers was that a "general statement of . . . illegal [espionage] activities would constitute a sufficient explanation . . . ," p. 2. The events of the July 17, 1942, meeting are listed in NARS, R.G. 59, 810.74/368, no. 1120, p. 1.

91. NARS, R.G. 59, 810.74/379, p. 1.

92. See NARS, R.G. 59, FW 862.20225/765, p. 2.

93. Ibid., p. 3.

94. República de Chile, Ministerio de R.R.E.E., *Archivo Confidencial-Sección Clave, Oficios Recibidos-Embajada en E.E.U.U.-1942,* no. 3628/85, June 18, 1942, Michels to the Foreign Ministry, pp. 1–7. The quoted statement is from p. 7.

95. Bohlen's explanation concerning PYL's disbandment and his own actions are explained in NARS, R.G. 59, 862.20210/11-2246, pp. 7–9. The quote is on p. 8.

96. About Mexican cooperation, see a letter from Inspector Boynton to Professor Rout, October 27, 1977. The arrangements in Brazil are discussed in NARS, R.G. 84 (Suitland, Maryland), 820.02 no. 10284, *Embassy Accomplishments Reports in Concessions and Privileges Gained from Brazil in Matters Relating to Hemisphere Defense, United States and United Nations Military and Naval Operations and Other Things*, pp. 15–16.

97. The proposal is discussed in detail in NARS, R.G. 59, 810.74/384, pp. 1–2.

98. NARS, R.G. 59, 810.74/391, N.P.O.-Confidential File no. 181, p. 1 and a letter from Roger L. Young to Professor Rout, October 8, 1981. Young disclosed that the intercepts were made and that the SIS/Chile had a special informant inside Transradio Chilena.

99. NARS, R.G. 59, 862.20210/11-2246, pp. 2 and 7, 810.74/346, no. 203, pp. 1–2, and 810.74/363A, no. 296, pp. 1–2.

100. NARS, R.G. 59, 810.74/381, enclosure 1, no. 393G, p. 1.

101. Ibid., enclosure 3, p. 3.

102. NARS, R.G. 59, 862.20210/2141, pp. 1–3.

103. Ibid., p. 3. See also 810.74/368, no. 1008, p. 1. The proposal was obviously discussed prior to July 15 because the State Department's instructions to Bowers expressing U.S. dissatisfaction with the proposal are found in NARS, R.G. 59, 810.74/346, no. 203, pp. 2–3. See also Bowers, *Mss. II*, Memorandum of Conversation with Señor Rodolfo Michels, July 22, 1942.

104. See NARS, R.G. 59, 810.74/408, no. 4095, p. 1, for the August discussions between Bowers and Barros Jarpa. Executive Decree 4516 (Ministry of the Interior) was issued August 12, 1942. The decree is vague enough to allow almost any interpretation. See República de Chile, *Diario Oficial de la República de Chile-1942*, vol. 65, section 3, July–September 1942, *Gazeta*, August 17, no. 19335, p. 2201.

105. Regarding U.S. commercial complaints and Chilean lassitude in preventing the sending of coded cables, despite Decree 4516, see NARS, R.G. 59, 810.74/368, no. 1005, pp. 1–2, and no. 1092, pp. 1–2.

106. See NARS, R.G. 59, 810.74/454, no. 1449, p. 1, and Bowers, *Mss. II*, letter to Welles, September 9, 1942, p. 1. Our suspicion is that the Chilean government promulgated the decree essentially to see whether the Axis embassies would obey it. It was another gesture designed to buy time.

107. NARS, R.G. 59, 810.74/480, pp. 1–3.

108. The beginning of negotiations with Cable and Wireless, Ltd., and RCA is found in NARS, R.G. 59, 810.74/288, pp. 1–2. The quoted material is from NARS, R.G. 59, 810.74/355A, no. 3046, p. 1.

109. See NARS, R.G. 59, 810.74/235, pp. 1–2, 810.74/384, pp. 1–4, and 810.74/412, pp. 1–3.

110. RCA seems to have gotten cold feet during early September 1942. For State Department threats, see NARS, R.G. 59, 810.74/412-2/5, pp. 1–2, and 810.74/410-3/6, pp. 1–2.

111. See NARS, R.G. 59, 810.74/496, pp. 1–2; 810.74/504, no. 163, p. 1, and no. 1607, p. 1; and 810.74/509, no. 1620, p. 1, and no. 1174, p. 1.

112. For the September 17 reply, see NARS, R.G. 59, 810.74/480, pp. 1–3. The quotation is on p. 2.

113. The hectic events of September 30–October 8, 1942, are delineated in detail in NARS, R.G. 59, 810.74/496, pp. 1–2; 810.74/498, pp. 1–4; 810.74/506A, no. 1891, pp. 1–2; 810.74/508, no. 1914, p. 1; 810.74/513, no. 1633, pp. 1–2; 810.74/518, no. 1652, pp. 1–2; and 810.74/520, pp. 1–2.

114. Regarding the Axis concern and quick recovery, see NARS, *DSGFOR*, T-120 series, roll 225, frames 171470-171499. Regarding sending cables via Argentina, see 171494, 171498, and 171499.

115. Bowers, *Mss. II*, letter from Franklin D. Roosevelt to Claude Bowers for presentation to Juan Antonio Ríos (letter dated August 11, 1942). Evidence that the pledge was given to Ríos is in NARS, R.G. 59, 810.74/485, no. 1581, section 2, p. 1.

116. Luning's agent number was found in U.S. Naval Department, Naval Historical Center, Washington Navy Yard, *Reports to Intelligence Sub-Office Bremen*, TM-15, reel 22, n.p.

117. The story of Luning's activity and his fate is related in *GELA*, pp. 195–196.

118. See ibid., p. 196, and FDRL, FDRP, OF-10B, no. 2262-G, box 34, J. Edgar Hoover to Harry L. Hopkins, October 13, 1942, pp. 1–2, and ibid., OF–10B, no. 2427-A, box 38, J. Edgar Hoover to Harry Hopkins, October 13, 1942, pp. 2, 4, and 7.

119. Ibid., OF-10B, no. 2258-A, box 33, J. Edgar Hoover to Harry L. Hopkins, October 2, 1942, p. 2.

120. See DGII, *Proceso seguido en Valparaíso,* vol. 11, pp. 2–4, which fails to denote any action was taken toward determining the veracity of the memorandum in question until October 10, 1942. See also República de Chile, Ministerio de Relaciones Exteriores, *Embajada en Washington-Oficios confidenciales, enviados y recibidos-1942,* copy 1, no. 331, November 4, 1942, pp. 3–4.

121. See FDRL, FDRP, OF-10B, box 34, no. 2263-A, J. Edgar Hoover to Harry L. Hopkins, October 16, 1942, pp. 1–2, which indicates Morales's dislike for Barros Jarpa. See also NARS, R.G., 711.25/10-2442, p. 2, which speaks of his ambition, youth, his ties with Ríos, and his perceived "instability." See also Great Britain, PRO, FO-371-30454-01999, A-3731/18/9, no. 50, enclosure, n.p., which gives background on Morales.

122. Indeed, Morales would definitely emerge as the strongest cabinet officer. See Great Britain, PRO, FO-371-22919-02057, A-1552/1552/51, p. 2, which indicates Morales's rise especially after Barros Jarpa's departure. See also Zúñiga and Meléndez, *Presencia de Juan Antonio Ríos,* pp. 75–86. Between April 1942 and April 1944, Ríos reshuffled his cabinet six times. Morales was the only man who was a member of all six.

123. On the Luning-Klaiber connection described here, see NARS, R.G. 59, 862.20225/718, no. 1694, section 1, pp. 1–2, and section 2, p. 1. The quote on the degree of the interrogation is from section 1, p. 1. The second quote is from section 2, p. 1.

124. See NARS, R.G. 59, 862.20210/11-2246, p. 8.

125. See NARS, R.G. 59, FW 740.0011 European War 1939/24637, p. 1. For the articles, see *El Mercurio,* Santiago, Chile, October 1 and 2, 1942, and *El Nacional,* Santiago, Chile, October 2, 1942.

126. See NARS, R.G. 59, 862.20225/715, p. 1, and 810.74/498, pp.4–5. Evidence that these materials were kept secret is found in NARS, R.G. 60, box 1, *Emergency—Advisory Committee,* p. 85.

127. Morales proceeded to mix the PYL and Luning cases together. Neither Luning nor anyone else involved in that case used a radio. See NARS, R.G. 59, FW 740.0011 European War/24637, pp. 1–2; FDRL, FDRP, OF-10B, no. 2427-A, box 38, p. 7; and Bowers, *Mss. II,* letter to Sumner Welles, October 5, 1942.

128. NARS, R.G. 59, FW 740.0011 European War/24637, p. 2.

129. The United States Department of State, *The Department of State Bulletin* 7, no. 177 (October 10, 1942), p. 810.

130. See NARS, R.G. 226, 24154-C, serial 695, p. 1.

131. Claude Bowers gave his frank views of Welles's speech, and admitted that he had received no advance warning, in Bowers, *Chile Through Embassy Windows,* pp. 109–10. See also NARS, R.G. 59, 711.25/10-2442, p. 2.

132. On the petroleum, lend-lease, and loan problems, see República de Chile, Ministerio de Relaciones Exteriores, *Archivo Confidencial-Sección Clave, Oficios Recibidos-Embajada en EEUU-1942,* no. 5037/132, October 16, 1942, Michels to the Foreign Ministry, pp. 11–12, and Bowers, *Mss. II,* letter from Franklin D. Roosevelt to Bowers, October 13, 1942.

133. República de Chile, Ministerio de Relaciones Exteriores, *Archivo Confidencial-Sección Clave, Oficios Recibidos-Embajada en EEUU-1942,* no. 5037/132, October 16, 1942, Michels to the Foreign Ministry, pp. 9–10. Quotation is from p. 10.

134. See NARS, R.G. 59, 862.20225/765, pp. 2–3.

135. See *El Mercurio,* Santiago, Chile, October 23, 1942.

136. DGII, *Proceso seguido en Valparaíso,* no. 90–42, vol. 11, no. 3335, Confidencial, October 23, 1942, order from Alfredo Rodríquez Mac-Iver, police superintendent of Valparaíso, to arrest Arnold Barckhahn, Bruno Dittmann, and Hans Hofbauer.

137. See República de Chile, Ministerio de Relationes Exteriores, *Embajada en Washington, Oficios confidenciales enviados y recibidos-1942,* copy no. 331, November 4, 1942, p. 3, for the quoted material.

138. On the virtual control of the CPD by the United States, see NARS, R.G. 59, 862.20210/2184, no. 108, p. 1. That the CPD would do essentially what Washington desired it to do is implied strongly in 862.20210/1996, letter from Sumner Welles to Jefferson Caffery, p. 1.

139. See, in particular, NARS, R.G. 59, 862.20225/761, no. 1892, section 2, pp. 1–4. Morales made it clear that the Ríos government considered the publishing of the document by the CPD a most unfriendly act. Ibid., section 2, p. 2.

140. That Welles was specifically talking about the coded cable traffic rather than the already terminated clandestine radio traffic is stated in Laurence Duggan, *The Americas: The Search for Hemispheric Security* (New York, 1944), p. 90. It is confirmed in Great Britain, PRO, FO-371-30438-07013, no. 10116/52/9, no. 153, section 3, p. 1.

141. See NARS, R.G. 59, 711.25/277, no. 4915 enclosure, p. 1. See also R.G. 59, 725.00/34, Memorandum of Conservation, by Acting Secretary of State Welles with Chilean ambassador, Rodolfo Michels, pp. 1–3. Note that while Welles originally utilized the Luning case as justification (711.25/284A-Circular Telegram, pp. 1–4), Spruille Braden demonstrated that such an explanation was totally useless, since Luning had no radio and he received and sent no radio messages to German sources.

142. See NARS, R.G. 59, 711.25/10-2442, p. 2. In a letter to Professor Rout, June 24, 1976, Ambassador Heath stated categorically that this was a major intention of Welles in making the speech. Ambassador Rodolfo Michels came to exactly the same conclusion. See República de Chile, Ministerio de Relaciones Exteriores, *Archivo Confidencial-Sección Clave, Oficios Recibidos Embajada en E.E.U.U.-1942*, no. 5037/132, October 16, 1942, Michels to the Foreign Ministry, p. 9.

143. This conclusion was also drawn by Sir Charles Orde. See Great Britain, PRO, FO 371-33919-02057, A1502/1552/51, p. 2.

144. NARS, R.G. 226, 24154-C, serial 695, pp. 1–2.

145. See NARS, R.G. 59, 711.25/277, no. 4915, enclosure, pp. 1–2. Other indications of Barros Jarpa's press campaign against U.S. policy, and Sumner Welles in particular, are found in Bowers, *Mss. II*, letter to Welles, November 7, 1942, p. 1.

146. For Orde's insightful analysis, see Great Britain, PRO, FO-371-30438-07013, no. 10116/52/9, no. 153, section 3, pp. 1–2.

147. The connection between the memorandum and the Law of External Security, Decree no. 7401 is demonstrated in Great Britain, PRO, FO-371-33919-02057, A1502/1552/51, section 1, p. 4.

148. In December 1942 Juan Ríos sent a small delegation to Washington to negotiate concessions in exchange for Chile's breaking of relations. The United States refused to consider making any concessions. See NARS, R.G. 59, 711.25/288A, p. 1, 711.25/309, pp. 1–2, 711.25/310, pp. 1–2, and 711.24/341, pp. 1–3.

149. Bowers, *Mss. II*, letter, Laurence Duggan to Bowers, January 21, 1943, p. 1.

150. NARS, R.G. 173, box 60, RID, folder: *Argentina*, "Data Revealing the Power of German Espionage," Frederick B. Lyon to G. E. Sterling, June 9, 1945, p. 7.

151. See *GELA*, p. 108, and DGII, *Proceso seguido en Valparaiso*, vol. 11, p. 24. Additional information regarding Reiners after he departed Chile was supplied in a letter from Heinrich (signed Enrique) Reiners, Santiago, Chile, to Professor Rout, October 15, 1978.

152. On Hans Blume, see NARS, R.G. 59, 862.20210/9-346, p. 8, and FDRL, FDRP, OF-10B, no. 2269-B, box 34, pp. 1–2. Blume's escape into Argentina is best described in 862.20210/7-2845, p. 1.

153. About the escapades of Knoll and his mistress, and his connection with German espionage, see NARS, R.G. 59, 862.20225/7-1245, p. 1, and 862.20210/2857, pp. 41–43.

154. See NARS, *DSGFOR*, T-120 series, roll 750, frames 355181-355182. The captured document was Johannes Szeraws's diary. See R.G. 165, box 967 (document marked *326, MID, 201, Szeraws, Johannes 2-3-43)*, J. Edgar Hoover to Adolf A. Berle, February 3, 1943, n.p.

155. See NARS, R.G. 59, 862.20210/2857, pp. 46 and 47 and 66–68.

156. Ibid., p. 66. The SIS/Chile wanted the matter pressed, but the Chileans declined to do so.

157. Ibid., pp. 48–49.

158. DGII, *Proceso seguido en Valparaíso,* vol. 11, pp. 20–26.

159. See NARS, R.G. 59, 862.20210/2857, p. 74, and DGII, *Proceso seguido en Valparaíso,* vol. 11, pp. 8–12, with quotations from pp. 10–12.

160. See NARS, R.G. 59, 862.20210/2857, pp. 16–17.

161. We wish to express our thanks to Dr. Gisela von-Mühlenbrock, legal specialist at the Hispanic-American Law Library, James Madison Building, Washington, D.C., who took a good deal of time explaining to us the peculiar eccentricities of the Chilean legal system. An English language description of the powers of the justice of the court is found in NARS, R.G. 165, box 982, *Clandestine German Radio "PYL"—November 6, 1942,* p. 15.

162. NARS, R.G. 59, 862.20210/2857, p. 17, and DGII, *Proceso seguido en Valparaíso,* vol. 11, p. 92.

163. Ibid., pp. 48, 92, and 170.

164. Ibid., pp. 195–197.

165. Ibid., p. 92, and NARS, R.G. 59, 862.20210/2857, pp. 18, 19, 30–31, 36, 49, and 63. See also NARS, R.G. 165, box 982, *Clandestine German Radio "PYL"—October 31, 1942,* pp. 4–6, 9–10.

166. República de Chile, *Diario oficial de la República de Chile—1941,* vol. 64, part 2, no. 18.847, April 8, 1941, p. 1073.

167. NARS, R.G. 59, 862.20210/12-844, p. 2.

168. The U.S. position is explained in detail in NARS, R.G. 60, box 7, file: *Committee for Political Defense—Country Study: "Chile,"* by Karl Lowenstein, May 1943, pp. 7–10, 27–30. In particular, Lowenstein reviewed the Chilean legislation and concluded that Decree 6026 was "amply sufficient" (p. 7) for dealing with the espionage problem.

169. See NARS, R.G. 59, 862.20210/2122 1/2, p. 4, and 862.20210/2857, p. 17.

170. DGII, *Proceso seguido en Valparaíso,* vol. 11, pp. 201–202.

171. NARS, R.G. 59, 862.20210/2857, p. 18. The legal attaché's report also states that the German embassy made determined efforts to get Kettler out, for "it would appear that they feared that he might reveal other incriminating information if he were questioned under proper circumstances."

172. DGII, *Proceso seguido en Valparaíso,* vol. 11, p. 202.

173. NARS, R.G. 59, 862.20210/2715, p. 1.

174. See NARS, R.G. 59, 862.20210/2541, p. 1, for the quoted material, and pp. 1–2 for the other parts of Heath's scheme.

175. NARS, R.G. 59, 711.25/278, p. 1, for the quoted material. See 711.25/277, memorandum, pp. 1–2, and /278, p. 1, for the Hull-Fernández discussions.

176. República de Chile, Ministerio de R.R.E.E., *Archivo Confidencial-Oficios de la embajada en los Estados Unidos, 1° Semestre-1943,* no. 274/124, Michels to the Foreign Ministry, October 6, 1943.

177. For Rockwell's blast, see NARS, R.G. 59, 862.20225/983, p. 4.

178. Bowers's report of his session with Fernández is in NARS, R.G. 59, 862.20210/2715, pp. 1–2.

179. For the CPD report, see NARS, R.G. 60, box 3, folder: *Emergency Committee for Political Defense: Chile—Follow-up—General—Latin American Section,* pp. 1–6. The report was completed in March 1944 and directed to Bowers in crude form. The quote is from NARS, R.G. 59, 710 Consultation (3) A/693, p. 1, which is Bowers's paraphrase of the CPD report.

180. See NARS, R.G. 59, 711.25/288, p. 3.

181. See NARS, R.G. 59, 862.20210/2857, pp. 1–2. The quoted material is from p. 2.

182. See NARS, R.G. 59, 862.20210/2769, pp. 1–2, and 862.20210/2857, p. 2.

183. See República de Chile, DGII, *Ordenes del Ministro Señor Baquedano y Oficios dirigidos al mismo con motivo del proceso 'Contra Bernardo Timmerman y Otros* (hereafter referred to as DGII, *Ordenes del Ministro Señor Baquedano*),' 1944–1945, vol. 42, no. 100, Garreton to Baquedano, April 12, 1944, pp. 717–718. The order also called for the arrest of Schulz-Hausmann, "Victor Vougha," and four other persons who were involved in espionage in Chile in 1943–1944.

184. See *GELA*, p. 112, for the December 6, 1944, opinion and the January 9, 1945, appeals panel decision.

185. See NARS, R.G. 165, G-2 Intelligence Division, *Latin America—Geographic*, subject file: 1940–46, file 64, 3112, J. Edgar Hoover to Brig. Gen. Carter W. Clarke, assistant chief of staff, G-2, p. 1.

186. Ibid., pp. 1–2.

187. See Zúñiga and Meléndez, *Presencia de Juan Antonio Ríos*, pp. 157–161.

188. Ibid.

189. On the detection of PQZ, see NARS, R.G. 173, RID, box 5, *Testimony of G. E. Sterling*, p. 24, and R.G. 59, 862.20210/2729, p. 2. On the FBI laboratory's inability to decode the PQZ messages until May 1944, see letter from Roger L. Young to Professor Rout, July 23, 1981, pp. 1–2. See also NARS, R.G. 59, 862.20210/4-2944, memorandum, Fletcher Warren to Adolf A. Berle, p. 2.

190. Bohlen's acquisition of the June 30, 1942, document has been previously discussed. How he learned that his cables were being read was never explained. That he learned this is specifically stated in NARS, R.G. 59, 862.20210/11-2246, p. 16.

191. See a letter from Roger L. Young to Professor Rout, July 23, 1981, p. 2. As of May 1944, the FBI had translated five PQZ messages. An explanation of the ingenious PQZ coding scheme is found in Appendix A of this work.

192. The background of Ludwig von Bohlen is found in NARS, R.G. 59, 862.20210/9-346, pp. 1–3, and 862.20210/11-2246, pp. 1–3.

193. Concerning Heise's activities, see *GELA*, pp. 116–117.

194. Concerning "Ina" and "Dunkel," see Ibid., pp. 116–117. About Bohlen's relationship with the pair, and his views of their personalities, see R.G. 59, 862.20210/9-346, pp. 6–7, and 862.20210/11-2246, pp. 10–11.

195. See NARS, R.G. 59, 862.20210/9-346, p. 7, and *GELA*, pp. 118–119. The names of the persons enlisted and the explanations for what they did are found in DGII, *Declaraciones de los implicados*, vol. 43, Secret Memorandum, "Sobre situación de detenidos en el norte del pais en relación con el proceso que instruye el Ministro Señor Baquedano," n.p.

196. The background data on Kunsemüller noted here is from *GELA*, pp. 121–122, NARS, R.G. 59, 862.20210/2729, pp. 21–22, and 862.20210/3-2444, pp. 7–10. See also DGII, *Declaraciones de los implicados*, vol. 43, n.p.

197. This specific declaration is found in NARS, R.G. 59, 862.20210/3-2444, p. 10.

198. Information concerning the training of Kunsemüller, who his superiors were, and what section he was responsible to is from NARS, R.G. 59, 862.20210/3-2444, pp. 10–12, and especially from letters from Roger L. Young to Professor Rout, October 8 and December 10, 1981.

199. On the beginnings of the Kunsemüller-Bohlen relationship, see NARS, R.G. 59, 862.20210/9-346, pp. 5–6. Kunsemüller gives his views of these circumstances in 862.20210/3-2444, pp. 14–15. RID interception of the PYL messages of March 10, 1942, and the first NOI message is reported in NARS, R.G. 173, RID, box 5, *Testimony of G. E. Sterling*, pp. 23–24.

200. See República de Chile, Ministerio de Relaciones Exteriores, *Oficios recibidos de la embajada de Chile en los Estados Unidos, del I al 200-1942*, no. 369/79, file E2-21-11-5, January 9, 1942, Michels to the Foreign Ministry, n.p.

201. See República de Chile, DGII, *1° Instancia-Corregir conforme a cuaderno original del proceso* (hereafter referred to as DGII, *1° Instancia*), p. 1903-B. See also NARS, R.G. 59, 862.20210/2729, p. 8.

202. NARS, R.G. 59, 862.20210/3-2444, pp. 10 and 15, and NARS, R.G. 59, 862.20210/2729, pp. 5–6.

203. Sources such as *GELA*, p. 122, are rather confusing concerning Kunsemüller's army status. More complete information, as presented here, comes from a letter from Roger L. Young to Professor Rout, October 8, 1981.

204. The number of broadcasts made and other data on NOI-GES is from letters from Roger L. Young to Professor Rout, July 13, 1981, p. 2.

205. See NARS, R.G. 59, 862.20210/9-346, p. 6, 862.20210/3-2444, pp. 15–17, and 862.20210/11-2246, p. 8.

206. NARS, R.G. 59, 862.20210/11-2246, pp. 8–9. The quote is from 862.20210/9-346, p. 6.

207. Copies of the PYL intercepts were found misplaced in DGII, *Proceso Seguido en Valparaíso*, no. 90–42, vol. 11, but the Chilean police allowed Professor Rout to examine them. Copies of NOI-GES messages are found in 862.20210/3-2444, pp. 15–17. Only a few of the coded cables are available in R.G. 59, 810.74/381, enclosure 3, pp. 1–6.

208. Bernardo Timmerman's recruitment is discussed by Bohlen in NARS, R.G. 59, 862.20210/11-2246, p. 11. A fuller explanation is found in DGII, *1° Instancia*, vol. 1, pp. 1900-B, 1901-A, and 1902-B.

209. Bohlen speaks of these orders in NARS, R.G. 59, 862.20210/11-2246, p. 11.

210. See NARS, R.G. 59, FW 862.20210/2868, letter to Cecil G. Lyon from William Andrews. This communication notes the Timmerman-Leiswitz connection, and implies that it had some sinister aspects.

211. NARS, R.G. 59, 862.20210/11-2246, p. 11. Bohlen admits his emotional entanglement with Miss von Plate in NARS, R.G. 59, 862.20210/9-346, p. 11.

212. About the circumstances of Timmerman's work for Bohlen in 1942, see ibid., pp. 11–12.

213. Regarding Timmerman's early years, see *GELA*, p. 125, and DGII, *Declaraciones de los implicados,* vol. 43, "Memorandum de 26 Febrero de 1944" (the interrogation actually began on 2/24/44), n.p.

214. Bohlen refers to a new code in NARS, R.G. 59, 862.20210/11-2246, p. 4. On its workings, see John Bratzel and Leslie B. Rout, Jr., "Abwehr Ciphers in Latin America," *Cryptologia* 7, no. 2 (1983): 140–142.

215. NARS, R.G. 59, 862.20210/11-2246, p. 11.

216. About Augusto Kroll's recruitment and beliefs, see NARS, R.G. 59, 862.20210/3-2444, pp. 20–22, and 862.20210/2729, pp. 25–26. His deposition is found in DGII, *Declaraciones de los implicados,* vol. 43, n.p. A more succinct history is found in DGII, *1° Instancia,* vol. 1, p. 1895-B.

217. A discussion of the new PQZ methods of organization and compartmentalization can be found in NARS, R.G. 59, 862.20210/3-2444, pp. 22, 28–29.

218. DGII, *Declaraciones de los implicados,* vol. 43, n.p.

219. NARS, R.G. 59, 862.20210/3-2444, p. 23.

220. About the background of Pérez until his sojourn in Chile, see NARS, R.G. 226, 1306-C, Office of Strategic Services, Research and Analysis Branch 2035, *The Discovery of a Nazi Spy Ring in Chile,* March 27, 1944, p. 13. See also R.G. 59, 862.20210/3-2444, pp. 29–31, and DGII, *Declaraciones de los implicados,* vol. 43, n.p.

221. See NARS, R.G. 59, 862.20210/3-2444, pp. 30–31, for Pérez's function in Chile, and p. 33, to note the rise in income.

222. Alberto Collel speaks of his connection with Col. Armando González in DGII, *Declaraciones de los implicados,* vol. 43, n.p. The Collel-Bruhn connection is noted in *GELA*, p. 126, and NARS, R.G. 59, 862.20210/3-2444, and 862.20210/2862, p. 1.

223. The transfer of the Hellemann group informants to Timmerman's control is noted in NARS, R.G. 59, 862.20210/3-2444, p. 38, and 862.20210/11-2246, p. 11. The names and confessions of these informants can be found in DGII, *Ordenes del ministro Señor Baquedano,* vol. 42, n.p. See especially memorandum 200, Hernán Barros Bianchi to Mr. Justice Luís Baquedano, September 1, 1944.

224. Hans Heinke's deposition (again, incomplete) is found in DGII, *Declaraciones de los implicados,* vol. 43, n.p. A broader picture is sketched in NARS, R.G. 59, 862.20210/3-2444, pp. 52–53.

225. A background of Ilse Dorrer is found in *GELA,* p. 127. Hans Heinke related his connection with this woman whom he refers to as "Señorita Ilse" in his statement of March 11, 1944. See DGII, *Declaraciones de los implicados,* vol. 43, n.p. See also NARS, R.G. 59, 862.20210/3-2444, pp. 44, 53–54.

226. About Krebs, Westmayer, and Kurt Vietl, and others who held equipment and funds, see *GELA,* pp. 129–130.

227. Ibid., p. 128.

228. Ibid., pp. 119–120.

229. See ibid., p. 130, and NARS, R.G. 59, 862.20225/7-2845, p. 2.

230. Ibid., p. 130. On her actions in warning persons that the DGII was moving to make arrests, see NARS, R.G. 59, 862.20210/8-945, p. 2.

231. See DGII, *Declaraciones de los implicados,* vol. 43, n.p. Here Heinke states that he paid Cespédes about $165–170 a month. This money was divided between Cespédes, a person who was a "prefect," and a third person who obtained shipping data. Evidence of Guillermo Gómez Rosenfelt's involvement is discussed in greatest detail in NARS, R.G. 59, 862.20225/4-2444, pp. 1–2.

232. See NARS, R.G. 59, 862.20210/2862, pp. 1–2, concerning Collel's admitted work for the U.S. military. Collel's function as a double agent was admitted by Colonel González, 862.20210/11-844, enclosure 1. We wrote to Colonel Johnson, now retired and living (as of 1977) in Camden, Maine. In a letter dated June 8, 1977, to Professor John F. Bratzel, Colonel Johnson stated that he had only "hazy recollections" of the problems of Axis espionage in Chile.

233. On the payment of funds to González by Augusto Kroll (for Timmerman), and the provision of U.S. documents to the PQZ groups by González (through Collel), see NARS, R.G. 59, 862.20210/2862, pp. 1–2, and 862.20210/11-644, enclosure 1, pp. 1–3.

234. This conclusion is based on a comparison of the charts denoting the size of Abwehr organizations in *GELA,* pp. 51, 67, 73, 78, 85, 89, 102, and 123.

235. For the PQZ group's 1943 expenses, see DGII, *1° Instancia,* vol. 4, pp. 425–428 (total is on p. 428).

236. The amount given to Timmerman was stated by Bohlen in NARS, R.G. 59, 862.20210/9-346, p. 10. The amount gathered in by the DGII was close to $202,000. See FDRL, FDRP, OF-10B, box 39, letter from J. Edgar Hoover to Harry L. Hopkins, March 31, 1944, p. 1.

237. This German goal was expounded upon in a letter from Maj. Oscar Reile to Professor Rout, September 28, 1977.

238. See NARS, R.G. 59, 862.20210, *Engels, Albrecht Gustav/71,* section 4, n.p.

239. See NARS, R.G. 59, 862.20210/2729, p. 9.

240. The full story of Emilo Schonherr's activities in the United States and his connection and reward by German intelligence is related in DGII, *1° Instancia,* vol. 1, pp. 1903-B, 1923-A, and vol. 3, p. 332. See also República de Chile, DGII, *Ordenes del ministro Señor Baquedano,* vol. 43, no. 83, Garreton to Justice Baquedano, April 4, 1944. For English language copies of the story, see NARS, R.G. 59, 862.20210/2729, pp. 8–9, and 862.20210/6-2444, Report of the Naval Attaché, June 19, 1944, p. 2, and 862.20225/4-2444, pp. 2–3.

241. DGII, *1° Instancia,* vol. 1, pp. 1922A-1925A and B provides information on the planes and models cited. A check of Leonard Bridgemann, ed., *Jane's All the World's Aircraft,*

1943/44 (London, 1945) demonstrates that the exact models listed were in production in 1943.

Information on the P-40 series is found in Joe Cristy and Jeff Ethell, *P-40 Hawks at War* (New York, 1980), pp. 54–70 and 127. On the P-39 series, see Lloyd S. Jones, *U.S. Fighters: Army-Air Force: 1925 to 1980's* (Fallbrook, California, 1975), pp. 95–97. Joe Cristy and Jeff Ethell, *P-38 Lightning at War* (New York, 1980) is the best study of that versatile craft. The G and H models produced in 1943 are discussed in ibid., p. 123. On the P-61A, see Lloyd Jones, pp. 161–163. (Material on the *Consolidated Vultee PB2Y-3* (Schonherr erred in the model number) can be checked in *Jane's All the World's Aircraft, 1943/44,* p. 177.)

242. About Lieutenant Sievers and his work for PQZ, see DGII, *Ordenes del Ministro Señor Baquedano,* vol. 42, no. 104, Garreton to Baquedano, April 17, 1944. See also NARS, R.G. 59, 862.20225/4-2444, pp. 2–3, and R.G. 165, box 967, *Chile-Axis and Subversive Activities General,* no. 4, "German Espionage Ring," n.p.

243. Details on the U.S./Chilean lend-lease agreement are found in the República de Chile, Ministro de R.R.E.E., *Archivo confidencial-Oficios de la embajada en los Estados Unidos—1° Semestre, 1943,* memorandum 224, Rodolfo Michels to the foreign minister, January 26, 1943. On the incident related here concerning the copied manuals, see DGII, *1° Instancia,* vol. 1, p. 1922-A.

244. See NARS, R.G. 59, 862.20210/2729, p. 7.

245. About the special courier delivery of microfilmed documents to Argentina, see *GELA,* pp. 125 and 134, and DGII, *Declaraciones de los implicados,* vol. 43, memorandum, February 22, 1944, n.p.

246. Regarding the background of this incident and the Chilean pledge to U.S. and British representatives, see NARS, R.G. 59, 701.6225/139, pp. 1–2, and enclosure 2, p. 2. See also 862.20210/2729, p. 17.

247. For Tovarías's explanation of events, see NARS, R.G. 59, 701.6225/140, enclosure 1, pp. 1–2, and 862.20210/2729, p. 17. Concerning the pro-Nazi sympathies held by Tovarías and his previous connection with Ludwig von Bohlen in Germany, see 862.20210/11-2246, p. 1.

248. Wolf's dual position as Dienststelle Ribbentrop and SD officer was noted and commented upon by Bohlen in NARS, R.G. 59, 862.20210/9-346, p. 11.

249. The Bohlen-Lange conflict is elaborated upon in ibid., pp. 8–10. In his second interrogation, Bohlen was more forthcoming in explaining his problems with and objections to Lange. See NARS, R.G. 59, 862.20210/11-2246, pp. 13–14. Regarding Bohlen's rebuff by Berlin in his efforts to keep Lange out of Chile, see DGII, *Declaraciones de los implicados,* vol. 43, memorandum from Eugenio Ellinger Knoll or Juan Valdés (Santana) or (Carlos) Martín Flores, March 17, 1944, n.p.

250. On Becker's plans and Lange's failures in Brazil, see NARS, R.G. 84, 820.02, box 533, *Memorandum—Johannes Siegfried Becker with Aliases,* April 18, 1946, pp. 13–16. For further details concerning Lange and Becker's Brazilian mission, see German Federal Republic, München, Institut für Zeitgeschichte, NG-4871, GZ. BL. Ph., *Interrogation of Karl Gustav Arnold* (hereafter referred to as *Interrogation of Karl Gustav Arnold*), November 20, 1946, pp. 9–11.

251. About the identity of Victor Vougha, see NARS, R.G. 59, 862.20210/11-2444, p. 1.

252. See NARS, R.G. 84, 820.02, box 533, *Memorandum—Johannes Siegfried Becker,* pp. 20–21, and DGII, *Declaraciones de los implicados,* vol. 43, memorandum from Eugenio Ellinger Knoll, March 17, 1944, n.p.

253. Heriberto Schlosser, Melitta Tietz, and several other collaborators and subagents recruited by Lange were all one-time employees of the Banco Germánico branch in Santiago. For more information on Schlosser and his wife, Gertrudis, see NARS, R.G. 59, 862.20210/8-445, pp. 1–3. On the role played by Aristides Parodi, see 862.20210/2883, enclosure 1, pp. 1–2. An explanation of how these ring members functioned together and their specific tasks is found in DGII, *Declaraciones de los implicados,* vol. 43, memorandum from Eugenio Ellinger Knoll or Juan Valdéz, March 30, 1944, n.p.

254. Regarding clerical mail recipients, see NARS, R.G. 59, 862.20210/8-145, p. 1, 862.20210/7-2845, pp. 1–2, and *GELA*, p. 135.

255. See DGII, *Declaraciones de los implicados,* vol. 43, memorandum from Eugenio Ellinger Knoll, March 17, 1944, n.p., and NARS, R.G. 59, 862.20210/3-2844, pp. 1–2, and 862.20225/7-1245, pp. 1–2. See also 862.20210/2880, p. 2, 862.20210/11-2246, pp. 14–15, and *GELA*, p. 135.

256. See NARS, R.G. 59, 862.20210/11-2246, p. 15, and *GELA*, p. 135.

257. On Pérez's dual role with the Abwehr and SD, see *GELA*, p. 126, and NARS, R.G. 59, 862.20210/3-2444, pp. 27, 31–32.

258. See NARS, R.G. 59, 862.20210/9-346, p. 8.

259. NARS, R.G. 59, 862.20210/9-346, pp. 8–9. Bohlen is quite specific in explaining what happened to him, and the vengeance of Lange. On the low opinions of Heinz Lange held by SS-Capt. Karl Gross and other SD chiefs, see *Interrogation of Karl Gustav Arnold*, p. 9. See also NARS, R.G. 84, 820.02, box 533, file: *Interrogations Made in Germany II, memorandum—Affidavit of Hedwig Sommer, 4 March 1946* (hereafter referred to as *Affidavit of Hedwig Sommer*), p. 8. The quote is from ibid.

260. See NARS, *DSGFOR,* T-120 series, roll 366, frames 291170-291175.

261. The events noted here are noted in NARS, R.G. 59, 862.20210/9-346, pp. 8–9, and *Affidavit of Hedwig Sommer,* pp. 7–8.

262. For this story, see NARS, R.G. 59, 862.20210/11-2246, p. 9, and 862.20210/9-346, p. 6. The essentials of the story are similar except the dates mentioned in /9-346 cannot be correct given the time the PQZ started transmitting. Secondly, in /11-2246, the person bringing the *Afu* back for the Abwehr was a Chilean consul. In /9-346, Bohlen said that he was told by a former German consul that a "Chilean citizen who had returned from Europe" was the man with the transmitter.

263. The transmitting problems are noted in ibid. (both reports, same pages). The June 18, 1943, PQZ-URK contact is noted in NARS, R.G. 59, 862.20210/2729, p. 2.

264. Concerning the new transmitter, the cessation of broadcasting, and the atmospheric problems, see NARS, R.G. 59, 862.20210/11-2246, p. 9, 862.20210/9-346, p. 6, and DGII, *Declaraciones de los implicados,* vol. 43, memorandum, February 22, 1944, n.p.

265. See NARS, R.G. 59, 862.20210/2844, p. 2, *GELA*, p. 130, and a letter from Roger L. Young to Professor Rout, July 23, 1981, p. 2.

266. Information on the number of attempts made, the first decipherment of a PQZ message, and the number of messages sent on the PQZ-URK circuit come from a letter from Roger L. Young to Professor Rout, July 23, 1981, p. 2. Additional verification of much of this information can be found in DGII, *Declaraciones de los implicados,* vol. 43, memorandum from Bernardo Francisco Timmerman Buschung, February 22, 1944, n.p.

267. The quote is from DGII, *Declaraciones de los implicados,* vol. 43, memorandum from Bernardo Francisco Timmerman Buschung, February 22, 1944, n.p.

268. A discussion and affirmation of this conclusion is found in NARS, R.G. 173, RID, box 5, *Testimony of G. E. Sterling,* p. 24.

269. Ibid.

270. On the work of George Fellows, and the location of the transmitter, see NARS, R.G. 59, 862.20210/2453, pp. 1–3, and 862.20210/2729, p. 3.

271. The basis for SIS surveillance and censorship of mail is found in La República de Chile, Ministerio de Relaciones Exteriores, *Cartas enviados correlativo y especial, A-Z—1943,* E-11-6-20a no. 80. This letter from Foreign Minister Joaquin Fernández to Albert Guani, dated April 9, 1943, gave Chilean permission to a February 1943 request of the Emergency Advisory Committee for the Political Defense of the Americas (CPD Committee) to allow U.S. functionaries with experience in matters of censorship "to check mail and other communications mediums."

272. NARS, R.G. 59, 862.20210/2729, p. 27.

273. Kunsemüller calmly described what he had done, and showed his interrogators the photo he took. See NARS, R.G. 226, 1306-C, *The Discovery of a Nazi Spy Ring in Chile,* R and A 2035, p. 12.

274. About Kunsemüller's smuggling career, see NARS, R.G. 59, 862.20210/2729, pp. 1, 12–16, 18–19. See also 862.20210/2731, pp. 1–3. Kunsemüller knew he was being tailed, and had spoken to an SIS/Chile informant about destroying the transmitter he had last used.

275. See letter of February 4, 1944, p. 2, from J. Edgar Hoover to Adolf A. Berle, attached to NARS, R.G. 59, 862.20210/2729, pp. 1–2.

276. The basis of this conclusion regarding the February 5, 1944, inaccuracies is based on a comparison of the list of suspects given in NARS, R.G. 59, 862.20210/2729, pp. 21–29, with the list of those mentioned as being detained and questioned in 862.20210/2861, pp. 4–7.

277. See NARS, R.G. 59, 862.20210/2807, p. 2 and 862.20210/2749, p. 1. The driving force behind the decision to act first was Foreign Minister Joaquín Fernández. He insisted that national security considerations and international commitments necessitated violating legal procedure, and agreed to take responsibility if the Chilean Congress demanded retribution.

278. The times listed for these lightninglike actions (especially in comparison with the PYL case) are found in NARS, R.G. 59, 862.20210/2731, p. 1, 862.20210/2752, pp. 1–2, and DGII, *Declaraciones de los implicados,* vol. 43, n.p.

279. Kunsemüller's full confession is found in DGII, *Declaraciones de los implicados,* vol. 43, memorandum, February 16, 1944, n.p. The information concerning the condition of the jail cells and the diabolical use of them by the DGII, plus the quoted material, is from NARS, R.G. 59, 862.20210/3-2444, p. 21.

280. Timmerman's near escape and capture are related in detail in DGII, *1° Instancia,* vol. 1, p. 1896-A.

281. Timmerman's first confession is found in DGII, *Declaraciones de los implicados,* vol. 43, memorandum, February 20, 1944, n.p. In it he claimed, among other things, that he had been recruited in August 1943 by an SD man, press attaché Wilhelm Hammerschmidt. The quote and the threat by Garreton are from NARS, R.G. 226, 1306-C, R and A 2035, *The Discovery of a Nazi Spy Ring in Chile,* p. 7.

282. Regarding Timmerman's cooperation and revelations to his interrogators, see ibid., pp. 7–8, NARS, R.G. 59, 862.20210/2282, p. 1, 811.515/2288, pp. 1–3, and *GELA,* pp. 125–126 and 129.

283. For Timmerman's second confession, see DGII, *Declaraciones de los implicados,* vol. 43, memorandum, February 21, 1944, n.p. Hans Heinke's statement is found in the same source, and the memorandum in which it is located is also dated February 21, 1944. Slightly varying confessions are found in NARS, R.G. 59, 862.20210/3-2444, pp. 40–45, 48–50, 52–54. For a breakdown of the funds uncovered, see NARS, R.G. 59, 862.20210/2802, pp. 4–5.

284. Concerning those who escaped to Argentina, see NARS, R.G. 59, 862.20210/11-1344, p. 4.

285. See NARS, R.G. 59, 862.20210/2807, p. 1. See also República de Chile, DGII, *Relacionadas con el proceso 'Contra B. Timmerman e otros'—PQZ Ano: 1944* (hereafter referred to as DGII, *Relacionadas con el proceso 'Contra B. Timmerman'*), vol. 35, n.p., which contains Chilean newspaper accounts of PQZ events.

286. The Eugenio Ellinger Knoll story is found in NARS, R.G. 59, 862.20210/2280, p. 1, 862.20210/2282, p. 1, 862.20210/2786, p. 1, and 862.20210/3-2444, pp. 54–55. A copy of Knoll's confession is in DGII, *Declaraciones de los implicados,* vol. 43, memorandum, March 17, 1944. This confession demonstrates that he had previous dealings with Jorge Dumont.

287. See NARS, R.G. 59, 862.20210/3-2444, p. 54, on Knoll in prison. His despondency, attempted suicide, and the quote concerning the DGII response is covered in DGII, *Declaraciones de los implicados,* vol. 43, memorandum, February 26, 1944.

288. This is evidenced in NARS, R.G. 59, 862.20210/2786, p. 1, and 862.20210/2880, p. 1.

289. See DGII, *Relacionadas con el proceso 'Contra B. Timmerman,'* vol. 35, n.p. The copies of the articles from *El Siglo* and *El Mercurio* were found here. The *La Nación* editorial was found in the March 8, 1944, edition.

290. See NARS, R.G. 59, 862.20210/2807, p. 2. For the names of those released, see DGII, *Ordenes del ministro Señor Baquedano,* vol. 42, n.p. See also memorandum 556, Jorge Garreton to Justice Baquedano, March 3, 1944.

291. See NARS, R.G. 59, 862.20210/2807, p. 2, and 835.01/205, pp. 1–2. Ríos's discussion with the chief justice is further elaborated, and the quoted statement is from Bowers, *Mss. II,* letter to Cordell Hull, March 14, 1944, p. 2. For Trucco's pledge to support government policy, see ibid. For Baquedano's lightninglike change of practice and his reversal of decision, see R.G. 59, 825.00/2102, p. 1, and 862.20210/2801, p. 2, and also DGII, *Declaraciones de los implicados,* vol. 43, n.p.

292. This was the perceptive opinion expressed in 1942 in NARS, R.G. 59, 825.00/1650, no. 3117, p. 2, and R.G. 226, no. 27439, n.p.

293. See La República de Chile, El Ministerio de Relaciones Exteriores, *Sección confiden-cial—Oficios de los misiones en Europa y Asia—1944,* no. 602/290, May 10, 1944, Manuel Bianchi to the foreign minister. See also Ministerio de R.R.E.E., *Sección confidencial—Oficios de en Embajada en E.E.U.U. y de lo UNRRA—1° Semestre, 1944, #561/27 (Estricta-mente confidencial) 3 de Marzo de 1944,* Michels to the foreign minister.

294. See NARS, R.G. 59, 862.20210/2802, pp. 6–7, and NARS, R.G 165, *Chile—Axis and Subversive Activities—General,* box 967, no. 65222, "Current Events, M/A Chile, German Espionage Ring," n.p.

295. See NARS, R.G. 59, 862.20210/2758, p. 1 and 862.20210/6-2444, report of the naval attaché, enclosure 1, p. 2.

296. See NARS, R.G. 59, 862.20210/4-2444, p. 2. The full interrogation and quote is found in DGII, *Declaraciones de los implicados,* vol. 43, no. 104, Jorge Garreton to Justice Baque-dano, April 17, 1944.

297. DGII, *Declaraciones de los implicados,* vol. 43, *Informe,* no. 83, April 4, 1944, Garreton to Justice Baquedano, and NARS, R.G. 165, box 967, "Chile-German-Nazi Organi-zation, N/A Chile #6479," n.p.

298. On González, his declaration to Baquedano, and his connection with Collel, see NARS, R.G. 59, 862.20210/11-644, no. 11045, pp. 1–2.

299. NARS, R.G. 59, 862.20210/2793, p. 1. The same statement is repeated but in a slightly different fashion in 862.20210/2807, p. 6.

300. This charge against the chief of staff and other unnamed high ranking military officers, is found in FDRL, FDRP, OF-10B, box 39, letter of March 31, 1944, J. Edgar Hoover to Harry Hopkins. See also NARS, R.G. 59, 862.20210/2864, p. 1.

301. NARS, R.G. 59, 862.20210/2793, p. 2.

302. See NARS, R.G. 59, 862.20210/2867, p. 1, 862.20210/2876, p. 1, and 862.20210/2878, pp. 1–2.

303. Ibid. See also NARS, R.G. 226, no. 94788, "Comments as Current Events #152," p. 6.

304. See NARS, R.G. 59, 862.20210/2878a, p. 1, and 862.20210/2944, p. 1.

305. See NARS, R.G. 59, 862.20210/2807, p. 6, and 862.20210/2864, p. 1, and FDRL, Harry Hopkins Papers, box 141, undated letter from J. Edgar Hoover to Harry L. Hopkins, and Bowers, *Mss. II,* memorandum, Donald Heath to Claude Bowers, January 23, 1944, p. 3.

306. NARS, R.G. 59, 862.20210/11-644, pp. 1–3 and enclosure 1, for the *El Chileno* newspaper article.

307. Letter from Roger L. Young to Professor Rout, July 23, 1981.

308. See DGII, *Declaraciones de los implicados,* vol. 43, no. 43, Garreton to Justice Baquedano, March 14, 1944.

309. See *GELA,* p. 127, and NARS, R.G. 59, 862.20225/4-2444, p. 1, for the quote.

310. See DGII, *Declaraciones de los implicados,* vol. 43, memorandum, February 28, 1944. Collel argues that his actions were supervised by Colonel González. No statement about working for the U.S. military attaché or spying against the U.S. embassy is found here. On the other hand, in NARS, R.G. 59, 862.20210/2860, p. 1, and 862.20210/2862, pp. 1–2, the SIS/Chile agent who was there when Collel was interrogated made reference to Collel spying against the U.S. and states that Collel confessed that González was paid off by the Germans.

311. See NARS, R.G. 59, 862.20210/2860, p. 1.

312. Ibid., and R.G. 165, box 968, "Comments on Current Events #152, Chile-7077-7152," p. 2.

313. NARS, R.G. 59, 862.20210/2793, p. 1.

314. The figure of ninety persons questioned is from FDRL, Harry Hopkins Papers, box 144, letter from J. Edgar Hoover to Harry Hopkins, June 14, 1944. The figure of sixty-one persons arrested is from NARS, R.G. 59, 862.20210/2861, pp. 4–7, and DGII, *Ordenes del ministro Señor Baquedano,* vol. 42, no. 200, Hernán Barros Bianchi, sub-commisario, to Luis Baquedano, September 1, 1944, n.p. *GELA,* p. 130, gives the figure as sixty-three.

315. The Martínez and Ulrich incidents are reported in NARS, R.G. 59, 862.20210/2861, p. 7.

316. Ibid. Señora Pederit de Reiners's connection with the PQZ ring is noted in NARS, R.G. 84, no. 64-3112, *Radio Station PYL,* J. Edgar Hoover to MID, January 4, 1946, p. 2.

317. Our copy of the Law of External Security is from Controlaría General de la República, *Recopilación de leyes por orden numérico con indices por número: Ministeríos y materias,* vol. 29 (Santiago, 1944), pp. 232–235.

318. DGII, *Ordenes del ministro Señor Baquedano,* vol. 42, no. 35 (confidential), Garreton to Justice Baquedano, March 14, 1944, n.p. See also NARS, R.G. 59, 862.20210/2807, p. 4.

319. See NARS, R.G. 59, 862.20210/3-2444, pp. 40–41, 46–48.

320. See NARS, R.G. 59, 862.20210/2884, no. 736, p. 2. For the background to these events, see 862.20210/2846, no. 457, no. 465, and no. 542.

321. This is from a letter dated May 4, 1944, attached to /2884. It was forwarded by C.B. Lyon to Adolf Berle.

322. Ibid. Attached to the letter mentioned was a note dated May 8, 1944, which stated that "Admiral Schuirman gave permission by telephone this p.m. about 4:00 to supply Chileans with copies."

323. See NARS, R.G. 226, OSS Confidential, C.I. 91277, no. 7077-152-WGS/DG/LWW/RMP/RCC/mm/ajs, August 21, 1944, (16) *German Espionage Case,* p. 6.

324. DGII, *Ordenes del ministro Señor Baquedano,* vol. 42, no. 69, Garreton to Justice Baquedano, March 28, 1944. Document bears the title, *Sobre anormalidas en las visitas a los detenidos que indica.*

325. NARS, R.G. 59, 862.20210/6-2444, no. 10070, enclosure 1, p. 1.

326. See NARS, R.G. 59, 862.20210/2807, p. 6.

327. NARS, R.G. 226, no. 1306C, R and A 2035, *The Discovery of a Nazi Spy Ring in Chile,* p. 10. Koch was the son-in-law of Carlos Ibáñez. See R.G. 59, 862.20210/6-2444, no. 10068, enclosure 1, p. 2. Koch had allegedly taken the case because of the appeal made by Timmerman's aunt and uncle. These two people had taken Koch when he was orphaned as a child and raised him.

328. Ibid., and R.G. 59, 862.20210/2807, p. 6.

329. NARS, R.G. 59, 862.20210/6-2444, no. 10068, enclosure 1, p. 1. Koch also added that it was totally unfair to punish only the civilians.

330. Koch hints at what his tactics would be in ibid., pp. 1–2. These are more clearly defined in R.G. 226, 1306-C, R and A 2035, *The Discovery of a Nazi Spy Ring in Chile,* p. 10.

331. For the denunciations of Jorge Garreton and the DGII, see NARS, R.G. 226, 1306C, R and A 2035, *The Discovery of a Nazi Spy Ring in Chile*, p. 10. See also R.G. 59, 862.20210/6-2444, no. 10070, and 862.20210/2873, no. 923, pp. 1–2.

332. NARS, R.G. 59, 862.20210/11-444, no. 1739, pp. 1–2. While in Buenos Aires, Garreton was beaten up by several persons who later turned out to be members of the Argentine police!

333. See NARS, R.G. 59, 862.20210/2765, pp. 1–2, for the quote. See 862.20210/2768a, no. 265, pp. 1–2, for the subsequent disillusionment.

334. For example, see NARS, R.G. 59, 825.00/2165, memorandum of conversation 21, enclosure 2, p. 1, 862.20210/2768a, no. 265, p. 2, FW 825.00/2077, pp. 1–2, and 862.20210/2878a, p. 2.

335. Washington's view of the PQZ investigation, and recognition that less than legal means had been used, is noted in NARS, R.G. 59, 862.20210/2749, p. 1, 862.20210/2807, p. 2, and 862.20010/6-2444, no. 10070, enclosure 1, p. 1.

336. See NARS, R.G. 59, 862.20210/11-1344, no. 11086, p. 1, and enclosure 1, pp. 2–4. See also 862.20210/1-1545, pp. 2–3.

337. República de Chile, Corte de Apelaciones de Santiago, Proceso 7–44, *Expediente de Bernardo Timmerman y Otros,* Procediente 1° Instancia, T-378, pp. 2034 and 2067.

338. Ibid., pp. 2098–2101.

339. See DGII, *1° Instancia,* vol. 1, pp. 2096–2100.

340. Ibid., pp. 2100–2101. In addition, Kunsemüller, Kroll, Heinke, and Knoll lost all civil rights, and became subject to expulsion, or revocation of citizenship upon completion of their penal sentences.

341. NARS, R.G. 59, 862.20225/6-1145, p. 2.

342. NARS, R.G. 59, 862.20225/10-445, no. no. 1273, pp. 1–3, 862.20225/10-945, pp. 1–4, and *GELA,* pp. 134 and 136. See also Appendix C in this volume, and DGII, *Declaraciones de los implicados,* vol. 43, n.p. See expulsion decree 4892, of October 4, 1945, for Eugenio Ellinger Knoll.

343. Some judicial action of this kind was hinted at in NARS, R.G. 59, 710.62115/7-2045.

344. See NARS, R.G. 59, 862.20235/7-2247, p. 1.

345. See NARS, R.G. 59, 862.20210/9-847, pp. 1–2.

346. See NARS, R.G. 59, 862.20225/2-248, no. 72, p. 1.

347. Information on Hans Blume is from a letter from Heinrich (Enrique) Reiners to Professor Rout, May 12, 1982. Information on Reiners himself: ibid. Information on Bernardo Timmerman is from an interview with Pedro Monteuffel, Detroit, Michigan, by Professor Rout, March 11, 1982. Information on Guillermo Kunsemüller is from interview with Dr. Fritz Hinzer, Santiago, August 24, 1978.

348. Letter, Krause to Professor Rout, *Deutsche Dienststelle,* VI/A-677, Berlin, West Germany, March 26, 1982.

349. República de Chile, Ministero de Relaciones Exteriores, *Oficios confidenciales enviados y recibidos—Embajada de Chile—1944,* no. 21, no. 50/4, and no. 52/19, Joaquin Fernández Michels, February 29, 1944, n.p.

350. República de Chile, Ministerio de R.R.E.E., *Sección Confidencial—Oficios de los embajada en E.E.U.U. e del UNRRA, 1° Semestre-1944,* no. 541/27, Rodolfo Michels to the foreign ministry, March 3, 1944, n.p.

351. See NARS, R.G. 59, 862.20210/6-2944, p. 1, and *GELA,* p. 120.

352. See NARS, R.G. 59, 711.25/97, pp. 1–2 for quoted material.

353. U.S. Department of the Army, Center for Military History, Washington, D.C., Historical Section, Caribbean Defense Command, *Chile and the War Effort,* 8–28, B.E. C-1, (Washington, D.C., 1946), p. 76. See also FDRL, Adolf Berle Papers, box 29, folder: *BOA-BOY,* letter to Ambassador Claude Bowers, August 3, 1944, pp. 1–2. Berle, his skepticism ill-concealed, argued that Chile could expect little more so long as it was not at war.

354. For these aid figures and comparisons, see United States of America, Export-Import Bank of Washington, *First Semiannual Report to Congress for the Period July–December 1945,* (Washington, 1945), p. 20, 41–43.

7

The Espionage War in Argentina: 1939–43

I. Introduction: The Purposes of Neutrality

One would not usually associate Sumner Welles, undersecretary of state, Adolf Berle, assistant secretary of state, Norman Armour, ambassador to Argentina, and Philip Bonsal, chief of the American republics desk, with what have come to be known as diplomatic dirty tricks. Nevertheless, the facts reveal that during the 1939–45 epoch, the Axis countries were not the only parties who cynically violated the normal rules of diplomatic behavior.

From the time of the overthrow of Pres. Hipólito Irigoyen by military elements in September 1930, elections in Argentina had been characterized by force and fraud.[1] Nevertheless, following his ascension to power via the same methods in October 1937, Roberto Ortiz defied the more reactionary elements in the coalition supporting him and moved to allow the winners in forthcoming elections to be decided by the free vote of the majority. The most conspicuous result of this policy change came in March 1940, when in the federal congressional elections, the opposition Radical party (actually a middle-class, middle-of-the-road party), aided by the Socialist party, gained control of the Chamber of Deputies, the lower house of the Argentine Congress.[2]

Despite the angry and open opposition of many of his erstwhile political allies, Ortiz was determined to persevere in the march toward electoral honesty. Alas, debilitation, in the form of a rapidly worsening diabetic condition and failing eyesight, made his continuation as chief executive increasingly doubtful.[3] Unable to effectively execute his duties any longer, on July 3, 1940, Ortiz handed over the reins of power to his arch-conservative running mate, Ramón S. Castillo.

Initially surrounded with Ortiz's partisans, Castillo found it wise to move cautiously, but in September 1940, he was able to name his own cabinet, and thereafter he demonstrated that the old method of political manipulation was once again standard operating procedure. In December 1940 and February 1941, he blatantly moved to ensure the election of candidates from the Concordancia (as his supporting coalition was called) in two provinces, acts which sparked violent reactions in the Chamber of Deputies. Determined to prevent the future from becoming a repetition of the past, when the Castillo government submitted its budget for the 1941 fiscal year, the Chamber of Deputies refused to pass it.[4]

This impasse soon became critical, and the situation was further exacerbated by the fact that in February 1941, the ailing Ortiz publicly criticized Castillo's antidemocratic activities, in effect, placing himself on the side of the governmental opposition.[5] That same month, however, an Argentine general told the U.S. military attaché, Maj. Robert Devine, that even if Ortiz were to regain his sight and reclaim his presidency, "nationalist military elements" would overthrow the government.[6] Thus, the stage was set for a major test of strength between prodemocratic and antidemocratic elements in Argentina.

The next round in the political struggle produced what was one of the most spectacular U.S. propaganda victories in Latin America prior to the attack on Pearl Harbor. On June 19, 1941, by a vote of ninety-five to one, the Chamber of Deputies voted to create the Committee for the Investigation of Anti-Argentine Activities, to be chaired by Raúl Damonte Taborda. As the group's inquiries would focus almost entirely on the continued activities of the officially outlawed (since May 15, 1939) Nazi party, it received the discreet assistance of both the United States and British embassies.[7] While the anti-Nazi fervor of the deputies was undeniable, so, too, was their intention of composing and orchestrating a concerto of criticism aimed at the internal policies of the Castillo regime. Aware of the deputies's intentions, Castillo declared that the executive branch of the government would provide no assistance to the congressional investigators.[8]

The disdain exhibited by the president only reinforced the determination of the Anti-Argentine Activities Committee to hand a smashing setback to Castillo and his administration. The opportunity arose obliquely when the U.S. State Department learned that via LATI a powerful radio transmitter had arrived in Brazil and was being forwarded, in three diplomatic bags, to Peru via Argentina.[9] On June 27, 1941, Philip Bonsal, chief of the American republics desk at the State Department, forwarded instructions to James Norweb, ambassador to Peru, regarding the eventual arrival of some German "excess baggage," and the latter swiftly made arrangements with the Peruvian government. Several days later, when the three bags were landed in Lima, customs officials seized them, insisting that they represented "excess baggage." Due notice was taken of the diplomatic seals, but the Peruvians were adamant; the bags had to be opened or sent back to where they came from.[10]

For three weeks, the German embassy cajoled, threatened, and connived, but Ambassador Norweb had done his work well; the bags remained at the Lima airport. In the interim, Sumner Welles completed certain negotiations with Juan Trippe, president of Pan American Airways, and instructions were sent to Ambassador Norman Armour in Buenos Aires for delivery to Anti-Argentine Activities Committee chairman Raúl Damonte Taborda.[11] On July 24, 1941, Erich Leinhos, an attaché at the German embassy in Peru, boarded a Pan American plane bound for Buenos Aires. The three bags bearing the radio equipment were marked as "diplomatic mail" and secured in the cargo hold. The plane made a refueling stop at Córdoba, Argentina, and while Herr Leinhos enjoyed a sumptuous lunch in the airport restaurant, Pan American officials stealthily removed the baggage from the plane. The pilfered goods were sped to Buenos Aires and delivered to a waiting group consisting of the Anti-Argentine Activities Committee, a federal judge, and Eduardo Bradley, chief of Pan American's Argentine division.[12] According to a report filed by Damonte Taborda with Ambassador Armour, hidden inside a part of the radio transmitter was "a secret code . . . as well as instructions for making transmissions to a foreign country."[13]

There remains some question as to whether there was any code in the bags,[14] but once the Germans learned that they had been victims of a clever ruse, their rage and fear incited desperate actions. On both July 26 and 27, Ambassador Freiherr von Thermann presented notes to Argentine Foreign Minister Enrique Ruiz-Guiñazú, complaining of the "surreptitious seizure of diplomatic mails," demanding restitution of the three bags, and punishment of the guilty parties.[15] Ruiz-Guiñazú pleaded ignorance, but the German ambassaor did not believe him. Convinced that a giant conspiracy was afoot, Thermann wired Berlin on July 27 that the embassy's secret papers and codes were being burned.[16] He soon discovered that he had acted prematurely, for the next day, the diplomatic baggage "burglary" was suddenly cleared up. Damonte Taborda delivered the radio equipment to the federal police and held a press conference concerning the actions his committee had taken.[17]

The resultant clamor and controversy, which continued for weeks, was the perfect background for the release of the Anti-Argentine Activities Committee's first report, dated August 29, 1941. This document was an unmitigated denunciation of the Castillo regime's alleged failure to interdict Nazi operations in the country. To be sure, the evidence was stretched to fit preconceived conclusions. Nevertheless, the document was powerful propaganda, and it served to enhance the position of the committee members as dedicated defenders of national sovereignty.[18]

Understandably, Castillo considered Damonte Taborda a lackey on Uncle Sam's payroll, and the whole affair simply another devious maneuver intended to undermine the Concordancia's hold on power.[19] But the position of the government was none too secure,[20] and any effort to discipline the committee could easily have been interpreted by the public as the castigation of Argentine nationalists at the urging of a foreign power. This would have been political suicide, a consideration of which Ruiz-Guiñazú candidly reminded the Germans. Thus, the foreign minister returned the disassembled transmitter (August 3) and watched as its parts were destroyed on embassy grounds. In private, he also made sympathetic noises concerning the devilish deeds of the congressional malefactors, but that was as far as he and Castillo were going to go.[21]

Freiherr von Thermann would undoubtedly have been willing to let the matter drop, but Foreign Minister Joachim von Ribbentrop demanded satisfaction. And so, throughout August 1941, the ambassador conducted an increasingly strident press campaign against Damonte Taborda. On September 15, 1941, on a motion by the Anti-Argentine Activities Committee, the Chamber of Deputies voted seventy-eight to one (with over seventy abstentions) to censure Thermann for overstepping his diplomatic privileges. Castillo angrily rejected all suggestions that the German be given his passport, but on November 16, the harried diplomat cabled Berlin that his position had become "impossible."[22] Ribbentrop finally consented to his return, but in retaliation, the Argentine ambassador to Germany was also sent packing. Germany and Argentina maintained diplomatic relations until January 1944, but after December 1941, neither country again exchanged ambassadors.

Following the announcement of Ambassador Thermann's definite departure, the State Department decided that one successful burglary justified another. On January 27, 1942, Adolf Berle sent a secret message to Norman Armour inquiring as to the possibility of having an agent open and examine Thermann's sealed luggage.[23] Armour's reply emphasized that although he did not oppose the idea, there was too little time to plan the careful execution of this gambit. Fortunately, perhaps, Berle decided not to press for the implementation of what he chose to call a "quiet endeavor."[24]

The "excess baggage" coup produced the scalp of a German ambassador, but U.S. officials were in error if they believed that they had cast no shadow. From Spain in March 1942, Thermann wrote a personal note to his "esteemed friend," President Castillo, in which he remarked that "the deputies [i.e., Raúl Damonte Taborda and his committee] acted dishonestly in this affair but ... we both know, my friend, who was really responsible for this tragedy...."[25]

Insofar as one was made at the time, the justification for this brazen action was U.S. concern over burgeoning Abwehr activity in Latin America. In January 1941, GBO had begun broadcasting from Mexico, and within six months, several other clandestine stations began operating in Chile and Brazil. The radio equipment known to be in the German diplomatic bags was believed destined to become the voice of another spy group.[26] Moreover, in July 1941, the same month as the incident in question, Janos Salamon and Miklos Sandor had employed the diplomat's cloak in slipping their transmitter past Brazilian customs officials. Given these considerations, U.S. concern was certainly justified.

Nevertheless, an equally relevant fact is that between September 1, 1939, and December 7, 1941, the United States did not find it necessary to execute an operation like that just described in Mexico, Brazil, or Chile. A critical factor in the U.S. decision was probably Washington's growing concern over the course and direction of Argentine policy. A number of historians have observed that, although Roberto Ortiz declared Argentina neutral, until he stepped down in July 1940, he demonstated in his public pronouncements a marked preference for the Anglo-French cause.[27] In secret, he did even more, for during the first ten months of the war in Europe, he passed on to the British, via his Foreign Ministry, data on suspected German agents. At the same time, and at the behest of British intelligence, the president ordered federal police to keep suspected V-men under surveillance.[28]

Ortiz was also a believer in the necessity of U.S.-Argentine cooperation in the defense of the Americas against possible Axis attack. It was through his intervention in July 1940 that the Argentine delegation ultimately moved to support U.S. initiatives at the Second Consultative Meeting of Foreign Ministers held at Havana, Cuba on July 21-30, 1940.[29] But this development would be the crest of Washington–Buenos Aires hemispheric cooperation; under Castillo, collaboration would steadily evaporate.

Resolution XVI adopted at the Havana conference espoused the basic principle that an attack upon one nation was an attack upon all of them. Still, this formal agreement did not represent an alliance since it established neither a defense plan nor the nature of mutual commitments to be undertaken. It was precisely to concretize bilateral defense arrangements that U.S. military and naval negotiating teams were sent to Brazil, Chile, Mexico, and Argentina in August and September 1940. But while Brazil and Mexico proved accommodating and Chilean officialdom reasonably frank, the discussions in Buenos Aires proved utterly disastrous. The commencement of secret negotiations had been sanctioned in August 1940 by the unabashedly anti-Axis foreign minister and Ortiz appointee, José María Cantilo. But by the time Lt. Col. Robert Christian and his assistants reached Buenos Aires on September 11, 1940, Cantilo was out of office, and a bitter struggle was going on between Argentine elements over naval and military cooperation with the United States.[30]

The U.S. military representative passed a month in aimless diversions before an Argentine delegation finally agreed to meet with him. Negotiations began on October 13, 1940, and collapsed the same day. In his official report, Christian observed that "the Argentine conferees were forbidden to make any staff agreements, sign any document or discuss any important points prior to a formal agreement between the governments of the United States and Argentina authorizing such action. . . ."[31]

U.S. naval negotiators arrived three weeks after Lt. Col. Christian, but discussions with their Argentine counterparts proved equally discordant. In an exceptionally shrewd analysis, Capt. W.D. Brereton, U.S. naval attaché in Argentina and a member of the naval delegation, concluded that the Argentinians believed that they were unlikely to be attacked. Moreover, in the event of a British defeat, lucrative commercial dealings with the Axis were bound to ensue; there was simply no reason for taking actions which a triumphant Rome or Berlin might construe as unfriendly.[32]

Interestingly, Rear Adm. Julian Foblet, chief of the Argentine naval negotiators, thought along similar lines, but his report drew markedly different
conclusions. Foblet doubted that the Axis planned to attack Argentina, but
if they did, he questioned whether the United States would be able to
provide effective assistance. Yet, the admiral's principal objection to the
discussions was political in nature. Because any defensive arrangement
with the United States meant the de facto abandonment of neutrality, Foblet was unwilling to take any action until Castillo openly declared himself
on this issue.[33] And since the acting president was unlikely to take such a
step, future bilateral talks were bound to be unproductive.

Not surprisingly, it was in the field of counterintelligence that the
failure of the bilateral talks proved most immediately troublesome. For
example, while the talks were supposedly secret, Argentine naval negotiators told Captain Brereton that they were reluctant to discuss any issues
of substance because they believed German V-men possessed the means
of discovering what was said.[34] In fact, the Abwehr probably knew little of
what had transpired, but until there existed a bilateral agreement sanctioning the establishment of a joint counterintelligence program, discovery of what the Germans did or did not know was unlikely to be attained.

It was the fear that no Argentine cooperation would soon be forthcoming which probably sparked the bizarre crusade subsequently
launched by U.S. diplomatic officials. In December 1940, Ambassador
Armour proposed a scheme whereby the embassy would develop and
direct an intelligence network in Argentina. The chargé d'affaires, R.
Stanford Tuck, was suggested as dispenser of a secret agent fund, while
Undersecretary Sumner Welles was asked to sanction the plan and devise
a means of covertly providing the cash. Welles did agree to consider the
scheme, but Ambassador Armour was not inclined to wait for his Washington superiors to make up their minds. Evidently he had already begun
building up a roster of agents, for in a message of January 7, 1941, he
asked for additional funds, and boasted that with a one-hundred-dollar
payment, a secret list of two dozen German spies had already been
obtained. The enthusiastic Armour went on to affirm that the procurer of
the secret document attested to its validity with an "unconditional mon-
eyback guarantee."[35]

In retrospect, the ambassador would have been wise to ask for a
refund, for only one name in this highly touted document proved to be
that of an Abwehr V-man.[36] More significantly, Armour's bid to become a
striped-pants spymaster somehow became known to the Argentine government. News of embassy wheeling and dealing in the intelligence
underworld was passed on from Minister of the Interior Miguel Culaciati
to Foreign Minister Julio Roca. The latter's terse and frosty commentary
was that intelligence activities conducted in Argentina by the U.S. embassy constituted "an unfriendly act."[37] Suffice it to say that the United
States was wise to make J. Edgar Hoover rather than Ambassador Norman

Armour its secret agent supervisor in both Argentina and the rest of Latin America.

Despite the aforementioned spate of cloak-and-dagger capers, Washington was earnestly seeking the "carrot" which would persuade Ramón Castillo to adopt a neutrality policy more in harmony with U.S. plans and purposes. Therefore, in 1940–41, economic loans for Buenos Aires were agreed to,[38] and an arms deal, without commitment for mutual defense, was being negotiated by Argentine-U.S. bargaining teams at the time of the Japanese attack on Pearl Harbor.[39] But with the official entry of the United States into the war, and the Castillo regime's successful blockage of U.S. diplomatic plans at the January 1942 Rio Foreign Ministers' Conference, friendly persuasion became passé. Confirmation of the new hard line was formally given when, on March 15, 1942, Sumner Welles told the Argentinians that if U.S. weaponry was desired, an appropriate quid pro quo would have to be forthcoming. He suggested that Argentina agree to supply naval escort for any American republics ships entering or leaving its territorial waters.[40]

One doubts that the undersecretary was surprised by the rejection of his suggestion. In any case, his April 3 response indicated that Washington would not have any weapons to sell to neutrals for a long, long time.[41] Moreover, the United States was already committed to supplying $200 million in military equipment to Brazil, Argentina's traditional enemy. Ramón Castillo might persist in refusing to cater to U.S. wishes, but the result for his country would be increasing military and naval inferiority vis-à-vis its Portuguese-speaking rival to the north.

In addition, the State Department believed that it possessed still another means for convincing Castillo of the imprudence of his foreign policy. Beginning in March 1942, Washington slowly but inexorably tightened the economic screws, reducing or canceling the shipment of industrial and consumer goods bound for Argentina.[42] Well aware that Buenos Aires might attempt to obtain the interdicted materials from other sources, the United States sought both British and Canadian cooperation in its effort to hamstring the Argentine economy.[43] Months would pass before this commercial blockade could have any serious effects, but Welles, Duggan, Bonsal, et al. seemed prepared to wait.

Ramón Castillo was resolved to bend to neither blockade nor blandishment, but the specter of a Brazil armed to the teeth with weapons Argentina could not obtain was something neither he nor the Argentine naval and military forces could countenance.[44] Since Nazi Germany was the only nation which conceivably might provide the desired weapons without demanding a political commitment, in February 1942, Buenos Aires initiated arms purchase queries in Berlin. Discussions went on through intermediaries until, in July 1942, Chargé d'Affaires Erich von Meynen was directly approached on the subject by one of Castillo's henchmen, chief of the federal police, Gen. Domingo J. Martínez. Then, after Brazil declared war on the Axis powers (August 22, 1942), Castillo dropped the mask entirely. Naval minister Rear Adm. Mario Fincati presented to German naval attaché, Capt. Dietrich Niebuhr, a specific list of naval and military equipment that Argentina was anxious to purchase.[45]

With its armies battling at Stalingrad in the USSR, and stalled at El Alamein in Egypt, the Third Reich had honeyed words but no tanks, submarines, or dive bombers to spare. In September 1942, Niebuhr was ordered to prolong the discussions, but to refrain from making any definite promises. He did his job superbly, but by October, under the weight of a welter of "maybes," the negotiations ground to a halt.[46] Castillo's failure won him no friends among the Argentine military and naval officer corps, and as a result, he would eventually pay the price.

While some might interpret this presidential quest for weaponry without strings as pro-German policy, certainly the most outspoken and convinced partisans of the Nazi cause were to be found not in the civilian government, but among the members of the Argentine armed forces. In explaining why this was the case, in March 1941, Maj. Emilio Loza, acting chief of Argentine military intelligence, told U.S. military attaché Lt. Col. Robert Devine that in addition to a long history of German-Argentine military relations, Berlin's support for Argentine hopes of territorial expansion was a critical consideration.[47] But such justifications do not explain certain kinds of relationships which developed between Abwehr personnel and Argentine military and naval figures. The most notorious agent in this regard would be a Nest Cologne, I-Wi section operative named Hans Leo Harnisch. This V-man cultivated the friendship of Capt. Eduardo Aumann, a *Volksdeutscher* who was naval aide-de-camp to President Castillo. In April 1943, Harnisch assisted Aumann in sensitive political discussions with Paraguayan military officials. Perhaps as a form of payment, Aumann placed Harnisch in contact with Rear Admiral Fincati, who agreed to allow an Abwehr agent to obtain cover as an operative of Argentine naval intelligence.[48] While it cannot be proven that this action was actually executed, the fact that it was even provisionally agreed to speaks volumes concerning the attitude of many naval and military officers toward Germany.

As for the subsequent activities of Captain Aumann, in the German Military Archives at Freiburg-im-Breisgau, there is an order dated January 25, 1944, which assigned this officer the task of creating an Abwehr network in Paraguay.[49] Twenty-four hours after this order was issued, Argentina broke diplomatic relations with the Reich, and there is no evidence that Aumann ever received or moved to execute it. But neither in Brazil, Chile, nor Mexico was a *Volksdeutscher* ever ordered by the Canaris organization to establish an espionage ring in a country other than his own. Clearly during the Castillo years, German intelligence and a number of Argentine naval and military officers enjoyed very close ties.

Despite this evidence, in assessing Argentine foreign and counterintelligence policies between July 1940 and June 1943, we conclude that such terms as *pro-Nazi, pro-Allied,* or even *pronationalist* tend to distort the situation. Perhaps the most perceptive insight in this regard was provided by a British specialist in Latin American affairs, J.V. Perowne. On February 5, 1943, Foreign Minister Enrique Ruiz-Guiñazú remarked to British ambassador Sir David Kelley that the war represented only a passing episode, and that Argentine policy was geared to deal with "permanent realities." What were these permanent realities? In Perowne's view, they "include[d] dislike of the Americans and annoyance at the American patronage of Brazil; admiration . . . for Fascist and Nazi methods . . . a desire to vary the Argentine market, and thus to escape, so far as possible, from Anglo-Saxon 'economic domination'; the comfortable conviction that we shall always need to sell them our manufactures and buy their meat, and that, if we don't buy their meat, it will be easy to sell it to Germany and Italy after the war. . . ."[50]

Even among the Radical party and the others who detested Castillo, there existed no desire to have Argentina formally become a combatant.[51] All agreed that Argentina should eventually line up with the winning coalition, but for Castillo and Ruiz-Guiñazú, the nation possessed some uniquely exploitable options. For example, in November 1940, Minister of War Gen. Juan Tonazzi told Walter von Simons, chief of Transocean, the German overseas news service, that in the future, Argentina would use this German agency to counteract United States influence in Latin America. Ramón Castillo personally supported this declaration, adding that in time he intended to utilize Transocean to further Argentine commercial and political influence, and "to protect the freedom of Latin America" against Yankee subjugation.[52] Thus, a German victory or a stalemate favoring the Reich was a development most likely to advance the possibilities of Argentine hegemony in South America.[53] Moreover, by the end of August 1942, the nations most prone to oppose Argentine aspirations, the United States and Brazil, were at war with the Third Reich. Eminently applicable was this variation on the old axiom: The enemy of my enemies is my friend.

Given these considerations, the prospect of significant U.S.-Argentine counterespionage collaboration against the Germans was bleak. Therefore, SIS/Argentina could expect little local assistance and, conversely, a good deal of indifference, factors which insured that the counterespionage struggle in Argentina would be most difficult.

II. The Trail of "Diego"

A COI confidential report of May 23, 1942, credited Maj. Gen. Günther Niedenführ with being "the most dangerous Axis agent in Latin America, if not the whole American continent," but it could relate nothing about the spy rings Niedenführ controlled or the agents he financed.[54] A number of postwar sources have accepted the description of Niedenführ as being very dangerous, concluding that until this soldier was repatriated, he was the chief of the Abwehr in South America.[55]

Since it is true that an *Ast* or *Nest* held the ultimate control over most of the FMKs in the Americas, the belief that Niedenführ controlled the Abwehr in South America is essentially inaccurate. On the other hand, Lt.

Comdr. Hermann Bohny, naval attaché in Brazil, considered Niedenführ only a co-director of the Abwehr groups in that country, and the naval attaché in Argentina, Kapitän zur See Dietrich Niebuhr, as his boss.[56] This perspective was shared by the air attaché in Chile, and creator of the PQZ ring, Lt. Col. Ludwig von Bohlen, who was told before he left for Latin America in 1941 that Niebuhr was his superior.[57] Finally, it was the last Reich ambassador to Argentina, Freiherr Edmund von Thermann, who, when asked in 1945 to name the Abwehr chief in Argentina, identified that man as Naval Attaché Dietrich Niebuhr. He never even mentioned Niedenführ.[58]

In 1945–46, United States interrogators formally questioned Niebuhr on three occasions. In the first sessions in October and November 1945, the German stated that his connection with Abwehr activities had been purely auxiliary. After reviewing the results of these question-and-answer sessions, J. Edgar Hoover told the Department of State that Niebuhr was lying. It was not until his third question-and-answer period in June 1946 that Niebuhr began to provide more reliable information and to admit that he had been more closely involved with intelligence activities. Nevertheless, the captain cleverly tried to lead the conversation along innocuous paths, much to the exasperation of his interrogators. Attached to the report of the June 1946 interrogation was a note written by an unknown observer: "I got the feeling that he [Niebuhr] was really laughing at us. . . . Getting the information you want out of him was like pulling teeth. . . ."[59]

Assigned to Abteilung I-M first under Konrad Patzig and then under Wilhelm Canaris, Dietrich Niebuhr ("Diego") got the job of naval attaché to Argentina, Brazil, and Chile in 1936. Making his headquarters in Buenos Aires, he spent the rest of the prewar years developing informants among the German residents in Argentina.[60] The naval attaché was also supplied with roughly $350,000, so that once Abwehr networks in Chile and Brazil started functioning in 1939–40, Niebuhr could finance these from his Argentine sanctuary.[61] (See Chart X for a representation of Niebuhr's organization in Argentina.)

Because his effectiveness as a military-political observer and clandestine financier was dependent upon his ability to maintain a low profile in his country of residence, there was too much at stake for Niebuhr to become directly involved in most intelligence operations.[62] The technique he developed which allowed him to continue his twin tasks while avoiding notoriety was to establish a series of front men who could carry out orders and, if necessary, shoulder the blame. Among the first of these enlisted were two naval reserve officers, Johannes Martin Müller and Franz Mammen, both of whom were named in October 1939 as assistant naval attachés. Initially, at least, Mammen's work was limited to the coding of messages sent in the naval attaché's cipher. This was not the case with Müller, who from the beginning functioned as a cutout for his chief. Nor would this separation of tasks last long, for by mid-1940,

CHART X

ABWEHR AND EMBASSY GROUPS IN ARGENTINA 1939-45

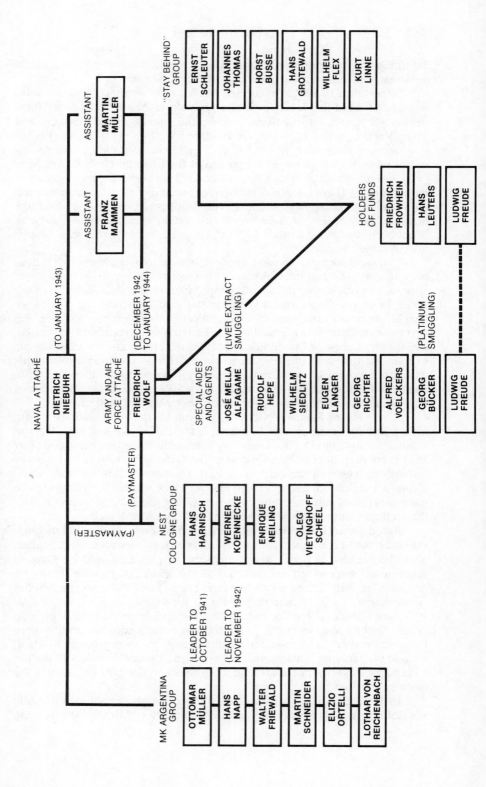

Mammen was working in collaboration with Müller directing confidential missions, making payments, and contacting informants.[63]

In addition to naval personnel, Niebuhr also utilized civilians who would do his bidding and allow him to remain in the shadows. As we have previously noted, two of these confidential agents, Alfred Voelkers and Thilo Martins, acted as go-betweens when meetings with Brazilian couriers became necessary in 1942. Others who undertook special assignments were Rudolf Hepe, an employee of the Antonio Delfino Company (a Hamburg–South America line affiliate), a textile company executive named Eugen Hans Langer, and the representative of a German tourist-cum-propaganda agency, Wilhelm von Seidlitz. Exactly when Niebuhr obtained the consent of these men to undertake clandestine assignments is not clear, but in December 1939, the attaché would manifest an urgent need for their services.[64]

The incident which would amply demonstrate both Niebuhr's skill as intriguer and the resourcefulness of his civilian lieutenants was the *Graf Spee* sailor escape operation. Following the much-publicized Battle of the River Plate on December 13, 1939, the pocket battleship *Graf Spee* sought to repair damages in Montevideo harbor. Unable to have the seventy-two-hour stay granted by the Uruguayan government extended, Capt. Hans Langsdorff concluded that he had steamed into a cul-de-sac. Convinced that even if he escaped the British men-of-war awaiting his exit more powerful units would destroy him on his homeward dash, Langsdorff ignominiously scuttled the *Graf Spee* on December 17. Several days later, he sought to atone for his errors by committing suicide.[65]

It was left to Dietrich Niebuhr to clean up the mess and see to the future welfare of the pocket battleship's crew. First, he had Rudolf Hepe arrange for Antonio Delfino Company lighters to bring one thousand *Graf Spee* crew members to Buenos Aires. The Ortiz government had not yet formally agreed to accept the crew in internment camps, and this precipitous action caused a storm to break over Hepe's head. But thanks to the judicious use of influence, and probably a large measure of "palm grease," the Delfino Company avoided further legal complications.[66]

Based on information he received from several sources and through visits to the internment camps by Lieutenants Mammen and Müller, Niebuhr decided that the Argentine security guards would do little to counteract determined escape efforts. Therefore, in January 1940, he proposed to Eugen Langer (code name: Eugen) and Wilhelm von Seidlitz (code name: Dicker) that they arrange for sailors to be smuggled as stowaways aboard Spanish and Portuguese freighters leaving Argentine ports. Other escapees were to be led over the Andes to Chile where Friedrich von Schulz-Hausmann would arrange for their passage to Vladivostok via Japanese freighters. "Eugen" and "Dicker" would obtain the false papers and passports, arrange for guides and safe houses, and pay the necessary bribes.[67]

In 1940, Eugen Langer conducted three escape expeditions to Chile via Bolivia, but his mysterious involvement in a political plot involving

Peruvian political exiles in Santiago made another trip to Chile dangerous.[68] Thus, the job of delivering *Graf Spee* escapees to Schulz-Hausmann
fell to a man whom Langer introduced to Niebuhr in 1940, and whose
work in Chile has been already discussed: Eugenio Ellinger Knoll, better
known as "Juan Valdéz."[69] Working independently of Seidlitz, Langer also
smuggled *Graf Spee* crewmen aboard Spanish ships in Buenos Aires and
Rosario. A dedicated worker, Langer appears to have done most of his
work for expenses for Niebuhr claims to have paid him no more than one
thousand dollars. This figure is suspect, however, because his co-conspir-
ator, Wilhelm von Seidlitz, allegedly collected seventy thousand dollars.[70]
Certainly a good deal of money wound up in a variety of Argentine,
Spanish, and German pockets, because without hefty expenditures, operations of this kind would never have succeeded.

From January 1940 to January 1943, nearly two hundred of the one
thousand interned *Graf Spee* crew members succeeded in returning to
the Third Reich, two-thirds from Argentine ports, and the rest via the
Pacific Ocean route.[71] This total represented less than 20 percent of the
total number of men interned in Argentina, but ninety of those who
escaped were either officers or skilled technicians.[72] In 1943, Anglo-
American protests and pressure on Franco's Spain, plus the fact that
Germany was losing the war, resulted in the termination of the project.
Nevertheless, the escapees included officers who subsequently became
U-boat aces, a consideration which made this an operation of which
Niebuhr could be justifiably proud.

What eventually proved to be the most critical clandestine activity
under Niebuhr's supervision was one which initially was of minor importance. This was the smuggling of mica, platinum, and industrial diamonds
through the British sea blockade and back to Germany. The method
employed was generally to give a package of these items to a crewman
aboard a Spanish or Portuguese freighter who, for one to two hundred
dollars, would deliver the package to an Abwehr agent in Spain. Since the
amount paid was two or three times the monthly salary of the average
Spanish or Portuguese seaman, the Germans had few problems finding
and developing reliable couriers.

To carry out the procurement of the strategic metals and the selection of the couriers, Dietrich Niebuhr again used Wilhelm von Seidlitz as
operational front man. The latter, in turn, depended upon two Spanish
subagents, Esteban Jesús Amorín (code name: Rodríguez) and Juan Antonio Prieto, to make contact with amenable sailors. But the efforts of
these men were matched by those of José Mella Alfageme, an alleged
Spanish military intelligence agent who admitted to shipping some one
and a half tons of liver extract (which was thought to improve night
vision, and thus be useful to pilots) to German agents in Spain. Mella
Alfageme carried on his activities from Argentina's second largest port,
Rosario, and regularly presented bills for his services to Niebuhr's assistant, Lt. Martin Müller.[73]

For most of 1941, quantities of mica, platinum, and industrial diamonds reached Germany via LATI airlines as well as by smuggling through the port of Buenos Aires.[74] Still, Germany's increasing war production needs, coupled with its inability to obtain these materials from virtually any other source, necessitated that a more prodigious acquisition effort be undertaken in South America. Chosen to lead the operation was an agent assigned to the I-L section of Ast Berlin, Georg Bücker. This V-man left for Argentina via LATI, but by the time he reached Buenos Aires in December 1941, Germany was at war with the United States, and the Italian transatlantic air service was about to be shut down. This situation left smuggling through Argentine ports as the most efficient way of shipping strategic minerals from South America to the Reich.[75]

The establishment of a safe means of delivery was important, but Bücker soon found himself facing critical procurement problems. Through a series of purchase contracts signed with South American countries in 1941–42, the United States had cornered the market in the legitimate mining of platinum.[76] By June 1942, the price of black market platinum reached two hundred dollars an ounce, and since there were other bidders in the contraband market, Bücker needed virtually unlimited funds; with Niebuhr acting as facilitator, these were obtained from commercial attaché Alfred Burmeister.[77] Burmeister committed suicide in May 1944, and since his records were destroyed, it is impossible to know the total of funds he made available. Nevertheless, postwar estimates indicate that at least $1 million worth of platinum, mica, and industrial diamonds were smuggled out of Buenos Aires aboard neutral shipping from 1941 to 1944.[78]

If general acceptance at the dinner tables and in the board rooms of both Argentine and German elites is considered to be a requisite for a master spy, then Hans Leo Harnisch (code names: Boss, Viereck) was the Abwehr's nonpareil in Argentina. A lawyer and businessman who immigrated in 1920, Harnisch became extremely well connected in capital city business and military circles, and gained an enviable reputation as a facilitator and expediter of difficult deals. Asked to negotiate a sensitive government-business arrangement in Germany, Harnisch departed for Berlin via LATI in June 1941. Shortly after his arrival in the Reich, he was approached by a "Dr. Kramer," probably the same officer who was Theodor Schlegel's controller (Capt. Georg Kraemer-Knott) and recruited as a V-man for the I-Wi section of Nest Cologne.

Charged with the task of reporting on U.S. and Argentine economic developments, Harnisch sent his reports to his controller by airmail and cable. When, in April 1942, "Dr. Kramer" decided that Harnisch's reports had become irregular, he contacted Niebuhr and asked him to look into the matter. The response given was that Harnisch believed the mail and telecommunications links with Europe were no longer secure, so that intercepted reports might result in his unmasking. Niebuhr's solution to the problem was simple: Harnisch would henceforth report to him, and he would send the information in his special code.[79] Certainly Nest

Cologne believed that the reports were valuable, because in May 1942, Niebuhr was ordered to pay Harnisch up to $14,200 in expense money. Harnisch received $2,500 on one occasion, and the balance was placed in a cash box to which the assistant naval attaché, Lt. Martin Müller, had the key. In this fashion, Niebuhr received regular reports from Harnisch, Nest Cologne received the information it was paying for, and all the parties involved were temporarily satisfied.[80]

While Dietrich Niebuhr got on well with Hans Harnisch, the bane of his existence as naval attaché was the Ottomar Müller–Hans Napp ring, euphemistically referred to at Ast Hamburg as MK "Argentina." It should be recalled that Friedrich Kempter, the erstwhile superior of these two men, believed Napp to be a knave. Niebuhr went Kempter one better, for he considered both men contemptible. Only grudgingly did he make the $150 payments each month which he had been ordered to provide in 1940, and he made no effort to disguise his distaste for the two men he considered to be unmitigated scoundrels.[81]

As long as the money rolled in and shipping news was sent to Kempter three times a week, Ottomar Müller and Hans Napp could thumb their noses at a fuming Niebuhr. In May 1941, MK "Argentina" grew to three members with the induction of Walter Friewald (code name: Tannin), a Paraguayan *Volksdeutscher* who had taken up residence in Buenos Aires. The new recruit had had some training as a deep sea diver and offered to serve the Reich by fastening bombs to the hulls of British ships.[82] But Ast Hamburg displayed a definite lack of interest in this proposal. Instead, it told Müller in August that it wanted a radio operator recruited, not a saboteur. In short, headquarters desired that MK "Argentina" become an FMK.

Ottomar Müller knew nothing about radiotelegraphy and he had no interest in improving his knowledge in that area. Instead, he stalled and complained for over two months, until Ast Hamburg decided that his usefulness was at an end. On October 25, 1941, a radio message received by Friedrich Kempter in Brazil and forwarded by airmail to Buenos Aires ordered that Ottomar Müller cease all activity, and it designated Hans Napp as chief of MK "Argentina."[83]

The new leader promptly called upon Niebuhr, who had been informed by coded cable of the change of command. Perhaps Ast Hamburg thought that Napp could be persuaded to build a radio station, because it authorized the naval attaché to pay him six hundred dollars immediately and a monthly stipend of five hundred dollars. In exchange for this increased salary, Hans Napp was prepared to do something other than vegetate. He recruited another network member, Martin Schneider, a headwaiter at a nondescript restaurant, who went daily to the harbor to observe shipping. Napp also moved his family into a sumptuous house in a Buenos Aires suburb and established a business front by renting offices in downtown Buenos Aires, a few doors from the British embassy. Between November 1941 and July 1942, he received thirty-five hundred dollars in salary, but he did not create a radio station. Instead, he sat at his desk in his office, clipping reports of arriving and departing Anglo-American vessels from the newspapers.[84]

It was the hint of possible danger which apparently caused Napp to reassess his commitment to the cloak-and-dagger life. With the break in relations between Brazil and Germany, Friedrich Kempter advised him that cables and mails were no longer secure, and that in the future, Napp should deliver shipping data to Captain Niebuhr. The MK "Argentina" boss held a hasty conference with the naval attaché (January 28) and agreed that the information would be delivered twice a week to the embassy porter in a sealed, unaddressed envelope.[85]

This arrangement continued until July 1942, when the Argentine government ordered the press to discontinue publishing news of the arrival and departure of ships of belligerent countries. With no more news to be obtained from the daily newspapers, Hans Napp decided that somebody else needed to be the boss and take the risks. He then introduced Martin Schneider to Niebuhr as the new MK leader. Still, Napp would continue in an advisory capacity, and thereby justify receiving a share of the monthly stipend. It is presumed that Schneider willingly accepted this new setup; in any case, the deliveries of envelopes to the embassy porter continued through October 1942.[86]

The record of MK "Argentina" is not merely uninspiring, it is one of unrelieved mediocrity. Dietrich Niebuhr would later establish that on one occasion, he told Hans Napp "to leave Buenos Aires for his own good."[87] It would be unfortunate for all concerned that Napp failed to heed this sage advice.

In a message dated July 13, 1942, Dietrich Niebuhr informed the Abwehr that his special spy fund was down to about ten thousand dollars in Argentine pesos.[88] Niebuhr had spent the money sustaining Abwehr networks in Brazil, Chile, and Argentina, directing the *Graf Spee* sailor escape operation, and conducting the contraband trade in strategic materials. Nevertheless, by July 1942, the naval attaché was out of favor in Berlin, and the reasons for his fall from grace were both tactical and philosophical.

As far back as August 1941, Ast Hamburg had been expecting a clandestine radio station to be built in Argentina, and rightly or wrongly, it had assumed that Niebuhr would assist either Ottomar Müller or Hans Napp in achieving this goal.[89] With the breakup of the Brazilian networks in March 1942, and the silencing of the Chilean radios by July, the Abwehr in South America was off the airwaves. This was a situation which neither Berlin headquarters nor the various *Asts* and *Nests* intended to tolerate. Thus, in July 1942, Ast Hamburg made its position crystal clear: It wanted Dietrich Niebuhr to quickly arrange for a clandestine radio station in the one country where it was still relatively safe to do so.[90]

Pressure from Hamburg engendered resistance from Niebuhr, and in light of the attaché's operating style, this was completely logical. Whether it was the *Graf Spee* sailor escape scheme or the smuggling of strategic materials, he had always acted from behind a screen of trusted front men.

If Niebuhr took over the task of creating an Abwehr clandestine radio station, in all probability he would have to junk his usual operational procedure. Moreover, the likelihood was great that he would become as deeply involved in the affairs of an Argentine FMK as Hermann Bohny had been with Gustav Engels's CEL organization. And if anything went wrong, he could expect that, at the very least, his tenure as naval attaché in Argentina would be summarily terminated.

Under interrogation in October 1945, Brig. Gen. Erwin Lahousen, long-time chief of the Abwehr's sabotage organization, provided what was probably the most incisive and enlightening explanation concerning the involvement of German service attachés in intelligence activities. Those who did not have espionage tasks to execute were considered to be "spotless"; those who undertook such assignments or who were ordered to do so were considered to be "stained."[91] Captain Niebuhr would never have been considered immaculate; still, for three years he had been prudent. By July 1942, however, the pressure of the war situation had downgraded the value of discretion. What the Abwehr wanted was for Niebuhr not only to become spotted, but to paint himself liberally with the tar brush. The future did not appear promising for Dietrich Niebuhr, but when the end finally came, he would have the satisfaction of knowing that he had not pulled the rug out from under himself.

III. Commencement of the Counterespionage War in Argentina

A. A Perilous Toehold: The SIS in Argentina

Although the first SIS/Argentina agent reached that country in September 1940, William Doyle did not reach Buenos Aires until May 1942, and his status as legal attaché was not fully recognized by the Argentinians for another six months.[92] As a result, the counterespionage war in Argentina would be conducted without the police cooperation prevalent elsewhere and under the direction of an official whose status the Argentine government seemed in no hurry to recognize.

The grilling of Friedrich Kempter in Brazil, plus the intercepted LIR-MAX messages, had revealed a great deal about the identities of the MK "Argentina" ring as well as Niebuhr's involvement.[93] As in Brazil and Chile, the United States was intercepting cables sent between Argentina and Germany, and although they could not decipher the Enigma-coded messages sent by Niebuhr, U.S. cryptanalytic specialists had little trouble decrypting the others.[94] Naturally, those persons mentioned in the deciphered messages came under suspicion, as did others like Friedrich von Schulz-Hausmann, whose activities elsewhere were reason enough for him to be kept under surveillance.

In addition, U.S. spy hunters were also the beneficiaries of plain blind luck. The source of their good fortune was Pablo Santiago Longhi (code name: Pablo), an Argentine bon vivant who lacked the means for maintaining the life style he craved. Returning to Buenos Aires in July 1941 after several years of living in Spain, Longhi promptly presented himself at the U.S. embassy. Claiming that he had been trained as a spy by the Abwehr, he proposed to become a double agent, loyal to the United States. Embassy interrogators suspected a trap and declined the offer. Thereupon, Longhi had to get along only on what the Germans paid him. Apparently they had some faith in him, for he was dispatched as a courier by Dietrich Niebuhr to Mexico and elsewhere in the Americas during the final months of 1941.[95] He was subsequently sanctioned as a cutout between Niebuhr and the Heinz Lorenz group in Rio de Janeiro, but the arrest of Longhi by Brazilian police in April 1942 canceled that operation.[96] On July 23, Niebuhr reported to Berlin that although "Pablo" was not blown, he should not be used for a while.[97]

For Longhi, enforced inactivity probably meant a reduced paycheck. In any case, this enterprising hustler once again contacted the U.S. embassy and this time the reaction was quite different. Legal attaché William Doyle needed all the assistance he could get, and of course, dollars spent just as well in Buenos Aires as German marks. In August 1942, the SIS/Argentina chief interrogated Longhi and learned that Dietrich Niebuhr's code name was "Diego."[98] The significance of this confirmation lay in the fact that despite intercepted radio and cable messages, the SIS was still somewhat uncertain as to whether "Diego" was Günther Niedenführ, Dietrich Niebuhr, a German bartender named Diego Meyer, or Pablo Longhi himself.[99] After Longhi provided his vital piece of intelligence detail, Dietrich Niebuhr became a primary target for SIS/Argentina.

Unfortunately for the United States, the acquisition of counterintelligence data in Argentina was not its only major difficulty. Embassy counsel Clifton P. English stated the problem succinctly when he wrote to a Washington associate in May 1942 that the embassy staff had no idea "what we are going to do if and when we get all the local [i.e., German] agents identified and located."[100] What English was emphasizing was that the Castillo regime was not collaborating in either the surveillance or detention of suspected spies. Indeed, in a meeting between Ruiz-Guiñazú and Ambassador Norman Armour on July 8, 1942, the foreign minister made light of any suggestions that the Abwehr was active in Argentina. He also made it painstakingly clear that unless the United States produced indisputable evidence that ship movement data were being cabled to Germany by Reich embassy personnel, and that this information actually caused the sinking of ships, Argentina would take no action.[101]

Of course, the United States could not reveal all it knew without indicating that it was intercepting Argentine cable traffic and raising the suspicion that it was doing so from Argentine territory. But since the Castillo government believed that the United States was intercepting international cable traffic,[102] Washington would have lost nothing by admitting the fact. The State Department was not inclined to do so, and although Ambassador Armour continued to make protests concerning Axis cable traffic to the Castillo government, his efforts proved unavailing.[103] Gradually, Armour reached the conclusion that even if irrefutable evidence was obtained proving that cabled information from Argentina directly resulted in the sinking of Allied ships, Ruiz-Guiñazú would do as little as possible to restrict Axis telecommunications.[104] In essence, good faith between U.S. and Argentine officials was made conspicuous by its near total absence.

Thus, when on October 8, 1942, Sumner Welles made his controversial indictment of Argentina and Chile for permitting "their brothers and neighbors in the Americas to be stabbed in the back by Axis emissaries," the goals were the same as in the Chilean case, but the expectations were somewhat different. Recall that after the initial violent reaction, Foreign Minister Barros Jarpa had been sacrificed, and by November 1, 1942, most of the PYL group was behind bars. Argentina, in contrast, was expected to be a much tougher nut to crack.

Unexpectedly, however, the usually cautious Ruiz-Guiñazú took steps which initially enhanced State Department plotting. Two days after Welles's speech, he unleased a caustic blast intimating that the undersecretary had been deplorably loose with the truth, challenged Welles to prove his charges, and reaffirmed Argentina's commitment to a policy of neutrality.[105] Washington meekly held its peace until November 1942, by which time Chile was finally undertaking the desired counterespionage activities. Then it struck with a vengeance.

B. *Heads, I Win, Tails, You Lose*

Enrique Ruiz-Guiñazú having opened his mouth wide, the United States made haste to push his foot into it by pressuring the Castillo government into drastically revising its foreign policy. The means to this end became a spy memorandum which, like the documents given Chile and Mexico in 1941 and 1942, identified German agents operating within the national boundaries and unsubtly urged that unspecified but stringent action be taken. But any resemblances between the Chilean and Mexican spy documents and "German Military Espionage in Argentina" were strictly coincidental. In fact, the compendium presented to Argentine officialdom on November 3, 1942, was, to an uncomfortable extent, an exercise in misinformation.[106] It listed thirty-two alleged Abwehr agents and divided these into four groups or networks. The errors, half-truths, and misstatements accumulate steadily thereafter:

(1) The memorandum affirmed that "some of the principal espionage agents are Nazi party leaders and are known as such."[107] But the study failed to demonstrate that any of the thirty-two persons named were or ever had been a Nazi party (AO) leader in Argentina.

(2) The memorandum insisted that "millions of dollars worth of ships, merchandise, petroleum, munitions and foodstuffs have been sent to the bottom of the sea due to the efforts of these agents." It further charged that "these agents are also directly responsible for the loss of the lives of hundreds of men, women and children who died when their ships were destroyed by German torpedoes."[108] But only one ship, the *Andalucia Star,* was mentioned as being sunk through the efforts of any of the spies mentioned.[109]

(3) The memorandum argued that "only the names of those are included regarding whom there is a reasonable certainty that they are to some degree guilty."[110] This statement did not square with several examples found in the body of the memorandum, and the case of Otto Hein is typical. Hein was listed as an agent even though the document admits that "nothing definite is known against him." As if to counter the question of why he was included at all, the writer or writers of the memorandum stated that "in view of his close connection with those involved, his name is submitted for what it is worth."[111]

(4) The leader of one agent network was stated to be Rudolf Hepe, the man who arranged for the delivery to Argentina of the *Graf Spee* crewmen. Named as chief of another Argentine ring was Friedrich Tadeo von Schulz-Hausmann ("Casero"), the founder of the Chilean PYL organization. The spy memorandum did not relate a single espionage activity conducted in Argentina by Schulz-Hausmann, and it failed utterly to establish any functional or administrative link between the alleged leaders and the alleged members of either group.[112]

(5) The memorandum contained no example of cabled shipping information sent from Argentina. The only evidence presented in this regard are shipping reports radioed from Brazil to Germany (over LIR-MAX) or from Chile to Germany (PYL-REW) between April and November 1941.

(6) Listed as "an important agent" under Dietrich Niebuhr was a German citizen allegedly named "Viktor Mann." The memorandum admitted that "the exact identity of this person was not known"; nevertheless, "there has come to the attention of the United States government a certain Viktor Mann or Victor Rudolf Mann, whose activities have attracted suspicions."[113] Approximately four months later, another report dealing with Argentine espionage affirmed that "Viktor Mann" was one of a string of code names used by another suspected agent named Hans Biebel (or Bieben).[114] But was Hans Biebel a German spy? Neither the final list of agents presented by the Argentine police in June 1945 nor the official FBI account of Abwehr activities published after the war listed either "Viktor Mann" or Hans Biebel.[115]

The weaknesses of this tissue of fiction, innuendo, and occasional fact become comprehensible if it is understood that despite its presumed focus, the memorandum was based almost entirely on information gleaned from non-Argentine sources. Presumably the inability to have a legal attaché assigned to the country prior to May 1942 plus the lack of cooperation by Argentine security forces were the factors which made a decisive difference. The only Argentina-based group which the SIS knew much about was the Müller-Napp organization, and once again, its principal information source was Friedrich Kempter, who was in prison in Rio de Janeiro.[116] A more appropriate title for the document would have been "German Military Espionage in Argentina as Discovered from Counterintelligence Activities in Chile and Brazil."

Certainly the vagaries and inaccuracies of the spy memorandum were well understood by United States officialdom,[117] but the truth or falsity of the document was secondary to its potential utility. That some of those mentioned in "German Military Espionage in Argentina" had never committed any acts of espionage in Argentina was immaterial. So was the fact that, like Chile and Brazil, Argentina had no law which covered espionage actions conducted against other states during a time when Argentina was not at war.[118] What Washington provided was a weapon: Argentina was expected to use it to begin destroying the German intelligence apparatus operating within its borders. Of course, if Argentina acted accordingly, it would necessarily arrest and/or deport a number of German citizens. As in the case of Chile, once such steps were taken, the termination of telecommunications connections and the severance of diplomatic relations with the Axis were actions which presumably must follow.

Still, given the past attitude of the Castillo government, even if this shabby excuse for a spy memorandum had been accurate and comprehensive, it was not certain that the scenario just presented would have become a reality. Therefore, Washington had readied a "persuader" to make certain that the Argentines would not fail to see the light. On the evening of November 4, 1942, in response to the undersecretary's invitation, Ambassador Felipe Espil visited Sumner Welles. The U.S. representative presented him with a copy of "German Military Espionage in Argentina" and promptly began criticizing Argentina for its failure to arrest V-men and to cut telecommunications links with the Axis nations. Ambassador Espil, an old hand at the diplomatic game of feints and gestures, got the point very quickly. According to Welles, "he [Espil] hoped earnestly that the document now communicated to the Argentine government will not be made public if the Argentine government took effective and prompt steps to correct the situation complained of. He said that publication of a document of this character could only increase bad feeling against Argentina within the United States and within the other republics. . . ." The undersecretary's reply was both classic and menacing: "The question of publication or non-publication of the document must be left open. . . ."[119]

Welles also informed Ambassador Espil that on the previous evening, a copy of "German Military Espionage in Argentina" had been presented to the foreign minister in Buenos Aires by the U.S. ambassador. Welles did not know, nor was the State Department immediately informed, that Norman Armour had not acted as the undersecretary believed. On November 3, 1942, the U.S. ambassador did hand a copy of the spy memorandum to an Argentine official—Minister of the Interior Miguel Culaciati, not Enrique Ruiz-Guiñazú.[120]

Over three decades later, in a private interview, Ambassador Armour explained the reasons for his independent action. In his view, the primary purpose of the spy memorandum was to have Argentina take counterespionage actions which Washington hoped would result in a radical change in the direction of the neutralist policy of the Castillo govern-ment. Armour believed that Ruiz-Guiñazú, no matter what the merits or demerits of the document, would work to thwart these goals. The United States might retaliate by embarrassing Argentina in much of the world press, but this would lead to neither the detention of additional German agents nor the achievement of the other policy goals. Armour viewed Culaciati as a responsible official who would seek to avoid having Argen-tina being held up for world censure. The ambassador concluded that his maneuver was successful, for after reading the memorandum, the minis-ter of the interior replied: "I'll take care of this," and asked that the United States take no action before he had had an opportunity to arrest and interrogate suspects.[121] On November 4, the spy memorandum was duly presented to the Argentine Foreign Ministry, and two days later, Armour was told that the Castillo government needed "time to complete investi-gations which premature publication would undoubtedly jeopardize."[122] Armour's response to Foreign Minister Ruiz-Guiñazú was that while he would recommend delay, everything depended upon the speed and energy manifested in moving against the Germans.

Norman Armour was as good as his word. He did suggest that the State Department give Argentina sufficient time to prove its intentions, but this suggestion did not gain favor with Sumner Welles. The undersec-retary's rather sharp response was that "the situation will still be totally unsatisfactory unless the Argentine government . . . undertakes, on its own initiative, to stamp out all of the Axis activities today going on in Argentina, many of which we have no knowledge of . . . ."[123] Washington never established the minimum requirements Argentina would have to meet in order to prevent the public release of "German Military Espio-nage in Argentina." But, it now believed it had sufficient leverage to call the tune. Buenos Aires would have to dance, sweat, and hope for the best.

C. *"An Admirable Form of Blackmail"*

Although the situation now necessitated that the Castillo regime take some public action, that government's primary concern remained the blunting of U.S. assaults on its neutrality posture. This meant that, ulti-mately, little more than a cosmetic counterspy campaign was all that was envisaged. Still, after Minister Culaciati promised Ambassador Armour rapid action on November 3, 1942, there was some initial cause for optimism. On November 5, Hans Napp's business office was raided, and in a desk, police found carbon copies of ship movement reports which referred to the recipient as "Attaché," or "Niebuhr." Like Joséf Starziczny in Brazil, Hans Napp had chosen to keep copies of his handiwork, and this security lapse would have far-reaching consequences. During the next twenty-four hours, Ottomar Müller, Walter Friewald, Martin Schneider, and two others associated with MK "Argentina," Lothar von Reichenbach and Helvecio Ortelli, were arrested and held incommunicado by the federal police of the city of Buenos Aires.[124]

The missing member of the MK "Argentina" cast of characters was Hans Napp, and for almost two weeks, the federal police in the capital city declared themselves unable to discover his whereabouts. This disclaimer was treated with a maximum of skepticism by legal attaché William Doyle, because from November 4–6, 1942, SIS/Argentina operatives had kept Napp under surveillance in his home. Only shortly before the federal police arrived to arrest him did Napp suddenly disappear. Convinced of collusion between the Abwehr agent and police elements in the capital, Ambassador Armour sought Minister Culaciati's permission to have two detectives of the Buenos Aires Provincial Police enter the Federal District and make the arrest. Culaciati agreed, and on November 18, Miguel Llorens Herrera and Jacobo Savaronsky, police detectives apparently on good terms with SIS/Argentina, entered the city limits and arrested Hans Napp—at his home.[125] Taken to La Plata, capital of the Province of Buenos Aires, Napp complained that since he bribed a Buenos Aires (i.e., city) police official, he had not expected to be arrested.[126] The provincial officers, however, had not been recipients of German money, and they were not inclined to listen to a great many evasive responses. Not surprisingly, a confession implicating Dietrich Niebuhr was obtained in forty-eight hours.[127] Only then was Hans Napp returned to Buenos Aires and incarcerated with his other MK "Argentina" cohorts.

If the arrest and detention of these Abwehr V-men seemed to be progressing propitiously from the U.S. point of view, SIS/Argentina chief William Doyle soon discovered that there was a definite limit to Argentine cooperation. Aside from the Napp arrest, Culaciati refused all offers of cooperation and rejected a request to allow SIS personnel to be present during the interrogation of prisoners. The minister of the interior told Armour that "he did not want it known that the Americans had anything to do with the matter [of espionage investigation]."[128] SIS/Argentina would have to stay on the sidelines, unable either to be a part of or to critically influence the investigatory and interrogative processes.

Not unnaturally, their lack of input caused some apprehension among U.S. onlookers, and their inquietude was heightened by the curious manner in which certain other aspects of the investigation were handled. In addition to Müller, Napp, and the four others allegedly involved with MK "Argentina," ten other persons named in "German Military Espionage in Argentina" were arrested and interrogated. Among these, Thilo Martens was asked a few perfunctory questions and then released. Rudolf Hepe denied that he had ever had anything to do with the *Graf Spee* crew escape efforts and stated that Capt. Dietrich Niebuhr was only a casual acquaintance. Friedrich Tadeo von Schulz-Hausmann disclaimed any connection with German intelligence and admitted only a "superficial acquaintance" with the naval attaché.[129] SIS/Argentina, when it obtained a transcript of these declarations, was rightly inclined to scoff, but, as Norman Armour reported to Washington, many of those questioned possessed "considerable influence" in Argentine social and political circles.[130]

Meanwhile, the intentions of the Castillo regime in conducting the spy investigation were becoming increasingly clear. Beginning on November 24, news releases concerning German espionage in Argentina received significant play in the national press.[131] Then, on December 4, 1942, a specially appointed federal prosecutor, Belisario Gache Pirán, delivered to Federal Judge Miguel Jantus a long memorandum summarizing the evidence against the six men being held, and emphasized that the confessions of Martin Schneider, Hans Napp, and Ottomar Müller had implicated naval attaché Dietrich Neibuhr. The judge conducted his own inquiry, and on December 10 issued a judgment concluding that there was sufficient reason to hold those arrested, and that Dietrich Niebuhr was certainly implicated.

Forthwith, Argentine attorney general Dr. Juan Álvarez called upon the Argentine Supreme Court "to request that the Castillo government, through the foreign minister, approach the German embassy in order to have the naval attaché place himself under the jurisdiction of the Supreme Court." The justices took this request under advisement and on December 22, a solid majority formally sanctioned the execution of this action.[132] That the Third Reich would allow Captain Niebuhr to be formally questioned by an Argentine court could hardly have been expected. The formal refusal from Foreign Minister Ribbentrop was presented on January 9, 1943, and two days later—again with a good deal of press coverage—Dietrich Niebuhr completed his rendezvous with calamity by being declared persona non grata. He departed Argentina aboard a Spanish steamer on January 30, 1943.

The Castillo government had judiciously manipulated the press in conducting its spy investigation and, as U.S. observers had to admit, reinforced the public's impression that the German espionage agents were all being deported or detained.[133] Not surprisingly, however, the State Department came to a vastly different conclusion and soon found itself faced with the prospect that it might have to make good its threat. On November 18, 1942, Sumner Welles had cabled Norman Armour that the spy memorandum would remain unpublished for now, but continued forbearance was contingent upon positive Argentine action. But exactly seven days later, Welles informed the ambassador that since the Castillo government apparently was going to "disregard the information" given to it, the State Department was contemplating the publication of the spy memorandum by the Emergency Advisory Committee for the Political Defense of the Americas (CPD).[134] Why the undersecretary suddenly changed his mind about Argentine intentions is not clear, but before the end of the year, Norman Armour, Lawrence Duggan, Philip Bonsal, and Carl Spaeth, U.S. representative in the CPD, would all question the wisdom of making this document public.[135] Assuming that one ever existed, a State Department consensus regarding the publication of "German Military Espionage in Argentina" and its utility as a persuasive weapon was swiftly eroding.

Ultimately, certain developments transpiring in December 1942 apparently made it seem incumbent that the State Department take some retaliatory action. For example, on December 7, Miguel Culaciati met Norman Armour and promised that Friedrich von Schulz-Hausmann and other *Reichsdeutschen* named in the spy memorandum would all be jailed or deported. The minister of the interior assured the ambassador that although there might not be sufficient proof to hold these people for trial, all that was necessary for their deportation was "enough evidence to satisfy his own conscience." He then assured Armour that sufficient proofs for the latter already existed.[136]

But other inner voices, or orders from higher officialdom, caused a change of plans. No one named in the spy document would be expelled from Argentina until 1944. Moreover, on December 16, 1942, the confessed agents implicated in the activities of MK "Argentina" were all released on bail and allowed to leave the environs of the federal capital.[137] Indeed, for one week after Napp, Müller, and the others were released on bond, Culaciati was still telling U.S. embassy officials that these persons were behind bars![138] In a report to the White House (December 7, 1942), J. Edgar Hoover argued that the Castillo regime intended nothing more than a cosmetic investigation and publicity campaign.[139] The events surrounding release of the MK "Argentina" six, plus Culaciati's inability to make good on his verbal promises, were strong indication that the FBI chief knew exactly what he was talking about.

In addition to the issue of German agent activity inside Argentina, for ten months the United States had been pressing Argentina to cut all telecommunications links with the Axis powers. Once again, Argentine actions followed a similar pattern. On November 10, 1942, Ruiz-Guiñazú intimated to Norman Armour that the privilege of sending cable and radio-telephone messages to their capitals might soon be prohibited to the Axis diplomatic missions.[140] Subsequently, however, the Argentinians regained their nerve, for on November 27, Ruiz-Guiñazú told Armour that telecommunications privileges could not be terminated without breaking relations with the Axis.[141] Finally, on December 30, Minister Culaciati issued new orders limiting the Axis diplomatic missions to the dispatch of one hundred coded word groups per day. This was not what Washington wanted, but it was as far as Argentina would go. On January 2, 1943, Welles cabled the embassy in Buenos Aires that Culaciati's December 30 announcement had left the United States with no alternative; Castillo, Ruiz-Guiñazú, and company must now be made to comprehend the depth of Washington's discontent.[142]

With the decision made, developments followed as in a chain reaction. On January 4, 1943, Carlos Dário Ojeda of Mexico, acting chairman of the CPD, received "Axis Espionage Activities in Argentina," a slightly rewritten version of the November 3, 1942, document. This revision contained no more proofs of charges than its prototype,[143] but the State Department seems to have had no doubts that the CPD would act in the manner desired. Indeed, on January 7, Welles received assurances that the CPD would make "Axis Espionage Activities in Argentina" public as soon as "Chile officially broke diplomatic relations with the Axis."[144] Since the CPD had not yet formally met to discuss the document so recently received, it is curious that such assurances could have been given so quickly; evidently, the fix was in, but the climax would not occur until the last days of January 1943. On the twentieth, Juan Ríos of Chile declared that his nation was breaking diplomatic relations with the Axis powers. The following day, Ramón Castillo announced that Argentina would persist in its neutrality policy, and on the twenty-second, the CPD voted to publish "Axis Espionage Activities in Argentina," which it did amid waves of publicity on January 28, 1943.

Argentine reaction to the CPD's actions was on one level predictably dyspeptic. Ruiz-Guiñazú condemned the January 4, 1943, document as "prejudicial and repugnant." Ambassador Adrian Escobar in Spain characterized the CPD's decision to publish the document as a cheap trick engineered from Washington, a conclusion to which Ambassador Felipe Espil cabled his general concurrence.[145] When called to the Argentine chancellery and quizzed about the matter on January 23, Ambassador Norman Armour's bland response was that his government believed the document should be published since it "affects the security of all the American republics."[146] Ruiz-Guiñazú found this explanation inadequate, and in a report to Ramón Castillo he concluded that "once more the fundamental dishonesty of Yankee diplomacy has manifested itself."[147]

But in dealing with what they viewed as a U.S.-inspired diplomatic offensive, the Castillo government did more than mutter darkly about Washington's perfidiousness. On February 1, 1943, all national radio stations were ordered to cancel scheduled broadcasts for one hour beginning at 9:15 P.M., to accord pro-government speakers an opportunity to attack the recently released CPD document and to praise the foreign policy of Ramón Castillo. The speeches were mocked in a U.S. embassy report as inept propaganda, but this observation was cautiously presented as being primarily an initial reaction.[148]

Whether the Argentine effort to discredit the January 4, 1943, memorandum succeeded cannot be proved one way or another. On the other hand, on February 6, 1943, Ambassador Norman Armour suggested to Washington as inoffensively as he could that release of "Axis Espionage Activities in Argentina" by the CPD had engendered neither new concessions nor additional cooperation.[149] What a British official had dubbed "an admirable form of blackmail"[150] had proven, in the end, to be pitifully innocuous.

D. *Dreams and Policies*

The salient problem with both the November 3, 1942, spy document and its January 4, 1943, revision was that they failed to prove the ship-sinking charges made by Sumner Welles in his speech of October 8, 1942. Foreign Minister Ruiz-Guiñazú had continuously insisted that he required proof that shipping information collected in Argentina and transmitted over telecommunications facilities in that country had directly resulted in the sinking of Allied ships.[151] In fact, a secret January 1943 State Department study admitted that only indirect evidence of this connection existed.[152] In 1982, the FBI informed us that conclusive evidence of this connection never had existed.[153]

Without the proverbial smoking gun, or at the very least, stronger evidence than that presented in the November 1942 spy memorandum, it was exceedingly presumptuous to assume that the Argentine government would take actions which would have terminated its commitment to a policy of neutrality. Furthermore, the United States was still maintaining an informal economic blockade of Argentina, and had never stipulated to Buenos Aires what the minimum requirements would be if the spy memorandum was to remain confidential.[154] In retrospect, the presentation of the November 1942 spy document and the threat to publicize it seem prompted largely by the implicit conviction that Argentina, like Chile, was now ready and eager to jump aboard the Allies' victory wagon. Possessed of "German Military Espionage in Argentina," Castillo could conveniently discover the unsanctioned presence of German agents, express disgust, shock, and dismay, and then sever telecommunications and diplomatic links with Germany.

The chief problem with this scenario is that Washington could not seem to understand that the goals and intents of the Castillo government were only partially affected by the shifts which had thus far taken place in the war situation. By December 1942, Ramón Castillo had indeed become convinced that the Axis might not win the war,[155] but this realization did not mean that the Allies must achieve a total victory over the Axis. From the chief executive's perspective, it was not yet in Argentina's interest to abandon its neutralist stance and embrace the cause of its perennial enemies, the United States of America and Brazil. Given these conditions, the spy memorandum could have only limited value as an instrument of either diplomatic utility or persuasion.

Meanwhile, convinced that the United States could force changes in Argentine counterespionage and foreign policy only through much more drastic economic and/or military action,[156] Ambassador Armour moved to de-escalate the situation. On February 5, 1943, he proposed that Washington henceforth ignore Buenos Aires as much as was diplomatically possible.[157] There was considerable merit in this proposal, but by the time a special group of State Department officials met on March 6 to formulate future U.S. policy initiatives toward Argentina, new developments had ruled out a serious consideration of Armour's proposal. A German clandestine radio network had been detected operating in Argentina. Not only were FBI code breakers unable to crack the cipher being used, but the RID direction-finding units indicated that the Germans were broadcasting from several different locations.[158] In 1940–42, Brazil had been the center of German espionage activity in South America; by 1943, Argentina occupied that position.

IV. The SD in Argentina

The "Bolívar" network represented the most ambitious and technically intricate radio scheme established by German intelligence in Latin
America during World War II. Its creation and operation proved conclusively that the Abwehr and SD could maintain cipher security despite
strenuous efforts by U.S. cryptologists to break the ciphers and decrypt
the messages. The brainchild of a young electronics mastermind named
Gustav Utzinger, "Bolívar" would also become striking evidence of the
rise of the SD as the preeminent German intelligence agency in the
Americas.

A. "Bolívar" and the Great Deception

Born Wolf Franczok in 1914, Gustav Utzinger saw duty as a reserve
officer in the German navy in Norway in 1940. Towards the end of the
year, he was released in order to complete work for his Ph.D. in electronics. Subsequently, he was hired by the Telefunken Corporation.
About the middle of 1941, the Reich Economics Ministery and Telefunken decided to send Utzinger to Brazil to obtain quartz crystals, and to
determine whether a new method of shipping them was possible.[159]
However, before he left Germany in September 1941, the Abwehr obtained Utzinger's commitment to provide technical assistance for its radio
networks in Brazil. The young technician agreed, but he didn't tell the
Canaris organization, the Reich Economics Ministry, or Telefunken that
the SD organization had already ordered him to assist in creating a
Sicherheitsdienst-controlled radio system in Brazil.[160] A man with three
missions, Utzinger's situation was further evidence of the ceaseless intrigue which characterized relationships between the German governmental and intelligence agencies.

Ever the resourceful workman, Utzinger managed to send several
shipments of quartz back to Germany, and in January 1942 he assisted
Benno Sobisch in the unsuccessful attempt to reactivate Freidrich Schlegel's transmitter. But under Heinz Lange's erratic leadership, the SD radio
scheme never got off the ground. In any case, once the arrest of the
Abwehr V-men began in March 1942, departure from Brazil became
imperative. Using a forged passport in the name of Juan Manuel Stewart,
Utzinger reached Argentina; there he tarried only long enough to make
contact with Telefunken officials before moving on to Paraguay.[161]

During his stay in Brazil, Utzinger had been introduced to several
Paraguayan officials visiting that country, and one of these, Maj. Pablo
Stagni, commander-in-chief of the Paraguayan air forces, made a definite
bid for his services. By May 1, 1942, Utzinger was comfortably ensconced
in Asunción, possessor of an appointment as chief radio engineer for
Paraguay's aerial arm. Washington was well aware of the pro-German
sympathies of many Paraguayan officers, and mindful of the fact that the
support it received from the Higinio Morínigo government was dependent upon the continuing supply of economic and military goods.[162]
Presumably the United States could have reacted unfavorably had it been

aware that its "friends" in Asunción were appointing German agents to major technical positions, but this prospective development does not seem to have bothered Pablo Stagni. In fact, although the Paraguayan major knew of Utzinger's SD connections,[163] he was instrumental in having the German also appointed professor of radio communications and meteorology at the Paraguayan Academy.[164]

The SD man's rise to prominence would be enhanced by the disasters which befell German intelligence throughout South America. When Utzinger fled to Argentina in March 1942, Dietrich Niebuhr learned of his arrival, but made no effort to engage his services. Four months later, with the inadequacies of the Hans Napp group evident and the Abwehr radio connections in Brazil and Chile destroyed, Utzinger became a truly indispensable man. When he visited Buenos Aires on holiday in July 1942, the naval attaché contacted him and insisted that it was his duty as a German to create a new radio link with the Reich. There was, however, one factor which threatened this prospective relationship even before it began to develop. Now that Niebuhr was insisting that Utzinger make his expertise available, Utzinger believed it necessary to inform the naval attaché of his SD allegiance.

Niebuhr shared Admiral Canaris's abhorrence for the Heydrich-Himmler organization, so he tried to find someone else to set up the new radio link. But his search was futile, and he was forced to employ Utzinger in order to get the job done.[165] Recall that for some months, Niebuhr had been under pressure from Ast Hamburg to aid in the erection of a radio network in Argentina. By July 1942, Nest Cologne was also pressing for a radio link with its man in Buenos Aires, Hans Harnisch.[166]

If Utzinger was planning and directing the creation of the system, the SD could be expected to demand the same privileges granted the Abwehr groups. Given Abwehr-SD antipathies, Nest Cologne, Ast Hamburg, and the Sicherheitsdienst were unlikely to cooperate, but Utzinger and Niebuhr had no intention of dealing directly with this conundrum. Nor did they have the resources necessary for constructing two or three autonomous radio networks. According to Utzinger, "a series of Potemkin villages were set up so that each agency might feel itself the 'owner' of its own radio station."[167] In fact, transmitters were established at different locations in Argentina, but only one of these was operated at any one time and all of them except one were essentially auxiliary stations. (See Chart XI.)

What had been a two-party line (i.e., for Ast Hamburg and Nest Cologne) became a three-party hook-up after January 1943, when Johannes Siegfried Becker took charge as SD chief in South America. Becker was also probably the first outsider to comprehend the nature of the deception which Utzinger and Niebuhr had perpetrated on the Abwehr and SD. He soon demanded a separate connection with Berlin, but to no avail. Utzinger was technically his subordinate, but the engineer's blunt appraisal was that for the foreseeable future, the "Bolívar" setup was all that was feasible.[168] As for the Abwehr, when Dietrich Niebuhr returned to the Reich in February 1943, German records indicate that his report

CHART XI

"BOLÍVAR" NETWORK

German Clandestine Radio Stations in Argentina, 1942-1944

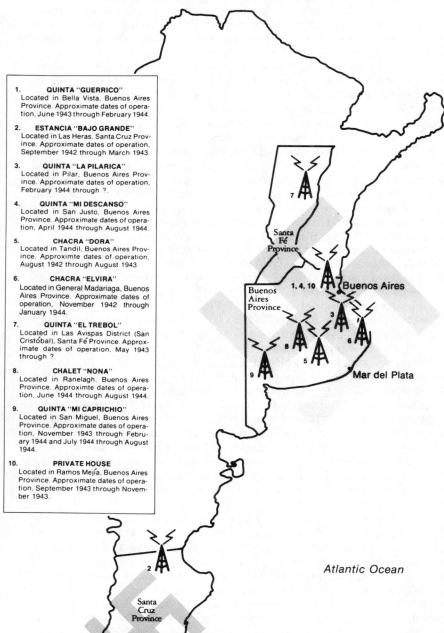

1. **QUINTA "GUERRICO"**
Located in Bella Vista, Buenos Aires Province. Approximate dates of operation, June 1943 through February 1944.

2. **ESTANCIA "BAJO GRANDE"**
Located in Las Heras, Santa Cruz Province. Approximate dates of operation, September 1942 through March 1943.

3. **QUINTA "LA PILARICA"**
Located in Pilar, Buenos Aires Province. Approximate dates of operation, February 1944 through ?.

4. **QUINTA "MI DESCANSO"**
Located in San Justo, Buenos Aires Province. Approximate dates of operation, April 1944 through August 1944.

5. **CHACRA "DORA"**
Located in Tandil, Buenos Aires Province. Approximte dates of operation, August 1942 through August 1943.

6. **CHACRA "ELVIRA"**
Located in General Madariaga, Buenos Aires Province. Approximate dates of operation, November 1942 through January 1944.

7. **QUINTA "EL TREBOL"**
Located in Las Avispas District (San Cristóbal), Santa Fé Province. Approximate dates of operation, May 1943 through ?.

8. **CHALET "NONA"**
Located in Ranelagh, Buenos Aires Province. Approximte dates of operation, June 1944 through August 1944.

9. **QUINTA "MI CAPRICHIO"**
Located in San Miguel, Buenos Aires Province. Approximate dates of operation, November 1943 through February 1944 and July 1944 through August 1944.

10. **PRIVATE HOUSE**
Located in Ramos Mejía, Buenos Aires Province. Approximate dates of operation, September 1943 through November 1943.

candidly admitted that the SD and the Abwehr were bedfellows in
"Bolívar."[169] Quite likely, the Abwehr leadership suffered some apprehension over the arrangement, but by 1943, the need to maintain contact
with agents in the Americas superceded any concern over how the
system had been created. The stark reality was that the war situation
caused both SD and Abwehr to implicitly accept a clandestine radio
arrangement which neither would have sanctioned under other circumstances.

Still another reason why the "Bolívar" scheme raised so few hackles
was that in security and administrative matters, Utzinger was careful to
maintain the illusion of separation. Those messages enciphered on Siegfried Becker's Enigma machine and intended for the SD were sent as "red"
dispatches. Before departing Argentina, Dietrich Niebuhr apparently gave
an Enigma device to Hans Harnisch. Messages enciphered on it and
intended for Nest Cologne were labeled "green" dispatches, while those
sent by either Niebuhr or his successor, Brig. Gen. Friedrich Wolf, were
called "blue" dispatches.[170] All of the messages transmitted were received
at the Ast Hamburg reception station, but "red" network missives were
sent on to Berlin undecrypted.[171]

In addition to these maneuvers, Utzinger worked hard at camouflag-
ing the "Bolívar" network. In August 1942, the first transmitter was set up
on a small farm near the city of Buenos Aires, and in November, a second,
also on a farm in the vicinity of the Argentine capital, began making an
occasional broadcast. Before the clandestine radio system was finally
broken up, some eleven different sites had been selected for broadcasting, and transmissions were actually conducted from nine of these. Some
sites were used for only a short time and then abandoned. For example, in
September 1943, a house near the police station in the town of Ramos
Mejía was rented by an Utzinger agent, and "at least six transmissions
were conducted from that site."[172]

In part, such activities were intended to prevent various spy chasers
from detecting what became the network's main station. It was located at
a farm (Quinta Guerrico) near the town of Bella Vista and over one
thousand messages were broadcast from this location from July 1943 to
February 1944. Here, a large transmitter was concealed in a pit beneath a
chicken coop, while the antenna was partially hidden amongst a grove of
trees. Nevertheless, the most effective disguise for the Quinta Guerrico
station was the fact that the farm was a functioning entity and remained a
profitable operation until its abandonment in February 1944.[173]

Even had Utzinger been superhuman, it would have been impossible
for him to recruit agents, buy farms, install transmitters, and repair
equipment all by himself. Moreover, he continued performing legitimate
radio repair work for the Paraguayan air force and for German companies
in Buenos Aires. Thus, he needed plenty of help, and thanks to fortuitous
circumstances, he got it. Georg Richter, a trusted contact of Dietrich
Niebuhr and business representative with the Siemens-Halske Company,
supplied much of the transmitting equipment.[174] Enrique Reinhard

Schibli, Werner Lorenz (code name: Enrique), Ullrich Fritz Daue (code name: Livio), and Felipe Imhoff were radio operators known to Niebuhr whom Utzinger recruited for the "Bolívar" system. Utzinger also used Hans Lieberth (code name: Don Juan) and Pio D'Negri, an Italian businessman, who turned a blind eye to the fact that the network's radio equipment was repaired and tested in his store. Another Italian, Antonio Solazzi, accepted Utzinger's money and opened a school where radio telegraphy and repairs were taught. There was nothing unusual about the school itself, but the same could not be said of the students, a number of whom were apprentice radiomen Utzinger planned to use as part of his clandestine radio operation.[175]

Another front into which the organizational chief poured money and eventually realized a handsome profit was a sporting goods store established in the Buenos Aires suburb of San Isidro, which was run by Hans Otto Schurer Stolle (code name: Alves). Customers would have been surprised to learn that the supposed owner, who had once been a journeyman soccer player, was a trained SD agent, and that the store was a drop where enciphered messages were brought for subsequent transmission. In addition, the store had a small basement storage room where repaired radio equipment was stored and kept ready for instant movement.[176]

In addition to these agents, Utzinger would eventually have a dozen others on his payroll, but his chief aides were two former PYL operatives who had fled from Chile, Hans Blume ("Flower"; Argentine code name: Raphael) and Johannes Peter Szeraws ("Esco"; Argentine code name: Pedro). Blume, aided by Friedrich Grimm and Wily Reichelt, was the group's chief radio repairman, while Szeraws was eventually acting second-in-command. Operating mainly out of his own home, Szeraws installed equipment, supervised the distribution of radio traffic, monitored the transmitting stations, and paid ring members.[177] In fact, in 1943, after Becker provided an Enigma machine for Utzinger, it became Szeraws's task to encipher many of the "red" messages.[178] In the history of German espionage in Latin America, no other persons played so significant a role in the functioning of two separate clandestine radio networks as Johannes Szeraws and Hans Blume.

As head of the "Bolívar" operation, Gustav Utzinger claimed that he received no salary for his efforts. Still, the salaries of perhaps twenty agents, the cost and maintenance of agricultural and other properties, plus the expense of radio equipment made the system an expensive proposition. From July 1942 until the end of the year, Utzinger enjoyed unlimited credit from Niebuhr.[179] Beginning in January 1943, he established an expense payment plan which divided costs thusly: attaché—54 percent, Harnisch—23 percent, and the Becker (SD) group—23 percent.[180] A meticulous keeper of records, Utzinger made sure that all the involved parties paid their assessed shares. Thus, money squabbles were usually avoided.

Not counting the 1942 expenses, the units serviced by the "Bolívar" system paid Utzinger (up to August 1944) over $62,500.[181] Of the other clandestine stations in South America, only Joséf Starziczny's CIT was nearly as expensive, but balancing the financial consideration was the fact that "Bolívar" also performed some unusual services. For example, on June 11, 1943, the military dictatorship of Gen. Pedro Ramírez (the Castillo regime was overthrown one week earlier) prohibited Axis diplomatic missions from transmitting any coded messages from Argentina.[182] Thereafter, all secret reports intended for the Reich Foreign Office were enciphered in the "blue" code and radioed via the "Bolívar" network.[183]

The emergence of this clandestine radio system caused the Argentinians no major concern, but for U.S. counterintelligence, it was a nightmare.[184] The FBI, for example, reported that a "Bolívar" transmitter was sometimes on the air as much as three consecutive hours at a time, and that the volume of traffic occasionally "resembled that of a commercial station."[185] In fact, between June 1943 and August 1944, twenty-five hundred separate messages were dispatched to Ast Hamburg.[186] This total was approximately six times the number of messages sent over Fredrich Kempter's LIR and seven times the number radioed over Friedrich Engels's CEL. Gustav Utzinger's clandestine radio system was one of the most active systems developed by German intelligence during World War II.

B. *Johannes Siegfried Becker's First and Second Comings*

An FBI study written in 1946 concluded that "any attempt to decide who was the most important German agent in the Western Hemisphere during World War II would find Siegfried Becker a leading candidate for the dubious distinction."[187] While Becker was on the wrong side, his capabilities as a spy no longer need to be denigrated by wartime rhetoric. This agent displayed unusual cunning, a grim tenacity of purpose, and a capacity to learn from his mistakes. Of these characteristics, the latter must be considered the most crucial, for after returning to Argentina from Europe in June 1940, Becker definitely made his share of miscalculations. Arriving in Buenos Aires as a diplomatic courier, Becker managed to bring through customs a trunk load of explosives which he intended to place aboard British ships. Somehow Ambassador Frieherr von Thermann discovered his intentions and demanded that the SD agent cease and desist, or play saboteur in some other country.[188] Becker stayed, and gathering information became the intelligence activity to which he henceforth limited his activities.

The sabotage affair made the SD man both well known and instantly unpopular at the German embassy, and he would have other problems as well. For example, Heinz Lange, who had preceded him to Argentina, was supposed to be Becker's assistant. Yet when Becker contacted his alleged underling, seeking to establish a general financial pool, Lange announced that while he would obey other orders, he would not turn over his money.[189] As for agent recruitment in Argentina, the only person whose services Lange and Becker were able to enlist was Wilhelm von Seidlitz, a man who was already working for Dietrich Niebuhr. In fact, Lange spent much of 1940 acting as Seidlitz's assistant in the *Graf Spee* sailor escape operation.[190] Plainly, the SD's South American effort did not begin in a very auspicious manner.

In October 1940, Becker left Argentina on a trip around South America, recruiting contacts in Rio de Janeiro, Lima, and La Paz. He also arranged for several LATI pilots in Rio to deliver his reports to Rome for mailing to Berlin,[191] only to discover that this method took time, and obtaining a response was by no means certain. The solution to this problem, in Becker's opinion, was the establishment of an SD radio station in Brazil, the most strategically located South American state. Therefore, in January 1941, Becker named Seidlitz head of the nonexistant SD network in Argentina, and ordered Heinz Lange to begin constructing a clandestine radio station and ring of agents in Rio de Janeiro. Becker himself planned to make that country his center of operations while he supervised the creation of a transcontinental network of informants.[192]

These were the plans, but Becker still failed to exhibit the qualities of a spymaster who conceivably might carry them out. Loitering around Rio, he became sexually involved with the wife of a Brazilian cabinet minister, who became pregnant.[193] He also got into the habit of throwing his weight around at the German embassy, a development which did not enthrall Ambassador Kurt Prüfer. After a noisy and bitter argument with Prüfer, Becker was told that his presence at the embassy would no longer be welcome.[194]

And if these personal problems were not enough, the organizational difficulties which beset him soon proved more than he could cope with. In October 1940, he had recruited two businessmen, Gerson Ganter in Lima, and Hellmuth Strehmel in La Paz, to act as informants, but neither man was providing the promised reports.[195] More significantly, Heinz Lange was aptly demonstrating that while he knew how to click his heels and spout National Socialist doctrine, setting up a radio station was a task beyond his powers. Finally, by mid-1941, both Becker and Lange had run out of money and were virtually living hand to mouth. Since the SD had not replied to frantic airmail requests for funds and skilled radio assistance, Becker decided to return to Germany and plead his case directly with his supervisors.

It is also possible that Becker's decision was partially motivated by another event as well. Alfred Engling, a German businessman with SD connections, had sent a blistering report to headquarters detailing Becker's sexual liaisons and denouncing him as a dangerous blunderer. Someone from SD headquarters in Berlin then phoned Becker over an open transatlantic line and ordered that he return home to answer charges.[196] Efforts to obtain a seat on an eastbound LATI flight proved unsuccessful, for without German embassy intervention the Italians were allotting all seats to their own nationals and preferred customers. Swallowing his pride, Becker approached Kurt Prüfer in June 1941 and sought to obtain a seat as a diplomatic courier. The ambassador agreed; he did not intend to refuse the SD man, thereby generating trouble with Berlin for himself. But even after agreeing, Prüfer let Becker wait for more than four months before actually arranging transport.[197]

In the interim, Becker's fortunes suddenly took a turn for the better. In August, an SD agent named Jonny Schnieter (code name: Karl) arrived with five thousand dollars for the group. The following month brought the appearance of Gustav Utzinger, who, along with Schnieter, became primarily responsible for establishing an SD-controlled transmitting station in Brazil.[198] Becker had hopes that these men would succeed; but he knew he would not be around to see any results. Prüfer finally pulled the necessary strings, and on October 22, 1941, Becker was able to leave for Berlin.

Back at headquarters, Becker seems to have had little trouble explaining away his Brazilian escapades. However, before he could return, LATI's Brazilian landing rights were terminated. From late December 1941 until April 1942, he saw combat with a Waffen-SS unit on the Russian front. He might well have remained there except that the SD, insisting that "it did not consider his mission terminated," demanded his retransfer.[199] As of April 1942, the Abwehr's Brazilian networks were in ruins, Utzinger, Lange, and Schnieter had fled to Paraguay, and the only reports reaching SD headquarters were coming from Wilhelm von Seidlitz in Buenos Aires. Despite these disasters, the SD leadership concluded that in the Abwehr's catastrophe lay the seeds of future success; now was the moment in which their organization might establish intelligence hegemony in South America! It would now become Becker's task to build an organization for which the SD would provide unlimited backing.[200]

This time, however, Becker's return to Argentina had to be carefully arranged, since his capture might result in the collapse of the entire operation. First, Hans Otto Schurer Stolle ("Alves"), a naturalized Argentine citizen who worked as an advisor for Section D/4 of Amt VI, was given six thousand dollars for Wilhelm von Seidlitz. Posing as a Spanish seaman, he reached Buenos Aires undetected in June 1942.[201] He told Seidlitz that Becker would return, but that he did not know when and how soon. Using the papers of José Luschnig, an Argentine *Volksdeutscher* who had joined the German army and been wounded on the Russian front, Becker made two trips to Spain. He reconnoitered the ports and made a courier traffic arrangement with Karl Arnold, an SD official in the Madrid embassy who would act as cutout between Berlin headquarters and Argentina. Becker also concluded that his José Luschnig papers might not be good enough to fool British inspectors at Gibraltar or Trinidad. His best hope of reaching his destination lay in once again becoming a stowaway.[202]

Returning to Germany in September 1942, Becker was given twenty thousand U.S. dollars and five thousand dollars in Swiss francs. He learned a special list of cryptographic abbreviations for radio work and was apparently given one or more Enigma coding machines. He was promised that seventy thousand dollars in credit would be provided by the German embassy for establishing a radio system, and was told "to concentrate on everything relating to the United States."[203] Becker was smuggled into Spain, and in December 1942 he stowed away aboard a Spanish freighter, the *Rita García*, which had docked at the port of Vigo. After being at sea for eight days, Becker revealed his presence to the captain, and agreed to pay a lump sum for passage to Buenos Aires and six pesetas a day for food. The Spaniard proved amenable, and on January 2, 1943, when the ship docked at Buenos Aires, crew members loaded him into a carton and whisked it through customs.[204] SS-Capt. Johannes Siegfried Becker had returned and was ready to commence his mission.

C. *The Becker Organization Emerges*

Becker's first act was to contact Wilhelm von Seidlitz, from whom he learned of Utzinger's radio network. Next, Becker visited the engineer, asserted his general leadership over all SD personnel in South America, and became a participant in the "Bolívar" system, designating Hans Schurer Stolle to act as contact man with Utzinger. On January 15, Becker traveled to the interior city of Mendoza to confer with Heinz Lange. The latter was ordered to establish an SD group in Chile, and Becker promised to dispatch some capable assistants once his own organization began functioning. As already noted in the chapter on Chile, he was as good as his word. But questions concerning long-term funding were fobbed off with vague promises. Becker gave Lange a measly five hundred dollars and sent him on his way; evidently, the insubordination of 1940 had not been forgotten.[205]

Returning to Buenos Aires, Becker turned his energies to creating the spy ring he and his SD superiors envisioned. (See Chart XII for a representation of the SD organization Becker eventually established.) Through Stolle he contacted a federal police official named José Calderón and obtained an identification card in the name of Rudolfo Juan Moore.[206] Next, he ordered Seidlitz's long-time henchman, Esteban Amorín, to establish an SD group in Uruguay. He personally recruited Hans Lieberth (code name: Juancito) and Hans Harmeyer, a German businessman Becker knew from prewar days. Others added to the organizational roster included Eugenio Prieto, another Seidlitz associate, Eduardo Leeb, Ernesto Ortiz de la Calle, Manuel de Miguel Arrastia (code name: Manolo), and Nicolás Quintana.[207] Initially, Wilhelm von Seidlitz functioned as number two man in the growing network, but gradually Becker concluded that this trusty agent had been active too long and was known to Anglo-American intelligence.[208] As the year 1943 passed, an increasing number of Seidlitz's duties became those of Hans Harmeyer.

Becker believed his organization to be incomplete so long as it was limited to Argentina, and an unexpected bonus for Becker was his

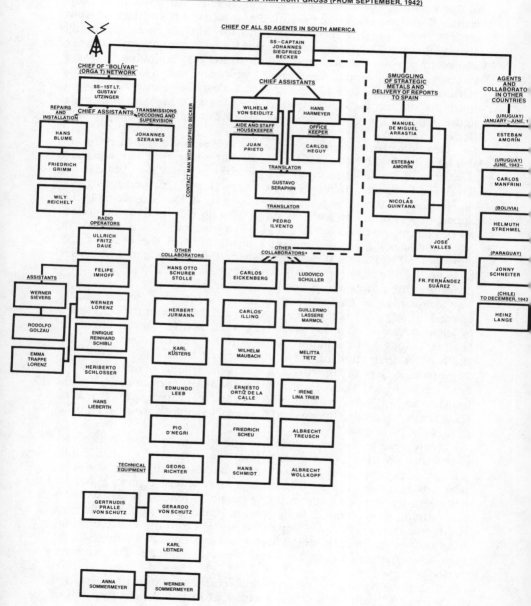

CHART XII

THE SICHERHEITSDIENST ORGANIZATION IN SOUTH AMERICA 1943–1945

CHIEF—AMT VI—SS—LT. COLONEL THEODOR PAEFFGEN

CHIEF—AMT VI/D4—SS—CAPTAIN KURT GROSS (FROM SEPTEMBER, 1942)

CHIEF OF ALL SD AGENTS IN SOUTH AMERICA

SS—CAPTAIN
JOHANNES
SIEGFRIED
BECKER

CHIEF OF "BOLÍVAR"
(ORGA T) NETWORK

SS—1ST LT.
GUSTAV
UTZINGER

CHIEF ASSISTANTS

REPAIRS
AND
INSTALLATION

CHIEF ASSISTANTS

TRANSMISSIONS
DECODING AND
SUPERVISION

HANS
BLUME

JOHANNES
SZERAWS

FRIEDRICH
GRIMM

WILY
REICHELT

RADIO
OPERATORS

ULLRICH
FRITZ
DAUE

FELIPE
IMHOFF

ASSISTANTS

WERNER
SIEVERS

WERNER
LORENZ

RODOLFO
GOLZAU

ENRIQUE
REINHARD
SCHIBLI

EMMA
TRAPPE
LORENZ

HERIBERTO
SCHLOSSER

HANS
LIEBERTH

OTHER
COLLABORATORS

HANS OTTO
SCHURER
STOLLE

HERBERT
JURMANN

KARL
KÜSTERS

EDMUNDO
LEEB

PIO
D'NEGRI

TECHNICAL
EQUIPMENT

GEORG
RICHTER

GERTRUDIS
PRALLE
VON SCHUTZ

GERARDO
VON SCHUTZ

KARL
LEITNER

ANNA
SOMMERMEYER

WERNER
SOMMERMEYER

CONTACT MAN WITH SIEGFRIED BECKER

CHIEF ASSISTANTS

WILHELM
VON SEIDLITZ

HANS
HARMEYER

AIDE AND STAFF
HOUSEKEEPER

OFFICE
KEEPER

JUAN
PRIETO

CARLOS
HEGUY

TRANSLATOR

GUSTAVO
SERAPHIN

TRANSLATOR

PEDRO
ILVENTO

OTHER
COLLABORATORS

CARLOS
EICKENBERG

LUDOVICO
SCHULLER

CARLOS
ILLING

GUILLERMO
LASSERE
MARMOL

WILHELM
MAUBACH

MELITTA
TIETZ

ERNESTO
ORTIZ DE LA
CALLE

IRENE
LINA TRIER

FRIEDRICH
SCHEU

ALBRECHT
TREUSCH

HANS
SCHMIDT

ALBRECHT
WOLLKOPF

SMUGGLING
OF STRATEGIC
METALS AND
DELIVERY OF REPORTS
TO SPAIN

MANUEL
DE MIGUEL
ARRASTIA

ESTEBAN
AMORÍN

NICOLÁS
QUINTANA

JOSÉ
VALLES

FR. FERNÁNDEZ
SUÁREZ

AGENTS
AND
COLLABORATO
IN OTHER
COUNTRIES

(URUGUAY, 1
JANUARY–JUNE, 1

ESTEBAN
AMORÍN

(URUGUAY)
JUNE, 1943–

CARLOS
MANFRINI

(BOLIVIA)

HELMUTH
STREHMEL

(PARAGUAY)

JONNY
SCHNEITER

(CHILE)
TO DECEMBER, 1943

HEINZ
LANGE

discovery that Helmuth Strehmel in Bolivia and Jonny Schnieter in Paraguay were still undetected and ready to cooperate with his plans. In
February 1943, Becker ordered both men to create independent networks in their resident countries, and to forward regular reports to a drop
in Buenos Aires.[209] His most curious confederate turned out to be Hans
Harnisch, the Nest Cologne boss in Argentina. Gustav Utzinger brought
the two men together in February, and the Abwehr man, apparently
sensing that the Canaris organization was losing its struggle with the SD,
agreed to provide political information to Becker. Undoubtedly aware
that his decision would have caused problems with his supervisors,
Harnisch did not bother to inform Nest Cologne of his new collaborator.[210] He did, on the other hand, assign Carlos Enrique Neiling (code
name: Charlie), a *Volksdeutscher*, as cutout between himself and
Becker.[211]

Pleased with his recruitment success, Becker decided in March 1943
that he needed both office space and a centralized location. Through Hans
Harmeyer, a workable solution was swiftly reached. As a publicist for
Bayer and Company, Harmeyer knew Carlos Heguy, a naturalized Argentine citizen of German origin, who had enjoyed indifferent success in the
import-export business. With Becker putting up eleven thousand dollars
for office rent and furniture, Heguy signed a lease and took possession of
adjoining offices in a building on Cangallo 439 in the heart of the
metropolitan banking and business district. Heguy conducted his affairs
daily until 4:30 P.M., scrupulously doing his best to remain as ignorant as
possible of the events transpiring in the other office.[212]

Maintaining an informal sort of business etiquette, Becker usually
opened his office only after Heguy had departed. He spent the next seven
or eight hours in company with henchmen like Harmeyer, Stolle, or
Seidlitz, coding and decoding messages to be sent or received via the
"Bolívar" system, studying materials received from other agents, and
formulating orders and instructions. But as the volume of materials to be
encoded increased, Becker realized that additional personnel who could
translate English into German would have to be enlisted. Again, thanks to
Hans Harmeyer, Pedro Ilvento and Gustavo Seraphin were soon enlisted
to perform these tasks.[213]

With more and more people using the Cangallo office, Becker decided that the late evening arrival and departure of a conspicuous
number of persons must eventually draw undesired attention. The solution was to establish a second headquarters where reports could be
delivered, translations made, and ring members hidden. It was Wilhelm
von Seidlitz who found a home on the Calle Oro in a middle-class
residential district. Juan Antonio Prieto moved into the house with his
wife and three children, but it was still large enough so that several
members of Becker's ring could live there comfortably for extended
periods of time.[214]

Before he became a stowaway and returned to Argentina, Siegfried
Becker had worked out a scheme with Karl Arnold for the dispatch of

messages and strategic minerals across the Atlantic, and in March 1943, the first messages were successfully exchanged.[215] In Buenos Aires, ring members Manuel de Miguel Arrastia, Nicolás Quintana, and Esteban Amorín made contact with amenable Spanish sailors and, for fifty to one hundred dollars, gave them packages to deliver in Spain. Increasingly, however, these men left the business of making contacts to a Spaniard named José Valles. An assistant press attaché with the Spanish embassy, Valles had developed reliable couriers on virtually all the Spanish vessels regularly calling at Buenos Aires. Furthermore, thanks to payments made to a customs police official with the unlikely name of Ramón Castillo, Valles could count on the noninterference of the Argentine authorities.[216] Thus, when a Spanish freighter known to have a courier on board docked at Buenos Aires, Valles (or a trusted aide) boarded the vessel and sought out the courier using the passwords, "greetings from José" or "greetings from Pepe" (i.e., from Johannes Siegfried Becker). The sailor replying to this salutation was then asked: "Have you brought something from over there?" The exchange of cash for a parcel or message would take place, and Valles would subsequently deliver whatever was turned over to Arrastia, Quintana, or Amorín. If Valles or a ring member failed to meet a courier, the latter was instructed in Spain to deliver whatever he had been given to Fr. Alfredo Fernández Suárez, a priest in the parish of San Miguel, who acted as a drop for the Becker organization.[217]

Reports intended for SD headquarters and small packets usually containing platinum or liver extract were delivered by Arrastia, Quintana, or Amorín to Valles, who entrusted these to his couriers. When the eastbound Spanish ship docked at Bilbao, Vigo, or Cádiz, one of Arnold's representatives would usually be waiting, the passwords being "greetings from Carlos" or "greetings from the fat man." If contact was not made, the sailor-courier was instructed to deliver whatever he was carrying to Jorge Demmel, owner of Bar Germania in Bilbao. The latter kept a supply of cash on hand and regularly delivered packages he received to Arnold in Madrid.[218]

While the system described was certainly crude, it functioned remarkably well until April 1944 when, under pressure from the Anglo-Americans, Spain ousted Valles from its Argentine embassy; still, Valles continued to operate some semblance of a courier service until 1945. Not counting payments to police and individual sailor-couriers, Valles is believed to have received at least $500 monthly from the Becker ring for his services.[219]

The purchase of strategic materials, the courier service, "Bolívar" system payments, plus the maintenance of a network which eventually included over fifty persons required heavy expenditures, but SS-Captain Becker regularly obtained the funds required. In addition to the $30,000 he brought with him, between June 1943 and June 1944, German embassy sources supplied an additional $250,000 in U.S. and Argentine currencies. Furthermore, Becker did not hesitate to demand financial assistance from the Argentine subsidiaries of Telefunken, Ferrostaal, Siemens-Holske, and Siemens-Shukert. At least $50,000 was obtained in this fashion, the parent companies obtaining repayment from the SD in Berlin. All told, between January 1943 and June 1944 Johannes Siegfried Becker's operation cost a minimum of $330,000. No other German spy network in the Americas was so liberally financed. Yet, if we are to believe Becker's deposition, the funds were spent almost as fast as they came in.[220]

Whether the SD received real value for the money expended remains a matter of some controversy. Once it became known that Becker would send messages via the "Bolívar" network, SS-Capt. Kurt Gross "leaned back and rubbed his hands together, anticipating the reception of some sensitive and interesting reports on the United States."[221] What the chief of Amt VI, section D/4 received were materials culled from *Time* and *Newsweek* and data concerning Argentine political affairs, the latter of which Gross neither expected nor desired.[222] But if Becker's immediate superior was unhappy, Gross's chiefs, SS-Lt. Col. Theodor Paeffgen and SS-Maj. Gen. Walter Schellenberg, seemed overjoyed that they could brag that an SD radio and information service was operational in the Americas. It was certainly with their recommendation that on June 21, 1943, Heinrich Himmler ordered placed in Becker's file (with a copy to be dispatched to him) a letter of special commendation for "exceptional broadcasting service."[223] Further evidence of the SD's high regard for this agent was soon forthcoming. Like other successful spy ring chiefs (Niebuhr, Kempter), Becker was awarded the War Service Cross, Second Class, with Swords. But shortly after the issuance of his letter of special commendation, Becker was also awarded the Iron Cross, Second Class.[224]

Possessing tangible evidence that the men in Berlin appreciated his efforts, it is small wonder that Johannes Siegfried Becker believed himself justified in planning far more ambitious operations. Recall that in June 1940, Ambassador Frieherr von Thermann, emphasizing the sensitivity of German-Argentine relations, had blocked Becker's plans to put bombs aboard British ships in Argentine ports. In July 1943, Becker again prepared an operation which, successful or not, would have a major effect on Argentine-German diplomatic relations. And this time he did not intend to concern himself with the complaints and protests of diplomats.

V. *Summary: A "No Win" Situation*

Until March 1942, Brazil had been the center of German intelligence activity in South America. In Argentina, the espionage threat, while significant, was still a secondary problem. But late in November 1942, the RID began picking up transmissions from the still embryonic "Bolívar" network.[225] On January 25, 1943, the existence of a German clandestine network in Argentina was confirmed for the State Department, along with the fact that the FBI code breakers were unable to decipher the messages.[226]

At this point, Welles, Hull, et al. may have concluded that this new development presaged the commencement of a new era in which Argentina would be the center of German intelligence operations in South America. If the United States expected to maintain even a modicum of Argentine cooperation, prudence dictated that it seek to improve relations with the Castillo government. Therefore, in February 1943, Ambassador Norman Armour was ordered to seek government cooperation in locating the clandestine German transmitters known to be operating in Argentina. Specifically, Washington wanted the military attaché, Col. John Lang, empowered to work in conjunction with Argentine security forces and to make use of special radio detection equipment that would be shipped to him. Not unnaturally, Castillo had neither forgiven nor forgotten the slap in the face administered by the CPD with Washington's encouragement. Probably, Foreign Minister Ruiz Guiñazú gloated a bit when on February 25, 1943, he presented a curt and categorical rejection of U.S. requests.[227]

In retrospect, the United States tried accommodation in 1941, menace and pressure in 1942, and humble supplication in February 1943; nothing worked. In our opinion, the only U.S. diplomat to emerge from this swamp of diplomatic failure with his striped pants relatively clean was Ambassador Norman Armour. An envoy whose talents were greatly respected by both his British counterparts and SIS/Argentina,[228] Armour believed that an amalgam of personal and psychological factors adversely affected Washington's relationship with Buenos Aires. Cordell Hull, he felt, "hated Argentina," while Sumner Welles was "primarily concerned with Brazil." No one "except maybe [Laurence] Duggan" could accept the notion that for the Argentines, World War II was simply not a struggle between good and evil. Especially after the Pearl Harbor attack, "the Argentines were always under fire at the State Department." These turgid comments aside, the strength of Armour's analysis lay in the fact that he had continually and correctly advised Washington that unless it intended to use its muscle decisively, a confrontational stance should not be adopted in dealing with the Castillo government. It is unfortunate that Hull, Welles, et al. failed to give greater credence to this sage advice.[229]

On the other hand, did Washington's clumsy stratagems and tunnel-visioned démarches really make that much difference? Is there anything to indicate that had the United States adopted a more flexible policy, Castillo would have reciprocated by conducting a more comprehensive counterespionage campaign? In a 1943 book, Foreign Minister Ruiz-Guiñazú insisted that the Argentine government intended to arrest and prosecute German spies,[230] but the events of the November 1942–June 1943 do not sustain this claim. Consider, in this regard, the case of Hans Napp and his associates. Arrested in November 1942, this gang of six was released on bail on December 16, 1942. Assuming that the Argentinians intended comparatively rapid legal action, in March 1943, the Abwehr ordered the German embassy in Buenos Aires to make $12,500 available for the defense of several of those arrested.[231] But prior to the overthrow of the Castillo government on June 4, 1943, no legal proceedings were initiated and no trial date was docketed. After investigating the causes of this legal inactivity, U.S. military attaché Col. John Lang concluded that "Castillo's crowd would willingly have whitewashed the whole affair." The judgment of this officer was perhaps prejudiced, but it is also true that in December 1942, a secret Argentine government source had told SIS/Argentina that Castillo did not intend to prosecute arrested German agents.[232] If inaction speaks louder than words, Colonel Lang, rather than Foreign Minister Ruiz-Guiñazú, provides the more credible analysis of the situation.

Of the other persons named in the November 3, 1942, spy memorandum, none were charged, and despite Minister Culaciati's promise to Ambassador Armour in December 1942, only naval attaché Niebuhr would soon be deported.[233] Furthermore, with the exception of Friedrich Grimm (March 5, 1943), Hans Zweigert (May 21, 1943), and two Spanish sailors who consorted with German agents, no additional persons were arrested for espionage activity before Castillo's overthrow.[234] In particular, the Grimm case is revelatory, because when this agent was arrested, "Bolívar" radio equipment was also confiscated.[235] Had they been so inclined, the police could have loosened Grimm's tongue and begun a roll-up of the Utzinger organization. Gustav Utzinger subsequently affirmed that early on, Argentine military and governmental officials knew about the "Bolívar" network and the location of several transmitters.[236] But here again, prior to Castillo's removal, Argentine officials took no action to interfere with the operation of the clandestine radio system.

A development upon which Utzinger did not later elaborate was the fact that in March 1943, his organization abandoned a broadcasting site near Buenos Aires precisely because "this station was detected by Allied direction finders."[237] In fact, the exact location of a "Bolívar" network transmitter was not achieved by U.S. radio location units before June of that year.[238] A likely supposition is that the warning was delivered by an Argentine source which had access to general intercept information being delivered to the Argentine government by Ambassador Armour.

But perhaps the most damning evidence against the Castillo government came from a former Argentine diplomat. Effective December 31, 1942, Isidoro Ruiz Moreno, legal advisor to the Argentine Foreign Office, resigned his post. Privately, he told a number of persons that the handling of the espionage issue was one of the fundamental reasons for his decision to withdraw. Ruiz Moreno held that while Argentina should resist U.S. pressure to break relations with the Axis, the Castillo government should have been equally concerned about the German intelligence operations in the country. He was convinced that the regime was not really interested in discovering the extent of German espionage penetration, for the truth might prove both embarrassing and politically damaging.[239]

Ruiz Moreno's conclusion seemed exceedingly accurate, for by 1943, political circumstances dictated that Ramón Castillo become more cautious about the evils he saw and heard. In April of that year, the Argentine president waved his magic wand, as it were, and produced the Concordancia's next presidential candidate, a sixty-six-year-old senator with a heart condition, Robustiano Patrón Costas. If Castillo was to successfully stage-manage the election of his chosen successor, controversial issues like the espionage question needed to be dropped into a deep pit and covered over—at least until the presidential elections of October 1943 were safely out of the way.

As for Patrón Costas himself, this politician from the northwest province of Salta was not ignorant of the swirling political and diplomatic currents affecting both his and the nation's future. Specifically, he had decided that a foreign policy change was inevitable. Even before his candidacy was officially announced, Patrón Costas secretly informed Ambassador Norman Armour in March 1943 that once he took office in February 1944, diplomatic relations with the Axis would be severed and sweeping action would be taken against all German agents in Argentina.[240] But whether he would have been able to execute these acts is totally hypothetical, for the day Patrón Costas was to be nominated at the Concordancia party convention (June 4, 1943), Argentine army units toppled the Castillo government. A previously drawn conclusion remains valid: Probably nothing except a total blockade or a military ultimatum would have forced Argentina to arrest all the German agents and sever diplomatic relations with Berlin. What is astounding, however, is that with the coming to power of a military regime, these issues would become even more tightly intertwined and diplomatically prevalent than ever.

Notes

1. Between 1880 and 1912, electoral fraud and manipulation had been a general practice. From September 1932 until June 1943, the so-called Concordancia dominated Argentine politics. This coalition was made up of the National Democratic party (NAP), and antipersonalist Radical party members. On the tactics used to ensure the election of conservative candidates in the presidential elections of 1931 and 1937, see Alberto Ciria, *Partidos y Poder en la Argentina (1930–1946)*, 2d. ed. (Buenos Aires, 1968), pp. 53–66. Methods and tactics are also discussed in George Pendle, *Argentina*, 3d. ed. (New York, 1965), pp. 74 and 81. A somewhat less condemnatory view of the electoral practices of 1931 and 1937 is presented in Arthur F. Whitaker, *Argentina* (Englewood Cliffs, New Jersey, 1965), pp. 89–90.

2. The best analysis of the March 1940 elections is found in National Archives and Records Service (hereafter referred to as NARS), R.G. 59, 835.00/849, no. 645, *Memorandum Regarding the Political Situation in Argentina*, pp. 1–6. After the final tabulation, there were seventy-six Radicals and five Socialists elected, while the government parties held seventy-seven seats. In the report, Ambassador Armour praised Ortiz and expressed the hope that the policy of rigging elections had come to an end. This election and its significance is also mentioned in Robert A. Potash, *The Army and Politics in Argentina: Yrigoyen to Perón* (Stanford, 1969), p. 114.

3. See John W. White, *Argentina: The Life Story of a Nation* (New York, 1942), p. 164, who suggests (perhaps unkindly) that Ortiz virtually ate himself into bad health.

4. See NARS, R.G. 59, 835.00/967, /969, /970, and /971. Elections in Mendoza (December 1940) and Santa Fé provinces (February 1941) were disputed, with Castillo taking steps to see that progovernment candidates were victorious. On the refusal of the Chamber of Deputies to pass the budget and their complaints regarding electoral fraud, see 835.00/971 and /975. The situation is also discussed, but with fewer specifics in White, *Argentina*, p. 169.

5. NARS, R.G. 59, 835.00/975, no. 121, pp. 1–2. Ortiz left no doubt concerning his views when he stated in a published interview that government power had been used "to legalize situations of violence and fraud in elections."

6. NARS, R.G. 59, 835.00/979, no. 141, pp. 1–2. The unnamed general states that since Ortiz did not represent the view of the Concordancia, he could not expect to return to power.

7. On the direct assistance of the British embassy's press attaché and others, see Great Britain, Foreign Office (hereafter referred to as FO) 371-25712-01940, registry number A6603/120/2, no. 122, June 26, 1941.

8. As evidence of this continuing struggle and the refusal of Castillo to cooperate with the committee, see NARS, R.G. 59, 835.00-MID/39, no. 1849, 835.00/971, p. 4 and R.G. 59, R and A Report no. 139, *Report on Anti-Argentine Activities*, October 27, 1941, pp. 3–4.

9. See NARS, R.G. 59, 701.6235/96, no. 772 and 701.6235/97, no. 776 of July 25–26, 1941. See also 701.6235/101, no. 2848, July 30, 1941, p. 2.

10. See unnumbered note from Philip Bonsal to George Gordon, chief of foreign activity correlation, and Sumner Welles, undersecretary of state. The note, dated June 27, 1941, was attached to 701.6235/101.

11. NARS, R.G. 59, 701.6235/101, no. 2848, pp. 2–3. As a result of meetings held between Damonte Taborda and Pan American officals S.J. Roll and Eduardo Bradley, the Argentine congressman was "instructed [by the Pan American lawyer] as to how the order should be worded to exonerate the company from any complicity." These arrangements were made known to and approved by the U.S. embassy. See pp. 1–3.

12. Ibid., pp. 2–3.

13. Ibid., p. 4.

14. See German Federal Republic, Bonn, Auswärtiges Amt, Büro Reichminister, RAM 27, *Akten Betreffend: Peru, Juni, 1937–Januar 1942*. In a message dated July 27, 1941, the German embassy in Peru specifically stated that there were no coded materials in these boxes.

15. NARS, R.G. 59, 701.6235/101, no. 2848, pp. 3–4.

16. German Federal Republic, Bonn, Auswärtiges Amt, Büro des Staatssekretars, *Akten Betreffend: Argentinien*, vol. 2, May 1, 1941–December 23, 1941, USTS VI.

17. NARS, R.G. 59, 701.8235/101, no. 2848, p. 4. The U.S. report notes laconically that the members of the committee made themselves "unavailable so that sufficient time would be had to give the contents of the packages a thorough examination."

18. The committee's first report is filed as NARS, R.G. 59, 862.20235/596.

19. See NARS, R.G. 59, 835.00/1145, no. 340, pp. 2–3.

20. In September 1941, the Castillo regime was buffeted by an air force officers' revolt. It failed, but the administration survived chiefly because of the efforts of former president Gen. Agustín Justo. See NARS, R.G. 59, 835.00/1086, MID 71, pp. 1–2.

21. German Federal Republic, Bonn, Auswärtiges Amt, Büro des Staatssekretars, *Akten Betreffend: Argentinien*, vol. 2, May 1, 1941–December 23, 1941, USTS VI. Thermann took pains to point out that the crisis had placed Damonte Taborda in a strong position.

22. See NARS, R.G. 59, 701.6235/115, no. 975, p. 1. On Thermann's problems and his deteriorating position, see German Federal Republic, Bonn, Auswärtiges Amt, Büro des Staatssekretars, *Akten Betreffend: Argentinien*, vol. 2, May 1, 1941–December 23, 1941, USTS VII. The Germans proposed the simultaneous exchange of new ambassadors, but Castillo didn't want to commit himself in writing. As a result, negotiations collapsed.

23. See NARS, R.G. 59, 701.6235/157, nos. 111 and 112.

24. NARS, R.G. 59, 701.6235/164, no. 199, p. 1, and 701.6235/157, no. 111, p. 1.

25. La República de la Argentina, Ministerio de las Relaciones Exteriores y Culto, *Guerra Europa*, cabinet 7, box 37, file 383, section 1, no. 146, Adrian Escobar to the foreign minister, March 28, 1942, n.p. This note was sent via diplomatic pouch for delivery to Ruiz-Guiñazú.

26. Interview of Ambassador Norman Armour by Prof. Leslie B. Rout, Jr., New York, New York, May 14, 1976. Then a spry, gracious man in his late eighties, Ambassador Armour recalled incidents after certain documents were shown him. His comment in this instance is ironic: "We did things [i.e., World War II] we probably wouldn't do today."

27. See NARS, R.G. 59, 835.00/48, no. 847, and 835.00/835, no. 733, pp. 1–2. Other studies of Ortiz's preference for the Anglo-French cause are Stanley E. Hilton, "Argentine Neutrality, September 1939–June 1940: A Reexamination," *The Americas* 22, no. 3 (January 1966), pp. 227–257, and Alberto Conil Paz and Gustavo Ferrari, *Política Exterior Argentina: 1930–1962* (Buenos Aires, 1964), pp. 53–56.

28. These reports were received and passed on through the office of Foreign Minister José María Cantilo. See La República de la Argentina, Ministerio de las Relaciones Exteriores y Culto, *Guerra Europa: Subditos de paises beligerantes sospechados de Espionaje*, cabinet 7, box 9, file 124, 1939, n.p. It is interesting to note that only persons believed to be German spies were subject to surveillance.

29. See Alberto Conil Paz and Gustavo Ferrari, *Política Exterior Argentina*, pp. 57–59, and Harold Peterson, *Argentina and the United States: 1810–1860* (Albany, 1964), p. 405. Consult in addition, United States Department of State, *Foreign Relations of the United*

States—1940, vol. 5 (Washington, 1959–1961), pp. 239–241 (hereafter referred to as FRUS). U.S. disgust with Argentine dilatory tactics is evident in the report of the U.S. military attaché, Maj. M.A. Devine, Jr. See NARS, R.G. 84, 820.02 (Suitland, Maryland), box 533, no. 6381, *Argentine-American Conversations*, October 22, 1940, pp. 1–4.

30. NARS, R.G. 84, 820.02 (Suitland, Maryland), box 533, no. 6381, *Argentine-American Conversations*, pp. 1–2. Part of the problem, however, was due to a State Department error. No one in the embassy in Buenos Aires knew exactly when Lieutenant Colonel Christian would arrive until the day before he was supposed to arrive (August 18, 1940). It was on September 25, 1940, that the new foreign minister, Julio A. Roca, agreed to begin negotiations.

31. The quote is from U.S. Army, Office of the Chief of Military History for the Army, 8-28, *Bilateral Staff Conversations with Latin American Republics*, appendix 1, pp. 1–2.

32. NARS, R.G. 38, Office of the Chief of Naval Operations, Division of Pan-American Affairs and U.S. Naval Missions, *Reports of Bilateral Staff Conversations*, entry 49, box 1, AIG-I/EF-5, serial no. 178, October 21, 1940. Capt. W.P. Brereton to Chief of Naval Operations (CNO), pp. 1–2.

33. La República de la Argentina, Ministerio de las Relaciones Exteriores y Culto, *Guerra Europa: Projecto del Gobierno de la Estados Unidos sobre defensa continental*, cabinet 6, box 35, file 192, no. 23A, naval minister to Foreign Minister Julio Roca.

34. NARS, R.G. 38, *Reports of Bilateral Staff Conversations*, OP-12-BG, HRM (SC) AIG-1/EF-5, serial no. 178, October 21, 1940, Capt. W.D. Brereton to CNO, p. 1.

35. This remarkable and bizarre series of incidents is reported in NARS, R.G. 59, 862.20235/375, pp. 2–3. For the January 7, 1941, message and the quote, see 862.20210/388, p. 2.

36. Ibid., p. 2. The man was Walter Giese ("Griffin"), who was a subagent of Friedrich Kempter's FMK "Brazil."

37. La República de la Argentina, Ministerio de las Relaciones Exteriores y Culto, *División Política*, cabinet 8, box 34, file 141, n.p. Unnumbered document sent by the chief of federal police in the capital to Foreign Minister Julio Roca. The comment was apparently written by Roca.

38. See *FRUS—1941*, vol. 6, pp. 387–401. A good discussion of the background of these negotiations is found in White, *Argentina: The Life Story of a Nation*, pp. 220–229. See also NARS, R.G. 59, 835.00 MID/39, no. 1849, p. 1, which explains why the $100 million loan was vetoed by the Argentine Chamber of Deputies.

39. On the origins of these talks and how they developed, see NARS, R.G. 59, 810.20 Defense/1098, pp. 1–3, 810.20 Defense/8-1941, no. 554, 810.20 Defense/ 1096, no. 511, and 835.24/157, pp. 1–3. These documents aptly demonstrate Argentina's near-paranoia concerning the nation's lack of modern military and naval equipment. Further background regarding the negotiations which followed can be found in 835.24/61, pp. 1–2, 835.24/177, no. 701, 835.24/195, no. 1161, and 835.24/345a. The Argentine view of these negotiations is well presented in Paz and Ferrari, *Política Exterior Argentina*, pp. 102–106.

40. See NARS, R.G. 59, 835.24/277, no. 201. Actually, Ambassador Armour had made the U.S. position very clear after the end of the Rio Conference of January 1942. See ibid., p. 3. On the anticlimactic convoy negotiations, see *FRUS—1942*, vol. 6, pp. 387–400. For Welles's formal reply to Argentine objections and complaints, see R.G. 59, 835.24/595A, pp. 1–7. The Argentine position is deftly analyzed in FW 835.24/534, pp. 1–4, and Paz and Ferrari, *Política Exterior Argentina*, pp. 112–118.

41. See NARS, R.G. 59, 835.24/595a, pp. 6–7.

42. On the economic blockade of Argentina beginning in March 1942, see NARS, R.G. 59, 835.24/386, /387, /389, /529, /592, /592a, /594, and 763½.

43. See NARS, R.G. 59, 835.24/386, /390, and /848. See also FW 835.24/1330, and 835.032/180. The British were loath to comply with U.S. policy and dragged their feet consistently. See Great Britain, FO 370-30314-01013, no. A3871/23/2 (pages alternately marked 86–89), and FO 371-33546-02057, no. A1393/283/2, n.p.

44. On shipments of lend-lease arms to Brazil, and Argentine fears concerning Brazilian superiority, see Glen Barclay, *Struggle for a Continent: The Diplomatic History of South America, 1917–1945* (London, 1971), p. 149; Harold Davis et al., eds., *Latin American Diplomatic History* (Baton Rouge, 1977), p. 230; Gary Frank, *Struggle for Hegemony: Argentina, Brazil and the United States during the Second World War* (Coral Gables, Florida, 1979), pp. 38–40, 45–47, and 99n.; Irving Gellman, *Good Neighbor Diplomacy: United States Policies in Latin America, 1933–1945* (Baltimore, 1979), pp. 190–191; and Potash, *The Army and Politics in Argentina*, pp. 167–169.

Argentine authors are more incisive in that they argue that if Castillo had obtained the weapons, the June 4, 1943, coup may well have been averted. See Paz and Ferrari, *Política Exterior Argentina*, p. 124, and Miguel Ángel Scenna, "El largo malentendido: El tiempo del enfrentimiento," *Toda es Historia* 2, no. 28. (August 1969), p. 82.

45. The high points of the German-Argentine arms negotiations are judiciously and briefly presented in German Federal Republic, Auswärtiges Amt, *Alten sur deutschen auswärtiges politik*, series E (Göttingen, 1969–1979) (hereafter referred to as *ADAP*, series E), vol. 2, p. 127, vol. 3, pp. 417–419, 419n., and 522–523.

46. Ibid., vol. 4, pp. 197–198.

47. NARS, R.G. 165, 2657–90(2), Military Attaché Report, no. 6555, March 18, 1941, p. 12.

48. On Harnisch's Paraguayan trip and activities, see NARS, R.G. 59, 862.20235/10-3147, pp. 11–12. The arrangements with Aumann and Fincati are detailed in R.G. 319, Federal Bureau of Investigation, *German Espionage in Latin America* (Washington, D.C., 1946) (hereafter referred to as *GELA*), p. 165.

49. See German Federal Republic, Bundesarchiv-Militärarchiv, Freiburg-im-Breisgau, *Bestand:* H 27/6, *Fremde Heere West: Personalkartei Lateinamerika* (to 1945), Amt. Ausl. Abw. Klg. Ausl., NR. 195/44 G.k.v. 25.1.44. Indisputable confirmation of the Harnisch-Aumann link is found in NARS, R.G. 84, 820.02 (Suitland, Maryland), box 533, File: *Interrogations Made in Germany—Interrogation of General Friedrich Wolf*, October 17, 1945, appendix D., p. xvi.

50. See Great Britain, FO 371-33546-02057, no. A1381/283/2, page is marked 23. Ruiz-Guiñazú had expressed similar ideas to British officials more than six months earlier. See FO 371-30315-01013, no. A889A/23/2, page is marked 113.

51. This general agreement had long been recognized by the Anglo-Americans. See NARS, R.G. 226, 1306-C, *Situation Report #4*, pp. 2–5, and Pendle, *Argentina*, p. 88n.

52. NARS, Auswärtiges Amt, *Documents Selected from German Foreign Office Records* (hereafter referred to as *DSGFOR*), T-120 series, roll 25, frame 26627.

53. Barclay, *Struggle for a Continent*, pp. 66 and 131–134. Frank, *Struggle for Hegemony*, pp. 86–88, Pendle, *Argentina*, pp. 82–86, and White, *Argentina: The Life Story of a Nation*, p. 304, are works which deal with Argentine expectations of achieving a position of leadership in South America, and its mistrust and suspicion of the U.S.A. and Brazil. Especially for evidence that Germany was to be used to aid Argentine aspirations, see *DSGFOR*, T-120 series, roll 25, frame 26627, and Great Britain, FO-371-30314-01813, no. A2106/23/2 memorandum, February 28, 1942, and FO-371-30315-01013, Registry A8894/23/2, minutes of the report, pp. 113–114.

54. See NARS, R.G. 59, 701.6235/193, p. 2. Document also bears the mark "COI-Confidential 8437-B."

55. NARS, R.G. 165, box 982, Military Intelligence Division (MID), *Axis Espionage and Propaganda in Latin America* (Washington, 1946), p. 34, argues that Niebuhr succeeded Niedenführ as "the ranking Abwehr officer in South America." See also David Kahn, *Hitler's Spies: German Military Intelligence in World War II* (New York, 1978), p. 76, who calls Niedenführ the head of German intelligence in South America.

56. Evidence that Bohny considered Niebuhr his superior is plentiful. See U.S. Department of the Navy, Naval Historical Center, Washington Naval Yard, *Files of the German Naval Staff, German Naval Attaché in Brazil* (hereafter referred to as *GNAB*), T-65, PG-32004, pp. 168 and 181–182. See also NARS, R.G. 319, *GELA*, p. 138, and R.G. 59, 862.20210, *Engels, Albrecht Gustav/71*, n.p., sections 5 and 14.

57. NARS, R.G. 59, 862.20210/9-346. p. 4.

58. See in particular, NARS, R.G. 59, 862.20235/7-1145, p. 4 and R.G. 84, 820.02, box 533, Report F-2328, *Interrogation of Edmund von Thermann, German Ambassador to the Argentine from 1934 to 1942: First Interrogation 10 May 1945*, p. 5, and *Second and Subsequent Interviews—12, 16, 21 May 1945*, p. 14.

59. See NARS, R.G. 59, *State Department—Special Interrogation Mission* (Dewitt Poole Mission) *Dietrich Niebuhr*, NI-WA 1946, box 3, PL-(GPD)-1-12-50, *Interrogation Sessions Held October 25, November 2 and November 6, 1945*. On Niebuhr's claim, see p. 2 of this document. J. Edgar Hoover's comments are found in R.G. 59, 862.20210/12-445, p. 1. A June 20, 1946, interview is listed in R.G. 238, CI-FIR/115, box 7, *Detailed Interrogation of Captain Dietrich Niebuhr* (hereafter referred to as NARS, R.G. 238, *Dietrich Niebuhr*, [1946]). The note quoted was signed ".W.," and attached to annex 1 of this report.

60. On Niebuhr's 1934–36 service in the Abwehr, the best source is NARS, R.G. 59, 862.20210/12-445, pp. 2–5.

61. NARS, R.G. 238, *Dietrich Niebuhr* (1946), p. 6. An additional $80,000 (200,000 RM) was delivered to Niebuhr by Maj. Heinz Junge in 1941.

62. This consideration is repeatedly emphasized in NARS, R.G. 84, 820.02, box 533, *CSDIC* (WEA), *Full Report on Gottfried Brandt, Friedrich Grimm, Wilhelm von Pochhammer, Lt. I.A. Franz Mammen, Oblt. d.R. Martin Müller, Heinrich Volberg*, February 28, 1946 (hereafter referred to as *Full Report on Brandt, Grimm, et al.*), pp. i–iii.

63. Ibid., pp. i and ii. See also NARS, R.G. 84, 820.02, box 533, PIR-119, *Preliminary Interrogation Report on Oblt.d.R. Johann Martin Müller*, February 21, 1946, pp. 3–5.

64. Evidence that these men performed missions for Niebuhr is found in NARS, R.G. 238, *Dietrich Niebuhr* (1946), pp. 10–12, and R.G. 319, *GELA*, p. 140.

65. The River Plate battle and the scuttling of the *Graf Spee* are well told in Richard Humble, *Hitler's High Seas Fleet* (New York, 1971), pp. 36–42, and Sir Eugene Millington Drake, ed., *The Drama of the Graf Spee and the Battle of the River Plate* (London, 1964).

66. On Niebuhr's use of Rudolf Hepe and the role of the Delfino Company, see NARS, R.G. 59, 862.20210/12-445, pp. 7–8 and 14–15.

67. Ibid., p. 8. On the enlistment of Langer and Seidlitz, see NARS, R.G. 84, 820.02, box 533 820.02, PIR-119, *Preliminary Interrogation Report on Oblt. d.R. Johann Martin Müller*, pp. 3 and 5, and R.G. 319, *GELA*, pp. 140, 169–170.

68. See NARS, R.G. 319, *GELA*, p. 134.

69. See NARS, R.G. 238, *Dietrich Niebuhr* (1946), p. 9. Niebuhr claims that he paid Eugenio Ellinger Knoll about $450 for expenses. It is not clear whether this was the total or the amount paid for each trip.

70. On fees spent in this operation, see NARS, R.G. 238, *Dietrich Niebuhr* (1946), p. 10. See also NARS, R.G. 84, 820.02, box 537, no. 10304, *Sworn Statement of Esteban J. Amorín*, May 8, 1947, p. 1 of enclosure.

71. See R.G. 59, 862.20225/155, p. 1, 862.20210/4-1046, p. 2, and R.G. 319, *GELA*, p. 140.

72. See NARS, R.G. 59, 862.20235/5-847, p. 1 of enclosure I.

73. On the strategic materials contraband trade, and the work of these men, see R.G. 84, *Full Report on Brandt, Grimm, et al.*, pp ii and iv–vi; ibid., box 537, no. 9774, *Sworn Statement of Juan Antonio Prieto*, May 1, 1947, p. 1 of enclosure; and R.G. 319, *GELA*, p. 140. See also R.G. 59, 862.20235/5-646, p. 2.

74. On LATI, see NARS, R.G. 59, 800.20210/786, p. 5.

75. On Georg Bücker, see NARS, R.G. 84, 820.02, box 533, *Re: General Friedrich Wolf*, October 17, 1945, appendix D, p. xvii, and R.G. 319, *GELA*, pp. 140–141.

76. Strenuous efforts were undertaken by the United States to assure that strategic materials would not be shipped to the Axis nations. For the agreements signed concerning platinum purchases at thirty-two dollars an ounce, see NARS, R.G. 59, 811.20 Defence (M) Colombia/30. For other agreements, see *FRUS—1941*, vol. 6, pp. 140–171, 357–387, and 538–551. See also vol. 7, pp. 40–55.

77. On Burmeister's role as supplier of funds for the strategic metals traffic, see NARS, R.G. 84, *Full Report on Brandt, Grimm, et al.*, pp. iv–vi; ibid., *Re: General Friedrich Wolf*, October 17, 1945, appendix D, p. ix; and particularly ibid., Report F.-2328, *Interrogation of Edmund von Thermann, German Ambassador to the Argentine from 1934 to 1942: Second and Subsequent Interviews—12, 16, 21 May 1945*, pp. 13–14.

78. This figure was supplied in a letter from Insp. Roger Young, FBI, to Professor Rout, October 26, 1982, and NARS, R.G. 59, 862.20235/5-646, p. 3. See also R.G. 59, 862.20210/ 2631, pp. 1–3.

79. On Harnisch's recruitment by the Abwehr, see NARS, R.G. 59, 862.20235/ 10-3147. Enclosure, *Report of Interrogation of Hans Rudolf Leo Harnisch, Wansee Internment Camp; July–September, 1947*, p. 5. Concerning his arrangements with Niebuhr, ibid., p. 6. Niebuhr had a naval *Enigma* machine and a code he described as "Schluessel M." See R.G. 59, *State Department—Special Interrogation Mission* (DeWitt Poole Mission) *Dietrich Niebuhr*, N1-WA 1946, box 3, PL-(GPA)-12-50, *Interrogation Session Held October 25, November 2 and November 6, 1945*, p. 7:

80. The order to provide money for Harnisch is from U.S. Department of the Navy, Naval Historical Center, Washington Naval Yard, Washington, D.C., *Files on German Naval Staff: German Naval Attaché in Argentina* (hereafter referred to as *GNAA*), confidential, OM/ TAM/244 T-67 series, PG-32010, frame 277. Niebuhr recalled paying Harnisch a $2,500 lump sum on one occasion. See R.G. 238, *Dietrich Niebuhr* (1946), annex 2, p. 10. On the special box kept for Harnisch with the remainder of his funds, see NARS, R.G. 84, 820.02, box 533, *Re: General Friedrich Wolf*, October 17, 1945, appendix D, p. xviii.

81. This is the amount Niebuhr claimed he paid these men. Testimony by Müller and Napp indicates a higher figure. See NARS, R.G. 238, *Dietrich Niebuhr* (1946), annex 2, pp. 11–12.

82. On Walter Friewald and his offer, see NARS, R.G. 319, *GELA*, p. 79.

83. The Abwehr apparently believed that Ottomar Müller's activities as a pro-German broadcaster had destroyed any further usefulness he may have had. For the messages surrounding his removal from active participation in MK "Argentina," see NARS, R.G. 59, 862.20210/2439, pp. 27–30. Müller himself believed that he was replaced essentially because he failed to take action in regard to the radio station. See NARS, R.G. 84, 820.02, box 537, no. 9883, *Enclosing Results of Interrogation of Ottomar Mueller*, May 13, 1947, enclosure no. 1, p. 1.

84. On the funds paid Napp, his activities and the recruitment of Schneider, see La República de la Argentina, Ministerio de las Relaciones Exteriores y Culto, *Guerra entre Estados Unidos y los Paises del Eje—1943*, file 1, annex 2, vol. 8, 1943, pp. 1–6 (pages are marked intermittently). This is actually Napp's testimony of November 21, 1942, to the federal capital police, Jefe de Sección Orden Social, La División de Investigaciones.

85. Ibid., p. 18.

86. These events are covered mainly in pp. 7–9.

87. NARS, R.G. 59, 862.20210/12-445, p. 12.

88. See *GNAA*, T-67 series, PG-32010, no frame number listed. The exact figure given was 40,939 pesos.

89. This conclusion is evident in the radio messages (Ast Hamburg to Kempter) of September 8 and September 29, 1941. See NARS, R.G. 59, 862.20210/2439, pp. 27–28.

90. That the Abwehr and especially Ast Hamburg were bringing great pressure on Niebuhr in this regard is evident from several sources. See NARS, R.G. 84, 820.02, box 537, no. 11158, *Report of Interrogation of Wolf Emil Franczok, Alias Gustav Utzinger* (hereafter referred to as *Interrogation—Gustav Utzinger*), October 24, 1947, enclosure 1, pp. 3 and 5, and enclosure 2, p. 2.

91. See NARS, R.G. 59, State Department Interrogation Mission (DeWitt Poole Mission) N1-WA, E#637, *Testimony of General Erwin Lahousen, Nuremberg, Germany, 31 October 1945*, p. 16. Speaking specifically about Niebuhr, Lahousen noted that from the Abwehr's perspective, the naval attaché in Argentina was reputed to be "one who helps us out."

92. Letters from Insp. Homer Boynton, FBI, to Professor Rout, January 25 and August 8, 1979.

93. NARS, R.G. 173, RID, box 60, Folder: *Argentina*, no. 4903, *Members of the German High Command Clandestine Radio Transmitting Groups in Argentina*, enclosure 1, pp. 1–6. See also R.G. 59, 862.20210, *Kempter, Federico/18*, pp. 14–16.

94. Proof that the U.S. was intercepting cabled messages sent from Argentina is in NARS, R.G. 59, 862.20210/599, p. 1, and 862.20210/118, nos. 406 and 521, and letter from Inspector Young to Professor Rout, August 6, 1982.

95. See NARS, R.G. 84, 820.02, box 533, Longhi, letter of February 4, 1942, Ambassador Norman Armour to Ambassador Jefferson Caffery. See also R.G. 59, 862.20210/4-1345, pp. 26–27.

96. See *GNAA*, T-67 series, PG-32010, frame number unintelligible, message NR. 1839/42.

97. See NARS, R.G. 59, 862.20210/1428, p. 1, 862.20210/4-1345, p. 68, and *GNAA*, T-67 series, PG 32010, no frame number, message NR. 2405/42.

98. See NARS, R.G. 59, 701.6235/194, p. 1.

99. NARS, R.G. 59, 862.20210/1428, no. 666, and no. 878, pp. 1–2.

100. NARS, R.G. 59, 862.20210/1658, p. 3.

101. See NARS, R.G. 59, 862.20210/2056, p. 102, and Enrique Ruiz-Guiñazú, *La política Argentina y el futuro de América* (Buenos Aires, 1944), pp. 122–123. The first provides a U.S. view of the July 1942 meeting, while Ruiz-Guiñazú gives his side in the book.

102. See *ADAP*, series E, vol. 2, p. 88.

103. On Argentina's refusal to have Trans-Radio International cut all links with the Axis nations in 1942, see NARS, R.G. 59, 810.74/346, pp. 1–2; 810.74/384, pp. 1–3; /463, p. 1; /556; /586, pp. 1–2; /675, p. 1; and especially /889, pp. 1–5.

104. Interview with former Ambassador Norman Armour by Professor Rout, New York, New York, May 14, 1976.

105. Ruiz-Guiñazú, *La política Argentina y el futuro de América*, pp. 122–123. See also NARS, R.G. 226, 27124-C, n.p. (report dated October 9, 1942).

106. See NARS, R.G. 59, 862.20210/1307, pp. 1–2, 862.20210/1409, pp. 1–2, and enclosure 1, pp. 1–6. See also 862.20210/2010, p. 1, which indicates that the FBI put together most of the memorandum at the request of the Department of State. The original FBI document covered Japanese as well as Italian espionage. As revised for Buenos Aires, only German espionage was covered.

107. See NARS, R.G. 59, 862.20210/1996, marked p. 3 (right-hand corner).

108. Ibid., p. 2 (p. 4 right-hand corner).

109. Ibid. p. 5 (p. 7).

110. Ibid. p. 2 (p. 4).

111. Ibid., enclosure to Espionage Group 1, pp. 8–9 (pp. 15–16).

112. Ibid., Espionage Group 3, pp. 1–2 (pp. 20–22), and Espionage Group 4, pp. 1–3 (pp. 24–26).

113. Ibid., p. 119.

114. NARS, R.G. 165, box 966, *Uncovering of German Espionage in Argentina*, February 24, 1943, p. 5.

115. See R.G. 319, *GELA*, which fails to mention either name in the text or index. See also R.G. 59, 862.20235/6-1645, no. 176, pp. 1–5.

116. See again NARS, R.G. 59, 862.20210/1409, enclosure 1, pp. 1–6.

117. Sumner Welles indirectly admits as much in NARS, R.G. 59, 862.20210/2013, no. 1867, p. 1. Furthermore, in 862.20210/2010, a letter to Adolf Berle from J. Edgar Hoover, October 22, 1942, Hoover states that "active investigations are pending."

118. This fact was well known to U.S. officials. Assuming that anyone was arrested and tried, the only charges that could be leveled were those covered by Article 219 of the Argentine Penal Code. See NARS, R.G. 59, 862.20210/2482, pp. 1–2.

119. This event is related in full in NARS, R.G. 59, 862.20210/2056, pp. 1–2. The quoted material is on p. 2.

120. Interview with former Ambassador Armour by Professor Rout, May 14, 1976.

121. Ibid.

122. NARS, R.G. 862.20225/771, pp. 1–2. Quote is on p. 1.

123. See NARS, R.G. 59, 862.20210/2019, no. 2183, pp. 1–3. Quoted material is on p. 2.

124. Franklin D. Roosevelt Library (hereafter referred to as FDRL), Harry Hopkins Papers, Hyde Park, New York, box 140, memorandum, Hoover to Hopkins, December 7, 1942, p. 1, and La República de la Argentina, El Ministerio de las Relaciones Exteriores y Culto, *Guerra entre Estados Unidos y los paises del Eje—1943*, file 1, annex 2, vol. 8, pp. 2–9.

125. These events are detailed in FDRL, Franklin D. Roosevelt Papers, OF-10 B, box 35, memorandum, J. Edgar Hoover to Harry Hopkins, December 15, 1942, p. 2, and FDRL, Harry Hopkins Papers, box 140, December 15, 1942, p. 2. NARS, R.G. 59, 862.20210/2088, p. 1, and R.G. 173, box 11, RID, Folder: *Argentina*, no. 7497, *Transmitting Resume of Confession of Hans (Juan Jacobo) Napp, German Agent*, November 27, 1942, p. 1.

126. NARS, R.G. 59, 862.20210/2088, p. 1.

127. The quote is from NARS, R.G. 59, ONI, Serial-R-262, Monographic Index Guide 104-500, Report R-260, November 28, 1942, p. 1.

128. See NARS, R.G. 59, 862.20210/2024, pp. 1–2.

129. For the statements of those mentioned, see *Guerra entre Estados Unidos y los paises del Eje—1943*, vol. 8, pp. 31–33, 48–49, and 52–53. See also NARS, R.G. 59, 862.20210/2125, pp. 6 and 9–11.

130. NARS, R.G. 59, 862.20210/2024, p. 2.

131. See *La Prensa*, Buenos Aires, November 24, 1942.

132. The legal events and the quoted material transpiring between December 10 and December 23, 1942, were provided to us in great detail in a letter from Inspector Boynton to Professor Rout, December 14, 1977. A less descriptive history of some of these events is found in *La Prensa*, Buenos Aires, December 23, 1942.

133. See, for example, NARS, R.G. 59, 835.00/1579, p. 2, and enclosure 1 to Dispatch 10655, pp. 2–4.

134. See NARS, R.G. 59, 862.20210/2050, no. 1782, p. 1, and 862.20210/2060, p. 1.

135. On the varying view of State Department officialdom concerning the value of publishing the spy memorandum, see NARS, R.G. 59, 862.20210/2048, p. 1, 862.20210/2089, no. 24801, p. 2, and 862.20235/1086, p. 1.

136. NARS, R.G. 59, 862.20210/2089, pp. 1–2.

137. NARS, R.G. 84, 820.02, box 537, no. 9883, *Enclosing Results of Interrogation of Ottomar Mueller, German Deportee from Argentina*, May 13, 1947, enclosure 1, p. 2, and 820.02, box 537, no. 10576, *Enclosing Report of Interrogations of Hans Jacob Napp, German Deportee from Argentina*, July 30, 1947, Enclosure 1, p. 2.

138. See NARS, R.G. 59, 862.20210/2114, p. 1, in which Armour reports that he received "confirmation today [December 23, 1942] from the Minister of the Interior" that Müller, Napp, Friedwald, Schnieder, and Ortelli were in jail, but that Reichenbach had been released.

139. FDRL, Harry Hopkins Papers, box 140, J. Edgar Hoover to Harry Hopkins, December 7, 1942, p. 6. See also NARS, R.G. 59, FW 862.20210/2093, pp. 1–3.

140. NARS, R.G. 59, 810.74/586, p. 1, and R.G. 173, box 11, Folder: *Argentina*, no. 7584, p. 1.

141. Ibid., p. 2.

142. NARS, R.G. 59, 862.20210/2060, no. 183, p. 1, and 862.20210/2146a, no. 4, p. 1.

143. For a copy of "Axis Espionage Activities in Argentina," see NARS, R.G. 60, box 1, Department of Justice, *Official Record of the Consultative Visit of the Emergency Advisory Committee for Political Defense in the United States*, envelope 1, *Annual Report—1943*, pp. 105–129. The number of alleged German V-men was reduced from thirty-two to twenty-seven. The document is critically analyzed by the British in Great Britain, FO 371-33546-02057, Registry A-1879/283/2, January 20, 1943.

144. NARS, R.G. 59, 862.20210/2144, memorandum to Duggan and Welles, and ibid., no. 13, p. 1. The argument for releasing the January 4, 1943, version of the spy document was that the material enclosed "affects the security of the entire hemisphere and thus in varying degrees, the security of each of the American Republics."

145. See NARS, R.G. 59, 862.20210/2168, no. 97, p. 1. The comments of Escobar and Espil are from *Guerra entre Estados Unidos y los países del Eje—1943*, R.E. no 57, Juan Escobar to Ruiz-Guiñazú, January 25, 1943, p. 72, and no. 86 (15), Espil to Ruiz-Guiñazú, January 21, 1943, p. 91.

146. Ibid., no. 822, memorandum, January 25, 1943, pp. 116–117.

147. Ibid., unnumbered note attached to memorandum, Ruiz-Guiñazú to President Ramón Castillo, February 4, 1943.

148. See NARS, R.G. 59, 835.00/1258, p. 2.

149. Ibid., pp. 2–3.

150. R. Henderson was the Foreign Office official who made this observation. See Great Britain, FO 371-30310-01013, registry no. A 10443/2/2, p. 1.

151. See NARS, R.G. 59, 810.74/888, p. 1, 810.74/899, p. 3, and 862.20210/2092, p. 1. In particular, Ruiz-Guiñazú insisted that the messages indicating Friedrich Kempter had been transmitting shipping data sent from Argentina meant nothing to him. He was only concerned about data sent from Argentina by cable or radiotelephone.

152. See NARS, R.G. 59, 810.74/938, p. 1, and 810.74/976, pp. 1–2.

153. Letter from Inspector Young to Professor Rout, August 6, 1982.

154. Interview with former Ambassador Armour by Professor Rout, May 14, 1976. Ambassador Armour stated that the State Department wanted Argentina to (a) break diplomatic relations, and (b) cut all telecommunications links with the Axis powers. His comments suggest that even had Argentina conducted a comprehensive espionage investigation, and not taken the political-diplomatic action desired, the U.S. might still have published the memorandum.

155. Ibid.

156. *DSGFOR*, T-120 series, roll 26, frames 27240–27242.

157. NARS, R.G. 59, 835.00/1358, pp. 3–4. See also memorandum by Laurence Duggan to L. Dreier, March 6, 1943, and appended to the document noted.

158. See 862.20210/2209, pp. 1–2, 862.20210/1-2543, pp. 1–2, 862.20210/2285, pp. 1–3, and 862.20210/2326, p. 1. Initially, it was believed that the Germans had established a portable station. By April 1943, RID had established that there were at least three stations in the network.

159. On Utzinger's background and the nature of his mission in Brazil for Telefunken and the Reich Economic Ministry, see NARS, R.G. 84, 820.02, box 537, no. 11158, *Interrogation —Gustav Utzinger*, enclosure 1, pp. 1–2.

160. On Utzinger's pledge to the Abwehr, see ibid., p. 25. Utzinger was exceedingly vague about his pledge to the SD, ibid., p. 2. German records demonstrate that Wolf Franczok was commissioned as *Untersturmführer* (SS-second lieutenant) on November 9, 1941, and *Obersturmführer* (first lieutenant) on April 20, 1943. It is doubtful that he would have been so promoted without some cognizance on his part that he was considered an SD operative. Information on Utzinger's promotions is from a letter, *Deutsche Dienststelle*, Krause to Professor Rout, VI/a-677, no. 157, March 26, 1982.

161. NARS, R.G. 84, 820.02, box 537, no. 11158, *Interrogation—Gustav Utzinger*, enclosure 1, p. 3. On Utzinger's mission for the SD, see R.G. 84, 820.02, box 533, *Memorandum —Johannes Siegfried Becker with Aliases*, April 18, 1946, p. 15.

162. On Utzinger's appointment in Paraguay, see NARS, R.G. 84, 820.02, box 537, no. 11158, *Interrogation—Gustav Utzinger*, enclosure 1, p. 3. On the strictly utilitarian attitude of the Paraguayans toward the war and their alliance with the United States, see Michael Grow, *The Good Neighbor Policy and Authoritarianism in Paraguay* (Lawrence, Kansas, 1981), pp. 69–70 and 75–76.

163. On the pro-Fascist sympathies of Pablo Stagni, see NARS, R.G. 59, 862.20210, Stagni, Pablo Major 8–944, pp. 1–2. See also a letter from the Honorable Willard Beaulac (former U.S. ambassador to Paraguay) to Professor Rout, October 6, 1977.

164. NARS, R.G. 84, 820.02, box 537, no. 11158, *Interrogation—Gustav Utzinger*, enclosure 1, p. 4.

165. Ibid., enclosure 3, p. 2.

166. Ibid., enclosure 3, pp. 3–4. While Harnisch was certainly the chief of the Nest Cologne group in Argentina, Utzinger states that Werner Koennecke made the payments and Carlos Neiling delivered the coded messages. For evidence of Werner Koennecke's 1942 purchases for the "Bolívar" system, see NARS, R.G. 319, *GELA*, pp. 154–156.

167. NARS, R.G. 84, 820.02, box 537, no. 11158, *Interrogation—Gustav Utzinger*, enclosure 3, pp. 2–3. Utzinger continued: "In practice, the 'telegraphic network' was composed of only one installation . . . with technical receivers for emergencies. . . ." See also enclosure 4, p. 6.

168. Ibid., enclosure 3, p. 3.

169. Ibid., enclosure 3, p. 2.

170. The best description of the "blue," "red," and "green" codes is in NARS, R.G. 84, 820.02, box 533, *Interrogation of Brigadier General Friedrich Wolf*, October 17, 1945, Appendix A, p. 3. For further explanation as seen from the German side, see NARS, *DSGFOR*, T-120 series, reel 366, frames 291160-291161.

171. NARS, *DSGFOR*, T-120 series, roll 366, frames 291161-291162. See also R.G. 84, 820.02, box 533, no. 11158, *Interrogation—Gustav Utzinger*, enclosure 1, p. 9.

172. On the construction of radio stations and the use of Ramos Mejía and other locations, see NARS, R.G. 173, RID, Folder: *Argentina, Data Revealing the Power of German Espionage* (hereafter referred to as *Data—German Espionage*), pp. 1–3.

173. Ibid., p. 2.

174. NARS, R.G., 319, *GELA*, p. 168.

175. NARS, R.G. 173, RID, *Data—German Espionage*, pp. 1–5, and R.G. 319, *GELA*, pp. 164 and 169–170.

176. NARS, R.G. 173, RID, *Data—German Espionage*, p. 5.

177. Ibid., pp. 6–7, and R.G. 319, *GELA*, pp. 170–171.

178. NARS, R.G. 173, RID, *Data—German Espionage*, p. 4.

179. Ibid., p. 6.

180. NARS, R.G. 84, 820.02, box 537, no. 11158, *Interrogation—Gustav Utzinger*, enclosure 1, p. 6. The actual formula was 7:3:3. Utzinger relates that each month he estimated expenses and assessed the three groups accordingly.

181. NARS, R.G. 173, RID, *Data—German Espionage*, p. 6. Utzinger gave his estimated 1943–44 expenses as $62,500, "excluding investments in furniture and one loan." The value of furniture seized by Argentine police from assorted broadcasting sites and hideouts was given as $3,500. Ibid., pp. 3–6.

182. See NARS, R.G. 59, 835.741/36, no. 1309, p. 1.

183. See NARS, *DSGFOR*, T-120 series, roll 366, frames 291161-291162.

184. See for example, NARS, R.G. 59, 800.76, Monitoring/576, p. 1, 862.20210/ 2326, pp. 1–2, and attached letter, Adolf A. Berle to James L. Fly, chairman, FCC, 862.20210/2403, pp. 1–3, and 862.20210/1-2543, pp. 1–2.

185. NARS, R.G. 319, *GELA*, p. 153.

186. Ibid., p. 149.

187. Ibid., p. 161.

188. See NARS, R.G. 84, 820.02, box 533, *Memorandum—Enclosing Affidavit of Hedwig Sommer*, March 4, 1946, p. 8. According to this witness, sabotage as well as political espionage was Siegfried Becker's view of his mission.

189. See NARS, R.G. 84, 820.02, box 533, *Memorandum—Johannes Siegfried Becker with Aliases*, April 18, 1946, pp. 8–9.

190. Ibid., pp. 8–10. Becker claims that Seidlitz had been the man he had told Heinz Lange to contact once he reached Buenos Aires. This suggests that Seidlitz was not actually recruited by Lange, but by Becker.

191. Ibid., pp. 10–11. The letters were to be delivered to Dr. Clara Fadda, secretary to Bruno Mussolini, then the president of LATI. Becker let the LATI pilots believe that the contents were love letters to Dr. Fadda. The lady was supposed to forward them unopened to a leather-goods shop in Berlin which was a drop for the SD. See German Federal Republic, Institut für Zeitgeschichte, München, NG-4871, *Interrogation Report of Karl Gustav Arnold*, November 20, 1946, p. 10.

192. For Becker's radio and Brazilian operational plans, see *Memorandum—Johannes Siegfried Becker*, pp. 13–14.

193. On Becker, Engling, and the affair with the wife of a Brazilian minister, see *Interrogation Report of Karl Gustav Arnold*, p. 11.

194. See NARS, R.G. 84, 820.02, box 533, *Memorandum—Enclosing Affidavit of Hedwig Sommer*, p. 8. According to this source, Becker virtually attempted to take over the embassy.

195. *Memorandum—Johannes Siegfried Becker*, pp. 12–13. Ganter was repatriated as a dangerous German national by the Peruvian government in January 1942.

196. *Interrogation Report of Karl Gustav Arnold*, p. 11. There is some disagreement here, for the aforementioned affidavit of Hedwig Sommer (p. 10) states that Becker's departure was tied to his fight with Ambassador Prüfer.

197. *Memorandum—Johannes Siegfried Becker,* pp. 14 and 16.

198. Ibid., pp. 14–15.

199. On Becker's service with a Waffen-SS unit and his transfer back to the SD, see ibid., p. 17. The quoted material is from the same page.

200. Ibid., p. 18. On the SD's growing interest in South American affairs, see *Interrogation Report of Karl Gustav Arnold*, pp. 11 and 14–15.

201. On Schurer Stolle's background and mission, see *Memorandum—Johannes Siegfried Becker*, pp. 17–18, and *Interrogation Report of Karl Gustav Arnold*, pp. 10 and 15. See also NARS, R.G. 319, *GELA*, p. 170.

202. On Becker in Spain and his contact with Karl Arnold, see *Memorandum—Johannes Siegfried Becker*, pp. 18–19, and *Interrogation Report of Karl Gustav Arnold*, pp. 17–18.

203. *Memorandum—Johannes Siegfried Becker*, p. 18. Becker was also told not to deal with the German diplomatic corps, and that he should "use discretion so as not to compromise his country." He was also to make a tri-monthly account of expenses and to finance a radio-telegraphic service. This order is further evidence that the SD did not know at that time what Utzinger and Niebuhr were up to.

204. See ibid., p. 20, for Becker's escape and landing in Buenos Aires.

205. The meeting with Lange is described in ibid., p. 21.

206. Ibid., p. 21.

207. See ibid., pp. 20–21, and NARS, R.G. 319, *GELA*, pp. 165–167 and 169.

208. Ibid., p. 24. See also NARS, R.G. 84, 820.02, no. 9706, box 537, *Enclosing Sworn Statement of Johannes Harmeyer*, enclosure 1, pp. 1–2.

209. *Memorandum—Johannes Siegfried Becker*, pp. 21 and 25–26.

210. On the Harnisch-Becker relationship, see ibid., pp. 22–23. For the same relationship from Harnisch's perspective, see NARS, R.G. 59, 862.20235/10-3147, no. 11208, pp. 13–14. Evidence that the Abwehr knew little or nothing about the Becker-Harnisch relationship or what Harnisch was actually doing is evident in NARS, *DSGFOR*, T-120 series, roll 366, frames 291162-291163 and 291169.

211. On the appointment of Neiling as cutout, see *Memorandum—Johannes Siegfried Becker*, p. 24.

212. Ibid., p. 24. For the views of *Johannes Harmeyer* on the enlistment of Heguy, see NARS, R.G. 84, 820.02, box 537, no. 9706, *Johannes Harmeyer*, enclosure 1, p. 1. Harmeyer insists that he, and not Becker, paid for the furniture. As for Heguy, Harmeyer made the following statement: "Heguy did not have the qualifications of a business manager . . . ," ibid.

213. See NARS, R.G. 84, 820.02, box 537, no. 9706, *Johannes Harmeyer*, enclosure 1, p. 2.

214. See NARS, R.G. 84, box 537, 820.02, no. 9774, *Enclosing Sworn Statement of Juan Antonio Prieto—May 1, 1947*, p. 3. Prieto here tells of his connection with the house, who visited it, and describes how Seidlitz requested that he take charge of running it.

215. *Interrogation Report of Karl Gustav Arnold*, p. 18.

216. Ibid., pp. 18–19, and NARS, R.G. 319, *GELA*, pp. 145–153, provides a somewhat different picture of the transatlantic courier operations.

217. *Interrogation Report of Karl Gustav Arnold*, pp. 18–19, and NARS, R.G. 319, *GELA*, pp. 147 and 150. Once Amorín was sent by Becker to Uruguay in February 1943, Manuel de Miguel Arrastia took over much of the courier traffic (i.e., using Valles as a middleman). If Fr. Fernández could not be found, sailors were to head for Boker and Company in Calle Moreno. This was the enterprise of which Hans Harnisch was president.

218. *Interrogation Report of Karl Gustav Arnold*, pp. 19–22. Arnold had four assistants who were in charge of this phase of the operation. The fat man in question was Jorge Demmel. According to Arnold, Demmel worked only for expenses and, later, a few bonuses. The other aides received twenty-five hundred pesetas a month.

219. On Valles's salary and 1944–45 adventures, see NARS, R.G. 319, *GELA*, pp. 147, 150, and 153.

220. On the funds received by Becker, see NARS, R.G. 319, *GELA*, pp. 156, 161, and 163. On funds obtained from Telefunken, Siemens, etc., see in particular, *Enclosing Affidavit of Hedwig Sommer*, pp. 7–8, and R.G. 84, 820.02, box 537, no. 11158, *Interrogation—Gustav Utzinger*, enclosure 1, p. 7, and *Memorandum—Johannes Siegfried Becker*, pp. 31, 35, 39, and 41. The problem is that the final amount given by the embassy is listed as $60,000 on p. 39, and $180,000 on p. 41. The data in *GELA* suggests that both figures are correct, making a total of $240,000.

221. *Enclosing Affidavit of Hedwig Sommer*, p. 2.

222. Ibid.

223. Our thanks to Daniel Simon, director, Berlin Document Center, Letter BDC/354/82/JG, May 25, 1982. Simon was kind enough to send a copy of *Befehlsblatt des Chefs der Sicherheitspolizei und des SD*, IV, no. 32, Berlin, July 3, 1943, p. 198, which contains the quoted citation.

224. Ibid. Letter included copies of Siegfried Becker's service record, and it records his recipiency of the Iron Cross, Second Class.

225. NARS. R.G. 59, 862.20210/2168, 862.20210/2209, and R.G. 319, *GELA*, p. 153.

226. NARS. R.G. 59, 862.20210/2209, 862.20210/2364, and 862.20210/1-2543.

227. On Armour's February 1943 efforts and Argentina's refusal, see NARS, R.G. 59, 800.76 Monitoring/570 through /576.

228. See NARS, R.G. 226, 27124-C, anonymous letter of October 3, 1942, n.p., and Great Britain, FO 371-30310-01013, Registry A-10240/2/2 (pages marked 53 and 55).

229. Quoted material and views are from an interview with former Ambassador Armour by Professor Rout, May 14, 1976.

230. See Ruiz-Guiñazú, *La política Argentina y el futuro de América*, pp. 122–128. The foreign minister does not discuss the question of the prosecution by the Argentine government of those arrested.

231. See NARS, *DSGFOR*, T-120 series, roll 750, frames 354331-354833 and 354838. The Abwehr wanted to pay only for the recognized V-men, specifically Müller, Napp, and Martin Schneider. The embassy in Argentina decided to put up defense money for all six involved.

232. See NARS, R.G. 165, Box 966, WD-, General and Special Staffs, *Folder: German Espionage, Argentina, 1942–43, et al.*, M/A, Argentina, no. 9279, August 14, 1943, p. 1. In December 1942, a U.S. intelligence source had predicted that the Castillo government would not prosecute Napp and the others involved. See NARS, R.G. 226, 28783-C, pp. 2–3.

233. This promise was reported in NARS, R.G. 59, 862.20210/2089, no. 2480, p. 1.

234. On the arrests of Zweigert, Grimm, and two Spanish seamen, see NARS, *DSGFOR*, T-120 series, roll 750, frame 354851. See also NARS, R.G. 165, box 966, MIS, G-2, *WDGBI NR 20-C*, March 15, 1943, p. 1; R.G. 226, 37908-C, n.p., FDRL, FDRP, OF-10B, box 37, J. Edgar Hoover to Harry L. Hopkins, August 11, 1943, pp. 1–30. See in particular, La República de la Argentina, Ministerio de las Relaciones Exteriorés y Culto, *Guerra Europa: Acusación de espionage contra Hans Zweigert y Francisco Javier Azarola*, cabinet 7, box 41, file 485, 1943, n.p.

235. See NARS, R.G. 173, RID, Folder: *Argentina*, "Data Revealing the Power of German Espionage," pp. 4–5, which reveals the work performed by Grimm for Utzinger.

236. See also NARS, R.G. 84, 820.02, box 537, no. 11158, *Interrogation—Gustav Utzinger*, enclosure 1, pp. 10–11.

237. NARS, R.G. 173, RID, "Data Revealing the Power of German Espionage," p. 2.

238. Ibid., p. 2. In fact, U.S. direction-finding equipment did not reach Argentina until after the June 4, 1943, revolution.

239. See NARS, R.G. 59, 862.20210/2199, pp. 1–3. Ruiz Moreno did talk to a U.S. official about his objections to the foreign policy of the Castillo regime. For his blunt declaration concerning the pro-Nazi sympathies of the Castillo government, see Isidoro Ruiz Moreno, *Historia de las relaciones exteriores Argentinas (1810–1955)* (Buenos Aires, 1961), pp. 316–317.

240. See NARS, R.G. 59, 835.40/1371, no. 9096, p. 1, and 835.00/1377. Through Federico Pinedo, a cabinet minister under Roberto Ortiz, Patrón Costas secretly communicated with Norman Armour. In the interview which took place on May 14, 1976 in New York City, the former ambassador to Argentina confirmed that Patrón Costas had made the promises noted. In Armour's opinion, this was one reason why the Grupo de Oficiales Unidos (GOU) did not want Patrón Costas either nominated or elected.

8

Climax of the Espionage War in Argentina: 1943–47

I. Introduction: The War Washington Didn't Win

Shortly before midnight on June 3, 1943, Pres. Ramón S. Castillo was awakened to receive a phone call from Minister Amadeo y Videla. Warned that unusual and threatening troop movements were taking place at the military bases on the outskirts of the city, Castillo hurriedly sent for Minister of War Gen. Pedro Ramírez. Earlier in the day, the president had decided to remove Ramírez, and calling on him now was really an indirect means of testing his loyalty. In any case, Castillo ordered Ramírez to the Campo de Mayo Army base, outside Buenos Aires, "to make an inspection and return to report."[1] Ramírez did as he was instructed. But he knew that a rebellion was brewing and his investigation was essentially perfunctory; he did little or nothing to defend the interests of the regime he was allegedly serving. When he reported to Castillo's executive office, the Casa Rosada, at 6:00 A.M. the next morning, troops were already marching toward the city. Ramírez told the president that resistance was useless. Castillo responded by denouncing Ramírez as a traitor, and ordering Gen. Rodolfo Marquez, army quartermaster, to arrest the minister of war. This proved to be virtually the last order Castillo ever gave as president of Argentina. With rebel troops advancing almost unopposed, at 9:25 A.M., the president and his cabinet boarded the minesweeper *Drummond* and sailed out into the River Plate. General Marquez was left behind to treat with the rebels, led by Brig. Gen. Arturo Rawson. Shortly after 11:30 A.M., Rawson radioed Castillo that further resistance was useless.

By noon on June 4, Buenos Aires was totally under the control of the rebels. At midday, Rawson enjoyed a victory lunch at the Club Militar in downtown Buenos Aires, and at 2:30 P.M., he entered the Casa Rosada. The following afternoon, a forlorn Ramón Castillo resigned, but Rawson would have litle time to savor his triumph. In proclaiming himself provisional president, the general angered and disappointed those who had expected either a three-man junta or Pedro Ramírez to take charge. Then, without consulting the colonels and majors who had formed the back-bone of the rebellion, Rawson appointed a cabinet which did nothing to inspire confidence in his judgment. Informed that he would have to reorganize his regime, Rawson refused, but not before allegedly threatening to shoot General Ramírez, whom he believed to be his chief opponent. On the evening of June 6, Rawson resigned, and on the morning of the seventh, Gen. Pedro Ramírez and his ministers took office.[2]

The significance of these events in Argentine history can hardly be overestimated. With three presidents in office in four days, some chagrined Argentinians wondered aloud whether their nation had sunk to the level of a banana republic.[3] The indisputable facts were that a seemingly stable, nominally democratic government had been overthrown virtually without a struggle, and power had passed to military rulers whose attitude toward the restoration of democracy was decidedly cynical.

The key conspirator in this whirlwind turn of events was Lt. Col. Enrique González, Ramírez's confidant and staff assistant. On or about May 26, 1943, he arranged a secret meeting between Minister of War Ramírez and several leaders of the Radical party. Since February 1943, Castillo had been smoothing the path for his hand-picked successor, Senator Rubustiano Patrón Costas. In considering Ramírez, the political logic was eminently comprehensible: with a general running on the opposition ticket, Castillo would have to abstain from using blantant vote-fixing tactics.[4] Ever the cautious one, Ramírez "didn't say yes and he didn't say no,"[5] but Castillo somehow learned of the negotiations, and that was the beginning of the end for Pedro Ramírez as minister of war. By the morning of June 3, 1943, Castillo was already maneuvering to replace him, and it was this action which was the proximate cause of the June 4 revolution.

Considering that Lieutenant Colonel González did not contact General Rawson until June 3, 1943,[6] he would have needed to be a magician in order to organize a rebellion which began less than twenty-four hours later. He was not, but in truth, he did not have to be. Enrique González, along with Lt. Col. Juan Perón and perhaps eighteen other colonels and majors, formed the directorate of a secret military lodge called the Grupo de Oficiales Unidos (GOU) or United Officers Group. Organized in 1942 and formally constituted in March 1943, the GOU was wedded to the concept of Argentine neutrality, contemptuous of democracy and civilian politicians, and anxious to get on with the creation of the powerful Argentina that they envisioned. A rebellion against Castillo had been projected for September 1943, and while the firing of Ramírez forced a premature move, it also gained the adherence of non-GOU officers whose support was necessary for the plot to succeed.[7]

Removing Castillo and inserting Rawson into the presidential office was hardly the final solution GOU adherents desired. But the new president's political clumsiness in appearing to monopolize the reins of power, his distinctly unpopular cabinet choices, and his refusal to reconsider his selections provided the GOU with a justification for advocating another change.[8]

Desirous of avoiding the fate of Arturo Rawson, General Ramírez allowed a trio of colonels to assist him in selecting his cabinet. One of the selectors was the ubiquitous Enrique González, who, in addition to becoming the chief of the presidential secretariat, arranged for GOU members to receive key assignments in the Ministries of War and Interior (i.e., police) and command of vital troop concentrations. Before the end of June, Col. Juan Perón, now second-in-command in the Ministry of War under Gen. Edelmiro Farrell, began replacing non-GOU base and troop commanders with officers who were loyal to the secret lodge. As a result of the events of June 3–6, 1943, Ramírez occupied the presidential chair, but the GOU was in the driver's seat.[9]

Although the threat of Ramírez's removal and the nomination of Patrón Costas as Concordancia presidential candidate had galvanized the disparate army officers into action, their preeminent grievance against Castillo was that his foreign policy had failed to provide Argentina with modern weaponry.[10] Still generally unknown is the fact that the seemingly fruitless 1942 arms negotiations with Germany did in fact produce minimal results. Working through a Swiss firm, German minister Erhard Morath and the Argentine military attaché in Berne, Lt. Col. Carlos Adolfo Wirth, managed to have a shipment of twelve antiaircraft guns sent to Argentina via Spain during 1943.[11] But in the meantime, Brazil was receiving millions of dollars worth of tanks, planes, and other military equipment through lend-lease. If Argentina was to maintain a military balance in South America, not twelve, but twelve dozen, modern antiaircraft weapons would have to be obtained from either the United States or the Axis powers.

From the commencement of his tenure in office, Pedro Ramírez was acutely aware that the longevity of his regime would depend, in large measure, upon his success in obtaining the weapons which the national armed forces craved. Within a week of his assumption of office, he proposed to dispatch a delegation to the United States for the expressed purpose of consummating an arms deal, but the State Department rebuffed this overture.[12] Cordell Hull, the hard-liner, and Sumner Welles, the apostle of Good Neighbor accommodation, were often at odds over policy, but in this case there was complete accord. Ramírez was told, therefore, that only after diplomatic relations with the Axis were broken and the German espionage organization in Argentina was liquidated would the United States discuss weapons sales and shipments.[13] Initially, Ramírez indicated his willingness to meet these demands, but GOU spokesmen were unalterably opposed. The exchange of diplomatic memoranda would continue into September 1943, but substantive bargaining over these issues never really began.[14]

Unquestionably, a significant reason for this disinclination to make any concessions was the fact that concurrent with its dealings with Washington, the Ramírez government was conducting secret but promising arms procurement negotiations with both Germany and Japan. Moreover, in July 1943, both Berlin and Tokyo appeared eager to sell weapons without requiring that Argentina modify its neutralist foreign policy. Unfortunately for Argentina, most of the details of these secret arms negotiations were being intercepted and revealed by "Magic," the system of cryptanalysis pioneered by U.S. code breakers in the 1930s.[15] Utilizing the information gleaned from decoded Japanese messages, the United States was able to hamstring an Argentine-German arms deal in October 1943, and also verify that SD agents and Argentine army officers had conspired with Bolivian nationalists in the overthrow of Enrique Peñaranda on December 20, 1943.[16] That the Bolivian regime was corrupt and repressive is undeniable, but Peñaranda had been clever enough to ally himself with the nations battling the Axis. Given participation in the cabal by elements hostile to the Allied war effort (i.e., German spies in Argentina), Washington was understandably alarmed and readied itself for a showdown with Buenos Aires.

With the war definitely going in favor of the Allies, it was not deemed necessary to fit the velvet glove over the mailed fist. On January 24, 1944, the Ramírez government was curtly informed that unless diplomatic relations were broken posthaste, the United States would recall its ambassador, freeze Argentine assets, and publish evidence of Argentine collaboration with German espionage elements. Foreign Minister Gen. Alberto Gilbert hastily capitulated, pledging that "stern measures" would be taken against "Axis collaborationists and others guilty of subversive activity."[17] On January 26, Argentina became the last Latin American republic to sever diplomatic links with Berlin and Tokyo. Not only did the United States achieve a policy goal it had sought since 1941–42, but, for the first time since the war began, it had bested the Argentinians in diplomatic struggle.

Had Cordell Hull been wiser, he would have marked time until the Argentinians indicated a willingness to reach some kind of general settlement. Instead, convinced that the Ramírez regime was on the run, Hull pressed his attack. On January 25, he cabled Ambassador Armour, demanding that the Argentinians disclose to the United States all data they possessed on German spies. Hull believed that such information would implicate persons high in the Ramírez regime. Therefore, the readiness to make this information available would be unassailable proof that Argentina had cast her lot with the anti-Axis coalition.[18]

It is difficult to believe that Hull really expected that Ramírez would turn over materials which implicated cabinet members, high-ranking army officers, and possibly even himself. Still, after a meeting with Hull on February 3, Ambassador Adrian Escobar cabled his principals in Buenos Aires that the secretary was determined "to force Argentina to publicly admit her sins."[19] By this time, SIS/Argentina sources were providing a steady stream of information concerning spy arrests, but Hull was not impressed. On February 5, 1944, he fired off another blast, excoriating Argentine counterespionage policies, and intimating that the desired housecleaning would never take place.

Seemingly, the residue of past strife between the United States and Argentina, and a sense of mutual suspicion exacerbated by the continued "Magic" intercepts,[20] made the differences between these two states insurmountable. But in analyzing the Department of State's position, a memorandum written by Assistant Secretary Adolf Berle late in 1943 seems particularly cogent. In explaining the situation to Undersecretary Edward R. Stettinius, Berle observed that "I think that Secretary Hull felt, and I feel that being nice to the Argentine Government got us nowhere . . . breaking relations with the Axis is now a secondary issue. The real question is whether Argentina is going fascist or not. . . ."[21]

Events in February 1944 gave some credibility to the Berle-Hull position. In breaking relations with the Axis, President Ramírez and Foreign Minister Gilbert had committed the unpardonable sin of bending under United States pressure. The GOU leadership split over this action, but Col. Juan Perón, director of the Secretariat of Labor and Public Welfare and assistant chief at the Ministry of War, rallied the disgruntled elements opposing the move away from diplomatic neutrality. On February 24, General Ramírez was coerced into ceding his executive powers to Vice-President and Minister of War Gen. Eldemiro Farrell. The GOU had lost its clout. But Juan Perón became the real power behind the scenes.[22]

For Cordell Hull, these February 1944 developments only served to confirm his prejudices. The secretary considered the Ramírez regime as odious, but the new Farrell government he considered to be blatantly pro-Fascist and totally unacceptable. On February 26, 1944, a circular telegram sent to the Latin American capitals alerted them to the fact that the United States considered the new rulers in Argentina to be a threat to hemispheric security. This was followed by another circular communiqué (March 15), which depicted Farrell and his cabinet as being "opposed to the break in relations with the Axis, and . . . anxious to overlook the existence of Axis espionage in Argentina."[23]

Taken together, these missives represented an oblique declaration of war upon an Argentine government in which Juan Perón was playing a steadily more prominent and visual role. Proposals calling for punitive measures were sifted and studied,[24] the culmination of this exploratory process being a long memorandum dated June 8, 1944. Beginning with an in-depth study of U.S.-Argentine relations since January, the document concluded that all improvements in Argentine policy vis-à-vis the United States were outweighed by Argentine failings. The document recommended that strong actions be taken to remedy this situation, but failed to establish a priority of action to be taken. Of major significance is the fact that fifteen of the twenty-four complaints presented by State Department analysts dealt solely with continuing espionage and smuggling activities, and the arrest of SIS/Argentina agents and informants.[25] From this docu-

ment, the outline of future Department of State policy becomes clear: a
wide-ranging assault was to be made on the Farrell government in an
attempt to force it to declare its unreserved adherence to the Allied
cause. As long as the Argentinians failed to destroy the German spy rings
operating in their country, the State Department could justify its actions
by insisting that this counterintelligence complacency represented a
threat to hemispheric security.[26]

Two weeks after the official release of this memorandum, Hull
commenced his diplomatic offensive. On June 22, the State Department
called upon Great Britain and the other American republics to demonstrate their disapproval of the Farrell regime by recalling their heads of
diplomatic missions in Argentina. Norman Armour departed Buenos
Aires, and the other ambassadors and ministers soon followed; by July 30,
the Paraguayan ambassador was the only American representative of that
rank still in the Argentine capital.[27]

With diplomatic isolation achieved, Hull next fired off his economic
heavy artillery. In August 1944, the United States Treasury prohibited the
removal from banks in this country of $200 million in Argentine gold.[28]
Next, the Department of State prevailed upon the British to delay the
signing of a new meat purchase contract with Argentina, and on September 4, "with a minimum of publicity," it put into effect a new series of
trade restrictions, and virtually prohibited entry of United States ships
into Argentine ports.[29] Four days later, Hull terminated his attack with a
vituperative speech in which he charged that Argentina had become the
"headquarters of the Nazi-Fascist movement in the Western Hemisphere."[30]

Up to this point, the secretary of state had displayed a careful use of
his economic and diplomatic options and, in gradually increasing the
pressure, an excellent grasp of tactics. It was the poverty of his overall
strategy which would ultimately undo him. From the beginning of this
struggle to force a change in Argentine foreign policy, the vital necessity
of British cooperation had always been evident.[31] But with an eye on
preserving his nation's postwar economic position in Argentina, Winston
Churchill dragged his feet. He refused U.S. suggestions that Britain also
freeze Argentine assets and only reluctantly agreed to support the informal blockade restrictions of September 4, 1944. But Hull soon discovered
that Churchill's acquiescence had been tongue-in-cheek. Within two
months, U.S. investigators knew with certainty that British shippers were
ignoring the agreed-upon embargo, and that Anglo-Argentine commercial
trade had increased considerably.[32]

Argentina could do nothing about its frozen gold assets, but the
soundness of its peso made smuggling an attractive alternative, and the
reshipment of prohibited goods through other Latin American republics
further undermined the effectiveness of the September 4, 1944, trade
restrictions.[33] Moreover, on October 17, the Farrell government announced that with most of the German agents detained, diplomatic
nonrecognition had lost its only justification. The Argentinians then

called for a meeting of American foreign ministers to resolve all causes of discord, a recommendation which Cordell Hull summarily rejected. The secretary refused to admit it, but the truth was that the promising anti-Fascist crusade launched in June 1944 had collapsed in four months.

Despite increasing criticism from the Latin American republics and a rising crescendo of voices calling for rapprochement with Argentina,[34] Hull remained inflexible. He had decided to resign in September 1944, and after Franklin D. Roosevelt's reelection, he could step aside (November 27, 1944),[35] head held high, his dignity seemingly intact. Still, someone else would have to clean up the shambles he had left behind. This task fell to Edward R. Stettinius, Jr., and Nelson Rockefeller, officially appointed on December 4 to the posts of secretary of state and assistant secretary for Latin American affairs, respectively.

Straightaway, Rockefeller sought to escape the cul-de-sac in which Hull's defective diplomacy had left him. After rejecting an Argentine proposal for an inter-American conclave, Rockefeller threw his weight behind Mexican foreign minister Ezequiel Padilla's call for an extraordinary meeting of American republics, to be held in Mexico City.[36]

As conceived by Padilla, this special conference was to deal primarily with economic problems and measures to strengthen the inter-American security system, but Rockefeller also viewed it as a way of disposing of the embarrassing Argentine question. During the first week of February, before the conference was scheduled to convene, Rockefeller secretly dispatched Adolf Berle, and later Rafael Oreamundo, a former Costa Rican diplomat and friend of Rockefeller, to Buenos Aires to negotiate an understanding with Juan Perón. The talks were conducted in an informal atmosphere, with the colonel quickly agreeing to enforce the 1942 Rio de Janeiro Conference accords dealing with spies and the control of Axis citizens, property, and press. He also promised to accept any requirements that the.upcoming Mexico City conference might impose upon a still neutral Argentina, but rejected a suggestion that before democratic elections were held, the Farrell government would turn over its power to the Argentine Supreme Court.

Both Berle and Oreamundo reported that Perón became increasingly expansive during the meetings, but the friendly atmosphere did not prevent him from demanding a heavy price for his collaboration. The United States had to agree to drop all economic sanctions against Argentina and to sell military equipment if and when Argentina might enter the war. But with the basic deal in place, the U.S. delegation could look forward to the Mexico City conference, confident that there would be no sudden shocks and that the Argentine problem would soon be effectively liquidated.[37]

The Inter-American Conference on Problems of War and Peace began in Mexico City on February 21, 1945. At its closing on March 8, the participants signed a document which became known as the Act of Chapultepec. This agreement bound the signatories to intensify their efforts to suppress Axis subversion (Resolution VII), recommended the negotiation and adoption of a hemispheric security pact (Resolution VIII), and sanctioned the liquidation of all business establishments owned or controlled by Axis nationals (Resolution XIX).[38]

Also included was the vague and tortuously worded Resolution LIX, which became Washington's vehicle for patching up its feud with Buenos Aires. Put forward as part of a prearranged plan, this resolution deplored Argentina's failure to take part in the conference or to align herself with the Allied nations against the rapidly collapsing Axis powers. At the same time, the resolution intimated that Argentina could end its diplomatic isolation by declaring war on Germany and Japan, and formally adhering to the Act of Chapultepec. In exchange, the United States would do what it could to see that Argentina became a member of the soon-to-be-founded United Nations organization.[39]

Having escaped with only the mildest of censures and aware that no watchdog provisions had been created for determining the extent of its future compliance, the Farrell regime could have chosen to strike a more conciliatory pose. Instead, it opted to remain defiant. For example, on March 27, 1945, Argentina declared war on Japan and upon Germany, but "only in view of the latter's position as an ally of Japan."[40] The American republics chose to ignore this premeditated slap in the face, and on April 4 allowed Argentines to adhere to the Act of Chapultepec. Five days later, most of the American republics and Great Britain resumed full diplomatic relations with Argentina.

Formal rapprochement between the United States and Argentina occurred on April 17, when a special commission headed by the chief of the American republics desk, Avra Warren, reached Buenos Aires. He conferred with Perón and other military men, and the February 1945 agreements were reviewed to the satisfaction of all parties. Warren side-stepped a request by Perón for immediate weapons purchases, but confirmed that Washington would eventually sanction arms sales. He promised that a new U.S. ambassador would reach Buenos Aires in May and accepted Argentine promises to arrest all spies and to liquidate the assets of Axis-owned businesses.[41]

Seemingly, Washington and Buenos Aires had finally agreed to kiss and make up, but disgruntled voices could still be heard carping away in the background. Adolf Berle bitterly opposed the mild proposals adopted for ending the imbroglio with Argentina, while in his *Memoirs*, Cordell Hull eschews any attempt to mask his rage and frustration:

> To me the recognition of the Farrell Regime through the estab-
> lishment of diplomatic relations, and the admission of that regime
> into ... the very United Nations for whose defeat it [Argentina] had
> hoped and worked ... was the most colossal injury done to the
> Pan-American movement in all its history.[42]

While neither of these men had anything to do with making the choice, neither Berle nor Hull could have been too unhappy about the man Rockefeller and Stettinius chose as the new ambassador to Argentina: Spruille Braden. Known for his brass-knuckled, straight-ahead style of diplomacy, Braden felt the men who chose him for the post had shown "moral flabbiness" in dealing with Perón. Even before he left for Buenos Aires, Braden publicly declared that he intended to push aggressively for free, democratic elections.[43] Given his attitude, it is hardly surprising that he rapidly became the center of a political storm which rocked both Argentina and the Department of State.

Arriving in Buenos Aires on May 19, "Cowboy" Braden, as British diplomats dubbed him,[44] immediately went on the attack. Resolution XIII of the Chapultepec document required all signatories to end government censorship and promote the "free exchange of information" among the people of the hemisphere. Since Argentina had adhered to this Act, but still was censoring the press and radio, Braden had a ready-made cause. In speech after speech, he blasted away at the military government's restrictions on the press and radio, called for democratic elections, and insinuated that the latter would be impossible if Perón was a candidate. These acts made him the darling of the diverse political elements opposed to the colonel and earned him Perón's implacable hatred.[45]

What might have happened had Braden remained in Buenos Aires even six months makes for interesting speculation, but in August, Nelson Rockefeller resigned his post, and the new secretary of state, James Byrnes, ordered Braden to take Rockefeller's place. The "Cowboy" was initially reluctant to return to Washington, but he eventually persuaded himself that the "battle of Buenos Aires" could effectively be sustained from the banks of the Potomac. Following his return on September 22, 1945, Braden urged Undersecretary of State Dean Acheson to cancel the conference tentatively scheduled for October 20 in Rio de Janeiro, dealing with the formulation of the Inter-American Treaty of Reciprocal Assistance (which would come to be called the Rio Pact). He argued convincingly that Argentina had reneged on its commitments undertaken when it adhered to the Mexico City agreement. Both Acheson and Byrnes agreed, and on October 2, the announcement was made canceling the inter-American defense pact conference until further notice.[46]

Following the completion of this blocking action, Braden was free to commence work on the vehicle with which his name has become most closely associated historically; this was *Consultation among the American Republics with Respect to the Argentine Situation*, more commonly known as the *Blue Book*. The origins of this controversial document appear to have been an FBI espionage report formulated in response to a State Department request in February 1945,[47] but actual work on the *Blue Book* did not begin until eight months later. On October 29, 1945, Secretary of State James Byrnes ordered Robert Murphy, United States political advisor in Germany, to excerpt from captured German records "all evidence of Axis activities in Argentina," and to search especially for evidence of Perón's links with SD and Abwehr V-men. The collected data was to be forwarded not only to Washington but to Buenos Aires, where it was to be checked and elaborated on by Acting Chargé d'Affaires John Cabot and SIS/Argentina chief James P. Joice. The *Blue Book* was, therefore, a document assembled in some haste, but one which was based upon an older, reasonably comprehensive investigatory report.[48]

Concerning the *Blue Book*'s contents, over one-third of its pages deal with German intelligence activity and the contacts and collaboration of Argentine military and government figures with SD or Abwehr agents.[49] Other topics dealt with are the alleged failure of the Farrell regime to close German schools, liquidate German-owned businesses, and close German-owned newspapers. Finally there is an essay dealing with the Nazi-Fascist character of the Argentine military government.

The *Blue Book* made interesting reading, but in light of the fact that it was released on February 11, 1946, roughly two weeks before the Argentine presidential elections, the crucial question quickly became: what were the State Department's motives in releasing it? There remains serious disagreement among the persons involved on this matter. Spruille Braden strenuously denied that the derailing of Juan Perón's presidential express was the goal of the *Blue Book*. On the other hand, John Cabot, the ranking diplomat in Buenos Aires at the time the Argentine presidential elections were held, does not seem to agree. Cabot, who was ambivalent towards the *Blue Book*, said "the *Blue Book* was a very slanted account of the cooperation between the Argentine authorities and German spies in an effort to smear Perón. . . ." Cabot disagreed with some of the document's other critics in that he felt that its errors of fact are relatively minor; it was the conclusions drawn from the information which he believed to be unjustified.[50]

Very likely, a mixture of motives sparked the final decision to release the document, and while it did generate shock waves, it did not induce the Latin American reaction which some State Department personnel certainly hoped it would.[51] In retrospect, Spruille Braden would have been fortunate if he had been able to borrow the crystal ball owned by Adolf Berle, a charter member of the "get tough with Argentina" school. After secretly meeting with Perón in February 1945, Berle had warned Nelson Rockefeller that within a year, elections would take place in Argentina, and Juan Perón would storm to the presidency.[52] On February 24, 1946, this is precisely what happened. Subsequently, Sumner Welles, contemplating the *Blue Book*'s release and the long struggle with Argentina, would write that the United States had suffered the "worst diplomatic defeat" in the history of Pan-American relations.[53]

Nothing deflates like failure, and with Perón as Argentina's chief executive for at least the next six years, Spruille Braden became an albatross around the State Department's neck. Both Pres. Harry S. Truman and James Byrnes were convinced that a policy change was now unavoidable, but liberal elements in the Democratic party remained adamant against any accommodation with Perón.[54] As a result, the Truman administration embarked upon a two-track Argentine policy. In speeches made on March 24 and April 1, 1946, Secretary Byrnes declared that until the

Argentine government proved that the denazification commitment made when it signed the Act of Chapultepec was effectively carried out, no hemispheric security pact could be negotiated.[55] But even as this rededication to moral principle was taking place, the president and his secretary of state prepared to board a train headed in the opposite direction, for on April 1, 1946, they nominated George Messersmith as Spruille Braden's successor in Argentina.

As U.S. ambassador to Mexico since 1942, George Messersmith had done well, but he was an enemy of Miguel Alemán, the minister of the interior, who was a sure bet to win the presidential election scheduled for July 1946. The Mexican government had tactfully suggested to Braden that Messersmith's presence would become intolerable,[56] and since his record was otherwise excellent, Messersmith was ordered to leave Mexico City and prepare for transfer to Buenos Aires. After his arrival in Washington on April 5, 1946, Byrnes and Truman huddled with their ambassador-designate and ordered him to "get this Argentine situation straightened out so that we could implement the military arrangements ... arrived at, at the Chapultepec Conference in Mexico City." The president and secretary both condemned Spruille Braden's conduct in Buenos Aires and promised complete support if, as Messersmith expected, major policy clashes with the assistant secretary for Latin American affairs were in the offing.[57]

The new ambassador to Argentina was certainly prescient, because he and Braden exchanged verbal jabs even before he left Washington. Nevertheless, the intriguing factor is that even though Truman and Byrnes promised Messersmith their unqualified backing, they continued to assure Braden that they were unswerving supporters of his uncompromising stance toward Argentine compliance.[58] Assuming that internal political exigencies necessitated these duplicitous doings, there was certainly some advantage in being able to plug a tough policy in Washington while Messersmith sought to butter up Perón in Buenos Aires. Depending upon where the advantage was seen to lay, Truman and Byrnes could eventually disavow either man; but they would have to proceed carefully lest the situation blow up in their faces.

Messersmith arrived in Buenos Aires on May 23, 1946. In the reports dispatched to Washington during the next seven months, the ambassador remained tirelessly optimistic that Perón would close all Axis educational facilities, confiscate all Axis-owned commercial enterprises, and deport all former German spies. His favorable presentations of Perónist Argentina were countered and contradicted by angry memoranda from Braden to Byrnes and Undersecretary Dean Acheson, which insisted that the Argentine president was feigning compliance, and nothing more. Indeed, in reading Messersmith's dispatches and Braden's rebuttals, the views expressed are so utterly at odds that it is sometimes difficult to believe that the two men were talking about the same country and the same chief executive.[59]

James Byrnes officially resigned on January 10, 1947. He left behind a Braden-Messersmith feud which had become vicious, personal and, worst of all, public.[60] George C. Marshall became secretary of state on January 21, 1947. With President Truman now allegedly referring to Messersmith as a "son-of-a-bitch,"[61] Marshall instructed Dean Acheson to end the war between the ambassador and the assistant secretary as circumspectly as possible. The decision reached was probably the only one feasible: both men would have to go.[62]

Unfortunately, solving State Department personnel problems did nothing to improve U.S.-Argentine relations or bring the Rio Pact meeting closer to realization. Aware that his administration was on the verge of suffering a diplomatic defeat, the president chose to take a personal hand in the diplomatic proceedings. On March 31, 1947, flanked by Tom Connally, a Democratic senator from Texas, Arthur Vandenberg, a Republican senator from Michigan, and Undersecretary Dean Acheson, Truman received Argentine ambassador Oscar Ivanissevitch at the White House. The president insisted that he wanted only the best relationship with Argentina. He declared that "everything" could be settled if Perón saw fit to deport an "additional 20 or 30 dangerous Nazi agents" still in Argentina. Since Invanissevitch was returning to Buenos Aires, Truman wanted his message personally conveyed to Perón.[63]

It would have been unusual for this kind of diplomacy to produce dramatic results, and the likelihood is strong that Truman was merely going through the motions in order to justify the near-inevitable surrender. The de facto response to this strategem was given about five weeks later. The State Department had consistently attempted to use the spy issue as a political weapon against Argentina; now Buenos Aires served up a taste of the same medicine. On May 6, 1947, Foreign Minister Juan Bramuglia directed Ambassador George Messersmith to tell his superiors that "so important a matter as the Rio meeting and defense pact could no longer be held up because a few enemy aliens had not been apprehended."[64] Bramuglia's next steps indicated that he was not bluffing. On May 21, the steamer *Río Teuco* departed for Europe carrying eight former Abwehr and SD operatives. Two days later in answer to a press conference question, Bramuglia solemnly declared that his nation had now met all commitments undertaken when it signed the Act of Chapultepec.[65]

Both Secretary of State George Marshall and Thomas C. Mann, chief of the River Plate Republics Division, doubted that Perón had made a good-faith effort to recapture or deport the Abwehr and SD fugitives in the country.[66] The reasons for their skepticism were persuasively presented, but by this time, Truman was prepared to recognize the fact that he did not—and probably never did—have a viable alternative. He may have been holding his nose, but on June 3, 1947, the president announced that Argentina had satisfactorily complied with the anti-Nazi provisions of the Act of Chapultepec.

The major problem disposed of, the smaller one could now be liquidated with dispatch; the same day Truman reported Argentine compliance, he also announced the resignations of Spruille Braden and George Messersmith.[67] The ambassador to Argentina had not been expecting the ax to fall so abruptly, so on June 6, he shot off an angry cable to George Marshall, sarcastically asking, "As I have not submitted any resignation to the President has my 'resignation' been accepted by him?"[68] Thus ended two reasonably successful diplomatic careers, and although Braden and Messersmith had no regard for each other, they both emphatically agreed that they had been shabbily treated by the president of the United States.[69]

Harry S. Truman did not mention such factors publicly, but there were several pressing reasons why he felt impelled to embrace the myth of Argentine compliance. By June 1947, even Spruille Braden was prepared to admit that the Soviet Union represented a greater threat to U.S. interests than that nation which couldn't or wouldn't find "20 or 30 dangerous Nazi agents."[70] Furthermore, the proposed Rio Pact (signed on September 2, 1947) would have been a useless instrument without the signature of Argentina, then the wealthiest and most influential Spanish-American republic. Cold War considerations were beginning to assert themselves.

The president was also silent about other pressures which in any case would have forced a major modification in the compliance posture of the United States. Former vice-president Henry Wallace might decry our cowardly abandonment of principle,[71] but in May 1947, over Washington's vigorous objections, the Clement Atlee government in Britain agreed to sell Argentina one hundred new jet fighter planes and nine warships.[72] This decision short-circuited U.S. policy, because with the British prepared to deliver Perón almost any military equipment he could pay for, Truman could no longer deny the Argentine arms market to eager U.S. military suppliers.[73] The English probably would have preferred to sell weapons to a leader who did not have a pro-Fascist reputation, but the prospect of sales and profits simply outweighed moral and other considerations.

Truman's declaration of Argentine compliance with the Chapultepec agreement was a convenient fiction intended to facilitate the start of the long-delayed Rio Pact meetings. This expeditious retreat served to obscure the definitive response to the compliance question which the Argentinians themselves would soon provide. Consider that on March 31, 1945, the Farrell government issued Executive Decree No. 7035/945, which created the Junta de Vigilancia y Diposición de Propiedad Enemigo or Board of Vigilance and Ultimate Liquidation of Enemy Property. In keeping with Resolution XIX of the Chapultepec accords, this organization was empowered to seize Axis-owned firms, liquidate their assets, and take whatever steps necessary to eradicate Axis influence. By July 1946, the board would claim that twenty firms formerly owned by Axis nationals and possessing assets of over $58 million had been taken over. But in the same report, members of the board complained that governmental intervention in the interest of favored parties, and lawsuits by owners of the intervened enterprises, had brought liquidation of assets actions to a virtual standstill.[74]

On July 25, 1947, six weeks after President Truman announced Argentina's satisfactory compliance with the Chapultepec resolutions, the Department of State sought information regarding the board's subsequent progress. Foreign Minister Bramuglia's reply was that an interim report was forthcoming and that the State Department would be informed when it was completed. Perhaps Bramuglia was sincere, but Argentine records fail to reveal when this report was either completed or issued. Just as important, as of July 1948, the Argentine Supreme Court still had not issued a definite ruling as to whether the board could proceed with the liquidation of seized Axis properties. Despite the lip service paid to inter-American concerns, the Argentine government never complied with the spirit of the Chapultepec accords.[75]

The truth is that once again, Washington's foreign policy makers had been outmaneuvered by their wily counterparts in Buenos Aires. But, in deciding to make peace with Perón, Truman demonstrated that he was prepared to accept the obvious: as far as Latin America was concerned, World War II was over.

II. The Hellmuth-Harnisch Affair

A. Background

The origins of the most spectacular spy saga in Latin America during World War II lay in events transpiring during Easter week (March 30–April 5) 1942. Osmar Alberto Hellmuth, a prosperous insurance salesman, traveled to the Province of Neuquén to inspect a coal mine and write a policy on that property. The trip from Buenos Aires took over thirty hours and early during the train ride, Hellmuth became acquainted with Brig. Gen. Pedro Ramírez, who was traveling west on an inspection tour. Hellmuth and Ramírez hit it off immediately, and the general subsequently invited the insurance man to join him and his aides in what became a nonstop railroad party. Ramírez, then a cavalry brigade commander, had no idea that in thirteen months he would become president of Argentina. Osmar Hellmuth would have laughed scornfully had anyone told him that in eighteen months he would first be made a diplomat and and then jailed as a spy. In fact, Ramírez and Hellmuth probably never met again. But the insurance broker would subsequently see a good deal of some of Ramírez's companions. In particular, he would come to be on intimate terms with three of the GOU's original integrants: Capt. Francisco Filippi, Maj. Mario Bernard, and Lt. Col. Enrique González.

Osmar Hellmuth was an Argentine citizen, born in Buenos Aires on November 23, 1908. His father was a German immigrant, and young Osmar learned both Spanish and German at an early age. In 1924 he entered the Argentine naval academy only to be sent packing two years later after he failed to pass a mathematics test. Disappointed over his failure to become a naval officer, Hellmuth drifted into the insurance business, where over the next sixteen years, he became prosperous as a claims adjuster and policy salesman. He joined the Argentine Yacht Club and became friendly with many British and German businessmen, one of whom was Hans Harnisch, a man whom Hellmuth had originally met in 1928. By 1942, Osmar Hellmuth had become a successful businessman, but one who longed to gain the renown and prestige which he believed a successful naval career would have allotted him. If and when opportunity knocked, he intended to seize it with both hands.[76]

Hellmuth's espionage involvement began about March 1943. At a dinner held at the Argentine Yacht Club, he encountered Hans Harnisch, general manager of Boker and Company, a hardware and steel machinery subsidiary of a German firm headquartered in Bonn. The two men spent some time talking and drinking and met again at several other yacht club dinners in March and April of 1943. At these subsequent meetings, Harnisch did a good deal of bragging about his intimate relations with SS-Maj. Gen. Walter Schellenberg, head of Amt VI of the SD, and other Nazi party bigwigs. These claims of connections did not seem improbable because recently, Harnisch's reputation as a "fixer" or facilitator had soared. In February 1943, the Castillo government asked the German businessman to assist in gaining the release of some Swedish newsprint for which Reich officials had refused to grant an export license. Since he succeeded, Harnisch became persona grata with the regime and was believed to possess plenty of clout in Nazi Germany.[77]

It is not clear whether Osmar Hellmuth knew that Harnisch was an Abwehr agent, but he told Captain Filippi, Major Bernhard, and Lieutenant Colonel González about Harnisch's SD connections; these GOU members apparently resolved to find out the facts. Their opportunity came when shortly after the June 4, 1943, military coup, Harnisch and Hellmuth crossed paths at still another social function. This time, however, the German began complaining. With the unexpected fall of Castillo, he no longer had close contacts in the ruling group, a most dreadful position for a "fixer" to be in. Hellmuth subsequently confessed that he "at once saw an opportunity for advancement" and acted accordingly. For some months, Juan Castillo had sought to persuade the Germans to issue a safe conduct certificate so that a six-thousand-ton tanker, purchased by Argentina from Greece and renamed the *Buenos Aires*, could sail for home. Hellmuth knew that for prestige reasons the Ramírez regime was desperately seeking to succeed where Castillo had failed. Thus, he asked the crucial question: Could Harnisch, with his powerful Reich connections, convince the Germans to allow the *Buenos Aires* to sail for Argentina?

The German was initially noncommittal, but he subsequently assured Hellmuth that he could indeed assist in making the proper arrangements. Next, Hellmuth set up a meeting which included himself, Harnisch, Filippi, Bernard, and González. By mid-June 1943, the trio of GOU stalwarts all held important posts in the Ramírez regime, so that if Harnisch could deliver on his promises, he would again become a man on the inside. In response to a query about the *Buenos Aires*, Harnisch declared that with his intervention the matter could be resolved instantly. Then, Lieutenant Colonel González dropped the other shoe: Could Harnisch, through his powerful friends, help the Ramírez government to negotiate an arms purchase with the Third Reich? The German cautioned that the Argentinians would probably have to send ships to Spain to transport what was purchased, but this, too, could be easily negotiated. González liked what he heard and promised to put Harnisch in contact with Ramírez himself.[78]

All the previous participants except Hellmuth were present at a meeting which took place at González's apartment on June 28, 1943. González reviewed Harnisch's promises of facilitation and indicated his satisfaction with the responses given. The highlight of the conclave, however, was the arrival of Pedro Ramírez himself. After expressing his distrust of U.S. policy toward Argentina and his disdain for Ambassador Norman Armour, Ramírez questioned Harnisch closely about the release of the *Buenos Aires* and the possibility of a German-Argentine arms deal. Satisfied with the responses given, the president promised the German his full support in executing both operations.[79]

Thereafter, Harnisch usually maintained contact with González through Hellmuth and he continually affirmed that with his help both issues would be successfully resolved once the Ramírez government sent a confidential envoy to Berlin. Hellmuth had visions of filling this role, but González initially gave him little encouragement. Argentina was then exploring the possibility of arms deals with both the United States and Japan, and no decision was to be made until all options had been fully investigated. But prolonged negotiations confirmed that the United States would provide weaponry only to those who declared war on the Axis, and that the Japanese never really intended to sell military or naval equipment to Argentina.[80] Germany might have lost the initiative on the battlefields of Europe, but it must be recalled that one small shipment (via Switzerland and Spain) of antiaircraft guns had already reached Argentina in 1943. Moreover, the Argentinians wanted the *Buenos Aires* released, and the ultranationalists of the GOU would only accept an arms sale which did not jeopardize their concept of neutrality. Given those conditions, the Harnisch offer became the only game in town.

B. *The Preparation*

The Ramírez government would subsequently tell the Germans that the refusal of the United States to make an arms deal which did not affect Argentine neutrality triggered the decision to send a special representative to Germany.[81] Perhaps this is so, but it would be mid-September 1943, before Osmar Hellmuth was called by González to meet the new foreign minister, Col. Alberto Gilbert. The two officials announced that Harnisch's good offices had been accepted and that Hellmuth, if he agreed, would be secretly sent to Germany to deal with the problem of the *Buenos Aires,* among others. The insurance broker accepted, but complained that because of the Anglo-American bombing campaign, he would not wish to accept a post in the Reich itself. González and Gilbert indicated that this would be unnecessary. Furthermore, if the negotiations proved successful, they assured Hellmuth that he would become "one of us."[82]

Whether this meant that Hellmuth would receive a prestige job in the Ramírez regime or merely sponsorship for entry into the most prestigious sailing clubs, and so forth, is not clear, but the promise proved sufficient. The insurance man formally agreed to become a confidential agent, and on September 25, he was given a diplomatic passport and made auxiliary consul in the Argentine Consulate-General in Barcelona. He was also handed a dossier containing all relevant information on the *Buenos Aires* and told that Admiral Benito Sueyro, the naval minister, would arrange for fueling the vessel and for obtaining a crew. Hellmuth was also instructed to attempt the recruitment of German technicians for Argentine arms factories, the transfers to be arranged by Capt. Eduardo A. Ceballos, the naval attaché in Berlin, who would also double as Hellmuth's assistant. In addition, the insurance-man-turned-diplomat was authorized to explain to the highest German authorities that even if Argentina found it necessary to break diplomatic relations, de facto contact with Germany would be discreetly maintained. Finally, he was ordered to sail aboard the Spanish liner, *Cabo de Hornos*, for the port of Bilbao on October 2, 1943.[83]

Possibly the most striking aspect of Hellmuth's instructions is that they reveal the deep distrust felt by the military regime for the Argentine diplomatic corps. For example, on September 26, 1943, Luís Luti, Argentine chargé d'affaires in Berlin, wrote Foreign Minister Col. Alberto Gilbert, predicting that by the end of 1944, the Allied nations would defeat the Third Reich. Luti would undoubtedly have been less candid had he known that since November 1941, the SD had been opening the Argentine diplomatic pouch and reading his anti-Axis commentaries.[84] The chargé would certainly have been disturbed had he known that Harnisch had discreetly but clearly indicated to the Argentines that Berlin preferred to have Luti replaced. And since he was a supporter of the Hellmuth mission, Colonel Gilbert could hardly have been overjoyed with Luti's report. Nevertheless, he and González decided to turn the situation to their own advantage. Hellmuth was now ordered to avoid contact with any Argentine diplomatic personnel in Germany except Captain Ceballos. At the same time, if Luti's dismissal became crucial to the release of the *Buenos Aires*, then Hellmuth was authorized to go to the embassy, confront Luti, and send him packing![85]

The decision to go forward with these arrangements implies that sometime prior to Hellmuth's acceptance, González obtained from Harnisch concrete evidence of his powerful German connections. As the insurance broker soon discovered, González already knew that Harnisch was, in fact, only the front man in this operation; the brains in the plot and the man with the influence in the Reich was really Johannes Siegfried

Becker. Hellmuth became privy to these developments on September 26, when he first met Becker at a luncheon given by Harnisch. Becker's instructions were simple enough: After the *Cabo de Hornos* docked at Bilbao, Hellmuth was to take a room at the Carlton Hotel. A day or so later, he would be approached by a man who would identify himself with the salutation, "Greetings from Herr Sigmund Becker." Hellmuth was to respond, "Ah yes, the Haupsturmführer" (i.e., SS-captain).

The identification formalities over with, the unnamed greeter would arrange for Hellmuth's German visa. Becker further instructed that Hellmuth would be flown to the Reich where his immediate Berlin contact was to be SD Amt VI chief, Walter Schellenberg. In addition, negotiations might be carried on with Heinrich Himmler, and there was even the possibility of meeting with the Führer himself! Everything had been prepared. All Hellmuth had to do was get to Spain and follow Becker's instructions.[86]

Well aware that the success or failure of his mission must have a decisive effect on Argentine-German relations, Hellmuth spent several days going over strategy with González and receiving instructions from Harnisch on how he was to conduct himself with SD leaders. Then, on or about September 29, 1943, González pulled another surprise. Nothing had been said for some time about arms negotiations. Now, Hellmuth was told that as soon as the tanker talks were successfully completed, he and Col. Alberto Vélez, the newly appointed military attaché to Spain and Portugal, were to jointly handle arms purchase negotiations. A large dossier of instructions dealing with the classes and types of armaments sought was shown to Hellmuth and then ordered placed in a diplomatic pouch to be carried by special courier to the Argentine embassy in Madrid.

In explaining why the weapons purchase deal was to be jointly handled, González explained that another individual was determined to muscle in on the secret mission. This was Col. Juan Perón, then assistant to the minister of war, Gen. Edelmiro Farrell. Perón had decided to send Vélez as the sole negotiator for the purchase of German weapons. González and Gilbert had vociferously opposed this plan, and the twin negotiator scheme was the result. Nevertheless, Perón had to be made part of the secret mission planning group, and it was he who was credited with the identification and access scheme which Hellmuth and Vélez were to use before the armaments dossier would be turned over to them. Upon successful completion of the tanker release negotiations, the duo was to meet in the Argentine embassy in Madrid. Before he left Buenos Aires Hellmuth was:

> shown a piece of lined cardboard which had been cut in half . . . one half would be placed in an envelope bearing his name in the diplomatic bag [the same with the weapons negotiation dossier], the other would be similarly forwarded in the name of Colonel Vélez; the dossier itself would be handed to them on their simultaneous production of the two halves of the card.[87]

In the final hours before his scheduled departure, Hellmuth received a generous letter of credit for his expenses and turned his business affairs over to Carlos Enrique Neiling ("Charlie"), who was the V-man Harnisch used to communicate with "Bolívar" network director, Gustav Utzinger. There were final conferences with Juan Perón and Siegfried Becker, but what irritated Hellmuth was the flood of last-minute personal requests which came from persons whom he could not afford to alienate. Making a bid for enhanced prestige, Hans Harnisch gave the confidential agent food parcels for both his mother and SD Amt VI boss, Walter Schellenberg. Enrique González wanted several publications on the aerial warfare in Europe and a "machine for removing hair from the nose." And as a personal favor, Naval Minister Adm. Benito Sueyro wished a greeting be personally delivered to an old friend in Barcelona. It was a slightly harried Osmar Hellmuth who, along with Colonel Vélez and several other Argentine diplomats bound for Europe, boarded the *Cabo de Hornos* on October 2, 1943.[88]

Although Hellmuth subsequently stated that he had had no qualms about undertaking this secret mission, by the time he left Buenos Aires, he should have. What had begun as a top-secret operation involving the negotiated release of a tanker had ballooned into a multifaceted affair, a situation which could easily compromise the security precautions taken. Yet, the most dangerous development from the latter perspective was the intrigue and back-stabbing engaged in by the Germans, who were involved in, or who believed themselves affected by this secret mission. On September 29, 1943, Colonel Gilbert called in German Chargé d'Affaires Erich von Meynen and told him that a "close friend of the Führer" had arranged for an "Argentine naval officer" (i.e., Osmar Hellmuth) to travel from Spain to Germany to purchase weapons and negotiate the release of the *Buenos Aires.* Gilbert estimated that the tanker talks would be completed in four days, and proclaimed himself to be optimistic about the success of the prospective weapons discussions as well.[89]

Erich von Meynen, officially informed of the Hellmuth mission seventy-two hours before the alleged naval officer was scheduled to sail, considered this entire operation a gross usurpation of Foreign Office prerogatives and was determined to stymie it. There is evidence that a German embassy source had learned of the Hellmuth mission several days before Gilbert talked to Meynen, and this discovery gave the chargé time to produce a surprise of his own. Meynen's first move was to enlist the assistance of a *Reichsdeutscher* named Ludwig Freude. The owner of a construction company and possibly the wealthiest German in Argentina, Freude's task was to find out who was the close friend of the Führer that Gilbert alluded to, and what could be done to prevent the execution of this mission.[90]

An extremely influential person, Freude promptly set about finding answers and came close to achieving Meynen's goal. First, he and military attaché Gen. Friedrich Wolf met with Minister of War General Farrell, Colonel González, and several other officers to discuss the Hellmuth mission. Next, Freude hosted a dinner party attended by Farrell, Foreign Minister Gilbert, Police Chief Gen. Domingo Martínez, and Col. Otto Vélez. Following the meal, Freude declared that he, too, was on excellent terms with the leader of the Third Reich. In his opinion, however, Osmar Hellmuth was not the kind of negotiator who would be welcomed in Germany; Col. Otto Vélez, the military attaché being sent to Spain and Portugal, was the man to negotiate the release of the *Buenos Aires*.[91]

At least one source argues that Enrique González was persuaded to reconsider sending the insurance broker,[92] but after a meeting of the Argentine principals involved, it was Juan Perón who prevailed. He informed Meynen and Freude that Osmar Hellmuth enjoyed the "absolute confidence of the Ramírez government."[93] On October 1, Gilbert and González, professing to be puzzled by the obvious conflict among the Germans, informed Hellmuth of the Freude-Meynen machinations. Straightaway the insurance broker, who feared his dreams of glory were about to be dissipated, called upon Harnisch and Becker. They reassured Hellmuth that the mission had not been jeopardized and that the SD would teach Meynen to ignore matters which did not concern him.

In keeping with the tragicomic atmosphere which surrounded this whole affair, Meynen somehow discovered that Hellmuth and Becker intended to make him suffer for his interference. In an October 3, 1943, report to the Foreign Ministry, he described the Hellmuth mission as being an SD escapade and added that the confidential agent en route planned to destroy his reputation.[94] In any case, news of Hellmuth's mission and impending arrival did nothing to brighten the outlook of Foreign Minister Joachim von Ribbentrop. Since May 1943, he had been receiving information which indicated that SD agents in Buenos Aires were acting as diplomats and making foreign policy decisions. Ribbentrop was convinced that unless the SD abandoned its adventures in diplomacy, an indiscretion would be committed which would destroy his own plans for keeping Argentina neutral. In an effort to keep Himmler's intelligence arm from trespassing on his ministry's turf, Ribbentrop demanded that the SD supply full details concerning the Hellmuth operation. If nothing else, once Ribbentrop received more data, he conceivably would be better able to prevent any blame for the feared fiasco from falling on his organization.[95]

Initially, the SD ignored all Foreign Office entreaties, but towards the end of October, it seems to have experienced some second thoughts about the feasibility of the entire operation. On October 25, Walter Schellenberg personally assured Ribbentrop that the SD had no intention of becoming a second Foreign Office. Ribbentrop remained unmollified until two days later, when Amt VI-D chief, SS-Lt. Col. Theodor Paeffgen agreed to discuss the Hellmuth mission with the head of the Latin American section of the Foreign Office, Otto Reinebeck.[96]

Whatever his instructions from Schellenberg were, Paeffgen proved to be both canny and candid. After assuring Reinebeck that the discussions with the Argentinians would be concerned only with the *Buenos*

Aires and weapons sales, the SD official surprised the diplomat by stating that his bosses didn't want Hellmuth to come to Germany either. He agreed that the Reich had no weapons to sell, no technicians to spare, and was unlikely to have a surplus of either for an indefinite period. Nevertheless, SD headquarters had to support the mission for the sake of maintaining an intelligence presence in Argentina. If the release of the *Buenos Aires* was refused, and possible weapons sales were rejected outright, a vengeful Argentine government might arrest all the SD agents in the country. Schellenberg and Himmler proposed to solve this ticklish situation by simulating cooperation and allowing the negotiations to drag on either until the war situation changed or the Argentinians lost interest.[97]

From Reinebeck's perspective, the talks proved shocking because of the SD's apparent ignorance of the factors involved in the proposed *Buenos Aires* release. Paeffgen professed to be unaware that in June 1943, chargé Erich von Meynen had sought and received a certificate from Berlin allowing the tanker to sail from Sweden anytime the Argentine government supplied fuel and a crew.[98] Yet the truth was that neither Paeffgen nor Reinebeck was fully informed, for although the SD and the Foreign Ministry were disposed to release the *Buenos Aires,* the German navy was not. An appeal to the Führer was necessary before Adm. Karl Doenitz grudgingly agreed to transfer control of the vessel. This event was accomplished on December 22, 1943, but by that time, other developments would make this accomplishment irrelevant.[99]

In retrospect, the Hellmuth affair became a not-so-secret mission carried out by an insurance broker who lacked diplomatic experience, with an Abwehr V-man (Harnisch) acting as cutout between the Argentine government and the SD chief in Argentina, Johannes Siegfried Becker. It was a mission in which the confidential agent was selected partially because if it failed, he could more easily be disowned. It was also a mission in which the confidential agent was being sent to obtain weapons the Germans did not have, and to negotiate with an intelligence agency which was primarily interested in buying time. It was a recipe for disaster.

C. *Squeeze Play*

In their analyses of Osmar Hellmuth, both British and German commentaries are in accord: This would-be diplomat was an "innocent abroad," who had nonchalantly dived into the murky waters of international intrigue without a life jacket. Hellmuth shrugged off his inexperience and explained his decision to become a confidential agent in this way: "I had a marvelous opportunity to go to Europe, free of expenses, with a good salary, on an extremely important mission, and with good prospects [of success]. I put it that no one in my position would have turned down this chance."[100]

On the other hand, if Hellmuth had been a believer in omens, he might have gotten off the vessel at the first opportunity and found some other means of reaching Europe. The *Cabo de Hornos* sailed on October

2, but in the River Plate estuary, its engines broke down and the liner limped into Montevideo harbor. On October 11, after repairs were made, the vessel moved on to Rio de Janeiro. On October 29, it reached Port of Spain, Trinidad. That same afternoon, British contraband control officers began combing the ship. Nothing of significance was reportedly found, but at 1:00 A.M. on October 30, British officials again boarded the vessel. Over Spanish protests and despite his diplomatic passport, they removed Osmar Hellmuth from the ship. The next morning, an RAF transport plane flew him to Bermuda. Three days later, the light cruiser HMS *Ajax* whisked him across the Atlantic, arriving at Portsmouth on November 12. Hellmuth was removed to a special camp, where British interrogators soon had him telling them what they wanted to know.[101]

If this ill-starred secret mission seemed a highly improbable venture even before it began, events transpiring after Hellmuth's capture mark it as one of the most unique in the annals of World War II. Not until November 4, 1943, did the Ramírez government receive a cable from Consul General Dário Quiroga in Trinidad, reporting that Hellmuth had been arrested.[102] Then, out of the blue, there arrived another cable on November 8, allegedly signed by Osmar Hellmuth, and listing Port of Spain as its place of origin. This message, addressed to Col. Enrique González, stated that British authorities were detaining him in Trinidad, and begged the colonel to intervene on his behalf.[103]

It is the dating of both messages and the place of origin of the second which is curious and, insofar as the Argentinians understood the circumstances, disturbing. Why did it take until November 4 for Consul General Quiroga to send a cable to Buenos Aires? Was Hellmuth still in Trinidad? Why hadn't he sent a cable before November 8? Were the cables held up? Hellmuth was, in all probability, aboard the *Ajax* on November 8, 1943. He could not have sent the cable that bears his name on that date. Nevertheless, it was not until November 17, 1943, that the Ramírez government finally obtained most of the facts. Edgardo Pérez Quesada was an Argentine diplomat posted to Lisbon who also sailed aboard the *Cabo de Hornos*. He covertly witnessed Hellmuth's forced departure during the early morning hours of October 30, and disembarking himself, he rushed to Consul General Quiroga's residence and reported the incident. The two men waited until a cable office opened, and then sent a message to Foreign Minister Alberto Gilbert. It was this cable, sent on October 30, which somehow took five days to reach Buenos Aires.[104]

Returning to the *Cabo de Hornos*, which sailed on November 1, 1943, Pérez Quesada informed other Argentine diplomats on board of Hellmuth's arrest and his own actions in alerting Quiroga. An attempt was made to have the captain of the ship radio a message ahead to the Argentine embassy in Madrid, but the commander refused to do so. Not until November 16, after the *Cabo de Hornos* reached Lisbon, was Pérez Quesada able to send a long cablegram and provide the Ramírez government with a reasonably complete picture of everything that had occurred.[105]

The cumulative effect of these relations must have caused Enrique González, Alberto Gilbert, and Pedro Ramírez to break out in a collective cold sweat. The British had obviously known a good deal about this supposedly secret mission and were prepared to run the risk of confrontation, for they had seized an Argentine diplomat, and somehow delayed the transmission of warning cables. Moreover, Hellmuth had most certainly talked, so that the British now possessed information which could be used to the detriment of the Argentine government. The Hellmuth mission, begun with such high hopes, had swiftly degenerated into an unmitigated debacle.

After some hesitation, Foreign Minister Gilbert started what he must have suspected was a hopeless effort to obtain Hellmuth's quick release. Wrapping himself in the cloak of righteousness, Gilbert cabled England on November 14, demanding that the British explain their "insolent attitude" and instantly release Osmar Hellmuth, who was described as a "career Argentine diplomat."[106] The ambassador to the Court of St. James, Miguel Carcano, promptly presented this formal protest to Foreign Office Undersecretary Sir Arthur Cardogan, but the British were one step ahead of the Argentinians. Cardogan listened to Carcano's measured protests, and on November 15 replied that the Foreign Office knew nothing whatsoever about an Argentine diplomat named Osmar Hellmuth![107]

This thunderclap, plus Pérez Quesada's aforementioned cable, made it evident that the British believed themselves to be in a position to extract some major concessions from Argentina. This suspicion was deepened when on November 25, Undersecretary Cardogan called in Carcano and announced that Hellmuth was, after all, a British prisoner. But when the Argentine ambassador sought to establish the captive's condition and whereabouts, Cardogan again displayed invincible ignorance.[108]

Two more weeks would pass before Foreign Secretary Anthony Eden summoned Carcano and delineated the British position. Eden began by categorically denying that his government had delayed the dispatch of cables from Trinidad, and refused to discuss Hellmuth's whereabouts. He did say that the British government believed Osmar Hellmuth was a "secret representative of a subversive German organization in Argentina." And this was not the only bombshell Eden exploded. Carcano was further informed that "before the departure of Hellmuth, the British Government was informed by a prominent member of the German colony in Buenos Aires that Hellmuth would soon travel to Germany via Spain in representation of a branch of the German espionage service in Buenos Aires."[109]

Gilbert and González had no difficulty concluding that the "prominent member of the German colony" fingered by the British foreign secretary was none other than Meynen's henchman, Ludwig Freude.[110] The trouble was that no one could be sure whether these revelations were genuine, or a clever move in a game of misinformation, intended to draw attention away from the real leak. Moreover, by declaring Hellmuth to be a German spy, was it possible that Eden was cautiously suggesting to the Ramírez government a means of escaping a difficult predicament with some semblance of its prestige still intact?

For Foreign Minister Gilbert, answers might be forthcoming if additional diplomatic fencing took place. On December 17, 1943, he proposed that the British release Hellmuth and turn over any evidence suggesting that he was, in fact, a German spy. In return, the Argentine government "would then be inclined [to] cancel Hellmuth's [diplomatic] appointment," and make him available for interrogation at a later date.[111] This proposal was promptly rejected. On December 26, Gilbert made what he must have considered to be his maximum offer: The British would provisionally release Hellmuth, but he would remain in England. Argentina would then discover (to its horror, of course) that Hellmuth was indeed a German spy. His diplomatic appointment would immediately be cancelled, the Argentines would pronounce themselves no longer interested in his fate, and acquiesce to Hellmuth's return to British custody for the war's duration.[112]

Initially, at least, Carcano seemed to have had great hopes that this formula would win British acceptance, for on December 31, 1943, he cabled Gilbert that only "technical difficulties" were delaying a favorable response to this proposal.[113] Why the Argentine ambassador was so optimistic cannot be gleaned from diplomatic records, for although the British Foreign Office considered the plan as an encouraging basis for further negotiations, the Home Office insisted that "legal difficulties" made it unfeasible.[114] Negotiations had moved away from square one, but settlement was nowhere in sight.

Left to themselves, London and Buenos Aires might have allowed the dickering to go on indefinitely, but menacing actions threatened by the United States over a concurrent problem with Argentina suddenly necessitated a full and rapid resolution of the Hellmuth affair. Shocked by "Magic" decodes which indicated Argentine-SD participation in the overthrow of the Peñaranda government in Bolivia (December 20, 1943), the United States moved toward a dramatic showdown with the Ramírez regime. Proposals calling for a diplomatic rupture with Argentina, the freezing of all Argentine assets in the United States, plus other economic sanctions, were accepted by Cordell Hull, and British support for these endeavors was earnestly requested.[115]

For the Churchill government, dependent on Argentine wheat and meat, and absolutely determined to preserve Britain's economic predominance in that country, Washington's decision to force the issue jeopardized both long- and short-term British interests. Thus, the consolidation of an accord that would head off a U.S.-Argentine clash became an urgent necessity. Sometime between January 10 and 17, 1944, an arrangement was hammered out, the underlying understanding being that the Argentinians would denounce Hellmuth and break relations with the Axis, or the British would tell the world about the confidential agent and his mission.[116]

For Ramírez and his aides, the exit offered was not to their liking, but it was the only conceivable means for avoiding even greater problems. On January 18, Col. Emilio Ramírez, chief of the federal police, received a secret order signed by Col. Enrique González which declared that Hellmuth was a German spy and ordered the arrest of all German agents found in the country.[117] Since Hans Harnisch and Enrique Neiling had already been in custody for two days, there remains the distinct possibility that this order was either postdated or placed in the record primarily to justify subsequent actions. On January 21, a presidential decree terminated Hellmuth's diplomatic appointment, and the following day, the Ramírez government officially announced that a wide-ranging espionage investigation was under way.[118]

The official commencement of a German spy hunt was apparently part of the deal established between Argentina and Britain, for on that same day, the Churchill government informed Washington that it could not participate in a program of economic sanctions directed against Argentina.[119] On January 23, Churchill attempted to soften the effect of the refusal by communicating directly with President Roosevelt. The prime minister assured FDR that he would work to avoid any public divergence of views. But he added, "How are we to feed ourselves plus the American Army for 'Overlord' [i.e., the invasion of Europe] if this [i.e., the meat supply] is cut? ... We can always save up and pay them back when our hands are clean."[120]

Despite British opposition, Washington was still determined to present the Argentinians with an ultimatum. As previously noted, on January 24, 1944, Ambassador Norman Armour confronted Alberto Gilbert and explained what steps the revolution in Bolivia was forcing Washington to take. The foreign minister's reply was that a spy hunt was under way and a break in diplomatic relations would soon be announced. Disaster had been averted, but Gilbert probably did not breathe easier until the next day when he received this cryptic cable from Carcano:

1. The British Government has resisted the application of economic sanctions [i.e., sought by the United States].
2. ... Authorized circles ... have *informed me that the Argentine Republic will break relations with the Axis.*[121]

General Pedro Ramírez could now publicly announce (January 26) his dismay at the discovery that Osmar Hellmuth was a spy, express indignation over the "systematic espionage activity" being carried out on Argentine soil, and justifiably break diplomatic relations with the Axis.[122] In his heart, he knew that Argentina had been dragooned into abandoning its neutrality policy; publicly, however, the regime had saved face.

This sequence of events probably gratified the British, but U.S. ambassador Norman Armour only realized what the salient issue was years later. Armour had assumed that the Argentinians would have been exceedingly concerned about U.S. anger over the overthrow of Peñaranda and the possibility of stiff economic sanctions. What gradually dawned upon him was that what the government really feared was public and officer corps reaction to the discovery that an arms procurement mission and an attempt to obtain the release of the tanker *Buenos Aires* had been badly botched. In the ambassador's view, the Hellmuth debacle, not the Bolivian coup, was the key to understanding the Argentine retreat.[123]

Unfortunately for Ramírez, González, and their coterie of supporters, this desperate démarche proved unavailing. Juan Perón had been involved in the Hellmuth mission, but in deciding to break diplomatic relations with the Axis, Ramírez apparently acted without previously consulting the colonel. When the latter learned what had been done, it is reliably reported that he went to the Casa Rosada with a loaded pistol, waved it in Ramírez's face, and declared, "You're through."[124]

Perón's action appears rash, but his position was buttressed by the fact that on December 29, 1943, military attaché Colonel Vélez had initiated arms purchase discussions with a Reich official in Madrid. Perón was therefore able to convince many disgruntled officers that as a result of the precipitous diplomatic break, Ramírez had jeopardized Argentina's opportunity for obtaining weapons without paying Uncle Sam's price. And Perón was correct in assuming that nationalist army officers were not going to tolerate that kind of behavior.[125]

Thus, a direct repercussion of the Hellmuth debacle was the February 24, 1944, fall of Pedro Ramírez, Two years later, the former chief executive gave a private interview to Brig. Gen. A.R. Harris, U.S. military attaché to Argentina, and categorically denied that Hellmuth was or had ever been an SD agent. He ruefully suggested that his regime would have been better off if the insurance man had been, in fact, an SD agent.[126]

D. *The Responsible and the Damned*

Pedro Ramírez would not be the only person for which the Hellmuth disaster would have far-reaching repercussions. For several people the time bomb began ticking on November 6, 1943. On that date, Johannes Siegfried Becker reported via "Bolívar" that Col. Arturo Brinkmann, a GOU member and chief of the military district of the province of Buenos Aires, had informed him of the confidential agent's arrest in Trinidad.[127] On the twelfth, another "Bolívar" message from Becker stated that González and Perón were the sources of reports which indicated that Hellmuth was in a "British concentration camp" undergoing "rough treatment."[128] Yet, concerning the future of SD activity in Argentina, Becker remained optimistic. A November 24, 1943, radio report from the SD spy leader indicated that Ramírez was considering the dispatch of still another special negotiator. This time, however, in the interest of security, the name of this person would not be revealed until said agent reached Europe and contacted Captain Ceballos, the Argentine naval attaché in Berlin.[129]

Despite these communications, no secret representative reached Germany in December 1943. Another "Bolívar" missive from Becker (January 16, 1944) affirmed that a recently appointed plenipotentiary would soon depart for Spain and the signal of his arrival would be the departure of naval attaché Captain Ceballos on a trip from Berlin to Madrid.[130] The trouble was that within ten days, diplomatic relations between Germany and Argentina would be severed. Thus, when Ceballos left the German capital, it was clear that he would not soon be coming back.

Did Pedro Ramírez actually intend to send another agent to negotiate an arms purchase deal? Or was Becker deliberately sending optimistic reports in an effort to magnify the importance of his operation and simultaneously make his superiors in Berlin feel more hopeful? It cannot be definitively stated whether either hypothesis is true, but by December 1943, one person uninterested in determining their veracity was Hans Harnisch. Since June 1943, this Nest Cologne V-man had sent no economic warfare news via "Bolívar," and he had earned a reprimand from his superiors for openly collaborating with the SD.[131] Since he failed to report on his role in the Hellmuth affair until October 17, 1943, it is likely that Harnisch believed that with the success of that mission, all would be well, and the Abwehr would see the wisdom of his actions.[132] But with Hellmuth's capture and the collapse of the operation, Harnisch's dream of expanding influence in Argentina and enhanced prestige in the Reich waned. Instead, he became the man most likely to be blamed for everything that had gone wrong.

Harnisch was granted an insight into his eventual fate on December 23, 1943. At that time, Maj. Mario Bernard called for Harnisch and took him to a private meeting with Col. Enrique González. This officer began by blaming chargé Erich von Meynen and Ludwig Freude for Hellmuth's capture, indicating that their loose talk or even premeditated treachery had been responsible for British discovery of the operation. González further vowed that these malefactors would be repaid.In the meantime, however, the gravity of the situation might require Argentina to take drastic steps; he therefore advised Harnisch to make himself as inconspicuous as possible.[133]

Probably because he wished to prevent outright panic, González assured Harnisch that no matter what happened, he would not be thrown to the wolves.[134] Still, twenty years residence in the land of the gaucho had conditioned the V-man to put little stock in such promises. Following his visit with González, Harnisch began taking precautions. He gathered together his Enigma coding machine, old messages, and secret papers, and delivered them to his longtime embassy connection, Lt. Martin Müller. Thus, when police secretly arrested him on January 16, 1944, they found no incriminating evidence.[135]

Seventy-two hours after Harnisch's arrest, chargé Meynen, who evidently had an informant in the police, cabled the news of this detention to Berlin. The German Foreign Office realized what was about to occur. Indeed, three days after the break in relations, Andor Hencke, chief of the Political Division of the Foreign Office, stated the problem with unexcelled clarity. The Hellmuth fiasco had placed the Ramírez regime in an equivocal position. It could feign righteous anger and sever diplomatic connections, or it could admit that secret negotiations had been carried on with Germany using SD agents as intermediaries. Since Ramírez was hardly a paragon of political courage, there was little doubt as to the choice he would make. As Hencke observed, "The arrest of Harnisch and the news in the [Argentine] press shows that the Argentine Government chose to take the first path. . . ."[136]

Throughout 1943, German foreign minister Joachim von Ribbentrop had maintained that the Reich had to be circumspect in its dealings with Argentina, for that country was "the last bridgehead [i.e., of the Axis] in the Western Hemisphere."[137] Now that it was gone, someone would have to bear the onus for this diplomatic setback; and since the Argentinians had made Harnisch a scapegoat, Ribbentrop decided that the disgraced V-man could successfully play the same role in Berlin. The justification for the plot he contrived was an allegedly unsolicited memorandum dated January 28, 1944, and written by the German ambassador in Spain, his brother-in-law, Hans Dieckhoff. This diplomat linked the unauthorized sabotage being committed by Abwehr agents in Spain with the Hellmuth-Harnisch affair and charged that the egregious blunders of the Abwehr had undermined the effort to keep Argentina neutral. Furthermore, unless the blundering stopped, Spain's neutrality would also be destroyed.[138]

Utilizing Dieckhoff's report, on January 30, Ribbentrop forwarded to the office of Field Marshal Wilhelm Keitel, chief of the German High Command, a splenetic tirade denouncing the Abwehr chief, Adm. Wilhelm Canaris. He condemned the unauthorized sabotage, but really zeroed in on the Hellmuth mission and Harnisch's alleged role in it. The continuous and unmitigated bungling by the Abwehr, Ribbentrop insisted, demonstrated conclusively that said intelligence organization must refrain from launching undercover operations in a neutral country without first consulting the chief of the diplomatic mission there.[139]

Keitel's reply on February 4 indicated that while he accepted the demand for greater coordination of effort, he rejected the idea that the actions cited were primarily responsible for Germany's deteriorating diplomatic position in either Spain or Argentina.[140] Apparently the foreign minister had assumed that this would be the nature of the reply, for in addition to Keitel, he was discussing these same issues with the commander of the SS and SD, Heinrich Himmler. In an undated memorandum sent to the *Reichsführer,* Ribbentrop made it plain that he knew that while Harnisch was an Abwehr agent, he had been working almost entirely for the SD since the middle of 1943. After dropping this oblique blackmail hint, Ribbentrop asked Himmler's help in making Canaris and the Abwehr accept his demand for greater coordination of intelligence and foreign policy goals in neutral countries.[141]

In analyzing the foreign minister's actions, it should be pointed out that in October 1943, the SD had given the German Foreign Office the pledge Ribbentrop now sought to extract from Canaris.[142] It is to be assumed that Ribbentrop was aware that an SD promise meant no more than what the SD wished it to mean at a given time. No doubt the foreign minister's personal dislike for Canaris acted as a goad, but in enlisting the aid of an intriguer like Himmler, Ribbentrop had joined forces with a man who wanted not only Canaris's head but his entire organization as well. And when on February 7, 1944, news reached Berlin of the defection of several Abwehr agents in Turkey, Himmler was ready to make his move. The unauthorized sabotage in Spain, the Hellmuth-Harnisch disaster, and the treason of the Abwehr operatives in Turkey were the final nails driven into Canaris's coffin.[143]On February 12, 1944, Hitler signed the order authorizing Canaris's removal, thus paving the way for the SD's swallowing of the Abwehr. Now Ribbentrop had only one intelligence organization to worry about; but the possibilities of obtaining SD cooperation with his policy plans would not improve as a result of Canaris's downfall.

Although they were deeply involved in the Hellmuth affair, the SD and the Foreign Office escaped all the repercussions of this calamity. In contrast, Canaris and the Abwehr had virtually nothing to do with the planning or preparation of this muddled mission, but they became the patsies. With the Third Reich losing the war, scapegoat politics had become standard operating procedure.

1. *The Hidden Triumph*

When Adolf Hitler was told of the British arrest of Osmar Hellmuth, he ordered a full-scale investigation. Specifically, the Führer wanted to know who had been responsible for sanctioning such a perilous mission and whether German (rather than Argentine) bungling had been primarily responsible for the debacle.[144] But with the Russians advancing in the East and the Anglo-Americans preparing their own attack on western Europe, Hitler's attention was soon diverted to more important issues and the inquiry was postponed. The fact is that the Germans never did discover how the British learned of the secret mission.

On the Argentine side, the explanation given by Foreign Minister Anthony Eden on December 10, 1943, seemed to cause Buenos Aires to conclude that Ludwig Freude and chargé Erich von Meynen were the sources of the leak. The few writers who have ever bothered to comment on this incident have either accepted this explanation or argued that the Argentine infighting over Hellmuth's appointment provided British agents with the information.[145]

Over thirty years later, declassified documents revealed what actually occurred. A November 1943 memorandum written by Maj. Gen. George Strong, assistant chief of U.S. Army G-2, reports that the Hellmuth case was broken by the British with U.S. assistance through methods involving "security precautions of the first order."[146] General Strong may well have been referring to "Ultra," the means by which British intelligence was able to decrypt signals coded on Enigma coding machines.[147] On the United States' end, it is not clear whether a message sent by Baron Tomii, the Japanese ambassador to Argentina, or a communication from

Baron Oshima, his counterpart in Berlin, provided the facts. In any event, "Magic" Summary Report No. 581 demonstrates that the details and goals of the Hellmuth mission were all known in Washington prior to October 29, 1943.[148]

III. The Climax of the Espionage War in Argentina

A. The Emergence of the Coordinación Federal

On September 4, 1943, J. Edgar Hoover directed a report to Assistant Secretary Adolf Berle which alerted the State Department to the fact that the Argentine government was establishing a special counterespionage force, and that a Lt. Col. Adolfo Udry was "already working on it."[149] The FBI chief was informed about Udry's activities, but he failed to tell Berle the name of that organization. Perhaps he did not know it, but there is no question that the Coordinación Federal would eventually make life interesting for the SIS agents stationed in Argentina in 1944–45.

The origins of the Coordinación go back to the last six months of the Ramón Castillo administration. This president had publicly taken the position that with the arrest of Hans Napp's sextet of amateurs, and the expulsion of naval attaché Dietrich Niebuhr, German intelligence operations in Argentina had been smashed. Of course, Castillo knew better; still, he was against taking any action which the potential opposition could depict as evidence contradicting his official position.[150] Thus imobilized, Castillo did nothing until the June 1943 revolution, which made a decision on his part unnecessary.

It fell to Pres. Pedro Ramírez to create a new counterespionage unit, but he put off taking concrete action until September 1943. At that time, Lieutenant Colonel Udry initiated provisional planning not only for a counterspy unit, but for a redesigned, federalized police arm. However, further action was forestalled by a tug-of-war developing between Ramírez on the one hand and Col. Juan Perón on the other. The president was leery of the rising star who headed the Ministry of War Secretariat. And since Udry was perceived as being a Perón protégé, his potential career as Argentina's chief counterspy was brought to a rapid and irreversible halt.[151]

With Udry exiled to a command in the province of Jujuy, Ramírez could now move to assure himself that the new federal police force would not come under Perón's sway. Decree No. 17550 of December 24, 1943, revamped the federal police force and gave it much broader national powers. At the same time, this decree made the federal police chief directly responsible to the president, not the minister of the interior. Selected as the first chief of this expanded force was a member of the GOU directorate who was increasingly antagonistic to Perón, Col. Emilio Ramírez.[152] Evidence that the colonel and the general with the same surname had struck a deal surfaced quickly. On January 9, 1944, Colonel Emilio Ramírez announced the creation of the Coordinación Federal, an agency whose purpose was "the suppression and prevention of espionage and counter-espionage in the country."[153] The first commander of this unit was another GOU insider, who also happened to be President Ramírez's son-in-law, Maj. Francisco Filippi.

Thanks to the organizational efforts of Lieutenant Colonel Udry, Major Filippi did not have to begin operations by enlisting and recruiting a brand new corps of officers. But neither would he enjoy a long tenure of office because on February 24, 1944, President Ramírez was deposed, and the following day, Juan Perón was able to replace Col. Emilio Ramírez with Col. Juan Filomeno Velazco. These actions presaged Filippi's imminent dismissal, and he was shortly thereafter posted to an army unit in the province of Río Negro. On February 26, Maj. Oscar Contal took charge as commander of the Coordinación Federal.[154]

Under its new commander, the Coordinación executed a number of successful counterespionage operations, and on January 1, 1945, this police force was made an independent entity, separate from the rest of the federal police structure.[155] Perón seemed satisfied with Contal's leadership, but the relationship between the two men cooled perceptibly, and on August 31, 1945, the major was unceremoniously removed.[156] Contal's departure was further evidence that staying on good terms with Col. Perón had become a requisite for aspirant young officers.

The Coordinación Federal was different from the Mexican, Brazilian, and Chilean security police contingents in that its counterespionage operations were directed not only at the Abwehr and SD, but against the British and North American intelligence organizations as well. It was this aspect which made the phase of the shadow war fought in Argentina in 1944–45 the most unusual in the Western Hemisphere.

B. *SIS/Argentina under Fire*

In response to an RID query, Adolf Berle replied on April 24, 1943, that "certain conditions beyond our control" prevented the SIS/Argentina organization "from moving about freely," and thereby locating the clandestine radio stations operating in Argentina.[157] Apparently with the removal of Castillo and the shipment of some radio detection gear to the Argentine army, the situation was altered, for on June 18, 1943, RID special agent John DeBardeleben was ordered to Buenos Aires. This was the same officer who had located the PYL transmitter in Chile and once again, DeBardeleben hoped to use intercept data being cabled from the RID in conjunction with his detection equipment in order to pinpoint the location of "Bolívar" transmitters.[158]

While the operation started with high hopes, before the month was over, Pedro Ramírez was actively exploring the possibilities of obtaining the release of the *Buenos Aires* and considering an arms purchase deal with the SD. Under those conditions, it was unlikely that the Argentine government was going to do much to assist in locating the "Bolívar" transmitters, since such action would certainly have aggravated relations with the Third Reich. Realization that he would receive only very limited assistance slowly dawned on DeBardeleben, and in a series of reports in July and August 1943, he complained bitterly to his director, George E. Sterling, and requested the dispatch of additional equipment.[159]

It was in September that the Ramírez regime began to manifest unmistakable opposition to DeBardeleben's investigation. The RID man wanted an automobile on which to mount a mobile detector, but the Argentinians refused to allow its entry. On September 9, the apartment of a U.S. vice consul—which happened to be the place where DeBardeleben maintained his equipment—was raided by Argentine police. When the embassy suggested that DeBardeleben be allowed to use a light plane in order to locate the "Bolívar" transmitters, the Argentinians vetoed that plan as well. By the end of the month, it was evident in Washington that if the 1942 Chilean success was to be repeated in Argentina, DeBardeleben would have to outmaneuver both the Germans and the Argentinians.[160]

What could not have been predicted was that the RID agent's hope of using a light plane would have a devastating effect upon the U.S. counterespionage effort in Argentina. Since permission to use the aircraft was refused, the U.S. military attaché, Col. John Lang, decided that it should be moved to Montevideo, Uruguay. But in attempting to take off from a Buenos Aires airport, the plane crashed, and its pilot, assistant military attaché Maj. Campbell H. Gould, was killed. Picking through the wreckage of the plane, an Argentine official found some suspicious materials and "reached the conclusion that Major C. H. Gould had carried out acts of espionage with knowledge of members of the American Embassy." Police investigators also examined the evidence and declared that "there exists in the country a vast network of North American espionage."[161]

The FBI had long been concerned over the possibility that an SIS/Argentina agent or informant would be arrested and made to tell all he knew. Indeed, a January 1944 report to J. Edgar Hoover by Insp. C. H. Carson warned of the "tremendous danger of one of our agents being picked up in Argentina, [and] tortured into a full confession ... with consequent publicity throughout the world. The repercussion of such an incident might be terrific insofar as Latin American relations are concerned."[162]

Unfortunately, this epistle of caution came too late, for the behavior of a couple of loose-lipped, hard-drinking SIS/Argentina informants had already furnished the Argentinians with leads they would not otherwise have enjoyed.[163] On January 11, 1944, the Argentinians struck. Exactly forty-eight hours after the official birth of the Coordinación Federal, that organization began a wave of arrests against SIS/Argentina, MI-6, and U.S. military attaché informants and agents. Fearing the worst, RID ordered John DeBardeleben out of the country on January 13, and he departed several days later.[164]

The task of saving both his own agents and the network of informants maintained by the military attaché fell on SIS/Argentina chief, legal attaché Francis Crosby, and he proved equal to the task. During January, he began secretly shuttling key agents and informants across the River Plate to Uruguay. "Crosby's Navy," as this escape operation was known, proved extremely successful, but with the departure of important operatives, the SIS/ Argentina was forced to curtail its activities.[165]

There can be no minimizing of the disastrous effects of the Coordinación Federal's war on Anglo-American counterintelligence. Between February and June, fourteen of Crosby's men were arrested and ten were jailed. During the same period, twenty-one agents controlled by either military attaché Col. John Lang or Britain's MI-6 found themselves imprisoned in Buenos Aires's Villa de Voto jail. Furthermore, the Coordinación strove to place informants inside the U.S. embassy, kept U.S. diplomatic personnel under close surveillance, and was believed to be opening "unaccompanied United States diplomatic pouches."[166]

Something like a thaw in this undercover war took place in August 1944, when an Argentine naval intelligence officer invited Crosby to send observers to witness a series of successful raids by the Coordinación against "Bolívar" stations. Still, on September 22, 1944, the military attaché sent a special report to Washington predicting that another wholesale attack on the U.S. intelligence network in Argentina was in the offing.[167] This forecast proved inaccurate, but J. Edgar Hoover decided that no extra risks should be incurred. Francis Crosby's replacement was dispatched to Buenos Aires in November 1944, but the new SIS/Argentina chief was not immediately designated as legal attaché. Instead, James Joice entered the country, apparently on a nondiplomatic passport, and his official succession to Crosby's office was not recognized by the Argentine government until June 5, 1945.[168]

Aside from dodging the persistent attacks of the Coordinación, the greatest difficulty experienced by SIS/Argentina in 1944–45 was that it was unable to interrogate the Abwehr and SD agents arrested during that period of time.[169] Not until the visit of the Avra Warren mission of April 17–21, 1945, did the SIS/Argentina receive an official (though incomplete) head count of the number of Abwehr and SD agents in Argentine prisons. In May, the last Anglo-American agents arrested during the first six months of 1944 were quietly released, and in June, Maj. Oscar Contal allowed the SIS/Argentina to enter the sealed German embassy and make a careful search for undestroyed documents.[170]

These developments proved to be the high point of U.S.-Argentine intelligence cooperation. In August, Washington began pressing Buenos Aires to deport the jailed German spies to the United States, a request that was rejected by the Farrell government. Following Major Contal's forced resignation on August 31, 1945, the intelligence relationship again deteriorated. There would be no more arrests of SIS agents; but neither would there be further collaboration. Instead there would be "fixed smiles and polite exchanges of opinion."[171]

An analysis of the work of the SIS/Argentina must emphasize that this intelligence group did comparatively little to assist in the arrest and detention of the German espionage rings operating in that country. Nor was the SIS unit able to accomplish a great deal in its effort to stop the smuggling of strategic materials from Argentine ports. But the SIS/Argentina did survive an attack intended to destroy it completely. No other SIS unit in Latin America would be able to make that claim.

C. *Argentine Spy Hunt: The First Round*

As of the end of 1943, the gods of espionage seemed to be smiling on Johannes Siegfried Becker. The SD chief, in addition to having a functioning clandestine radio system and a developed network of agents, was also receiving useful information courtesy of Britain's MI-6. The origins of this last development lay in Becker's decision to replace Esteban Jesús Amorín as subchief in Uruguay. In Becker's opinion, Amorín had spent entirely too much of the network's funds on wine, women, and other pleasures in Montevideo, and so in June 1943, the Spaniard was replaced by a Swiss-born recruit named José Pfeffer. Returning to Buenos Aires, Amorín continued to work with the Becker group as a contact man with the Spanish sailors involved in the contraband traffic between Spain and Argentina. It was in the execution of these duties that Amorín was approached by MI-6 agents who wanted details concerning the *Graf Spee* sailor escape operation and SD activities in the River Plate republics.[172]

Dealing with any kind of double agent is a dangerous game, but when Amorín told Becker of the British contact, the SD leader ordered Amorín to take the British money and function as a counterfeit traitor. A mixture of truth and falsity was to be fed to the British contact man (known as "Mr. Rubio"), and the money received—at least most of it—went into the SD treasury. There is no way of determining how much truth Amorín told the British, but the SD definitely gained certain advantages from the informational exchange. For example, in December 1943, Amorín warned Becker that both the organization's safe house on the Calle de Oro, as well as Becker's place of residence, were known to both British intelligence and the Argentine police. Acting on this data, Becker secretly rented a hideout in another part of the city. Then using another agent as a "beard," he purchased a second safe house in a Buenos Aires suburb. By the end of December 1943, Becker was paying for two apartments for himself and two residences for his agents, but before another month had passed, both alternative locations would be in use.[173]

There is still another reason why Becker believed that he and his organization were doing well. Possibly through Hans Harnisch, sometime after June 4, 1943, Becker established a working relationship with an Argentine military officer of German parentage, Col. Arturo Brinkmann. Using Juan Bove Trabal, a Uruguayan, and Guillermo Lassere Marmol, a restaurant waiter, as cutouts, Becker received through Brinkmann messages from Argentine government figures and details concerning foreign policy decisions.[174] Brinkmann was probably the officer who relayed the news of Hellmuth's arrest and, later, of the Ramírez government's alleged decision to send another confidential agent to negotiate an arms deal.[175]

Nevertheless, the colonel was hardly performing these friendly actions simply because he was sympathetic to national socialism. Arturo Brinkmann, in addition to being a GOU stalwart, was commander of the province of Buenos Aires military district and chief of a supersecret Argentine army intelligence group, whose primary task was to monitor Anglo-American intelligence activity.[176] In return for his services, he demanded information from Becker on Argentine political dissidents in Montevideo and comprehensive reports on Esteban Amorín's contacts with British intelligence.[177] Indeed, by February 1944, Amorín was in direct contact with Brinkmann and providing details which might not even have been given to Becker. Still, possessing a pipeline into the highest realms of the Argentine military hierarchy, the SD leader believed that he would be able to avoid the kind of sudden, sweeping stroke which had obliterated the Abwehr groups in Brazil in March 1942. Manifesting a confidence which would subsequently prove unjustified, Becker radioed via "Bolívar" that Colonel Brinkmann was, for all practical purposes, "one of its [i.e., the SD's] agents."[178]

The repercussions of the Hellmuth mission and the forced alteration of Argentine foreign policy reawakened Becker to the grim facts of espionage life. On January 16, 1944, both Hans Harnisch and his recruit, Enrique Neiling, were taken into custody. Possibly through his connection with Brinkmann, Becker learned immediately of these detentions. That same evening, he moved to the new apartment rented at the end of December 1943. Orders were given for the destruction of incriminating materials at the Calle Cangallo headquarters, and through a friendly Coordinación officer, Pedro Andrade, the following message was delivered to Harnisch: "We'll do everything for you. Greetings, Pepe" [i.e., a code name used by Becker].[179]

Brave words certainly, but following a short lull during which President Ramírez broke diplomatic relations with the Axis, the Coordinación Federal would make life miserable for Abwehr/SD V-men. On January 29, Manuel de Miguel Arrastia, a colleague of Esteban Amorín in arranging contraband shipments, became the first member of the Becker group to be jailed by Argentine police. Over the next thirty days, the Coordinación Federal arrested 146 persons whom it listed as spy suspects.[180] As opposed to the counterespionage burlesque performed under Ramón Castillo from November 1942 to January 1943, Argentine authorities this time seemed determined to destroy the German intelligence operations in the country.

In fact, only about forty-one of those arrested were Abwehr or SD agents,[181] but the Coordinación promptly impressed upon all those detained that evasion and resistance to interrogation could be both painful and ineffective. Hans Harnisch, for example, was placed in solitary confinement for seventy-four hours, given little food or water, and when he tried to sleep, police officers beat on the bars of his cell every ten minutes in order to keep him awake. This forty-six-year-old man was in a state of total collapse when a prison doctor managed to force a halt to these mind-bending tactics.[182]

Even under these circumstances, though, Harnisch was fortunate. It would have been interesting to know where this prison doctor was when Herbert Jurmann was interrogated. A caretaker on a farm where a "Bolívar" transmitter was located, Jurmann, who was arrested on February 15, was at best a minor figure in the Becker organization. Nevertheless, his evasive answers to questions infuriated his interrogators, who proceeded to use the electric prodding iron in order to speed up the flow of revelations. Early on the morning of February 18, following another session with this diabolical instrument, Jurmann committed suicide.[183]

This prisoner would not be the only one upon whom the electric prod was used; yet, the most revealing aspect of the interrogation process had nothing to do with either the number of prisoners quizzed or their brutal treatment. Under both the Ramírez and Farrell regimes, the Coordinación's most difficult task was probably the management of the details revealed in the confessional declarations. Thus, when Hans Harnisch was told to confess, he wrote a veritable epistle implicating President Ramírez and Col. Enrique González, explaining their roles in the Hellmuth case. At least two of the officers who read this declaration were shortly thereafter removed from this interrogation unit, and Harnisch was personally told that he had "better forget about his deposition." It was also after this incident that the aforementioned torture of Harnisch began.[184]

Similarly, Esteban Jesús Amorín also discovered that declarations implicating Argentine officials might produce unpleasant results. This V-man was promised protection by both Colonel Brinkmann and his British contact, "Mr. Rubio." In addition, Major Filippi, then the Coordinación chief, promised that Amorín would experience only routine questioning. Amorín therefore turned himself over to Coordinación officials on February 23. The next day, Ramírez turned over the reins of power to Gen. Edelmiro Farrell, and shortly after that, Major Contal replaced Filippi. Taken aback by this rapid turn of events and convinced that Contal would honor no understanding previously reached, Amorín panicked and wrote a confession naming several police and customs officials as recipients of payoffs from Becker. To his chagrin, Amorín quickly learned that this declaration proceeded to earn him the rough treatment he had been trying to avoid. For the German agents arrested in January–February 1944, truth could have painful consequences; cooperation in the orchestration of confessions ultimately made life much less complicated and painful.[185]

Meanwhile, Johannes Siegfried Becker was hard at work doing what he could to assure the salvation of the bulk of his organization. Since he was sure that the deceased Jurmann as well as others had talked, the transmitting and receiving equipment had to be moved from several farms into secondary sites long ago selected for that purpose. Thus, after a temporary interruption, by March 1, the "Bolívar" network was again broadcasting regularly, a convincing demonstration of the resiliency of the SD organization in Argentina.[186]

In contrast, the Coordinación sweep of January–February 1944 seriously impaired the functioning of other German networks. With the exception of Werner Koennecke, by February 1, 1944, all of Hans Harnisch's ring was behind bars. Also adversely affected was the tiny group of informants and aides originally controlled by naval attaché Dietrich Niebuhr's replacement, Brig. Gen. Friedrich Wolf. Realizing that diplomatic links with the Reich would eventually be severed, early in 1943, Wolf began planning what he called a "stay behind" organization, and chose an old friend he had known in Chile, Ernst Schleuter (code name: Jacobo), to direct it. On January 26, 1944, General Wolf put his plan into effect. He gave Schleuter two Enigma coding machines, placed him in charge of the embassy informants, and ordered that all information subsequently collected be given to Gustavo Utzinger for radio transmission.

The most controversial aspect of Wolf's last-gasp maneuvers was the financial arrangements he made for his new intelligence group. Schleuter himself received sixty-two hundred dollars, but a total of forty-four thousand dollars was divided among three German citizens, Hans Leuters, Friedrich Frohwein, and Ludwig Freude. Schleuter would be able to draw funds from the trio of trustees at any time by approaching them and uttering the code words, "Diana Dog." Over the next eighteen months, Schleuter spent much of the money held by these men, but he does not appear to have sent any message via the "Bolívar" system. Still, since Schleuter had neither radio telegraphy training nor microdot-making equipment, our suspicion is that General Wolf hardly expected much in exchange for his money. The funds were available, and by creating a special group, when the military attaché returned to the Reich in July 1944, he could tell his superiors that he had done his utmost to assure the continued transmittal of intelligence information from the Western Hemisphere.[187] In short, an espionage group was created and funded primarily for the purpose of making its creator appear both dedicated and effective.

The wave of arrests which characterized the Coordinación's assault on the German intelligence organization petered out in March 1944. Argentine government propaganda may have convinced many of the citizens that the maximum steps were being taken to destroy the German spy network in the country, but both London and Washington remained openly skeptical.[188] In the meantime, the Germans, who were quite displeased over the counterspy campaign, informed an Argentine official in Spain that the *Buenos Aires* would be released if and when the jailed V-men were set free.[189] In sum, the blow against German espionage failed to placate the Anglo-Americans, but succeeded in displeasing the Germans. If the Farrell government intended to make its counterspy campaign pay diplomatic dividends, it would eventually have to make somebody happy, or at least less suspicious.

C. *Argentine Spy Hunt: Second Round*

Between March and the end of July 1944, not one member of the SD organization in Argentina was known to have been arrested by the Coordinación Federal.[190] This lack of action remains difficult to explain because the Coordinación certainly obtained useful information from those agents captured in January and February. Furthermore, this agency continued to press its campaign against Anglo-American intelligence. It may be, therefore, that this lull was chiefly caused by the continued deterioration in U.S.-Argentine diplomatic relations, plus the Department of State's unceasing denunciation of the counterespionage campaign the Argentines were conducting. As Col. Juan Perón confided to the Chilean military attaché in April 1944, the Farrell government could not survive if it appeared to be bending under pressure from the United States.[191] Purposeful inaction became a way of demonstrating to the world that Argentina intended to follow an independent course in the execution of its foreign and counterspy policies.

In contrast, the Germans perceived the relaxation in the campaign against their agents as being executed for entirely different reasons. Early in March 1944, the SD connection with Colonel Brinkmann, temporarily moribund, was resuscitated. According to a Becker message radioed via "Bolívar" on the eighteenth, Brinkmann informed him that the break in diplomatic relations had been accomplished in an illegal manner and thus the German government should disregard it. Argentina was still interested in purchasing weapons and was considering the dispatch of a special representative to Spain, who would maintain de facto relations with the Reich.[192] Encouraged by this news, the SD chiefs in Berlin decided to put into motion a plan they had been considering for some time.

For many months, Amt VI-D chief SS-Lt. Col. Theodor Paeffgen had been convinced that indifferent equipment, poor transmission techniques, and a shortage of highly trained personnel were factors limiting the effectiveness of the "Bolívar" broadcasts from Argentina. Thus, in June 1943, SD headquarters ordered that a secluded spot on the Argentina coast be found where a U-boat could land men and special equipment. Becker assigned this task to Wilhelm Seidlitz, and he selected the ranch of Carlos Eickenberg, a Bolivian millionaire who had made financial contributions to the Becker ring.[193]

No action was immediately taken, but Otto Reinebeck, the German Foreign Office's chief specialist in Latin American affairs, soon gave his support to the idea. In a September 30, 1943, memorandum, he suggested that the German navy be requested to make available a U-boat to deliver SD technicians and equipment to Argentina.[194] A series of conferences involving SD, Foreign Office, and German naval officials was held in October 1943, but the latter poured cold water on the proposal. Admiral Doenitz would release a submarine only if Ribbentrop would take full responsibility for the loss of the craft.[195] But since the SD was supplying the men and the equipment, the foreign minister saw no reason for putting his head in a possible noose; instead, he demanded that the SD accept joint responsibility for the mission, or allow it to come directly under Foreign Office control. The upshot of this quarrel was a development Doenitz may have foreseen; SD headquarters radioed Becker towards the end of October and declared the U-boat supply project temporarily cancelled.[196]

Some five months later, the relaxation of the spy hunt and the March 1944 reports attributed to Colonel Brinkmann caused the SD to begin reevaluating the situation. Without the Foreign Office, it would proceed with the resupply mission, and in view of the disagreements of October 1943, a U-boat was not requested. The yawl *Santa Barbara* (ex-*Passim*), commanded by Heinz Garbers, had successfully delivered two V-men to Brazil in May 1943; it would now serve as the means of executing still another transatlantic mission. Summoned to Berlin at the beginning of April 1944 were Walter Burckhardt (real name: Waldemar Boettger; code name: Cobija) and Alphonse Chantrain (real name: Josef Schroll; code name: Valiente), the former being an electrical engineer, the latter an Abwehr agent and Luxembourg national specially trained in radio transmitting and microdot work. They were ordered to assist Gustav Utzinger in improving "Bolívar" broadcasts, to deliver funds to Becker, and if possible, to begin the creation of a separate clandestine radio network.[197]

The two men proceeded to Arcachon, France, where they boarded the *Santa Barbara*. They brought with them radio equipment, a new microdot machine, from $60–100,000, mostly in English pound notes, and ten large containers of valuable pharmaceutical chemicals and supplies.[198] The last-named items were to be sold to the Bayer and Merck Company subsidiaries in Argentina or placed on the black market for sale. The estimated value of these drugs in Buenos Aires in 1944 was $238,000, a sum sufficient to keep the Becker group solvent and, at the same time, finance any organization Burckhardt and Chantrain might be able to build.[199]

With Heinz Garbers at the helm, the *Santa Barbara* sailed from Arcachon on April 26, 1944. The voyage was uneventful, and radio contact between the ship and a "Bolívar" station was established several days before the yawl reached Punta Magotes, less than thirty kilometers from the location originally selected by Wilhelm Seidlitz in 1943. Contact with a reception committee led by Gustavo Utzinger was accomplished during the night of July 2–3, 1944, and the disembarkation of Burckhardt, Chantrain, and their equipment was successfully accomplished. Nevertheless, Garbers was in for a shock, for Becker had decided that the *Santa Barbara* ought to take three men who wished to leave Argentina back to Germany. Anxious to make the transatlantic trip east were radiomen Felipe Imhof and Werner Sievers, and the first SD agent ordered to South America, Heinz Lange.

After fleeing from Chile, Heinz Lange, his mistress, Melitta Tietz, and radioman Heriberto Schlosser, reached Buenos Aires late in December

1943. Their arrival, however, did little to enthuse Johannes Siegfried Becker. Schlosser was pressed into service as a member of Utzinger's coterie of radiomen, but Señorita Tietz lacked similar skills and Lange was now a twice-failed spymaster who was known to the Argentine police. Becker's solution to the problem was to find his old colleague a place to stay in a Buenos Aires suburb, provide him with $2,700 for expenses, and order him to stay out of the way. Spurned and resentful of what he considered uncomradely treatment, Lange sent radio messages via "Bolívar" pronouncing himself tired of the cloak-and-dagger game and anxious to join an SS combat unit.[200]

There would be no response to this request, but on June 20, Becker told Lange to prepare for a long trip. With Imhof and Sievers, he was put aboard the *Santa Barbara*, along with several sacks of reports, packets of platinum, industrial diamonds, and tins of Brazilian coffee being sent to SD headquarters as a present from Becker.

Even before the *Santa Barbara* reached Argentina, the Anglo-American landings at Normandy had made a return to the port of Arcachon impossible. Heinz Garbers radioed German naval headquarters for instructions and was told to head for the Spanish port of Vigo, where he anchored on September 17, 1944. Both the U.S. and British ambassadors demanded that the ship, crew, and passengers be detained, but the Franco government decided that it owed Hitler one more favor. On November 15, 1944, a German plane flew the *Santa Barbara* passengers and crew from Madrid to Berlin. The SD assigned Lange as SS-Captain Gross's chief assistant at Amt VI, D/4, a post he held until the Russians overran Berlin.[201]

With the bombs falling night and day and the Russians moving ever closer on the eastern front, SD headquarters in Berlin was certainly no paradise. Still, Walter Burckhardt and Alphonse Chantrain would rapidly discover that Argentina was a place where German agents were no longer welcome. The Coordinación record states that not until July 24, 1944, were the locations of the new "Bolívar" broadcasting sites discovered,[202] but this claim is flatly contradicted by other Coordinación documents.[203] What is likely is that Contal had been ready to pounce for some time, and on July 24, the Farrell government finally allowed him to take action.

The whirlwind attack on the Becker organization opened on July 29, 1944, when Argentine agents grabbed Ullrich Fritz Daue in the process of sending messages to the Ast Hamburg reception station.[204] Ever mindful that the State Department had consistently questioned the authenticity of the Coordinación's January–February campaign, careful consideration was given the task of demolishing any prospective allegations that the Argentines were merely going through the motions. On August 1, 1944, Navy Lieutenant Ernesto Greenwald contacted SIS/Argentina chief Francis Crosby and invited him to send observers to monitor raids on German spy nests.[205] Of those who participated, one agent observed that "the raids were efficiently conducted, but who was kidding who[sic]? Those guys [i.e., Argentinians] obviously knew for a long time where the spy radios were located."[206]

Sitting down to breakfast on August 18, Gustavo Utzinger learned that he had company. Officers of the Coordinación Federal proved themselves hospitable; they let him finish his meal before hustling him down to police headquarters.[207] Both Walter Burckhardt and Alphonse Chantrain were still at large, but, by means of a clever ruse, the police obtained the location of their hideout from Utzinger.[208] Burckhardt was arrested on August 22. Chantrain evaded the hunters for an additional forty-eight hours, but he was eventually found drowning his sorrows in a bar; officers trailed him to the home of Johannes Szeraws, where they arrested both men. Optimistic even in the face of disaster, an SD report issued on September 30, 1944, claimed that "Bolívar" messages were still being transmitted from Argentina.[209] This was possible, but the likelihood is that if any signals were still being sent, the man tapping the radiotelegraph key was under the control of Argentine security forces.

Between July 29 and August 29, 1944, thirty-four SD agents and informants plus fifty-five transmitters and receivers were bagged by the Coordinación Federal.[210] The situation after September 1 was that, except for Johannes Siegfried Becker and a handful of others, the SD apparatus had been effectively wiped out. Becker dyed his hair darker, grew a mustache, which he also colored, and changed his address four times during the next seven months. He maintained contact with several of his former aides and attempted to continue sending microdot messages to Spain through a priest, Fr. Fernández Suárez.

Living the life of a recluse, Becker became totally dependent upon Melitta Tietz, Heinz Lange's former mistress, who now beguiled another crestfallen spymaster with her assorted charms. The lady regularly made large purchases of food and beverages, but since nobody ever saw her "husband" and she held no job, her apparent wealth of funds made someone suspicious. Coordinación Federal agents put Señorita Tietz under surveillance, and when she went shopping on April 16, 1945, police entered the apartment she had just left and found Becker.[211]

Between October 1942 and July 1944, some twenty-five hundred messages were sent over the "Bolívar" network and received by the Ast Hamburg reception station.[212] Unfortunately, many of these messages provided information of questionable value, and no effort was made to respond to many important questions for which Berlin wanted answers. For example, a December 8, 1943, message directed Becker to "find out all you can about United States flying units in South America . . . strength, bases, equipment, and number. . . ." The "Magic" summary of December 12, 1943, reveals that Berlin informed the SD in Argentina of its "urgent need" for information concerning "U.S. aircraft attack procedures on both surfaced and submerged submarines."[213] An examination of "Bolívar" transmissions between December 1, 1943, and July 19, 1944, failed to demonstrate that responses to these commands were ever provided.[214] The fact is, Johannes Siegfried Becker never had, and never developed, a means of obtaining sensitive information from U.S. sources. To that extent, the "Bolívar" system did not fulfill its potential.

But even though the clandestine radio service was a partial failure and the Hellmuth mission an unmitigated disaster, the Becker ring must be considered a successful organization. Where it distinguished itself was in the smuggling of large amounts of badly needed platinum, mica, liver extract, and industrial diamonds through the Anglo-American blockade to Germany via Spain. By 1943, the Abwehr and the Becker groups had become the only suppliers for these items in the Americas, and the Reich's major source of non-European acquisition as well.[215]

From this perspective, the decline of the Becker group began not with the Hellmuth disaster, but in November 1943, when British inspectors at Trinidad seized a three-hundred-thousand-dollar shipment of platinum hidden aboard a Spanish ship. Smarting from this loss, on December 8, the Abwehr ordered Georg Bücker to temporarily cease platinum purchases and shipment.[216] At that time Becker was having few problems, but he concluded that if there was a leak somewhere in the Abwehr smuggling group, his organization would soon be affected as well. Quietly, he ordered Esteban Amorín, Nicholás Quintana, and Manuel de Miguel Arrastia, the trio whose job it was to contact Spanish sailors, placed under special surveillance.[217] But, as matters developed, this precaution proved to be of little value. All three men were jailed during the January–February 1944 counterespionage sweep and, with their incarceration, the SD strategic minerals smuggling program was crippled. After April 1944, stricter measures taken by the Franco government also took their toll, and the smuggling program gradually died.[218]

The other casualty of the July and August 1944 spy arrests was the arms negotiation talks which Col. Alberto Vélez, the military attaché who was supposed to have worked with Hellmuth, had been conducting with German representatives since December 30, 1943. Berlin had merely been stringing the Argentinians along, and it is difficult to believe that a shrewd and ruthless operator like Juan Perón was not aware of this fact. Still, continuing the arms talks apparently served internal political goals until mid-1944.[219] Thereafter, the Normandy landings and the Russian summer offensive made it clear that the thousand-year Reich would be lucky to last another twelve months. In the game of international politics, nobody mourns a loser. Under those circumstances, a relationship with Hitler's Germany lost the psychological and material significance it might once have held.

The final arms meeting occurred in Madrid on September 26, 1944, between Colonel Vélez and Rheinhard Spitzy, a representative of the Skoda Union Armaments Works. The German noted that the recent arrests of Germans in Argentina was considered by the Reich to be an unfriendly act. Vélez's rejoinder was that his government had been seeking weapons for months, but was now inclined to believe that the Germans did not and would not have any for sale.[220] For a change, both sides were right.

IV. The Legal Escapade

A. Making It Up as You Go Along

With the arrest of Gustav Utzinger and thirty other agents in July and August 1944, the Coordinación Federal had only to find Johannes Siegfried Becker in order to put an end to German espionage activity in Argentina. As in February 1944, the Argentine counterspies were not squeamish about persuading prisoners to be more cooperative. Thus, when Gustavo Seraphin was picked up on January 13, 1945, he was sweated by his inquisitors and then threatened with the electric prodding iron. Terrified, the prisoner slashed one of his wrists in his cell, but the police intervened in time and prevented him from committing suicide.[221]

Seraphin escaped a session with the fiendish electrical device, but Juan Antonio Prieto would not be so fortunate. Arrested on February 24, 1945, Prieto was repeatedly jabbed with the prod, and then denied food and water for three days. Intensive interrogation continued with relay teams for several more days until Prieto attempted suicide. He, too, was prevented from taking his life, but his mental and physical condition was such that he had to be transferred to a prison hospital, where he remained for eight months.[222]

If there be any excuse for the brutality inflicted upon Seraphin and Prieto, it was that the Coordinación officers believed that these two men either knew where Becker was hiding or that they possessed information which could lead them to the elusive spy chief. Unfortunately, no such explanation is applicable in the case of Hans Lieberth, a caretaker on one of the farms where "Bolívar" transmitters were operated. According to the subsequent testimony of this prisoner, the prodding iron was freely applied to his genitals and, in addition to skin burns, for some months he was convinced that he had been rendered impotent.[223]

In retrospect, the use of torture probably had an insidious motivation because the mere threat of the use of the electric prod was enough to make fearful prisoners adjust and readjust their confessions as the occasion warranted. That there would be such a need was a factor quickly demonstrated. On August 23, 1944, with Utzinger only recently captured, and Szeraws and Chantrain still at large, Colonel Perón paid a visit to Coordinación headquarters. He closeted himself with Major Contal and laid down the following guidelines: All confessions obtained were to be "touched up" so that references to contacts with Argentine military officers and Argentine, Bolivian, and Paraguayan political figures or dealings with German-owned commercial firms were removed.[224]

On August 25, Contal called in Gustavo Utzinger and candidly explained the situation. The confessions would have to be adjusted in accordance with the prescriptions laid down by Perón. Since Utzinger, second in command to Becker, was the most important agent captured, Contal wanted him to convince the other captives to be accommodating in this matter. The Coordinación chief promised better treatment, a reduction in the level of harassment, and the early release of persons whom he concluded might not be V-men after all.[225] Convinced that there really was no feasible alternative to this proposal, Utzinger issued a written statement, which the Coordinación circulated among the prisoners. It specified that the recently captured spies could truthfully admit their activities, but that there was to be no mention of contacts with Argentine military or political figures, German-owned business firms, or other intelligence agencies. Lt. Alfredo Ossinde was given the task of censoring the confessions and sewing them together, while another officer, Pedro Andrade, passed among the prisoners, urging upon them the wisdom and necessity of following Utzinger's orders.[226]

This series of actions was primarily intended to protect the Farrell government and the army from embarrassing revelations, but Perón had concerns of a more personal nature as well. Arrested on August 29, 1944, Werner Koennecke was the last member of the Harnisch ring taken into custody. Naval attaché Capt. Dietrich Niebuhr had long suspected that Koennecke was really a double agent loyal to the British, and in 1943, the Argentine government temporarily suspended his pilot's license for flying over a restricted military zone. Hans Harnisch would adamantly insist that Koennecke was the true author of many of the "Boss" and "Viereck" radio messages, while the expressed judgment of SIS/Argentina was that Koennecke was, at best, an unreliable schemer.[227] Nevertheless, the agent in question had one priceless advantage which rendered all these negative factors irrelevant: He was the son-in-law of millionaire Ludwig Freude.

The emergence of Ludwig Freude, and the nature of his influence over Juan Perón, remains one of the unsolved mysteries of Argentine politics in the 1940s. In December 1943, Col. Enrique González had resolved to make Freude pay for his suspected treachery in the Hellmuth affair. With the official creation of the Coordinación Federal, one of the first commands given Maj. Francisco Filippi was to arrest and interrogate Ludwig Freude. But Minister of Public Works Gen. Juan Pistarini's threat to resign blocked the execution of this order, and it was this same officer who allegedly brought Perón and Freude together.[228]

No clearer example of the operation of a Perón-Freude axis is to be found than the Werner Koennecke case. On August 30, 1944, the day after Koennecke's arrest, Vice-President and Minister of War Perón ordered Major Contal to bring the prisoner to his ministry office. Koennecke was asked whether he was connected with German secret intelligence, and he categorically denied such a relationship. Contal objected to this procedure, but to no avail. Koennecke swore he was not involved, and Perón ordered his release.

A disgusted Oscar Contal still refused to release the prisoner, his excuse being that Perón would have to provide written confirmation of the ministry meeting and the sanctioned release. Naturally, the colonel had no intention of leaving behind any evidence that potential enemies could someday use against him. Instead, he waited until a period of days early in 1945 when Contal was away from the capital, and his assistant,

Capt. Abel Rodríguez, was temporarily in charge. Koennecke was then sprung, and Contal was presented with a fait accompli.[229]

According to postwar testimony, the German agents held by the Argentine counterintelligence agency were instructed that in their confessional statements, any charges against Koennecke were to be blamed on Hans Harnisch instead.[230] While this claim sounds suspicious, certain discoveries give credence to the charges. First of all, no record of Koennecke's arrest or interrogation was to be found in the Argentine records, and more significantly, none of the confessions released by the Coordinación even mention his name![231] Finally, FBI records reveal nothing more than the fact that Koennecke's release from jail was believed to have occurred sometime between July 30 and October 10, 1945. There is, however, additional information which suggests that Koennecke was actually released from detention prior to July 30, but was carried on the roster of prisoners after he was, in fact, at liberty. Werner Koennecke became the V-man who vanished and who took his dossier with him.[232]

All this reshaping of confessions and modification of statements came to a halt, and the process had to be started all over again after Johannes Siegfried Becker was arrested in April 1945. In a rancorous mood, Becker drew up a declaration which ran over three hundred pages and implicated numerous Argentine military and political figures. Evidently he was persuaded to change his statement, because the final confession was boiled down to fifty pages, and with the exception of Pedro Andrade, no Argentine police or military collaborator was mentioned. The confessional problem settled, Becker's condition of imprisonment steadily improved, and in the months that followed, he, too, became an intimate of Ludwig Freude.[233]

At the same time Coordinación Federal agents were fabricating and refabricating confessions, they were also busy making advantageous financial arrangements. Items like Gustavo Utzinger's microscope and stamp collection and the personal possessions of other prisoners became the property of Coordinación agents. Of greater importance is the fact that confiscated funds came to be viewed as spoils of war. Argentine records reveal that roughly sixty thousand dollars in English pounds, U.S. dollars, and Argentine pesos were taken from agents and suspects arrested between August and October 1944. Both Major Contal and Captain Rodríguez attempted to acquire some of these funds for themselves; the major managed to acquire some, but the captain got caught in the act.[234]

The largest swindle, however, occurred with the sale of the drugs brought off the *Santa Barbara* by Burckhardt and Chantrain. The Coordinación claimed that the value of the drugs was about $52,000, told the Uruguayan police that $125,000 was the true worth of these "vitamins," and possibly underestimated their price on the open market by 200 percent.[235] Early in 1945, a rigged auction was conducted in which the Bayer Company subsidiary in Argentina bought all the drugs for $36,200. Of course, the price was scandalously low, but in the end, the joke was on the Germans. By Executive Decree No. 16743/945 of July 7, 1945, the Bayer firm was taken over by the Argentine government. The legal battle over the liquidation of the firm's assets continued into 1948; in the meantime, the Coordinación was left in possession of the drugs and presumably the $36,200.[236]

In addition to arranged confessions and sharp financial dealings, there would be significant legal chicanery as well. The previously mentioned stay-behind group, conceived by Gen. Friedrich Wolf and led by Ernst Schleuter, contributed nothing tangible to the effort of the German intelligence apparatus in Argentina. Still, this did not prevent Schleuter from contacting Ludwig Freude, one of the trustees of the espionage funds turned over by General Wolf, and obtaining $10,500 between July and December 1944. Not until September 1945 did the Coordinación arrest Schleuter, Horst Busse, Johannes Thomas, and the other two financial trustees, Hans Leuters and Friedrich Frohwein. All of these persons were decreed to be undesirables, and on February 15, 1946, they were put aboard the steamer *Highland Monarch* and whisked back to Germany[237]—all, that is, except for the final member of the group, Ludwig Freude. (See Appendix D.)

In a special meeting held on September 6, 1945, U.S. ambassador Spruille Braden obtained from Foreign Minister Juan J. Cooke a pledge that Ludwig Freude would be arrested. But on September 19, Cooke told Braden that Freude had too many influential friends to be either arrested or deported.[238] After the U.S. ambassador departed on September 22, the State Department instructed its chargé, John Cabot, to tell the Argentine foreign minister: "This Embassy considers its efforts to have Freude interned a crucial test case, in that it will show whether the Nazi machine in Argentina can be broken. . . ."[239]

The man who was the object of this attention was no doubt informed of U.S. demands and promptly took steps to disrupt any deportation action. On September 21, Freude petitioned the Federal Court of San Juan province to allow him to take the oath of citizenship. Freude claimed to have filed for citizenship in this jurisdiction on May 8, 1935; ten years had passed, but now he wanted to complete the process of becoming an Argentine national.

Unexpectedly, Judge Gutiérrez threw sand in the gears and temporarily foiled this legal maneuver. British and North American sources may have alerted Gutiérrez to the fact that on November 20, 1937, Freude had sworn allegiance to the Reich and obtained a passport at the German embassy in Buenos Aires. At any rate, the judge stated that by waiting over a decade to complete the process of naturalization, Freude had demonstrated contempt for the nation. He further cited Executive Decree No. 6005 of November 27, 1943, which suspended the granting of naturalization documents for the duration of the war. Thereupon he rejected Freude's petition to take the oath of citizenship.[240]

The German promptly appealed his case to the Federal Court of Appeals of the province of Mendoza. Meanwhile, a power struggle in

Buenos Aires climaxed with Perón's fall from power, his arrest, and ultimately his triumph over his enemies (October 12–17, 1945).[241] During this tumultuous period, Freude allegedly offered to hide the colonel and supposedly managed to destroy a signed executive decree ordering his own deportation.[242] With Perón's reconquest of power, Freude's legal situation took a turn for the better. On December 18, 1945, the Mendoza Court of Appeals reversed the San Juan court's decision and confirmed the citizenship petition of May 8, 1935. Still, since government pressure was widely believed to have influenced this judgment, the magistrates themselves suggested that a federal inquiry into Freude's wartime activities would be in order.[243]

Following the February 24, 1946, balloting, Juan Perón became president-elect of Argentina, and on March 18, the British and United States governments took the joint step of asking Argentina to deport Ludwig Freude. The request was taken under advisement but subsequent developments should have indicated to Washington and London that they were wasting their time. In April 1946, Rudolph Freude, Ludwig's son, was named the new president's secretary, while on May 17, the elder Freude threw a massive birthday party for Eva Perón.[244] The official investigation into Ludwig Freude's wartime activities began on May 21, and given the developments cited, only the naive could have failed to correctly predict the outcome.

The procedure by which this investigation was conducted further substantiates the conclusion that the entire affair was an orchestrated whitewash. The prosecuting attorney never introduced the testimony of Ernst Schleuter into the record and sought no depositions from Erich von Meynen or Osmar Hellmuth. Perhaps the most revealing comment was the observation of one of the judges that the primary reason for this inquiry was "the complaints expressed by the embassies of the United States and England. . . ." Once a sufficient interval had passed, on October 23, 1946, the Argentine government announced that the investigation had cleared Freude, and it issued a decree to this effect.[245] The United States was hardly in accord with this pronouncement and Assistant Secretary of State Spruille Braden was particularly upset, for he discovered that Ludwig Freude had gained citizenship without ever having appeared in the San Juan Federal Court.[246] John Cabot, chargé d' affaires in Argentina in 1945–46, summed up the situation succinctly three and one-half decades later: "We tried to get Freude deported but Perón was able to thwart us."[247]

In Mexico in 1946, the Avila Camacho government did what it could to conceal the fact that some Germans scheduled for deportation managed to buy their way off the list. In Chile in 1944, President Juan Ríos did whatever he could to hide the connection between Bernardo Timmerman and the Army Officer Corps. But nowhere were so many military figures as deeply involved with German intelligence as in Argentina. The reality of the situation was that the protection of reputations made legal invention a continuing necessity and torture a convenient persuader.

Even then, various contradictions and questionable acts could not be covered up or explained away. These were simply ignored. Such were the policies which set the stage for the commencement of the Argentine spy trials of 1946–47.

B. *Judicial Tangle and Political Dilemma*

Despite the Argentine declaration of war in March 1945, a full and comprehensive listing of imprisoned German agents was never made available to U.S. intelligence.[248] Washington wanted the captured agents shipped to the United States for interrogation, but given the doctored confessions and the governmental complicity in the activities of these agents, Argentine reluctance to cooperate is quite understandable. Still, the termination of state of siege provisions on August 6, 1945, forced the Farrell government to take some long-delayed actions regarding the status and fate of the prisoners. On August 31, 1945, in federal court in the capital city of Buenos Aires, Judge Horacio Fox placed the prisoners under the jurisdiction of the court and charged them with violating Article 219 of the penal code, which stipulated that a person could be jailed for up to eight years for carrying out activities which jeopardized Argentina's diplomatic relations with friendly powers.[249] Like Brazil and Chile, Argentina had no peacetime espionage statute.

After examining the evidence provided on October 10, Judge Fox ruled that it was sufficient to justify the prosecution of fifty foreign nationals and eleven Argentine citizens. Of this number, fifteen (all Germans) were to be held in police custody, three would remain hospitalized, but forty-three others were to be given provisional liberty.[250] (See Appendix D.) This last order was promptly set aside, for on October 11, 1945, state of siege regulations were reimposed throughout the country.

In public speeches and radio addresses given on November 12 and November 19, 1945, Foreign Minister Juan Cooke emphatically reiterated his government's determination to comply with commitments undertaken when it had adhered to the February 1945 Act of Chapultepec. Specifically, Cooke held that in pledging to destroy "Axis centers of influence," as it was stated in Resolution VII, Argentina must not only try spies, but swiftly expel from its borders all foreign nationals believed to have collaborated with the Axis. In line with these intents, Executive Decree No. 27.921 was issued on November 7, 1945; it named ten persons as recently detected German spies or undesirables and ordered them deported.[251]

The first group ordered repatriated was scheduled to leave aboard the USS *Red Jacket* on December 1, 1945, but legal action requesting the issuance of habeas corpus writs stymied this action. After hearings in several federal courts, in January 1946, the petitions for writs were refused, and additional decrees issued on February 8 and 12, 1946, increased the number scheduled for expulsion. On February 15, 1946, the English steamer HMS *Highland Monarch* sailed from Buenos Aires for Hamburg, carrying twenty-nine undesirables.[252]

But it was soon evident that some persons who were ordered deported would nevertheless avoid the transatlantic trip back to a ruined Germany. Named in either the November 7, 1945, or February 8 and 13, 1946, expulsion orders were Georg Bücker, the Abwehr's chief platinum smuggler, Carlos Eickenberg, the Bolivian millionaire who had aided Johannes Siegfried Becker, and Karl Conrad Reidel, another wealthy businessman. No official explanation for their reprieves was given, but aside from the Coordinación's alleged inability to find these people, the most consequential factor these men had in common was their friendship with that man of mysterious power, Ludwig Freude.[253]

The deportation effort against undesirables had commenced with rather spotty results. Unexpectedly, it was soon brought to a complete standstill. Executive Decree No. 4840/946, issued on February 13, 1946, ordered the expulsion of Claus Joachim Watjen, a German businessman then living in the city of Buenos Aires. The Argentines apparently knew that Watjen had been a member of Friedrich Tadeo von Schulz-Hausmann's PYL ring. Operating out of the North German Lloyd Shipping offices in Callao, Peru, Watjen sent shipping information to Chile, from where it had been forwarded to Germany via the ring's clandestine transmitter. In December 1941, Watjen joined Schulz-Hausmann as an executive with Bromberg and Company, headquartered in the Argentine capital. He was not arrested during the 1942 or 1944 spy investigations and escaped police detention until February 23, 1946. It was shortly before his arrest that lawyers brought suit seeking a cancellation of the deportation order.

Both the federal court and the federal appeals court in the capital found in favor of the Farrell government, but the Argentine Supreme Court reached a different conclusion. In a decision issued May 8, 1946, the high tribunal ruled that under the Law of Residence, the chief executive of the nation could expel any foreign alien whose activities were judged inimical to the security of the nation. But first, the litigant would have to be informed of the charges brought against him and given an opportunity to present his case against the execution of the deportation decree.[254]

The net effect of this decision was to give any person named in a deportation decree ample opportunity to either slow the legal process to a crawl, or publicly reveal information which the government wanted to be kept secret. Nevertheless, what proved devastating was the effect the Watjen decision would have upon the case against the sixty-one persons charged with violation of Article 219 of the penal code. To be sure, this spy trial had never really gotten under way. First, Judge Horacio Fox had struggled for over four months to obtain the facts and to issue a ruling concerning the status of prisoners' property confiscated by Coordinación officers. Proceedings were further delayed by the stalling tactics of Octavio Rivarola, the barrister hired to defend most of the prisoners. Paid forty thousand dollars up front by Ludwig Freude, Werner Konnecke, and

Johannes Siegfried Becker,[255] Rivarola quickly demonstrated why he was worth such an enormous fee.

In Executive Decree No. 4842/946 of February 14, 1946, the Farrell regime ordered the deportation of all alien spies arraigned on October 10, 1945. The expulsion order was to be executed only after the trial was over, and according to government lawyers, it was intended essentially to keep most of the spies in jail once the state of siege was again lifted. But one week after the Watjen decision was handed down, Rivarola approached the bench and demanded writs of habeas corpus for all the non-Argentine prisoners. He argued that since the state was simultaneously trying prisoners it intended to deport, a grave injustice was being perpetrated. At the very least, he insisted, the defendants must be released so that they might effectively take issue with the deportation order already promulgated.[256]

Apparently Judge Fox was sympathetic to what he had heard, because on May 31, 1946, he found in favor of Rivarola's request; by June 10, most of the prisoners had been placed at liberty. On July 12, the court of appeals reversed Fox's action, but on August 21, the Argentine Supreme Court reversed the ruling of the court of appeals. Accepted was the argument that the deportation order was merely a utility device intended to prevent unlawful flight by the spy trial defendants. Nevertheless, the justices of the Supreme Court concluded that "the aliens brought for trial cannot be expelled by the Executive Power . . . until such time as the case is closed, and in the case of condemnation, until such time as the sentence is fulfilled."[257]

This Supreme Court decision presented Juan Perón, president of Argentina since June 4, with a serious difficulty. He could continue the spy trial or hold hearings in order to proceed with the deportation of the spies, but he could not do both simultaneously. If either the trial or the deportation hearings dragged on indefinitely, certain kinds of revelations could still cause him plenty of trouble. Then there were also international considerations. From August 1945 to August 1946, not one German spy had been convicted, and only twenty-nine undesirable aliens had been deported. With the United States pressing for the expulsion of six times that number of Germans,[258] Argentina needed to maintain the appearance of complying with its Chapultepec promises. Nevertheless, the court actions indicated that the legal process would be arduous, and further evidence of the collusion of Perón and others with the SD might leak out. If, on the other hand, the president could gain control over the final disposition of the spies, the legal process could be carefully controlled and swiftly completed. And that is exactly what Perón decided to do.

C. *"Thick" Air and Thin Numbers*

The tactical means for resolving the spy problem was Executive Decree No. 18480/946, officially issued on November 15, 1946. This edict provided for the arrest and deportation of fifty-three foreign nationals, forty-four of whom had been placed at liberty as a result of the habeas corpus decisions of May through August 1946 (see Appendix D). No provision was made for either a judicial or administrative hearing prior to deportation, and in that sense, the order represented total defiance of the Supreme Court's ruling in this matter. Even more significantly, with this stroke of a pen, Perón could now manipulate and liquidate the issue as he deemed fit.[259]

Orders to begin arresting those named in the decree were immediately issued, but the usually competent Coordinación Federal suddenly demonstrated a peculiar inability to locate the persons wanted. In the light of certain developments, the reason for this failure became increasingly clear. For example, on November 3, 1946, Hans Harnisch was personally telephoned by Capt. Abel Rodríguez, Coordinación chief, and told to find a safe hiding place. On November 6, Gustavo Utzinger received word that prudence dictated that he depart posthaste for the interior of the country. On November 7, in the office of lawyer Octavio Rivarola, Juan Antonio Prieto was told that he would be arrested in eight days unless he moved away from the capital. Among others, Johannes Harmeyer, Carlos Manfrini, Gustavo Seraphin, Wilhelm Maubach, Esteban Amorín, and Johannes Szeraws were forewarned either by the police, Rivarola, or another former spy.[260]

Even some of those who failed to heed the early warnings could still count on the benevolent assistance of Coordinación personnel. On November 6, Becker telephoned Alphonse Chantrain and announced that "the air" was "thick" and it was time to "travel."[261] The trouble was that Chantrain had both a sweetheart and a well-paying job in Buenos Aires and no inclination to leave either. At least, that was his feeling until 6:00 A.M. on November 20, when a Coordinación officer came to his door. After identifying himself, the officer declared, " 'What Alphonso, are you still here?' " The policeman told Chantrain that he had been ordered to arrest him, and that he would return a little later.[262] In the interim, Chantrain made himself scarce and departed for the home of a friend over two hundred miles away.

In addition to these examples of purposeful inefficiency, there were others which suggest that more formal arrangements were occasionally made. Indicative are the cases of two Spaniards, Nicolás Quintana and Manuel de Miguel Arrastia, who had been important cogs in Becker's smuggling operation. These men decided to flee not to the interior but even farther—all the way back to Spain. Quintana approached a friend in the National Chamber of Deputies, obtained a false passport, and left Buenos Aires aboard a Spanish freighter in November 1946.[263] Miguel Arrastia decided that the phony document route was not for him. He went to the Spanish embassy to obtain the necessary clearances, and when he was told that the Coordinación considered him a fugitive, he replied that the necessary steps for his departure had already been taken. The embassy validated his passport, and although police checked the embarking passengers to prevent the escape of fugitives, Miguel Arrastia sailed aboard the *Monte Amboto* on December 16, 1946.[264]

Given these blatant examples of chicanery and corruption, it is hardly surprising that after thirty days, only fourteen of the fifty-three persons ordered deported in the November 15, 1946, decree had officially been found. The Argentine government apparently deemed prompt expulsion more important than numbers expelled, for on December 21, 1946, thirteen of these fourteen were packed off to Germany aboard the SS *La Pampa* (see Appendix D). In fact, the speed of departure helped to mask the clever charade that the Perón regime was perpetrating. Only nine of the thirteen fugitives deported had been involved in Abwehr/SD operations in Argentina in 1943–45, and of them, only Esteban Amorín and Juan Prieto had been important members of the Becker organization. The Argentinians had provided bodies, but as one U.S. interrogator noted, virtually all of these were "quota fillers," not key espionage personnel.[265]

Before *La Pampa* sailed, however, Octavio Rivarola, seemingly displeased that any of the fugitives were being deported, went to court seeking writs of habeas corpus for nine persons. The desired orders were issued in federal court in Buenos Aires in January 1947, and on February 8, the federal appeals court in the capital issued its strongest prohibition yet. It flayed the Perón government for deporting Esteban Amorín, Ferdinand Ullrich, and Fr. Fernández Suárez without holding a deportation hearing, and ordered that this trio must be disembarked at an Argentine port. Nevertheless, the naval minister, undoubtedly acting on presidential orders, defied this injunction.[266] As part of its general plan to manipulate and liquidate the spy issue, Perón presented the judges with a fait accompli, and then demonstrated his determination to defy unfavorable court orders.

With these acts, Perón was also attempting to portray internationally the image of an embattled president struggling to overcome a reactionary judiciary in order to effect Argentine compliance with the Chapultepec agreement. U.S. ambassador George Messersmith was an unabashed advocate of this view, but State Department leaders were more concerned with the Coordinación's failure to apprehend both additional fugitives and the more important spy ring leaders.[267] This skepticism was fortified by the fact that the department was in possession of intelligence reports which the passage of time demonstrated to be increasingly accurate. For example, in September 1945, the military attaché in Argentina, Col. John Lange, had predicted that Perón and the other military chiefs would allow only a few minor agents to be sacrificed.[268] The United States also enjoyed some unexpected good fortune in that in May 1946, the SIS/Argentina secured the services of an "Argentine of German extraction" who had been "a member of the [Hans] Harnisch organization until his arrest in January, 1944." This informant was probably Enrique Neiling ("Charlie"), whose first report was delivered shortly after Perón's inauguration. According to Neiling, Coordinación chief Capt. Abel Rodríguez owed his job to Perón, and was in deep debt to Ludwig Freude. In May 1946, Rodríguez had promised the former German agents that he would do "everything in his power" to prevent their deportation or conviction, and it was unlikely that he would make such a promise without the approval of his chiefs. Neiling also predicted that unless Perón suddenly demanded action, only a token number of spies captured in 1944–45 would suffer any penalty.[269]

For United States policy makers, these and other intelligence reports only fortified the prevailing conviction that Peronist actions masked an evident insincerity.[270] The problem, however, was that unless Washington was prepared to risk another confrontation on the spy issue, nothing of importance could be done about the situation. Meanwhile, aware of United States skepticism and mistrust, Perón moved toward the full and final settlement of the spy issue. Implying that he blamed the Coordinación Federal high command for the failure to locate the fugitive spies, on February 1, 1947, he replaced Captain Rodríguez with Maj. Miguel Bietti.[271] Two days later, Hans Harnisch was arrested, and on April 1, Gustavo Utzinger, who was tired of hiding, gave himself up. Abel Rodríguez's demotion did not, however, mean that his friends and protectors had turned their backs on him. He resigned from the Coordinación, but he soon had another well-paying position on the payroll of the man who apparently had a great deal to say about who would be caught: Ludwig Freude.[272]

The deportation of Harnisch, Utzinger, and six others aboard the *Río Teuco* on May 22, 1947, marked the end of Argentina's compliance push. Perón had gone through the motions and the United States could call for the inauguration of the Rio Pact meetings. Still, the unvarnished facts were painful. Not one of the alien Abwehr or SD agents arrested after January 1, 1944, was ever convicted. Furthermore, as a consequence of the November 15, 1946, deportation order, a total of twenty-one persons were repatriated to Germany. Still, this number represents only about 40 percent of the total named in said decree, and only seventeen of these people belonged to spy networks which operated in Argentina after 1942. For Juan Perón, it had been a remarkably cunning performance. He had prevented the revelation of additional evidence of collusion with the SD until it could do him no harm[273] and simultaneously made the United States government eat crow.

Following the signing of the Rio Pact on September 2, 1947, Argentina moved expeditiously to liquidate the spy question. The final legal step took place on November 10, 1947, when the federal appeals court in the city of Buenos Aires dismissed charges against thirty-five foreign-born persons indicted on espionage charges in October 1945. The justices of the court ruled that the state had failed to provide adequate proofs and had been "reticent in pressing its case." Both the state and the justices—but not the press—conveniently chose to overlook the fact that among those on hand to hear the decision were nine persons whom the Coordinación Federal claimed it had been unable to find in May 1947 (See

Appendix D). The mask of compliance had not only been removed, it had been trampled upon.[274]

Since none of the alien Abwehr or SD agents captured in 1944–45 were convicted, it was a foregone conclusion that the eleven Argentine nationals who were also on trial would escape any legal penalties. These individuals had been allowed to post bail following the raising of state of siege provisions on February 22, 1946, and with the court decision of November 10, 1947, all charges against them were dropped.

Paradoxically, perhaps, the only spy trials to be completed in post-war Argentina involved two nationals who were arrested by the British: Ernst Hoppe and Osmar Hellmuth. Born in Germany and naturalized in Buenos Aires in 1936, Ernst Hoppe had returned to the Reich in 1939 and remained there for four years. According to British intelligence, Hoppe was recruited by the SD and ordered to supervise the landing and safekeeping in Argentina of gold, jewels, and other valuables worth at least $2.5 million. These valuables were to be transported across the Atlantic by U-boat, and presumably represented the booty of Nazi leaders who were intent upon starting over after the Third Reich collapsed. But on October 19, 1943, when the Spanish ship upon which Hoppe was returning reached Gibraltar, the British arrested him and hustled him off to England for interrogation.

Repatriated to Argentina on October 27, 1945, Hoppe was put under arrest, and Foreign Minister Juan Cooke told U.S. embassy officials that a denaturalization suit would soon be initiated. Actually, no judicial action commenced before February 1947. No sooner had the trial begun than the federal prosecutor, Belisario Gache Pirán, informed Judge Horacio Fox that while evidence of Hoppe's recruitment had been requested, neither the British nor the United States had provided any. All Hoppe had to do was to deny that he had ever been an SD agent, and the trial ended.[275]

The case against Osmar Hellmuth should have been a different matter, because the Ramírez government claimed to have obtained proof that Hellmuth was a German agent. Upon returning to Argentina on October 25, 1945, Osmar Hellmuth had a private meeting first with Ludwig Freude and then with Colonel Perón;[276] only then was he taken into police custody. His trial was delayed until November 12, 1947, and by that time, President Perón had already demonstrated his intention to swiftly liquidate the matter. On December 30, 1947, a federal court in the capital ruled that Hellmuth's protestations of innocence had not been disproven by the prosecution. He, too, walked away free.[277]

Considering that the Coordinación Federal's first campaign against German espionage was launched in connection with the Hellmuth disaster, it was fitting that the final espionage-related prosecution ended with this trial. Moreover, Hellmuth had never been a German spy, and his only crime was being caught in the middle. Thus, the verdict reached in his trial, for whatever reason it was reached, became one of the few examples of justice to emerge from this muddled and manipulated legal masquerade.

1. *Where Are They Now?*

Ludwig Freude, who was intimately involved in spy matters, died in 1952, allegedly after being poisoned. A kinder fate awaited former GOU strongman and Hellmuth affair organizer, Col. Enrique González. On May 20, 1949, Perón named his old comrade in conspiracy national director of migrations; a year later, he became national director of the Argentine Atomic Energy Commission, a post he held until 1952.[278] His whereabouts and activities after 1952 are unknown.

The subsequent history of the deportees is interesting in that, despite their experiences in Argentina, a fair number of them did their best to return as soon as they could. Alphonse Chantrain was prevented from leaving Europe in September 1947, but in 1949 he succeeded. Walter Schwaiger did so in 1953, Albert Voelckers came back in 1954, and Gustavo Utzinger migrated to the province of Córdoba in 1960. Hans Harnisch remained under the scrutiny of Argentine intelligence, which reported that, in 1948, he was enjoying business success and had ingratiated himself with Robert Murphy, a political advisor to the United States military government in Germany.[279]

Possibly the most vexing question that remains is: What happened to Johannes Siegfried Becker? Both the CIA and FBI claim that they have no post-1946 data on this former spymaster.[280] There has been at least one erroneous account of Becker's postwar activities,[281] and the Coordinación Federal, without explaining how it obtained the information, declared that Becker left Argentina in July 1947.[282] Of course, U.S. intelligence was skeptical, and a secret report dated September 4, 1947, is the best source of information now available. It revealed that Becker had been positively identified as living on a farm in the province of Santiago del Estero. He was reputedly under the protection of Col. Aristobulo Mittlebach, a one-time GOU stalwart and well-known Perón loyalist. The report further stated that it was unlikely that Mittlebach would be sheltering Becker without the Argentine president's consent. Scrawled across the bottom of this report was the cryptic comment: "Could be true, but what can we do about it?"[283] It had taken Washington an inordinate amount of time to recognize and accept the obvious answer.

D. *Summary: The Permanent Enemy*

While his stubborn stand on compliance and his personal antipathy for Perón have made Spruille Braden a figure of ridicule among some historians,[284] certain aspects of his analysis should be recognized as sound. Specifically, one of the premises championed by Braden was that a Fascist regime in Argentina, led by a clever politician like Juan Perón, represented a "threat to the peace of the nations of the hemisphere."[285] If one substitutes "the interests of the United States" for the "peace of the hemisphere," then Braden's view may be considered prescient. Evidence of this conclusion is to be seen in a top secret study prepared by Brig. Gen. Carlos von der Becke for Pres. Pedro Ramírez in November 1943.

At the time he wrote "Political-Military Considerations of the Countries at War," von der Becke was chief of staff of the Argentine army. In February 1945, he became commander-in-chief. In April 1946, the Farrell government sent von der Becke to enlist General of the Army Dwight D. Eisenhower's support for Argentine purchases of United States military equipment. Much to the chagrin of the Department of State, Eisenhower conferred with the Argentinian, and pronounced him "quite a guy."[286] Suffice it to say that the Argentine army commander was an impressive and influential figure, and when he expressed his views, a good many military men paid attention.

It is precisely for these reasons that "Political-Military Considerations" ought not be dismissed as the mad musings of a general staff officer who had lost touch with reality. The document was partially concerned with the struggle being fought in Europe, but its major relevance is that it is a directive for future Argentine conduct. Even a cursory reading of the document demonstrates that while von der Becke sympathized with Germany, his basic conclusion was that by late 1943, Adolf Hitler had lost the war. On the eastern front, the Wehrmacht could only hope to stop the Red Army steamroller by retreating to the Reich's "natural frontiers." As for the western front, von der Becke viewed the Italian campaign as a misguided sideshow, but predicted an Anglo-American invasion "through the north of France during the summer of 1944." Since the continental landings would probably be successful, Germany could stave off disaster only if the Grand Alliance collapsed, or if the Führer was able to negotiate a settlement with the allied powers "before the end of 1944."

If the Reich suffered total defeat and occupation, von der Becke predicted a rapid collapse of the Grand Alliance and Soviet occupation of Poland and the Balkan states. The United States would move to check Russian aspirations, a step which would necessitate its military presence in Europe for an indefinite period. War between the United States and Russia was a probability, and von der Becke predicted its outbreak no more than seven years after Germany had been defeated.

For Argentina, the post-World War II world would definitely be a dangerous place. To survive, the nation would have to industrialize rapidly, while diplomatically playing the U.S.A. and USSR against each other. Still, a war between the United States and the Soviet Union could, in the long run, serve the interests of Argentina. If the nation managed to stay neutral while building up its industrial plant, the way would then be clear for the creation of a "coalition of South American nations under Argentine leadership." Such a bloc would finally be able "to challenge Yankee domination of the hemisphere."[287]

What made "Political-Military Consideration of Countries at War" particularly relevant is that the ideas it expressed closely coincided with the views of Juan Perón. He was also convinced that rapid industrialization was the only way in which Argentina could escape superpower domination after World War II. Like von der Becke, Perón believed that World War II would probably be followed by World War III. Rio Pact or no Rio Pact, his intention was to maintain a policy of neutrality while maneuvering astutely among the belligerents. If all went well, then Argentina must emerge as the leading power in South America and possibly the leading nation in the Hispanic world.[288]

What all this meant in terms of the 1942–47 situation was that since the United States was the nation most directly frustrating the ambitions of Argentine nationalists, the United States became Argentina's number one enemy. Unless the United States continuously exerted an overwhelming amount of economic and diplomatic pressure, it could expect nothing except half-hearted and inconsistent counterespionage cooperation from any Nationalist regime in Buenos Aires. The same would be true for spy conviction and deportation matters, and the overall settlement of U.S.-Argentine differences would be impossible except on Argentine terms.

Spruille Braden is to be credited in that his actions in 1945–47 demonstrated his awareness of the attitude of the Argentine Nationalists. His essential difficulty, however, was that Argentina was no banana republic. Any decision to force a change in its attitude and policy would have necessitated a major reallocation of economic resources, a sustained diplomatic campaign in Latin America, and a confrontation with Great Britain. Except in the Hellmuth affair, the United States was never prepared to make that kind of commitment. The resultant disappointments and frustrations are evidence of what happens when the United States underestimates the power and determination of the opposition, and attempts to win a major diplomatic victory on the cheap.

Notes

1. The report of events utilized here is the July 13, 1943, report of Ambassador Sir Donald Kelly to Anthony Eden, the foreign minister. We believe this report to be the most accurate produced and unmatched as a source of factual information concerning the political events of June 3–6, 1943. See Great Britain, Foreign Office, FO-371-33514-02057, no. 6530/11/2. On the decision to drop Ramírez on June 3 and the testing of his loyalty, see p. 3. (Hereafter, Foreign Office documents will be referred to by their FO number alone.)

2. For the events related, see ibid., pp. 3–6. On Ramírez's activities during the period June 3–4, see Robert A. Potash, *The Army and Politics in Argentina: 1928–1945* (Stanford, 1969), pp. 198–199. On the problem of General Rawson, see ibid., pp. 204–208, and Miguel Ángel Scenna, *Los Militares* (Buenos Aires, 1980), pp. 191–192.

3. FO-371-33514-02057, no. G530/11/2, p. 6.

4. There is a disagreement among sources concerning who offered the nomination to Ramírez and whether the offer was completely genuine. FO-371-33514-02057, no. G530/11/2, p. 2, names three important Radical party figures who attended the meeting and concludes that a genuine offer was made to Ramírez. Potash, *The Army and Politics.* pp. 190–191, states seven Radical deputies were at the meeting, but names none of those in the British account and finds that the offer made was unofficial.

5. The quotation is from Miguel Ángel Scenna, *Los Militares,* p. 192.

6. Concerning the late date of this action and the fact that Ramírez knew about what González intended to do, see Potash, *The Army and Politics,* pp. 192–193.

7. There is no adequate history of the GOU. The best history available is in ibid., pp. 184–190. George I. Blanksten, *Perón's Argentina* (Chicago, 1953), pp. 47–49, provides a copy of a document allegedly written by Perón and circulated among GOU adherents in May 1943. It stressed authoritarian standards and admiration for Fascist goals and methodology.

8. The removal of Rawson, the GOU's role in this scheme, and Rawson's problems are covered in Potash, *The Army and Politics,* pp. 204–208, and Scenna, *Los Militares,* p. 192.

9. GOU gains and additional influence under Ramírez are discussed in full in Potash, *The Army and Politics,* pp. 208–213.

10. On the failure to obtain weapons and the complaints of the military, see FO-371-33514-02057, no. 6530, pp. 1 and 3, Alberto Conil Paz and Gustavo Ferrari, *Política Exterior Argentina: 1930–1962* (Buenos Aires, 1964), p. 104, and Arthur Whitaker, *The United States and Argentina* (Cambridge, Mass., 1954), p. 114.

11. See National Archives and Records Service (hereafter referred to as NARS), R.G. 84,820.02, box 533, *Interrogation of Otto Reinebeck* (no TC number), January 24, 1946, p. 10. Apparently the U.S. interrogators were loath to believe this statement and so Reinebeck reaffirmed it, adding the names of those found in the body of this page. See NARS, R.G. 84,820.02, box 53, *Interrogation of Otto Reinebeck,* TC-20977, January 27, 1946, p. 2.

12. On Ramírez's plan to send a representative to Washington as an arms negotiator, see NARS, R.G. 59, 835.00//1582 (memorandum, Duggan to Welles). See also Conil Paz and Ferrari, *Política Exterior,* pp. 130–131.

13. See NARS, R.G. 59, 835.00/1556, pp. 1–3. See also attached memorandum (same number, dated June 10, 1943), Duggan to Bonsal, which is the basis of the subsequent Hull message to Armour. For the Welles memorandum to Armour, see R.G. 59, 711.35/194.

14. On Ramírez's problems and GOU opposition to his plan to break relations, see NARS, R.G. 59, 835.00/1643, pp. 1–2. See in particular, Potash, *The Army and Politics*, pp. 218–219. Various commentaries on U.S.-Argentine discussions are to be found in Conil Paz and Ferrari, *Política Exterior*, pp. 128–133, Sir David Kelly, *The Ruling Few* (London, 1953), pp. 297–298, and Enrique Ruiz Guiñazú, *La política Argentina y el futuro de América* (Buenos Aires, 1944), p. 113.

15. On German intentions to sell weapons to Argentina in July 1943, see NARS, Auswärtiges Amt, *Documents Selected from German Foreign Office Records* (hereafter referred to as *DSGFOR*), T-120 series, roll 762, frames 356225–356226. The Japanese, rather cynically, were prepared to offer the Argentines anything. See United States War Department, Office of the Assistant Chief of Staff, *The Magic Documents: Summaries and Transcripts of the Top Secret Diplomatic Communications of Japan: 1938–1945* (hereafter referred to as *Magic Documents* (Washington, D.C., 1980), reel 3, frames 0506–0515.

16. On SD and Argentine participation in the Bolivian revolt of December 1943, see Franklin D. Roosevelt Library (hereafter referred to as FDRL), Harry Hopkins Papers, box 141, report, Hoover to Harry Hopkins, December 22, 1943. Solid evidence is supplied in *Magic Documents*, reel 7, report no. 633, frame 0823.

17. Hull's decision to freeze Argentine assets (later rescinded) is reported in Laurence Duggan, *The Americas: The Seach for Hemisphere Security* (New York, 1949), pp. 91–92. It is also referred to in NARS, R.G. 59, 835.00/2899, p. 1. The events of January 24, 1944, are explicated in 835.00/2273, pp. 1–4. The quoted material is from p. 3.

18. See NARS, R.G. 59, 835.00/2275, p. 3.

19. See Cordell Hull, *The Memoirs of Cordell Hull* (New York, 1948), vol. 2, p. 1391, which gives a straightforward (but incomplete) report of what the secretary said that he said. See República Argentina, Ministerio de Relaciones Exteriores y Culto, *Acuses de Recibios, Asuntos Varios y de Caracter general*, cabinet 7, box 46-D, case 1, file 589, vol. 1, *Decreto y Comunicaciones*, Escobar to the Foreign Ministry, no. 206, n.p.

20. *Magic Documents*, reel 7, report no. 681, frame 0377, and report no. 714, frame 0687. These reports indicate that even after diplomatic relations were broken, Juan Perón and other Argentinians desired to remain on good terms with the Axis.

21. NARS, R.G. 59, 835.00/2162.

22. The story of the split in the GOU and the forced resignations of Gilbert, González, and Ramírez is related in Potash, *The Army and Politics*, pp. 231-237.

23. See NARS, R.G. 59, 835.00/2659 A, p. 2.

24. See NARS, R.G. 59, 800.20235/438, and especially FW 835.00/2824, pp. 1–5, and 835.50/189.

25. NARS, R.G. 59, 835.00/186, pp. 1–6.

26. See ibid., FW 835.00N/186, and in particular, República de Chile, Ministerio de Relaciones Exteriores, *Oficios confidenciales enviados y recibidos—Embajada de Chile en E.E.U.U.—1944*, confidential report no. 1022/79C, August 9, 1944, n.p. This document, a report of an interview between the Chilean ambassador and the departed Argentine ambassador, demonstrates conclusively that the Latin Americans were aware of U.S. tactics. Further corroboration of the Hull scheme was supplied in an interview with Ambassador Norman Armour by Professor Leslie B. Rout, Jr., May 14, 1976.

27. Concerning the June 22 circular cable and the U.S. drive to have all the Latin American republics withdraw their chiefs of diplomatic missions from Buenos Aires, see NARS, R.G. 59, 835.00/6-2244. For the U.S. coordination of effort and means employed to achieve this goal, see 835.01/6-2044, /6-2344, /6-2644, /6-2744, and /7-144. On the departure of all except the Paraguayans, see FW 835.01/7-2544. Concerning the U.S.-British friction over this issue, see FO-371-37704-02231, no. AS3666/78/2, and R.G. 59, 835.01/7-1744, pp. 2–4.

28. The order blocking movement of Argentine gold is reported in *The New York Times*, August 17, 1944, and alluded to in NARS, R.G. 59, 835.00/8-444, p. 3. This action is also mentioned in Hull, *Memoirs*, vol. no. 2, pp. 1402–1403.

29. NARS, R.G. 59, 835.50/9-444, no. 1378, pp. 1–4. The quote is from p. 3. On British agreement to go along on the meat contract and the embargo proposal, see 835.24/9-444, and 835.00/9-1644.

30. *The New York Times*, September 8, 1944. For similar public comments made by Hull blasting Argentina, see NARS, R.G. 59, 835.00/9-1644, p. 1.

31. Hull was to repeat this conviction on several occasions. See Hull, *Memoirs*, vol. 2, pp. 1419 and 1421. See also NARS, R.G. 59, 835.01/6-2944, p. 1, and 835.01/7-1744, pp. 1-4 and 835.01/7-3144, no. 6074, p. 1. Note also, FDRL, *The Presidential Diaries of Henry J. Morgenthau, Jr.*, reel 2, vol. 5, frame 1349.

32. On British failure to cooperate with U.S. plans, see NARS, R.G. 59, 835.00/9-1644, 835.01/10-1044, and 740.35112A/12-1644.

33. On the smuggling of contraband between Argentina and other Latin American republics, see NARS, R.G. 59, 835.24/2723 and 835.24/9-2244. See also 835.50/11-2444, 835.50/12-1244, 811.20 Defense (M) Brazil /5486, /5488, and 811.20 Defense (M) Brazil /8-2644.

34. On the restlessness of the Latin American republics and their growing opposition to the non-negotiation policy, see NARS, R.G. 59, 835.00/ 7-2444, pp. 1–2, and especially, República de Chile, Ministerio de Relaciones Exteriores, *Oficios confidenciales enviados y recibidos—Embajada de Chile—1944*, 3448/112, November 2, 1944, pp. 1–9, and confidential report no. 2545/116, November 17, 1944, pp. 1–5.

35. FO-371-37702-X/17-0308, #AS2818/78/2. The views expressed by the specialists of the South American Department of the British Foreign Office were candid. On May 6, 1944, a Mr. Allen wrote: "The present roughshod policy of the United States with regard to Argentina is entirely subordinated to the vote-getting necessitites of the election year and the Administration's bid for the favours of the Press. . . ."

36. The United States took the position that only those nations which had declared war on the Axis could attend the Mexico City conference. Argentina retaliated on January 12 by declaring that it would abstain from any further Pan American meetings. For these dealings, see NARS, R.G. 59, 710 Conference W and PW/1-1745, and 710 Conference W and PW/1-1845. See also J. Lloyd Mecham, *The United States and Inter-American Security, 1889-1960* (Austin, 1961), pp. 246–249, and especially Arthur P. Whitaker, "Pan-American Politics and Diplomacy," in *Inter-American Affairs: An Annual Survey #5*, ed. Arthur P. Whitaker (New York, 1946), pp. 2–13.

37. These secret meetings between Perón and Rockefeller's personal envoys were first mentioned in Sumner Welles, *Where Are We Headed?* (New York, 1946), p. 206. For Adolf Berle's report, see FDRL, *The Diaries of Adolf Berle*, roll 5, frames 1122–1130. The full story is in Irving Gellman, *Good Neighbor Diplomacy: United States Policies in Latin America, 1933–1945* (Baltimore, 1979), pp. 200–201 and 207.

38. For these resolutions, see Pan American Union, *Inter-American Conference on Problems of War and Peace, Mexico City, February 21 – March 8, 1945: Report Submitted to the Governing Board of the Pan-American Union by the Director General* (Washington, 1945), pp. 1–60 (especially 28–29, 30–32, 47–49, 59–60) and 133–134.

39. On the prearranged deal and the significance of Resolution LIX, see Whitaker, "Pan American Politics and Diplomacy," pp. 14–16.

40. See República Argentina, Ministerio de las Relaciones Exteriores y Culto, *Asuntos Varios-1945*, cabinet 7, box 45-D, file 589, see no. 37, War Decree—Law no. 6945/45. Article II declared war on Japan; Article III is the quoted phrase. The philosophical significance of this declaration is that Argentina is saying that it has no quarrel with Germany; it is declaring war on the Third Reich only because the Reich is an ally of Japan.

41. On the Avra Warren Commission's activities, see NARS, R.G. 59, 711.35/4-2145, and 711.35/4-2345. More informative is in República Argentina, Ministerio de las Relaciones

Exteriores y Culto, *Guerra entre EEUU y los paises del Eje*, cabinet 7, file 26, vol. 12, "Actitud de la República Argentina–Misión Avra Warren." Spruille Braden is particularly caustic in his summation of the work of the commission. See Spruille Braden, *Diplomats and Demagogues: The Memoirs of Spruille Braden* (New Rochelle, N.Y., 1971), p. 320.

42. That Berle continued to despise Perón and describe the Farrell regime as Fascist is evident from FDRL, *The Diaries of Adolf A. Berle*, reel 5, frames 1129 and 1132–1137. His opposition to the compromise policy backed by Rockefeller and Stettinius is evident in FO-371-45015-02375, no. AS1349/317/51, p. (marked) 59, and especially FO-371-45015-02375, no. AS1550/317/51, p (marked) 119. Hull's statement is found in Hull, *Memoirs*, vol. 2, p. 1408.

43. Braden makes his intention of pushing a hard line unmistakably clear in *Diplomats and Demagogues*, p. 319. The best explanation of why Braden was selected is found in Gary Frank, *Juan Perón vs. Spruille Braden: The Story Behind the Blue Book* (Lanham, Maryland, 1980), pp. 56–57 and 135–136.

44. See FO-371-44690-02397, no AS5647/12/2, memorandum, n.p. It should be noted that Sir David Kelly, long-time British ambassador in Buenos Aires, personally liked Braden. See Sir David Kelly, *The Ruling Few* (London, 1952), p. 307.

45. On Braden's crusade to smash Perón, see Braden, *Diplomats and Demagogues*, pp. 322–328. A more objective study of these events is found in Frank, *Juan Perón vs. Spruille Braden*, pp. 57–86.

46. Braden gives his explanation of these events in *Diplomats and Demagogues*, pp. 355–356, and says the final decision was made by Harry S. Truman. Dean Acheson, *Present at the Creation: My Years in the State Department* (New York, 1964), p. 188, emphasizes the idea that Braden was responsible for persuading Byrnes and Truman to go ahead with the cancellation.

47. The FBI report is found in FDRL, Harry Hopkins Papers, box 140, FBI report of February 22, 1945. We suggest that pp. 1–15 of this report be compared with United States Department of State, *Consulation Among the American Republics with Respect to the Argentine Situation* (Washington, D.C., 1946), pp. 5–34.

48. For Byrnes's order to Murphy, see NARS, R.G. 59, 862.20235/11-2945, no. A-239. The role played by John M. Cabot and James Joice in assembling the *Blue Book* (advice, double-checking, etc.) is noted in NARS, R.G. 59, 862.20235/1-1446, no. 135, 862.20235/1-2341, no 173, and 862.20235/1-2946, no. 313.

49. See specifically, pp. 5–34 of *Consulation among the American Republics with Respect to the Argentine Situation*.

50. For Braden's opinion, see Frank, *Juan Perón vs. Spruille Braden*, pp. 104–105. The quotation and other material on John M. Cabot is from a letter by him to Professor Rout in July 1979 (undated).

51. Argentine response was relatively restrained. See *La Prensa*, February 13, 1946, and *La Nación*, Buenos Aires, Argentina, February 14, 1946. For other press commentary, see NARS, R.G. 59, 835.00/2-2346, nos. 132, 154, and 233, and 835.00/2-2546, nos. 135, 214, and 583. See also 835.00/2-2846, no 117.

52. FDRL, *The Diaries of Adolf A. Berle*, roll 5, frames 1125–1130, and 1135-1136.

53. Welles, *Where Are We Headed?*, p. 230.

54. The role played by left-wing elements in the Democratic party plus the continuing opposition of the liberal press to any accommodation is noted in several sources. See *The New York Times*, April 17, June 12, and September 30, 1946. See also Ernest R. May, "The Bureaucratic Politics Approach: U.S.-Argentine Relations, 1942–1947," in *Latin America and the United States: The Changing Realities*, ed. J. Cotler and R. Fagan (Stanford, 1974), pp. 133 and 154, Sumner Welles, *Where Are We Headed?*, pp. 219–220, and the George Messersmith Papers, University of Delaware, Newark, Delaware, ND 2007, pp. 10, 16–19, and 25–26.

55. See NARS, R.G. 59, 711.35/3-1846. and 710 Consultation 4/4-146 Circular Telegram. This message was sent out to U.S. embassies on April 1. It was officially announced on April 8, 710 Consultations 4/4-846.

56. Letter from the Honorable Spruille Braden to Professor Rout, December 8, 1977.

57. The George Messersmith Papers, ND 2007, pp. 1 (quotation) and 3. See also pp. 7 and 9, where Truman, Byrnes, and Messersmith join in criticizing Braden. The "complete support" declaration is also on p. 9.

58. On the clash between Messersmith and Braden in Washington, see George Messersmith Papers, ND 2007, pp. 12–14. Messersmith insisted that Truman and Byrnes promised him total support. Braden insisted exactly the opposite in *Diplomats and Demagogues*, pp. 358 and 361, and his letter of December 8, 1977.

59. For evidence of the Braden-Messersmith differences of opinion and their growing antipathies, see NARS, R.G. 711.35/6-1546, 711.35/6-2546, no. 230, and 835.00/8-1546, no. 583. Messersmith's criticisms of past policies and Braden's angry responses are found in 835.00/7-2246, memorandum, 835.00/8-1646, and 711.35/10-246 AW, 835.00/10-1546, no. 1004, and 862.20235/11-646, no. 378.

60. See *The New York Times*, January 2, 8, 14 (columns by James Reston), and 24, 1947, and NARS, 862.20235/2-1347, no. 1830, pp. 1–3, FW 862.20235/2-1347, and 835.60/2-747.

61. Quote is from a letter by the Honorable Spruille Braden to Professor Rout, December 8, 1977. Braden recreated this incident, emphasizing the president's use of salty language, in his *Diplomats and Demagogues*, p. 363.

62. Dean Acheson speaks of these events in *Present at the Creation*, pp. 189–190.

63. See NARS, R.G. 59, 711.35/4-247, no. 252, the quoted matter being from p. 2. This story also appeared in rather graphic detail in *La Nación*, Buenos Aires, July 29, 1972.

64. See NARS, R.G. 59, 862.20235/5-747, memorandum, p. 1. See also 862.20235/5-847, pp. 6–9, for Messersmith's supportive statements.

65. See NARS, R.G. 59, 862.20235/5-2347, no. 626.

66. See NARS, R.G. 59 862.20235/5-747, no. 395, 862.20235/5-847, no. 404, and especially Thomas Mann's comprehensive 711.35/5-1347, memorandum to Braden.

67. See *The New York Times*, June 4, 1947. In *Diplomats and Demagogues*, pp. 365 and 370, Braden explains that Messersmith was supposed to be removed, with his resignation being announced on June 30, 1947. Instead, a White House secretarial error necessitated that both actions be announced at once.

68. See George Messersmith Papers, ND 1293, p. 3.

69. See, in particular, ibid., ND 2006, p. 4, and ND 2007, p. 31. Braden, *Diplomats and Demagogues*, p. 370, leaves no doubt as to his feelings toward Truman.

70. For Braden's comment, see *The New York Times*, June 10, 1947.

71. Ibid., June 12, 1947.

72. See United States Department of State, *Foreign Relations of the United States—1947* (Washington, 1972—1973), vol. 8, pp. 171–172 and 221–225. On the naval purchases, see NARS, R.G. 84, 820.02, box 537, file 830-1947, no. 2471, p. 1.

73. See May, "The Bureaucratic Politics Approach: U.S.-Argentine Relations, 1942–1947," p. 148, and NARS, R.G. 84, 820.02, box 537, no. 824, p. 1.

74. On the junta's activities, see La República Argentina, Ministerio de Relaciones Exteriores y Culto, *Asuntos Varios—1945*, cabinet 7, box 46-D, file 589, no. 37, deals with confiscated companies whose funds were supposed to be liquidated. See also *Guerra entre EEUU y los paises del Eje*, file 26, vol. 19, annex 14 (1946), "Memorandum de la Embajador de EEUU sobre liquidación de la Compañía de Seguros Germano-Argentina." On other liquidations and U.S. protests, see NARS, R.G. 165, box 967, MID, *Axis Espionage and Propaganda in Latin America* (Washington, 1946), p. 98.

75. See La República Argentina, Ministerio de Relaciones Exteriores y Culto, *Guerra entre EEUU y los paises del Eje*, file 26, vol. 19, annex 25, 1947, n.p. The failure of the Supreme Court to rule on these issues is also noted here.

76. For this background story, see NARS, R.G. 820.02, box 533, *Report on the Case of Osmar Hellmuth* (hereafter referred to as *Case of Osmar Hellmuth*), pp. 2–4.

77. Ibid., p. 5. Apparently Capt. Eduardo Aumann, naval adjutant to Castillo, suggested that Harnisch involve himself in this affair. See NARS, R.G. 59, 862.20235/10-3147, no. 11208, p. 11.

78. *Case of Osmar Hellmuth*, pp. 5–7.

79. NARS, *DSGFOR*, T-120 series, reel 762, frames 356225–356226. See also R.G. 59, 862.20235/10-3147, no. 11208, p. 9.

80. On the U.S. position, which never actually changed from 1942 on, see NARS, R.G. 59, 711.35/184, pp. 1–4, and 835.00/7745, pp. 1–7. On the Japanese, see NARS, 835.24/7-2743, pp. 1–4, and *Magic Documents*, reel 3, frames 0506–0515.

81. See German Federal Republic, Bonn, Auswärtiges Amt, Abteilung Inland IIg, 105, *Akten Betreffend: Südamerika Tätigkeit des SD, der Abwehr, der Agenten und Polizeat-tachés, 1943–1944* (hereafter referred to as Inland IIg, 105, *Polizeattachés*), pp. 259833 and 259834.

82. *Case of Osmar Hellmuth*, p. 7.

83. Ibid., pp. 7–8.

84. For Luti's report, see La República Argentina, Ministerio de Relaciones Exteriores y Culto, *Guerra Europa-Informaciones de caracter general enviados por nuestra embajada en Alemania*, cabinet 7, box 16, file 161, Año 1942-43, Tomo III, #401, Luti a Gilbert, 26 de Septiembre de 1943, pp. 9-12. For the evidence of German interception, see German Federal Republic, Bonn, Auswärtiges Amt, Abteilund Inland IIg, 455, *Akten Betreffend: Südamerika SD-Meldungen aus Südamerika, 1940–43*, pp. E211020–E211022.

85. For these details, see *Case of Osmar Hellmuth*, p. 10. Ceballos was to be named to replace Luti if Hellmuth decided that Luti had to be replaced.

86. *Case of Osmar Hellmuth*, pp. 8–9.

87. The arms negotiation details and the quotation are from ibid., p. 10.

88. Ibid., pp. 11–12.

89. For Meynen's report of these events, see Inland IIg, 105, *Polizeattachés*, pp. 259818–259819. On Meynen's intention of preventing the mission, see ibid., pp. 259832–259833.

90. *Case of Osmar Hellmuth*, pp. 9–10, and NARS, R.G. 59, 862.20235/11-3147, no. 11208, p. 9. On Ludwig Freude's background, see R.G. 84, 820.02, box 533, no. 1166, November 6, 1946, pp. 3–4.

91. See NARS, R.G. 59, 862.20235/10-3147, no 11208, p. 9, *Case of Osmar Hellmuth*, pp. 9–10, and R.G. 84, 820.02, box 533, file: *Interrogations Made in Gemany, Interim Report of the Case of General Friedrich Wolf*, appendix C, p. VII, and Inland IIg, 105, *Polizeattachés*, pp. 259832–259833.

92. See NARS, R.G. 59, 862.20235/10-3147, no. 11208, p. 9.

93. See NARS, R.G. 84, 820.02, box 533, file: *Interrogations Made in Germany of Otto Reinebeck*, TC 21540, February 4, 1946, p. 11. Another verification of Peron's critical role is found in ibid., File: *Interrogations Made in Germany of Otto Reinebeck*, n.d., TC 20565, p. 5.

94. See Inland IIg, 105, *Polizeattachés*, p. 259814. Only a summary of the October 3, 1943, cable still exists. The memorandum covering its contents was sent to Counsellor Reinebeck.

95. See NARS, R.G. 84, 820.02, box 533, *The Case of General Friedrich Wolf*, appendix C, p. III, and *Interrogations Made in Germany of Otto Reinebeck*, TC 21540, February 4, 1946, p. 5.

96. Inland IIg, 105, *Polizeattachés*, pp. 259831 and 259835.

97. For the Paeffgen-Reinebeck conversations and the details noted, see NARS, R.G. 84, 820.02, box 533, *Interrogations Made in Germany of Otto Reinebeck*, TC 21540, February 4, 1946, p. 12.

98. NARS, R.G. 84, 820.02, box 533, *Case of General Friedrich Wolf*, appendix C, p. VII.

99. See NARS, R.G. 59, 862.20235/4-2646, *Testimoney of Andor Hencke*, TC 21537, p. 6. See also, *Magic Documents*, reel 8, frames 0254–0255.

100. NARS, R.G. 84, 820.02, box 533, *Case of General Friedrich Wolf*, appendix C, p. VII. According to Wolf, Hellmuth was "an innocent abroad, badly informed and very trusting." The English interrogators concluded that "as an amateur diplomat he was very much the innocent abroad. . . ." See *Case of Osmar Hellmuth*, p. 13.

101. *Case of Osmar Hellmuth*, p. 13. This was probably Camp 020, near London.

102. La República Argentina, Ministerio de Relaciones Exteriores y Culto, *Detención Consul Hellmuth*, cabinet 7, box 44 (no file number), 1943, telegram 3048, Consul-General Dário Quiroga to the foreign minister, November 4, 1943.

103. Ibid., telegram 00127, Hellmuth to González, November 9, 1943.

104. Ibid., telegram 1096, Pérez Quesada to Gilbert, November 17–18, 1943, no. 1100, November 18, 1943, and no 1102, November 19, 1943, Pérez Quesada to Gilbert.

105. Ibid., telegram 1100, November 17–18, 1943, and no. 1102, November 19, 1943, Pérez Quesada to Gilbert.

106. Ibid., telegram 696 (also numbered 190), Gilbert to Embassy, November 15, 1943. Gilbert demanded that the British respect the "inviolability" of Hellmuth's person and allow him to continue to Spain.

107. Ibid., telegram 1090 (also numbered 275), Carcano to Gilbert, November 15–16, 1943.

108. Ibid., telegram 1120 (also numbered 290), Carcano to Gilbert, November 26, 1943.

109. Ibid., telegram 1177 (also numbered 298), Carcano to Gilbert, December 10–11, 1943, 3 pp. Obviously Carcano was shocked, for he immediately sought new instructions.

110. Ibid. Additional evidence that the Argentians thought this and informed the Germans of their suspicion is seen in Inland IIg, 105, *Polizeattachés*, p. 259911. This memorandum dated January 29, 1944, specifically names Ludwig Freude as the tip-off man.

111. *Detención Consul Hellmuth*, telegram 748 (no. 205), December 17, 1943, Gilbert to Carcano. See also telegram 1203 (no. 307), December 22–23, 1943, Carcano to Gilbert.

112. The proposal was found in FO 371-37666-02237, no. AS126/4/2, minutes written by J.V. Perowne, January 5, 1944.

113. *Detención Consul Hellmuth*, telegram 1232 (no. 313), December 31, 1943, Carcano to Gilbert.

114. FO 371-37666-02231, no. AS126/4/2, minutes written by J.V. Perowne.

115. On the proposed sanctions, see the interview with Ambassador Norman Armour by Professor Rout, New York City, May 14, 1976. See also NARS, R.G. 59, 835.00/2899. On the role of the Bolivian revolution in strengthening U.S. resolve to punish Argentina, see 835.00/2258, no. 8461, pp. 5–6, and especially 835.20224/1, no. 13597, pp. 1–2. See also *Magic Documents*, reel 7, frame 0823, and reel 8, frames 0115–0119.

116. It is our conclusion that serious negotiations leading to the liquidation of the Hellmuth problem began after January 10, 1944, because that is the date of a message from Carcano to Gilbert in which the ambassador reports that British intelligence has no intention of allowing Hellmuth to be released. See *Detención Consul Hellmuth*, telegram 58 (also numbered 9), Carcano to Gilbert, January 10, 1944. Evidence of the nature of the deal between Argentina and Britain comes from two diplomatic sources. The most complete is República de Chile, Ministerio de Relaciones Exteriores, *Sección Confidencial de la Embajada en Estados Unidos, 1° Semestre, 1944*, no. 277/13, *Misión Hellmuth*, January 31, 1944, pp. 1–7. Ambassador Michels gives as his source the Argentine counselor (embassy in the

United States), Rudolfo García Arias. The second major source is Inland IIg, 105, *Polizeat-tachés*, NR. 4 (document also marked V.St.S pol NR. 28), pp. 259893 and 259894.

117. For these events, see *Detención Consul Hellmuth*, unnumbered, strictly confidential memorandum dated January 18, 1944.

118. News concerning Hellmuth's alleged membership in a German spy ring and the commencement of a large-scale spy hunt was announced by the Argentine government on January 21. See La República Argentina, Ministerio de Relaciones Exteriores y Culto, *Memoria del Ministerio de Relaciones Exteriores y Culto, Años 1943–1944* (Buenos Aires, 1945), pp. 32 and 34. The same announcement is noted in NARS, R.G. 59, 702.3552/3, no. 192, pp. 1–3.

119. República de Chile, Ministerio de Relaciones Exteriores, *Sección Confidencial de la Embajada en Estados Unidos, 1° Semestre, 1944*, 277/13, *Misión Hellmuth*, Michels to the foreign minister, January 31, 1944, p. 1.

120. FDRL, *Map Room Messages of President Roosevelt*, reel 3, message 552, frames 0802–0803.

121. *Detención Consul Hellmuth*, telegram 138 (also numbered 24), Carcano to Gilbert, January 25, 1944. The underlining of the terms was apparently supplied by someone in the Argentine Foreign Office.

122. *Memoria del Ministerio de Relaciones Exteriores y Culto, Años 1943–1944*, pp. 35–37.

123. Interview with Ambassador Armour by Professor Rout, May 14, 1976. A similar recognition concerning the predominant importance of the Hellmuth problem is found in Potash, *The Army and Politics*, p. 231.

124. See the interview with Ambassador Armour by Professor Rout, May 14, 1976.

125. See NARS, R.G. 59, 862.20235/2-2046, no. 565, pp. 1–8, and 862-20235/4-2046, TC 21542, *Interrogation of Walther Becker*, pp. 1–4. On December 29, 1943, Col. Alberto Vélez began meeting with Reinhard Spitzy, representative in Spain and Portugal of Waffen-union Skoda–Bruenn. See also NARS, *DSGFOR*, T-120 series, reel 762, frames 356197, 356198, 356220–356222, and 356240. See also Potash, *The Army and Politics*, p. 252. So long as the talks did not collapse, Perón's stock remained high with those officer elements who were unwilling to compromise with the United States in order to receive lend-lease weaponry.

126. See NARS, R.G. 165, box 2611, report R-102-46, I.6., file 3164.0600, *Latin America Subversive—Argentina*, n.p.

127. See NARS, R.G. 84, 820.02, *Interrogation of Theodor Paeffgen*, TC-21322, February 4, 1946, pp. 8–9, and particularly, *Interrogation of Otto Reinebeck*, TC-21540, February 4, 1946, p. 15. The man who acted as cutout between Brinkmann and Becker apparently was Alberto Bove Trabel. See NARS, R.G. 59, 862.2035/1-1546 (marked FBI-2-558 and 2-559), special report from legal attaché James P. Joice, Jr.

128. Inland IIg, 105, *Polizeattachés*, p. 259825. See also NARS, R.G. 84, 820.02, *Interroga-tion of Otto Reinebeck*, TC-21540, February 4, 1946, p. 15.

129. Inland IIg, 105, *Polizeattachés*, pp. 259839–25940. This message was sent to the SD from Argentina on November 24, 1943. Amt VI chief Schellenberg informed the German Foreign Office of this information on December 3.

130. NARS, R.G. 242, ML-171a, roll 23, message no. 525, n.p.

131. NARS, *DGSFOR*, F-120 series, reel 366, frames 291160–291163.

132. Ibid., frame 291162.

133. NARS, R.G. 59, 862.20235/10-3147, no. 11208, p. 10.

134. see NARS, R.G. 84, 820.02, box 533, *Interrogation of Otto Reinebeck*, TC-21540, February 4, 1946, pp. 14–15.

135. NARS, *DSGFOR*, T-120 series, reel 366, frame 291163. Harnisch claimed that he turned in his equipment only as a precaution.

136. Inland IIg, 105, *Polizeattachés*, pp. 259892–259893.

137. NARS, R.G. 84, 820.02, box 533, *Interrogation of Otto Reinebeck* (no TC number), January 24, 1946, p. 6.

138. On German sabotage in Spain in 1943–1944, Franco's displeasure, and Dieckhoff's complaints, see Heinz Höhne, *Canaris: Patriot im Zwielicht* (München, 1976), pp. 515–521.

139. NARS, *DGSFOR*, T-120 series, reel 366, frame 291168.

140. Ibid., frames 291153–291155. All that Keitel really agreed to do was to inform the chief of diplomatic mission in a neutral country of Abwehr attack plans.

141. Ibid., frame 291169.

142. NARS, R.G. 84, 820.02, box 533, *Interrogation of Otto Reinebeck* (no TC number), January 24, 1946, pp. 7–8.

143. Höhne, *Canaris,* pp. 524–525.

144. See NARS, R.G. 59, 862.20235/4-2046, TC-22636, *Interrogation of Andor Hencke,* January 2, 1946, p. 5.

145. See Potash, *The Army and Politics,* pp. 231–232, and Conil and Paz Ferrari, *Política exterior,* p. 138.

146. NARS, R.G. 59, 702.3552/11-2343, p. 1.

147. On "Ultra," see Peter Calvocoressi, *Top Secret Ultra* (New York, 1980), and Frederick W. Winterbotham, *The Ultra Secret* (New York, 1974).

148. *Magic Documents,* reel 8, frames 0617–0618.

149. See NARS, R.G. 319, MID 370.95, 360.2 to 383.3, box 176, memorandum, J. Edgar Hoover to Adolf Berle, November 4, 1943, p. 1.

150. The view and attitude of Ramón Castillo are discussed rather guardedly in La República Argentina, Ministerio del Interior, Policía Federal, *Memoria: Correspondiente al Año 1945* (Buenos Aires, 1950), pp. 11–13.

151. See NARS, R.G. 165, G-2, *Regional File, 1933–44, Argentina,* file 5930, box 101, military attaché report, March 3, 1944. In fact, Udry's only real political friend may have been Castillo.

152. See *Memoria: Correspondiente al Año 1945,* p. 16, for the details of the December 24, 1943 decree. See also Potash, *The Army and Politics,* p. 229n. On Emilio Ramírez's growing disenchantment with Juan Perón, see ibid., pp. 228–229 and 261.

153. *Memoria: Correspondiente al Año 1945,* p. 17.

154. On the replacement of Emilio Ramírez, see Potash, *The Army and Politics,* p. 229n. On Filippi's removal and dispatch to a post far away from the capital city, see NARS, R.G. 54, 862.20235/10-3447, no. 11208, enclosure 4, p. 2, and enclosure 5, p. 2.

155. *Memoria: Correspondiente al Año 1945,* pp. 17–18.

156. On Contal's problems with Perón, see NARS, R.G. 59, 862.20210/10-3147, no. 11208, enclosure 4, p. 3. See also R.G. 165, box 2611, G-2 Intelligence, entry 77/regional file, *Latin America—Subversives,* no. R-693-45, WD 209506, October 12, 1945.

157. NARS, R.G. 59, 862.20210/2326.

158. Concerning DeBardeleben's purpose and plans in Argentina, see NARS, R.G. 59, 862.20210/2364, /2447, /2461, and /2887.

159. See NARS, R.G. 59, 862.20210/2539, /2539a, /2541 1/2, and /2551.

160. See NARS, R.G. 59, 862.20210/2540 and /2655.

161. The story and the materials quoted here are from La República Argentina, Ministerio de Relaciones Exteriores y Culto, *Guerra entre E.E.U.U. y las paises del Eje: Actuación de la República Argentina,* memorandum, file 26, vol. 20, p. 13.

162. Information was supplied by letter from FBI Inspector Roger Young to Professor Rout, April 22, 1983.

163. See NARS, R.G. 59, 862.20235/1282. Proof that these loquacious individuals were part of the U.S.intelligence apparatus was made evident when these names were checked against the list found in NARS, R.G. 59, 862.20210/4-2145, no. 17783, enclosure 4.

164. On the quoted material and the arrest of SIS/Argentina agents, see the letter from Inspector Young to Professor Rout, April 22, 1983. On DeBardeleben's departure, see NARS, R.G. 59, 862.20210/2698.

165. Don Whitehead, *The FBI Story* (Bantam edition, New York, 1958), p. 268. Whitehead describes the surreptitious escape by sea as being effected by "Crandall's Navy." Whether by intent or accident, the name is incorrect; it should be "Crosby's Navy." See the letter from Inspector Boynton to Professor Rout, September 23, 1977.

166. See NARS, R.G. 59, 835.00/7-444, no. 717, pp. 1–3, for a listing of the total arrests between January and the end of June 1944. For the diplomatic pouch quote, see 835.00N/186, pp. 3–4.

167. NARS, R.G. 59, 862.20210/9-2244, no. 16155.

168. This information on the arrival and activity of Joice was provided by Source T, a former SIS/Argentina agent who was stationed in that country in 1944–1945. Letters to Professor Rout, March 4, 1980 and April 8, 1980.

169. See NARS, R.G. 59, 835.00N/186, p. 3.

170. See NARS, R.G. 59, 862.20210/4-2145, enclosure 4, and R.G. 59, 862.30235/5-1145, no. 961. See also letter from Source T, March 4, 1980, which states that U.S. agents were secretly allowed to enter and search the closed German embassy. He did not, however, provide an exact date. NARS, R.G. 173, FCC-RID, box 11, folder: *Argentina*, Letter, C.P. English to G.E. Stirling, July 7, 1945, indicates that the shuttered "German Embassy residence" was entered and examined on June 12–13, 1945. The possibility is strong that Source T simply misnamed the place examined.

171. This was the point made by Source T, letter of March 4, 1980. See also NARS, R.G. 59, 862.20235/8-245, no. 1735.

172. See NARS, R.G. 84, 820.02, box 533, *Memorandum, Johannes Siegfried Becker with Aliases*, pp. 32–33, and R.G. 59, 862.20235/4-1045, no. 5683, p. 4.

173. On Amorín's contact with British intelligence and Becker's moves, see NARS, R.G. 84, 820.02, box 533, *Memorandum, Johannes Siegfried Becker*, pp. 32–33, and R.G. 59, 862.20235/4-2347, no. 9666, enclosure 1, pp. 4–7.

174. Contacts with Brinkmann by these two agents of the Becker ring are acknowledged in NARS, R.G. 59, 862.20235/4-1847, 9610, p. 2, and R.G. 84, 820.02, box 533, ACC no. 59A 543, *Folder-Brinkmann* (1946), *Memorandum*, January 15, 1946, pp. 1–2 and especially 862.20235/4-2347, no. 9666, pp. 1–2 and enclosure 1, pp. 5–6.

175. See especially, NARS, R.G. 84, 820.02, box 533, *Interrogation of Otto Reinebeck*, TC 21540, February 4, 1946, p. 15.

176. Ibid., and R.G. 59, 862.20235/4-2347, no. 9666, p. 5.

177. *Memorandum, Johannes Siegfried Becker*, pp. 32–33, and NARS, R.G. 59, 862.20235/4-2347, no. 9666, p. 5.

178. See NARS, R.G. 84, 820.02, box 533, *Interrogation of Hans Haack*, TC 20565, n.d., p. 4.

179. *Memorandum, Johannes Siegfried Becker*, p. 33.

180. See copy of press release by the Argentine subsecretary of information, February 29, 1944, NARS, R.G. 165, box 967, *File: Germans Arrested in 1944 for Nazi Espionage*, and ibid., Special Intelligence Branch, AIS, SS-2143, March 11, 1944.

181. the list of those apprehended between January 29 and February 29, 1944, was from special FBI file no. 64-27943, provided by Inspector Boynton. The names found on one list were then compared against the list of German agents held in June 1945 (NARS, R.G. 59, 862.20235/6-1545, no. 178, n.p.), and with the list of January 25, 1946 (R.G. 84, 820.02 [861.5], *Arrest and Parole of Axis agents*, no. 712, pp. 1–2).

182. On the treatment of Harnisch in prison, see NARS, R.G. 59, 862.20235/10-3147, no. 11208, pp. 17–18. See also R.G. 165, box 966, *File: Argentina-Germany and Nazi Who's Who*, military attaché report, no. 10556, March 4, 1944, p. 1.

183. NARS, R.G. 84, 820.02, box 537, no. 11158, *Interrogation of Wolf Emil Franczok, alias Gustav Utzinger*, October 24, 1947, enclosure 2, p. 1.

184. See NARS, R.G. 59, 862.20235/10-3147, no. 11208, p. 17, and R.G. 165, box 966, *File: Argentina-Germany and Nazi Who's Who,* military attaché report no. 10566, March 4, 1944, p. 1.

185. NARS, R.G. 59, 862.20235/4-1847, no. 9610, pp. 3–4, and 862.20235/4-1247, no. 9666, pp. 5–7.

186. *Memorandum, Johannes Siegfried Becker,* pp. 33–37, and R.G. 59, 835.00/2376A, 862.20210/2583, 862.20235/4-1045, no. 5683, p. 13.

187. On Wolf's "stay behind" group, see NARS, R.G. 84, 820.02, box 533, *Interrogation of General Friedrich Wolf,* appendix B, p. 5. appendix D, pp. 11 and 13–14.

188. Concerning U.S. disbelief, see NARS, R.G. 59, 835.00/2376A, no. 266, p. 4, R.G. 165, box 967-SS-3901, military attaché report, April 17, 1944, and 835.00N/186, p. 2. For the British opinion, see FO 371-37726-X/M 03010, no. AS977/145/2.

189. See German Federal Republic, München, *Institut für Zeitgeschichte,* NG-4871, *Interrogation of Karl Gustav Arnold,* pp. 39–40. The official was Argentine naval captain Eduardo Ceballos, former naval attaché to Germany.

190. This conclusion is based on data found in FBI, Bureau Description File no. 64-27943, Subject: *German Agents in Latin America,* n.p.

191. See NARS, R.G. 59, 835.00/2849, no. 9682, pp. 2–3.

192. See NARS, R.G. 84, 820.02, box 533, *Interrogation of Otto Reinebeck,* TC 21540, February 4, 1946, p. 20.

193. Inland IIg, 105, *Polizeattachés,* pp. 259794–259797. On the SD order to Becker to find a place for a U-boat landing, see NARS, R.G. 84, 820.02, box 533, *Memorandum, Johannes Siegfried Becker,* p. 31.

194. Inland IIg, 105, *Polizeattachés,* pp. 259794–259795 and 259808–259809.

195. Ibid., pp. 259808–259809.

196. NARS, R.G. 84, 820.02, box 533, *Memorandum, Johannes Siegfried Becker,* p. 31.

197. On the orders given Burckhardt and Chantrain and their backgrounds, see NARS, R.G. 59, 862.20235/4-1045, 5683, pp. 18–19, *Memorandum, Johannes Siegfried Becker,* p. 39, and R.G. 165, *Axis Espionage and Propaganda in Latin America,* p. 63.

198. In NARS, R.G. 59, 862.202.35/4-1045, no. 5683, p. 19, Burckhardt states that he and Chantrain carried roughly one hundred thousand dollars in English pounds. R.G. 84, 820.02, box 537, no. 11158, *Interrogation of Wolf Emil Franczok,* p. 16, puts the amount at fifteen thousand pounds, divided into fifty packets of thirty ten-pound notes. This represents the low figure of sixty thousand dollars. NARS, R.G. 165, box 966, MID, *Axis Espionage and Propaganda in Latin America,* p. 63, gives the figure of twenty-five thousand pounds (i.e., one hundred thousand dollars).

199. No source explains what these drugs and chemicals actually were. On the value of these products, see NARS, R.G. 84, 820.02, box 537, no. 11158, *Interrogation of Wolf Emil Franczok,* p. 15. Here the value is given at one million Argentine pesos (about $238,000 at 4.2 Argentine pesos per dollar).

200. On Lange and Becker and their problems, see NARS, R.G. 59, 862.20210/6-745, n.p. (pages not marked consecutively), and R.G. 84, 820.02, box 533, *Memorandum, Johannes Siegfried Becker,* p. 30.

201. NARS, R.G. 59, 862.20210/6-745, n.p., and R.G. 84, 820.02, box 533, *Memorandum, Johannes Siegfried Becker,* pp. 36–37, and 862.20252/1-2545, no. 3902, enclosure 4, pp. 1–2. See also R.G. 59, *Interrogation of Dr. Theodor Paeffgen, State Department Special Interrogation Mission,* N1-WA, box 3, 1945–1946, pp. 5–6.

202. La República Argentina, Ministerio de Relaciones Exteriores y Culto, *Guerra entre E.E.U.U. y los países del Eje,* file 26, vol. 20, annex 10, no. 273, pp. 5–6.

203. Ibid. In this collection (see also annexes 20 and 30) are photographs of the raided farms and the seized radio equipment. On the back of several of the photographs, the dates when they were allegedly taken are listed. Several of these were marked "Junio" (June).

204. See NARS, R.G. 59, 862.20235/4-1045, p. 67.

205. On the Argentine invitation to participate in the raids of August 1944, see NARS, 862.20210/8-144, no. 1234, pp. 1–2, 862.20210/8-1744, no. 1305, 862.20210/8-1944, no. 2871, and 862.20210/8-2144, no. 1315.

206. A report from RID buttresses this conclusion. See NARS, R.G. 59, 862.20210/8-1744, no. 1305. The quote is from the Source T letter, March 4, 1980.

207. La República Argentina, Ministerio de Relaciones Exteriores y Culto, *Guerra entre E.E.U.U. y los paises del Eje,* file 26, vol. 20, annex 10, no. 273, p. 2. The U.S. story of these arrests can be found in NARS, R.G. 59, 862.20235/8-2944, enclosures 1–5.

208. See NARS, R.G. 59, 862.20235/4-2947, no. 9725, p. 6. The trick employed was to have a policeman pass himself off as a German and gain Utzinger's confidence by claiming to be sympathetic, and by promising to carry a message to Burckhardt.

209. See German Federal Republic, Bundesarchiv-Militärarchiv, Freiburg-im-Breisgau, Bestand: H27/6, *Attache-Abeteilung Pr. Pressetätigkeitsbericht für die Zeit von 1-9-30.9.44.*

210. *Guerra entre E.E.U.U. y los paises del Eje,* file 26, vol. 20, annex 2, pp. 3–4. See also NARS, R.G. 59, 862.20235/4-1045, no. 5683, no. p. 17.

211. For details of the pursuit and capture of Johannes Siegfried Becker, see NARS, R.G. 84, 820.02, box 533, *Memorandum, Johannes Seigfried Becker*, pp. 43–44.

212. See NARS, R.G. 242, ML-171a, roll 23, n.p.

213. See *Magic Documents*, reel 7, Magic summary no. 622, frame 0721, and summary no. 624, frame 0731.

214. NARS, R.G. 242, ML-171a, roll 23, n.p. All replies on this roll were carefully scrutinized, but all results were negative.

215. See NARS, R.G. 319, *German Espionage in Latin America* (hereafter referred to as *GELA*), pp. 144–146 and 153–162. See also German Federal Republic, München, *Institut für Zeitgeschichte,* NG-4871, *Interrogation Report of Karl Gustav Arnold*, pp. 19–20.

216. *Magic Documents*, reel 7, frames 0915–0916.

217. NARS, R.G. 59, 862.20210/6-745, n.p.

218. See *GELA*, pp. 144–146, and R.G. 59, 852.20225/1-2545, enclosure 2.

219. See Potash, *The Army and Politics*, p. 252, and NARS, *DSGFOR*, T-120 series, reel 761, frames 356107–356198.

220. Ibid., frames 356204–356206.

221. For Seraphín's confession, see NARS, R.G. 59, 862.20235/4-1045, no. 5683, pp. 30–35. On Seraphín's attempted suicide, see 862.20233/3-1245, no. 5561, p. 4.

222. NARS, R.G. 84, 820.02, no. 9774, box 537, *Sworn Statement of Juan Antonio Eugenio Prieto*, May 1, 1947, enclosure 1, p. 4.

223. For Lieberth's testimony, see NARS, R.G. 84, 820.02, no. 10549, box 537, *Report of Interrogation of Hans Lieberth*, May 8, 1947, p. 1, and enclosure 1, p.3.

224. See R.G. 84, 820.02, box 537, no. 11158, *The Interrogation of Wolf Emil Franzcok*, enclosure 4, pp. 5 and 13.

225. Ibid.

226. Ibid., enclosure 4, pp. 6–7, and R.G. 59, 862.20235/10-3147, no. 11208, p. 25.

227. For these statements on Koennecke, see NARS, R.G. 59, 862.20235/8-2944, enclosure 1, p. 2, 862.20235/10-3147, no. 11208, pp. 15–16, and R.G. 84, no. 820.02, box 537, no. 11158, *The Interrogation of Wolf Emil Franczok*, enclosure 3, pp. 3–4.

228. NARS, R.G. 59, 862.20235/10-3147, p. 23 and enclosure 6, p. 2.

229. See NARS, R.G. 84, 820.02, no. 10826, *Interim Report of Interrogation of Hans Harnisch, Wolf Franczok, alias Gustav Utzinger, and Josef Schroll, alias Alfonso Chantrain,* August 30, 1947, enclosure 2, p. 3, and also R.G. 59, 862.20235/10-3147, no. 11208, p. 25.

230. See NARS, R.G. 84, 820.02, box 537, no. 11158, *Interrogation of Wolf Emil Franczok*, p. 20, and 862.20235/10-3147, no. 11208, p. 25.

231. After a methodical search of Argentine Foreign Office records in 1978, we can say categorically that there is no record of an interrogation of Werner Koennecke available. A search of the Civil and Diplomatic Records Branch conducted by the authors with the assistance of archivist Kathy Nicastro produced no information not already found in 862.20235/8-2944, enclosure 1, p. 2. The only FBI material available is insignificant. See *GELA*, p. 166.

232. See FBI, file 64-27943 (dispatch 17175, p. 2), and NARS, R.G. 84, 820.02, box 537, *Arrest and Parole of Nazi Agents*, no. 712, January 25, 1946, p. 3, 862.20235/6-1545, p. 2, and 862.20235/10-3147, no. 11208, enclosure 6, p. 5.

233. On the reshaping of confessions after the arrest of Becker, see NARS, R.G. 84, 820.02, no. 10826, *Interim Report of Interrogation of Hans Harnisch*, etc., pp. 2–3. On the reduction of the confession to about fifty pages, ibid., p. 2. On the growing relationship between Johannes Siegfried Becker and Ludwig Freude, see R.G. 84, 820.02, box 537, no. 11158, *The Interrogation of Wolf Emil Franczok*, pp. 20–21, and also R.G. 59, 20235/4-2347, no. 9666, p. 9.

234. For the total sum reported, see La República Argentina, Ministerio de Relaciones Exteriores y Culto, *Guerra entre E.E.U.U. y los países del Eje*, file 26, vol. 20, annex 3, *Policía Federal, Coordinación Federal*, no. 273, annex 10, n.p. On the theft of goods and money by various officers, see NARS, R.G. 84, 820.02, box 537, no. 1158, *The Interrogation of Wolf Emil Franczok, alias Gustav Utzinger*, p. 10, and enclosure 6, pp. 1, 2, and 6. See also R.G. 59, 862.20235/4-2147, no. 9617, p. 3.

235. See NARS, R.G. 59, 862.20235/4-1045, no. 5693, pp. 21–22. The figure given the Uruguayan police is from 862.20233/3-1245, no. 5561, p. 5. The high figure is from R.G. 84, 820.02, box 537, no. 11158, *The Interrogation of Wolf Emil Franczok*, p. 15.

236. On the phony sale of the drugs and the retention of the money by the Coordinación Federal, see, NARS, R.G. 84, 820.02, box 537, no. 11158, *The Interrogation of Wolf Emil Franczok*, pp. 15–16. On the nationalization of Química Bayer and the long court fight into 1948, see La República Argentina, Ministerio de Relaciones Exteriores y Culto, *Guerra entre E.E.U.U. y los países del Eje*, vol. 19, annex 20, 1947, n.p., and annex 24, 1947, n.p.

237. See NARS, R.G. 59, 862.20235/11-646, no. 1166, pp. 2–3, 862.20235/4-848, pp. 4–5, and R.G. 84, 820.02 (800-Compliance), box 533, no. 378, November 27, 1946, pp. 1–2.

238. See NARS, R.G. 165, box 2611, G-2 Intelligence, *Entry 77/Regional File, Latin America, Subversive*, no. 2097, September 1945, p. 1, and R.G. 59, 862.20235/9-2145, p. 1.

239. NARS, R.G. 84, 820.02 (800-Compliance), box 533, no. 378, November 27, 1946, p. 3.

240. See NARS, R.G. 59, 862.20235/11-646, no. 1166, p. 4, for the May 8, 1935, filing, the October 27, 1943, decree, and decision of September 21, 1945. The passport data is from *The New York Times*, March 19, 1946.

241. For the best description of the power struggle of October 9–17, 1945, and of Perón's early defeat and final triumph, see Potash, *The Army and Politics*, pp. 266–282.

242. On the offer of a place to hide, see NARS, R.G. 59, 862.20235/11-646, no. 1166, p. 7. For the burning of the deportation orders, see R.G. 59, 862.20235/10/3147, no. 11208, p. 24.

243. NARS, R.G. 59, 862.20235/11-646, no. 1166, pp. 4–5. According to Hans Harnisch, the Mendoza decision was rigged with Perón pulling the strings. See especially 862.20235/10-3147, no. 11208, p. 24.

244. See NARS, R.G. 59, 862.20235/7-746, and R.G. 84, 820.02, box 1930, *Folder: 820.02— 1946*, no. 2813, May 17, 1946, attached to memorandum dated January 2, 1946, from Mr. Post to John Cabot. On Rudolf Freud's position, see Robert D. Alexander, *Juan Domingo Perón* (New York, 1965), p. 213.

245. See R.G. 84, 820.02 (800-Compliance), box 533, no. 378, November 27, 1946, p. 5, for the Schleuter and Wolf controversies and the quote.

246. This revelation came secretly from Carlos del Campillo, an Argentine federal appeals court judge. See NARS, R.G. 59, 867.20235/10-246, p. 2.

247. Letter from the Honorable John Cabot to Professor Rout, June 13, 1979.

248. See NARS, R.G. 59, 862.20235/6-1545, no. 126, pp. 1–5. On June 16, 1945, the SIS/Argentina obtained a list that was allegedly complete and authentic. In fact, it was neither.

249. NARS, R.G. 165, box 2611, G-2 Intelligence, *Entry 77/ Regional File, Latin American Subversive*,200348, R-620-45, September 7, 1945.

250. For evidence of the judge's procedural action, see NARS, R.G. 862.20235/12-745, pp. 1–4.

251. See NARS, R.G. 59, 862.20235/12-745, p. 4, *La Nación*, Buenos Aires, Argentina, May 24, 1947, and La República Argentina, Ministerio de Relaciones Exteriores y Culto, Dirección de Informacion al Exterior, *Nota de su Excelencia el Señor Ministro de Relaciones Exteriores y Culto, Dr. Juan I. Cooke, dirigida en nombre del gobierno Argentina a los representantes diplomáticos Americanos acreditados en la República, el 24 de Marzo de 1946, exponiendo los puntos de vista del gobierno Argentina ante las aseveraciones del "libro azul"* (Buenos Aires, 1946), pp. 32–38.

252. A list of these deportees is found in NARS, R.G. 59, 862.20235/5-1247, no. 249, p. 2.

253. On the escape of Eickenberg and Bücker from deportation despite the issuance of deportation orders, see R.G. 59, 862.20235/2-1546, A-172, and NARS, R.G. 165, box 2611, *G-2 Regional File, 1933-44, Folder: Latin American Subversive—Argentina*, military attaché to MID, no. 105-46, February 19, 1946, p. 1. Further information on this trio is found in 862.20235/10-3147, no. 11208, pp. 19 and 25, enclosure 2, p. 3, and 862.20235/4-2347, no. 9666, p. 12.

254. For the Claus Watjen story, see NARS, R.G. 84, 820.02, memorandum, box 533, May 11, 1946, and R.G. 59, 800.20210/6-2546, no. 229, pp. 1–3, and enclosure 1, pp. 1–4. The case is explicated in full in República Argentina, Ministerio de Justicia e Instrucción Pública, *Fallos de la Corte Suprema de Justica de la Nación* (Buenos Aires, 1948), vol. 204, pp. 616–617.

255. See NARS, R.G. 84, 820.02, box 537, no. 1158, *The Interrogation of Wolf Emil Franczok*, enclosure 6, p. 3. See also R.G. 59, 862.20235/4-2147, no. 9619, enclosure 1, pp. 1–2, and 862.20235/4-2347, no. 9666, p. 9.

256. NARS, R.G. 59, 862.20235/4-546, and /6-2646, and /9-2046, p. marked "16" on the unconstitutionality of decree no. 4842/946.

257. See NARS, R.G. 59, 862.20235/9-2046, no. 821, enclosure 2, p. 10. A more complete summary is found in República Argentina, Ministerio de Justicia y Instrucción Pública, *Jurisprudencia Argentina*, vol. 3 (Buenos Aires, 1946), pp. 739–742.

258. NARS, R.G. 59, 862.20235/4-1046, enclosure to dispatch 2483, p. 1.

259. See La República Argentina, Ministerio de Relaciones Exteriores y Culto, *Guerra entre E.E.U.U. y los paises del Eje*, file 26, vol. 21, pp. 14–15.

260. NARS, R.G. 59, 862.20235/4-1847, no. 9610, p. 2, 862.20235/4-2347, no. 9666, p. 9, and 862.20235/10-3147, no. 11208, p. 27, and enclosure 7, p. 1.

261. NARS, R.G. 84, 820.02, no. 10826, box 533, *Interim Report of Interrogation of Hans Harnisch*, etc., enclosure 1, p. 2.

262. Ibid.

263. See NARS, R.G. 59, 862.20235/4-2347, p. 11.

264. Ibid.

265. A list of those arrested after thirty days is found in NARS, R.G. 84, 820.02, box 537, file marked: *Arrest and Parole of Axis Agents*, December 6, 1946. The unfavorable comment noted is from ibid., no. 10826, box 533, *Interim Report of Hans Harnisch*, etc., p. 1.

266. NARS, R.G. 59, 862.20235/2-1247, no. 1844, p. 1.

267. Ibid., and 862.20235/2-1347, no. 1850, p. 2. Opposing commentaries are found in 711.35/3-3147, no. 332, 835.40/2-747, Memorandum, Braden to Acheson, and 711.35/2-2147.

268. NARS, R.G. 165, box 2611, G-2 Intelligence, *Entry 77/Regional File, Latin America Subversive*, 1715-210887, Argentina no. 930; September 29, 1945.

269. NARS, R.G. 84, 820.02, box 532, *Arrests and Parole of Axis Agents*, July 17, 1946, pp. 1–2.

270. See, for example, NARS, R.G. 59, 862.20235/7-2546, pp. 1–3.

271. See NARS, R.G. 59, 862.20235/4-2347, no. 9666, p. 12, and 862.20235/10-3147, no. 11208, p. 20, on Captain Rodríguez's removal.

272. See NARS, R.G. 59, 862.20235/10-3147, no. 11208, pp. 22 and 27–28, and R.G. 84, 820.02, box 537, no. 1158, *The Interrogation of Wolf Emil Franczok*, enclosure 5, pp. 2–4.

273. Of the people deported, the pair who could provide the most damaging testimony, Utzinger and Harnisch, were not turned over to U.S. interrogators until June 26, 1947. By that time, both Truman (June 3) and the State Department (June 10) had declared themselves satisfied with Argentina's compliance. See NARS, R.G. 59, 862.20235/7-1547.

274. NARS, R.G. 59, 862.20235/4-848, no. 332, p. 3. See especially *La Prensa*, November 11, 1947.

275. For the Ernst Hoppe story, see NARS, R.G. 59, 862.20235/1-846, no. 1736, and 862.20235/10-2945, no. 2710. The court case is in La República Argentina, Ministerio de Relaciones Exterories y Culto, *Guerra entre E.E.U.U. y los paises del Eje*, file 26, vol. 20, annex 7, 1947, Ministry of Justice and Public Education, file 02098/947, n.p.

276. NARS, R.G. 59, 862.20235/10-3147, no. 11208, p. 23.

277. NARS, R.G. 59, 862.20235/1-748, no. 15, and *The New York Times*, January 1, 1948.

278. On Ludwig Freude, see Ladislas Farago, *Aftermath: Martin Bormann and the Fourth Reich* (New York, 1974), pp. 207 and 226. On Enrique González, see La República Argentina, Archivo Nacional, Buenos Aires, Department of Photography, case 745.

279. On the return of the persons mentioned to Argentina after 1949, see German Federal Republic, West Berlin, *Deutsch Dienststelle*, Geschaftszeichen VI/A-677, letter to Professor Rout, March 26, 1982. On Hans Harnisch, see La República Argentina, Ministerio de Relaciones Exteriores y Culto, *Guerra entre E.E.U.U. y los paises del Eje* (no year listed), Coordinación Federal to the foreign minister, no. 1775, September 24, 1948, pages marked 20–21.

280. Letter from Inspector Young to Professor Rout, October 26, 1982, and letter from Larry R. Strawderman, CIA, to Professor Rout, March 14, 1983.

281. A good example is Vincent and Nan Buranelli, *Spy/Counterspy: Encyclopedia of Espionage* (New York, 1981), p. 27. This account has Becker being deported back to Germany in late 1945.

282. See NARS, R.G. 59, 862.20235/7-1147, p. 1.

283. NARS, R.G. 84, 820.02, box 533, folder: *Whereabouts of Formerly Deported Axis Personalities*, September 7, 1947. On Mittlebach's GOU connection and Perónist loyalty, see Potash, *The Army and Politics*, pp. 185, 210, 215, and 272.

284. See Conil Paz and Ferrari, *Política Exterior*, pp. 160–161, Blanksten, *Perón's Argentina*, pp. 415 and 437–438, and Marvin Goldwert, *Democracy, Militarism and Nationalism in Argentina, 1930–1966: An Interpretation* (Austin, 1972), p. 92.

285. See the letter from the Honorable Spruille Braden to Professor Rout, December 8, 1977. See also Frank, *Juan Perón vs. Spruille Braden*, pp. 87–88. Virtually the same thing is said in *The New York Times*, January 6, 1946, and *Consultation Among the American Republics*, pp. 2 and 17–18.

286. Braden, *Diplomats and Demagogues*, p. 366.

287. For the von der Becke report, see La República Argentina, Ministerio de Relaciones Exteriores y Culto, *Dirección de Asuntos Políticos: Commentarios sobre la Guerra*, "Consideración política-militar de los paises en lucho," cabinet 7, box 50, file 633, November 20, 1943, pp. 1–7 for the quoted materials.

288. On Perón's certainty of continued great power warfare, see NARS, R.G. 59, 835.20/123, enclosure 3, pp. 2–3. On the comments concerning World War II and Argentina's neutrality, see Blanksten, *Perón's Argentina*, pp. 411–414 and 423–424, and Alexander, *Juan Domingo Perón*, p. 214–215.

9

Conclusion

I. Operation "South Pole" and Other Failures

In May 1939, Army Lt. Joachim Rudloff, traveling in mufti, reached Buenos Aires and promptly closeted himself with naval attaché Capt. Dietrich Niebuhr. Rudloff was bringing word of the intention of Col. Erwin Lahousen, commander of Abwehr Abteilung II, to create a super secret sabotage unit which would be separate from all Abteilung I (secret intelligence) groups, and responsible only to Berlin headquarters. Lahousen assumed that although the South American governments might be indifferent to most German intelligence activities, these same regimes would feel threatened once British ships began blowing up in their harbors. Hence, Lahousen's intention of creating a select group of saboteurs, unknown to other Abwehr networks and therefore relatively safe from hostile penetration.[1]

Of course, recruiting the kind of operatives needed would require, among other things, a knowledge of those *Reichsdeutschen* who might make good saboteurs. Since Lahousen lacked such information, Rudloff's task was to obtain the names of potential recruits from Niebuhr. How many of these were passed on by the naval attaché is unknown, but in May 1939, Rudloff enlisted Karl Otto Gohl, a German engineer working for the Brazilian government, and Albert Julius von Appen, a Hamburg-American shipping line inspector in Valparaíso, Chile. Both men agreed to travel to Germany for training at the Abwehr sabotage school at Charlottenburg, in Berlin, and to assist in the enlistment of other potential saboteurs.

By January 1940, these men had returned (via the USSR and Japan) to their homes in Chile and Brazil. Six months later, they were joined by Georg Konrad Friedrich Blass (code name: Dr. Brown), a self-proclaimed university professor who had been selected by Lahousen as sabotage chief for South America. Summoning his charges to Rio de Janeiro in June 1940, Blass explained that operations against British shipping could begin only after he received a communication from Berlin which included the word *cyclops*. Each of the various regional leaders would be informed of this development by means of a telegram which extended birthday greetings. In the meantime, they were to remain inactive and, most of all, unknown to other Abwehr units.[2]

On November 23, 1940, Blass sent a coded cable to Abteilung II stating that Operation "South Pole" (i.e., the placing of bombs aboard British freighters in South American ports) could begin at any time.[3] At that time, "Dr. Brown" commanded a network of almost thirty agents. The principal operatives were:

> 1. Karl Otto Gohl (code name: Hirsch), who was the chief of operations in Brazil.
> 2. Kurt Heuer (code name: Hirth), who was stationed in Callao, Peru.
> 3. Albert Julius von Appen (code name: Apple), who was the chief of operations in Argentina, Chile, and Peru.
> 4. Boris Dreher (code name: Bohrer), who was stationed in Santiago, Chile.
> 5. Rudolf Max Poensgen (code name: Karl Wehrt), who was stationed in Cali, Colombia.
> 6. Hans Lahrius (code name: Peter Paul), who was stationed in Barranquilla, Colombia.
> 7. Ernst Gerhard Roggemann (code name: Gersten), who was stationed in Caracas, Venezuela.
> 8. Wilhelm Lange (code name: Fish), who was stationed in Buenos Aires, Argentina.[4]

Despite Blass's optimism, Abteilung II headquarters never sent the *cyclops* message. As far back as February 1940, Dietrich Niebuhr had advised Lahousen that Operation "South Pole" would cause violent reactions by the South American governments, and the result would be that the collection of intelligence (i.e., ship arrivals and sailings, war production news) would be adversely affected. In other words, the Abwehr in South America could blow up ships or obtain intelligence information, but the existing situation did not allow for the effective execution of both tasks simultaneously. With these alternatives established, Niebuhr did not hesitate to state his preference. At that time, both Wilhelm Lange and Julius von Appen were demanding permission to start planting bombs; it was also in February 1940 that Niebuhr asked for and received a temporary restraining order affecting those two agents.[5]

Interestingly, Georg Blass claims that after he had been in Brazil for a year, he sent a message to Abteilung II urging the postponement of "South Pole."[6] Conceivably, Niebuhr's opinion may have had some impact, but the more potent inhibitors were probably Admiral Canaris's alleged aversion for the sabotaging of shipping and the German Foreign Office's hope of maintaining Latin American neutrality in the conflict.[7] In essence, a complex of circumstances and higher priorities kept "South Pole" on the shelf until the virtual severance of effective communications between the Reich and South America made effective implementation of the scheme improbable.

For doing nothing except remaining potentially ready to act, Berlin paid Georg Blass and his aides $105,000 in 1939–1941.[8] Yet what these men did on their own may accurately depict both the possibilities and limitations of "South Pole," had it been executed. For example, Wilhelm Lange, sabotage leader in Argentina, was determined to take action. Despite Niebuhr's February 1940 prohibition, but with Albert von Appen's connivance, Lange arranged to have two bombs placed aboard the British freighter *Gascony*. On June 10, one of these exploded, damaging the ship's engines, blowing a hole in its hull, and killing the Argentine stevedore who brought the bomb on board. This incident sparked a special police investigation, and instead of praise and a medal, Lange's actions earned him a scathing denunciation from Niebuhr and a subsequent reprimand from Blass.[9]

The only other known operations were undertaken by Karl Otto Gohl in Brazil. In November and December 1939, he attempted to put delayed action bombs aboard two British vessels, but they do not appear to have exploded. Four years later, after Brazil had declared war on the Reich, Gohl and Blass conceived of a plot to blow up the Cubatão hydroelectric plant, then the largest in Brazil, and a major source of light and power for the state of São Paulo. The inability to obtain enough explosives without alerting the suspicions of the police foiled that proposed action, but Gohl wasn't through yet. With the aid of two assistants, he planned to dynamite the water pipes at the Cubatão plant. The explosives were actually taken to the plant site, but "circumstances arose which caused Gohl to abandon the plan." If any additional sabotage operations were attempted by the "South Pole" ring, they remain unrecorded.[10]

Amazingly, the detection and apprehension of the Abwehr sabotage group occurred largely by accident. Albert von Appen contacted Johannes Szeraws, and on March 24 and April 24, 1942, the PYL radioman sent two messages from "Apple" intended for Abteilung II. The first informed headquarters that Kurt Heuer in Peru was being repatriated to Germany via the United States, and the second asked that money be sent directly to Chile, since "Apple" claimed to be low on sabotage funds.

The response that came from Berlin on May 1, 1942, was loaded with displeasure. Appen was criticized for revealing his identity to an Abteilung I unit (i.e., the FMK "Valparaíso" group) and for using that unit's radio facilities, and he was ordered to break off all contact. The fears of Abteilung II headquarters proved justified, for the RID intercepted all these messages, and the FBI Technical Laboratory quickly deciphered them. Still, conclusive evidence was lacking, and while the SIS/Chile believed that von Appen was "Apple," the Chilean DGII questioned the man on October 27, 1942, and then released him.[11]

The dénouement of this situation came in January 1945, when Chile declared war on the Axis, and a number of mysterious ship fires took place in Valparaíso, Coquimbo, and Antofagasta. Just as Niebuhr had predicted in 1940, the Juan Ríos government suspected that German saboteurs might be causing these "accidents." A German national and AO member, Albert von Appen had been relegated from Valparaíso to a small town in Chile early in 1943. In March 1945, he was suddenly ordered to Santiago where, on the twenty-fifth of that month, he was grilled continuously for seventeen hours. Not surprisingly, he cracked, and since he knew all about the sabotage operations in the various South American states, the DGII was able to complete the roll-up of the sabotage group simply by sending on the names to security police in Colombia, Brazil, and Argentina. In less than a month after von Appen's confession, virtually all of the "South Pole" agents were behind bars.[12]

This hapless history of the "South Pole" ring bears consideration chiefly because of what it reveals about the overall problems of German intelligence in Latin America from 1939 to 1945. For example, it is difficult to believe that the Abwehr leadership was oblivious to the fact that the sabotage ring's activities might seriously affect other intelligence efforts. If, in fact, the sabotage ring was worth creating and deploying, then it should have been put to use. On the other hand, if Abteilung II believed that conditions militated against activating the sabotage unit (as Niebuhr had advised in February 1940), then there was no reason to send Georg Blass to supervise "South Pole" activities. The Abwehr leadership in Berlin seemed unable to coordinate its Latin American operations or understand what had to be done in order to attain the ends desired.

Another of the "South Pole" unit's preeminent difficulties was its continuing inability to obtain instructions from Berlin. Recall that in May 1942, Abteilung II criticized Albert von Appen for using the PYL transmitter to send out information. Appen's actions proved fatal, but the question is: Since the "South Pole" group had no clandestine radio of its own, how else was "Apple" going to get in touch with Berlin?

Berlin headquarters had supplied the South American sabotage group with a drop address in Rome, but with the British intercepting and scrutinizing transatlantic mail, the security of this link became highly questionable. Furthermore, Appen could not have known it, but with the United States intercepting transoceanic cable traffic, that means of communication was no longer secure, either. After the war, Georg Blass would lament to his captors that once Brazil broke relations with Germany in January 1942, communications with his superiors in Berlin became virtually nonexistent.[13] His contention, which would appear to be justified, was that Abteilung II created a South American ring and then left it in the lurch when communications difficulties developed.

In fact, not only Abteilung II, but the entire Abwehr operation in Latin America suffered grieviously from transatlantic communications difficulties. Given the Anglo-American control of the sea, air, and communications links, by 1941 the most secure means of passing sensitive information between Germany and South America had become the clandestine radio. With so much dependent upon secure radio communications, only the strongest ciphers should have been employed in transatlantic radio traffic. Instead, the primitive ciphers utilized were easily broken and, as a result, the Abwehr networks in Brazil, Chile, and Mexico were cut to pieces. Why were such weak codes used for so long in 1941–42? Certainly logistics was partially responsible for the problem. This contention was buttressed by naval Capt. Herbert Wichmann, commander of Ast Hamburg during World War II, who explained to us that the Abwehr "did not have the opportunity to get good codes to the individual V-men in South America."[14]

The point Wichmann made is highlighted by the fact that Albert von Appen and Karl Gohl, the only "South Pole" recruits to study sabotage techniques in Germany, received a total of five days' training each.[15] Much as these agents were not really trained saboteurs, the Abwehr was simply not ready to fight the kind of struggle it would eventually be asked to fight. With Hitler planning a short, continental campaign, the weaknesses of the Latin American networks were not so obvious, nor so important. But when the war did not end in the winter of 1940–41, and the Atlantic Ocean became a decisive theater of conflict, the shortcomings of the Latin American Abwehr groups became glaringly apparent and practically irreparable. There was no time to give the agents better training or stronger cover identities, nor supply them with large amounts of sophisticated equipment. Forced to undertake critical functions in a region where a major intelligence campaign had not been expected, the Abwehr could have committed fewer errors, but eventual defeat could never have been prevented, merely postponed.

As for the SD, serious involvement in Latin America came too late to be considered as anything but a stopgap measure. Political intelligence was the SD's forte, but within months after his January 1943 return, Johannes Siegfried Becker probably knew that there was no way he was going to obtain much secret data about U.S. political activity. But with the Abwehr organization faltering, Becker's de facto job became the maintenance of both the strategic metals traffic and the "Bolívar" radio network. As a rescuer, he enjoyed some success, and his fanatical leadership reenergized the German intelligence apparatus in Argentina.

But holding the line was not sufficient action for Becker, an activist with a decided taste for political intrigue. Using the Hellmuth mission as the prime example, it seems evident that Becker's operational theory was that any action which fostered Argentine nationalism would exasperate the United States, possibly distracting Washington's attentions from the European theater of war. While the theory is simplistic, the critical problem was that Becker was a true believer; apparently, he never imagined that Germany lacked weapons to sell. As for the tanker *Buenos Aires*, even if the Germans pledged to release it, no assurance was given that the vessel would obtain fuel, a crew, or permission to go through the Anglo-American blockade unscathed.

SD headquarters in Berlin could have corrected Becker's obliviousness. It should have taken the time to find out whether the German navy really intended to release the *Buenos Aires*. But to do any of these things would have necessitated facing the problem of whether the proposed mission should have been sanctioned. It would also have forced the SD to take a good look at the Reich's real position, and raised serious questions about the purpose and prospects of its South American operations. Naturally, the SD was unprepared to do these things. Thus, ideological considerations dictated that the tail be allowed to wag the dog, even though this was in the interest of neither the SD nor the Reich.

Perhaps a fitting judgment concerning SD and Abwehr operations in Latin America is this: The German intelligence services were able to attract and recruit some capable personnel, but they did not often use them to the best advantage.

II. From SIS to CIA

On May 25, 1940, Adolf Berle expressed satisfaction that President Roosevelt was feverishly pushing ahead with defense mobilization plans. At the same time, the assistant secretary's comments were freighted with a good deal of apprehension. In his opinion, many of the actions taken were of the helter-skelter variety and devoid of any consideration of possible consequences. He feared that the nation must eventually pay for both its lack of preparation and its subsequent rush to repair its deficiencies.[16]

When one recalls the rather informal manner in which the SIS was created, Berle's apprehensions seem partially justified. J. Edgar Hoover won his fight to control the new service, but his capabilities as a counterspy czar were unknown. Furthermore, no plan for coordinating the activities of SIS agents with Latin American diplomatic staff requirements was even considered until mid-1941. As for the legal attachés eventually assigned to these posts, many lacked both regional experience and the necessary linguistic skills.

Fortunately this makeshift organization would receive decisive support from other quarters. The legal attachés were often inexperienced and hastily trained, but they were the representatives of the predominant economic and military power in the hemisphere. This meant that, except in Argentina, they could count on receiving at least minimal cooperation from the security forces of the country to which they were assigned. Equally important was the fact that these attachés would regularly receive copies of decoded Abwehr messages from the FBI Technical Laboratory and priceless information based on the "Magic" intercepts. Provided with the ability to look over the Germans' shoulders, as it were, the SIS was able to compensate for nearly all of its otherwise critical deficiencies.

While the technical advantages played a big role in the undercover struggles, the human factor should not be underestimated. SIS agents received vital information, but days and weeks of tailing suspects and checking out clues would be necessary before a German spy ring was fully uncovered. Several legal attachés—specifically Gus Jones in Mexico,

Jack West in Brazil, and Francis Crosby in Argentina—demonstrated unusual talents, proving themselves to be counterspy masters with a knack for the job. For the others, patience, determination, and strong, comfortable shoes were the factors which produced favorable results. In sum, technical brilliance in cryptography and radio interception plus hard work by field agents proved to be the unbeatable combination which made victory possible.

While he may be the man some Americans love to hate, the bulk of the credit for the defeat of the German intelligence services in Latin America has got to be given the man who put the SIS together, J. Edgar Hoover. Yet the FBI boss's most prudent decision was possibly the product of his oft-manifested egoism. Recall that in 1940–41, Hoover fought a running battle with MID representative Brig. Gen. Sherman Miles over the division of authority for intelligence activities in Latin America. SIS leaders and military attachés did effectively cooperate in the countries where they were stationed, but Hoover refused to grant a special area of precedence to military attachés, and thereby dilute his absolute authority in Latin American intelligence affairs.

Obviously, the United States and German situations were different. Still, the fact to be recognized is that the division of authority between the Abwehr and SD did nothing to enhance the performance of either group in Latin America. In Argentina, for example, where cooperation of a sort was sometimes achieved, separate smuggling organizations were maintained until 1944, and a fictitious division of "Bolívar" network responsibilities was necessary in order to obtain the sanction of the rival chiefs in Berlin. Hoover's problems were not comparable, but he could and did move his agents around at will,[17] demonstrating a measure of flexibility which would not have been available to him had it been necessary to consult the State Department, ONI, or MID before taking such steps. Particularly when such incidents as the Heinz Lange-Ludwig von Bohlen contretemps are reviewed, the advantage of having a single regional authority with primary responsibility for intelligence affairs would seem indisputable.

Former SIS operatives with whom we communicated were unanimous in their pride in their World War II efforts, insistent that their activities were limited to counterespionage, and devoted to J. Edgar Hoover.[18] Nevertheless, few of these former operatives were anxious to detail their post-1946 experiences. A basic reason for their reticence was certain changes which occurred after September 1945. At that time, United States leaders concluded that some unified, worldwide secret intelligence mechanism ought to be developed to further the security of the nation. Among the losers in the struggle to hang on to an intelligence fiefdom was J. Edgar Hoover. Between July 1946 and April 1947, the new Central Intelligence Group (CIG) proceeded to replace the SIS organization south of the Rio Grande.[19]

Amazingly enough, the last post taken over by the CIG, Port-au-Prince, Haiti, was then directed by the first legal attaché to Brazil, Jack

West.[20] With his departure in mid-March 1947, the SIS saga came to an end—but only legally and administratively. When some SIS officers departed, they turned over to their CIG replacements not just office and equipment keys, but lists of informants, and other data as well. Indeed, some SIS officers and informants joined the CIG, remaining with the organization when it was folded into the CIA in July 1947.[21] Thus, although no one could have foreseen this development in 1940, the success of the SIS laid the groundwork for the emergence of the CIA in that area of the world.

Particularly since the 1970s, there has been a great deal of public and private debate over the morality and utility of CIA operations in Latin America. While the utilitarian criticisms may be valid, there is a historical perspective to the issues which often seems largely ignored. Admittedly, the SIS was intended primarily to act as a counterespionage outfit, but there was nothing in the June 24, 1940, order of Franklin D. Roosevelt that specifically limited it to this role. With a cold war on the horizon, with Latin America a good bet to become an area of U.S.-Soviet conflict, and given the 1940–45 intelligence success in the region, the continuation of clandestine activity became a foregone conclusion. The SIS passed away, ultimately to be replaced by the CIA, which continues to perform the regional tasks which the U.S. leadership deems necessary.

III. The "Right" Price

In *Axis Espionage and Propaganda*, published by MID in 1946, the unnamed author (or authors) made it clear that he considered the level of counterespionage cooperation received in Mexico, Chile, and Argentina to be inadequate.[22] One former assistant attaché who had worked in Chile explained that "those [DGII] people acted as if they had all the time in the world. . . . It gradually dawned on some of us that for them, this was no big deal. . . . It wasn't any skin off their backs if the Nazis got caught or not. . . ."[23] In fact, this last observation goes directly to the heart of the matter. The Nazi dogma about the master race, the blatant anti-Semitism, and the unmitigated claims of territorial domination caused many North Americans to believe that the Third Reich was the incarnation of evil. In Latin America, things were quite different. Anti-Semitism was not necessarily unfashionable, and pro-Facist sympathies were widely expressed. Moreover, some of the German V-men were nationals of the countries in which they operated, and the general understanding was that the intelligence activities being carried on were directed only against the United States and Great Britain. The attack on Pearl Harbor undoubtedly generated sympathy for the United States, but with the Japanese on a rampage in the Pacific and the Nazis still advancing in Russia and North Africa, many Latin Americans preferred to hedge their bets until they could be sure of siding with the winners. Finally, the war would have to end some day, and based on past experience, the Germans had been both good customers and good immigrants. With the possible exception of Brazil, whose expeditionary force suffered heavy casualties, the people of Latin

America did not conceive of World War II as a moralistic crusade. Indeed, given the enormous cultural and psychological differences, the wonder is that some U.S. intelligence personnel expected much more than the indifferent collaboration they often received.

As far back as 1940, U.S. policy makers had become quite aware that if they wanted effective cooperation from the Latin American republics, they would have to provide loans, arms, or some other important *quid pro quo*. Legal attaché Jack West rapidly discovered that if he wanted secret information, he would have to pay for it. While the *Blue Book* and the Act of Chapultepec embodied some highly commendable ideas, it is likely that the Coordinación Federal would have found more German spies if Perón had received a World War II surplus tank for each spy delivered. In the eyes of our poorer, weaker hemispheric partners, the United States was simply too rich and powerful to be an altruistic crusader; where moral suasion is unlikely to produce results, the discreet purchase of favor became a reasonably credible practice.

These observations may have some relevance to contemporary affairs, for in our view, discord rather than harmony has been the normal state of United States-Latin American relations. Given the cultural differences and the huge disparities in economic and military power, it could hardly be otherwise. If the United States hopes to obtain certain kinds of collaboration from Latin American states, it must provide aid packages and other persuaders as an integral part of its policy. And we have little doubt that one of the areas in which the circumspect purchase of favor will continue to be made is in secret intelligence.

Notes

1. República de Chile, Dirección General de Información e Investigaciones (hereafter referred to as DGII), *Grupo de Saboteadores*, vol. 45, pp. 21–23. See also National Archives and Records Service (hereafter referred to as NARS), R.G. 165, box 966, MID, *Axis Espionage and Propaganda in Latin America* (Washington, D.C., 1946), p. 40, and R.G. 59, 862.20210/4-445, no. 11886, enclosure 3, p. 1.

2. On "Dr. Brown," see DGII, *Grupo de Saboteadores*, vol. 45, pp. 57 and 282. See also NARS, R.G.59, 862.20210/4-345, no. 827, enclosure 1, pp. 1–2. On the activation code word, *cyclops*, see DGII, *Grupo de Saboteadores*, vol. 45, p. 70.

3. This information comes from p. 103 of General Lahousen's diary. A search of files in German Federal Republic, Archiv. Institüt für Zeitgeschichte, München, produced the page from which we quoted. Our thanks to Dr. Hermann Weiss of the Institüt für Zeitgeschichte staff. The material was forwarded in a letter to Prof. Leslie B. Rout, Jr. (Az:AB III, We/s), August 8, 1977.

4. The basis for this list was information found in DGII, *Grupo de Saboteadores*, vol. 46, p. 417.

5. Ibid., vol. 45, p. 217, and vol. 46, pp. 404–405. See also NARS, R.G.59, 862.20210/4-445, no. 11886, enclosure 3, pp. 1–2.

6. NARS, R.G.165, box 966, *Axis Espionage and Propaganda in Latin America*, p. 41, and R.G.59, 862-20210/4-545, p. 1.

7. On Canaris's supposed opposition to sabotage operations, see Karl-Heinz Abshagen, *Canaris* (London, 1968), pp. 187–188. For an explicit statement of the German Foreign Office position, see NARS, R.G. 84, 820.02, box 533, *Interrogation of Otto Reinebeck* (no TC number), January 24, 1946, p. 6.

8. See NARS, R.G. 59, 862.20210/4-545, p. 1, and R.G. 165, box 966, *Axis Espionage and Propaganda in Latin America*, p. 203.

9. On the *Gascony* affair, von Appen's support, and the Argentine investigation, see ibid., p. 41, and also DGII, *Grupo de Saboteadores*, vol. 46, pp. 406-408.

10. For the attempts on the two British vessels, see DGII, *Grupo de Saboteadores*, vol. 45, p. 282. The Cubatão plot is described in NARS, R.G. 59, 862.20210/4-945, pp. 1–2. See also R.G. 319, *German Espionage in Latin America* (Washington, D.C., 1946), p. 202 for the quoted material.

11. The three radio messages in question are found in NARS, R.G. 59, 862.20210/5-345, no. 12043, enclosure 2, pp. 2–3.

12. On von Appen's arrest and interrogation, see NARS, R.G. 59, 862.20210/4-445, no. 11886, enclosure 1, pp. 1–2. For evidence of the assistance given by Chile in informing the other Latin American republics, see DGII, *Grupo de Saboteadores*, vol. 45, pp. 195–196.

13. Ibid., vol. 45, p. 282, and NARS, R.G.59, 862.20235/5-345, no. 12043, enclosure 2, pp. 4 and 31.

14. Letter, Kapitän zur See a.D. Herbert Wichmann to Professor Rout, July 13, 1982.

15. On the five days of training, see NARS, R.G.59, 862.20210/4-945, p. 2 and 862.20210/5-345, no. 12043, enclosure 2, p. 10.

16. Franklin D. Roosevelt Library, Hyde Park, New York, *The Diaries of Adolf A. Berle*, reel 2, frame 0658.

17. Letter, Jack West to Professor Rout, November 8, 1978. This retired agent explained in detail how agents were moved around to fit the needs of the situation.

18. We hereby note that not one of the former SIS informants we questioned was in any way critical of Hoover. For better or for worse, few leaders we have ever heard of have been able to inspire that kind of loyalty.

19. On the rise of the CIG, see Thomas F. Troy, *Donovan and the CIA: A History of the Establishment of the Central Intelligence Agency* (Frederick, Maryland, 1981), pp. 360–362 and 395.

20. See letter, Jack West to Professor Rout, January 25, 1979.

21. On the CIG's end and the beginning of the CIA, see Troy, *Donovan and the CIA*, pp. 394–410. Evidence that some SIS personnel joined the CIA came from the Source T in a letter to Professor Rout, March 4, 1980.

22. NARS, R.G. 165, box 966, *Axis Espionage and Propaganda in Latin America*, pp. 38–41.

23. Letter from Source T to Professor Rout, March 4, 1980.

Appendix A

German Spy Ciphers

When World War II began, the Germans lacked established spy networks in all of Latin America except Chile. With great speed, but not always with great care, the German military intelligence service worked to remedy this situation. Initially, little thought was given to radio communication, but the slowness of the mail and the speed of the war eventually required that it be used. Enormous effort was put into the production and establishment of clandestine transmitters, including the dispatch of personnel and equipment from Germany. The skill that marked the construction of radios, however, was not matched by the selection of ciphers.

The most common type of cipher employed in Latin America was the single columnar transposition. This weak system was used by the Mexican network and important segments of the Brazilian and Chilean spy networks. It is not strange that this cipher dominated secret communications, since this type had been used extensively in World War I, and many of the German agents in Latin America were veterans of that war. Unfortunately for the Germans, after the Radio Intelligence Division (RID) of the Federal Communications Commission began intercepting the enciphered messages in 1941, the Treasury Department and, later, the FBI Technical Laboratory had little difficulty in deciphering them.

Other networks received different ciphers, but they were still inadequate. A case in point is the CEL network, the principal Brazilian espionage organization. In an attempt to increase the secrecy of messages, Berlin gave the leader of the group, Albrecht Engels, a strengthened variation of the single columnar transposition. In order to encipher, Herbert von Heyer, CEL's executive officer, obtained his key letters from an anthology he referred to in his confession as *The Collected Works of German Authors*. He chose the page number at random and transmitted this information to his controllers in Berlin by means of an extra code group placed in a prearranged position. This indicator group gave the page number of the key through numerical equivalents of letters, whereby *A* was 1, *B* was 2, and so forth. Consequently, page 147 would be ADG. A fourth letter was added as padding.

The last letter of the five letter group indicated which of eight checkerboard grilles that had earlier been sent by microdot to Brazil was to be used. In each, a quarter of the squares were randomly blacked out. In writing his message, von Heyer would fill in only the open squares and later add dummy letters to the empty spaces. In the example below, the alphabet is used. Berlin would know which grille was in service and could therefore ignore the padding.

3	13	19	1	15	16	5	2	6	9	17	4	14	18	11	7	8	12	20	10
C	R	U	A	T	T	F	B	G	L	T	D	R	T	O	G	J	P	Y	N
F	M	O	U	R	X	S	C	O	N	O	R	E	X	P	Q	R	A	N	X
D	T	X	U	S	E	V	E	V	N	X	Y	E	W	A	R	S	X	A	G
O	X	X	O	U	R	X	F	Y	A	T	Z	H	W	R	S	A	X	B	C
B	R	O	U	G	D	H	E	T	X	F	O	F	R	T	G	H	H	S	O
N	X	T	H	I	S	X	C	O	N	I	Y	I	N	E	N	T	J	K	X
A	X	N	E	W	X	N	A	T	I	O	N	X	X	X					

The darkened letters represent "the pad." The "pad" represents letters added to prevent the decryption of the letters. The message would then be sent by columns. It appears here in its final version: UUOUH ECEFE CAFDO BNARY ZOYNS VXHXN OVYTO TORSG NRSAH TNNAX NIXGC OXPAR TEXAX XHJMT XRXXE EHFIX RSUGI WXERD SXOXT FIOXW WRNXO XXOTN NABSK.

The use of the grille afforded relatively little extra protection to Engels's messages. What is extraordinary is that a revolving grille cipher was not used. The eight checkerboards with one quarter of their cells blacked out (in a revolving grille, one quarter are open) seem to suggest that something like that was planned, but never put into practice. If there was a reason for this otherwise inexplicable lapse, it may be that the Germans believed that their Latin agents would mishandle a more complicated cipher.

As weak as these ciphers were, the Abwehr added to their lack of security by using a constant block size of twenty spaces. This made the anagrammatizing required to decipher any messages much easier. The biggest mistake, however, was in the choice of key books. In a burst of cleverness, Abwehr leaders chose a set of books composed of pirated U.S. and British classics known as the Albatross series. Because these books could not be sold in the U.S. or Great Britain, the Germans reasoned that they would not be available to the Allies. The 1940 desertion of William G. Sebold, however, gave the United States an early clue to the Nazi system. As described by Paul A. Napier, the head of the cryptology section for the FBI, his organization simply read the list of books available in the series on the back of the one edition they had, and then sent off to neutral

European countries for a complete set. Consequently, once one message was broken and the page number found, it took only a few minutes to discover the key book.

There was one cipher the FBI never had the opportunity to break. The standby German agent in Brazil, Werner Waltemath, was captured before he was able to contact his home station. He had a relatively unusual cipher, which he referred to as a "comb" code, that possessed some of the strengthening elements of Engels's grille system but without the grille.

To obtain his key, Waltemath was supposed to use the book *Pagel in Glueck.* He would add twenty to the day of the year to obtain the key page. On April 12, the 102d day of the year, he would use page 122. He would then write the first twenty-six letters on the key page along both the top (horizontal) and left (vertical) axes of a grid. He would write the alphabet over the key letters, and then number the key letters in alphabetical order. The only function of the vertical key and the straight horizontal alphabetical listings was to establish the comb, or blacked out section. The comb was determined by crossing out all the spaces to the right of the alphabetical position of the key letter. To illustrate, the first key letter is *H* in the example below (vertical column). All the spaces in the first horizontal row that are to the right of the *H* are blacked out. Likewise, all the spaces in the second row of the grid are blacked out to the right of the *E* in the alphabetical row.

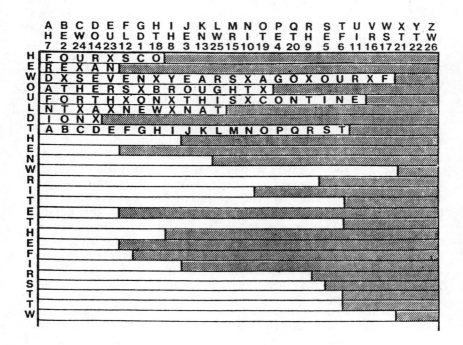

The message is then written into the open spaces horizontally, with *X*s placed between each word. If the final row used for the message is not completely filled in, then *X*s would be added until all the spaces in that row were filled. The next row is used simply for padding. To encipher the material, Waltemath would start with the column numbered 1 and, reading down, would write the letters horizontally. Column 2 would continue in the same pattern, but it and all even numbered columns would be read from the bottom up. Hence, the message in our sample grid would be as follows: CNXOE GBOTO TXEOE OTNJP OGOIS TNUFR DAFNI AIXXR YXTRN XTXRE FNXSE SAUHA KDXAT EEARS HSMXF HWNBX OAXCO QNOXN VRHXE CNXRH SXURG ITLXX.

Not all ciphers were of the single column transposition type. At least two Chilean-based networks used varieties of polyalphabetic substitutions. When, for example, Guillermo Kunsemüller of GES-NOI sat down to encipher, he began by opening his book *Soñar la Vida* (*To Dream Life*), by Carmen de Icaza, to the appropriate page; this he determined by adding his birthday to the current date, and then adding that sum to the month. He then numbered the letters of the first phrase to send basic data. If, for example, the line was:

It has been determined that
12   345   67   8   9   0

the opening, which included the hour of the message, day of the message, total number of letters, and the number of the message would appear as follows:

PAGE	DATE	HOUR	LETTERS	NUMBER
21---	03---	17---	89---	245---
TIABC	RHDEF	IEGHI	NDJKL	TASMN

The above indicates that page 21 was the key page, that it was the third of the month, the seventeenth hour, and that there were eighty-nine letters in message 245.

With the preliminaries completed, Kunsemüller's next task was to determine the index letter and where the key began. The index letter corresponded directly to the day of the month. The first day of the month was *A*, the second *B*, and so forth. After the twenty-sixth, the two digits comprising the date were added together. Thus, the twenty-seventh equaled 9, or the letter *I*; the thirty-first would be 4, or *D*. To find the start of his key, Kunsemüller, beginning with the first letter on the key page, would count the same number of letters into the text as the page number of the page. If the key page was page 21, his key would start with the twenty-second letter on the page.

With this information at hand, Kunsemüller would turn to his sliding scale. For example, if it was the third day of the month, he would place the third letter of the alphabet, *c*, over the first letter of the plain text; the letter *c* would be the index letter for the entire message encipherment. If the text to be enciphered was "Four score and seven years ago," the *c* would lie above the *F*. Then, by utilizing the text of page 21 beginning with the twenty-second letter, he could encipher his message. If the twenty-second letter was *O*, for example, the first letter of the key phrase "order to secure diplomatic recognition," then the first cipher letter would be *R* (its derivation is illustrated below).

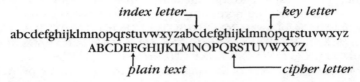

To determine the next cipher letter, Kunsemüller moved the sliding scale so that the index letter, *c*, rested above the second letter of plain text *O*. Then, the second letter of the key phrase, *r*, would be located on the sliding scale, and the second cipher letter would be found directly below, in this example, letter *D*.

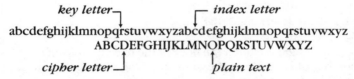

He would follow this procedure until the entire text of the message was encoded, which in the case of our example would be as follows: RDVTH TAHGA FSUFB RWKOY IYAVQ.

PQZ, another Chilean radio network, had a similar cipher. Instead of one book, PQZ used thirteen, each of which had a separate indicator and key word. "Jimmy," for example, meant the book *L'ombre del'Amour* and key word *panamericakurs* were to be used. Apparently, the sender could use either a book-based running key as in the GES example or use the quicker key word. The latter system would, of course, repeat in a regular pattern, but is easier to use. Index letters were derived in the same manner as GES-NOI. Instead of using a slide, the PQZ used a cipher disk with mixed alphabets.

A polyalphabetic substitution code is certainly breakable, and the ones described here are hardly extraordinary or new, but the FBI never broke them. The major reason, besides the strength of the codes, was that the FBI's resources were concentrated on other, more immediate, problems. Thus, PQZ enjoyed privacy in its conversations until a number of agents were captured and forced to divulge their ciphers.

Probably the worst cipher used in Latin America was one invented by an Abwehr agent sent to Brazil, Othmar Gamillscheg. This luckless V-man simply padded his messages with the same ten-figure number, pi

(3.141592653). For example, Gamillscheg's code name, "Grillo," would be sent as follows:

$$
\begin{array}{cc}
 & \begin{array}{ccc} 1 & 2 & 3 \end{array} \\
G + 3 = J & (H, \ I, \ J) \\
R + 1 = S & \\
I + 4 = M & \\
L + 1 = M & \\
L + 5 = Q & \\
O + 9 = X &
\end{array}
$$

The problem was that since the pad recurred, common phrases such as closings were always coded the same way. "Grillo" had the distinction of having his cipher broken not only by the United States, but also by Great Britain, Brazil, and rival German networks.

While the German ciphers did improve during the war, considerable damage to their networks resulted from the Anglo-Americans being able to read the early spy messages. In the opinion of Dr. Erich Huttenhain, head of analytical cryptanalysis for the German military (Gruppe IV of OKW/Chiffrierabteilung) during World War II, a lack of knowledge was at the root of the problem. Too many of the people working in cryptanalysis had only a slight understanding of their craft.

Appendix B

Persons Convicted in the Brazilian Spy Probes and Trials in 1942–45

	Sentence	Date of Conviction
Engels-Bohny (CEL) Group		
Eduard Arnold	25 years	October 6, 1943
Rudolph Heinrich Ehrhorn	25 years	October 6, 1943
Albrecht Gustav Engels	30 years	June 28, 1943
	3 years	October 6, 1943
	(A 30-year consolidated sentence was imposed on December 21, 1943)	
Herbert Julius von Heyer	20 years	June 28, 1943
	(A 25-year consolidated sentence was imposed on December 21, 1943)	
Heinz Otto Hermann Lorenz	25 years	June 28, 1943
Carlos Francisco Frederico Meyer	8 years	October 29, 1943
Hans Otto Meier	20 years	October 29, 1943
Hans Kurt Meyer-Clason	20 years	October 29, 1943
Hans Sievert	20 years	October 29, 1943
Kurt Weingartner	20 years	October 28, 1943
Capt. Tulio Regis do Nascimento Group		
Walther Becker	25 years (in absentia)	June 28, 1943
Hermann Bohny	25 years (in absentia)	June 28, 1943
Alvaro da Costa e Souza	25 years	June 28, 1943
Valencio Wurch Duarte	25 years	June 28, 1943
Heinz Ehlert	25 years	June 28, 1943
Oswaldo Riffel França	20 years	June 28, 1943
Gerardo Melo Mourão	30 years	June 28, 1943
Tulio Regis do Nascimento	30 years	June 28, 1943
Kurt Prüfer	25 years (in absentia)	June 28, 1943

	Sentence	Date of Conviction
Frank Walter Jordan (LFS) Group		
Julius Wilhelm Baum	8 years	May 28, 1943
Afonso Digeser	8 years	May 28, 1943
José Gnecco de Carvalho	8 years	May 28, 1943
Hans Holl	8 years	May 28, 1943
Frank Walter Jordan	20 years	May 28, 1943
Walter Moll	14 years	May 28, 1943
Eduardo Pacheco de Andrade	8 years	May 28, 1943
Herbert Max Winterstein	8 years	May 28, 1943
Friedrich Kempter (LIR) Group		
Carlos Fink	7 years	October 29, 1943
Karl Eugen Haering	20 years	October 29, 1943
Friedrich Kempter	25 years	October 6, 1943
Heriberto Othmar Müller	8 years	October 29, 1943
Othmar Gamillscheg (JOH) Group		
María José Soares Gamillscheg	4 years	October 29, 1943
Othmar Gamillscheg	25 years	October 6, 1943
	(A 30-year consolidated	
	sentence was imposed	
	on December 21, 1943)	
Adalberto Wamser	25 years	October 6, 1943
Janos Salamon (HTT) Group		
Jofre Magalhães dos Santos	25 years	October 29, 1943
Ellemer Nagy	25 years	October 6, 1943
Janos Salamon	30 years (in absentia)	December 21, 1943
Schlegel (Radío "Carola") Group		
Erwin Backhaus	8 years	November 19, 1942
Nicholaus von Dellinghausen	8 years	November 19, 1942
Theodor Friedrich Schlegel	14 years	November 19, 1942
	(A 30-year consolidated	
	sentence was imposed	
	on December 21, 1943)	
Karl Thielen	8 years	November 19, 1942
Rolf Trautmann	8 years	November 19, 1942
Gustav Utzinger	8 years (in absentia)	November 19, 1942
The Starziczny-Uebele (CIT) Group		
Euclides de Albuquerque	8 years	October 29, 1943
Max Bernhardt Bartels	20 years	October 29, 1943
Heinrich Bleinroth	25 years	October 6, 1943
José Ferreira Dias	7 years	October 29, 1943
Wilhelm Gieseler	20 years	October 29, 1943

	Sentence	Date of Conviction
Antonio Gonçalves da Cunha	20 years	October 6, 1943
Antonio Gonçalves da Silva Barreto	7 years	October 29, 1943
Galdino Francisco de Medeiros	7 years	October 29, 1943
Karl Muegge	25 years	October 6, 1943
Martin Peter Petzold	20 years	October 29, 1943
Joaquim Pinto de Oliveira	20 years	October 6, 1943
Albert Schwab	25 years	October 6, 1943
Joséf Jacob Starziczny	30 years	October 6, 1943
(listed in the trial records and sentenced as Niels Christian Christensen)		
Karl Hans von den Steinen	25 years	October 29, 1943
Hans Ulrich Uebele	25 years	October 29, 1943
Otto Uebele	8 years	October 29, 1943
Fritz Weissflog	25 years	October 29, 1943
Emil Wohlmann	7 years	October 29, 1943

Werner Waltemath (INC) Group

Paulo Griese	25 years	December 28, 1943
Hans Christian von Kotze	27 ½ years (in absentia)	December 28, 1943
Werner Christoph Waltemath	27 ½ years	December 28, 1943

Wilhelm Koepff and Marcus Baarn

William Marcus Baarn	27 ½ years	May 22, 1945
Wilhelm Heinrich Koepff	27 ½ years	May 22, 1945

Appendix C

Persons Implicated or Convicted in the Chilean Spy Probes and Trials of 1942–45

I. Persons named in the June 30, 1942, Spy Memorandum

	Nationality
Juan Aguilera	Chilean
Arnold Barckhahn	Chilean
Kate Berg	German
Hans Blume	German
Maj. Ludwig von Bohlen	German
Frederick Clarke Carr	U.S.A.
Bruno Dittman	German
Fr. Túlio Franchini	Italian
Jorge Hasseldieck	German
Hans Hofbauer	German
Kurt Irritier	German
Arturo Neef	German
Isabel Pederit de Reiners	Chilean
Heinrich Reiners	German
Friedrich Tadeo von Schulz-Hausmann	German
Emilio Simonsen	German
Johannes Szeraws	German
Guillermo Zeller	Chilean

Note: Frederick Clarke Carr fled to Argentina in November, 1942. He seems to have boasted about obtaining information for Bohlen from his daughter, who worked in the American embassy in Ecuador, but was unable to do so. Thereafter, Bohlen kept clear of him. See NARS, R.G. 165 (Suitland, Maryland), 3610, no. 201 file, Clarke, Federico. Title: *Federico Clarke (Carr) With Alias, Santiago, Chile,* pp. 1–6. See also GELA, pp. 106–107.

II.   Persons arrested or indicted as a result of Proceso 90-42 (PYL case)

	Nationality	Eventual Action Taken
Juan Aguilera	Chilean	Released
Albrecht Julius von Appen	German	Released; rearrested in 1945; interned in the U.S.A.
Arnold Barckhahn	Chilean	Released
Kate Berg	German	Released
Ernesto Brandes	Naturalized Chilean	Released
Walter Brandes	Naturalized Chilean	Released
Otto Buchholz	German	Relegated to Salamanca, Chile, for the duration of the war.
Juan Cuneo	Italian	Released
Bruno Dittman	German	Released
Fr. Túlio José Franchini	Italian	Questioned in Ecuador in 1943; no legal action taken.
Jorge Hasseldieck	German	Relegated to Limache, Chile, for the duration of the war.
Hans Hofbauer	German	Indicted
Kurt Irritier	German	Released
Horst Kettler	German	Allowed to leave Chile.
Werner Nahr	German	Released
Arturo Neef	German	Released
Otto Osterloh	Naturalized Chilean	Released
Carlos Reiher	Naturalized Chilean	Released
Isabel Pederit de Reiners	Chilean	Released
Emilio Simonsen	German	Relegated to Limache, Chile, for the duration of the war.
Ernst Seeman	German	Released
Kurt Wandell	German	Released
Erich Wichmann	German	Released
Guillermo Zeller	Chilean	Released

III.   Persons convicted as a result of Proceso 7-44 (PQZ case) and their sentences following appeal

	Nationality	Original Sentence (6/7/45)	Sentence After Appeal (10/4/45)
Guillermo Kunsemüller	Chilean	7 years	3 years, 1 day
Bernardo Timmerman	Dual German-Chilean Citizenship	5 years	2 years

	Nationality	Original Sentence (6/7/45)	Sentence After Appeal (10/4/45)
Eugenio Ellinger Knoll	German	4 years	541 days
Hans Heinke	German	4 years	541 days
Augusto Kroll	German	4 years	541 days
Jorge Ebensperger	Chilean	3 years	240 days
Waldemar Koesser	German	3 years	240 days
Walther Thieme	Chilean	3 years	95 days
Hilda von Plate Timmerman	Chilean	2 ½ years	541 days
Ana Bradenkamp de Helleman	German	2 years	541 days
Lucinda Silva Vargas	Chilean	2 years	541 days
Ilse Blanca Dorrer	Chilean	541 days	100 days
Carlos Bruhn	Chilean	541 days	Sustained
Armando Cespédes	Chilean	541 days	Sustained
Eduardo Drust	Chilean	541 days	Sustained
Karl Ernst	Chilean	541 days	Sustained
Eugenio Fraumeni	Chilean	541 days	Sustained
Hans Graner	German	541 days	Sustained
Raúl Malvino	Chilean	541 days	Sustained
Francisco Humberto Pérez	Paraguayan	541 days	Sustained
Diego Fajardo	Chilean	541 days	Absolved
César Frias	Chilean	541 days	Absolved
Franz Hilger	Chilean	541 days	Absolved
Claudio Krebs	Chilean	541 days	Absolved
Gerado Krebs	Chilean	180 days	Absolved
Carlos Orrego Renard	Chilean	61 days	—
Guillermo Reichmann	Chilean	Absolved	—

Notes: (1) The following persons, as a result of their reductions in sentence, were considered to have completed their time in jail: Ilse Dorrer, Jorge Ebensperger, Eugenio Ellinger Knoll, Waldemar Koesser, Augusto Kroll, and Walther Thieme.

(2) The Ríos government did not appeal the appellate court decisions of October 1945 to the Chilean Supreme Court.

(3) The sources for the sentences and convictions are NARS, R.G. 59, 862.20225/6-1145, pp. 1–3, and 862.20225/10-945, pp. 1–3.

Appendix D

Persons Indicted as Spies by the Argentine Government, 1945–46

Group I—Foreign agents charged on August 31, 1945, with violation of Article 219 of the Penal Code, and released on a *habeas corpus* writ in June 1946

Agent	Nationality	Approximate Date of Arrest	Status as of June 1947
Esteban Amorín*	Spanish	2/1/44	Deported on the *La Pampa*
Manuel de Miguel Arrastia*	Spanish	1/29/44	Left in December 1946 on his own, aboard the *Monte Amboto*
Federico Bade*	Chilean	8/29/44	"At Liberty"**
Hans Blume*	Chilean	8/22/44	Departed on his own to Chile, July 1947.
Johannes Siegfried Becker*	German	4/16/45	Fugitive
Walter Burkhardt* (Waldemar Boettger)	German	8/23/44	Fugitive
Alphonse Chantrain*	Luxembourg	8/23/44	Deported on the *Río Teuco*
Ullrich Guenther Daue*	German	8/3/44	Fugitive
Luísa Matthies de Daue*	German	8/3/44	Fugitive (released under doctor's care; she was an invalid).
Karl Fandrich*	German	4/1/45	Fugitive
Alfredo Fernández Suárez*	German	2/29/45	Deported on *La Pampa*
Johannes Harmeyer*	German	2/5/44	Deported on *La Pampa*
Hans Harnisch*	German	1/16/44	Deported on *Río Teuco*
Rudolf Hepe	German	3/23/45	Released from prison due to imminence of death (confined to mental hospital)
Kurt Horstenmeyer*	German	8/22/44	Fugitive
Karl Küsters*	German	8/23/44	Fugitive
Eugen Hans Langer*	Czech-oslovakian	8/29/44	Fugitive

Agent	Nationality	Approximate Date of Arrest	Status as of June 1947
Karl Leitner*	German	11/28/44	Deported on *La Pampa*
Hans Lieberth*	German	8/3/44	Deported on *Río Teuco*
Willi Lindestruth*	German	3/23/45	Deported on *La Pampa*
Ema Lorenz*	German	8/3/44	Fugitive
Werner Lorenz	German	8/3/44	Fugitive
Carlos Manfrini Castro	Uruguayan	1/5/45	Deported on *La Pampa*
Wilhelm Maubach*	German	3/24/45	Died on December 17, 1946
Juan Prieto*	Spanish	2/24/45	Deported on *La Pampa*
Nicolás Quintana Moreno*	Spanish	2/8/44	Left for Spain using a forged passport in October 1946.
Willi Reichelt*	German	8/23/44	Fugitive
Friedrich Scheu*	German	8/23/44	Voluntarily left for Paraguay
Anton Scheurle	German	?	"At Liberty"** (Imprisoned as of April 26, 1945).
Enrique Schibli*	German	8/13/44	Fugitive
Gertrudis Hostovsky de Schlosser*	Chilean	2/11/44	Voluntarily left for Chile, July 1947
Heriberto Schlosser*	German	2/11/44	Voluntarily left for Chile, July 1947
Gerhard von Schutz*	German	8/23/44	Fugitive
Gertrudis Pralle von Schutz*	German	8/23/44	Fugitive
Walter Schwaiger*	German	8/25/44	Deported on *La Pampa*
Martin Kurt Schwartz*	German	8/23/44	Fugitive
Wilhelm Seidlitz*	German	2/5/44	Fugitive
Gustavo Seraphin*	Romanian	1/7/45	Fugitive
Anna Assmann de Sommermeyer*	Polish	8/17/44	Deported on *La Pampa*
Werner Sommermeyer*	Polish	8/17/44	Fugitive
Melitta Tietz	Chilean	4/16/45	"At Liberty"**
Albrecht Treusch*	German	?	Deported on *Río Teuco*
Irene Lina Trier	German	8/23/44	Released from prison because of imminence of death
Ferdinand Ullrich*	German	2/16/44	Deported on *La Pampa*
Gustavo Utzinger* (Wolf Franczok)	German	8/17/44	Deported on *Río Teuco*
Olegario Vientinghof Scheel*	Russian	1/21/44	Fugitive
Alfredo Villa Alvarez*	Spanish	1/5/45	Fugitive
Margarita Meta Wilkening*	German	3/9/45	Fugitive

Group II—Argentine nationals charged with violation of Article 219 of the Penal Code, released on bail in February 1946, and freed of all charges in November 1947

Agent	Approximate Date of Arrest	
Pedro Andrade	1/ 7/45	
Olga E. Bade	8/23/45	
Oscar Bade	8/23/45	
Carlos Illing	2/23/44	
Pedro Illvento	2/15/44	
Guilliermo Lassere Marmol	3/30/45	
Edmundo Leeb	8/22/44	
Lina Maurer	?	
Enrique Pablo Neiling	1/16/44	(Originally listed as a person to be prosecuted, by November 1947, Wollkopf's name had been dropped from the list of Argentines still being prosecuted)
Ludovico Schuller	2/10/44	
Hans-Otto Schurer Stolle	2/ 8/44	
Alberto Wollkopf	3/22/44	

Group III—German agents and collaborators who, while never indicted, were ordered deported

	Nationality	Arrested	Date(s) on Which Deportation Was Ordered	Status as of May 1947
Ramón Baulenas Salas	Spanish	2/10/44; released—5/8/44	11/15/46	Deported to Chile; returned by Chileans 7/22/47
Georg Bücker*	German	2/8/44; released—date unknown	2/7/46 and 11/15/46	"At Liberty"**
Horst Hermann Busse	German	9/7/45	11/7/45 and 1/18/46	Deported on *Highland Monarch*
Carlos Gustavo Eickenberg	Bolivian	2/5/44; released—date unknown	2/8/46	Voluntarily left for Bolivia
Wolf Herbert Freudenberg*	Chilean	2/14/44; released—5/8/44	11/15/46	Deported on *La Pampa*
Friedrich Frohwein	German	9/7/45	11/7/45	Deported on *Highland Monarch*
Hans Leuters	German	9/7/45	11/7/45	Deported on *Highland Monarch*
José Mella Alfagame	Spanish	2/8/44; released—date unknown	1/18/46	Deported on *Highland Monarch*
Ino von Roland*	German	3/21/44; released—5/8/44;	11/15/46	Deported on *La Pampa*
Georg Richter*	German	2/12/44; released—5/8/44	11/15/46	Deported on *Río Teuco*
Ernst Schlueter	German	9/7/45	11/7/45	Deported on *Highland Monarch*
Albert Voelckers*	German	2/12/44; released—5/8/44	11/15/46	Deported on *Highland Monarch*

Group IV—Convicted spies and their sentences for violation of Article 219 of the Penal Code

	Nationality	Arrest	Sentence	Final Disposition as of May 1947
Rosendo Almozara	Spanish	5/11/43	12/10/43—two years	
Francisco Javiar Azarola	Spanish	5/19/43	None	Shipped back to Spain, 1/15/44
Walter Friewald	Paraguayan	11/5/42; rearrested—1/23/44	2-year sentence given on 6/21/44. Sentence confirmed after appeal on 7/26/45; parole granted on 11/29/45	Officially deported to Paraguay, 5/4/46
Ottomar Müller*	German	11/5/42; rearrested—1/23/44	Same as Friewald except that the original sentence was for three years	Deported on *La Pampa*
Hans Napp*	German	11/19/42; rearrested—1/23/44	Same as Friewald	Deported on *Río Teuco*
Martin Schneider	Argentinian	11/5/42; rearrested—1/23/44	Same as Friewald	
Hans Zwiegert	German	Taken into custody 2/23/44; officially arrested—3/15/44	12/1/44—two years sentence raised to four years on 7/26/45	Ordered deported, 11/17/47

Group V—Agents from Groups I and II found not guilty by the Federal Appeals Court decision of November 10, 1947

Group I
Manuel de Miguel Arrastia
Federico Bade***
Luísa Matthies de Daue
Karl Fandrich***
Alfredo Fernández Suárez
Johannes Harmeyer
Rudolf Hepe***
Kurt Horstenmeyer
Karl Küsters
Karl Leitner
Willi Lindestruth
Ema Lorenz***
Werner Lorenz
Carlos Manfrini Castro
Wilhelm Maubach
Juan Prieto
Willi Reichelt***
Friedrich Scheu
Anton Scheurle
Heinz Schibli
Gertrudis Hostovsky de Schlosser
Heriberto Schlosser
Gerhard von Schutz***
Gertrudis Pralle von Schutz***
Walter Schwaiger
Martin Kurt Schwartz
Gustavo Seraphin
Anna Assmann de Sommermeyer
Werner Sommermeyer
Albrecht Treusch
Irene Lina Trier
Ferdinand Ullrich
Olegario Vientinghof Scheel
Alfredo Villa Alvarez
Margarita Meta Wilkening***

Group II
Pedro Andrade
Olga E. Bade
Oscar Bade
Carlos Illing
Pedro Illvento
Guilliermo Lassere Marmol
Edmundo Leeb
Lina Maurer
Enrique Pablo Neiling
Ludovico Schuller
Hans-Otto Schurer Stolle
Alberto Wollkopf

The *Highland Monarch* sailed from Buenos Aires for Hamburg on February 15, 1946. The *La Pampa* sailed from Buenos Aires for Hamburg on December 21, 1946. The *Río Teuco* sailed from Buenos Aires for Antwerp on May 22, 1947.

*Indicates that a particular alien was named in Decree 18.480 issued by President Perón. Of this group, as of May 23, 1947, 22 were still fugitives, 21 were deported, 7 were said to be voluntarily repatriated, or in any case to have left Argentina, and 2 were described as being "At Liberty."
**"At Liberty" indicates that despite the fact that a deportation order had been issued, the person in question was not going to be deported. No reason was given for this special status.
***According to a newspaper account, these persons were in attendance when the judicial decision was handed down on November 10, 1947.

Source: FBI Special File 64-27943, NARS R.G. 59, 862.20235/5-1247, no. 2491, and 862.20235/5-2347, no. 2599.

Glossary

Abwehr. The German military intelligence organization.

Ast. Abwehrstelle. Name for the twenty-four or so intelligence stations which usually controlled the agents, and sent them to the Americas, Europe, Asia, Africa, etc.

Abteilung. The Abwehr headquarters section. There were four *Abteilungen,* all located in Berlin and subdivided into smaller units.

AO. *Auslandsorganisation.* This is the name given by the Nazi party to those party branches that were located outside of the Reich. Nazis overseas did not belong to a "home" Nazi party unit; their membership was shifted to that of the umbrella organization which directed all overseas party activities.

Auswärtiges Amt. The German Foreign Office.

BSC. British Security Coordination. After the arrival of Sir William Stephenson in New York in May 1940, British MI-6 agents and activities in the Americas came under Stephenson, and were referred to as BSC.

CPD. The initials by which the Emergency Advisory Committee for Political Defense of the Americas was better known. This group was created as a result of a resolution passed at the Third Conference of Ministers of Foreign Affairs of the American Republics, held in Rio de Janeiro in January 1942. Headquartered at Montevideo, Uruguay, the group consisted of seven member nations. Its ostensible purpose was to improve and coordinate hemispheric defense against espionage, sabotage, and propaganda by Axis agents. The members of the committee were Argentina, Brazil, Chile, Mexico, the United States, Uruguay, and Venezuela. The CPD functioned in such a way so as to mobilize the power of public opinion in the Americas in order to bring pressure against those nations and governments which were lax in conducting counterespionage activities.

Cutout. An agent who acts as a go-between for two other agents.

DGII. Dirección General de Investigaciones e Identificaciones. This was the Chilean security agency primarily concerned with counterespionage activity.

DOPS. Delegacia Especial de Ordem Política e Social. This was the Brazilian political police agency. Counterespionage activity in Brazil was primarily their concern.

Drop. Intelligence slang for a person or place to whom secret reports, documents, etc., can be safely sent. The materials can then be picked up by another agent, or forwarded to an espionage headquarters.

FMK. Funkmeldeköpfe. A network of V-men who were connected with the controlling *Ast* by means of radio. The *FMK* generally took the name of its chief or the area where it operated.

Integralistas. Or Greenshirts. This was a right-wing political group in Brazil. It was opposed to Getúlio Vargas, and since Vargas was seen as pro-American, they were anti-American and sometimes pro-Axis as well.

Jefatura de Servicios de Viligancia Policía. Headquarters for Services of Police Vigilance. Established in February 1942 to execute counterespionage work in Mexico.

Legal attaché. A diplomatic post created in Latin American embassies in 1941. Legal or civil attachés were in reality FBI agents whose task was to coordinate and control counterespionage and antisabotage efforts in Latin America.

MK. Meldeköpfe. An information center, a spy center, a headquarters, etc. In South America, a network of agents in a particular country was generally described as a Meldeköpfe. For example, MK "Argentina."

MID. Military Intelligence Division, G-2 Section of the U.S. Army. All military attachés sent their reports to this office.

Nest. Nebenstelle. These are substations which were under the administrative direction of an *Ast.* Many of these (like *Nest* Bremen) were virtually independent and controlled their own agents.

ONI. Office of Naval Intelligence of the U.S. Navy. All naval attachés sent their reports to this office.

Reichsdeutscher. A person who is of German citizenship, or who travels on a German passport.

RID. Radio Intelligence Division. This was a section of the FCC specifically created in July 1940 to monitor and locate clandestine radio broadcasts emanating from or being received in the Western Hemisphere.

SIS. Special Intelligence Service, established by J. Edgar Hoover in July 1940 specifically for Latin American work. In 1941, each legal or civil attaché became the SIS director in the Latin American republic in which he was stationed. Units are referred to by country. For example, SIS/Brazil, SIS/Mexico, etc.

Volksdeutscher. A person who may be a German culturally, or born of German parents, but who is actually a citizen of some Latin American country.

V-man. *Vertrauensmann,* or confidential agent or informant. This was the term used by the Germans to describe their operatives.

Bibliography

I. Archival Collections and Unpublished Documents

Argentina

Archivo de Ministerio de Relaciones Exteriores y Culto, Buenos Aires. Under the general heading *Guerra Mundial IIa* are a series of forty volumes including file 1, *Guerra entre Estados Unidos y los paises del Eje,* and file 26, *Guerra entre E.E.U.U. y los paises del Eje.* Files 95, 124, 161, 192, 197, 318, 485, and 486 are entitled *Guerra Europa,* and include over fifty volumes. File 589 is entitled *Asuntos varios de caracter general,* and 633 is called *Dirección de los asuntos políticos.* There are also several volumes that have no file numbers.

Brazil

Arquivo Nacional de Rio de Janeiro, Rio de Janeiro. Included in this archive are Seção de Poder Judiciário, Tribunal de Segurança Nacional, Processo 2.996, *Processo—Crime de Frank Walther Jordan e otros.* 2 vols. Another valuable collection is Processo 3.093, *Niels Christian Christensen e otros.* 16 vols. 2 appendixes.

Arquivo Superior Tribunal Militar, Brasilia, D.F. This repository contains Processo 3.293, *Tulio Regis do Nascimento e otros.* 8 vols.

Fundação Getúlio Vargas, Rio de Janeiro. The major collections are *Arquivo Osvaldo Aranha* (correspondence, 1941–1944) and *Arquivo Getúlio Vargas* (communications, 1939–1943).

Chile

Archivo de Ministerio de Relaciones Exteriores, Santiago. For documents relating to foreign affairs see:

—*Espionaje Alemán en Chile* (1942). (Please note that this folio is marked "conf R.")

—*Embajada en Washington—Oficios confidenciales enviados y recibidos* (1942).

—*Oficios recibidos de la Embajada de Chile en los Estados Unidos (del 201 al 400)* (1942).

—*Archivo Confidencial-Sección Clave-ofic., recibidos—Embajada en E.E.U.U.* (1942).

—*Embajada de Chile en Washington—Oficios confidenciales enviados y recibidos* (1943).

—*Archivo Confidencial—Oficios de la Embajada en Estados Unidos, 1° semestre* (1943).

479

—*Canje Diplomático Chile-Alemán*, vols. 1-2 (1943–44).
—*Embajada de Chile—Oficios recibidos de la Embajada de Chile en E.E.U.U.* (1-246) (1944).
—*Sección Confidencial de la Embajada en Estados Unidos, 1° semestre* (1944).

Dirección General de Investigaciones e Identificación (Department 50), Santiago. Three volumes are listed under Proceso 90-42. The exact title is *Informe sobre actividades nazis en Chile*, vols. 1, 5, and 9, plus 2 annexes. See also Proceso 7-44, *Contra Bernardo Timmerman e otros*, vols. 35, 42, 43, 44, and 2 annexes; all volumes have additional separate titles; the two annexes are marked "*1° a Instancia.*" On Chilean saboteurs, see *Grupo de Saboteadores*, vols. 45–46.

Ministerio de Justicia, Archivo Judicial, Santiago. On court decisions, see *Corte de Apelaciones de Santiago*, Proceeding T-378, Case no. 7-44. *Expediente de Bernardo Timmerman y otros.*

German Federal Republic

Bundesarchiv, Koblenz. Document R58/1217, *Reichssicherheitshauptamt VI-E.*

Bundesarchiv-Militärarchiv, Freiburg-im-Breisgau. *OKW/Amtsgruppe Auslandsnachrichten und Abwehr.* RW 5, Vol. 118. *OKW/Generalstab, Fremde Heere West.* H 27/6, *Lateinamerika* (to 1945), *Amt. Ausl.*

Institut für Zeitgeschichte, München. NG-4871, *Eidesstattliche Erklärung Karl Friedrich Arnold*, Berlin, November 20, 1946.

Politisches Archiv des Auswärtiges Amt, Bonn. See:
—*Büro Reichsminister*, RAM 27, Akten Betreffend: *Peru*, June 1937–January 1942.
—*Büro des Staatssekretärs*, Akten Betreffend: *Argentinien*, vol. 1, April 1938–April 1941; vol. 2, May 1–December 23, 1941.
—*Büro des Staatssekretärs*, Akten Betreffend: *Brasilien*, vol. 1, April 1938–April 1941.
—*Büro des Staatssekretärs*, Akten Betreffend: *Chile*, vol. 1, April 8, 1939–June 30, 1942.
—*Büro des Staatssekretärs*, Akten Betreffend: *Mexiko*, August 24, 1939–September 28, 1942.
—*Büro des Staatssekretärs*, Akten Betreffend: *Südamerika Allgemeines*, vol. 1, December 1938–May 1943.
—*Politische Abteilung, Pol. I M 169*, Akten Betreffend: *Abwehr-Allgemein*, vol. 12, March 3–November 11, 1941.
—*Abteilung Inland IIg 105*, Akten Betreffend: *Südamerika, Tätigkeit des SD, der Abwehr, der Agenten und Polizeiattachés*, 1943–44.
—*Abteilung Inland IIg 455*, Akten Betreffend: *Südamerika, SD—Meldungen aus Südamerika*, 1940–43.

Staatsarchiv, Nürnberg. *KV-Anklage*, Bestand: *Interrogations*, P-1, no. 1145a, April 15, 1947 (Theodor Paeffgen); R-1, no. 2856, July 16, 1948 (Heinrich Rüdt von Collenberg); and T-1, no. 2147, October 10, 1947 (Edmund Freiherr von Thermann).

Great Britain

Public Record Office, London. The authors used a great number of documents from the Foreign Office (FO) 371 file for the following countries: Argentina, Bolivia, Brazil, and Chile. Individual document numbers are cited in the notes following each chapter.

Mexico

Archivo General de la Nación, Mexico City, D.F. *Archivo del Presidente Manuel Ávila Comacho, Audiencias III.*

Secretaría de Relaciones Exteriores, Archivo General, Mexico City, D.F. (Some volumes are marked "Archivo Histórico."):
—File I/131/4329, Topográfica (archival locator number) 344–54
—File III/323(43)/6, Topográfica 2411–24
—File III/323(73)/76, Topográfica 2418–10
—File III/323(73)/76, Topográfica 2419–61
—File III/655.2(72)/10, Topográfica 1329–12
—File IV/323(43–72)/180, Topográfica 4178–9.

United States of America

Department of the Army, Office of the Chief of Military History of the Army, Washington, D.C. See:
—8–2.8BA—*Bilateral Staff Talks with the American Republics.* 2 appendixes.
—8–2.8BE—*Chile and the War Effort.*

Department of the Navy, Naval Historical Center, Washington Navy Yard, Washington, D.C. Office of Naval Intelligence, ONI/TAM/244, *Files of the German Naval Staff, German Naval Attaché Reports.* T-65 through T-67, PG-32004–32010 (microfilm).

Franklin D. Roosevelt Library, Hyde Park, New York. See:
—Harry H. Hopkins Papers. Boxes 140–141
—Henry Morgenthau Papers. Vol. 451
—Henry A. Wallace Papers. Box 117
—Franklin D. Roosevelt Papers. Office File 10B, boxes 22–39.

National Archives and Records Service, Washington, D.C. Records used in this study came from the following record groupings:
—RG 38: General Records of the Chief of Naval Operations
—RG 59: General Records of the Department of State
—RG 60: General Records of the Department of Justice
—RG 84: Records of the Foreign Service Posts of the Department of State (in Suitland, Maryland)
—RG 165: Records of the War Department, General and Special Staffs
—RG 173: Records of the Radio Interception Division (RID), Federal Communications Commission
—RG 226: Records of the Office of Strategic Services (OSS)
—RG 238: National Archives Collection of World War II Crimes
—RG 242: National Archives Collection of Foreign Records Seized.

II. Private Repositories

Claude D. Bowers Papers. Manuscripts Department, Lilly Library, Indiana University, Bloomington, Indiana. Bowers Mss. II (1939–44).

George F. Messersmith Papers. University of Delaware, Newark, Delaware. ND file nos. 1859, 1893, 1977, 2002, 2007, 2018, and 2026.

III. Personal Interviews

Tobias Barros Álvarez
The Honorable Norman Armour

III. Personal Interviews cont.

The Honorable Willard Beaullac
Donald C. Bird
The Honorable Philip Bonsal
Gen. Andrew Goodpaster, U.S.A. (Ret.)
Dr. Fritz Hinzer
Gerardo Melo Mourão
Harold Midkiff
Dr. Gisela von Mülenbrock, legal specialist, Library of Congress, Washington, D.C.
Victor Paz Estensoro
Elpídio Reali
Dr. Leandro Telles
Jack West
(N.B.—In addition to these people, the authors also interviewed twelve former
    SIS operatives, two diplomats, and two former Abwehr operatives. However,
    these persons agreed to be interviewed only if their names were withheld.)

IV. Correspondence (Acknowledgeable sources only)

Capt. D.C. Allard, U.S.N.
Sir Richard Allen
Arthur Baker
Berlin Document Center, Berlin, German Federal Republic
Insp. Homer Boynton, Public Affairs Office, FBI
The Honorable Spruille Braden
William C. Bradley
The Honorable John M. Cabot
William B. Caldwell
The Rev. Charles Conaty, O.M.I.
Cecil M.P. Cross
Deutsche Dienststelle, Berlin, German Federal Republic
The Honorable Donald R. Heath
Henry D. Heckster
H. Montgomery Hyde
Hugh Jenks
Col. Wendell G. Johnson, U.S.A. (Ret.)
James P. Joice
Dr. David Kahn
Dr. Maria Keipert, Auswärtiges Amt, Bonn, German Federal Republic
Friedrich Kempter
Hans Kurt Meyer-Clason
Morris G. Moses
Dr. Gisela von Mülenbrock, legal specialist, Library of Congress, Washington, D.C.
Col. Oscar Reile, German army (Ret.)
Enrique Reiners
Hans Ulrich Uebele
John N. Vebber
Jack West
Robert W. Wall
Kapitän zur See a.D. Herbert Wichmann, German navy (Ret.)
Insp. Roger S. Young, Public Affairs Office, FBI

V. Official Published Documents

Argentina

La República Argentina. Ministerio de Justicia e Instrucción Pública. *Fallos de la Corte Superior de Justicia de la Nación*, vol. 204. Buenos Aires, 1948.

——————. Ministerio de Justicia e Instrucción Pública. *Jurisprudencia Argentina*, 3 vols. Buenos Aires, 1946.

——————. Ministerio de Relaciones Exteriores y Culto, Dirección de Información al Exterior. *Nota de su Excelencia el Señor Ministro de Relaciones Exteriores y Culto, Dr. Juan I. Cooke, dirigida en nombre de gobierno argentino a los representantes diplomáticos americanos acreditados en la República, el 24 de Marzo de 1946, exponiendo los puntos de vista del gobierno argentino ante las aseveraciones del "Libro Azul."* Buenos Aires, 1946.

——————. Ministerio de Relaciones Exteriores y Culto. *Memoria del Ministerio de Relaciones y Exteriores y Culto, Años 1943–1944.* Buenos Aires, 1945.

——————. Ministerio del Interior, Policía Federal. *Memoria: Correspondiente al año 1945.* Buenos Aires, 1950.

Brazil

A República do Brasil, Ministério das Relações Exteriores. *Comercio exterior do Brasil: 1937–1939.* Serviço de Publicações. Rio de Janeiro, 1940.

Estado de São Paulo, Superintendência de Segurança, Política e Social de São Paulo. *A rede de espionagem nacista chefiada por Niels Christian Christensen, Relatório apresentado pelo Dr. Elpídio Reali.* São Paulo, 1943.

Chile

República de Chile. *Recopilación de leyes por orden numérico con indices por numeros: Ministerio y Materias*, vol. 29. Santiago, 1944.

German Federal Republic

German Federal Republic, Auswärtiges Amt. *Akten zur Deutschen Auswärtigen Politik, 1918–1945,* Series E, 8 vols. Göttingen, 1969–79.

Great Britain

Her Majesty's Stationery Office. *Documents on German Foreign Policy, 1918–1945, from the Archives of the German Foreign Ministry,* 13 vols. London, 1949–64.

United States of America

British Foreign Office/U.S. State Department, German War Documents Project. *Documents Selected from German Foreign Office Records* (microfilm), T-120 series, reels 25, 225, 366, 691, 733, 761, 762, and 1054. Washington, D.C., 1958– .

Franklin D. Roosevelt Library. *The Diaries of Adolf A. Berle* (microfilm), 8 reels. Hyde Park, New York, 1978.

Paul Kesaris, ed. *Maproom Messages of President Roosevelt, 1939–1945* (microfilm), 9 reels. Frederick, Maryland, 1981.

——————. *The Presidential Diaries of Henry Morgenthau, Jr., 1938–1945* (microfilm), 2 reels. Frederick, Maryland, 1981.

Pan American Union. *Inter-American Conference on Problems of War and Peace, Mexico City, February 21–March 8, 1945: Report Submitted to the Governing Board of the Pan American Union by the Director-General.* Washington, D.C., 1946.

United States Army, Military Intelligence Division, National Archives and Records Service. Record Group 165, box 982, *Axis Espionage and Propaganda in Latin America.* Washington, D.C., 1946.

United States Department of State. *Consultation Among the American Republics with Respect to the Argentine Situation,* publication 2437. Washington, D.C., 1946.

———. *Foreign Relations of the United States, American Republics* (vols. for 1937–48). Washington, D.C., 1953–64.

——————. *Report of the Delegation of the United States of America to the Inter-American Conference for the Maintenance of Peace.* Washington, D.C., 1937.

——————. *Report of the Delegation of the United States to the Eighth International Conference of American States.* Washington, D.C., 1941.

——————. *Twenty-Third Report to Congress on Lend-Lease Operations,* publication 2707. Washington, D.C., 1946.

——————. *United States Department of State Bulletin,* vols. 5–9. Washington, D.C., 1941–46.

United States Navy, Naval Historical Office, Office of Naval Intelligence. *United States Naval Administration in World War II.* Washington, D.C., 1954.

United States War Department, Office of the Assistant Chief of Staff. *The Magic Documents: Summaries and Transcripts of the Top Secret Diplomatic Communications of Japan, 1938–1945* (microfilm), 14 reels. Washington, D.C., 1980.

VI. Books

Braden, Spruille. *Diplomats and Demagogues: The Memoirs of Spruille Braden.* New Rochelle, New York: Arlington House, 1971.

Conil Paz, Alberto, and Gustavo Ferrari. *Política exterior argentina: 1930–1962.* Buenos Aires: Editorial Huemul, 1964.

Drake, Paul W. *Socialism and Populism in Chile, 1932–1952.* Urbana: University of Illinois Press, 1981.

Frank, Gary. *Struggle for Hegemony in South America: Argentina, Brazil and the United States during the Second World War.* Coral Gables, Florida: Center for Advanced International Studies, 1979.

Gellman, Irwin F. *Good Neighbor Diplomacy: United States Policies in Latin America, 1933–1945.* Baltimore: Johns Hopkins University Press, 1979.

Hilton, Stanley. *Suástica sobre o Brasil: A História da Espionagem Alemã no Brasil, 1939–1944.* Rio de Janeiro: Editora Civilização Brasileira, 1977.

Pommerein, Reiner. *Das Dritte Reich und Lateinamerika: Die deutsche politik gegenüber Süd- und Mittelamerika, 1939–1942.* Düsseldorf: Droste Verlag, 1977.

Potash, Robert A. *The Army and Politics in Argentina, 1928–1945.* Stanford: Stanford University Press, 1969.

Ruíz Guiñazú, Enrique. *La política argentina y el futuro de América.* Buenos Aires: Librería Huemul, 1944.

Volland, Klaus. *Das Dritte Reich und Mexiko: Studien zur Entwicklung des deutsch-mexikanischen Verhältnisses 1933–1942, unter besonderer Berücksichtigung der Ölpolitik.* Frankfurt-am-Main: Peter Lang, 1976.

Index